OXFORD STUDIES IN DEMOCRATIZATION

Series editor: Laurence Whitehead

The New Politics of Inequality in Latin America: Rethinking Participation and Representation

OXFORD STUDIES IN DEMOCRATIZATION

Series editor: Laurence Whitehead

Oxford Studies in Democratization is a series for scholars and students of comparative politics and related disciplines. Volumes will concentrate on the comparative study of the democratization process that accompanied the decline and termination of the cold war. The geographical focus of the series will primarily be Latin America, the Caribbean, Southern and Eastern Europe, and relevant experiences in Africa and Asia.

The New Politics of Inequality in Latin America

Rethinking Participation and Representation

EDITED BY

Douglas A. Chalmers, Carlos M. Vilas, Katherine Hite,
Scott B. Martin, Kerianne Piester, and Monique Segarra

OXFORD UNIVERSITY PRESS
1997

Oxford University Press, Great Clarendon Street, Oxford OX2 6DP

Oxford New York
Athens Auckland Bangkok Bogota Bombay
Buenos Aires Calcutta Cape Town Dar es Salaam
Delhi Florence Hong Kong Istanbul Karachi
Kuala Lumpur Madras Madrid Melbourne
Mexico City Nairobi Paris Singapore
Taipei Tokyo Toronto
and associated companies in
Berlin Ibadan

Oxford is a trade mark of Oxford University Press

Published in the United States
by Oxford University Press Inc., New York

except where stated, © the several contributors, 1997

British Library Cataloguing in Publication Data
Data available

Library of Congress Cataloging in Publication Data
The new politics of inequality in Latin America : rethinking
    participation and representation / edited by Douglas A. Chalmers . . .
    [et al.].
        (Oxford studies in democratization)
        Includes bibliographical references.
        1. Political participation—Latin America. 2. Representative
    government and representation—Latin America. 3. Poor—Latin
    America—Political activity. 4. Equality—Latin America.
    5. Democracy—Latin America. 6. Social change—Latin America.
    I. Chalmers, Douglas A. II. Series.
    JL966.N49 1997 323'.042'098—dc20 96–29002

    ISBN 0–19–878184–9 (hb.) ISBN 0–19–878183–0 (pbk.)

Typeset by Graphicraft Typesetters Ltd., Hong Kong
Printed in Great Britain
on acid-free paper by
Biddles Ltd., Guildford and King's Lynn

Preface

In 1991, graduate students and faculty at Columbia University's Institute of Latin American and Iberian Studies began a series of exchanges on the relationship among social change, equity, and the democratic representation of Latin America's poor majority. The group launched the Inequality and New Forms of Popular Representation Project, a collaborative research effort to explore the repercussions of the troubling paradoxes of the 1980s: the dual processes of formal democratization and heightened social inequality; the rise of several new civil society movements in the context of authoritarianism; the apparent weakening of those movements as democratic institutions returned to the fore; and the general increase in violence which has accompanied nominally democratizing regime transition. The first conclusions from our discussions were that existing approaches were not adequate, that there were many excellent researchers doing very good work, and that we needed to bring together this fresh empirical research and develop new ways of thinking about these paradoxes.

During the 1992 Latin American Studies Association Congress, members of the Inequality Project publicly proposed collaborative research, and the proposal attracted interest from students of political economy, social movements, and political parties around the region. In 1993, approximately seventy scholars participated in a workshop at Columbia to explore the questions of popular participation and popular representation using eight country cases—Argentina, Brazil, Chile, Colombia, Ecuador, Mexico, Paraguay, and Uruguay. Working groups were established among scholars and their US, Latin American, and Canadian affiliates to maintain contact and share research. The empirical work also expanded to include study of Guatemala, Nicaragua, and Uruguay. In March 1994, Project participants returned to Columbia to present their work in a two-day public research conference, 'The Politics of Inequality in Latin America'. Thirty-two papers were presented over a series of eight sessions. Working groups then met for in-depth critique of the papers, and an editorial board formed to select papers for revision and publication.

The major product of this several-year project is this volume, *The New Politics of Inequality in Latin America: Rethinking Participation and Representation*. Parts I through III of the volume focus on popular sector strategies to gain representation, social movement–political party relationships, and the immense challenges to popular participation when confronted with immiseration and violence. Parts IV and V examine the structures, patterns, and arenas of popular representation which have emerged or are emerging in the region. The chapters explore policy-making, new forms of popular representation, and the search for progressive alternatives to neoliberalism at subnational, national, and transnational levels.

The introductory and concluding essays which frame this volume reflect what Kathryn Hochstetler (Chapter 5 of this volume) terms the rich and varied interpretive 'lenses' for viewing the many realities of contemporary Latin America. Carlos Vilas's introduction focuses on the complex webs of social matrices which shape the lives of Latin America's popular sectors and which lie at the heart of any conceptual formulation of prospects for popular sector participation. The conclusion, written by Douglas Chalmers, Scott Martin, and Kerianne Piester, proposes that in the wake of the decomposition of traditional structures of popular representation (i.e. populism, corporatism), there are elements which suggest that new, 'associative' networks are becoming structures for representation. Together, the essays offer ways to conceptualize what are new as well as old or hybrid empirical phenomena for the region. Overall, the chapters of the volume continue to convey the paradoxes and contradictions prevailing in Latin America. On the one hand, they suggest the persistence, even the deepening, of social fragmentation and disarticulation and, therefore, of the obstacles to popular sector participation in any traditional sense. On the other hand, the essays document emerging forms of representation which may provide fertile ground for new and vibrant democratic practices.

The members of the Inequality Project believe that the inequality of the 1980s and 1990s comes at a time when governments have turned away from many of the tools they might have used to promote equality in the past, and when the organizations traditionally able to make demands on governments in the name of the poor are in exceptional disarray. Given sharpened inequality and the risks to social and political stability that such inequality engenders, the task facing many Latin American countries is not just finding short-term policies to alleviate poverty, but effective means of integrating the popular sectors into politics and society, so as to ensure, through their participation, that they will secure their rights as well as give their support to new political and economic institutions.

This Project has benefited from the support of a number of individuals and organizations. In particular, we would like to acknowledge the contribution of Ambassador Paolo Janni, Italy's former Permanent Observer to the Organization of American States, who, as a member of the Board of Guarantors of Columbia University's Italian Academy for the Advanced Study in America ensured support for the Project from the Academy. We would also like to thank Mary Uebersax and the North-South Center of the University of Miami for their strong contribution. Finally, the Project received welcome support from the Inter-American Development Bank, the Organization of American States, the William and Flora Hewlett Foundation, the Center for International Business Education of Columbia University, the New York Consulate of Mexico, and the United States Department of Education.

We would additionally like to thank the scholars who contributed to our Project with their participation and advice: Ana María Bejarano, Maxwell Cameron, Maria do Carmo Campello de Souza, Miguel Carter, Jorge Castañeda, José Luís

Coraggio, Margaret Crahan, Enrique de la Garza, Alvaro Díaz, Susan Eckstein, Vanna Ianni, Pedro Jacobi, Robert Kaufman, Peter Kingstone, Deborah Levenson-Estrada, Amy Lind, Laura MacDonald, Javier Melgoza, Joan Nelson, Philip Oxhorn, Julia Paley, Charles Reilly, Ian Roxborough, Cynthia Sanborn, William Smith, João Paulo Candia Veiga, and Kay Warren.

Furthermore, this project would not have been possible without the technical assistance and support of several individuals, including Susan Burgerman, Eric Carlson, Tom Giles, Andrea Hetling, Kent Kirschner, Steven Leslie, Alfred Montero, Judy Rein, and the program assistants at the Institute of Latin American and Iberian Studies of Columbia. We should also like to thank Columbia's Center for Social Sciences, which supported work on the project under the auspices of its Workshop on Identities, Institutions, and Representation. Finally, we thank Oxford University Press's Tim Barton, Jenni Scott, and our two anonymous readers, and we thank Oxford's Democratization Series editor Laurence Whitehead for believing in the importance of the Inequality Project and this book.

Katherine Hite

New York
February 1996

Contents

Notes on Contributors

KATHLEEN BRUHN is Assistant Professor of Political Science at the University of California, Santa Barbara. She has just completed *Taking on Goliath*, a book about the origins and consolidation of the Party of the Democratic Revolution in Mexico, forthcoming from Pennsylvania State University Press.

JO-MARIE BURT is a Ph.D. candidate in Political Science at Columbia University and acting assistant editor of *NACLA Report on the Americas*. She has written several articles about political violence, human rights, and grassroots organizing in Peru. She is currently participating in a comparative research project on the role of non-governmental organizations in shaping grassroots practices in Latin America.

DOUGLAS A. CHALMERS is Professor of Political Science at Columbia University and Director of its Institute of Latin American and Iberian Studies. Chalmers has authored several articles on political institutions and the state in Latin America, and he is co-editor (with Maria do Carmo Campello de Souza and Atilio Borón) of *The Right and Democracy in Latin America* (Praeger). He received his Ph.D. from Yale University. Chalmers's recent research has focused on transnational linkages and on Mexico, where he taught at the Colegio de México and where he led a team of researchers investigating the role of non-governmental organizations in that country.

MARÍA LORENA COOK is Assistant Professor at the New York State School of Industrial and Labor Relations, Cornell University. She earned her Ph.D. in Political Science at the University of California, Berkeley. She has written on Mexican state–labor relations and popular movements and is the co-editor of *Regional Integration and Industrial Relations in North America* (Institute of Collective Bargaining) and *The Politics of Economic Restructuring: State–Society Relations and Regime Change in Mexico*, and the author of *Organizing Dissent: Unions, the State, and the Democratic Teachers' Movement in Mexico*.

LILIA FERRO-CLÉRICO is Assistant Professor at the School of Social Sciences of the Universidad de la República, Uruguay. She received her MA in International Relations at Johns Hopkins University's Paul H. Nitze School of Advanced International Studies (SAIS) and her Ph.D. in Law from the Universidad de la República, Uruguay.

FERNANDO FILGUEIRA received his BA in Sociology at the Instituto de Ciencias Sociales at the Universidad de la República Oriental del Uruguay and is currently a Ph.D. candidate in the Sociology Department at Northwestern University. He has worked and published on issues of democracy, labor, and welfare in Uruguay and Latin America. He recently contributed to the book *El largo adiós al país modelo: Políticas sociales y pobreza en el Uruguay* (Peithos), with a historical analysis of the development of the welfare state in Uruguay.

JONATHAN FOX is Associate Professor of Social Science at the University of California, Santa Cruz, in the Latin American and Latino Studies Program. He is author of *The Politics of Food in Mexico: State Power and Social Mobilization* (Cornell University Press), editor of *The Challenge of Rural Democratisation: Perspectives from Latin America and the Philippines*

(F. Cass), and co-editor of *Transforming State–Society Relations in Mexico: The National Solidarity Strategy* (University of California, San Diego). He is currently finishing a co-edited volume: *The Struggle for Accountability: NGOs, Social Movements and the World Bank* (forthcoming).

ERIC HERSHBERG is Director of the Program on Latin America at the Social Science Research Council. He received his Ph.D. in Political Science from the University of Wisconsin-Madison in 1989, and has written extensively on the political economy of democratization and development in Southern Europe as well as in Latin America. He is co-editor, with Elizabeth Jelin, of the collection of essays entitled *Constructing Democracy: Human Rights, Citizenship and Society in Latin America*, published by Westview Press.

KATHERINE HITE is Associate Director of the Institute of Latin American and Iberian Studies at Columbia University, where she received her doctorate in Political Science in 1996. Her recent article, 'The Formation and Transformation of Political Identity: Leaders of the Chilean Left, 1968–1990', appeared in the *Journal of Latin American Studies*, and she is currently at work on citizenship formation issues in both democratizing and consolidated democracies. Hite teaches Columbia's undergraduate seminar in Latin American studies as well as college lecture courses on democracy and authoritarianism.

KATHRYN HOCHSTETLER is Assistant Professor of Political Science at Colorado State University. She received her Ph.D. in Political Science from the University of Minnesota in 1994, and continues to research and write about social movements, political participation, and democracy.

MARGARITA LÓPEZ-MAYA is Investigating-Professor at the Centro de Estudios del Desarrollo (CENDES) of the Universidad Central de Venezuela. She received her Ph.D. in Social Science from the Universidad Central de Venezuela. Her work has focused mainly on the socio-historical and political analysis of contemporary Venezuelan society. She is co-author of *De Punto Fijo al Pacto Social: Desarrollo y hegemonía en Venezuela 1958–1985* (Fondo Editorial Acta Científica Venezolana) and *El tejido de Penélope: La reforma del Estado en Venezuela 1984–1989* (CENDES), and author of *El Banco de los Trabajadores de Venezuela: ¿Algo más que un banco?* (Universidad Central de Venezuela) and *Los Estados Unidos en Venezuela: 1945–1948 (revelaciones de los archivos estadounidenses)* (forthcoming).

SCOTT B. MARTIN is a Ph.D. candidate in Political Science and Research Associate at the Center for Social Sciences, both at Columbia University. His dissertation focuses on the social construction of unions and industrial governance in the Brazilian automotive sector, with comparative reference to Mexico and advanced industrial countries. He also directs two research projects based at the Institute of Latin American and Iberian Studies at Columbia examining, respectively, industrial governance in Mexican automobiles and economic governance in Latin America and Southern Europe in cross-regional perspective. Mr Martin has published articles on unions and industrial restructuring in Brazil in the *NACLA Report on the Americas* and the Brazilian journal *Lua Nova*. He has taught courses in Latin American politics at Columbia and New York Universities and in industrial relations at the Mexico City campus of the Instituto Tecnológico y de Estudios Superiores de Monterrey.

M. VICTORIA MURILLO is a Harvard Academy Scholar at the Center for International Affairs at Harvard University. She received her Licenciatura in Political Science at the

Universidad de Buenos Aires and is a Ph.D. candidate in the Department of Government at Harvard University. She is completing a dissertation on the impact of union responses to market-oriented reforms implemented by labor-based parties in Argentina, Mexico, and Venezuela.

WILLIAM R. NYLEN is Assistant Professor of Political Science and Chair of the Latin American Studies Program at Stetson University in Deland, Florida. He has also taught at Harvard and Northeastern Universities and has published several works on neoliberalism and business–class politics in Brazil. Ongoing work includes case-studies of local governance by the Workers' Party in Brazil and a study of political organization and mobilization of non-elite capital in Brazil in the 1970s and 1980s.

ALDO PANFICHI is Professor of Sociology at the Universidad Católica of Peru, and a doctoral candidate in Sociology at the New School for Social Research. His areas of research interest and publication include Peruvian urban history, contemporary politics, and popular culture. His most recent publication is a co-edited collection of social history research entitled *Mundos interiores: Lima 1850–1950* (Universidad del Pacífico).

JORGE PAPADÓPULOS has published several articles on decentralization and social policies and is the author of *Seguridad social y política en Uruguay* (CIESU). He is preparing his Ph.D. dissertation, 'Democracy and Neoliberalism under Stress: The Politics of Security in the Southern Cone', at the Department of Political Science, University of Pittsburgh.

ANTHONY W. PEREIRA is Assistant Professor of Political Science at the Graduate Faculty of the New School for Social Research, New York City. A graduate of the University of Sussex (England) and Harvard University, he has published articles on regime change, development, labor, and land issues in Latin America. He is the author of *The End of the Peasantry* (University of Pittsburgh Press, forthcoming), a book about the rural labor movement in north-eastern Brazil, and is currently researching legacies of authoritarianism in Brazil and the Southern Cone.

KERIANNE PIESTER is a Ph.D. candidate in the Department of Political Science at Columbia University. She is currently completing a dissertation on social welfare reform in Mexico and its impact on the changing structure of relations between the state, non-governmental, and popular organizations. She has ongoing research interests in social welfare restructuring and the politics of reform in developing countries. She has lectured on Latin American politics and Inter-American relations at the University of Pennsylvania and Columbia University.

PAULO SÉRGIO PINHEIRO is currently United Nations Special Rapporteur on the Situation of Human Rights in Burundi. He is a professor of Political Science and Director of the Center for the Study of Violence at the Universidade de São Paulo, Brazil. In addition, he is the author of several books and articles on social history and human rights, including 'The Legacy of Authoritarianism in Brazil', in Stuart Nagel (ed.), *Latin American Development and Public Policy* (St Martin's Press). He has taught at Columbia University, at the École des Hautes Études en Sciences Sociales, Paris and, during 1995, at the Kellogg Institute, University of Notre Dame.

KENNETH M. ROBERTS is Assistant Professor of Political Science at the University of New Mexico. He earned his Ph.D. in Political Science at Stanford University, and has written on political parties and the impact of neoliberalism on political representation in Latin America. He is currently writing a book on the modern Left and social movements in Chile and Peru.

MONIQUE SEGARRA is a Ph.D. candidate in the Department of Political Science at Columbia University. Her dissertation examines the construction of what she terms 'welfare networks', involving new practices among non-governmental organizations, international organizations, and the state in social service and welfare provision. Segarra is analyzing the impact of this institutional reshaping on how popular sector interests are represented within the process of state reform in Ecuador, and she has conducted comparative field research on these questions in Guatemala and Bolivia.

MELINA SELVERSTON is a doctoral student in the Political Science Department at Columbia University. She is currently completing her dissertation, 'Politicized Ethnicity and the Nation State: The Indigenous Movement in Ecuador'. She was the South America correspondent for *Native Nations* magazine.

CARLOS M. VILAS is Research Professor at Universidad Nacional Autónoma de México. He is the author of numerous articles and books, including *State, Class and Ethnicity in Nicaragua* (Lynne Reinner Publishers) and *Between Earthquakes and Volcanoes: Market, States and the Central American Revolutions* (Monthly Review Press). His current research focuses on the ongoing restructuring of state/market/civil society relations in Latin America and its impact on processes of democratization.

PETER WINN was educated at Columbia and Cambridge Universities and has taught Latin American history at Princeton, Yale, Wellesley, Tufts, and the Universidad de la República in Montevideo, Uruguay. His publications include *Weavers of Revolution* (Oxford University Press), an oral history of Allende's Chile, and *Americas* (Pantheon Books), the companion volume to the PBS television series, for which he served as the Academic Director. He has also published a book and articles on Britain and Uruguay and co-edited two volumes on Uruguay and democracy. During 1993 and 1995 he was a Fulbright Lecturer in Uruguay.

DEBORAH J. YASHAR is Assistant Professor of Government and Social Studies at Harvard University. She is the author of *Demanding Democracy: Reform and Reaction in Costa Rica and Guatemala, 1870s–1950s* (forthcoming by Stanford University Press). She has written on democratization, social movements, and state violence. Her current research focuses on the rise of indigenous movements in Latin America and the relationship between identity politics, democratic representation, and political participation.

List of Figures

List of Tables

Introduction

1 | Participation, Inequality, and the Whereabouts of Democracy

Carlos M. Vilas[1]

This book deals with the vicissitudes of democracy and political participation in Latin America, in settings where civic institutions exist alongside strong social and economic inequalities, where the state has changed its structure and redefined its functions, and where violence remains a key resource for many actors. It is also a book about some of the current popular strategies devised to overcome the most harmful aspects of the new setting and its new definition of winners and losers.

Through case-studies of nine countries—Argentina, Brazil, Chile, Ecuador, Guatemala, Mexico, Peru, Uruguay, and Venezuela—the book analyzes the tensions faced by actors (parties and unions) that in the past attempted to sustain some degree of articulation between political institutions and social demands, and who now harbor often uneasy relationships to the state and social activism propelled by new modes of popular organization (environmentalists, indigenous organizations, human rights organizations). The relationship among social actors, political organizations, and the state is discussed in relatively stable institutional contexts as well as in environments plagued by open violence and generalized instability. Aside from exploring the disjunctures between new actors and old organizations, the book debates recent attempts to reach a new articulation between the two, including: trade union efforts to adapt to the new characteristics of the labor market and to economic restructuring; the emergence of political organizations that seek an elusive equilibrium among party structures, electoral procedures, and popular movement autonomy; and the appearance of renewed forms of traditional caudillismo.

The chapters in this volume explore different ways of tackling a number of topics that constitute the agenda for contemporary studies of popular participation and democracy in Latin America. Some chapters emphasize the importance of historical and cultural processes of state construction and their relationship to society. Others address the advantages and limitations of different ways of conceptualizing

[1] I am grateful for the comments and stimulus of Katherine Hite, Monique Segarra, Scott Martin, and Mireille Szynalski, and for the support of Douglas Chalmers. None of these individuals is responsible for the limitations of this text. The editors would like to thank Eric Hershberg for his translation of this chapter.

democracy and citizenship. Several chapters focus on the persistence of violence as an element in society and in political regimes and as a resource rationally mobilized by certain actors in particular circumstances; they examine insecurity and fear as ingredients and catalysts for collective action. Finally, many authors explore the issue of identities and the reconfiguration of social and political actors, as well as the impact of identity construction on state organization and the building of the political system. Any discussion that seeks to be relevant to political participation and democracy in contemporary Latin America must incorporate each of these elements.

The first part of this introduction discusses some of these issues: (1) the modes and dimensions in the making of a popular identity and its demands and strategies for social and political participation; (2) the difficulties of recent processes of democratization in incorporating new demands for participation and in giving institutional weight to social identities behind these demands; (3) the impact of social fragmentation on the constitution of civil societies and citizens' politics, and the role of the state and increasing globalization in the development of specific modes of participation; and (4) the significance of inequality and impoverishment in shaping political environments and outcomes in the search for alternative forms of social and political participation. The second part of the chapter places the various contributions to the volume in the context of the considerations outlined above.

One gets the sense that the sincere enthusiasm fueled by processes of democratization and the emergence of 'new' actors with diverse demands for participation triggered a sort of academic amnesia regarding what was already known about Latin American societies and democracy, about its conditions, actors, and consequences. Francis Fukuyama may have believed that history is over, but a great deal of literature on the topics addressed in this volume gives the impression that history never existed, and that for analysts and the actors being studied, history starts now.[2] It is for this reason that the following discussion seeks to specify not only the fragmentation and profound transformations which have been taking place and are under way, but also the elements of continuity and permanence, of the sometimes ominous, sometimes encouraging, stubbornness of actors; of whirlwinds of change intertwined with the daunting inertias of a complex reality. Above all, this chapter highlights the capacity of men and women to seek forms—heroic and perverse—of individual and collective participation, forms that allow them to attain (or maintain the illusion of attaining) a more honorable life, one that nourishes, sustains, and gives real meaning to democracy.

1. Popular Participation: Identities and Strategies

A variety of forms of popular organization and mobilization contributed to ending the military regimes in Argentina, Brazil, Chile, and Peru, and to a degree, to

[2]   Stiefel and Wolfe point to a similar 'disregard of even recent history' in studies on popular participation (Stiefel and Wolfe 1994: 3).

the opening of strongly authoritarian systems, like Mexico's. Simultaneously, the new organizations called for an expansion of the democratization agenda, towards issues of social welfare and a variety of concerns that had traditionally remained marginal, such as identity, the environment, and ageing, among others. These aspects provided the principles of identification and articulation of 'new' actors. Gender or ethnicity, for example, became issues for democratic participation because they were the principles by which social groups articulated and identified themselves. The identification of a given area as problematic opened the way for the definition of 'new' actors.

The emergence and activism of such actors contrasted with the less visible role carried out by more traditional organizations, such as unions and some parties (Calderón *et al.* 1992; Slater 1994). This is not incompatible with the fact that many of these movements and expressions of social activism had well-defined social profiles. Referring to Western Europe, Habermas (1981) and Offe (1988) both point out that at the core of 'new' social movements is the 'new middle class' (professionals, technicians . . .), accompanied by elements of the old middle class and peripheral groups outside the labor market (the unemployed, students, housewives, retirees . . .). In any case, these are none of the central classes of capitalist society. Frank and Fuentes (1989) compare the development of these movements in the 'West' and the 'Third World'. In the former, they note the dominant role played by the middle classes, while the latter exhibits a more popular character. They also point out that these movements frequently have middle-class leadership, and that in this respect they resemble the worker and peasant movements that preceded them. I have (1994) concluded, in turn, that these actors' activism corresponds principally to the sphere of the poor and the powerless, and that even with regard to 'broad' issues (human rights, ethnicity, gender, ecology . . .), there is a strong presence of actors from the spheres of the poor and the oppressed.

Indeed, the majority of the cases studied in the specialized literature addresses this atmosphere of the masses, the impoverished, and the politically or culturally dominated, including violent forms of collective action. These encompass peasant and labor movements; mobilizations against military regimes, economic policies, and external debt; Christian base communities; neighborhood movements; guerrilla organizations; human rights mobilizations; women's movements; environmental activism; and ethnic movements. Issues that have no precise socioeconomic referent—gender, sexual orientation, ecology, human rights—eventually refer to a climate of institutional oppression that links them to the dimension of oppression peculiar to mass poverty. These issues are subsequently joined with— and are eventually articulated through—social movements that emerge from the multiple manifestations of poverty. The issue is clear in the arena of human rights. An overwhelming majority of the victims of human rights violations belong to the world of the poor and the oppressed: half of those detained and disappeared during Argentina's 1976–83 military dictatorship were workers, and two-thirds were wage-earners; 70 per cent of those who died or were disappeared between 1979 and 1982 at the hands of the military and death squads in El Salvador were peasants;

more than 80 per cent of the victims of human rights violations in Guatemala during the 1980s were indigenous peasants and rural and urban laborers (Figueroa 1991; Vilas 1994, 1995a). Similar findings exist with respect to ethnic (Urban and Scherzer 1991; Solares 1993) and women's movements (Alvarez 1990; Fisher 1993; Radcliffe and Westwood 1993).

The widespread social mobilizations of recent decades thus highlight the importance of the 'popular', meant here as the intersection of economic exploitation, political oppression, and poverty. In Latin America the 'popular' is a mixture of socioeconomic, political, and cultural elements. The 'popular' encompasses but is not limited to poverty. Incorporating also a political and cultural dimension, the 'popular' includes middle-class groups mobilized not so much by strictly economic demands as around calls for democratization, public freedoms, and citizenship rights. The political and the cultural dimensions of the 'popular' imply a self-identification of subordination and oppression (labor, ethnic, gender . . .) in the face of a domination that is articulated by exploitation (insufficient income, meager wages, denial of a dignified life or prospects for the future) and is expressed institutionally, through insecurity, arbitrariness, and socially biased coercion. It therefore implies some type of differentiation and, ultimately, opposition to established power. In particular it signals opposition to the institutions and organizations that represent and articulate exploitation and domination in its various forms.

Differentiation and opposition are not unidirectional; the plurality of expressions of domination orients collective action towards a multiplicity of targets, most obviously the state, but also political parties, trade unions, non-governmental organizations, or international organizations. Nor does the state act with a single voice with respect to these demands. Some state agencies may be seen as more sensitive allies or interlocutors than others. Similarly, collective action refers to dimensions of the private sphere—violence against women and children, sexual orientation, the household division of labor—as well as to the public sphere. In fact, the very differentiation between public and private spheres is subject to question, in that public participation of some actors is conditioned by relations of power and divisions of labor in the private sphere. Taken as a whole, these factors establish a tension between the differentiation of the 'popular' in terms of a plurality of identities, and the unity of the 'popular' as a function of shared conditions of oppression, exploitation, and impoverishment.

The multiple directions of collective action imply the multiple dimensions of that action, ranging from demands for institutional participation to the search for forms of coordination or cooperation among institutional actors, and to protest movements and appeals to direct action. Processes of democratization in Latin America have had difficulty integrating the agendas and dynamics of social movements, and social movements themselves, into the constitution and functioning of institutions. Representative democracy is related uncomfortably to social participation. Political and institutional rigidities that impede incorporation of their agenda tend to relegate social movements to the sphere of social protest and pressures from outside the political system. The ineffectiveness of institutional actors in processing the demands of social movements undermines the representative basis of the democratic regime and reinforces the institutional marginality of these movements.

The conjoining of oppression, exploitation, and poverty in the construction of a popular subject means that the popular is constituted on the basis of multiple reference points situated in a complex web of complementarity and contradiction, in which subjects 'choose' those ingredients that best express their condition of oppression and exploitation. In some cases, the popular is constructed around class identities, in others it is based on ethnic referents, while in still others gender or symbolic elements become central. Other referents are articulated around these, in addition to the fact that specific modes of insertion into the labor market, differences in access to economic resources, and particular positions in power relations influence how actors build their own notions of gender, ethnicity, class, or other categories. No identity is definite or static; what remains permanent for the popular subject is oppression and exploitation in a context of poverty, even though the phenomenology of each of these dimensions, and the perspectives through which actors approach, conceptualize, and experience them, are contingent.

The emergence and activism of social movements allowed for the manifestation and acknowledgment of a wide range of actors as sources of collective action. This is at the same time a distinct way of conceptualizing and practicing citizenship. The revolution of identities makes explicit the multiple ingredients—in addition to socioeconomic or class status—that play a role in the constitution of citizenship: the right to civic equality is claimed together with, and intertwined with, the right to acknowledge differences (de Sousa Santos 1994). Moreover, this multiplicity of social identities marks a clear counterpoint with the legal unidimensionality of political citizenship: the multiplicity and complexity of the popular in the face of the literalness of citizenship; the democratic character of identity construction and of efforts to imbue identities with an institutional presence; and the authoritarian nature of an institutional democracy that reduces, denies, and homogenizes the richness of social diversity. When an indigenous child is prohibited from speaking his or her own language in school, or is taught that what he or she speaks is a dialect, this child is being taught that there are first-class and second-class languages, first-class and second-class language speakers, and that the child's father, mother, brothers and sisters, and all those like him or her, are second-class people. When children witness a man (the father, uncle, or boyfriend) inflict abuse on their mother or sister, they are learning the legitimacy of gender violence—one as victimizer and the other as passive victim. All this and much more is perfectly compatible with democratic institutions and representative politics. But what kind of citizenship, what sense of participatory efficacy, can develop in such a setting?

The tension between citizenship and people can be interpreted as a tension between two dimensions of democracy. On the one hand, citizenship refers to a group of free and independent individuals who enjoy rights of participation that compensate for, and at the same time conceal, actual socioeconomic inequalities. On the other hand, relationships of oppression, poverty, and exploitation restrict the effective exercise of these rights of citizenship. In Latin America, formally democratic institutions and procedures and the constitutional enunciation of citizenship rights exist alongside the persistent devaluation of indigenous people, women, the poor, and the young, all of whom confront objective barriers to participation in the institutional context of a state and a democracy which in practical terms mostly works as tailor-made for men, for whites or mestizos, for those who have stable jobs, for adults. This is not to deny the real advances made in these domains, but it forces us, as Melina Selverston puts it in her chapter, to qualify our assessment of the democracies under discussion here.

REALLY EXISTING DEMOCRACIES

Some years ago, in a provocative piece, the Mexican sociologist Pablo González Casanova asked: 'When we talk of democracy, what are we talking about?' (González Casanova 1986). The question remains valid because a great deal of the current discussion about processes of democratization in Latin America, about the real or supposed consolidation of democracies, or the evolution of a post-transitional phase, involves theoretical and conceptual questions, and definitional ones as well. What democracy are we talking about? The answer is by no means straightforward; a historical and comparative perspective indicates that, independently of textbook definitions, people place very different things under the rubric of democracy.

The literature on transitions to democracy in Latin America placed virtually exclusive emphasis on electoral regimes and on certain aspects of institutional arrangements. The shortcomings of the institutional dimensions of the transitions to democracy, which some authors recognized, did not open the way for an exploration of other aspects or components of democratization. The conventional focus made sense in light of the political referents of the discussion. The issue was above all transitions from military regimes—many of them savage and systematically repressive—to civilian governments, in a context of economic crisis and popular mobilization. The military dictatorships of Argentina, Brazil, Uruguay, or Chile were not overthrown by popular mobilizations or uprisings, but such mobilizations, from massive and persistent street protests to plebiscites, were important ingredients in the eventual withdrawal of the military. Hence as well the preoccupation with governability during transitions, and the recommendations that amounted basically to lowering the level and volume of popular mobilization in order not to overburden the new and presumably inexpert governments that had emerged from elections, and not to alarm the authoritarian actors who had reluctantly receded from the institutional arena. As often occurs, analyses of what is became indistinguishable from proposals for how one would like things to be.[3]

From this perspective, the governability of democracies depended on the effectiveness of political control over popular movements and the political or social organizations that expressed them. At the risk of oversimplification, it can be said that these were democracies that, from below, included individual electoral participation to choose, in a framework of competition between parties, elites who negotiated from above and competed among themselves in keeping with a set of rules and procedures established in accord with prevailing relations of (political, military, and economic) power. In addition to defining the 'how' of democracy, these rules defined the 'what' as well. They established which issues could be legitimately posed and which ones could not, that is, they defined which issues were democratic and which ones were not.

In general these transitions were consolidated in electoral terms and in terms of their respect and effective practice of individual liberties. It is important to point out that this apparent triumph of liberal democracy—as opposed to a social democracy of destabilizing consequences—in reality amounted to *less* than liberal democracy, in that liberal democracy includes, in addition to elections, questions as important as the rule of law, government accountability for its actions, an effective balance among the executive, legislative, and judicial branches, and military subordination to civilian rule. These are equally important issues for a democratic regime—even in their restricted institutional observance—yet they remained largely outside the debate about transitions.

The conceptualization of democracy as a system of rules and procedures made it possible for democracy to become compatible with the persistent veto of the military, as in Chile; with authoritarian educational systems, as in Peru and Ecuador; with impunity for repressive acts, as in Guatemala; with manipulation of public insecurity; and with the authoritarian discourse of a number of political leaders, as in Peru and Argentina. This literature reproduced as academic analysis the level, scope, and limitations of the real processes of transition; it accompanied them and gave them an academic expression, but in general it was unable to anticipate the obstacles that fledgling democracies faced or the bottlenecks in which they would become enclosed. The practical realization of the concept predated its academic rationalization. Unable in its theoretical reflections to get beyond what the processes being analyzed had amounted to in practice, this literature even presented as a virtue what was in the best of cases a product of necessity and, in the worst of cases, a vice.

The not always explicit theoretical referent for this literature on transitions is found in the Schumpeterian version of democracy (Schumpeter 1950) and in its

---

[3] The most representative and important work from this perspective is of course O'Donnell, Schmitter, and Whitehead (1986). On the 'overburdening' of political institutions as a threat to democracy, see Samuel Huntington (1968).

more elaborated version as polyarchy (Dahl 1971). Both place emphasis on a set of rules and procedures developed on the basis of a framework of freely formulated consensus. It is debatable whether this approach is relevant to analyzing processes of democratization in Latin America, or elsewhere, for that matter (see for example Gould 1988; Weffort 1984, 1992; Mayorga 1992; Cueva 1994; Parry and Moran 1994). The contemporary use of the model of polyarchy produces as many headaches and indulges in as many inconsistencies as were raised a century ago by attempts to appeal to the Federalist Papers for interpreting the constitutions of oligarchic states in South America, or the British Crown's aspiring to implant the principles of the Westminster system in its Caribbean colonies.[4] There is no more brutal a negation of polyarchy than the mono-archy of weapons and money that Yashar presents in her discussion of Guatemala, nor any more perverse than that of the 'everyone for him or herself' on the streets of São Paulo or Rio de Janeiro, the dispersion of violence and corruption in Brazilian politics (Pinheiro), or the quest for new saviors of the fatherland in Peru (Panfichi). The studies contained in this volume highlight the enormous distance that can exist between institutional design and political practice, and the entirely possible coexistence of democratic political institutions and authoritarian behavior—of state agencies as well as of social actors.

The importance of institutions for political regimes is something that was stressed by both nineteenth-century German *Staatsrecht* and French *droit publique*, and that every good law student knows well. Its relevance for political analysis depends on the capacity of institutional approaches to recognize the matrix of power relations that characterizes particular institutional arrangements (Rueschmeyer *et al.* 1992: 5–6). Stated succinctly, an institution is a patterned social practice enforced by law. In every society there exists a great deal of social practices, but not all of them are legally patterned and enforced, and many are even prohibited. Relations of power, the dominant culture, historical and ecological conditioning factors—all determine which practices and social relations will receive institutional status, which will not, and which will be punished. Institutions are not a *datum* but rather a *constructum*; institution-building, when it is effective, is the result of a particular configuration of power relations. At the risk of sounding trivial, it is worth recalling that the legal expression of a relation of power does not strip that relation of its nature, that is, of a relation of domination and subordination, command and obedience. Nor does it eliminate the inequality of access to resources upon which that relation is constituted. Several chapters in this volume focus on the complex causation between political and social organizations, relations of power, and institutions.

At the same time, neo-institutionalist perspectives and studies of actors' everyday rationale highlight the fact that the real functioning of institutions is linked

---

[4] Analysis of the 'export of democracy' is beyond the scope of this introduction. Lowenthal (1991) offers a series of essays on the reappearance of this theme in US foreign policy.

intimately to history, culture, and the specific characteristics of a society.[5] Political institutions condense, in the specific mode in which they operate, the values, memories, attitudes, fears, and expectations of a society: the collective imagination, in the sense conveyed by Castoriadis (1975). People create and recreate institutions through practice, and different people (by class, ethnicity, gender, generation . . .) recreate them differently. This point is emphasized in Scott's research (Scott 1985, 1990), but it is by no means confined to subordinate groups or to the social sphere. Alberto Fujimori and Carlos Menem illustrate the multiple manners through which it is possible to adapt electoral mechanisms and relations between the executive and the legislature to their own political designs.

To point out the inadequacies or shortcomings of procedural perspectives on democracy and participation should not be interpreted as disdain for the institutional importance of one or the other. In casting light upon a wide range of subjects that the literature did not adequately take into account, this book goes beyond purely institutional perspectives and proposes a less complacent interpretation of the societies and the political systems of the countries that it analyzes. It also brings in the necessary ingredients for the process of building the institutions of democracy in such a way that takes account of the history and culture of the societies and the social actors. The volume suggests that the frontiers between democracy and authoritarianism, between participation and exclusion, tend to be less precise and more complex than we usually think.

The emphasis on rules and procedures leaves aside the configuration of power relations and overlooks the modes in which actors interpret rules, negotiate around them, and apply them as a function of power resources which are distributed *unequally*. As Nun (1993) aptly pointed out, democratic transitions had a relation of familiarity with regard to the theoretical paradigm: they resemble democracies and exhibit elements of democracy but they are not democracies. Just as the market is present not only under capitalism, elections are not exclusively a characteristic of democracy: Somoza in Nicaragua, Stroessner in Paraguay, the Salvadoran colonels and the Guatemalan generals—all resorted routinely to elections that nevertheless did not modify the dictatorial character of the regimes in question. 'Reactionary despotism' was the term Baloyra (1983) used to define the mixture of electoral procedures and effective authoritarianism.

There have been numerous critiques of the procedural definition of democracy,[6] but in general they lacked the influence and support attained by the above-mentioned literature—in some cases, because the critiques failed to provide a conceptual alternative; in others, because they were dismissed lightly as disqualifications of 'really existing democracies', and even as evidence of an authoritarian perspective. Interestingly, some of the more recent re-elaborations of the literature

---

[5] See for example Putnam (1993); Joseph and Nugent (1994). From a different but complementary perspective, see Corrigan and Sayer (1985). *El laberinto de soledad* by Octavio Paz remains a most insightful appraisal of these issues.

[6] The most important Latin American work is Cueva (1988); see also MacEwan (1988).

12 Carlos Vilas

on transitions return to many of the issues posed by those critical perspectives: power relations, the question of the state, the representation of social actors, long-term historical factors (O'Donnell 1991, 1993*a*, 1993*b*, 1995; Cavarozzi 1992*a*; Schmitter 1993). Taken together, these re-elaborations may be interpreted as an *ex post* recognition that a meaningful discussion of democracy cannot be isolated from a consideration of the conditions for democracy—an observation which in fact applies to any political regime.

To focus on democracy as a set of institutional procedures is, clearly, a question of convention. In abstract terms one convention is worth as much as any other, but things change when one moves from the abstract to the specific, that is, to consider the capacity of one or another convention to take into account the directions and possible outcomes of political processes. The current state of the literature on democratic transitions, and the multiplicity of more or less imaginative adjectives with which the literature attempts to specify that 'relation of familiarity' that Nun points to, reflects the cul-de-sac in which these processes—of which the literature was an academic expression—now find themselves: 'protected' democracies; 'low intensity' democracies and citizenships; 'delegative' democracies, 'lended' democracies, etc. In light of the consolidation of electoral methods for voting upon and replacing governments, it can be affirmed simultaneously that Latin America would be 'beyond transitions to democracy' (Cavarozzi 1992*a*) or in need of a 'second transition' (O'Donnell 1993*b*) to overcome the shortcomings of what, it now seems, was only a 'first transition'. Schmitter, in contrast, points to the possibility of a reconceptualization of democratic regimes by analytically breaking them down into a plurality of 'partial regimes' of unequal and asynchronic consolidation. This would enable one to take into account the difficulties faced by democracies in giving representation to social actors that demand participation (Schmitter 1993).

Recognition that there is a coherent relation between social structures and political regimes is as old as political theory itself: for Aristotle, democracy, as form of government, is above all a societal condition. From Lipset and Barrington Moore, Jr., onward, empirical studies confirm the existence of what, with the resources of his era, Montesquieu labeled *l'esprit des lois*: the correspondence among economic, social, and even ecological structures and political regimes (see Helliwell 1994). But the likelihood of constructing democracy, or any other political regime, refers as well to the relations of power between actors and coalitions of actors as they are constituted and unfold in the economic and social sphere. This power-oriented perspective introduces two specific issues into the analysis of democratization processes: (1) the state, as a product of particular relations and balances of power between social and political actors; and (2) the international articulation of domestic relations of power—a theme that acquires growing significance with the expansion of globalization processes and free-trade agreements. At the same time, a power-oriented perspective emphasizes political decisions and their impact on prior balances and configurations of power, rather than restricting the analysis to institutional procedures for decision-making.

From this perspective, the questioning to which the transition literature made itself susceptible stems from the formalism of its institutional analysis much more than from institutional analysis itself. The questioning refers to the relevance of the political and historical-cultural assumptions it adopts concerning such issues as the processes of state formation in Latin America, the existence of genuine civil societies in many of these societies, and the existence, extent, and nature of processes of individuation upon which the concept of democracy is based. In other words, if political institutions express relations of power that evolve historically and culturally in particular socioeconomic, domestic, and international settings, not just any type of institution is relevant for all types of societies. The political dynamics and their rules will always remain subject to adaptation by actors in specific settings.

STATE, SOCIAL FRAGMENTATION, AND PARTICIPATION

The focus on political institutions as a product of power relations, and as a dimension of the history and culture of a society, links the analysis of political participation to the manner in which the state has been constituted and is recreated by distinct actors and their interaction. The specific macrosocial and macropolitical factors that intervened in the formation of the state in Latin America are multiple and well known: the colonial imposition of a political power with aspirations to unity *vis-à-vis* the multiple fragmentations of space and populations; the institutional invisibility of ethnic differentiation as a condition for the enactment of institutional racism; the subordinate articulation of the region *vis-à-vis* the world system. These elements, among others, shaped the formation of states and their changing relations with society, as well as the contemporary organization and operation of political regimes.[7]

Jo-Marie Burt questions analyses of Sendero Luminoso that place excessive weight on the territorial factor. She is correct to point out that Sendero eventually became an organization with a nearly nationwide presence, including an important penetration into poor neighborhoods in Lima. It is equally true, nonetheless, that Sendero emerged as an organization and spent the critical years of its initial consolidation in areas of Peru where the institutional presence of the state was most fragile. There exists an extensive bibliography that points out that revolutionary organizations and social rebellions tend to begin in frontier areas, or in areas less exposed to rapid reactions of the state apparatus (Wolf 1972; Winocur 1980; Vilas 1995a). In addition, a weakly integrated territory favors the regional or local persistence of social and political institutions and practices that officially do not exist from the point of view of the central authorities.

[7] On the spatial expansion of state power, see for example Slater (1989) and Brading (1991). On the ethnic question, see Urban and Scherzer (1991).

In multi-ethnic societies like those in the Andes or in Meso-America, different ethnic groups tend to be concentrated in specific areas, testimonies to the persistence of forms of social and political organization that may have little to do with the rationale of the modern state. Ethnicity has to do with symbolic elements of culture (beliefs, language, dress) but also with specific relations to nature (access to means of production, modes of economic or labor organization . . .) and to political power. In rural indigenous communities there can be electoral processes similar to those that are organized in an urban white or mestizo society; political parties can have a presence and activity in the communities. But it is doubtful that elections and parties will have the same meaning that they are given by mestizo voters in cities. A very plausible hypothesis might be that during what may be a long period, indigenous political institutions, loyalties, and authorities will continue to function, adapting themselves in a subaltern though vigorous way to the 'official' institutions.

The tensions, goals, and conflicts of popular participation and its relation with processes of democratization are a part of the problematique that arises from the contrast between the principle of unity typical of the modern state (such as it developed in England and France) and the profound fragmentation of Latin American societies. In turn, this fragmentation is a product as much of structural historical factors as it is an effect of political decisions (Aguiar 1990; Barbin 1991). Modernization in Latin America was a result of its external insertion, but the presence of traditional groups remained strong, above all in the area most closely linked to the international market: export production. The brutal exploitation of the labor force in the rural world and in mining constituted one of the supportive bases for world capitalism and for the reproduction of peripheral societies. Commodities were produced by a labor force that had not been fully commodified. In these conditions, there exists a close interdependence between backwardness and modernity that is evident in changing ways throughout the history of the region. In the sixteenth and seventeenth centuries it entailed slavery in mines and plantations integrated into European mercantile capitalism. Later on it involved servitude and peonage as a counterpart to industrial and financial capitalism. Dependent on the international market, Latin American capitalism developed in the sphere of circulation before doing so in the sphere of production, a situation that challenged attempts to interpret the patterns of Latin American development through a linear projection of the theoretical analyses rooted in European experiences. For the British economy, as for the United States and Japan, the international market was fundamentally an extension of its domestic markets. For Latin American capitalism, domestic markets are extensions of the international market.

The instability of political regimes in Latin America stems from this structural heterogeneity, which blends in a conflictive manner distinct forms of organization of the economy and of social relations (Pinto 1973; Thomas 1984). In such a structure, class domination is combined with racial and gender discrimination and with networks of kinship and lineage groups which together generate an extremely complex and weakly articulated matrix of relations of production, power, and social prestige. The state, through its agencies and policies, must contribute to the reproduction of an extraordinarily complex structure marked by tensions, conflicts, and contradictions of a very uneven nature, extent, and content. At the same time, the state must promote adaptation or transformation of that structure in response to changes in the world system. The conception of the state as an 'ideal collective capitalist' (Jessop 1982) is only partially pertinent here, since it neglects the fact that, along with the regulation and reproduction of social relations of advanced capitalism, state agencies and policies reproduce these other relations as well as the forms of social organization into which they are integrated.

This complex structural matrix is reinforced by some recent aspects of globalization: flexible accumulation, de-skilling of the labor force, polarization of income and technical progress, and the dispersion of levels of productivity, all of which nourish social and cultural fragmentation. This structure presents a conflictive and weak articulation among distinct forms of production and different modes of social organization, criteria of authority, and patterns of rationality. This matrix imprints on the state a particular combination of strength and vulnerability. Strength, in the sense that its coercive and repressive character must remain permanently exercised in order to guarantee that tensions resulting from its complex social base do not open the way to ungovernability or to the dismembering of the polis. Vulnerability, because of the fragmentation of opposed interests in the social body, which makes extremely fragile the achievement of a basic consensus and the granting of a minimal legitimacy to political power, its apparatuses, and functionaries. In other words, it imperils the conversion of power into authority. The weak base of consensus reduces the efficacy of institutional mechanisms for the processing of conflicts.

The conditions of social fragmentation, the persistence of communal affinities, and the international political and economic context favor a relation of non-correspondence between state and nation, between political geographies and historical-cultural identities. In addition, the growing globalization of the market and its actors—firms—clashes with the domestic character of the political system and its actors—parties, unions, and public bureaucracies. Moreover, the constitution of the 'national' dimension becomes a function of state mediation *vis-à-vis* the international system; the external articulation is the instance upon which certain actors ground their economic and political primacy as well as their eventual conversion into 'nationally' dominant groups. The dominant class within a nation is the group that can assure for itself the function of articulation with the international system. In these conditions, political responsibility shifts from the relationship between leaders and their domestic constituencies to the relationship between leaders and actors in the international arena. The strategic character of external relationships for the consolidation of domestic domination reduces the relevance of actors and their political participation in the internal market, thus calling into question the extent of rights of citizenship. It is not trivial to recall that processes of extending these rights—universal male suffrage, female suffrage, rights of organization—coincided with political strategies of social integration. Now, subordination of the domestic to the international market—deregulation, liberalization of trade and investment, financial conditionalities—subordinates, in turn, rights of political and social participation and resuscitates, in the new context, characters and political practices from the past: saviors of the fatherland, delegations of power, control and subordination of courts, among others.

Finally, in multi-ethnic societies, like those of the Andes and Meso-America, the definition of the nation assumes a particular kind of political and cultural domination which excludes from the nation the ethnically dominated groups. For example, the concept firmly implanted until very recently in most countries in the region, of an 'official language' (i.e. Castilian), discriminates against those 'dialects' and people that have not been socialized in the 'official language'. The delimitation of the nation is a merely territorial issue; the modern Latin American state is by definition, if not by historical formation, a 'nation-state' at the heart of which there coexist nations with unequal degrees of institutional recognition. Selverston shows how the construction of an indigenous identity in Ecuador involves a questioning of the putatively national and democratic character of the state, as it demands the transformation of both state structure and functioning.

The establishment of the modern state and its institutions involves the imposition of a specific type of domination and a particular form of legitimacy. Max Weber's 'rational-legal' legitimacy clashes and becomes intertwined with other types of domination and other forms of legitimacy, which express the heterogeneity of the social structure and the plurality of modes of social organization and political authority. The notion of citizenship is central to the official concept of the political system and refers to the subject of the nation-state and of democracy. Yet citizenship coexists with and is articulated through practices of clientelism and patronage, with patrimonialist and charismatic modes of exercising power, at the same time and in the same territory. Plurality of structure is expressed in a strong dose of particularism, as each social group pressures the state to obtain direct benefits. The idea of common goals and national interests, the possibility of presenting one's own objectives and interests as general interests, is inherently relative and tied to positions of power. In Latin America, it depends above all on the capacity of the state, its agencies, and its bureaucracy, to reach unstable and precarious equilibria in that context of overlapping pressures. For social groups with other referents and forms of organization, the idea of 'order' implicit in the concept of the nation-state can be synonymous with chaos and violence.

Every state encompasses by definition a form of imposition and some potential for compulsion. As the social system of domination develops and becomes stable, it is possible to extend the realm of consensus between dominators and dominated, and on this basis to construct the political institutions of the system. Yet this is not simply a matter of reaching agreement on the 'rules of the game', as observers frequently assert. Rather, it entails agreement on the foundations of political organization that enable the state to become a representative—real or virtual, effective or symbolic—of the entire society, a representative that the society recognizes as such and through which, to a greater or lesser degree but always to some degree, society feels expressed. In Gramscian terms, it is the conversion of domination into hegemony, and hegemony, again following Gramsci, is above all a historical-cultural process. The fragmentation of Latin American societies complicates enormously the achievement of this consensus around fundamental issues and the negotiation of a constitutional pact—in the substantive sense Ferdinand Lassalle assigned to the term constitution—upon which political coexistence can be forged. In many Latin American countries, including several of those considered in this book, dominant classes behave not as hegemonic but rather as conquering classes.[8] Domination is not cultural but coercive, and this is exacerbated in situations of crisis, when the economy operates as a zero-sum game in which surplus that goes to the international market is extracted at the expense of the domestic market, and income that is transferred upward no longer trickles down to those at the bottom. The tensions and instability that result from all of this are accentuated by the pace of economic transformations propelled by the international market. The timing of the economy is above all the timing of the international market and, in particular, of developed societies with their technological and financial leadership. Changes resulting from the transnational expansion of capitalism are imposed at a frenetic pace from the perspective of domestic actors and, above all, of the popular classes. The outcome is a profound disjuncture between formal institutions and social practices and, once again, between legality and legitimacy, and between politics and culture. The *México profundo* of Guillermo Bonfil Batalla, or the Peru of the *zorro de abajo* of José María Arguedas, experience these changes at a pace that is apparently more gradual and is in any case distinct. This opens greater opportunities for adaptation, processing, and eventually, for resistance.

This amount of tension creates opportunities for the entrenchment of political systems in which corporatist expressions of group interests—targeting state agencies—come to predominate over the formal institutions of a democracy of citizens organized through political parties. The political efficacy of pressure on state agencies and bureaucracies tends to displace the logic of the market onto the management of public resources. Despite neoliberal rhetoric, the capacity to influence decision-makers becomes an asset equally or more valid than efficiency in the management of the firm. Prebendalism, rent-seeking, and corruption are elements of the overall layout as much as private entrepreneurship, productivity increases, or technological innovation. The capacity to influence decisions of functionaries is not limited to economic compensation; relations of kinship and friendship, ethnicity, and regionalism tend to become as important as pecuniary resources for obtaining favorable decisions. All of this takes place in a framework

---

[8] I have borrowed this expression from the Brazilian sociologist Octavio Ianni.

of short-term time horizons and instability that narrows further as changes in the international system alter alliances and reduce the margin for maneuvering. Furthermore, the current bias of the global economy toward short-term financial investment increases the volatility of institutional settings and policy.

This network of basic loyalties and of mechanisms for participation operates relatively independent of political regimes and exhibits an extraordinary capacity to adapt to democratic as well as authoritarian regimes. Moreover, the characterization of a political regime as democratic or authoritarian reflects standard criteria that frequently become marginal, or affect only tangentially, this fundamental core of the social matrix of solidarities and relations of authority. It would be wrong, however, to focus on that matrix as an obstacle to democratization, though surely it does challenge the type of democratization entailed by the transitions considered in the conventional literature on the topic—a point discussed by Jonathan Fox in his chapter. One reason for the success of compensatory programs like PRONASOL in Mexico seems to be precisely its ability to integrate these mechanisms of participation with the state agencies and particular public policies, as discussed by Kerianne Piester. The chapters in this volume by Anthony Pereira, Kathryn Hochstetler, María Cook, Melina Selverston, and Monique Segarra point to the versatility of social actors, their ability to build associative networks, and their capacity to combine a very wide range of forms and strategies of participation, including a capacity to relate to state agencies.[9]

The fragmentation of society into different types of communities, ethnic and racial, local or regional, kinship-based, etc., is indicative of an incomplete process of social individuation. By this I refer to the process of constituting a society on the basis of personally free and independent *individuals*, whose social existence, rights, and obligations are not linked to their belonging to intermediate bodies (townships, kinship, profession) or to any other mechanic solidarities, in the Durkheimian sense. The process of individuation is one of the prerequisites for the existence of a civil society, and its principal engine is the gradual universalization of market relations. Thus, not every society is a civil society. Similarly, citizenship is not simply the recognition of formal rights but rather the outcome of a process—neither necessary nor inevitable—of particular, historically constituted political, economic, and cultural conditions (Van Gunsteren 1994; Turner 1993). The effective exercise of citizenship rights, and the mode of their exercise, is linked to the existence of the conditions that contribute to the formation of civil society: instrumental rationality, personal autonomy, resource endowments, and formal equality among individuals.[10]

In societies where communal identities are strong and the process of individu-

---

[9] Hoben and Hefner (1991) and Mazlisch (1991) discuss at length the articulation between the conventionally 'traditional' and the conventionally 'modern'.

[10] It is worth noting that this was a classist and androcentric conception of citizenship and civil society, which required the secular struggles of organized labor, socialist parties, and feminist movements in order to be overcome.

ation is weak, real inequalities are expressed transparently as formal inequalities. In these cases, one does not find political regimes of citizens, but rather what Gellner calls 'government by network'. Institutional rules are less important in these situations than personal arrangements and connections based on reciprocities, real or symbolic, explicit or implicit. Party loyalties matter to the extent that they correspond to personal, family, ethnic, or similar solidarities (Gellner 1994: 26). Current events and disclosures in Mexico prove that beneath the framework of the most modern-oriented formal civic institutions, clientelism and patronage relations tend to persist. Relations of friendship or kinship can open or close access to positions of power more effectively than legal provisions or party affinities.[11] Yet this opposition between individuation and organic networks should not be overemphasized nor presented as a total incompatibility. As Tarrow and others point out, one of the features in the initial stages of collective action is the mobilization of traditional networks (friends, relatives, neighborhoods . . .) in order to join processes that go far beyond the borders of kin or village community (Tarrow 1994, ch. 1; Vilas 1995a, ch. 1; also Seligman 1992, ch. 1). It is worth noting that this phenomenon is *not* exclusive to Latin America or to the developing world. What is perhaps uniquely Latin American, however, is that the slow individuation of society—inhibiting a more decisive development of a civil society from below—is combined with restrictions that many formally democratic regimes place on the generation of participatory associations and organizations independent of state agencies—restrictions 'from above' to the development of civil society.

The persistence of clientelist patterns of exercising political power, or the rise of new forms of clientelism, suggests a distinctive type of relationship between state and society. The private appropriation of public resources that clientelism implies calls into question the conventional separation between the public and the private. The (neo-)patron administers resources at his or her disposal as a function of particularist objectives, in the same way that the (neo-)client uses his or her vote as a function of equally particularist and short-term objectives. The *volonté générale* in these conditions, unlike that portrayed by liberal ideology, is an aggregation of micro-motivations and micro-rationalities. It is essential to point out that these aspects of clientelism are intertwined with the development of citizens' politics, and that they are found at the collective and not just at the individual level—as Jonathan Fox discusses in a later chapter in this volume.[12]

Regardless of whether the environment is one of citizenship, clientelism, or a mixture of both, political participation is participation in processes and institutions

---

[11] For example, Chalmers (1972); Guasti (1977); Rouquié (1982); Ai Camp (1982); Hermet (1983); Zeitlin and Radcliff (1988); Selby *et al.* (1990); Deere (1990); Edie (1991); Gil *et al.* (1993). The operation of modern parties on the base of clientelist relations and networks of particularist loyalties is, unfortunately, absent from the recent literature on the institutionalization of party systems. See for example Mainwaring (1988); Mainwaring and Scully (1994). Martz (1992) is an exception.

[12] Vilas (1993) notes the presence of neoclientelist elements in relationships between certain social movements, NGOs, and state agencies.

in which relevant decisions are taken about life, about welfare, about what people consider important. The mode of constitution of the state and its relations with society—the disjuncture between formal institutions and relations of power—displaces decisions toward spheres beyond the reach of popular participation. Democratic participation refers substantively to participation in decision-making processes. It assumes that democratic procedures lead to the adoption of democratic decisions, since the relation of representation links electors and representatives. Nevertheless, some scholars point out the growing disjuncture between procedures and decisions: either because decisions that are adopted have little to do with procedures (Franco 1994), or because new democracies conceal decision-making processes that, as in the past, take place elsewhere (Weffort 1992). For example, in almost every Latin American country, processes of economic adjustment and restructuring, which so severely altered people's living conditions, were carried out as a result of decisions taken, fundamentally, without consultation with the citizenry or meaningful participation by legislative bodies. The re-establishment of constitutional supremacy of civilian governments over the military is compatible with the preservation of a *de facto* veto power for the military (Loveman 1994). Privatizations of state enterprises were carried out insulated from public debate, parliaments, and even the stock exchanges.[13] Since democracy refers to something more than the police not repressing citizens, what does this insulation from vital discussions have to do with a democratic regime? Nevertheless, this 'reclusion' of policy from public control and participation does not apply equally to all: the declining involvement of unions and civic associations in public policy debates contrasts with the maintenance, and at times the strengthening, of participation by business associations or particular firms (Vilas 1994).[14]

The dislocation between representative institutions and political decisions, between the spheres in which people participate and the spheres in which decisions are made which determine living conditions for those same people, expands with the advance of processes of globalization and with the increasing weight of multilateral financial organizations which design the economic and social policies of states and impose rigid conditionalities upon them. The delegation, in the best of cases, or the loss, in most instances, of responsibilities and competencies that were once associated with the concept of sovereignty, and their transfer to international agencies, displaces the relation of political accountability to the outside. The state and its agencies cease to be accountable *vis-à-vis* their citizens; now they are responsible to international organizations (Held 1989, ch. 8; Held 1992: 360 ff). Governance becomes the central preoccupation of political analyses (Leftwich

[13] A specialized publication referred eloquently to the privatization of Telmex, the Mexican telecommunications firm, as 'a very private affair' (*Latin Finance*, 34, Mar. 1992). On the Argentine case, see Schvarzer (1993).

[14] Journalism is sometimes better than scholarly analysis at quickly detecting changes in political processes and contexts. Rodríguez Reyna (1993) discusses, for the Mexican case, what he terms the 'privatization of politics'.

1994; Williams and Young 1994; dos Reis Velloso 1994). This can be considered progress in the reports and recommendations of international bankers, but it is hardly such a thing from the perspective of political science. As noted above, it looks a great deal like a regression to the themes and approaches of the nineteenth century. Extracted from the context of relations of power, politics becomes public administration, and state activity is reduced to a set of rules, procedures, and legal institutions.

PARTICIPATION, INEQUALITY, AND POVERTY

> There has to be some economic and educational justice. We can't talk about holding hands and being friends when you have a job and I don't.[15]

The depth of social inequalities and the massive extent of impoverishment call into question the real existence of citizenship rights and foster forms of social and political confrontation with, or at the margins of, the institutional framework of democracy. This is not a new issue, but it has assumed dramatic proportions over the past decade. The Latin American population living in conditions of poverty grew during the 1980s by 80 million 'new poor', of whom 48 million live in cities. At the beginning of the 1990s, there were 196 million Latin Americans living in poverty, or 46 per cent of the total population (CEPAL 1992). During the past decade, Latin America has produced poor people at twice the pace of its total population. The entire Latin American population grew by 22 per cent while the poor increased by 44 per cent. This 'exclusionary style of development'—or 'development *cum* social exclusion' as several international organizations call it—conspires against the integrative principle which is implicit in every definition of citizenship or democracy (though cases and processes of accelerated and broad social exclusion do also occur in conventionally democratic political regimes) (Tenti 1993; Wolfe 1994; Silver 1994).

However it is defined (even in its minimal, procedural sense), democracy is an inclusive regime. It involves participation of all citizens in a polis that is seen as belonging to all—the res *publica* of the Romans or the Anglo-Saxon *commonwealth*. But the polis can hardly be considered as belonging to everyone when the principle of citizenship (as a synthesis of rights of participation and obligations of contribution) and the underlying idea of equality must coexist with profound and apparently growing inequalities in most countries, and with growing numbers of citizens who fall below the poverty line as a result of the restructuring of economies, changes in labor markets, the reform of the state, and the shifts in public policies. A movement of perverse causal reciprocity takes place in which inequality

---

[15] Statement of a black woman in Los Angeles, reported in the *New York Times*, 18 Apr. 1993, section A1.

Table 1.1. Changes in income polarization in some Latin American countries[a]

		(1) Lowest 20%	(2) Mid 60%	(3) Highest 20%	(4) (3 : 1)	Top 10%
Argentina	1986	5.0	54.9	40.1	8.0	34.1
	1991	4.6	42.5	52.9	11.5	36.9
Brazil	1983	2.4	35.0	62.6	26.1	46.2
	1989	2.1	30.4	67.5	32.1	51.3
Chile	1992	3.3	36.3	60.4	18.3	45.8
Guatemala	1981	5.5	39.5	55.0	10.0	40.8
	1989	2.1	34.9	63.0	30.0	46.6
Mexico[b]	1984	4.8	45.7	49.5	10.2	—
	1989	4.4	42.1	53.5	12.1	—
	1992	5.0	40.8	54.2	10.8	38.2
Peru	1985–6	4.4	43.7	51.9	11.8	35.8
Venezuela	1989	4.8	45.7	49.5	10.3	34.2

[a] Household income
[b] *Source*: Mexico's Instituto Nacional de Estadística, Geografía e Informática.
Source: World Bank.

increases poverty and poverty expands inequalities, and in which economic growth and growing poverty become entirely compatible (Vuskoviç 1993; Altimir 1994). What are the possibilities of consolidating political democracy when nearly half the population does not even earn the minimal benefits of development?[16]

Table 1.1 shows that in several Latin American countries considered in the essays that make up this volume, income polarization and resulting social inequalities increased over the last two decades. In Argentina, extreme income inequalities grew by almost one half in five years. In Brazil, they expanded by one-fifth during the 1980s, and in Guatemala they tripled over the same period. In Mexico, extreme inequalities diminished slightly in 1992 if compared to 1989, but remained deeper than in 1984. As illustrated by daily life in any Latin American metropolis, such extreme levels of social polarization militate against the possibility of developing an idea or feeling of common belonging. Those at the bottom are convinced that their needs, their insecurity, their lack of a place under the sun, result from or are in some way associated with the ostentatious prosperity of those

[16] The causal relation between inequality and poverty makes for a different situation from that which was evident a couple of decades ago, when the zero-sum quality of redistributive struggles was linked to the recessive phase of the economic cycle. Now things are different: the recuperation of growth does not imply the return to a cooperative framework. The growth of employment lags behind GDP growth, de-skilling of jobs downgrades wages and salaries, social spending is restricted, and income distribution not only does not improve but may even become more regressive. Unfortunately, these transformations of the economic dynamic are still not acknowledged in discussion of the linkages between the market economy and structural reforms to democratic politics: see for example Smith *et al.* (1994*b*) and the individual chapters included in their edited volume.

at the top. The latter, for their part, believe with equal conviction that resentment by those at the bottom imperils their lives and their fortunes, and they experience every demand of the former as a threat to their own well-being.

Anywhere, increased inequality and poverty are associated with growing levels of insecurity and violence, and Latin America is no exception. In Brazil and Guatemala, social polarization forms the background for the violence of everyday life, street children, gang warfare, police brutality and impunity. In Peru, the confrontation between Sendero Luminoso and the army placed many people in the middle of a shoot-out that seemed foreign to them. The demand for security and stability is especially intense in the 'hell of the poor', as it was labeled by Teffel (1969). The instability and insecurity that dominate the lives of the urban poor led Adler Lomnitz to refer graphically to them as the urban variant of hunting and gathering bands, which confronted the challenge of survival 'with the only resources at their disposal, their astuteness and their social solidarity' (Adler Lomnitz 1975: 96). The impact of 'structural precariousness' on the political behavior of the population that lives in these conditions was also discussed by Menéndez Carrión in her study of electoral support for Velasco Ibarra in Guayaquil (Menéndez Carrión 1989).

The dramatic rise of several mavericks in Latin American electoral politics (Fujimori, Collor de Mello, Menem) calls attention to the subjective factors that intervene in the gestation of popular support for these leaders: insecurity, uncertainty, and the search for defensive mechanisms, which always pave the road for the search, or acceptance, of political strongmen. These factors should not be seen as curiosities or as quaint aspects of underdevelopment. In the political philosophy of Thomas Hobbes, what moves people to constitute the state is precisely the search for security and the defense of their rights: 'the foresight of their own preservation, and of a more contented life thereby' (Hobbes 1973: 87). And indeed, everyday life in the Latin American world of joblessness, poverty, homelessness, and violence is highly reminiscent of Hobbes's state of nature, where there is 'no Society, and what is worst of all, continued feare, and danger of violent death; and the life of man, solitary, poore, nasty, brutish and short' (Hobbes 1973: 65). To the extent that each individual relates directly to the state, there is no place for civil society. As the image of the Leviathan suggests, the state is the exact sum of the individuals and exercises unmediated power over them. There are no rights *vis-à-vis* the state, nor legal constraints on its power.

It is worth emphasizing the contrast between this absolutist version of the political contract and that of the social contract, as a step prior to political contract, as introduced by John Locke half a century and a revolution later. For Locke, individuals are constituted as citizens first in civil society, which afterwards delegates specific powers to the state, powers that as a result are born limited by this delegation by civil society (Locke 1947). In Hobbesian theory, as in the real world of Latin American poverty today, the state is the absolute state, holding the power of ordering and organization. In populist or developmentalist conceptions of state–society relations, based on Keynesian–Fordist perspectives and strategies of extensive development, the 'contract' between the state and the popular classes was expressed on an everyday level through four basic public institutions: the school, the hospital, public works and employment, and the police. In the neoliberal conception, public works and employment retreats, schools do not function, and hospitals close. The 'self-management of civil society' is basically a *bellum omnia contra omnes*, an 'everyone for herself or himself', and relations between the state and the popular classes are processed primarily through the coercive apparatuses of the state. The popular classes become *classes dangereuses*.[17]

The descent into this condition of poverty and insecurity severely affects the principle of citizenship as formulated by Anglo-Saxon liberal political theory and exported to Latin America. According to this theorization, individual actors are the constitutive elements and effective political actors of a democratic regime. The foundation of democratic political life resides in the autonomy of the individual. In contrast, the destructuring impact of the economic crisis and downward social mobility shift people toward the strengthening of communitarian identities: what Geertz (1973) called 'primordial attachments' or what Bourdieu (1980) called 'retreat to the *habitus*', the household, kinship or ethnic group, communal allegiances.

This retreat takes place in a context in which, as noted above, the process of individuation of society is still incomplete and develops in a manner distinct from that which occurred as a result of capitalist development and the universalization of market relations (Franco 1993). As a result, it is a more rapid return to communitarian identities but also a more difficult one. It is more rapid because where communal structures persist, or where there is a non-stabilized urban demography, one never finishes leaving or separating from the spheres and forms of organization to which one returns. And it is more difficult because it involves a defensive attitude that places additional demands on communitarian structures that find themselves subjected to severe pressures by the very restructuring of the economy and the reorientation of state agencies. The family is as much a support as a burden; the traditions and rites of community generate solidarity at the same time as they create expenses. In this defensive movement, the solution of everyday problems becomes the central focus of actors; the rationale of political behavior is determined above all by the ability of individual and collective action to achieve material sustenance and a minimal level of security.

The growing number of countries where electoral procedures are implemented means that in today's Latin America there are more citizens than ever, but there are also more poor people than ever. Under these conditions, a democracy of first- and second-class citizens emerges, as one can see from the degree of public

---

[17] According to a recent census of the incarcerated population in Brazil, 95 per cent of the more than 126,000 inmates throughout the country lived in absolute poverty prior to their detention. According to this study, the 'typical Brazilian inmate' is male, black, illiterate or semi-literate, is imprisoned for the first time, and lacks money to pay for a lawyer; the most frequent crime is robbery or theft. *Excelsior* (Mexico City), 9 Aug. 1993.

consternation and the rapid state intervention provoked by the exercise of violence against some (for example, the kidnapping for ransom of a businessman) and the indifference towards the violence exercised with impunity against others (for example, the murder of a worker or student, or the rape of an indigenous woman). What democracies are we talking about in these contexts of broad and apparently growing social polarization, of people who surround their homes with electric fences and night watchmen so that the homeless are not tempted to stick their noses (or their hands) in? Pinheiro's answer is that we are dealing with 'democracies without citizenship', as the basic conditions for the exercise of citizenship are denied systematically to millions of men and women—a peculiar democracy indeed!

This line of argument should not, however, lead us to a dualist approach to the social fabric, in the manner of abstract Marxism (bourgeoisie/proletariat), nor to the operational categories of international organizations (poor/non-poor). In the real world there is much more than poor people and non-poor people, bourgeois and proletarians. For above all in Latin America there are the middle classes, which inspired a voluminous literature during the 1950s and 1960s, and which enjoyed much of the benefits of extensive growth, the broadening of the educational system, and the expansion of the public sector. The middle classes participated actively in the mobilizations of 'new' social movements, and today they are victims of privatization, deregulation, declining social spending, and of the increasingly open jaws of social polarization—in a kind of revival of the torment of Túpac Amaru exacerbated by the centrifugal tendencies of neoliberalism. Table 1.1 shows that in several countries the greater concentration of income in the highest levels of the social structure occurred not at the expense of the poorest, from whom it is difficult to extract any more, but at the expense of those in the middle. An important and usually very aggressive part of the 'new poor' in Latin America is recruited from these urban middle-class sectors, including those who are relatively well educated and informed. These are the students without diplomas, professionals without patrons, technicians without techniques, families without homes, small businessmen without businesses.

Social polarization is reinforced by state policies, which have abandoned countercyclical measures and operate now in the same direction as the market: they concentrate and strengthen towards the top; they disorganize towards the bottom. Extreme social polarization reduces the range of state policy instruments and their capacity to maintain inequalities within certain limits. Social polarization seems to be a process that feeds off itself. This turns the middle classes into the turkey at the neoliberal banquet, a circumstance that contributes to the explanation for the disenchantment and disillusion that reaps so many of their literary representation. Tax reforms are successfully resisted by the groups with highest incomes, who in principle could contribute more, and prove meaningless for actors with the lowest incomes, from whom it proves impossible to extract any more. Tax policy is thus aimed at the middle groups, from whom it is still possible to extract resources, and who offer little resistance. It is noteworthy in this regard that the few tax reforms adopted in recent years have consisted of the introduction of value added and other indirect taxes, which play an increasing role in tax collection, while taxes on property and income weigh very little. Indirect taxes are tied to consumption of goods and services with low income-elasticity of demand that make up a larger proportion of the consumption basket of families as their level of income diminishes. Thus, middle- and low-income families are forced to pay comparatively more for a state that spends comparatively less to meet their needs. Contrary to what is suggested by liberal democratic theory, in Latin America those who make decisions do not pay, and those who do pay do not make decisions.

A 'NEW POLITICS' OF INEQUALITY, OR MORE OF THE SAME?

To what extent or in what sense are we facing something really new, or are we just witness to an updating of well-known ingredients of the Latin American political *longue durée*? Increasing poverty and social polarization have been going on for more than a decade, and the gap between formal political institutions and actual political behavior is not an uncommon feature of Latin American politics.

Political changes—as well as changes in other dimensions of life—do not happen out of the blue; new events, actors, processes, or settings take place in a progressive way, intertwined with the inertia of already existing ingredients. Separating the new elements from the old and renewed ones is neither an easy task nor is it frequently a useful one. More often than not, what is novel lies in a particular combination of specific factors, rather than in the particular intervening 'pieces'.

O'Donnell's characterization of 'delegative democracies' is a pertinent case in point. 'Delegative democracy' has been suggested by O'Donnell as a new type of political regime that fits recent social and economic changes in a number of Latin American countries—a suggestion accepted in several chapters in this book. 'Delegative democracies' combine a number of well-known traditional ingredients of Latin American politics—such as caudillismo, patron–client networks, parliamentary subservience to the executive, insulation of key decisions from the public debate, lack of accountability of top government officers—with electoral processes (the 'first transition' to democracy) and a delegation of power on behalf of the president, who is thereby entitled to conduct government affairs 'as he or she sees fit' (O'Donnell 1991, 1995). What enables O'Donnell to conceptualize these regimes as democracies is the appeal to elections. It is this specific procedure which places this particular 'political animal' within the realm of democracies, distinguishing it from the 'bureaucratic-authoritarian' regimes of the recent past—which, as O'Donnell admits, share a number of traits with so-called delegative democracies.

The very notion of a 'delegative democracy' poses a number of conceptual issues which I cannot address here.[18] In any case, O'Donnell himself does not make clear whether he is actually identifying a new type of political regime, or just recording the re-emergence, in an electoral setting, of long-standing ingredients of political culture and history.[19] The answer is not an easy one, particularly when one considers the Mexican case—which O'Donnell once again excludes from his discussion, as he previously did when writing about bureaucratic authoritarianism. As a matter of fact, every ingredient of delegative democracies is present in the Mexican political regime, from increasingly competitive elections to systematic congressional subordination to the executive, to little if any public accountability of government officials—including the accepted non-accountability of the incumbent and former presidents. The Mexican regime pre-dates the 1980s economic crisis; some academic approaches have referred to it as a non-military case of bureaucratic-authoritarian regime (Reyna and Weinert 1977), notwithstanding its regular appeal to elections. Mexico has been changing over the last two decades, yet the most relevant changes seem to be more in academic approaches to the political regime than to the regime itself, or even to an implicit equation between further democratization and opposition parties winning elections. Certainly, Mexico's official political discourse conceals what Menem and Fujimori's rhetoric exposes or even exaggerates; and Carlos Salinas de Gortari's outlook was much more sophisticated than those of his South American colleagues. However, economic and social policies implemented by all of them stem from the same conceptual and ideological blueprint, as do the respective institutional settings of personalized leadership and strongly centralized decision-making, as well as a complex private/public mix where family and relatives' businesses mingle with government affairs.

What is new in these 'delegative', semi-authoritarian, election-based regimes, refers less to their institutional make-up than, first, to the content of the decisions made by office-holders; second, to relations between political institutions and society; and, therefore, third, to the way power relations are institutionally expressed and processed.

As stated above, electoral support for some variant of capitalist rule is not news in Latin America. Rather, the novelty lies in consistent electoral support for governments implementing neoliberal programs as a specific, exclusionary variant of capitalist economics and political rule. Pre-1980s attempts at neoliberal designs were conducted in heavily authoritarian institutional settings, usually involving

[18] For example, who is the active subject of delegation: the voters? the parliament? Is delegation an empirical fact or a theoretical assumption, such as the 'social contract' in liberal political theory, or the *Grundnorm* in Hans Kelsen's legal philosophy? Or is it just a metaphor? Are we dealing with an empirical/hypothetical/metaphorical act of delegation or with a particular version of standard 'elitist democracy', as addressed in either Przeworski (1991*a*: 10 ff) or Held (1992: 175 ff)? To what extent are these 'delegative democracies' different from traditional strong presidential regimes, such as those in Mexico, or even in the Dominican Republic during Joaquin Balaguer's governments?

[19] The depth of these doubts is illustrated by the fact that the 1995 English version of O'Donnell's piece reproduces almost verbatim the original 1991 Brazilian version.

military coups and *de facto* governments (Sheahan 1980; Waisman 1987; Pion-Berlin 1989; Collins and Lear 1995). Political repression of unions and progressive political parties enabled a drastic recomposition of the profit rate, and the abolition of individual rights and imprisonment or killing of citizens were employed to build a free economy. Quite to the contrary, what we are witnessing from the late 1980s on is neoliberal economics *cum* electoral politics and party competition, and a more effective enactment of civic and individual rights.

Does this mean that after being fed up with populist demagoguery and unfulfilled promises of sustainable welfare, the citizenry, particularly low- and middle-income citizens, eventually realized the virtues of a market economy and the evils of corporatism and state interventionism? Such is the assumption of both neoliberal policy-makers and international financial agencies (Lindenberg and Devarajan 1993; Williamson 1993; Haggard and Webb 1994).[20] However, this assumption is not supported by the empirical evidence, stemming, for example, from post-electoral field surveys, and cannot be treated as other than a hypothesis to be tested. It is hard to state in an aprioristic manner what people are thinking about when they vote for a particular candidate, what they see in, or expect from, him or her. Do people see in Menem the political umbrella for Cavallo's *plan de convertibilidad* or, on the contrary, its political counterbalance? Or do they just see the presidential candidate of the Justicialista Party, or the strongman equating himself with price stability? Is Fujimori the maverick of neoliberal restructuring, or the man who defeated Shining Path and thus afforded voters some longed-for basic stability in their lives? The analysis is further complicated by the fact that 'the people' involves such a variety of labor, gender, class, ethnic identities, allegiances, and combinations. In fact, we do not have enough evidence either to directly link massive majorities for Menem or Fujimori to a particular economic policy design, or to reject such an association. We only have a general coincidence, not a specific relation which isolates other intervening factors. Moreover, what we do know is that, whenever neoliberal programs have been explicitly submitted to public scrutiny through a vote (as in the December 1993 Uruguayan plebiscite, or in the November 1995 Ecuadorian referendum), they have been rejected and defeated—a point which is partially discussed in Filgueira and Papadópulos's chapter.

Be that as it may, these centralized regimes—just when decentralization becomes one of the catchwords of neoliberal reforms—give concrete expression to the neoliberal aspiration of 'insulating technical decisions' from particularistic, short-sighted societal pressures (World Bank 1993; Haggard and Kaufman 1995*a*). Alongside the celebration of democracy, 'delegative' regimes afford the institutional setting to advance policies and decision-making which in the past were insulated from middle- and low-income groups through overt authoritarianism or dictatorship. By the same token, they sponsor an unprecedented marriage of majority

---

[20] The title of Haggard and Webb's book (*Voting for Reform*) is tricky; the book does not deal with electoral processes where neoliberal reforms are involved, but with administrative dealings.

rule, even openly popularistic styles, with exclusionary economic designs. As long as there are elections, there is a democratic ingredient. So long as key decisions are insulated from public discussion, and opposing or merely alternative views are prevented access to public consideration or are officially discredited, there is an authoritarian appeal to democratic institutions.[21] Yet, delegative 'insulation' is uneven and works in a different fashion and to a different extent with regard to different actors. Shrinking parliamentary and political party involvement in policy-making affects the average citizen much more than it does those who are high above the average, namely, the most strategic actors of neoliberal economics. Lobbying, 'media politics', or bribery, strategies not available to every actor in the political system, substitute for open party competition.

These and other changes in the current political setting referred to in previous sections evolved as a follow-up, and to a great extent as an outcome, of what Cavarozzi has termed 'the exhaustion of the state-centered matrix' in Latin America, pointing to the state/market/society framework which developed in countries such as Mexico, Brazil, Argentina, Chile, and Uruguay beginning in the 1930s (Cavarozzi 1992*a*). This in turn may be interpreted as a dimension of technological, political, and economic shifts in the world system. Yet it would be excessive to understand this as an outright transition towards a 'market-centered matrix'. What we are witnessing is in fact a restructuring of state–market relations that involves a redefinition of power relations among social, economic, and political actors (Ibarra 1990; Vilas 1993, 1995*c*). Such a restructuring involves the state's withdrawal at the microeconomic level, for example through privatization of government-owned assets, as well as at the macroeconomic level, such as through financial and trade deregulation. This is simultaneous with increased intervention in other macroeconomic processes, e.g. fixing exchange and interest rates, setting the conditions for privatization (including who is going to compete for what assets, in what terms, and with what chances to succeed), and directing public foreign indebtedness towards specific goals. It also involves microeconomic state intervention on behalf of particular firms, as in the current case of the Mexican government's salvation of recently privatized banks.

There is no doubt that today's Latin American state is smaller than two decades ago; yet just as important as this reshaping of state agencies is the redefinition of the actors who are the recipients of state intervention—which has to do with shifts in power relations. To this extent 'state reform' involves the dismantling or severe transformation of institutions that, in the previous political-economic and cultural setting, fostered social participation together with both direct and indirect income distribution as core dimensions of political democratization. The 'retreat of the state' exposes low- and middle-income actors to a market whose biases toward multinational firms, financial investment, and large capital owners are now unchecked. According to some interpretations, these biases become politically

---

[21] For a lengthy discussion see Vilas (1995*b*); Panfichi and Sanborn (1995).

reinforced by the new 'public/private mix', despite compensatory efforts such as those discussed by Monique Segarra in her chapter on Ecuador's social investment funds.

These shifts in power relations may be interpreted as a case of 'political attrition'—albeit an attrition with regard to specific, popular actors, which is combined with renewed political support for big business, financial speculation, and the like. Accordingly, the affected actors—consumers, workers, women, indigenous populations—tend to look for different scenarios and organizational arrangements to advance their own demands, from NGOs and new associative networks to armed confrontation intended to force governments to the negotiating table, as in Chiapas.

As conventional institutional politics recedes with respect to popular actors, the social realm enhances itself. While politics at the state-national level becomes reoriented to meet the 'global' agenda, local-level politics turns out to be an increasingly expressive setting for popular participation—the 'niche' for politics 'from below'.

However, there is not enough evidence to support an interpretation of the ongoing popular shift towards the social sphere as a more or less permanent retreat from politics. Both the Brazilian experience of PT and the more recent case of Guatemala's Frente Democrático Nueva Guatemala show an ongoing, complex, and uneven process in which social movements' retreat from politics and search for alternative channels, such as NGOs or direct action, is followed sooner or later by the construction of new types of political organizations. In this way, entities such as the PT and FDNG, or the Venezuelan Causa R, or even the proposed 'Frente Zapatista de Liberación Nacional' tend to overcome previously existing tensions between movements and traditional political parties.

2. Participation and Representation

Economic, political, and institutional transformations that took place at the end of the 1980s and early in the 1990s introduced a variety of changes in Latin American political actors. Economic restructuring, the consolidation of the institutions of representative democracy, the reform of the state with its emphasis on deregulation and privatization, and external rearticulation, dramatically changed the context for collective action and contributed to a redefinition of winners and losers. The change in context decisively affected the attitudes and behaviors of individual and collective actors. Adjustment to the new economic and institutional environment encompassed 'new' actors—particularly the array of social movements that had become one of the most active protagonists of democratization processes—as well as 'traditional' ones, like political parties and labor unions.

THE ADJUSTMENT OF ACTORS: UNIONS

The first part of this volume discusses three cases of 'traditional' social actors attempting different ways of adapting to the new environment. The growth of informal employment, the contraction of stable wage employment, and the decline of mechanisms of tripartite (government–business–unions) collective bargaining, have called into question the projects and union strategies that prevailed until recent years. Economic adjustment and state reform have dealt severe blows to Latin American unions at a moment when the wounds have not yet healed from the economic crisis of the 1980s and the authoritarian regimes of the recent past. The chapters by Scott Martin, Victoria Murillo, and Anthony Pereira discuss the role of those elements in Brazil and Argentina which led to different strategies to adapt to a context that was hardly favorable to traditional union strategies. The authors show that, even in the most difficult circumstances, unions attempt to adapt and seek to maintain an active role in the labor market. In this search for alternatives, particularly relevant roles are played by the ingredients of working-class political culture as they emerged from the previous era, the organizational structures and internal democracy of unions, and the type of relationships that are forged among unions, firms, and the state.

In Argentina, the strategy that Murillo calls 'organizing autonomy', and that others might consider simply as a metamorphosis of the union into a business enterprise, pushes some unions to participate in the process of privatizing state enterprises and the pension and retirement systems, buying up part or all of the assets of formerly state-owned firms. This primarily involves organizations that in the past had a fluid relationship with the state because of the economic sectors in which they operated or because of ideological agreement with governing teams, and whose rank and file were severely reduced by the economic crisis and by the process of privatization itself. Several unions that chose this strategy had been very important strongholders of populist corporatism and long-standing targets of criticism from independent unions for their lack of political autonomy or for the lack of transparency in the way they administered their funds. Murillo describes the variants of this strategy, which opens a new organizational and operational dimension for these groups at the same time as it calls into question the accuracy of continuing to consider them standard unions. The issues of labor and social conflict, around which unions were created as mechanisms for defending their members, are transferred inside the union itself once the latter takes on the role of entrepreneur. In any case, this strategy presents new issues regarding the relationship between these unions/entrepreneurs and their members/employees.

Scott Martin focuses on one process of union adaptation to the new conditions of accommodation through negotiation with the corresponding business associations, aiming toward a reactivation of production and markets that distribute profits to workers and their organizations. Several elements analyzed by Martin highlight the uniqueness of the Brazilian case. These include the stable and active commitment of the Brazilian state to industrial growth and industrial exports, and at the same time as its consideration of the internal market as a dynamic component of development; the existence of a new generation of industrial workers and a new type of union organization which, without repudiating corporatist elements in government's and business strategies, emphasize union autonomy and manage to combine confrontation with bargaining in its relations with the state and firms; and a sustained growth of the industrial proletariat and of union membership throughout the decade.[22] The reforms introduced by the Fernando Henrique Cardoso administration partially modified this panorama without altering it fundamentally. The long strike by oil workers in 1995 did not succeed, but Cardoso's government chose to use its greater leverage at the end of the strike to begin a period of reflection on the reshaping of government–union relations instead of an offensive on union involvement in policy-making.

Pereira's chapter analyzes changes experienced by rural unions in the Brazilian north-east and calls attention to the ability of popular organizations, and the participation they foster, to introduce changes in their structure and strategies that were not foreseen in the literature on social movements. In particular, the analysis forces us to reconsider part of the accepted wisdom on populist regimes and corporatism with regard to popular organizations. The case of Pernambuco suggests that the rural labor movement was more pluralist and autonomous *vis-à-vis* the state during the populist period than during the process of democratic transition of the 1980s and 1990s, when the rural union movement remained much more subordinate to the state and took on a more decidedly classist character. According to Pereira, changes in the rural class structure and in the strategies of mobilization under the military regime can explain 'the construction of an "old" movement on the foundations of a "new" one'. His analysis also questions an assertion common to much of the literature on new social movements, which suggests that ties with the state automatically negate movements' potential for confrontation.

THE ADAPTATION OF ACTORS: PARTIES AND MOVEMENTS

Challenges have been equally daunting for political parties and social movements. In countries such as Argentina, Brazil, Chile, Guatemala, and Peru, the re-establishment of representative democracy returned political parties to the center of political activity and restored their traditional role of aggregating social interests and mediating between society and the state. At the same time, the restora-

---

[22] According to ILO records, between 1980 and 1992 Brazil's economically active population grew by 188 per cent (35 million) and employment in manufacturing almost tripled (198 per cent or 8.4 million). Union membership increased from 1.6 million workers in the aftermath of the 1964 military coup, to 14 million by the mid-1980s. In Mexico, in contrast, manufacturing employment declined by 1.3 million workers from 1988 to 1992 (ILO, several years).

tion of representative democracy privileged a specific mode of participation—the vote—subsuming the plurality of social actors under the unifying principle of citizenry. The new institutional context lacked specific space for social movements, and in practice they were reduced to roles as outside pressure groups. In this way, a disjuncture occurred between the broad character of social movements which had promoted democratization and the restrictive character of the emerging democratic regimes, even of those which resulted from those very mobilizations. In particular, there was tension between the democratic principle of majority rule and the decisions—political, economic, diplomatic, etc.—that were adopted by government agencies and political elites. Of course, there is tension in any democratic system between the principle of participation, which refers to the meaningful involvement of the citizen, and the principle of representation, involving delegation, but in Latin America this was exacerbated by economic restructuring and the deepening of social inequalities. Tensions emerged as well between social movements that espoused a broad agenda for democratization, and 'official' actors in electoral politics—parties—which often had a much more narrow agenda.

The second section of the book explores the tormented relationship between parties and movements from a variety of different but complementary perspectives. Focusing on the evolution of the environmentalist movement in Brazil, Hochstetler highlights the capacity of some social movements to adapt to changing situations to play a variety of political roles (interest representation, definition of identities, institutional transformation of the state, generation of an informal polity) and to promote a broad repertoire of strategies that include institutional and non-institutional options. Hochstetler also examines the difficulties of the state and of left political organizations in accepting these movements' claims for autonomy: proposals for alternative forms of treating the biosphere question have involved developmentalist assumptions shared by the Right and the Left alike, challenging traditional modes of relating state and society. In a similar vein, Selverston examines the way in which indigenous mobilizations and organization in Ecuador arise to promote the recognition of a social and cultural identity, questioning the organization and functioning of the state and of political and economic domination. Selverston discusses the tension between a focus on class and a focus on ethnicity that characterizes indigenous mobilizations, and she points to the role of political and economic factors in the construction of new social and cultural identities. Identity becomes much more than a symbolic question; it is transformed into a weapon for critique and advancing alternative proposals for the multiethnic reconstitution of the state and not only for the reform of the political regime.

The chapter by Aldo Panfichi explores the factors that shape the decision of impoverished urban masses to opt for personalist political leaders who are relatively marginal to the party system and representative institutions. Such factors include (1) a sharp and accelerated deterioration in their living conditions, which fosters a sense of insecurity and instability; (2) the inability of traditional political actors (parties, unions, government agencies) to reverse the situation or to make it less severe, which translates into a sense of frustration or disenchantment toward those actors; and (3) a political tradition or style that emphasizes the efficacy of 'strong' leaders to solve the problems of the people. As Panfichi points out, there is a parallel of sorts between Alberto Fujimori and Abimael Guzmán, the 'President Gonzalo' of Sendero Luminoso. In addition to personal biographies distinguished by marginality with respect to 'official' politics, the organization led by Guzmán was an effective alternative of confrontation with the state for sectors of the urban and rural popular classes. This issue is a central point in Burt's chapter. To be sure, the methods usually resorted to by Sendero were brutal and out of proportion, but it is not unreasonable to accept that in contexts defined by violence and racism—itself a form of violence—Sendero's performance may seem less bizarre. In any case, it is important to emphasize a certain pattern in the political behavior of the urban poor in Peru, who follow options that emerge, at least initially, as alien and opposed to 'the system'. This was true of the Peruvian generals in the 1960s and 1970s, of Alfonso Barrantes and Izquierda Unida for a very brief period in the 1980s, and of Fujimori and Sendero more recently (Cameron 1991*a*, 1991*b*; Panfichi and Francis 1993). The case of Fujimori is not unique, although it is the most successful; the career of Fernando Collor de Mello turned out to be much more brief and less spectacular, but there are macrosocial as well as personal factors which liken him to Fujimori (Oliveira 1992; Moisés 1993) and, in a sense, to Carlos Menem in Argentina as well (Novaro 1994).

The psychosocial elements that lend support for these strongmen reflect very concrete situations. Fear is fear of hunger, of joblessness, of the abuse of power by police or vigilantes. People do not invent fear; things that cause fear or generate insecurity are integral to their everyday experience. As remarked earlier in this chapter, poverty and insecurity frequently seed the ground for authoritarianism.[23] In fact, there also exists the phenomenon of a state policy of promoting fear. Consider, for example, Carlos Menem's insistence on presenting himself as the sole alternative to the return of hyperinflation; or the 'selective' punitive actions in Argentina against critical journalists or members of the opposition; or the never complete disappearance of impunity and of repressive parastatal groups.[24]

Nevertheless, not everything is fear and insecurity. It is possible to distinguish two moments in the support for these neocaudillos of neoliberalism. At first emotional factors appear determinant. But at second glance it seems that a more instrumental-rational approach becomes privileged: the effectiveness of the

---

[23] A USAID-sponsored survey recently conducted in the Dominican Republic shows that what may be called 'benevolent authoritarianism'—i.e. the belief that only a strong leader can take care of the people's problems and improve their lots—is stronger amongst the poor than among the middle or upper socioeconomic levels; among Blacks; among women; in people with lower educational levels; and in the young and the elderly—i.e. among those who are trying to enter the labor market and those who are leaving it with empty hands (see Duarte *et al.* (1995)).

[24] Pion-Berlin (1989) studies the creation of fear in Argentina and Peru as a rational state strategy, and analyzes its linkages with particular strategies of economic policy. Rodríguez Kauth (1994) conducts a provocative discussion of the issue.

leader in resolving or managing some of the most urgent problems of the impoverished urban people. Support is forged emotionally, but it is maintained and nourished by a system of trade-offs between services and loyalties. In the final analysis, it involves a traditional political relationship in a context that is not traditional. We no longer find the typical populist caudillo who links himself emotionally to the masses to incorporate them in a subordinate manner to a style of extensive and mobilizing development (full employment, import substitution, expansion of social services, social security).

Rather, these are neocaudillos who seek to create mechanisms to enhance the prospects for governability in a political and economic context that must combine the principle of majority rule with evidence that profits accrue to minorities. This is a rare combination, attained through dramatic drops in inflation rates, high rates of economic growth, and productivity increases, together with frozen or receding real wages, shrinking employment levels in the formal labor market, and targeted social policies aimed at several of the issues around which the poor tend to mobilize: land titles, personal security, and access to basic services, such as electricity, sewage, and running water.

The chapters by Kathleen Bruhn and Margarita López-Maya consider two cases in which the search for alternatives is directed toward organizational actors. Both Mexico and Venezuela experienced economic crises and dislocations which severely eroded living conditions for broad sectors of the working and middle classes, with the existing political system demonstrating the inability or the unwillingness to face the problem. In contrast with Peru, however, in Mexico and Venezuela the existence of a more solid political system operated in such a way that the search for alternatives was directed toward political organizations that, despite what some analysts have seen with consternation as a reemergence of personalist leaderships (Zermeño 1989), represented a 'new' type of actor. Focusing on the case of the Mexican left, Bruhn explores the achievements and frustrations of efforts to establish stable relationships between popular movements and left parties. Such relationships would enable movements to incorporate their perspectives into parties, rather than simply 'lending' them their votes, and would lead the parties to project social demands beyond the local and state levels. In short, it is the old and always complex problem of how to blend participation and representation. In the case that Bruhn studies, the difficulties derive from the new and not fully structured character of the Party of the Democratic Revolution (PRD), as well as from the fragmentation of social movements, and the intelligent, effective state response of deepening fragmentation while providing compensation through direct relationships between movements and government agencies.

López-Maya, in turn, reconstructs the long and little-known process of formation of 'Causa R', a party that resists easy labeling in conventional ideological terms, and that has succeeded in its efforts to capture growing portions of the citizens' vote (in contrast to the 'social vote' discussed by Bruhn). The citizens' vote of Causa R is not socially random, but it is processed and expressed in a looser tie with social movements, and in the 1994 elections it was linked closely to the growing level of urban street protest. The chapter by López-Maya highlights at the same time the significance of institutional factors in favoring or impeding the advance of particular political organizations.

The case analyzed by Bruhn contrasts with that discussed by William Nylen in this same volume. Mexico's strong political centralism and the extremely close relationship between the PRI and the state reduces the outreach of regional politics and the effective functioning of a municipal level of government. Moreover, political violence reaches its peak at the municipal level. In contrast, processes of political decentralization and municipalization were always more advanced in Brazil, enabling the local level to overcome many of the conflicts between parties and movements that proved particularly difficult to resolve at the national level. The local focus of government action permits closer monitoring by social organizations and generates a more dynamic interaction between them and government agencies. The experience of municipal administration of the Frente Amplio in Montevideo, as is discussed by Peter Winn and Lilia Ferro-Clérico, can be seen in a similar vein.[25] At the same time, ties between the local government and local organizations of the governing party to national structures provide some room for maneuver with respect to broader policy issues—external debt, public spending, price policy, deregulation, among others—that affect local life but which grassroots social organizations have little capacity to act upon directly.

The comparison between the cases of the PRD and Causa R also illustrates the importance of the timing factor for the formation and consolidation of political alternatives, an issue that is often overlooked by the short-term bias of academic analyses. Today Causa R is clearly one of the axes of Venezuelan politics, much in the same way as the PT is in Brazil. Yet, very few academic observers assigned any importance to the PT twenty years ago, or to Causa R fifteen years ago. Saviors of the fatherland arise overnight; organizations do not. It is important to keep this in mind so that the conclusions we extract today from the performance of the Mexican PRD—or Frente Grande in Argentina, or Papa Egoro in Panama, or FDNG in Guatemala—are not (for better or worse) refuted a few years down the road.

PARTICIPATION AND VIOLENCE

The monopoly on the legitimate use of violence is one of the basic attributes of any modern state. This is not exactly the case in Latin America, where for reasons that we cannot discuss here, the state admits recourse to violence by private actors and is not in a condition to prevent or repress it. To the extent that the legitimate monopoly over violence is part of the definition of the borders between state

---

[25] Schönwälder (1993) refers to these same issues in the case of Lima.

and society, the private recourse to violence and the privatization of state violence point to the existence of forms of state–society relations that establish a particular problematique and demand specific treatment. Part III addresses some aspects of this issue regarding the use of public violence as a power resource; the privatization of state violence that is focused upon particular social actors; and the recourse to violence by social actors as a rational option for survival—a *rational* option that is not necessarily a *voluntary* option.

According to Deborah Yashar, in Guatemala state violence is one of the fundamental axes around which politics is organized. Whether openly or under cover of civilian institutions, military authoritarianism as a quintessential expression of state power drives popular organizations to act at the margins of the political system, in virtual clandestinity or at least extra-legality, in ways better suited to rallies of protest than to participation. Yashar compares popular mobilizations in the 1940s that overthrew the Ubico dictatorship with those of today; she finds elements of strong continuity in the state's use of violence. Violence expresses the class character of state domination in Guatemala, for this is a state that, as Yashar describes it, has a rifle in one hand and money in the other. At the same time, violence is the predominant form of interaction between the state and elites on the one hand and popular social actors on the other. Yashar shows that this type of state–society relationship does not prevent popular protests from opening significant spaces to voice their opposition while it limits their achievements, since state violence keeps the marginality of popular organizations with respect to the political system, and complicates democratization of the popular organizations themselves. However, a new political setting seems to have emerged through the government/URNG peace talks, which involve a number of sensitive social, economic, and ethnic issues. The November 1995 general elections introduced a new political coalition of popular organizations (the aforementioned FDNG), which received about 10 per cent of the national vote, elected six parliamentary representatives, and in addition gained seats in some twenty municipal governments.

Paulo Sérgio Pinheiro focuses on a similar theme but places greater emphasis on the role of the state—a 'soft' state despite its huge bureaucratic size—and on the autonomy and impunity of repressive agencies. Pinheiro underscores the real possibility of legal recognition and exercise of political and civil rights in settings where basic human, social, and economic rights are systematically violated. The progressive, sequential expansion of citizenship, as portrayed by T. H. Marshall's theory of social citizenship, is called into question. This is not only because, as the Peruvian sociologist Carlos Franco notes, in Latin America social citizenship often preceded political citizenship or was obtained simultaneously with it (Franco 1994), but also because, as emerges from Pinheiro's analysis, there exists a profound gap between one and the other, in the context of a democratic institutional framework.

Jo-Marie Burt's discussion of Sendero Luminoso affirms the existence of a system of interactions with the population in the territory in which Sendero operates. This enables Burt to dismiss characterizations of Sendero as simply a terrorist organization, to examine the mechanisms and rationality that people saw in Sendero, and to investigate the role of the latter in supplying some 'goods' and 'services' (social discipline, transparency in the use of community resources, security *vis-à-vis* the state). Burt acknowledges the repulsion generated by the tactics Sendero employed to provide these services—though she somehow downplays the authoritarianism implied by the self-attribution of the right to reward, condemn, and assassinate—and analyzes this dimension of the problem by exploring the rationality that, in addition to fear, is found among the popular sectors that lent their support to Sendero Luminoso. Hers is an enquiry that, in the institutional conditions prevailing today in Peru, is itself considered to be subversive.

Violence is not, to be sure, a tactic used only by the state. The chapters in this section show that under some circumstances violence becomes a means of survival for some actors in the world of poverty and oppression and constitutes the environment in which their everyday life unfolds. But the notoriety of violence in the world of the poor should not blind us to the use of violence by elites. This is not only because elites maintain their privileged ties to the coercive agencies of the state—as various chapters in this book point out—but also because Latin American elites take advantage of the tenuous frontier that separates legality from illegality: 'white guards', financial scandals, 'narco-politics', corruption (see for example Little 1992; Ellner 1993*a*; Flynn 1993). Fox discusses the impact of the Zapatista Army on the ongoing process of democratization in Mexico, through a gun-supported process of dialogue involving segments of civil society in addition to government and guerrillas.

The chapters by Panfichi, Bruhn, López-Maya, and Fox, as well as those in the subsequent section, offer a more nuanced approach to the question of the supposed 'disenchantment' or 'disillusionment' with politics which some scholars consider to be a reaction to the frustration of expectations for overarching, structural change, as advanced by the radical Left (Lechner 1990: 103–18). Without denying that this attitude characterized important segments of the Latin American intellectual community, the chapters by Panfichi, Bruhn, and López-Maya offer a different perspective. In the poor neighborhoods of Lima, in the social movements of Mexico, or in the electorate of Causa R, one does not find much disenchantment, or if it is there, it is above all disenchantment with a certain way of doing politics. Frustration is displaced by a redefinition of loyalties and options and by the search for another way, a more efficacious way, of doing politics. The indigenous people of Ecuador, or the ecologists of Brazil, seemed much more enthused than disenchanted with the efficacy of political action.

In a similar vein, the chapters by Nylen and Winn and Ferro-Clérico point to the successful efforts to activate municipal politics as an arena for combining representative and participatory democracy. The situation of social organizations and the politically active is quite different in Brazil and Guatemala. The environment analyzed by Pinheiro—one of violence, corruption, and massive misery

—features active political involvement and the legitimation of institutional political competition to determine the direction of society. Studies on the vote for Collor de Mello suggest that this legitimacy is accorded equally by actors in 'formal society' and those who survive in 'informal society', though here as well one can infer the difficulties facing formal political organizations in seeking to attract the vote of the informal society.

In Guatemala, by contrast, repressive violence and the shortcomings of political parties and the electoral process seem to lead many people to political abstention or to transfer their energies toward organizations of civil society with marginal effectiveness, nonetheless, in influencing the course of events. The activation of these organizations, as Yashar shows, was of fundamental importance in aborting the Fujimori-style coup attempt of Serrano. It has so far been unable, however, to neutralize the pirouettes and metamorphoses of Ramiro de León Carpio, the man whom the mobilization of civil society installed in the presidency because of his previous record in defense of human rights, and who since his rise to the presidency has become a firm supporter of the civil defense patrols that he condemned as ombudsman.

SEARCHING FOR A WAY OUT

In recent years, a number of academic observers and political actors have considered the social democratic option as an answer to the current setting of social inequality and political tension and to the failure of more radical alternatives. 'Social democracy' as a concept and as a political formula comes from the European political tradition. As such, attempts to impose the concept on Latin America risk ambiguity and political imprecision. The chapters by Kenneth Roberts and Eric Hershberg focus on this question. Roberts discusses the structural constraints for Latin America regarding such an option; the present moment of globalization of the world economy reduces the room for autonomous 'national' economies and the capacity for state intervention. In addition, the weakness of union movements throughout most of Latin America reduces the centrality of workers as key actors in the European social democratic experience. Roberts points out that the notion of social democracy for Latin America comes at a time when its very practice is receding throughout Europe. One could add that while in Europe social democracy represented a proactive political strategy for workers, in Latin America it appears as a defensive retreat from the now dismissed radical options.

Hershberg, in turn, compares the Spanish and Chilean transition processes, emphasizing the social democratic resonances of some of their principal protagonists—the Socialist Workers Party of Spain and the Chilean Socialist Party—and the negotiated character of both processes. Hershberg also signals the difference between the two countries' economic conditions at the time of the transitions. Hershberg stresses the ability of the Chilean democratic coalition to negotiate tax reform with the Chilean right which permitted the government to finance anti-poverty programs and a modest rise in real wages and employment levels for Chile's workers. Although income distribution in Chile is extremely polarized (see Table 1.1), these reforms contributed to strengthening the legitimacy of the political regime in a context of union weakness and the lack of more radical alternatives.

Uruguay is a country in which political democratization was not accompanied by the broad adoption of market-oriented reforms. Fernando Filgueira and Jorge Papadópulos explain this infrequent situation as due to the capacity of the popular sectors to have a voice in key government policy issues, and not just in the election of those making these decisions. The Uruguayan case is a good illustration of the endurance of a welfare state political culture among large sectors of the citizenry. It is possible that this is also characteristic of other Latin American countries, as suggested by rallies and protests against some of the most severe structural adjustment reforms. The peculiarity of the Uruguayan case lies in the existence of institutional mechanisms for direct democracy which allow citizens to express their views in an efficacious manner. Moreover, the particularity of Uruguay's role in the subregional economy—as a financial market and tax haven for hot money—may also be playing a role in the state's ability to maintain a more traditional relationship with civil society, through a relatively broad array of welfare services funded with the revenues from this prosperous financial intermediation.

Discussion over a social democratic alternative lends itself to a not always conscious meshing of objective analysis and ideological concerns: is what we are calling a 'social democracy' really, in fact, a social democracy? The question is not a rhetorical one, since in the past we tended to speak of 'socialism' in Central America and of 'fascism' in the Southern Cone. Given the specificities of social and political development in Latin America, is it not inevitable that social democracy would be distinct from a European variant? Is it possible to be social democratic in political terms and not be so in terms of social reforms and economic policies? Are we arguing about political processes and regimes, or are we just arguing about ideological labels?

The last section of the book brings together several chapters which focus on the search for ways which combine the institutions of representative democracy with mechanisms for social participation. Nylen and Winn and Ferro-Clérico examine experiences of municipal government in Brazil and Uruguay. Over the last decade, the Latin American left has 'discovered' local government as an arena to experiment with and learn from direct involvement in governance, including budget management. It has been a concrete opportunity to demonstrate the left's efficacy in government problem-solving without necessarily abdicating its general ideological commitments to social transformation. The authors also analyze in precise terms the complex question of political party–social movement relations, particularly the dynamic between the principle of the representative nature of electoral politics and the movements' demands for direct participation, which left political parties themselves claim to support. Certainly a country is far more than the sum of its municipalities. Nevertheless, the two chapters open the terrain for a discussion of the articulation between representation and participation involving greater levels of complexity and reach—both in geographic and thematic terms.

María Cook's chapter moves in such a direction. NAFTA involves a drastic redefinition of the economic space of North America and the potential constitution of a new sphere for popular and union mobilization. Until now worker movement weakness in each of the countries has impeded its ability to take advantage of the new situation; NAFTA provisions on labor rights were among the weakest in the accord, as were those related to environmental protection. Nevertheless, Cook's discussion contributes to reorienting the predominant focus on globalization and regionalization processes; instead of focusing solely on attacks against citizens' social rights, she suggests a different lens which examines scenarios for turning threats into possibilities. Setbacks become opportunities for popular actors to define new strategies and objectives and create new kinds of alliances and solidarities.

Left parties and social movements are not the only actors who have had to adapt and respond to new circumstances. Governments and multilateral financial agencies have also had to propose alternatives for social participation in order to address some of the most severe problems created by economic restructuring and market-oriented reforms. Governments and donor agencies have stressed the need to address extreme poverty, appealing to grassroots and community efforts to execute compensatory projects and to achieve cost-saving results. From 1988 to 1994, the Mexican government's PRONASOL, or Solidarity Program, was the star example of such efforts. Today PRONASOL has fallen from grace along with the administration and officials who initiated the program, and it clearly seems that not all PRONASOL's resources went toward its declared objectives. Nevertheless, it enjoyed enormous popularity among international agencies and the academic community, and several Latin American governments found PRONASOL a source of inspiration for their own efforts.

Kerianne Piester presents an articulate discussion of PRONASOL, of the variety of objectives it pursued, and of the relational mode between the state and civil society that the program engendered. Her chapter analyzes a situation which contrasts with that discussed in the chapter by Monique Segarra. In Ecuador the social investment program defined a space for state–civil society relations where nongovernmental organizations (NGOs) acquired important space, encouraging government agencies to focus more attention on specific programmatic objectives as well as a better involvement of the affected population. Apparently there was also better fiscalization of assigned and executed resources. This did not take place in Mexico, a country where only recently did the state accept NGO activity and where the way in which PRONASOL was implemented contributed to the emergence of renewed modalities of clientelism and political favoritism.

Today's democracies in Latin America combine elections, participation, and violence in scenarios of strong social polarization and precarious reactivation of the economy. The history of these democracies did not begin with the military's retreat from the exercise of government, nor with the landing of technocrats from multilateral financial agencies. The chapters of this book attempt to address the current stage in this long, at times traumatic, and inevitably unending process.

PART I. Traditional Actors, New Settings

2 | Beyond Corporatism: New Patterns of Representation in the Brazilian Auto Industry

Scott B. Martin[1]

For roughly two years starting in late 1991, metalworkers' unions, auto companies, and state agencies in Brazil engaged in an institutionalized process of comprehensive negotiation of industrial policy issues in automobile manufacturing within the 'sectoral chamber' (*câmara setorial*) of the automobile industry. The two national accords and spirit of greater collaboration generated through the chamber yielded dramatic results—lower real auto prices, a recovery and subsequent boom in domestic auto sales and production, improvements in real wages and job security for workers, a much greater role for unions in shaping workplace and sectoral governance, and substantial advances toward the modernization of Brazil's heretofore backward industrial park in autos. Shifting priorities and personnel led the state slowly to withdraw, from late 1993 on into 1994, from the auto chamber as well as from identical tripartite arrangements established in other sectors in emulation of the auto experience. Yet all the available evidence suggests that the advances in establishing more cooperative and innovative governance arrangements between labor and capital and suppliers and producers, initially engendered through the chamber, continued and were reinforced in 1994 and 1995 even after the breakdown of formal tripartism.

Viewed in the context of trends in popular participation and representation in both Brazil and the Latin American region more generally, the auto chamber exhibited many novel and even unprecedented aspects. To begin with, such formal tripartite negotiating arrangements bringing together labor, capital, and state agencies on a more or less equal footing were viewed as highly evocative of European-style

[1] Funding for this research was provided by the Fulbright-Hays program, the Inter-American Foundation, and the Organization of American States. Generous support was also provided by the Center for Social Sciences and Institute of Latin American and Iberian Studies at Columbia University, as well as the Centro de Estudos da Cultura Contemporânea (CEDEC) in São Paulo. The author would like to thank his fellow editors as well as Bob Kaufman, Mark Kesselman, Peter Kingstone, Al Montero, Vicky Murillo, Bill Smith, Harrison White, and João Paulo Veiga for their helpful comments on earlier versions of this chapter. Any shortcomings are solely the responsibility of the author.

'democratic' (or 'societal') corporatism (Arbix 1995; Cardoso and Comin 1993; Diniz 1994; Martin 1994). The anomaly lies in the fact that societal corporatism stands in sharp contrast with Latin America's, and especially Brazil's, heritage of authoritarian or 'state' corporatism, particularly in the labor sphere.[2] What is more, cooperative endeavors of this sort had never been attempted at the sectoral level in Brazil and had failed roundly at the national level when, on various occasions, the governments of José Sarney (1985–90) and Fernando Collor (1990–2) attempted to negotiate social pacts (e.g. Roxborough 1992*a*, 1992*b*). Nor did the auto industry present itself as a propitious candidate for negotiating such sectoral 'pacts', given its legacy of private consultations (and conflicts) between large multinational manufacturers and state regulators; conflictual relations between parts suppliers and manufacturers (Shapiro 1994); and sharp antagonism between labor and capital dating back to the second half of the 1970s (Humphrey 1982; Silva 1991).

Another unusual feature of this negotiating forum was that perhaps its most active and enthusiastic participants were militant unionists from the Unified Workers' Central (Central Única dos Trabalhadores, or CUT) led by the metalworkers' union of São Bernardo do Campo and Diadema, which represents auto and other metalworkers in Brazil's largest industrial belt located just outside the city of São Paulo. Both this peak organization more generally and this particular union were key protagonists of the unprecedented upsurge in labor militancy experienced by Brazil throughout the 1980s (Noronha 1991). Moreover, the more equitable and participatory governance arrangements that auto unionists helped forge through their involvement in the auto chamber stand out in the comparative context of Latin American processes of industrial restructuring. Though extensive evidence is lacking, the extraction or imposition of major labor concessions on enfeebled, conciliatory, or non-existent unions is generally seen as the dominant, if not universal, trend in the region from the 1980s onward. Indeed, some scholars (e.g. Zapata 1993: 141–53) even speak of a general contemporary 'crisis of unionism' in Latin America.

The Brazilian auto chamber thus raises many explanatory and analytical puzzles that have strong comparative relevance. To what extent does the societal corporatist framework capture the origins and dynamics of the chamber? How can one explain the emergence—and subsequent breakdown—of tripartite concertation in a country and a region that lack a democratic corporatist legacy and instead possess a strong heritage of state corporatist domination of unions and of behind-closed-doors relationships between large oligopolistic firms and the state?

[2] The seminal contemporary monograph on corporatism in comparative politics is Schmitter (1974), in which the distinction between 'state' and 'societal' variants is made. Among the more influential studies on corporatism in Latin America are Collier and Collier (1979), the various essays in Malloy (1977), Stepan (1978), and Wiarda (1981). For a recent survey of the concept in Latin American studies see Collier (1995), and for a more general survey of its use in comparative politics see Chalmers (1985). Important treatments of corporatism in Brazil may be found in Erickson (1977), Mericle (1977), and Schmitter (1971).

More broadly, what are the general implications of the auto chamber for union strat-egy, industrial policy, and popular participation and representation in Latin America? In this chapter, I will attempt to provide firm responses to questions about the rise of the chamber and the proper analytical framework for studying it. However, given the fact that field research for this project focused mainly on the period through 1993[3] as well as the ongoing nature of experimentation with new forms of governance in the Brazilian auto sector at the time of this writing in early 1996, my discussion of the breakdown of the chamber and the broader implica-tions of this experience will be more tentative and brief.

The central argument is that the conceptual apparatus of societal corporatism—particularly its intermediate, or 'meso'-level, variant—is useful only for the very limited purpose of characterizing the formal structure of the auto chamber and distinguishing it in a general way from pluralist forms of interest representation. Both the structure of group interests and the form of policy-making that charac-terized the chamber differed from the defining features of societal corporatism. In the context of Brazil and its auto industry, this chapter demonstrates that two key preconditions for sector-wide negotiations were (1) the recent establishment or prior existence of representative associations of capital and labor that were legitimate in members' eyes and (2) incipient bonds of trust among competing actors that had emerged through iterative encounters. Further, I suggest that the opera-tions of social network ties, partly along the lines of the 'associative network' model proposed by Douglas Chalmers, Kerianne Piester, and myself in the con-cluding chapter of this volume, were fundamental to the rise, evolution, and fall of the sectoral chamber and the dynamics of parallel and continuing negotiations within the auto industry. In the conclusions I sketch out some of the possibilities and perils inherent in the pursuit by popular actors of cooperative approaches based on proactive strategies.

Overview of the Sectoral Chamber

Before acquiring the tripartite form and policy-making importance that would char-acterize them beginning in late 1991, sectoral chambers in Brazil, including the auto chamber, had passed through various phases. Originally created in 1988 by the José Sarney government (1985–90) as fora of state–business discussion on indus-trial policy within 'production chains' (*cadéias produtivas*), the chambers nonethe-less became *de facto* mechanisms for negotiating and administering price controls under anti-inflation plans. During the Fernando Collor government (1990–2), the

---

[3] I conducted field research in Brazil in stints of varying length spanning the period from 1986 to 1992. In addition, I draw in this chapter on secondary sources and primary documents that, with great generosity, were compiled for me under the auspices of the CEDEC during 1993.

chambers initially were renamed 'executive groups for sectoral policies' (*grupos executivos de políticas setoriais*) and were assigned the task of defining modernization strategies at the sectoral level. Given various difficulties, including deepening economic crisis, the chambers did little of consequence in this phase and generally were inactive. However, beginning in March 1991, they reacquired their original name and finally took on a formal legal status, becoming responsible for the gradual liberalization of price controls enacted under the Collor government's antiinflation programs. Moreover, by virtue of an amendment successfully attached to the legislation by Workers' Party Deputy Aloísio Mercadante, the chambers formally returned to their original tripartite formulation, including unions. Nonetheless, in practice the chambers continued to function almost exclusively as 'bipartite' business–government bodies. The São Bernardo metalworkers' union participated in a single meeting of the auto chamber, in April 1991, withdrawing when state and business officials were unwilling to add employment and wage issues to the agenda. In September of that same year, the final measures freeing auto prices were adopted and, with its narrow mission accomplished, the auto chamber lapsed into inactivity.

A series of events that took place between September and November of 1991 led to the reactivation and restructuring of the auto chamber, which resumed activity in December as a fully tripartite entity charged with establishing an industrial policy for the auto sector that would be consistent with macroeconomic stabilization efforts. In the midst of a deepening recession, near-record unemployment rates, and persistent rumors of other plant closings, Ford announced in October that it was shutting down its engine plant in São Bernardo.[4] With 700 jobs on the line, a small delegation of unionists and Workers' Party officials (including the deputy mayor of São Bernardo) travelled to Detroit, where it unsuccessfully lobbied Ford executives to reconsider their decision. Despite this setback, personal contacts generated by the trip together with the widely publicized woes of the auto industry created the conditions for what would prove a fateful meeting between union president Vicente Paulo da Silva, widely known as Vicentinho, and Economics Minister Marcílio Marques Moreira, shortly after the former's return to Brazil.

Two points of agreement came out of the meeting: first, the Minister would make a public appeal to Ford to reconsider the plant closing and second, (pending the acceptance of business officials) the sectoral chamber of the auto industry would be reopened as a tripartite forum to discuss and negotiate the whole gamut of issues related to the future of Brazil's auto industry. While the first point was mainly a symbolic gesture, which did not prevent Ford from following through on its plans to close the plant a few months hence in February, the second had momentous

[4] Unlike the other Ford plants in Brazil, this plant had not come under the management of the holding company Autolatina, which was created through a 1986 merger of Volkswagen and Ford's operations in both Argentina and Brazil. The joint venture was eliminated in 1994, as the two companies resumed separate operations.

consequences. With auto sales at historical lows and losses piling up, auto makers and parts manufacturers quickly agreed to participate, and the chamber resumed meetings in mid-December 1991, 'reborn' as a tripartite negotiating forum for industrial policy-making.

THE MARCH 1992 AGREEMENT

Given the severity of the problems confronting the industry and in the cooperative spirit of this new endeavor, the participants in the revived and restructured auto chamber adopted several procedural innovations. Instead of proceeding directly to point-by-point bargaining, they agreed to spend several weeks in formulating a joint diagnosis of the industry's ills. Based on evaluations submitted by all the actors—including a long and detailed report prepared by the union's technical staff—and subsequent discussions, a joint statement detailing major problem areas was adopted. Among the problem areas identified were the high prices and low quality of Brazilian vehicles; the absence of low-price models accessible to middle- to lower-income Brazilian consumers; poor performance in export markets; the lack of sustained investment in technological and organizational modernization; among the world's highest sales taxes on vehicle purchases; the devastating impact of rising vehicle imports under the gradual tariff liberalization program adopted in 1990; antiquated industrial relations arrangements; and, more generally, the absence of a coherent and coordinated national policy for the country's largest industrial sector. Grouping these problem areas into broad thematic divisions, the participants then agreed to decentralize negotiations into a series of six working groups that would meet frequently in either São Paulo or Brasília.[5] In practice, these groups often came to be dominated by mid-level officials with particular expertise in the policy areas in question. Periodically, the plenary, made up of the top labor, business, and state officials, would convene to assess progress made in the working groups and to try to hammer out a comprehensive accord.

After just over three months of intensive meetings and negotiations within this complex structure, involving hundreds of individual participants, a crucial phase was reached and a final plenary session was called in Brasília. In order to create as propitious an environment as possible for smooth deliberations, the Secretariat of Commerce of Industry—the Economics Ministry agency in charge of coordinating state participation in the chamber—hired a management consulting firm that specialized in the art of negotiations. The firm helped organize the physical environment for the meetings—which did not take place in official government buildings—trying to create as casual, relaxed, and non-hierarchical an atmosphere as possible. Nonetheless, there were tense moments in the talks as the

---

[5] The subject areas were the internal market; foreign trade; taxes; investments; technology, quality, and productivity; and labor relations.

tantalizing possibility of an agreement loomed larger. For instance, the auto manufacturers, still represented collectively by the outgoing president of their sectoral association, a noted hard-liner with an abrasive personality, decided to disavow his leadership and to replace him on the spot with the association's president-elect, a younger reformist with a reputation as a 'bridge-builder'. Moreover, according to subsequent accounts by participants, the personal intervention of the charismatic Commerce Secretary Dorothéia Werneck, a young economist tied to the Brazilian Social Democratic Party, was also crucial in ensuring the success of negotiations.

Finally, after several days of talks in Brasília, an accord designed to reactivate the struggling industry was signed by all the participating organizations on 27 March 1992. The centerpiece was an immediate, one-time 22 per cent reduction in the price of new cars and light commercial vehicles, carefully engineered through a combination of cuts in federal and state auto sales taxes and in the profit margins of manufacturers, parts makers, and car dealers. This decline in real auto prices was to be maintained by allowing prices to rise only in line with input costs in the future.[6] Since workers in the auto sector (like elsewhere in the Brazilian economy) had suffered sharp losses in real wages as well as significant lay-offs amidst the post-1990 recession and since labor costs represented a small fraction of overall production costs, additional labor sacrifice was neither possible nor necessary. Rather, unions won two important victories in the auto accord, with firms agreeing to maintain existing employment levels and fully to index wages to monthly inflation. However, in order to give the accord the opportunity to stimulate consumption and hence production, labor negotiators agreed to put off the renegotiation of their annual contract, which formally expired on 1 April, for three months. With the initial success of the accord, the participants agreed in June to extend all its provisions through the end of 1992. At about the same time, moreover, labor and business negotiators reached collective bargaining accords that provided for not only a renewal of wage-indexation and job-security clauses but also substantial real wage increases. However, the federal government made only piecemeal progress toward meeting its pledge to ease credit terms for auto purchases.

The March 1992 auto agreement had the important effect of stabilizing the troubled industry, producing an initial boom in sales and then a levelling off in the latter part of the year. Overall, total retail sales for the year—including the disastrous three months prior to the agreement when thousands of unwanted cars were being stockpiled—fell by a modest 4.3 per cent, far below the steep declines predicted before the accord and the sharp drops registered in 1990 and 1991 (*O Estado de São Paulo*, 12 Jan. 1993, p. 10). By virtue of a large increase in exports, moreover, overall production levels actually increased by some 15 per cent, returning to 1986 levels and reversing their large 1991 decline (*Veja*, 18 Nov. 1992, p. 85).

---

[6] Given that Brazil's inflation rate was running roughly at a 20 per cent clip *per month*, it was a given that nominal prices would continue to rise and the goal was to achieve a cut in *real* (i.e. inflation-adjusted) prices.

Workers also benefited, as employment levels remained virtually steady, declining only by virtue of natural turnover. Real wages also recovered slightly, thanks to indexation and real wage increases. Meanwhile, several other sectors of the Brazilian economy, such as computers and the electrical and electronic industries, attempted without success to emulate the example of the automotive accords through the revival of their sectoral chambers in tripartite form.

Although the chamber's six working groups continued to meet throughout the rest of the year, few additional agreements were reached after the March accord, due in part to the growing political uncertainty that engulfed the country with the rapid unfolding of Collor's impeachment crisis from April to October.[7] The most important accomplishments in this connection were a gradual easing of credit conditions for carbuyers and export-incentive legislation that was submitted to the Congress (though never passed). Nonetheless, chamber participants drew upon some of the ideas and proposals discussed in the working groups in the second set of national agreements, to which I now turn.

THE FEBRUARY 1993 AGREEMENT

After a brief period of uncertainty when Vice-President Itamar Franco assumed the presidency following Collor's departure from office in October 1992, the new government decided to move ahead with the sectoral chambers. Coordinating responsibilities were assigned to the Ministry of Industry, Commerce, and Tourism, one of the three new ministries created from the dismemberment of the former 'superministry' of economics. In the words of a Ministry of Industry report, the government objective was the following: 'To promote sectoral accords, seeking negotiated alternatives among business, workers, and the government for the restructuring of industrial complexes and the modernization of labor relations.'[8] The plenary of the auto chamber resumed meetings in November 1992.

The chamber participants' progress toward a comprehensive agreement was sidetracked temporarily in the early weeks of 1993. In keeping with his unpredictable governing style, President Franco made an off-the-cuff remark that it would be a good idea if Autolatina, the Ford–Volkswagen joint venture, were to bring back the old Beetle model (known in Brazil as the Fusca), which had been discontinued in Brazil in 1986. Taking the President at his word, the company quickly put together a proposal whereby the Fusca, as a low-priced 'people's car' (*carro popular*), would be granted a complete federal sales-tax exemption. Fiat and General Motors

---

[7] In March of that year, a corruption scandal centered on influence trafficking in Collor's inner circle erupted, resulting in a congressional investigation, a protracted civic pro-impeachment campaign, and Collor's impeachment in October.

[8] Ministério da Indústria, do Comércio e do Turismo, Secretaria de Política Industrial, *Evolução dos Acordos Setoriais*, Aug. 1993, p. 3.

then rushed to demand the same treatment for their low-budget cars. These direct business–government negotiations produced company-specific understandings reached outside the chamber with each of the three major auto makers, whereby *carros populares* equipped with small motors were exempted from federal sales taxes in return for company commitments to meet certain job-creation and production targets for these vehicles. The episode left the unions in a curious position. On the one hand, they had initiated the debate about changing the 'production mix' of auto makers toward lower-cost vehicles that could expand the very restricted domestic market; workers and unions also stood to benefit enormously from the new jobs that might be created through a boom in the production of people's cars. On the other hand, unionists expressed concerns about the agreements' focus on engine size rather than price as the defining criterion for determining fiscal incentives; the technological 'step backward' represented by the revival of the Beetle; as well as the principle of bilateral, extra-chamber negotiations between business and the state. Nevertheless, political pragmatism prevailed, since the agreements were hailed by the public and consumers rushed to dealers to buy cars whose prices, now without federal taxes, were suddenly at only two-thirds or less of previous levels. Moreover, since the bilateral accords were in keeping with the general objective of promoting the domestic market and promoting low-budget cars was a high priority on the chamber's negotiating agenda, they ended up actually *reinforcing* rather than undercutting the chamber participants' efforts to forge a new industrial policy for the auto sector.

After three months of negotiations, the chamber participants reached another comprehensive sectoral accord on 15 February 1993. This time, the São Bernardo union and the auto makers', autoparts', and auto dealers' trade organizations were joined by a wide range of other signatories: the national and state metalworkers' organizations of the Central Única dos Trabalhadores (CUT); unions belonging to the rival labor central, Força Sindical; twenty-four other sectoral associations and business *sindicatos* representing various automotive suppliers; and officials from four government ministries.[9] Moreover, the agreement was much more complex and far-reaching than its predecessor,[10] encompassing both a short-term demand stimulus package and a medium- to long-term industrial restructuring program. Again, the principal provision was a negotiated price cut for automobiles, achieved through further federal and state sales-tax reductions, another pruning of profit margins, and pledges of price relief from automotive suppliers. Depending on the engine size of the car, the overall cut in consumer prices varied from 10 to 15 per

---

[9] The CUT organizations were the National Metalworkers' Confederation and the State Metalworkers' Federation of São Paulo. Additional sectoral suppliers' associations included tires, glass, plastics, foundries, and paint products, among others. On behalf of the federal government, the ministers of industry, treasury, labor, and planning were all signatories. In addition, treasury secretaries from three states (São Paulo, Minas Gerais, and Bahia) participated in the negotiations as observers.

[10] The sheer size of the Feb. 1993 document testifies to its complexity—14 pages, including 8 clauses and 20 articles, as opposed to the 2 pages and 7 simple items of the sectoral agreement reached in Mar. 1992.

cent.[11] Other demand-stimulation measures included extending the maturity length of consumer consortia and proposals for tax reductions and easier credit facilities for the purchase of tractors, buses, and agricultural machinery. (Some of the latter proposals ended up being adopted in January 1994 by the 'spin-off' sectoral chamber for tractors and agricultural machinery.) Given the recovery and expected boom in auto sales, the second auto agreement maintained monthly wage indexation and established a medium-term program for real wage increases: through three annual raises of 6.27 per cent each in real terms (the first taking effect immediately), purchasing power was to be restored to its April 1989 level by March 1995. Unlike its predecessor, the February 1993 accord established clear medium- and long-term goals for the industry. An ambitious calendar of graduated production targets was established through the year 1999, with an overall goal of expanding auto production from 1.1 million vehicles in 1992 to 2 million a year by the end of the century. In the area of job creation, the parties established an objective of creating 4,000 new manufacturing openings, 5,000 in sales and distribution, and another 82,000 in parts and related sectors—all by the end of 1994. To achieve these production and employment goals, an overall investment target of US$20 billion was set for the remainder of the century, half of which was to come from manufacturers.[12] To this end, auto companies agreed to disclose their total investments every six months and a working group was established to study ways of improving private financing of automotive investments.

Several provisions of the second auto accord were designed to spur modernization efforts: (1) a review of companies' research and development activities; (2) the establishment of an industry body to harmonize quality evaluations, help bring production up to internationally accepted quality standards, and study other issues related to quality and productivity; and (3) the creation of a joint labor–business body to oversee progress on employment and production goals. The agreement's separate labor protocol was to last for thirty months, making it, as Industry Minister José Eduardo de Andrade Vieira noted, the 'longest labor accord of all time in Brazil' (*Folha de São Paulo*, 9 Sept. 1993, II-2), a country where collective bargaining contracts traditionally are reviewed annually. Moreover, the protocol provided for the gradual unification of collective bargaining dates for the many different unions representing workers in auto manufacturing, autoparts, foundries, and other supplier industries across different municipalities in the industrial state of São Paulo, the heart of the auto industry.

The second auto accord produced dramatic immediate results in 1993. Overall production levels reached an annual national record of 1.38 million vehicles, over

[11] The object of this measure was to stimulate consumption and production of 'lower-end' models that would be more accessible to Brazilian consumers than the 'high-end' models in which Brazilian producers increasingly had specialized since the 1980s.

[12] The other $10 billion was to be divided up as follows: $6 billion from parts manufacturers, $1 billion from tire makers, and a combined $3 billion from foundries, steel makers, raw materials providers, and auto dealers.

28 per cent above 1991 levels and 30,000 beyond even the ambitious goal set by the February accord (*Folha de São Paulo*, 6 Jan. 1994, I-3). Sales to the internal market increased by 40 per cent and surpassed the previous record set in 1980.[13] The autoparts sector also expanded rapidly, registering a 25 per cent jump in overall sales revenues and a 20 per cent rise in export revenues (*Folha de São Paulo*, 20 Jan. 1994, II-7). Since the auto industry as a whole accounts for somewhere around 10 per cent of GNP, the auto sector's growth also contributed to Brazil's modest economic recovery; the gross domestic product grew by 1.5 per cent in 1993, reversing its 1992 decline of 1 per cent (*New York Times*, 3 Jan. 1994). By one estimate, the auto industry alone accounted for at least one-third of the country's 10 per cent rise in industrial GNP for the year (*O Estado de São Paulo*, 3 Jan. 1994, p. 7).

The second agreement also brought considerable material gains for workers during 1993. Given the combination of continued indexation, the 6.3 per cent across-the-board raise in April, and additional company-specific raises and bonuses that many workers received later, real wages rose sharply for auto workers; by one estimate, purchasing power increased 30 per cent in the autoparts sector.[14] Employment levels also grew by 4.8 per cent in autos (*Folha de São Paulo*, 6 Jan. 1994, I-3) and 3 per cent in auto parts (*Folha de São Paulo*, 20 Jan. 1994, II-7).

Meanwhile, sectoral chambers in other manufacturing and service sectors proliferated in 1993, many but not all of them with full tripartite participation.[15] In August 1993, the Ministry of Industry reported that twenty-five such bodies were 'active',[16] though in only three besides automobiles were sectoral agreements reached—shipbuilding, toys and cosmetics, and agricultural equipment and machinery.

REQUIEM FOR THE SECTORAL CHAMBERS

At the same time that actors in other sectors found it difficult to emulate the auto industry's success, the auto chamber itself increasingly lapsed into inactivity over the course of late 1993 and on into 1994. Since Fernando Henrique Cardoso had moved from Foreign Affairs to Finance Minister in mid-1993, economic policy-

[13] The total number of vehicles sold in the domestic market was 1.017 million. *O Estado de São Paulo*, 3 Jan. 1994, p. 7. Had it not been for a large fall in exports—due mainly to a sharp decline in vehicle imports by neighboring Argentina under the South American Common Market—production levels would have been considerably higher.

[14] The estimate is by Cláudio Vaz, president of the autoparts' association Sindipeças. *Folha de São Paulo*, 20 Jan. 1994, II-7.

[15] In Aug. 1993, CUT-affiliated unions were participating in five chambers (automotive complex, electrical-electronic complex, shipbuilding, construction, and software) and making 'embryonic efforts' to participate in four others (chemical complex, capital goods, steel, and household appliances). See the CUT research institute DESEP, 'Câmaras Setoriais: Para Além do Complexo Automotivo', *Textos para Discussão* 6: 2–3.

[16] Ministério da Indústria, do Comércio e do Turismo, Secretaria de Política Industrial, *Evolução dos Acordos Setoriais*, Aug. 1993, p. 3.

makers within the Franco government had begun to act and speak with two different voices about the chambers. Cardoso's high-level deputies began to criticize publicly the notion of sectorally specific state policies, even while the Ministry of Industry and Commerce (formally charged with coordinating state participation in the chambers), the Labor Ministry, and other segments of the state apparatus continued to promote and defend them enthusiastically as a very useful policy instrument for promoting the modernization of production and of labor relations. As the months passed, Cardoso and his coterie increasingly became the lead players in economic policy-making and came to subordinate all other policy considerations to their efforts to formulate a strategy for handling four-digit annual inflation rates. In retrospect, one can now say that the ultimate fate of the chambers, in terms of the *de facto* withdrawal of the state from active promotion and participation, was sealed with the adoption of the anti-inflation currency reform program known as the Real Plan, in May 1994. However, there was no definitive announcement of the shift in state policy or cancellation of the chambers. Indeed, there was an unsuccessful effort to create a sort of macro 'chamber of chambers' late in the Franco government in order to coordinate sectoral strategies with macroeconomic priorities; moreover, as legal instruments the *câmaras* still exist legally under the Cardoso government (January 1995–present) and, occasionally, voices are heard inside and/or outside the state, calling for their revival. Rather, state withdrawal, already evident before the Real Plan but hastened by its adoption, manifested itself gradually, in a series of state actions that chipped away—deliberately or not—at the autonomy and scope of chamber negotiations.

As the forerunner and virtual paradigm for tripartite chambers, the auto chamber exemplified most vividly the gradual erosion of state support going back to 1993. In addition to the state's reluctance to negotiate new national accords despite strong labor and business support for efforts along such lines, its actions on two particular issues—trade and wages—undercut both the substance and spirit of tripartite cooperation. Given Finance Ministry opposition to pushing a specific bill addressing the needs of an individual sector, the export-incentive legislation approved by the chamber and submitted to the Congress in 1993 did not have the strong, united support of the Franco government and thus went nowhere. Moreover, with the initial success of the Real Plan, tensions between state officials, on one hand, and labor and business, on the other, exploded in September and October of 1994 over the issue of wage increases. Despite the fact that further real wage hikes were both called for under the terms of the 1993 accord and eminently justified by dramatic increases in productivity in the booming sector, the Finance Ministry (by then vacated by presidential candidate Cardoso and in the hands of Ciro Gomes) puts its foot down, fearing the demonstration effects of auto-sector raises elsewhere and wishing to wring wage-related inflationary pressures from the economy at all costs. Moreover, the tool chosen by the federal government to force auto makers not to give raises was to speed up by several months a cut in tariffs on auto imports, from 35 to 20 per cent, that was scheduled as part of the gradual liberalization program adopted by the Collor government and essentially kept in place throughout the sectoral chamber. This unilateral measure contravened both the spirit of tripartism as well as the substance of a *sectoral strategy premised on linking gradual trade liberalization with rapid and collaborative productive modernization efforts to make the auto sector more competitive.*

Finally, the new Cardoso government took further measures that effectively completed the state's withdrawal from tripartism in autos (and any other sector). With domestic auto sales booming under the combined weight of first price cuts through the sectoral chamber and then the dramatic drop in inflation under the Real Plan, auto makers had strained to expand production and productive capacity fast enough to keep up with demand throughout 1994. Spurred by continued tariff reductions and by their appeal and sheer novelty for consumers in a long-protected market, imports surged to fill some of the gap, increasing their share of the now greatly expanded domestic market to roughly a quarter by the end of 1994 (Shapiro 1995: 32). By the time Cardoso took office in January 1995, the rapidly unfolding financial crisis that had erupted the previous month in Mexico had made the new government's policy-makers extremely sensitive to the need to reduce the record current-account deficits the country was now running due to the post-Real consumption boom. To this end, they swallowed their strong pro-market convictions momentarily and adopted the 'emergency' measure of returning auto tariffs to 32 per cent. With the country's now insatiable appetite for imports remaining whetted and given the reluctance to use other measures to cut the trade deficit that might undermine price stability (such as a large devaluation), the Cardoso government then acted in April to raise tariffs on not only autos but also a variety of other big-ticket consumer durables to a whopping 70 per cent, again as an explicitly 'temporary' measure. In neither of these cases were business and labor actors in the auto sector consulted prior to the adoption of the measures. These tariff increases were reversed partially in the second half of the year, as international pressure on the Brazilian government mounted (particularly within the newly created World Trade Organization) and as tight-credit, high-interest policies adopted at mid-year put the brakes on the consumption boom and lessened the perceived need for protection.

Joint appeals by business and labor actors in the auto sector—as well as by industrial interests more generally—for a revision of tight-credit policies fell on deaf government ears throughout the second half of 1995. Nor did periodic calls by unionists and business leaders in autos and other sectors for a revival of sectoral negotiating fora, with the aim of discussing the emerging new issues facing them, merit a favorable response—either in the latter stages of the Franco government or the first year of the Cardoso government. Hence, at the time of this writing, the auto and other chambers clearly are dormant. However, given the many incarnations that they have gone through over the past four governments and Brazil's rapidly changing political and economic context, it would be premature to write them off as being altogether 'dead'.

THE LEGACY OF THE SECTORAL CHAMBER

Before proceeding to consider how tripartism arose and functioned in the Brazilian auto sector and what relationship it may have to the societal corporatist framework, it is important to underline the legacy left by this experience. If this legacy is not understood properly, one can appreciate neither the larger analytical implications of this experience for the study of political representation in Brazil and Latin America more generally nor its practical consequences for actors in the Brazilian auto industry as they approach the *fin de siècle*.

Numerous studies of the sectoral chamber experience have appeared in the last few years (Arbix 1995; Cardoso and Comin 1993; Martin 1994 and forthcoming; Diniz 1994; Guimarães 1994; Oliveira 1993; Salgado 1993*a* and 1993*b*). With the exception of the work of Salgado, two common conclusions emerge from this body of scholarship. These conclusions also tend to be confirmed by a very recent survey of trends in the Brazilian auto industry by Helen Shapiro (1996), another recent study by Caren Addis (1995), and impressionistic accounts that have appeared in the Brazilian and international press (e.g., *The Economist*, 27 Apr. –3 May 1996, pp. 72–3). A first major conclusion—and legacy—is that the chamber occasioned a massive spurt of productive modernization in the Brazilian auto industry, whose scope and intensity probably are unprecedented in the sector's history and which has continued *despite and well after* the breakdown of tripartism. To be sure, the verb 'occasioned' is chosen deliberately, for strict causation is difficult to establish in such matters and other factors—such as Brazil's sheer size, the rapid expansion of the new South American Common Market (Mercosur), and macroeconomic changes—clearly have contributed to these trends. Yet, there can be no doubt that unprecedented steps have been taken since 1992 in the Brazilian auto industry to introduce or expand innovations in the organization of production that are consistent with 'cutting-edge' practices in worldwide management— 'Just-in-Time' inventory control systems, 'relational' subcontracting involving close integration between suppliers and final producers, work teams and other forms of greater worker involvement in shop-floor decision-making, and the like. Moreover, overwhelming evidence indicates that, as a result of these innovations, the quality and international competitiveness of Brazilian vehicles and auto parts have improved dramatically during this period, thus putting Brazil back at the center of existing market participants' global and regional export strategies and leading both them and several new entrants (like Hyundai, Peugeot, Kia, and possibly Toyota) to announce or consider plans to set up additional plants in Brazil in the near future. Most crucially for the present study, quality and productivity enhancements have emerged not through unilateral decisions or impositions by particular firms but rather through novel and increasingly cooperative government arrangements at several levels—within firms (especially between workers and managers), between suppliers and final producers, and between labor and capital at the overall sectoral level.

By all indications, these new governance arrangements were given a tremendous boost by the sectoral chamber negotiations. By virtue of the communicative processes the auto chamber engendered among competing actors, the deficiencies and sticking points it revealed in existing production systems, and the expanded time horizons and reinvested profits that the 1992 and 1993 accords produced, sectoral negotiations acted as a powerful catalyst for the search for new forms of cooperation at the level of production. This is not to suggest that cooperation in production ineluctably flowed from cooperation in industrial policy-making. Rather, what seems evident is simply that successful sectoral negotiations increased both the perceived need for, as well as the probability of success of, the establishment of more cooperative governance arrangements in production; they did not determine such an outcome. As will be made clear in the following sections, relationships among actors at the level of production in the period leading up to the rise of tripartism in late 1991—although in some cases manifesting modest improvements—still tended to be of an adversarial, 'arms-length' variety. Had the crisis of the sector continued to deepen and extended on at least through the macroeconomic relief provided by the 1994 Real Plan—as a counter-factual 'rerunning' of recent Brazilian economic history suggests it would have—then more plant closings and job losses doubtless would have taken place, as multinational actors exercised their 'exit' option. Therefore, conflicts among remaining actors likely would have taken on an increasingly bitter and 'zero-sum' character, as the survival of each encouraged unilateral, 'beggar-thy-neighbor' strategies by all, which were suboptimal in the collective sense. Under such a scenario, it is questionable how many actors—workers, middle-level managers, multinational auto makers, small- and medium-size domestic parts manufacturers, etc.—from the 1990–1 'game' of managing rapid decline would have even survived to play the post-Real 'game' of managing expansion and modernization. Such was the depth of the industry's prior crisis—and such the impact of the sectoral chamber in changing fundamentally the nature of the context in which sectoral actors competed and cooperated from 1992 onward.

The second legacy of the auto chamber—and a second lesson emerging from the aforementioned studies—concerns the novelty of the forms of interest representation and policy-making that it embodied within the political contexts of both Brazil and its auto industry, in particular, and Latin America, more generally. The sectoral chamber flew in the face of many established political 'traditions' and/or practices in Brazilian politics and policy-making. From the standpoint of state–labor relations, the participation of unions as a formal co-equal of business and government representatives contradicted not only half a century of domination and subordination through state corporatist controls but also the traditional marginalization of unions from decision-making on issues beyond the level of plants located in a narrow territorial base (i.e. municipalities). In the context of industrial relations, unions' active participation in the tripartite forum stood at loggerheads with their historic weakness *vis-à-vis* employers; the still incipient character of collective bargaining institutions; and the virulent confrontations that had characterized union efforts to overcome these limitations—and to blunt firms' uni-lateral restructuring initiatives—from the late 1970s on throughout the turbulent 1980s.

In the sphere of intra-business ties, the chamber marked a departure in the historically asymmetric and often antagonistic ties between a handful of huge, oligopolistic multinationals producing final vehicles and engines and the much more diverse group of many firms—both foreign and domestically owned and ran-ging from small to large—who supplied them with auto parts (Addis 1995). In the realm of state–business ties, private actors had always sought and sometimes suc-ceeded in shaping state decision-making, through a combination of pressure and back-room deal making with individual and collective action through officially sanc-tioned sectoral *sindicatos* (Shapiro 1994). Yet what was novel about the sectoral chamber was the fact that the state granted business leaders the formal, legal right (and consequent legitimacy) to help shape policy on a broad range of sectoral issues through highly structured and publicly visible channels involving the co-equal par-ticipation of unions and of competing segments of the auto industry. Finally, from the point of view of the state, the kind of coercively compelled negotiations that historically lay at the heart of Brazil's state corporatist forms—and that underlie, for instance, Mexico's recent experiences with so-called 'pact making'[17]—were absent from the sectoral chamber. The latter tripartite forum was created by the voluntary consent of all the actors and—as will be made clear below—however much these actors still were organized within a legally regulated framework they possessed a high degree of autonomy in running their internal affairs and in 'articulating interests' *vis-à-vis* public authorities. In all the above senses, the auto chamber was an unprecedented departure for politics and policy-making in Brazil—and a highly unusual one in a Latin American region with a weak heritage of democratic tripartism and a recent history of marginalization of organized—especially popular sector—interests from the policy-making process.

Toward an Alternative Explanatory Framework

How can the emergence and dynamics of such a novel form of political repres-entation and policy-making be explained and understood? To what analytical cat-egory can this experience be assigned? The most common approach to date (Arbix 1995; Cardoso and Comin 1993; Diniz 1994; Martin 1994) has been to place the

[17] The heavy degree to which the Mexican state regulates and controls the organization of busi-ness and especially labor interests, and the lingering authoritarian characteristics of the Mexican polity, give the pact negotiations in that country a decidedly different cast from that of the Brazilian auto negotiations. Hence, however much 'play' of interests there may be in the former process, it is of a distinctly lesser magnitude and qualitatively different order—that is, much closer to the pure type of 'state corporatism'. For a contrary view on Mexico, see Roxborough (1992*a* and 1992*b*).

sectoral chamber squarely within the analytical framework of democratic or societal corporatism—also known as 'liberal' or 'neo-'corporatism (Schmitter 1974; Schmitter and Lehmbruch 1979; Lehmbruch and Schmitter 1982; Berger 1981; Offe 1985a; Wilson 1983). However, upon closer examination it is apparent that such efforts at classification obscure more than they illuminate, conflating form with substance.

DEPARTURES FROM THE SOCIETAL CORPORATIST MODEL

In his now classic definition, Philippe Schmitter defines corporatism in the following terms:

a system of interest representation in which the constituent units are organized into a limited number of singular, compulsory, noncompetitive, hierarchically ordered and functionally differentiated categories, recognized or licensed (if not created) by the state and granted a deliberate representational monopoly within their respective categories in exchange for observing certain controls on their selection of leaders and articulation of demands and supports. (Schmitter 1974: 93–4)

Schmitter's distinction between 'state' and 'societal' variants of corporatism essentially turns on the degree of control from above exercised by state authorities through such structures—extensive in the former, negligible in the latter. In many formulations, moreover, democratic corporatism constitutes, or is closely associated with, a particular form of policy-making that is sometimes called 'concertation',[18] in which state and societal actors jointly formulate and/or implement and enforce authoritative public policies through structures with corporatist features.

It is also important to highlight other features of the corporatist framework as it evolved in the 1970s and 1980s. Initially, the concept was employed to highlight institutionalized relationships of bargaining among centralized or 'peak' interest organizations at the macro level. However, empirical studies revealed a high degree of 'hybridization' of corporatist (in both variants) and non-corporatist structures in most extant polities. A dominant view emerged in the literature that this was not an 'all-or-nothing', system-level concept but rather a matter of degree that refers to *sub*systems of the larger polity (Collier 1995). In this connection, the notion of meso-corporatism was developed by a number of authors to capture the particular dynamics of structured intermediate-level processes of interest representation

[18] Though the 'first wave' of the literature on neocorporatism in the 1970s was characterized by a polarization between those (led by Schmitter) who treated it as a mode of interest intermediation and others (led by Lehmbruch) who viewed it as a form of policy-making, a certain convergence occurred during the 'second wave'. The two came to be seen either as close theoretical 'cousins' (e.g. the essays in Lehmbruch and Schmitter 1982) or as part of one and the same phenomenon (e.g. the essays in Cawson 1985). While acknowledging the fact that there may be instances of concertation outside formal corporatist structures and that the corporatist structuring of interests may exist without formal societal participation in policy-making, I will adhere to the latter view, which sees a strong elective affinity between (societal) corporatism and concertation.

and policy-making circumscribed to a specific branch of the economy, geograph-ical region, or issue area (e.g. the essays in Allen and Riemer 1989 and in Cawson 1985, as well as Cawson 1986, Wassenberg 1982). Among advanced industrial countries, the existence of corporatist arrangements on this subsystem level was noted both as an additional feature of some polities with strong 'macrocorporatist' characteristics as well as a trait in certain circumscribed portions of other polities lacking in such general characteristics.

Key concepts for the corporatist literature are 'exchange', which is explicitly part of Schmitter's definition, and 'centralization', which is conveyed by his use of the term 'hierarchically ordered'. The first suggests that corporatist relation-ships are suffused with a logic of accommodation between competing interests and conflict resolution. The classic examples were the 'quid-pro-quo' bargains in which unions agreed to forgo 'excessive' wage increases that might spur inflation in return for state and managerial guarantees of employment security and some-times full employment. The second concept highlights the fact that corporatist ties link together large collective actors whose top leaders 'mediate' between the external environment and their members, needing to 'deliver' the compliance of their members in order to make enforceable bargains with other actors and also requiring the resources that they obtain from these bargains in order to maintain their positions of authority and organizational wherewithal. In this connection, it is worth noting that, in explaining the conditions for the emergence of neocorporatist arrangements, theorists placed overwhelming emphasis on *formal institutional vari-ables*, particularly related to centralization.

Both the 'group structure' and the organization and dynamics of negotiations in the Brazilian auto chamber departed in important ways from the societal cor-poratist framework. Turning first to the organization of labor and business actors participating in the chamber, it is clear that they diverged in important ways from the general requisites articulated by Schmitter and shared by neocorporatist the-orists. Traditionally, under Brazil's state corporatist structure, workers and busi-ness *sindicatos* were not only created by the state but also regulated heavily by it—financed through a compulsory tax levied on workers and firms (respectively); holding a monopoly on representation within particular sectors and territorial units; hierarchically ordered into state federations and a peak national confedera-tion based on branch of activity; strongly circumscribed in their internal proced-ures and subject to legal state intervention and oversight; and so on. (Although the extraction of 'dues' was 'compulsory', formal membership in unions was not —with membership ratios typically very low—and the incidence of 'active' mem-bership in business organizations was often quite minimal.) However, the com-bination of increased efforts to democratize *sindicatos* from within, dating back to the 1970s, with legal reforms adopted in the 1988 constitution created a consider-ably more fluid and less strictly regulated organizational environment for business and labor. With regard to the latter, the state lost the legal power to recognize (or de-recognize) *sindicatos*—opening up the possibility of competing organizations within a given jurisdiction—and to intervene in internal affairs, such as elections. The fact that after 1988 most business and labor organization continued to operate within unitary structures that were *internally competitive* but did not involve *competition between rival organizations within particular jurisdictions* thus must be seen as a function of organizational legacies and choices made by leaders, rather than as an artefact of state laws and regulations. Moreover, while the compulsory tax continued under the new constitution, some larger business and labor organizations moved partially or—in the case of the São Bernardo metalworkers' union—completely to voluntary assessments on members. Such moves were part of ongoing internal reform movements, which pushed for the creation of more democratic and participatory internal structures in many *sindicatos*.

In the case of the São Bernardo union that led the labor delegation within the sectoral chamber, reform movements dating back to the recapture of unions from state-dominated bureaucrats in the late 1970s led not only to the consolidation of transparent electoral procedures, but also the creation of an extensive series of channels of participation and representation not contemplated in labor law, such as worker-elected shop-floor works councils (*comissões de fábrica*). Moreover, like many of its CUT allies, the union had increased membership markedly over the course of the 1980s by conducting unionization drives. Moreover, the extensive territorial and sectoral structures of worker representation developed by the CUT were created in defiance of existing laws and still possess no formal legal standing. Nonetheless, these CUT organizations participated in the 1993 chamber negotiations alongside their member unions.

On the business side, the two key segments present in the negotiations, auto makers and parts manufacturers, each were represented in the chamber negotiations by both their official *sindicatos* and their parallel voluntary associations. Since the 1970s, voluntary sectoral associations gradually had emerged alongside these official business organizations throughout much of Brazilian industry. The two often 'fused' in practice, through joint elections, shared directorates, and the following division of labor: *sindicatos* negotiated with labor unions (given their legal power to sign contracts) while associations handled other sectoral business, such as technical assistance and lobbying (Kingstone 1994*b*). Such was the case with the two most important sectoral actors in the auto negotiations—the auto makers' association (Anfavea) and *sindicato* (Sinfavea) and the autoparts' association (Abipeças) and *sindicato* (Sindipeças). Moreover, both Anfavea/Sinfavea and Abipeças/Sindipeças underwent elections around the time of the revival of the chamber in which young 'reform' candidates calling for more activist, professional, and accountable sectoral leadership had succeeded in defeating 'old-line' incumbents (Kingstone 1994*b*).

To summarize the points made thus far, then, labor and capital organizations participating in the sectoral chamber were 'voluntarily singular'; 'compulsory' mainly with respect to dues (and with notable exceptions even there on the union side); externally 'non-competitive' but internally competitive; and quite autonomous in their internal life. All of these features constitute important departures from Schmitter's definition in terms of the structure of interests. And what of the centralized or 'hierarchically ordered' character of interest associations, to which Schmitter and other theorists of neocorporatism assigned such importance? On the business side, despite the presence of the official *sindicatos* and parallel voluntary associations—with their elected leadership, professional staff, etc.—some large firms also sent their own representatives and observers to the talks. On the labor side, changes were evident over the course of the negotiations. For the March 1992 accord, the São Bernardo union—which also represents workers from the neighboring municipalities of Diadema and, since the mid-1993 unification of the two unions, Santo André—was the only bargaining agent for labor; given the enormous number of auto sector workers concentrated in the so-called 'ABC' region—comparable in numbers and concentration to Detroit in its heyday—the union dominated the labor movement in that branch of the economy. It also had the formal support of two other CUT-affiliated unions from other municipalities.[19] For the negotiations leading up to the February 1993 accord, the union was joined by the metalworkers' confederation and state federation from the CUT's weakly centralized national structure and by three member unions of the rival Força Sindical, but nonetheless continued to be the principal negotiator. Hence, labor representation in the sectoral chamber displayed a mixture of horizontal coordination among unions and other 'sub-peak' entities belonging to a weakly centralized national organization, cooperation among 'sub-peak' entities belonging to rival national labor organizations, and *de facto* leadership by a single but very large local union. This pattern differed greatly from the strongly centralized national confederations and sectoral federations that were the quintessential protagonists of European neocorporatist arrangements. In sum, then, the structure of labor and capital interests participating in the Brazilian auto chamber was much more fluid and dynamic, much less rigid and hierarchical, than that which, by definition, characterizes neocorporatist interest intermediation. Even allowing for the fact that considerably less state control and greater societal autonomy are central to the democratic variant of corporatism, these departures from definitional norms are sufficiently great as to raise serious questions about the utility and propriety of classifying the chamber negotiations as neocorporatist.

In addition to the group structure of the auto negotiations, the character and dynamics of the chamber itself also departed sharply from democratic corporatist notions of centralized bargaining and exchange. While a logic of give-and-take and compromise inevitably was present, there was also an important element of what Chalmers, Piester, and I call, in the concluding chapter to this volume, 'cognitive politics'. That is to say, debate, exchanges of information and ideas, and some

---

[19] These were the unions of neighboring Santo André, which in 1993 fused with the São Bernardo union, and of Betim in the state of Minas Gerais, located in the industrial zone outside the city of Belo Horizonte.

amount of social learning all took place, as illustrated by the emphasis on continuous working-group discussions and on formulating common agendas prior to entering into concrete negotiations. A clear reflection of the new 'intersubjective' ties forged through the chamber is provided by the many new ties and arrangements forged at the level of production that were alluded to earlier. That is not to say that 'deals' were not cut and 'horses' were not traded, but rather to suggest that, in the course of the protracted and complex discussions, actors were forced to defend their objectives and proposals and confront new ideas, issues, and information they had not considered before. Inevitably, unexpected coalitions and connections between issues were formed and, in some cases, actors' minds were changed, or at least their priorities were reordered. Given the fact that the fundamental goal that was shared and articulated by all actors—the 'modernization' of the sector—involved a whole set of changes in attitudes and practices that could not possibly be enshrined fully in a written agreement, efforts to define, refine, and operationalize this complex and contested concept constituted the enduring 'subtext' of the entire negotiating process.[20]

The importance of the cognitive dimension of the chamber deliberations stems in large part from their loose and decentralized structure, which itself constitutes yet another departure from societal corporatist definitions. Not only did many negotiations take place through decentralized working groups within the chamber, but there were also additional 'layers' of negotiations on related issues at the firm and collective-bargaining levels that were linked, albeit only informally, with peak sectoral negotiations through the chamber. The sectoral chamber was thus but one part—however crucial—of a *multi-tiered, non-hierarchically ordered negotiating process*.

In sum, then, despite having a formal structure of tripartite representation and policy-making superficially reminiscent of meso-corporatism, the sectoral chamber differed strongly from the latter's characteristic centralized and monopolistic structures of interests and bargaining. Perhaps one crucial reason for the more flexible and decentralized structure and character of negotiations in the sectoral chamber is the distinct nature of the challenges its participants confronted. In contrast to the demand-management-centered problems that neocorporatist arrangements were called upon to resolve in the post-war period and especially in the 1960s and 1970s in various parts of Western Europe, the Brazilian auto industry in the early 1990s faced simultaneous demand-side challenges of *stimulation* together with supply-side challenges of *technological and organization modernization*. The

---

[20] For instance, an important goal of managers is to improve worker contributions to the enhancement of productivity and quality, through some combination of re-skilling, multi-tasking, teamwork, and employee suggestions on how to reorganize work processes generated by 'hands-on' experience. While various measures and procedures designed to improve workers' contributions in these areas may be negotiated and agreed upon, the quality of the efforts they expend is ultimately a subjective and individual attribute that cannot fully be 'commodified' and 'exchanged' through collective or other forms of bargaining.

centralized rigidity of peak national and sectoral bargaining seems well suited to the former, but distinctly ill suited to the latter. Indeed, it is instructive that, in European countries and sectors where such centralized arrangements have long been present, strong pressures for greater decentralization to the local and plant levels have been experienced in recent years as demands for more rapid and thoroughgoing productive restructuring have mounted (Hyman 1994; Katz 1993; Kern and Sabel 1991; Locke 1992).

Despite the lack of fit of the sectoral auto negotiations with neocorporatist formulations, they nonetheless exhibited a blurring of state–society boundaries through joint policy formulation, a feature that is shared with corporatism and distinguishes the sectoral chamber from the arms-length character of ties between states and fully autonomous groups characteristic of liberal-pluralism. If the pluralist model does not help to understand the rise and characteristics of the chamber, the question then arises, what alternative approaches are possible? In the following section, I seek to sketch out a tentative answer to this question.

ELEMENTS OF AN ALTERNATIVE FRAMEWORK: ASSOCIATIONAL GOVERNANCE, TRUST, AND NETWORKS

The first step towards developing an alternative framework involves returning to the puzzles with which the chapter opened, which center on how actors managed to overcome a heritage of state corporatist control (especially of labor), unrepresentative organizations, and secretive dealings between large firms and the state, as well as a recent history of conflict in labor relations and supplier–producer ties. The foregoing discussion suggests that, in the context of Brazil and its auto industry, overcoming two types of obstacles was an essential *precondition* for the establishment of the particular form of loosely structured and cognitively dynamic negotiating arrangements that took hold—unrepresentative, top-down internal governance structures within organizations and weak and often conflict-ridden ties among competing actors. On the first point, it seems fairly straightforward that organizations of capital and labor that do not command a fairly high degree of legitimacy and authority in the eyes of their memberships will not be able to negotiate flexibly and creatively. In the particular case of business organizations, leaders' need for support is strengthened by an additional factor—as Offe and Wiesenthal (1985) note, it is firms who control the most important decisions in question (investment, production, use of labor power, etc.) rather than business associations. Hence, the ability of the latter to control the actions of individual firms, especially larger and powerful ones, through bureaucratic 'command and control' is circumscribed severely. However, it is equally important to point out that the particular form taken by efforts to make labor and business organizations more participatory and effective was quite consequential—*rather than pulverizing or splintering them, reformers strengthened mechanisms of internal accountability and external coordination across organizational boundaries* (i.e. among union entities and between business *sindicatos* and associations). Such reforms facilitated greatly the flexible, multi-tier negotiating process of which the chamber was a part and which it helped engender.

On the second point, it is logical to expect that mutual enmity among competitors—what some analysts call 'mistrust'—may raise the perceived costs attached to acts of cooperation as well as make it much more unlikely that cooperative approaches to common problems even will be considered. As it has come to be defined and employed, the concept of 'trust' denotes the willingness to make oneself vulnerable to the actions of an adversary, in the expectation that cooperation by the adversary will leave one (and perhaps both) better off than before (Coleman 1990; Gambetta 1988; Luhmann 1979; Putnam 1993; and Sabel 1992). This quality is generally held to be a useful—and sometimes indispensable—'lubricant' for turning conflictive or competitive relationships between political or social actors into more cooperative ones.

My field research produced considerable evidence that an important wellspring for the experimentation with new forms of bargaining that underlay the initiation of tripartite bargaining in late 1991 was subtle ongoing changes in relationships between managers and unionists. These changes, which I characterize as a move from 'antagonism' to 'adversarialism', generated a belief by both parties that the other was sufficiently trustworthy to justify taking a chance on opening a new negotiating front, whose form was without precedent and whose consequences were unforeseeable. The proximate cause of this bilateral search for new forms of cooperation was, of course, the common perception of crisis and expectation of imminent disaster for the industry if urgent remedial steps were not taken. Yet, crisis alone does not necessarily engender cooperation, despite the tendency of analysts to assign primary or exclusive explanatory weight to that factor in explaining the emergence of cooperation in Brazilian autos (Arbix 1995; Cardoso and Comin 1993; Diniz 1994; Oliveira *et al.* 1993). As Golden (1990) notes in the West European context, for instance, even militant unions facing what they perceive as certain defeat often may 'stick by their guns' for what may be perceived as eminently rational reasons.[21] Moreover, given the highly conflictive prior history of labor relations in both the auto industry and Brazil as well as the CUT's long-standing commitment to autonomy and militant strategies, the establishment of tripartism was a strongly counter-intuitive development—a sharp discontinuity in previously existing social relations—that demands a powerful explanation.

Oliveira *et al.* (1993) very aptly describe capital–labor relations in the auto industry from the late 1970s onward as a 'conflictive relationship of nullification

---

[21] Golden's argument is that unions persist in militant action despite certain defeat when their primary aim of organizational maintenance is perceived to be served by efforts that will enable them to shape what might be called 'the terms of defeat' (in the case at hand, this involves who will be dismissed and who retained in the context of massive work-force reductions).

of "the other"' (quotes mine). Such a description could easily be extended to state–labor and capital–labor relations in general. The CUT, founded in 1983, inherited the new unionist movement's posture of militant opposition toward both capital and the state, and its union affiliates were at the center of the unprecedented levels of labor mobilization experienced by Brazil in the 1980s, including the country's first two general strikes since the opening decade of this century. Echoing the generally antagonistic attitude of the state toward the CUT, the business community, particularly the powerful São Paulo State Federation of Industries (FIESP), took a more 'hard-line' attitude toward unions in the mid-1980s, after having shown an incipient openness to dialogue and negotiation in the early 1980s. Auto companies were part of this trend. Only a few years after they had (under strong union pressure) agreed to create the country's first worker-elected works councils, auto makers began resorting to former practices of firing union militants and even, in the case of Ford, dismissing the entire worker-elected factory commission in 1986. Given the explosive combination of a hard-line management and militant, well-organized metalworkers' unions, the auto industry was the scene, particularly from 1985 to 1987, of strikes that were veritable pitched battles—often lasting for weeks and involving worker occupations, harsh public recriminations by managers and unionists, and even incidents of sabotage.

Where Oliveira and other analysts of the sectoral chamber go astray is in failing to explore carefully events in the industry in the last few years before the chamber became tripartite, which suggested a subtle incipient shift away from unmitigated confrontation. From June to December 1992, I conducted research on the São Bernardo union and on labor relations in a large auto manufacturing factory within its jurisdiction, carrying out extensive interviews with scores of workers, unionists, and management officials.[22] These conversations (which built upon earlier fieldwork on the industry conducted by the author in 1986 and 1990) revealed that, since the period of acute conflict during the second third of the 1980s, supervisors had become less authoritarian; lay-offs had ceased to be used as a disciplinary measure and had become subject to negotiation; and the relationship between management and the works council, though by no means free of conflict, had become more 'professional' and subject to institutionalized procedures. These changes can be attributed to a combination of learning from the painful lessons of earlier struggles on both sides and of turnovers in managerial personnel and plant activist ranks that had brought to positions of authority individuals less identified with the earlier period of antagonism.

While moves toward dialogue were at first uneven and by no means irreversible, they took on greater urgency around the turn of the decade, as the company became

---

[22] In addition to a skill-stratified 'mini-sample' of thirteen workers, my plant-level research included interviews with roughly a dozen plant unionists (between past and present factory commission members and worker-elected members of the CIPA, the bilateral internal accident-prevention commission) and an approximately equal number of management officials, divided between production supervisors and industrial relations officers.

more serious about worker involvement in quality control and the crisis of the auto industry deepened. Informants on both sides confirmed in 1992 that, to borrow the words of one unionist, 'now for everything the *comissão* is sought out beforehand', in the sense of being consulted or notified of major workplace decisions affecting workers.[23] However, despite the fact that the works council no longer opposed management's participation and quality programs, a policy of full-scale participation had not been adopted due to internal divisions on this issue.

Interviews with informants outside the above plant suggested that the shop-floor changes that I observed were part of a larger, ongoing process of evolution in labor relations in Brazil's auto industry. The national human resources manager for the company that owned the factory in question told me, in August 1990, that both unions and managers had developed a greater 'awareness' of the need for improved dialogue (personal interview, 23 Aug. 1990). He also said that he had developed good working relationships with not only Vicentinho but also union leaders from the Força Sindical, which represented workers at some of its other plants.

Interviews with São Bernardo union officials in 1990 and 1992 also revealed that the union had softened its once strident opposition to auto companies' programs of worker involvement by the start of the new decade and had begun actively to encourage unionists and workers to participate in efforts to improve productivity and quality control by 1992. The union's shift in posture had the objective of shaping and contesting management decisions, as well as turning quality and participation programs into mechanisms for improving working conditions. The labor relations director of another auto plant in São Bernardo confirmed this change in union policy, noting that Vicentinho frequently justified this by using the phrase, 'we're not defending the industrialist, we're defending the industry' (personal interview, 27 Mar. 1992). Much like informants at the other factory, this manager indicated that, during his two years at the plant, the previous 'situation of confrontation' had been overcome and negotiations with unionists had become 'very frank, transparent, and mutually respectful'. Similarly, he noted that the two sides were operating under a tacit understanding that disputes would be negotiated before unionists would organize any sort of job action.

In sum, *well before* the time of the automotive chamber negotiations, São Bernardo unionists and auto companies had transformed what was once a 'total, no-holds-barred war' into an emerging institutionalized dialogue wherein the 'use of force'—in the form of punitive measures—was becoming more of a last resort for both parties. That is, 'sworn enemies' were becoming more akin to 'adversaries'. In terms of union strategy, I have characterized this shift as a move from 'oppositional militancy' to 'innovative militancy', borrowing terms developed by Chris-

---

[23] A second-term council member, interview with the author, 11 Nov. 1992, São Bernardo do Campo. Examples of decisions on which the commission were consulted routinely during the period of my research were transfers of workers to other factories, ways of cutting back working time to compensate for reduced demand, disciplinary problems with individual workers, and changes in physical layout to accommodate new machines.

topher Allen in the European context.[24] I have also shown how this shift was driven more generally by processes of learning structured through social networks of communication, inside and outside the union, which linked the leadership to rank and file, plant activists, labor-oriented non-governmental organizations, other CUT unions, international labor confederations, and Workers' Party activists (Martin 1995).

The specific arguments regarding business–labor relations presented here appear to be more generally valid with respect to the changing character of bilateral ties within the industry and to the state. Elsewhere (Martin 1995), I have cited evidence indicating that there were important ties—both personal and political—between unionists and business officials, on one hand, and a reformist clique who entered the Economics Ministry and its Secretariat of Industry and Commerce in 1991 amidst a general cabinet reshuffle. Further research is necessary to determine whether or not more trusting bonds also had begun to emerge in producer–supplier relations prior to the onset of tripartism. The general hypothesis is that, when actors took the historic step of establishing a tripartite chamber, they were taking a 'leap of faith' but not a 'leap in the dark'. *Iterative encounters among them had generated a realistic belief in the possibility of exploring unorthodox forms of cooperation like tripartism.* In particular, the actors had a reasonable basis, in the trustworthiness demonstrated in recent times by their adversaries, for judging that the latter would not take advantage of concessions made or weaknesses exposed in the course of negotiations. Hence, for each, 'taking a chance' on cooperation presented itself as a propitious course with which to experiment. With time, of course, successful negotiations generated increasing degrees of mutual trust and, as implied above, the latter may well have had positive 'spill-over effects' that help account for the subsequent (and still ongoing) strengthening of governance arrangements in the productive system.

The emphasis on ties among actors and internal governance arrangements within organizations dovetails closely with the proposed analytical model of so-called 'associative networks' in the concluding chapter of this volume. These are held to be a novel, non-hierarchical type of structure of representation (often involving popular actors) in which state and societal actors join together to shape public policy. In so far as the sectoral chamber brought participants together voluntarily, on formally equal footing, and with no restrictions on exit, it shares this basic non-hierarchical feature. Moreover, other distinctive features of this model of flexibly structured representation—the diversity of participants, frequent institutional reconfiguration, an emphasis on cognitive politics, and less rigid inequalities—are all manifested rather clearly in the sector-wide auto negotiations and the larger process of joint policy-making and governance to which it contributed. Indeed, as a hypothesis that merits further research, I would argue that the sectoral chamber

---

[24] Martin 1995. For Allen (1990: 70 n. 15), 'oppositional militance' refers to 'traditional, defensive, anticapitalist militance, unable (or unwilling) to formulate an alternative to the status quo within capitalism'. He defines 'innovative militance' as 'the use of union mobilization that points to a strategy and tactics that can be used for more potentially transformative purposes'.

as part of a larger sociopolitical process may be traced along the following lines: from (1) emerging trust-based social networks connecting competing actors within the sector and between it and the state (1990–1); to (2) the establishment and initial success of an associative network expressed organizationally through (but not limited to) the formal structure of the chamber (1992–3); to (3) the positive feedback effects of sector-wide negotiations on social networks of production and the creation of new governance arrangements on that level (1992–4); and finally to (4) the demise of the chamber due in large part to the absence of network ties between chamber participants and the new cohort of policy-makers who entered the government in 1993 with Cardoso; and (5) the underlying persistence and ongoing strengthening of production-level networks, now with few or very weak ties to state actors (1994–5).

Conclusions: Implications for Popular Sector Strategy

The experience of the Brazilian sectoral chamber and its aftermath suggests both the promises and perils associated with new structures of popular representation premised on extensive cooperation with more powerful elites and on pro-active popular strategies. One promising aspect is clearly the opportunity that these structures may afford to shape state policies in a more progressive and beneficial direction. In the case at hand, analysts such as Shapiro (1996) and Castañeda (1993*a*, 1993*b*) have noted that the reactivation, boom, and restructuring of the industry represented a novel and successful sectoral effort to combat the devastating impact of trade liberalization measures adopted unilaterally and in a vacuum by Collor; in essence, *unilateral neoliberal measures begat cooperative and collective efforts to embed expanding market relations in concrete social ties and institutional arrangements of governance.* This effort was accomplished through negotiated policies premised on collaborative modernization efforts, a gradualist approach to tariff-cutting, and a judicious mixture of domestic and international demand. Without entering into the debate on economic alternatives to neoliberalism, it is worth mentioning in passing that the unusual characteristics of the Brazilian auto industry—its size, central national importance, the level of organization of its actors, etc.—may well make it difficult to generate in other sectors or countries the same degree of focused attention and effort that underlay the chamber's brief but notable success. Another promising dimension of the chamber and its aftermath was that this experience also enabled unionists to secure an important role in shaping governance arrangements at the level of production. This ensured that they would be involved in the design and implementation of the type of innovations—flexible work weeks, teamwork, and the like—that often are being adopted in unilateral and exploitative fashion, not only in contemporary Latin America but throughout the world system.

The perils associated with cooperative forms of interest representation and the pursuit of proactive strategies are also highlighted by this study. Some of the wage gains secured by unions were undercut by state policy shifts, while firms failed to meet their employment-creation targets, instead relying more on overtime and intensification of work rather than on new hires. Moreover, when tight credit led to a dip in consumption toward mid-1995, some 150,000 layoffs ensued in the following months (Shapiro 1996: 32), though some were reversed later under innovative firm-level accords combining a flexible work week (varying between 46 and 38 hours) with a reduction in use of subcontracted, non-unionized labor. Two lessons for popular actors in comparable situations seem to emerge: (1) the need to push for goals and timetables backed by stronger oversight and enforcement mechanisms on controversial or difficult items, and (2) the importance of developing and acting upon as clear a reading as possible on the pattern of divisions and alliances within the state apparatus regarding issues of immediate concern.

Finally, this study clarifies two important dimensions of cooperative situations that are misunderstood frequently by both critics and advocates of new popular strategies. First, the road to such situations is paved not simply with good intentions or with innovative proposals, but also with the ongoing construction of interlocutorial ties with competing and often more powerful actors. When such actors do not recognize a popular organization's legitimacy or value as an interlocutor and persist in unilateral and confrontational strategies—as Brazilian firms did throughout the 1980s—that organization has little choice but to stand its ground and 'fight', intelligently picking its battles, to achieve the respect it deserves. Had Brazilian auto unions not blunted the impact of unilateral restructuring initiatives over the course of the 1980s throughout protracted, often bitter, struggles, for instance, it is clear that they would not have earned the grudging recognition that was an *essential* precondition for the dynamic of growing cooperation that ensued in the 1990s.

The final point is that the meaning of cooperation for popular organizations must be clarified and put into proper perspective. It entails not the abandonment of militant actions, but rather a more conscious harnessing of such actions in the service of well-defined goals of substantive and procedural reform. In the case at hand, unionists did not cease to go on strike and stage job actions when necessary; rather, these became political tools used selectively to enforce deals, break deadlocks, and so on within a complex, multi-tiered negotiating process. Nor does cooperation entail a renunciation of transformative goals, at least those lying short of revolutionary upheaval. Rather, the ultimate cost for militant popular actors comes in the form of accepting a greater institutionalization of conflict resolution through cooperative arrangements. It is against this cost, as well as the benefits and disadvantages of perceived alternatives to pursuing cooperation through pro-activism, that popular actors in any given setting must weigh the potential gains associated with obtaining access to vital decision-making centers through the establishment of more regularized ties.

3 Union Politics, Market-Oriented Reforms, and the Reshaping of Argentine Corporatism

M. Victoria Murillo[1]

Introduction

In the 1980s and 1990s, Argentina joined the wave of Latin American countries initiating programs of economic stabilization and structural reform. In 1989, in the midst of a hyperinflationary crisis, Argentina's second democratic administration since the transition of 1983 took office. President Raúl Alfonsín from the Radical party was replaced by President Carlos Menem from the labor-based Peronist party. President Menem reversed previous Peronist economic policy preferences for government economic intervention, expansionary policies, and import substitution industrialization by committing his administration to economic stabilization and a structural reform of the Argentine economy. The Argentine union movement had cemented its historic allegiance with the Peronist party on those previous policies, which included protectionism and Keynesian demand management, labor-based social benefits, and state regulation of the labor market favoring the organization of labor. The withdrawal of the state from economic activities, coupled with the policy shifts of the Peronist party, constitutes a fundamental challenge for the Argentine union movement.

This chapter focuses on union strategies to respond to the reshaping of state institutions affecting union constituencies, organizational structures, and relations with the Peronist party during the first administration of President Menem (July 1989–July 1995). The diverse strategies pursued by Argentine unions to face these challenges included opposition, loyalty, and organizational autonomy—of which the latter was most innovative. The main argument of the chapter is that the strategy of organizational autonomy was a direct response to the new distribution of union power resources (industrial, political, and organizational). These resources resulted from the new political and economic conditions that accompanied the

[1] The author would like to thank Ernesto Cabrera, Jorge Domínguez, Virginie Guiraudon, Robert Kaufman, Steve Levitsky, Scott Martin, James McGuire, Ian Roxborough, and William Smith for their comments on this chapter.

process of structural reforms. Organizational autonomy as a strategic response was also shaped by organizational legacies, including legal structures for labor organization favoring their interests in industrial policy. Organizational autonomy entailed the development of new resources adapted to the new environment of market competition. This strategy brought about a reshaping of state–union relations in such a way that unions partially evolved away from their corporatist dependence on state regulations and towards the ownership and administration of production and consumptive activities. From this perspective, the Argentine case broadens the horizon of alternatives for unions facing the challenge of stabilization and structural reforms, thus recasting established understandings of relationships between labor-based parties and affiliated unions.

The chapter is divided into four sections: a theoretical justification of my approach; a description of the main reforms and their consequences for unions; an analysis of how unions reacted to the withdrawal of the state, emphasizing organizational autonomy as a main strategy; and an explanation of the conditions that induced diverse union strategies.

1. Structural Reforms and State–Union Relations

I use the case of Argentina to introduce an argument about the conditions that shape union strategies in a corporatist context of labor regulation modified by market-oriented reforms implemented by a labor-based party. I also use this case to analyze the impact of the union strategy of 'organizational autonomy' on state–union relations.

Charlotte Yates (1992) points out that unions' strategic capacity to pursue a chosen strategy is influenced by immediate political-economic conditions and union resources. Following that argument and Jeannette Money's (1992) assumption that union leaders seek to maximize membership, I focus my study on the factors that shape the strategic capacity of unions rather than on their internal decision-making processes. My emphasis on external constraints to union strategies rather than internal dynamics derives from the fact that union decision-making in Argentina is dominated by national leaders. As Yates explains, the elements that define relations between rank and file and leadership—membership access to decision-making and mobilization of internal union opposition, centralization of union resources by the leadership, and channels of communication to connect leadership with rank and file—are skewed by labor regulations in favor of national leaders' control over rank and file and local leadership. I analyze how the change in political-economic conditions affected union resources and, thus, the capacity of unions to pursue their preferences. Moreover, I also analyze the organizational character of unions and its impact not only on union capacities, but also on the pre-eminence of industrial over universal preferences.

To understand the impact of shifting political and economic conditions on union resources and strategic capacity, I use a variation of Korpi's (1978) concept of the 'power resources' of the working class. Since the focus of my analysis is unions, I consider the distribution of 'power resources' not only in its political and industrial dimensions, but also in its organizational dimension. Organizational resources include elements such as finances, structure, and leadership patterns (Moe 1980), as well as the provision of selective incentives by the organization. Organizational resources can originate in the industrial or political arena, but they can also develop in a third arena: that of profit-seeking activities. Workers traditionally have been consumers of selective incentives developed to solve the problem of labor organizations (Olson 1971) or to provide services for their members as a complement to industrial representation. However, unions can expand their provision of services outside the segment of consumers constituted by their members, and they can also seek business profits to increase or maintain organizational resources that can be used in the provision of selective incentives or in the other arenas. I argue that the decision to use or invest in any type of resource[2] depends on both the immediate political and economic conditions pointed out by Yates, as well as the impact of organizational legacies and the previous experiences with each type of resource on the part of the national union movement.[3]

The Argentine union movement has been affiliated with the Peronist party since the origins of the party and this alliance was expressed in a corporatist framework of labor regulations that subsidized and controlled labor organization (Collier and Collier 1991). Moreover, this regulation strengthened industry-wide union organizing by guaranteeing monopolies of representation, financial autonomy, and provision of services at the industry level (as analyzed in the next section). Corporatist labor regulations endow union leaders with a degree of autonomy from labor market conditions. The use of political resources replaces that of industrial resources and results in institutions that enhance union influence (Pizzorno 1978). However, the current processes of structural reform and industrial restructuring challenge this institutionalized influence and induce unions to adopt different strategies to confront these threats.

Claus Offe (1985b) and Charles Sabel (1981) point out the different interests of leaders and rank and file and the ways in which participation in corporatist institutions resolves the tension between the need for workers' militancy to reach compromises with employers and the requirement of containing this same militancy in order to maintain the labor concessions that have been granted in exchange.

---

[2] Korpi (1985: 38) defines investment in power resources as 'present sacrifices through the conversion of resources in ways which can increase future benefits. At least four major forms . . . [are the] development of channels for the mobilization of power resources, creation of institutions for decision-making and conflict regulation, conversion of power resources from more costly to less costly types, and the fostering of anticipated reactions.'

[3] The impact of organizational boundaries and institutional legacies on union strategies for advanced capitalist countries has been analyzed in the recent work of the new historic institutionalism (e.g. Golden and Pontusson 1992; Thelen 1993; Rothstein 1992).

Moreover, political exchanges tend to be preferred to industrial exchange when labor-based political parties are in government, because union leaders' uncertainty about the future fulfillment of compromises is reduced (Przeworski and Wallerstein 1982) and, thus, they are more prone to control labor unrest. Besides, labor-based parties are more likely to grant state guarantees that reduce the need of union leaders to resort to worker militancy. However, Collier and Collier (1977) point out that in Latin America, these state institutions can be double-edged and accompanied by formal requirements that make labor leaders more dependent on the state. In addition, if institutions are modified, union leaders with a demobilized rank and file are very exposed to the loss of these state guarantees (Offe 1985b). This situation of institutional transformation was experienced by the Argentine union movement during the first administration of President Menem. Before analyzing the impact of these market-oriented reforms on union resources, the next section briefly reviews Argentine labor regulation and its impact on union capacities and preferences.

NATIONAL INDUSTRIAL UNIONS AS THE LOCUS OF POWER

The organizational boundaries and the institutional legacies that delimit the authority of national leaders and the financial strength of national industrial unions in Argentina are remarkably important in defining the prevalence of industrial interest and in shaping the strategic capacities of such unions. Three main laws established the structure of the Argentine union movement: Law 23,551 on professional associations, Law 14,250 on collective bargaining, and Law 23,660 on welfare funds.[4] These laws were re-enacted during the 1983–9 Radical administration because they had been suspended by the previous military regime.

The law on professional associations established a pyramidal organization for unions, based on the monopoly of one union per activity or industry, with high authority levels granted to the national union leadership and very reduced autonomy for local unions and shop-floor delegates, especially in the case of *uniones*. National leaders also collect union dues and welfare funds' compulsory fees by a system of automatic retention at the source by the employers (Laws 14,250 and 23,551).[5] The law on collective bargaining required employers to negotiate per industry

[4] Union-administered welfare funds provide mandatory health services to every worker of the industry according to Law 18,610 of 1970. Welfare funds expanded to other activities as well, such as tourism, recreation, complementary pensions, and educational and training services. State support of these activities can be traced, however, to Decree 30,655 of 1944, which promoted the provision of health and other social services for workers.

[5] The fact that Law 14,250 excluded unions from paying taxes when developing activities that benefit their members may have enhanced the development of welfare funds. The health and social services provided by these union-administered welfare funds became selective incentives despite the requirement that welfare funds provide health to workers regardless of union membership status. In many cases, membership in unions increased the range of available health services and opened social services to workers.

with the national union that held the monopoly of representation recognized by the state, and established the right of unions to negotiate with employers the retention of extraordinary quotas, which applied to members and non-members alike because the outcome of collective bargaining includes every worker. This legal scheme provided national industrial unions with high levels of authority and the opportunity to expand the activities of their organization around welfare funds and to use their organizational resources even when the party was banned. However, it deprived the national peak labor association (General Confederation of Labor or CGT) of authority over national industrial unions and financial and organizational means. This structure resulted both in high levels of control over rank and file by leadership, and in a union movement divided across industrial lines due to the restriction of competition within every industry. This type of organization also enhanced the prevalence of industrial over general interests because the peak labor association that could have subsumed diverse industrial concerns into a more general one to respond to a more diversified constituency lacked authority to control national industrial unions.

The next section analyzes the impact of economic reforms on unions and their constituencies, as well as the different union responses to the institutional changes involved in the reform process.

2. Argentine Economic Reforms

In 1983, after seven years of authoritarian rule, Argentina re-established democracy. The new Radical administration under President Alfonsín was faced with a long-term economic crisis deepened by the shock of the debt crisis. The effects of the economic crisis on workers included increasing unemployment (especially in the industrial sector), deteriorating wages, a declining labor share of the GDP, and increasing income inequality (Marshal 1989; W. Smith 1992). Wages did not decline uniformly across all sectors. Unskilled workers, workers in the public sector, and those in the less dynamic industries suffered the largest decline in real wages and living standards (Minujin 1993; Becaria and Orsatti 1990; Marshal 1989). President Alfonsín unsuccessfully attempted to stabilize the Argentine economy starting in 1985, when he launched the Austral Plan. His stabilization efforts encountered the opposition of the Peronist CGT, which organized thirteen general strikes against his economic and wage policies. Meanwhile, the Peronist legislators opposed the few privatization projects submitted to Congress by this administration.

By the end of the Alfonsín administration in 1989, unemployment and underemployment had risen while real industrial wages had sharply declined (Indec 1993a). A Peronist administration was elected to replace the Radical government in the midst of a deep fiscal crisis and hyperinflation that sharply eroded the purchasing power of wages. President Menem's inauguration was pushed forward by five months and he committed his government both to a stabilization program and to a structural reform of the public sector that would change the state's role in the regulation of markets. After Menem was inaugurated, Congress passed the Law of State Reform and the Law of Economic Emergency. This legislation attacked the fiscal deficit by reducing state expenditures and reforming the tax system while also introducing the privatization of public enterprises, trade liberalization, and a tax reform. At the beginning of 1991, a new Minister of the Economy, Domingo Cavallo, initiated a stabilization program that established a parity conversion between the peso and the dollar, with the legal commitment to back any monetary emission with dollar reserves in order to halt inflationary expectations. Seeking to reduce the public budget deficit, he accelerated the privatization process, cut back state expenditures, and increased tax revenues.

The consequences of these policies for workers and unions were diverse. Wage-earners benefited from reduced inflation while the impact of wage restraints varied according to activity. Real industrial wages maintained a declining trend (see Table 3.2 and Fig. 3.1) that showed the erosion of unions' industrial strength, although there was variation across sectors (Indec 1993a, 1995a). Unemployment and underemployment grew after 1991, with unemployment reaching a peak of 18.6 per cent of the economically active population in May 1995 (Table 3.1). Moreover, according to Gonda (1995), between the start of the adjustment program based on dollar parity (March 1991) and May 1995 more than 594,000 jobs were lost, about half of those by lay-offs. This reduction in employment was particularly sharp for state employees, railroad workers, city workers, and textile workers (54 per cent of job losses). In addition, according to official figures for 1993, half of those dismissed were never officially notified and 62 per cent of those did not receive severance payments, while 89.5 per cent were not paid unemployment insurance (Indec 1994). The state of the labor market affected both workers, through increasing job competition, and unions, through a decline in membership and an erosion of their industrial resources. In the public sector, privatization and adjustment processes were an important cause of job losses and the real income of public administration employees dropped.[6] The decline in public sector wages and employment was especially painful in the poor north-western provinces, where a large proportion of the population is employed by the provincial public sector.

Unemployment and job loss caused by privatization affected unions through a reduction in membership and industrial resources. In addition, decrees that

---

[6] In 1989 there were 302,600 employees in state-owned enterprises. In 1993, 103,500 of them lost their jobs or accepted early retirement (*Página 12*-CASH, 20 Mar. 1994). Moreover, 107,000 civil servants from the provincial and municipal governments were dismissed between 1989 and 1992, according to a World Bank Report (McGuire 1994). In addition, between 1989 and 1993 the national bureaucracy lost 672,754 civil servants (Indec 1994), while the wages of those in the administrative career system created in 1991 dropped by almost 15 per cent between 1992 and the end of 1994, according to the official statistics of the Ministry of Labor (Ministerio de Trabajo 1994b).

Table 3.1. Urban employment and unemployment rates during the first Menem administration (July 1989–July 1995)

Date	'Activity'	Employment	Unemployment	Underemployment
Oct. 1989	39.3	36.5	7.1	8.6
May 1990	39.1	35.7	8.6	9.3
Oct. 1990	39	36.5	6.3	8.9
June 1991	39.5	36.8	6.9	8.3
Oct. 1991	39.5	37.1	6	7.9
May 1992	39.8	37.1	6.9	8.3
Oct. 1992	40.2	37.4	7	8.1
May 1993	41.5	37.5	9.9	8.8
Oct. 1993	41	37.1	9.3	9.3
May 1994	41.1	36.7	10.7	10.2
Oct. 1994	40.8	35.8	12.2	10.4
May 1995	42.8	34.9	18.6	11.3

Source: Instituto Nacional de Estadísticas y Censos, Encuesta Permanente de Hogares, Información de Prensa, Oct. 1993 and May 1995. These rates concern the EAP (economically active population), which is composed of all the people with a job or actively searching for one. The activity rate measures the ratio of the EAP to the total population. The employment rate measures the ratio of the employed to the total population. The unemployment rate measures those that lack a job but are not seeking one. The underemployment rate measures those that work less than 35 hours a week (Indec 1993*b*, 1995*b*).

Table 3.2. Basic real wages achieved by collective bargaining for industrial and construction workers (general average, 1988 = 100)

Month	Skilled	Unskilled	Month	Skilled	Unskilled
Nov. 91	75.4	75.5	Jan. 94	73.4	73.9
Dec. 91	75	75.1	Feb. 94	73.4	74
Jan. 92	73.1	73.4	Mar. 94	73.4	73.9
Feb. 92	71.8	72	Apr. 94	73.5	74
Mar. 92	70.5	70.7	May 94	73.3	73.8
Apr. 92	70.2	70.4	June 94	73.1	73.5
May 92	70.5	70.7	July 94	72.6	73
June 92	70.4	70.5	Aug. 94	72.5	72.9
July 92	69.3	69.6	Sept. 94	72.1	72.5
Aug. 92	68.5	68.7	Oct. 94	71.9	72.3
Sept. 92	68.5	68.6	Nov. 94	73.2	73.9
Oct. 92	67.8	68	Dec. 94	73	73.7
Nov. 92	67.6	67.8	Jan. 95	72.1	72.9
Dec. 92	67.6	67.8	Feb. 95	72.1	72.9
Jan. 93	67.2	67.4	Mar. 95	72.5	73.2
Feb. 93	66.8	67.1	Apr. 95	72.2	72.9
Mar. 93	66.7	66.8	May 95	72.2	72.9
Apr. 93	66.1	66.3	June 95	72.3	73.1

Source: Ministerio de Trabajo y Seguridad Social (Indec 1993*a*, 1995*a*).

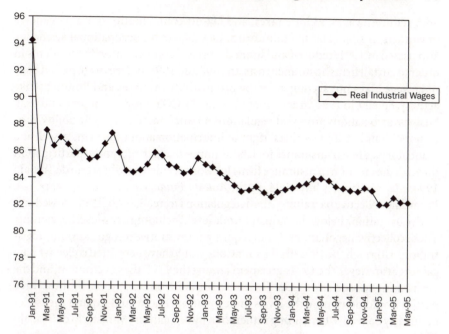

Fig 3.1. Real monthly industrial wages, 1991–1995

linked wage increases to productivity and restricted strike activity undercut union capacity to maintain workers' real incomes through collective bargaining (Table 3.2). Furthermore, the earlier economic crisis and the opening of the economy to international trade induced a segmentation of firms within activities according to levels of competitiveness. This segmentation made it difficult to sustain the traditional national strategies of national industrial unions. Since union leaders were aware that these reforms affected union resources, they tried to use their remaining resources to influence the design of the new institutions in order to safeguard organizational capacities. That is, they invested in certain kinds of resources. They focused on the reform of labor market regulations (including those affecting labor organization), the privatization of public enterprises, and the deregulation of social security and health services because these are reforms that have a strong impact on union resources and capacities. They affect the main laws regarding union organization and financial support (described above).

A SHIFTING SCENARIO FOR ARGENTINE UNIONS

The labor regulation reforms of the first Menem administration were centered on employment, collective bargaining, and union organization; they impacted the institutions that frame union action. Employment Law 24,013, passed in 1991, introduced numerical and pay flexibility through temporary hiring contracts with reduced wages, welfare taxes, and lay-off compensation for a percentage of workers in small and medium firms. Law 24,028 on occupational accidents, also passed in 1991, reduced and limited workers' compensation for accidents in order to curtail firms' insurance costs. In 1990 and 1991, decrees were passed banning wage hikes not accompanied by productivity increases and limiting strike activity. Finally, in 1994 an agreement among the CGT, the government, and peak business associations proposed regulations on work-force and pay flexibility, professional training, and workers' right to information about the firm, as well as a mandatory system of insurance for labor injuries that permits union participation through the creation of insurance firms for work accidents (Ministerio de Trabajo 1994*b*; *La Nación*, 25 July 1994, p. 14; *Ambito Financiero*, 2 Aug. 1994, p. 14). Regarding collective bargaining, the deregulation Decree 2,284 of 1991 allowed collective bargaining below the industry-wide level, including firm-level bargaining. Those collective negotiations do not require administrative recognition, only registration. Although the 1993 draft Labor Code would have permitted collective bargaining at any level, the 1994 agreement among the CGT, the government, and the peak business associations specified that a commission constituted by these three parties would determine the levels of negotiation, and would expand the topics defined by collective bargaining rather than by regulation (Ministerio de Trabajo 1994*a*).

The main consequences of these employment and collective bargaining reforms were the increasing use of lower-level negotiations for collective bargaining (although national unions tended to represent the labor side even at lower levels of negotiation), and the increasing inclusion of productivity and flexibility clauses to reduce labor and production costs in recent collective agreements.[7] Additionally, the impact of the new political-economic conditions on strike activity can be seen in a decrease in the number of strikes since the beginning of the administration, and especially after the second half of 1990 (McGuire forthcoming). The impact on job competition, wage restraint, and strike activity eroded the capacity for worker mobilization and, hence, union industrial resources. However, industrial resources may be open to redefinition if collective bargaining ends up allowing unions to acquire a new role in the definition of work conditions. Moreover, mandatory insurance for work accidents may enable unions to provide this privately administered service to workers, thus increasing union organizational resources (*Ambito Financiero*, 2 Aug. 1994, p. 14).

Regarding union organization, the project to reform Law 23,551, which would have decreased the obstacles to forming new union organizations and to challenging

[7] The negotiations between employers and unions that occurred between April 1991 and July 1994 introduced many clauses concerned with productivity and flexibility. They referred to increases in production capacity and work time (6 per cent); to the reorganization of work (functional flexibility, reform of hierarchies, and negotiation over working methods) (20 per cent); to the reduction of wage costs (numerical and pay flexibility) and other costs (schedule reorganization, distribution of vacation time, technological innovations, and labor peace clauses) (27 per cent); and to work incentives (18 per cent) (Deibe *et al.* 1994).

the monopoly of representation, was modified to restrict union competition only at the confederation level. Although it would have maintained authority prerogatives for national industrial unions, union pressures deterred any reform of regulations on union organization during this period. The privatization of state-owned enterprises had two consequences for unions. On the one hand, union dues and welfare funds dropped with decreased numbers of members. On the other hand, privatization increased the opportunities to generate union resources because it introduced a system of employee ownership administered by unions,[8] and opened the possibility for unions to purchase stocks in privatized firms in their industries.

The reform of the union-administered health system affected the law on welfare funds, one of the main pillars of organizational strength of industrial unions. Fee collection was transferred from unions to the state by Decree 1,325 of 1991, returned to the unions with state administrative surveillance in 1992,[9] and later transferred to the tax collection agency. Decrees 9 and 576 of 1993 abolished workers' compulsory affiliation with the welfare fund of their respective union. However, due to union pressure, the competition among welfare funds was limited to those administered by unions, and mergers were allowed and encouraged. Moreover, although this system was scheduled to enter into force in April 1993, it was not implemented during this administration due to unions' procedural objections. This delay was used by unions to modernize and prepare the merger of welfare funds' services in order to be able to compete within the new institutional framework. Finally, motivated by budgetary concerns, Decree 2,609 of December 1993 reduced employers' mandated contributions to union-administered welfare funds and the intermediation of the tax collection agency. This process eroded one of the main sources of union financial resources. The reduction in employer contributions affected every union, and was designed so as to be compensated by government money if welfare funds proved well administered (Ministerio de Trabajo 1994a). Yet, rich and efficiently administered welfare funds fared much better than those of low-wage workers or those which were poorly administered. When competition is open, outcomes are also likely to be diverse.

Law 24,241 of 1993 opened the social security system to competition among privately administered retirement funds (AFJyP) while maintaining a state-administered system.[10] Since union pressure resulted in the authorization of union participation (including permission for union employees to work as dealers of retirement funds), the reform of the social security system opened opportunities for some unions. Some established retirement funds; others began charging a fee for

---

[8] The law of state reform that introduced this system did not mandate union administration of the employee-owned stocks, although this was a widespread practice. Perhaps this practice was enhanced by the fact that until shares were paid fully by employees their administration had to be unionized by law.

[9] The director of the regulatory authority of welfare funds has been a union leader since then and until the end of the period.

[10] Individuals are able to choose if they want to remain in the state-administered system, rather than being automatically moved to the privately administered system of individual capitalization.

advising their members on their choice of retirement fund with the possibility of future capitalization of cumulated fees; and still others have planned to offer life insurance to the retirement funds (*Página 12*-CASH, 3 May 1994, p. 9; 8 May 1994). However, others opposed or were unable to participate in the process.

In short, the consequences of these institutional reforms were twofold. On the one hand, they introduced work-force and pay flexibility and increased job competition and heterogeneity among union members. Hence, it became more difficult for unions to represent their constituencies. On the other hand, these reforms introduced new fields for union negotiation while maintaining union organizational schemes. Moreover, they generated opportunities for the development of union organizational resources based on activities opened by structural reforms. The next two sections focus on union responses, especially on the unions whose strategy to respond to the reduction in union membership and in the size of their monopolized market of selective incentives was to broaden the market for their services from their members to all consumers or to enter new profit-making activities.

3. Alternative Union Strategies under Menem's Administration

In contrast to the thirteen general strikes called by the CGT against President Alfonsín, the CGT organized only one strike against the first Menem administration. Strike activity decreased and was concentrated in the sectors that were sharply affected by the liberalization of international trade (textile, metallurgical, automobile), and in the public sector: teachers and public and judicial employees (protesting wage restraint), and railroad, state steel, and telephone workers (protesting privatization). The union movement developed three main strategies to face the challenges posed by this administration: opposition, loyalty, and organizational autonomy. The first produced resistance to the reforms while the other two resulted in a limited opposition that allowed negotiations between unions and the government.

OPPOSITION

At the beginning of the Menem administration, labor's peak confederation split into a supportive confederation (CGT-San Martín), an oppositional confederation (CGT-Azopardo), and a third group of independent unions. Although the oppositional CGT limited its antagonism to one large demonstration and public declarations against the economic program, some of its more militant unions (teachers, state employees, metalworkers of Villa Constitución) organized numerous strikes. This minority of militantly oppositional unions in the CGT-Azopardo abandoned the CGT after its reunification in 1992, and joined together under the CTA

(Argentine Congress of Labor).[11] The CTA has maintained its antagonistic stance toward the government since then and, although it was unable to modify government economic policies or stop privatization, it led provincial demonstrations of discontent against public sector adjustment.

Beginning in late 1993, strikes and sometimes violent demonstrations by public employees took place in the north-western provinces of Argentina and spread to other provinces. The CTA gained influence in the inter-union organizations that emerged in the provinces of Santiago del Estero, La Rioja, and Salta.[12] At the same time, a group of Peronist unions, composed mainly of transport unions, gathered under the banner of the MTA (Movement of Argentine Workers) and joined the CTA in militant opposition. Together the groups staged a march from the provinces to Buenos Aires on 6 July and a national strike on 2 August 1994 (*Página 12*, 7 July 1994). In addition, the CTA and the MTA recommended that their members remain in the public social security system rather than become incorporated into the privatized system (*Página 12*-CASH, 8 May 1994).

LOYALTY

A group of unions that assembled under the CGT-San Martín and joined the re-united CGT chose to support the government initiatives in exchange for political appointments and privileged relations with the executive. For example, leaders of one of the two state employees' unions (UPCN), water provision workers, telephone workers, meatpackers, textile workers, construction workers, chemical workers, pasta industry workers, lifeguards' unions, railroad workers, and state oil workers were appointed by President Menem to the regulatory authority of welfare funds, although some of these unions have developed the alternative strategy of 'organizational autonomy'. 'Loyalist' union leaders were those who employed their remaining political resources to retain part of their short-term political privileges rather than adapt the strategies of their union to the new political-economic conditions.

ORGANIZATIONAL AUTONOMY

A group of large unions, generally representing well-paid workers who used to be in the public or protected sector, have chosen to develop a new strategy. This

[11] The CTA was formed by one of the public employee unions (ATE), the public teachers' union (CTERA), a local branch of the metallurgic workers (UOM-Villa Constitución), and the small maritime workers and pneumatics workers' unions.

[12] The CTA also claimed that it represented other social sectors affected by the adjustment program besides workers, among them unemployed workers and pensioners. For that reason, its strategy was based on the search for social support and demonstrations, especially within the local community, to complement industrial action (author's interview with Victor DeGennaro, Secretary General of CTA, 26 June 1995).

strategy is linked to the tradition of investing in organizational resources (mostly through union-administered welfare funds that provide social services for their members in what used to be called 'multiple action unionism'). However, these union leaders have gone further than their predecessors, having opened to different degrees their services and activities (previously restricted to members) to other segments of society, in some cases through market mechanisms.

The main unions in this group remained independent during the CGT split and joined the reunified CGT after 1992. They lobbied for the implementation of institutional reform along lines that would allow them to expand their organizational resources. They attempted to compensate for the loss of political resources produced by the combination of the abolition of their quota of representation in electoral candidacies within the party and policy shifts by the party that strained its historical alliance with the unions. These organizations had a strong influence in the reunified CGT, and all the secretaries general of the reunified organization during this period belonged to unions from this group.[13]

Both 'loyalist' and 'autonomous' unions joined the CGT as it reunited in 1992 to confront the government threat to union control over welfare funds. They organized a general strike and temporarily regained the right to collect welfare fees for the unions, as well as salvaging their welfare funds from debts dating to the 1970s. In early 1994, when the government decreed the reduction of employer taxes for union-administered welfare funds, the CGT responded by threatening a second general strike for January 1994. The strike was avoided by the government's promise to compensate welfare funds with state resources and to cover the debts acquired by welfare funds during the period of hyperinflation (*La Nación*, 13 Jan. 1994, p. 1).[14] In July 1994, the CGT signed an agreement with the government and the peak business associations. The CGT obtained a government commitment to introduce legislation for employee-owned stock in private enterprises; for compensating the reduction of employers' contribution with welfare funds; for a state-funded unemployment program that would grant union-administered welfare funds the provision of health services for unemployed people; and for mandatory occupational

[13] Some of these unions previously had joined a group that negotiated with the Radical government to ease the passage of laws on professional associations, collective bargaining, and welfare funds that had been suspended by the military government and whose reform is under discussion now. Among the national unions that adopted the strategy of organizational autonomy were the unions of private hospital workers, bank clerk employees, electrical energy workers, insurance employees, automobile workers, state oil workers, retail clerks, and railroad workers. All these unions have more than 25,000 members. The metallurgic workers union (UOM) can also be included in this group, although it is comparatively underdeveloped in the implementation of organizational autonomy. In addition to participating in the restoration of labor regulation, some of these unions—electrical energy workers, oil workers, retail clerks, automobile workers, and metallurgic workers—obtained from the Alfonsín administration wage raises that exceeded the limit set by the administration in 1986 (Carpena and Jacqueline 1994).

[14] Additional pressure was put on the union leaders by tax investigations into the administration of welfare funds, unions, and even the personal finances of union leaders.

accident insurance that could be provided by union-administered insurance firms (Ministerio de Trabajo 1994*a*).[15]

The CGT also obtained from the government a delay of welfare fund deregulation, the right to participate in social security privatization, and a halt to a reform of professional association and collective bargaining laws that would have challenged their monopoly of representation. Particular unions negotiated the workers' share in employee stock ownership programs derived from privatization, credits for the creation of firms employing former workers of privatized firms, and the opportunity to purchase assets in their sectors. As a result, opposition to government policies by the CGT was very limited. Unions pursuing the strategy of organizational autonomy took the greatest advantage of the negotiations over the implementation of institutional changes. At the same time, they contributed to the increasing differentiation among unions as a result of the process of structural reform.

Before analyzing the conditions that induced unions to pursue such a strategy, the next section will provide empirical evidence of the strategy of organizational autonomy and of how these unions transformed themselves under the new institutional framework negotiated with the government.

ORGANIZATIONAL AUTONOMY: BROADENING THE HORIZON OF UNION ALTERNATIVES

Argentine unions became Peronist under the influence of state institutional privileges which guaranteed labor-based benefits for workers and enhanced the organizational strength of industrial unions. Even after Perón was ousted in 1955, national industrial unions emphasized political tactics seeking institutional guarantees for their gains (e.g. Law 18,610 on welfare funds sanctioned by a military government in 1970). This was done partly to compensate for the absence of political resources stemming from the electoral proscription of the Peronist party.

During the Menem administration, union political resources that traditionally had been important when the Peronist party was in power—especially in the 1973–6 period—were eroded by the Peronist policy shift. Meanwhile, most of the industrial resources unions that had developed under a closed economy were weakened by the opening of the economy, by the new labor regulations, and by the increase in unemployment. This situation turned the most influential group of Argentine unions towards the strategy of organizational autonomy. This strategy entailed developing organizational resources so as to take advantage of market activities in an attempt to increase union autonomy from declining state guarantees. Union leaders explained this strategy in terms of the benefits accruing to the

---

[15] At the end of the administration, none of these promises had become law, although the latter was passed by Congress before the end of 1995.

remaining union members, in the form of both collective goods and selective incentives. In this way, the mobility of selective incentives provided and financed on a market basis, rather than exclusively by union constituencies, compensated for the threat that numerical flexibility posed to union membership and welfare funds. Yet, these unions did not become completely business-driven, in the sense that their profit-making activities were related to their sectors or to the social services they traditionally provide for members. Union leaders legitimized their activities as a continuation of the multiple action unionism of early Peronism that took advantage of acquired experience.

Examples of this 'marketization' of unions include: purchasing firms in their sectors; creating retirement funds to participate in the privatization of social security; establishing firms that provide services to privatized enterprises and jobs to former employees of those companies; reorganizing welfare funds to compete for health care provision; and managing the employee-owned stock of privatized state enterprises (charging their fee from dividends) (*El Cronista Comercial*, 26 Oct. 1993, p. 6; *Página 12*-CASH, 20 Mar. 1994 and 8 May 1994). That is, they invested in new 'power resources' that are easier to move and to apply in the new institutional context created by structural reforms. I will illustrate this strategy of organizational autonomy with a brief analysis of four national unions that have adopted it: the Federation of United Unions of State Oil Workers (SUPE), the Federation of Electricity Workers (FATLyF), the Union of Railroad Workers (Unión Ferroviaria), and the Federation of Commerce Employees.

SUPE set up 215 firms that hired 7,194 laid-off workers, and was in the process of establishing another 39 firms utilizing 663 workers slated for dismissal (SUPE 1993). The national union, together with the regional union and the workers, bought part of the YPF (public oil corporation) fleet and shares of an oil equipment firm (*La Nación*, 2 Aug. 1993). SUPE was also planning to manage the workers' 10 per cent stake in YPF privatization. It also charged a fee to a private retirement fund for referring union members to it and started organizing a welfare fund for the workers of the newly created firms (*Página 12*-CASH, 8 May 1994; personal interview with Alejandro Betancourt, Secretary of Social Affairs for SUPE, 1 August 1995). Antonio Cassia, Secretary General of SUPE (and Secretary General of the unified CGT since 1994), argued that, as strikes had become ineffective, union participation in the privatization process was the only alternative left by state reforms to combat both unemployment and the decline in financial and political power of the organizations that support workers' demands (personal interview, August 1993).

FATLyF held real estate, health and tourist services, housing projects, and a complementary retirement fund. This union bought 40 per cent of the stock in nine energy generators in the Argentine north-west, 33 per cent of the stock in four energy generators in the Argentine south, and 20 per cent of the stock in the Sorrento energy generator in Rosario. It also obtained the concession of the state monopoly of coal exploitation, and participated in partnerships that bought 90 per cent of the stock in three energy generators in Santa Fé and Paraná, and the company that distributes energy in the Argentine north-east. In addition, it bought a bank, organized a retirement fund with other unions that included insurance and automobile workers, reorganized its welfare fund, administered employee-owned stock of fifteen privatized companies, and had a director in the energy transportation employers' association (personal interviews with Alejandro Mirkin, Under-Secretary of Energy, 8 August 1995, and with Néstor Calegaris, Secretary of Energy Policies for FATLyF, 1 August 1995; *Clarín*, 8 Aug. 1993, 11 May 1994, and 29 June 1994; *Ambito Financiero*, 29 June 1994; *El Cronista Comercial*, 26 Oct. 1993; *Página 12*, 7 Feb. 1993; *Página 12*-CASH, 20 Mar. 1994).

In 1993, while a leader from this union was Secretary General of the CGT, the FATLyF National Congress decided to 'find, analyze, select and implement entrepreneurial projects . . . directed toward the general market, in addition to our members, with the object of generating economic resources that will be applied to the organization's social promotion and assistance services . . . [and to] participate in the modifications of the social security system and, especially, in the welfare funds system' (FATLyF 1993). Carlos Alderete (Secretary General of the Federation) and Néstor Calegaris (Secretary of Energy Policies) argued that participation in the privatization of energy generators was a way of achieving worker participation in management, influencing national energy policies, reducing the social costs of privatization, and preventing the decline of organizational resources (personal interviews, August 1993).

Unión Ferroviaria started several initiatives, such as the administration of a number of cooperative workshops for the maintenance of trains in Santa Fé, and considered purchasing cargo and passenger train lines in the north-west. The union was also planning to administer the employee-owned stock in privatized railroads, according to its secretary of organization, Armando Matarazzo (personal interview, August 1993). In addition, the Tenth General Assembly of union delegates decided to 'form any type of commercial companies oriented toward the maintenance or defense of employment, as well as the improvement of working conditions', as well as to participate in the privatization of the General Belgrano railroad line, retaining 51 per cent of the share for the union (Unión Ferroviaria 1993), although the latter effort did not come to fruition.

The Argentine Federation of Commerce Employees—which owned a sports complex, a number of hotels, housing projects, and part of an insurance company and manages a complementary retirement fund for its members—planned to expand the services of its welfare fund, to create an insurance firm for occupational accidents co-administered with employers, to start a credit card project, and to participate in life insurance services for the newly created retirement funds (*La Nación*, 2 Aug. 1993; *El Cronista Comercial*, 26 Oct. 1993; *Página 12*, 19 July 1994; FAECyS 1994). Its Secretary General, Armando Cavalieri, claimed that entrepreneurial activities 'allow the union to have financial support that will imply an improvement of service for members' (*La Nación*, 2 Aug. 1993). He also argued that these initiatives would produce 'unions that will be more independent from the state and the party' (personal interview, July 1992).

These union leaders have attempted to confront the impact of structural reforms, the erosion of their influence in the Peronist party, and the decline of union membership and strike activity by increasing their reliance on market mechanisms. They claimed to be protecting their organizations because these organizations provide workers with collective goods (e.g. employment) and services (e.g. retirement funds). The following section analyzes the consequences of this strategy for union members.

CONSEQUENCES AND RISKS OF ORGANIZATIONAL AUTONOMY

The consequences of this innovative strategy for wage-earners are still unclear. The collective bargaining contracts signed by these unions have followed the same trend towards flexibility of industrial relations that most recent contract negotiations have (Ministerio de Trabajo 1993b). A brief comparison between previous collective contracts and current ones for the same four unions that are pioneering organizational autonomy provides some illustrative evidence.

In the case of SUPE, the clauses on employment stability, educational benefits, the promotion ladder, health care, and preferential hiring for workers' relatives included in the 1975 collective contract with the public oil enterprise did not reappear in the 1993 collective contract with Naviera Sur Petrolera SA (the privatized fleet from YPF which was jointly purchased by SUPE, the State Oil Fleet Union, and employees); instead, it establishes some forms of numerical flexibility. The concessions that FATLyF had obtained in 1975—clauses on employment stability, a fixed work schedule, additional vacation and employer's contribution to the union-administered welfare fund beyond those required by law, a union-administered complementary retirement fund, and union participation in hiring and promotion processes and in the distribution of scholarships for technical studies—did not reappear in the 1992 agreements signed with Edelap SA, Edesur SA, Central Puerto SA, Central San Nicolás, and Central Pedro de Mendoza (privatized electricity distribution and generation firms). In contrast, they introduced the modernization of work organization with clauses aimed at rewarding productivity, instituting functional flexibility, numerical flexibility, increases in work time, modifications of vacation schedules, provisions for the solution of labor conflicts, as well as training and bilateral negotiations regarding work methods.

The new 1993 collective contract between Unión Ferroviaria and the private firm 'Buenos Aires al Pacífico-San Martín' suppressed wage indexing and reduced a number of occupational categories included in the 1975 agreement with the public railroad company. The 1993 collective agreement between the Federation of Commerce Employees, the Argentine Chamber of Commerce, the Business Chamber of Commercial Activities, and the Argentine Union of Commercial Entities modified the

1975 collective contract in the measurement of salaries; introduced a provision for resolving labor conflicts and a term limit for the agreement; and opened the possibility for provincial, local, and firm-level collective negotiations.

It is still too early to draw implications from this strategy of organizational survival for the welfare of union members. According to union leaders, this strategy would benefit union constituencies by preserving employment and improving or maintaining union selective incentives with the new financial development of organizations that were under financial stress. Moreover, the new union activities may lead to the creation of new arenas for discussion of work conditions, such as boards of directors or employers' associations. In addition, union management may speed the introduction of productivity concerns into labor organizations, redefining the character of industrial resources for unions that may begin to exercise greater initiative in terms of industrial restructuring. On the other hand, distortion of representation may occur; organizational well-being does not necessarily result in the immediate welfare of members, although the risk of rank-and-file discontent may act as a deterrent to excessive distortion of representation. Tensions between the interests of workers and union leaders seem more likely to arise if the organization experiences market failures that endanger work conditions and job security for the employees of union-owned firms as well as the selective incentives that unions offer to their constituencies. In addition, the productivity concerns of union administration may produce tension between union managers' interest in fulfilling the preferences of their customers in a competitive market and the interest of workers in job stability.

4. Union Strategies and the Reshaping of Corporatism: Understanding the Emergence of Organizational Autonomy

Offe (1985b), Streeck (1984), and Pizzorno (1978) argue that political guarantees increase union leaders' dependence on the state, and augment their autonomy from the rank and file and from the conditions of the labor market. Leaders choose to collaborate in corporatist arrangements to avoid the tension between their need to show the mobilization power of their constituencies and to restrain them in exchange for concessions, but this weakening of their 'industrial resources' becomes dangerous when the state starts to withdraw its corporatist guarantees (Offe 1985b). Within a shifting corporatist framework, Argentine unions used diverse strategies to respond to the challenge of the new political-economic conditions created by structural reforms. This variation can be explained by the impact that the distribution of union resources, affected by historical legacies and new political-economic conditions, had on unions' strategic capacity.

In Argentina, the new political-economic conditions and the earlier hyperinflation sharply affected industrial resources. The rapid drop in purchasing power and job uncertainty created by hyperinflation undermined worker mobilization. During the first Menem administration, worker militancy was also affected by the growth of unemployment and the expansion of temporary contracts which increased job competition. Decrees also limited strike activity and banned wage hikes not correlated with productivity growth. Further, the government was determined to confront strikes against privatization and public wage restraint. In addition, the impact of trade opening on the economy resulted in a segmentation of industries that has made developing national industry-wide strategies more difficult. Yet, the diversification of worker preferences did not sufficiently spark the widespread development of decentralized strategies.[16] These political-economic conditions explain the erosion of unions' industrial resources and the difficulties unions had in relying on the militancy of their members.

Regarding political resources, union influence on the Peronist party was reduced because of the role they played in the 1983 electoral defeat; this contributed to displacing union leaders from party hierarchies and to modifying the system that granted unions a third of all positions on the party's list of electoral candidates (McGuire 1991*b*). Moreover, the Peronist party supported the unions when they opposed the Radicals' attempts to stabilize the economy with wage restraint; but this policy alliance was broken when stabilization and structural reforms were carried out by the Peronist party. In addition, union leaders could hardly threaten the party with their withdrawal. The virtual monopoly of the Peronist identity over the labor movement undermined any serious threat from unions to transfer their loyalties to other parties because of the difficulty of constructing an alternative identity, for either members or leaders. Moreover, at the beginning of the administration, union leaders were afraid to undermine the government of their allied party and lose even their dwindling access to policy-making. For that reason, opposition came from union leaders who defected from Peronism and switched their allegiance to FREPASO (a loose center-left coalition that included many former Peronist leaders).

With regard to organizational resources, hyperinflation led to a deterioration in union finances because it affected dues and welfare contributions administered by unions, both of which were deducted from declining real wages. However, the government agreed to cover the debts acquired by welfare funds between July 1989 and April 1991 (*La Nación*, 13 Jan. 1994, p. 1). Moreover, structural reforms did not threaten the authority of national leaders, and created new incentives for the development of new union structures, such as the administration of employee-owned stock, participation in the private social security system, and the opportunity to purchase companies in their sectors. The main threat to their financial power was the opening of the health care market to private competition, which

[16] The resistance to decentralization is explained by the previous experiences of national leaders with challenges to their authority which emerged from the shop floor and local organizers in the 1960s and 1970s.

abolished the monopoly of every union over the workers in its industry. However, this challenge was reduced to internal competition among unions and it was not implemented during this period. In addition, large unions had a historical legacy of prior experience with the use of organizational resources, even when no political resources were available. These resources developed mainly around union-administered or co-administered welfare funds. These welfare funds originated in the early practices of firms and unions that provided social services for their workers before the emergence of Peronism. Beginning in 1944, these practices were promoted by the state under the auspices of Decree 30,655 of 1944, which created the Commission of Social Services and special laws that guaranteed funding for certain activities. According to Bunuel (1992), after the fall of Perón in 1955 the social services of welfare funds relied on collective bargaining. Law 18,610 of 1970, sanctioned by a military regime, made welfare funds compulsory providers of health care for every activity and granted them the collection of fees. This law enhanced the development of union-provided social services since, in most cases, there was no separation between union and welfare fund administration. Hence, organizational resources—finance, structures, selective incentives, leadership patterns—largely were preserved by unions, who took the opportunities available under the new political-economic environment to protect them.

Despite these common conditions and legacies, not all Argentine unions adopted the same strategy to confront the challenge of structural reform. Different combinations of union resources and organizational legacies resulted in diverse union strategies. A strategy of opposition was chosen by some militant unions, mainly in the public sector (i.e. teachers and public employees), which formed the CTA. These union leaders radicalized their position under the pressure of militant rank and file particularly threatened by unemployment and wage restraint. These union leaders had a tradition of militancy from the Alfonsín period and have participated in the creation of FREPASO. Thus, they were more independent of the party in government and had alternative political resources. The two main unions, CTERA and ATE, also lacked the tradition of welfare fund administration because their members tended to belong to the welfare funds of provincial governments, rather than to a national one. In addition, since they represented public sector employees, they were not monopolistic in their activities and had to compete for their constituencies with other unions that leaned more towards the government and had better access to organizational resources. What they offered as an alternative was to turn to industrial resources and worker militancy.

The loyalist unions that preferred negotiation with the government chose the strategy of increasing their dependence on the state and exploiting the Peronist identification of their members in order to compensate for the weakening of their industrial resources. Since they had inherited fewer organizational resources than their counterparts pursuing the strategy of organizational autonomy, they were able to take less advantage of the new opportunities created by structural reforms. However, they started to imitate the strategy of organizational autonomy when the CGT negotiated incentives for the marketization of union organizations that allowed their participation (e.g. participation in the privatization of social security and administration of employee-owned stock).

A combination of organizational legacies and conditions created by the reforms allowed some unions to follow the strategy of organizational autonomy. These unions had developed larger welfare funds than the others during the previous period, and for that reason they were endowed with *financial means, administrative structure*, and leaders with *managerial expertise* that enabled them to take advantage of the opportunities created by the reform process. These unions' welfare funds expanded because of their large membership or the better conditions that they were able to obtain by being in the protected sector or in public enterprises. These unions also had obtained better terms in their collective bargaining contracts than their counterparts during the previous period of a closed economy and had developed large organizations that provide better selective incentives to their constituents. This situation induced their leaders to preserve these large organizations, which were threatened by a decline in resources from union dues and welfare fees, since the new contracts were not as generous and employers' contributions were reduced. Their previous expertise in the privatized sector and the need to speed the process of privatization gave them a perfect opportunity to negotiate the conditions for the survival of their organizations with a Peronist government. The negotiations have been carried out by the CGT, whose leadership was dominated by this group following its reunification. A consequence of this strategy to introduce market competition among unions will be an increasing differentiation and rivalry among unions in seeking the best negotiating conditions, and an increase in industrial concerns over affairs of the union movement as a whole. This consequence is related to the industrial organization of Argentine unions and to a lack of sanctioning power and organizational development on the part of the CGT that might have enabled it to impose universalistic views over its industrial members.

Organizational autonomy substituted for the decline in industrial and political resources with an increase in their organizational resources. Instead of depending on state guarantees to augment their organizational resources as they had done before, these unions have relied on market mechanisms promoted by structural reforms. As selective incentives and business profits are complementary financial resources for any organization (Moe 1980), these union leaders chose to compensate for the decline in members' dues and welfare contributions with business profits. At the same time, their organizations purchased privatized firms with the combined objective of preserving employment (a collective good), providing selective incentives to their members, and increasing their dwindling financial resources by competing in the market.

Table 3.3 summarizes the argument concerning the impact of resource distribution on union strategies. The political conditions created by the state reforms themselves and the economic conditions provoked by the crisis together with historical legacies of organizational development explain the emergence of the

Table 3.3. The impact of resource distribution on union strategies

	Opposition	Organizational autonomy	Loyalty
Political resources	alternative political identity	Peronist identity	Peronist identity
Organizational resources			
Finances	low development	high development	low development
Structure	low development	high administrative development	low development
Leadership	militant legacy	authority and managerial expertise	authority but low managerial expertise
Industrial resources	low in public sector and heterogeneous in others	heterogeneous	heterogeneous and low in public sector

strategy of organizational autonomy. Thanks to lessons learned from the experience of a prior weakening of their political resources during the Peronist proscription (1955–73), unions started to develop an 'institutional pragmatism' (James 1988) that facilitated their organizational development based on state guarantees under the law of welfare funds. In addition, although the Peronist government provided them with fewer political resources than previous administrations, it was still prone to negotiate the implementation of structural reforms, if the unions limited their opposition. This situation, along with the decreasing power of worker mobilization, induced some unions to exchange the state for the market as their future source of 'organizational resources'.

Yet, many questions remain unanswered. What are the consequences of this strategy? Will the experience of union and employee ownership induce a faster involvement of unions with productivity concerns? Will their active role in industrial restructuring balance the burden of hard times with the promise of future profit distribution after restructuring increases international competitiveness? Although consequences are still unclear, the significance of the strategy of organizational autonomy has been demonstrated by its influence on the leadership of the reunified CGT as well as by the CGT's commitment to defend union structures and organizational resources during this period.

Concluding Remarks

Corporatist union movements in other countries face similar challenges of institutional transformation produced by structural reforms. Different distributions of union resources, affected by political-economic conditions and historical legacies, can produce diverse union strategies to confront the transformation. In the case of Argentina, political resources were fundamental in impelling unions toward strategies of opposition or negotiation, whereas organizational resources were central in influencing whether unions could pursue a strategy of organizational autonomy.

By promoting union participation in market mechanisms, the Argentine strategy of organizational autonomy could broaden the range of union alternatives for confronting structural reforms. However, the conditions created by structural reforms implemented by a labor-based party are not sufficient for inducing unions to pursue this strategy. The emergence of organizational autonomy must be accompanied by organizational legacies that provide unions with both funds and expertise to start the process of achieving autonomy from the state. At the same time, their industrial interests must remain unrepressed by a peak organization with universal concerns based on a membership that is more heterogeneous than that of industrial or enterprise unions (perhaps by virtue of its lack of sanctioning power over members, as was the case of the CGT). Other unions with an adequate structure and organizational development may take the opportunity to negotiate the implementation of institutional reforms in order to reshape their relationship with the state by starting new enterprises under the conditions created by structural reforms. This alternative is particularly advantageous for those large and relatively homogeneous unions like industrial or enterprise unions. This is especially so if they possess adequate financial and organizational development (which, in turn, may be related to the real wages of members and the existence of institutional tools to guarantee the collection of fees), as well as managerial expertise (e.g. union-administered pension funds, health insurance, union-administered unemployment insurance).[17] For these kinds of unions, the horizon of choices seems wider when they are in the position of negotiating the institutional transformation included in structural reforms, especially because labor-based parties are more prone to promote employee or union ownership to increase the acceptability of their policy shifts and to maintain their electoral coalitions. In short, in the age of less state and more market, the strategy of organizational autonomy allowed some Argentine union leaders to preserve their organizations through the marketization of corporatism.

[17] The experience of some Mexican unions, like the telephone workers during the Salinas administration, resembled, to a certain degree, the strategy of organizational autonomy, since they chose to reform their organizational structure to provide new social services to their members, taking advantage of the new political-economic conditions created by structural reforms (e.g. administration of employee-owned stocks). These unions, too, were able to negotiate based on a comparative homogeneity of membership and the lack of membership in a peak organization that imposed universal concerns over industrial interests.

4 The Crisis of Developmentalism and the Rural Labor Movement in North-East Brazil

Anthony W. Pereira

Introduction

The Brazilian transition to democracy was more gradual, evolutionary, and continuous than any other in Latin America. The formally democratic regime that was more or less in place by 1985 had many links, not only to its military predecessor of 1964–85, but with the populist Second Republic of 1946–64. A high level of continuity also characterized forms of popular representation in Brazil. In the late 1970s and early 1980s, for example, a revitalized urban labor movement took on a democratizing and oppositional role, much as it had done after the expansion of the electorate in the late 1940s (French 1991).

Such continuities are harder to find in the case of rural labor. On the surface, the post-1979 rural labor movement looks nothing like its populist predecessor. The embryonic populist movement was essentially led from above, with intense competition for leadership between the Communist Party, the Catholic Church, and the first organizations to claim and win the right of association for peasants and rural workers on a broad scale, the Peasant Leagues. The Peasant Leagues were voluntary organizations that had no formal link with the state; a large repertoire of collective action; weak links with political parties; many urban, middle-class leaders; a multi-class membership; and little or no central coordination of what were essentially local struggles. Peasant League leaders mobilized thousands of rural poor in direct actions such as land occupations that demanded a redistribution of land 'by law or by force', without compensation to large landowners.

The Brazilian rural labor movement of the 1980s and early 1990s is dominated by the Confederation of Agricultural Workers (Confederação dos Trabalhadores na Agricultura, CONTAG), an organization that contrasts sharply with the Peasant Leagues. It is formally included within the state's corporatist labor structure, has a narrow repertoire of collective action, strong links with political parties, is led mainly by professional union officials who have peasant and worker backgrounds, and is centrally coordinated at the national level. CONTAG mobilizes thousands of workers in legal strikes every year, and pressured the federal government, mainly by parliamentary means, to enact a modest 1985 agrarian reform proposal that was begun, and later all but abandoned, by the federal government (Pereira 1992).

The case of rural labor in Brazil is a reminder that forms of popular representation can change in ways unimagined by the literature on new social movements. The latter envisages a transformation of 'old' class politics into 'new' non-class politics in which 'a multiplicity of social actors' representing local gender, ethnic, neighborhood, and other identities compete within 'a fragmented social and political space'. Old social movements were narrowly ideological, political, and oriented to state power, while new social movements are just as likely to be cultural as political, preoccupied with 'identity' as much as with winning material concessions, and more concerned to maintain autonomy from the state than old social movements (Escobar and Alvarez 1992: 3).

The rural labor movement in Brazil, however, was more pluralistic, more autonomous from the state, more clearly a multi-class or even a non-class movement in the populist period than it became in the 1980s and early 1990s. Its trajectory was thus almost the reverse of the one described by the new social movements literature. Despite this fact, the movement, firmly embedded within the corporatist labor structure, was able to develop its own strategy and win significant rights for its members in some localities. Social movements that are 'old' and linked to the state are not, therefore, necessarily uncombative or incapable of generating social change.

The historical evolution from Peasant Leagues to unions in the coastal sugar zone of the north-eastern state of Pernambuco illustrates this point. Pernambuco was the site of the first Peasant League and the focus of much of the populist mobilization around agrarian issues in the early 1960s. Pernambuco's state federation FETAPE (Federação dos Trabalhadores na Agricultura do Estado de Pernambuco) is also one of the most powerful and active in Brazil, symbolized by the fact that the president of CONTAG from 1968 to 1989, and again from 1992 to 1994, was from Pernambuco.

The argument made here is that changes of both rural class structure and mobilization strategies under the military regime explain the construction of an 'old' movement on the foundations of a 'new' one in Pernambuco. Section 1 summarizes the Pernambuco rural labor movement in the populist period, while the changes mentioned above are analyzed in Section 2. The third section examines the crisis of developmentalism, the shift from import-substitution to an export-oriented strategy in the 1980s that it provoked, and what this shift meant for rural labor in Pernambuco and Brazil.

1. Populism

Like other populist regimes, the Brazilian Second Republic incorporated urban labor, but excluded rural workers and peasants (Collier and Collier 1991). A Ministry of

Labor was established in 1930 (Hall and Aurélio Garcia 1989: 171–2) to oversee a process of state-controlled unionization, and 1,262 unions for urban workers were registered by 1960. But only sixteen rural labor unions were registered in the whole of Brazil during the same period (IBGE 1991: 425).

The first major mobilization of rural labor during the Second Republic took place outside the corporatist labor system, in the form of Peasant Leagues. The Leagues were a reaction against the loss of access to land on the part of plantation workers, tenants, sharecroppers, and smallholders in the Brazilian north-east as large sugar estates expanded in the 1950s (Maybury-Lewis 1994: 64–6). Most observers misunderstood these organizations as constituting a purely peasant movement (see Fonseca 1962; Pearson 1967; Hewitt 1969; Morães 1970; Huizer 1972; Julião 1972; Page 1972; Forman 1975).[1] But the Leagues, at least in Pernambuco, were as much proletarian as they were peasant in character. The most active Leagues were located in the sugar zone, where wage laborers predominated, rather than the neighboring *agreste* region, where peasant smallholders constituted the majority of the population (Azevêdo 1982: 73; Price 1964: 42; Hewitt 1969: 374).[2]

This fact helps to explain why the rural trade union movement, organized in the early 1960s by the Catholic Church and the Communist Party (PCB) and oriented mainly to wage laborers, quickly outstripped the Leagues. Unions had state resources, an advantage that the Leagues did not. The unions' successful organization of a strike in 1963 in Pernambuco proved their effectiveness to plantation workers. The 1963 strike and its aftermath, in which wages rose by 80 per cent, was experienced by many workers as a defining moment of liberation, recognition of citizenship, and entrance into the consumer market (many workers bought their first bicycles and radios after the strike). Pernambuco union leaders also participated in the foundation of the national confederation of rural workers, CONTAG, in the same year.

The Pernambuco sugar zone was, and is, characterized by a very heterogeneous work-force and a complex spectrum of labor relations. Workers differ from one another in terms of their place of residence (on the plantation itself, in the towns of the sugar zone, or the interior), the legality of their employment (legal workers are entitled to state benefits that illegals do not enjoy, although illegals can often earn slightly higher wages), and the permanence of their employment (seasonal vs. year-round). Permanent employees in the sugar mills constitute a relatively

[1] There is a large literature on why and how peasants should be defined. One tradition identifies peasants primarily in cultural terms as 'part societies with part cultures' (Forman 1975: 247). I here define peasants in economic terms, as rural cultivators who have access to land and who engage in small-scale production, mainly with family labor. Workers, on the other hand, derive most or all of their income from wages. In the Pernambuco sugar zone, tenants, sharecroppers, and small landowners are peasants; wage workers are permanent or temporary employees on the sugar estates. The *moradores*, resident workers on the sugar estates discussed later, are in between the peasantry and the proletariat, with both a land and wage relationship to the landowner.

[2] The contrary assertion that the Peasant Leagues mainly attracted peasants rather than wage workers is found in Correia de Andrade (1994: 208).

privileged segment of the work force (Leite Lopes 1978), while migrant workers from the interior, who usually work illegally only for the duration of the harvest, constitute the least privileged end of the labor market. In between, seasonal and/or illegal workers who reside in the towns of the sugar zone have less security than permanent workers, some of whom (*moradores*) reside on the plantations and have access to subsistence plots of land. The differences between employers in the sugar zone, ranging from sugar mills owned by large industrial conglomerates to small cane planters with a few hectares of land, adds to the complexity and diversity of labor relations there.

The repertoire of collective action (Tilly 1986) of the rural movement in the early 1960s was eclectic, reflecting its affinity with the new social movements of contemporary social scientific literature. It included land occupations, marches, court cases, and local strikes. While the Leagues, guided by an ideology of *agrarismo*, focused their attention on land tenure, the unions, reflecting the then-dominant labor ideology of *trabalhismo*, accepted the existing distribution of land and pressured the state to grant rural workers the benefits that had been gained by urban labor. Unions and Leagues thus constituted competing and overlapping organizations with different sorts of appeals; many rural workers were members of both organizations at the same time. Actions by both the unions and the Leagues frequently met with violence on the part of landowners, who saw mere state recognition of the Peasant Leagues and unions' right to organize as a threat to their livelihood and way of life, and lamented the breakdown of the paternalistic social relations and worker deference that their own capitalist expansion had provoked.

Most landowners strongly supported the 1964 military coup that brought a new order to the countryside. The Army, police, and landowners broke up the Peasant Leagues, ransacked their headquarters, and hunted down their members. The newly purged Ministry of Labor then extirpated the influence of the Communist Party from the trade unions, replacing leaders and leaving the organizations in the hands of the Church. The military regime that formed after the coup denounced the populism of the post-war Second Republic, and embarked on a new project of authoritarian developmentalism that transformed the country.

2. Authoritarian Developmentalism

More so than its populist predecessor, which could also be called developmentalist, the military regime of 1964–85 based its legitimacy on its ability to modernize the country, measured in terms of economic growth. In the view of its leaders, modernization required 'order', the subordination of popular interests to a strong centralized state which claimed a monopoly of technical expertise and information. The military's Cold War doctrine of national security decreed that any kind of 'subversion', defined selectively and flexibly as circumstances changed, would not be tolerated within popular organizations.

However, by 1980, the authoritarian regime faced a wide array of popular movements ranged against it, including an expanded and revitalized rural labor movement. The explanation for the emergence of this movement offered here hinges on two sets of changes: in economic structures and interests, and forms of popular organization and self-expression. Both of these transformations were influenced by the developmental state's intervention in processes of economic development and popular representation, in which some of the most important effects of these interventions were unintended. The first set of changes was caused by the state's policies of agricultural modernization, and the second was a consequence of the state's creation of a rural welfare program administered by the trade unions. Within this context, a combative labor movement emerged that, while more firmly embedded within the corporatist labor structure than before, was more effective at gaining the recognition of collective rights for its members.

AGRICULTURAL MODERNIZATION

The developmental strategy adopted after the coup involved the repression of popular organizations, stronger central control over the economy, the expansion of the state-owned sector, and the promotion of big capital, both domestic and transnational (much of which continued to be protected) at the expense of small business. Foreign direct investment, mostly from the United States, increased markedly after the coup. As in other newly industrializing countries such as South Korea, state control over finance proved to be one of the keys to development (Woo 1991). In agriculture, the regime's provision of cheap credit to large producers led to considerable investment in chemical fertilizer and pesticides, machinery and implements, and more land.[3] As a result of the agricultural credit expansion, large estates modernized their holdings, and land concentration increased.[4]

In the sugar sector, the populist policy of 'balanced development' enforced by the state institution that regulated sugar production, the Sugar and Alcohol Institute (Instituto de Açúcar e Álcool, IAA), was reversed. This policy had tried to balance the interests of north-eastern sugar producers against those of their São Paulo counterparts, and the interests of sugar mill owners (*usineiros*) against those of plantation owners (*fornecedores*). After the 1964 coup, the military regime

---

[3] Subsidies to agriculture remained high in the 1970s. Credit (generally furnished on favorable terms by state development banks) represented 23 per cent of the total value of agricultural production in 1970, 33 per cent in 1973, and 57 per cent in 1977 (Araújo 1983: 303). Another part of the regime's development strategy in agriculture, its attempt to increase agricultural efficiency through taxation, failed due to lack of enforcement.

[4] The concentration of landholding in Brazil increased from a Gini coefficient of 0.858 in 1970 to 0.871 in 1980 (Bittencourt and Khan 1988: 27). In 1975 sugar cane had the highest concentration of land (with a Gini of 0.929) of nineteen crops surveyed, including soybeans, coffee, and wheat (Hoffman and da Silva 1986: 153 and 155).

instituted a policy that clearly favored big capital (including the *usineiros*) and the Paulista producers (Ramos and Belik 1989: 204).

Under the military, São Paulo sugar producers, already blessed with advantages over their north-eastern rivals, thrived.[5] They established their own organization, COPERSUCAR, which eventually eclipsed the north-eastern-controlled IAA, in terms of its technical and administrative capacity, becoming a flagship for the sugar industry. The politically well-connected Paulista producers achieved an average yield per hectare almost 50 per cent higher than that of the Pernambuco growers and had higher-capacity mills. In 1960 São Paulo produced 60 per cent more than Pernambuco producers; in 1985, it produced over five times as much, with a total labor force of about the same size as Pernambuco's (Ramos and Belik 1989: 208–9; IBGE 1985, Number 21: 122 and Number 14: 100).

Paulista production might well have spelled extinction for north-eastern producers if the sugar sector had depended solely upon market forces. But it was highly protected and subsidized by the state, both in the south and the north-east. The most notable example of this was the creation of the PROÁLCOOL program in response to the massive increase in oil prices in 1973. PROÁLCOOL, which replaced gasoline with alcohol made from sugar cane, began in 1975 as a bailout to the sugar industry and developed into a full-blown energy policy. It rescued the vulnerable north-eastern sugar mill owners, converting them from an export enclave to producers intimately tied to the dynamic industrial economy of the south (Barzelay 1986; Demetrius 1990). In effect, it compensated them for deteriorating conditions in global markets by giving them a captive, regulated domestic market with steadily increasing demand. As a result, the Pernambuco sugar zone underwent a period of major capital investment, changes in production processes, improvements in labor productivity, and tremendous increases in the output of sugar cane. Overall, production in the state increased fivefold in the 1960–89 period.

This picture contradicts the stereotype of the north-east as a stagnant agricultural backwater. Clearly, the north-eastern producers were still less efficient than producers in the south, and were subsidized more heavily than their southern counterparts. However, in this period, the north-eastern sugar sector experienced modernization at a rate comparable to that in the south.[6] The social costs of these changes in production processes were considerable: thousands of workers were displaced as employment per hectare decreased, contributing to the great streams of migrant labor that flowed from the north-east to the south and west of Brazil in the 1970s and 1980s.

---

[5] The advantages of the São Paulo producers over their north-eastern rivals included greater proximity to the heart of Brazil's mass market, more access to capital, greater links with the farm equipment industry, a flatter terrain that allowed for the easier introduction of machinery, and a better-organized labor market (Ramos and Belik 1989: 202).

[6] In using the term modernization, I do not mean to evoke the assumptions or teleology of modernization theory. I am using the term in a technical way to refer to the movement of agriculture towards more capital-intensive, commercial, and mechanized forms of production, as opposed to labor-intensive and subsistence forms.

By the late 1970s, the majority of Brazil's new automobiles were designed to run on alcohol rather than gasoline.[7] A government decree set the price of alcohol below gasoline prices, to ensure domestic demand. Sugar cane production for alcohol in Pernambuco rose dramatically as a result, from 335,872 tons in 1979 to 8.5 million tons in 1987, or a 25-fold increase (IAA 1987). The expansion of sugar output also benefited some rural workers. The number of permanent workers in the sugar zone increased from 74,590 to 108,379 between 1960 and 1980. At the same time, the number of temporary workers declined from 91,637 to 58,859. Permanent workers' share of total employment thus rose from 45 to 65 per cent.

This means that the ratio of labor to land declined. Between 1960 and 1980 alone, the ratio dropped from 0.422 to 0.316 (Anderson 1990).[8] Modernization had made sugar production less labor intensive. As labor costs declined as a proportion of total costs, landowners became more willing, when they were pushed, to concede to the wage demands of trade unions. And state subsidies and guaranteed prices gave them the means to make such concessions.

Modernization was therefore a mixed blessing for labor. While the total number of jobs remained more or less constant (Cabral 1984–6: 172–3), opportunities for year-round, secure employment and positions requiring new skills increased considerably between 1960 and 1980. Real wages, although still low, also increased steadily in the 1970s.[9] Therefore, despite its marginalization of many, modernization did not polarize the class structure. It instead created a number of new technical and supervisory positions within the plantation and sugar mill labor force, as well as opportunities for small cane growers to supply the mills.

These changes in class structure influenced the rural labor movement, attenuating its radicalism and reducing its threat to Pernambuco's landowners. Many newly secure employees who might otherwise have turned against the economic status quo saw themselves as its beneficiaries. These people, an influential minority amidst an impoverished majority, served as a brake on demands for land redistribution during the revival of democratic politics in the 1980s. The result was a labor movement in which the interests represented were more monochromatically working-class than they had been in the diffuse, multi-class, and more spontaneous movement of the early 1960s. Thus, as Paige argued, increasing capital investment and technological improvements paved the way for the emergence of a militant

---

[7] This situation later changed. In the first half of 1994, only 16.5 per cent of Brazil's new cars were alcohol-fuelled. From 'Queda Livre', *Correio Popular* (Campinas), 11 Aug. 1994, p. 1.

[8] Permanent employment actually declined between 1960 and 1970, but rose considerably in the 1970s, making the overall trend positive. It declined again in the 1980s.

[9] In Pernambuco between 1966 and 1979, average real wages for permanent agricultural workers increased by 4.4 per cent per year (compared to 4.5 per cent for the same category of workers in Brazil as a whole), while those of temporary workers increased by 5.6 per cent per year (compared to 6.3 per cent in Brazil as a whole). The gap between urban and rural wages narrowed considerably in Brazil during this time (Barros *et al.* 1983: 315–16). The extent to which these wage gains were captured by Pernambuco's sugar zone workers, whose earnings were often reduced by employers' manipulation of the piece-rate system, is unclear.

but reformist labor movement in Pernambuco's sugar cane fields (Paige 1975: 49–51). However, contrary to Paige's account, that process was neither ineluctable nor purely market-driven. State intervention influences how economic change affects social movements in the countryside.

CHANGES IN INTEREST REPRESENTATION

Structural factors in the economy of the Pernambuco sugar zone—continuing proletarianization, a rise in permanent employment, and a decrease in the labor to land ratio—made it more likely both that a working-class (rather than a peasant) trade union movement would emerge, and that it would be grudgingly acknowledged and bargained with by landowners in the 1980s. However, structural features of the local economy do not explain everything about the rural labor movement in Pernambuco. While structural change affected the interests of individuals in the sugar zone, it in itself did not directly lead either to the organization of people with common interests or to their mobilization (Tilly 1978: 52). Katznelson reminds us that proletarianization is 'not a sufficient condition' from which it is possible to 'infer ways of life, dispositions, or collective action' of workers (Katznelson and Zolberg 1986: 14). We therefore must, in our explanation, take account of factors other than the ones so far discussed, including the nature of political institutions and ideology.

At the macro level, the rural labor movement in Pernambuco was affected by the larger political system, or the political opportunity structure (Kitschelt 1986). Thus, while the capacity to organize a large-scale strike may have existed for several years in the 1970s, such a strike was only attempted in late 1979, after a substantial opening (*abertura*) by the military regime and the example provided by successful, and defiant, strikes by metalworkers in the ABC region of São Paulo in 1978 and early 1979 (Sigaud 1980).

In addition, military rule in Brazil exhibited a higher degree of continuity with the prior populist regime than did its counterparts in Uruguay, Argentina, and Chile. It might even be said that it engaged in a kind of populism of its own. While most of its populist practices were reserved for the middle class, such as in its expansion and subsidy of federal universities and underwriting of low-cost housing programs (Melo 1993), some were directed, albeit within a highly controlled structure, to organized labor. Trade unions were not, as they later were in Argentina under the junta of 1976–83, made illegal. While many of their leaders were replaced, a prerogative which the military regime could exercise simply by invoking prior legislation, the unions themselves were allowed to continue exercising their 'legitimate', economic functions. In practice strikes were prohibited, collective bargaining was replaced by labor court decrees, and union political activity was repressed, but unions as organizations were allowed to exist. In the limited political space allowed by the military regime, unionists could rebuild, attract members, and plan for the future.

At the micro level, rural unions were transformed significantly, beginning in the early 1970s, with the creation of rural welfare programs. The military regime established medical and dental programs (FUNRURAL/PRORURAL) that union leaderships could choose to administer (Maybury-Lewis 1994: 39–45). Unlike patronage programs controlled by Brazilian unions in the populist period, or by unions, for example, in Argentina, these resources were not centralized but instead distributed at the local level (Erickson 1977: 8–10, 62–3; James 1988: 165–8). The programs boosted the resources available to rural unions, providing them with a powerful magnet to attract members and encouraging the establishment of new unions in counties (*municípios*) that did not previously have them. As a result, the foundation of rural unions shot up in the 1970s, until in 1988 CONTAG was the largest confederation in the Brazilian labor system, with 22 state federations, 2,747 unions, and almost 10 million members on its books (IBGE 1991: 425).[10] In Pernambuco, the number of unions in the sugar zone increased from 32 in 1964 (Price 1964) to 45 in 1988.

The welfare programs, far from leading to a thoroughly controlled and uncombative type of rural unionism, led to a resurgence of militancy, symbolized by the Pernambuco sugar workers' 1979 strike, the first large-scale rural strike since the end of the populist regime in 1964. Other researchers have discovered similar examples in which popular movements 'navigate within the system and turn attempts at control into material to use in fortifying their autonomy' (Starn in Escobar and Alvarez 1992: 105; see also Anastasia 1994). How this occurred deserves some analysis.

In purely material terms, the welfare programs provided the unions with a financial base that had previously been lacking. Rural unions are usually much less able than their urban counterparts to raise funds through voluntary union contributions, due to the poverty and dispersion of their members. The welfare programs, by inserting dental and medical services into the unions (legal services already existed), attracted members and raised the level of finances available through voluntary contributions. This money was used to host training for union leaders at the state federation and confederation level, as well as the CONTAG congresses that brought thousands of rural unionists to Brasília every five years. Combined with rising levels of education in the rural areas, this produced a better-educated, more powerful, and at least potentially more combative labor leadership.

The welfare programs also led to a process in which rights to welfare services

[10]   At the end of 1994, CONTAG claimed to have 3,000 member unions. However, the unions' membership figures should be taken with a grain of salt, because the names of people listed in the registry who have died, moved away, or changed jobs are rarely removed. Also, absolute membership figures do not indicate rates of active participation in the unions, in which, for example, participation in elections is relatively low.

engendered a discovery of, and demand for, the labor rights that had been suspended in practice by the military regime. Labor leaders, in explaining the basis of legal workers' new individual rights to medical and dental services, were led to the collective right to strike, the right to the minimum wage, and other labor rights complementary to the social rights enshrined in the welfare programs.

On a cultural level, the rural labor leader became a sort of secular priest or preacher (many leaders had acquired their positions through association with the Catholic Church; a few were evangelical Protestants). The fact that the unions they controlled were some of the few sites in rural areas, along with churches, that directed resources to the rural poor and spoke in their name, gave them tremendous influence over their memberships. Freed from the burden of daily work in the fields, able to travel to other parts of Brazil, generally more politically knowledgeable and well connected than their members, trade union leaders (the team of elected, full-time officials responsible for the management of each local union) could shape the ideological outlook of the workers in their areas. Because they decided who was a legal rural worker, and thus who was eligible to the union's free medical and dental services, the leaders were important figures in their communities.

Language is particularly important for popular social movements that cannot count on the power of wealth, tradition, or military force (Bowles and Gintis 1986: 155). Trade union leaders spoke to the highly diverse collection of workers in their area, in an attempt to meld it into a cohesive body, influencing attitudes in a variety of settings. In informal talks with workers in the fields, in union meetings, in assemblies to which the entire union membership was invited, and in rallies open to the general public, unionists honed their speaking skills and helped to shape local perceptions of politics.

The language of union leaders varied. Some appealed to a common status as wage laborers, the untrustworthiness of the landowning employers (*patrões*), and the need for worker solidarity and collective action. Others favored the language of *agrarismo*, reminiscent of that of the Peasant Leagues, stressing members' fellowship in a broader category of 'little people' in the countryside who must work the land themselves, as opposed to the large landowners who avoid physical labor.

In addition to speeches, leaders drew on popular culture to attract, mobilize, and influence members. During strikes, bands often played music at union headquarters. Also as part of the strike, FETAPE, the state federation in Pernambuco, distributed song lyrics that were sung at union assemblies. These lyrics were similar to those of popular songs sung in the area, published as *folhetos* or *literatura de cordel* (Borges *et al.* 1986). They emphasized a common identity, as in the following lyrics, from a union song entitled 'I am a Cultivator': 'I am bought for one hundred grams of smile | I am worried by a grain of treason | I run from he who has a smooth face | My face is full of wrinkles'. These songs also emphasize the injustice of large landowners, as in 'Our Rights Will Come': 'Just because you have much land and many | Cattle, you deny the worker, | This poor nobody. But watch out . . . one | Day in the cemetery | Our flesh will mingle. | The grave will be your home | The worm your companion | Life will disappear | There, there is no use for money. | I want to hear your defense, | Where will be your wealth | Which bought the whole world?"[11]

Partly because they reflected and celebrated cultural forms popular in the Pernambuco sugar zone, union leaders were able to transform a bureaucratic system for the distribution of patronage into a genuine social movement. With new material, organizational, and cultural resources at their disposal, they staged nine major strikes in eleven years between 1979 and 1989.

There are thus two main reasons why their movement looked different from its precursor of the early 1960s. Both were results of state policies. The first of these is agricultural modernization, involving an increase in the capital-intensivity of production and a decline of the relative importance of land and labor as costs. Agricultural modernization led to a structural transformation of landholding and the diminution of that class of cultivators to whom the Peasant Leagues had appealed—tenants, sharecroppers, and renters with insecure access to land. At the same time, it led to the consolidation of the classes that are the mainstay of CONTAG, small farmers and rural workers.

The second factor that explains the nature of the revived rural labor movement is the creation of social welfare programs administered by the unions. The welfare programs gave the union movement an unparalleled opportunity to attract members, found new unions, and organize themselves. It also spawned the development of a cadre of professional union leaders who were well connected with the political system, well trained, and who had a strong incentive to defend worker rights and mobilize their members. The programs, designed by the authoritarian state essentially to dampen potential rural protest against its agricultural modernization policies, and to prevent union militancy, thus had an unintended consequence: the emergence of a large, nationally coordinated, and oppositional rural labor movement that regained the right to strike and stood ready to play a role in the democratization of Brazilian politics.

3. The Crisis of Developmentalism

By the beginning of the 1980s, it became clear that the model of development pursued by the military regime was exhausted. The regime faced an enormous debt burden, a chronic fiscal deficit, a large number of bloated state-owned enterprises, and an inefficient industrial sector that depended heavily on government protection and largesse. In response, the military regime began to jettison

---

[11] These are just two stanzas of the eight contained in the song. The song was sung at a union assembly in Nazaré da Mata on 2 Oct. 1988, when about 600 members of the union came to discuss and vote on the strike. The union had printed the lyrics and distributed them to those at the meeting; the song (and others) were sung with musical accompaniment.

import-substitution policies and state-led growth in favor of export promotion and the beginnings of economic liberalization.

Organized labor in Brazil was a major victim of these adjustment policies, as it was in the rest of Latin America (Roxborough 1989). In the sugar sector, while PROÁLCOOL was maintained, various pressures made the position of labor unions difficult. Subsidized credit to agriculture declined sharply due to the state's fiscal problems, and world market prices for most agricultural commodities stagnated or declined. As in other agricultural areas, the vulnerable north-eastern sugar producers reacted by squeezing labor; the number of permanent jobs in the Pernambuco sugar zone declined in the 1980s.

In this climate, the revitalization of Brazil's rural union movement in the 1980s was a remarkable achievement, unmatched by its counterparts elsewhere in Latin America.[12] However, in Pernambuco, rural labor experienced three incorporations that, in the literature on the new social movements, might have been expected to reduce its authenticity and oppositional force. It was incorporated into a system of bargaining over wages supervised by the state, in which the fulfillment of some of its demands was achieved at the cost of a tacit acceptance of a reformist strategy. Second, it became part of the personal following of a politician, Miguel Arraes, who controlled an effective electoral machine and who won the election for governor of the state in 1986 and again in 1994. Finally, it merged with the broader political struggle of Brazil's Workers' Party (PT) in the 1989 and 1994 presidential elections (Hellman in Escobar and Alvarez 1992: 53). Despite all of these accommodations, the movement succeeded in restoring to tens of thousands of workers a right denied them under fifteen years of dictatorship, the right to collective bargaining. The collective contract, negotiated annually in the sugar zone, was probably more important to rural workers' daily lives than the federal constitution. And through union elections, workers could choose who was to represent them in those negotiations.[13]

The rural movement that emerged in Pernambuco during this period did not share all of the preoccupations of the 'new' or 'authentic' unionism of southern and south-central Brazil, as typified by the metalworkers' unions of São Paulo's ABC region. Activists in the new unionism looked somewhat askance at what they regarded as the old unionism of CONTAG and its affiliated state federations. Whereas CONTAG leaders were associated with the pre-Medellín Catholic Church, the new unionism was linked to the post-Medellín Church of liberation theology.

---

[12] In Chile, for example, after 16 years under Pinochet in 1989, only 30,000 out of 450,000 agricultural workers were unionized, whereas 253,000 had been unionized before the Pinochet coup in 1973. The figures from 1989 are from James Petras, 'Chile's Exploited Farm Workers', in *Christian Science Monitor*, 11 Apr. 1989, p. 18, and the figures from 1973 are from Loveman (1976: 289). Overall unionization in Chile declined from 24.8 per cent in 1964 to 9.4 per cent in 1986. Rural labor in Argentina was also weakened by the general decline in unionization under military regimes. In 1960, 45 per cent of the rural labor force was unionized, compared to 30 per cent in 1989 (Maybury-Lewis 1994: 11–12).

[13] Admittedly, the elections are indirect. Union members vote for their local union leaders, who in turn vote for the leaders of the state federation, FETAPE.

The new unionism also urged the abolition of the union tax, the system of mandatory union dues collected and administered by the state, on the grounds that it represented unwelcome state paternalism. They made this demand because urban unions, such as the metalworkers, generally raised their own voluntary contributions and felt financially strong enough to sever their connections to the state. Rural unions, much more fragile financially, strongly resisted the idea of the end to the union tax.[14]

For the new unionists, CONTAG had many leaders who were *pelegos*, complacent officials interested in managing the welfare bureaucracy at their control but unwilling to confront employers on behalf of workers. The Pernambuco rural workers' unions, while perhaps not widely considered to be complacent in this manner, were still not unequivocally part of the renovation that had taken place in industrial unionism; many of their leaders had acquired their positions in the early years of the dictatorship.[15] In addition, the Workers' Party (PT), a party founded in 1980 by a coalition including 'new' unions, made few inroads in Pernambuco. Like most of the rest of the north-east, clientelism remained a strong feature of political parties there, older political forces prevailed, and PT candidates received few votes. While PT candidate Lula did win the 1989 presidential election in the Pernambuco sugar zone, he did this largely because he received the endorsement of Miguel Arraes.[16] Arraes enjoyed a high degree of loyalty on the part of the rural trade union movement, mainly because of his historic role, as governor before the military coup, in granting state recognition to the rural labor federation and supporting some of its demands.

Formally, the system of collective bargaining in the Brazilian sugar sector is similar to that which exists in the automobile sector, described elsewhere in this volume by Scott Martin. However, bargaining takes place at the state level, without the sectoral concentration that has been achieved in autos. In addition, employer–employee relations are still highly conflictual, with none of the shared consensus, professionalism, and worker participation that Martin found in the automobile sector. This is not because institutions of class compromise do not exist, but because the conditions within the sugar sector—for example, the precariousness

---

[14] While 64 per cent of urban unions reported in 1988 that 80 to 100 per cent of their members had paid their union contributions, only 6 per cent of rural unions reported the same. In contrast, 71 per cent of the rural unions got dues from fewer than 40 per cent of their members, while only 16 per cent of the urban unions reported this (IBGE 1991: 426). The fact that most rural unions represent many widely scattered peasants who do not earn wages is the main reason for their difficulty in garnering voluntary union dues.

[15] For a good discussion of the new unionism, see Margaret Keck, 'The New Unionism in the Brazilian Transition' (Stepan 1989). Many of the leaders of the Pernambuco sugar zone's rural unions had been active in the movement in the 1960s; some had also been members of the Peasant Leagues. For the fifty union leaders I interviewed there in 1988, the average time in the unions was nineteen years. Three leaders had actually started as 'interventors', officials appointed by the military regime to replace union leaders ousted in the wake of the 1964 military coup.

[16] Lula won 54 per cent of the second-round presidential vote in the sugar zone, compared to 39 per cent for his rival, Collor de Mello; he also won the state as a whole by a narrower margin of 40 per cent to 39 per cent. Source: Tribunal Regional Eleitoral, Recife, 1989 election results.

of the PROÁLCOOL program, the weak financial state of many producers, the predominance of unskilled labor, and high rates of seasonal unemployment—are an unfavorable basis for the kind of cooperation and 'innovative militancy' that the auto workers' unions engage in. Evidently, the new forms of labor–management relations that have evolved in high-technology sectors are not easily transferred to more traditional industries.

Partly for this reason, the Pernambuco movement falls short of the highest aspirations of those extolling both new, non-class social movements and the new unionism. The degree of democratic inclusion that FETAPE was able to achieve, even under the governorship of a protective leader, Miguel Arraes, was limited. Squatters claiming land rights, women, seasonally unemployed cane cutters, illegals (*clandestinos*), and peasants from the interior, most of whom were nominally part of the unions' membership base, received much less of the attention of the federation than its prime constituency: permanently employed field workers in the sugar sector. (Illegal workers constitute up to half of the work-force in Pernambuco's cane fields, revealing the extent of informal work relations within even a highly organized and militant work-force.) Even for its main constituency, FETAPE lacked the resources and connections to ensure the *enforcement* of the labor contract throughout the sugar zone; instead, local unions had to struggle largely on their own to get landowners to comply. And FETAPE was unable to get the state to prevent, or even to investigate and prosecute, landlord violence against workers.

This violence, usually carried out by landlords' hired gunmen or members of the military police, was aimed in Pernambuco at active union members and leaders, and workers involved in disputes with employers. It affected every rural union in the sugar zone and, because the police and judiciary rarely investigated, let alone prosecuted, these crimes, spread a climate of fear among the plantations. This picture is matched in many other parts of rural Brazil, ranging from Pernambuco, where the violence mostly relates to employer–employee conflicts, to frontier areas such as southern Pará, where smallholders are threatened by representatives of large estates, to Acre, where rubber tappers confront ranchers.

However, rural violence was not the major issue raised by the rural labor movement of the 1980s. Land reform was; it was this issue that ostensibly tied the many disparate strands of the movement together. The movement rallied behind the land reform plan announced by the civilian government of José Sarney in 1985, and gathered over a million signatures in favor of land reform when the Constituent Assembly was formed in 1986. CONTAG's stance on the issue was moderate; it supported parliamentary action in favor of land redistribution, but opposed illegal occupations and other forms of direct action designed to force the government's hand. Because of this, and the tendency of many local rural unions to avoid direct engagement in the struggle of the rural poor for land, new organizations within the rural labor movement arose in the 1980s. Joining the Catholic Church's Pastoral da Terra (Land Pastoral), which had been active in the countryside since 1975, were new entities such as the Movimento Sem Terra (MST, Landless Workers' Movement), founded in 1984, and the Movimento por Terra, Trabalho, e Liberdade (Movement for Land, Work, and Liberty), created in 1992. These organizations speak for the landless and try to help them occupy and win legal title to land.

However, the forces in favor of land reform suffered a serious political defeat in 1988 when the final draft of the new constitution made it harder to expropriate land than had been possible under the military regime's 1964 Land Statute. The rhetorical centerpiece of the rural labor movement had thus been rejected, and CONTAG's slogan—'there is no democracy without agrarian reform'—could only be interpreted as a condemnation of the undemocratic character of the new civilian regime.

Nevertheless, the failure of the agrarian reform initiative was not due entirely to the strength of its opponents. Much has been made of the phenomenal growth of the UDR, the Democratic Rural Union (União Democrática Ruralista), a well-funded organization of landowners that lobbied against the reform plan in the Constituent Assembly.[17] The importance of the UDR is not to be denied, but CONTAG itself was divided over the issue of land redistribution. Almost two-thirds of union presidents within CONTAG are small *owners* of property, making their attitude towards state expropriation and redistribution of privately held lands somewhat ambivalent.[18] In principle, small producers are exempt from land reform, but some of them still saw such measures as the 'thin end of a wedge' and identified more with other landowners than with the landless. This contradiction between small proprietors and wage-earners even caused a *de facto* separation of the São Paulo rural workers' federation, in the late 1980s, into two organizations, one, unofficial, representing wage workers, and another, official entity representing small farmers (Correia de Andrade 1994: 214).

The division within CONTAG on the land issue was revealed in the 1989 election results. Research on those results shows a striking inverse relationship between *município* population and the vote for conservative candidate Collor de Mello (Avelar 1990: 45).[19] CONTAG's almost 10 million members reside mainly in small *municípios* where support for Collor de Mello was strongest. Therefore, a significant percentage of CONTAG's members must have voted for a presidential candidate clearly opposed to agrarian reform, against his opponent who supported it.

The ambiguity with regard to land distribution could also be seen in the

[17] The UDR, formed almost immediately after the announcement of the 1985 agrarian reform plan, grew from 50,000 members in that year to 250,000 by 1988 (from *Veja*, 11 Nov. 1987, p. 30). It is now virtually inactive; in October 1994 the UDR leadership was discussing disbanding the organization.

[18] In 1988, 57.8 per cent of all CONTAG presidents were reported to be small landowners (*pequeno produtores*). In contrast, only 13.5 per cent were wage workers, while 8.7 per cent were renters (*arrendatários*) and 9.2 per cent were sharecroppers (*parceiros*) (IBGE 1991: 430). Generally, rural workers' unions in Brazil include as members any landowners who do not employ wage workers on their property. Landowners who do employ workers are required to join the rural employers' union (*sindicato*).

[19] The grand exception to this pattern is the city of São Paulo, the largest in the nation, where Collor de Mello won.

Pernambuco sugar zone. There, the state federation stood mainly for wage workers, but it was tied to a confederation, CONTAG, in which land reform was officially the main plank of the movement. When landless peasants seized privately owned land outside the capital city of Recife in 1988 and demanded government expropriation of, and their settlement on, the land, FETAPE was initially hesitant to support them because the state governor, Miguel Arraes, opposed the occupation.

In the cultural realm, ambiguity abounds as well. While FETAPE used songs to try to create a common identity, the identity most usually invoked was the old *agrarista* image of the Peasant Leagues, rather than a working-class identity predicated on a common experience as wage laborers. The Peasant League slogan, 'agrarian reform by law or by force', was still used by the unions. Furthermore, union songs are full of references to peasant, rather than worker identities—'us' is invariably a cultivator, a poor person, a person with callused hands, rather than a wage-earner. Among over two dozen union songs collected in the sugar zone, only one—'I am Going to Stay on this Side', very similar to the US labor song 'Which Side are You on'—clearly projected a working-class identity by specifically mentioning a strike and employers.

The reason for the durability of a peasant identity in the sugar zone, despite widespread proletarianization and the formation of an almost exclusively working-class movement, can be ascribed to a number of factors. First, there is a disjuncture between economic and cultural production. Popular songs remain popular, despite their declining relevance to contemporary economic realities. Second, while FETAPE is primarily a workers' movement, it is subordinated to a confederation, CONTAG, dominated by small landowners. Finally, small landowners and rural workers who would like to become small landowners do form part of the community, and the membership base, within which FETAPE leaders work. A peasant identity therefore provides them with a more inclusive category, and allows them to concentrate their confrontational tactics during the strike on large landowners employing relatively large numbers of workers.

The future of interest representation in the Pernambuco sugar zone depends on the fate of its sugar sector. Neither land redistribution nor extensive public works programs, both FETAPE demands, seem likely, given the power of Pernambuco's landed oligarchy and the fiscal crisis of the Brazilian state. However, the current Brazilian government might pursue more of the same in the north-eastern sugar zone—the maintenance of the PROÁLCOOL program, and continued financing for the modernization of sugar production. Because the IAA is virtually moribund, this would result in more vertical integration of production, more mechanization, and declining employment levels in Pernambuco. If FETAPE clings to its corporatist role and bargains only for higher wages, it might eventually find itself eclipsed by a new movement, outside the corporatist labor structure, claiming to speak on behalf of those marginalized by agricultural modernization. While the space for such a movement is easy to conceive, the particular form such a movement would take is hard to imagine.

A second scenario in the sugar zone would occur if the Brazilian state decided to dismantle the PROÁLCOOL program. Petrobrás, the state oil monopoly which administers the program, might welcome such a move. The current low international price of oil makes PROÁLCOOL uneconomic, and the Brazilian government's efforts to cut deficit spending might also put pressure on the alcohol program. If PROÁLCOOL were to be significantly reduced, the relatively inefficient north-eastern producers might face collapse, and go the way of many Caribbean sugar producers.

In such a context, the rural labor movement might return to the 'politics of despair' that has afflicted the north-east in past eras. The democratic consensus that currently prevails between landowners and union leaders would collapse. As in the 1960s, widespread demands for land could surface, and spontaneous incidents of direct action on the part of an idled labor force could occur. In such a setting, rural laborers might create something that looked much more like a new social movement than does the current network of unions. Glimpses of such a possibility could be seen in March 1993, when 1,000 sugar cane workers occupied the state agricultural secretariat in Recife. They demanded that the state redistribute uncultivated land to workers and create more public works jobs.[20] In response, the state government did create some public works jobs on a temporary basis, but it left the land issue untouched.

Nationally, it seems that the crisis of developmentalism revealed deep contradictions within CONTAG. Able to unite a wide variety of interests against the dictatorship in the 1970s, the confederation found itself internally divided once that common threat had disappeared in the mid-1980s. Then-CONTAG president José Francisco remarked despairingly in 1987, 'Before, in the darkness of the dictatorship, we . . . would end up finding a way, some space. Today we are having difficulty finding the way to this space within the democratic transition. It is such a complicated, illogical transition that we ask if we are living in a transition to democracy or incorporating the behavior of the dictatorship.'[21] Such frustration is understandable. No urban labor confederation faces problems of coordination comparable to CONTAG, which is supposed to speak for small landowners, colonists, renters, sharecroppers, and temporary and permanent workers all over the country. The confederation's defeat on the agrarian reform issue in 1988 showed up its ambivalence about land redistribution, and the ineffectiveness of its use of the populist rhetoric of *agrarismo* to mobilize workers and farmers

---

[20] The occupation took place on 29 March; from James Brooke, 'In Brazil, Too, the Withered Land Cries for Rain', in the *New York Times*, 8 Apr. 1993. In the same month, in the interior of the north-east, the situation was much worse. Hungry peasants and workers looted food supplies in dozens of towns. In response, then-President Itamar Franco allocated $180 million to create 1 million public works jobs—a fraction of the $1.2 billion in federal credit that went to sugar cane growers for the 1993 harvest. From 'Desespero no Sertão', in *Veja*, 24 Mar. 1993, pp. 78–80 and Business Monitor International Ltd. (1993: 118–19).

[21] Quoted in 'Reforma Agrária: Traição Por Decreto', in *O Trabalhador Rural*, the CONTAG newspaper, Nov. 1987, p. 4.

facing complicated issues of labor representation and agricultural policies. While CONTAG represented an admirable unity of the rural lower classes in the face of authoritarian repression in the 1970s, in the 1990s a more pluralistic organizational form might better serve the variety of interests included in its cumbersome institutional body. Some kind of democratic reform of the corporatist labor structure, along the lines suggested by Scott Martin elsewhere in this volume, definitely seems to be needed—and would provoke great changes—in Brazil's countryside.[22]

Because of CONTAG's limitations, local movements such as those of the landless, rubber tappers in Acre, cultivators threatened by the construction of dams, and women have moved outside the formal union structure to organize their interests. A prime example of this is the MST, whose slogan is 'occupy, resist, and produce'. Emerging out of a land occupation in the southern state of Rio Grande do Sul in 1979, the MST claimed responsibility for eighty-nine squatter settlements in twenty-two of Brazil's twenty-six states by the fall of 1995. The organization's militancy and tactics often provoke severe repression from landowners and military police, but they get governmental attention and, sometimes, results—results that would not arise from merely waiting for the slow agrarian reform bureaucracy to redistribute land. In September of 1995, MST coordinator Gilberto Portes warned the government of Fernando Henrique Cardoso that if it did not keep its promise of settling 40,000 landless families on land by the end of the year, the MST would double the number of its land invasions (Villar 1995: 6–7). While it is unclear whether this threat could be carried out (the government, for its part, could not meet its target, due to the ease with which landowners delayed and blocked expropriations in court), it contrasted with the more moderate stance of CONTAG, whose president, Francisco Urbano de Araújo, was a member of the president's party.

Conclusion

The two main reasons why Brazil's contemporary rural labor movement looks different from its precursor of the early 1960s are the modernization of agricultural production and the implantation of welfare services within the trade unions. Both changes owe much to deliberate state policies, albeit policies that had unintended outcomes. Labor resistance, when it resurfaced in the more liberal political climate of the 1980s, took new directions as it came up against altered economic and organizational structures. This case-study is another illustration of the truism that state policies and institutional forms influence patterns of popular protest.

[22] Boito makes an argument in favor of the abolition of Brazil's current corporatist labor system, including the mandatory union tax and the principle of one union per category of worker in a given territory (*unicidade*) (Boito 1991). An argument for the contrary view in support of more modest modifications of the system is found in Gacek's book (Gacek 1994) and Scott Martin's chapter in this volume.

The trajectory of the rural labor movement in Pernambuco is an ambiguous one. The movement gained autonomy from societal elites (renegade landowners, the Church, the Communist Party) only by accepting incorporation into the state. Both kinds of linkages involved constraints, but the movement was still able to achieve some of its goals despite state incorporation. This outcome contradicts a recurring fallacy in the literature on new social movements and civil society, that linkage to the state automatically nullifies any potential for authentic and oppositional action on the part of social movements. That literature, derived from European societies with strong states, has been carelessly applied to quite different social realities. In Latin America, the state is extensive but weak, and nowhere more so than in the countryside (O'Donnell 1993*d*). Its ramshackle institutions allow for considerable representation of popular interests, conflict, and compromise. 'Old' corporatist unionism, and not just 'new' social movements, some of which are quite slight and transitory, can play a role in democratic consolidation.

The point here is not that new social movements have not arisen in Latin America. However, what has not been sufficiently recognized is that their ability to organize in areas already dominated by corporatist structures tied to the state is limited. In Brazil, new social movements have had a tremendous impact on the way the interests of slum dwellers, women, and blacks have been represented, because none of these interests had been formally incorporated into the state. In the case of rural labor, which was incorporated, the room for growth of new social movements has been much less extensive.

In Pernambuco, organizations representing peasants and expressing their desire for land have been marginalized, not because peasants there have completely ceased to exist, but because organizations of this type were violently abolished by the military regime. Subsequently, the implantation of welfare programs into the unions raised the costs of entry into the 'market' of rural labor representation, deterring competitors to the unions. The welfare programs also empowered a new category of professional union leaders, connected to the state, with a high degree of influence over their members, little interest in challenging the distribution of property rights, and the responsibility of representing rural labor as workers, in a way analogous to their counterparts in urban unions. These union leaders directed what was now an 'old' social movement that repeatedly used a single repertoire of collective action—the strike—in a stable, ritualized pattern of annual class conflict. The unions helped those workers who could benefit from wage increases—in particular, permanently employed field hands—to achieve some measure of citizenship, dignity, and economic improvement.

However, the crisis of the military regime's developmentalist policies made the role of Brazilian rural labor leaders increasingly difficult. The union movement was revitalized at a time when state subsidies to agriculture were slashed, and the import-substitution policies of the past were replaced by a more open, export-oriented (and less successful, in terms of growth) model of development. This meant that labor's new freedoms to organize were exercised in an increasingly lean environment, as the state attempted to ride out the debt crisis by curbing domestic demand, ratcheting down wages, and increasing trade surpluses that provided the foreign exchange for debt repayment.

In highlighting the movement's modest victories, we should not forget all those who are frequently excluded from the current, dominant forms of popular representation in rural Brazil: women, children, migrants, landless peasants, squatters, illegal workers. The union song 'I am a Cultivator' eloquently expresses the dilemma of citizenship for the millions of rural poor who have not been effectively granted the right to political consultation: 'I am a Brazilian only when it is time to vote.' Barrington Moore's tranquil assertion that democracy is best served by the disappearance of the peasantry (Moore 1966: 429) reflects the developed world's comfortable history, in which agricultural modernization occurred at a time when surplus labor could readily be absorbed by industry. Those conditions do not exist in contemporary Latin America.

The emergence of new forms of interest representation in the countryside is vital if the negation of citizenship rights by economic marginalization, landlord violence, and misery is to be curbed. In Brazil, the continuation of capital-intensive modernization in agriculture without countervailing policies of social assistance could return the country to the 'politics of despair', involving struggles over land-use rights, that have recurred for centuries. Involving trade unions and other organizations in a creative adaptation that ends the privileged status of crops such as sugar, and employs the land in new and more socially productive ways, would be one solution, albeit an improbable one, to the conditions of violence and marginalization that currently exist.

PART II. Searching for New Forms of Participation

5 | The Rise of Causa R in Venezuela

Margarita López-Maya[1]

Introduction

This chapter analyzes the rise of an alternative popular actor in the Venezuelan political system, Causa Radical, better known as Causa R. This organization first emerged on the Venezuelan political scene following the 1988 national elections, when the party won three seats in the Chamber of Deputies. The first elections for state governors, held in December 1989, led to victory for Andrés Velásquez, its candidate for the state of Bolívar. Three years later, in 1992, municipal and state elections enabled Causa R to retain that office, and increase its hold over mayoralties and city councils throughout the state. One of its more charismatic leaders, Aristóbulo Istúriz, whose political career began as a leader of the Venezuelan teachers' association, earned a surprising victory in the contest for mayor of Caracas. This provided an additional impulse to the organization, and running as its presidential candidate in the December 1993 elections, Governor Velásquez obtained 22 per cent of the vote in a tight race among four candidates.

To understand the remarkable and growing role of Causa R, we must take into account the severe sociopolitical crisis that has affected Venezuela in recent years. This crisis was expressed most dramatically in the 'Caracazo' of 1989 and two failed coup attempts which took place in 1992. Yet this is not a sufficient explanation: the process of state reform which has unfolded since the mid-1980s, and the evolution of Causa R itself from its origins in the early 1970s to the present, are key to explaining the party's recent success.

The first part of this chapter briefly reviews the decentralizing reform implemented at the end of the 1980s. The second part describes the birth and evolution of Causa R through 1989, when it began its sustained transformation into a political party, first at a regional level and then on a nationwide basis. The third section follows the development of Causa R since 1989, analyzing its triumphs in various elections and identifying shifts in its discourse which have resulted from the rapid expansion of its influence in the Venezuelan political system. The final section offers some conclusions about the rise of Causa R and its future as a representative of popular sectors in national politics.

[1] The editors would like to thank Eric Hershberg for his translation of this chapter.

1. Reform of the State and Decentralization[2]

The emergence of Causa R was facilitated enormously by the process of state reform initiated in 1984 by the decree establishing the Presidential Commission for State Reform (COPRE). The reforms, which were enacted in 1988 and 1989, following numerous delays, helped to establish new channels of mediation between state and society during a period when a critical economic situation and the deterioration of traditional political parties threatened to bring about the collapse of the political democracy that had functioned in Venezuela since 1958.

Indeed, since the close of the administration of Social Christian President Luis Herrera Campíns (1979–83), Venezuelan society increasingly exhibited signs of disequilibria, which directly undermined the prestige of hegemonic actors. Relations among these actors were characterized by growing tensions derived from government efforts to bring about changes in the economic model. The 1982 takeover of the Banco de los Trabajadores de Venezuela revealed the first in a series of corruption scandals; in February of the following year the national currency, the bolivar, was devalued following twenty-two consecutive years of stability, a measure that for many observers symbolized the end of an era during which Venezuela prospered through oil rents.

These developments led the candidates in the 1983 presidential campaign to promise solutions to overcome the crisis. The eventual winner, Jaime Lusinchi of Acción Democrática (AD), offered a Social Pact, consisting of a negotiated accord between the state and the various organized social forces. In the short term the Pact aimed to resolve the economic crisis, and in the longer term it purported to correct the social and political ills which affected Venezuelan society.

In December 1984 the newly elected president fulfilled his campaign promise by decreeing the creation of COPRE and naming thirty-three members representative of elites across the Venezuelan political spectrum. With a mandate to advise the Executive on any matters requested of it, and to develop comprehensive proposals for state reform, COPRE worked intensively from its creation to the end of the Lusinchi administration in early 1989. In 1985 it drafted a series of reports offering a comprehensive and coherent diagnosis of the principal obstructions to sociopolitical development in Venezuela as they had emerged since 1958. At the same time, building on consultations with individuals and organizations from all sectors of the political arena, in 1986 COPRE began to present the Executive—and thus shape public opinion—with a series of proposals that had generated a strong consensus within the Commission. From the outset, COPRE emphasized that the decentralization of power was an essential aspect of any expansion and rationalization of democratization. From 1986 onward, decentralization emerged as

---

[2] This section summarizes freely the results of research carried out by the Area Sociopolítica of CENDES, portions of which have been published in at least three publications, including López-Maya *et al.* (1989); Gómez Calcaño and López-Maya (1990), and López-Maya (1991). Citations are provided for texts other than those mentioned above.

one of the crucial elements of state reform in Venezuela. Three COPRE documents merit attention as critical elements to the development of major proposals for decentralization.

In May 1986, COPRE published its first document entitled 'Proposals for Immediate Political Reforms' (COPRE 1986). Beginning with proposals to democratize parties and to modify existing electoral mechanisms, the document went on to propose the implementation of a constitutional provision, suspended since 1961, which called for direct elections of governors of federal entities or states. For COPRE, the failure to apply this provision both contradicted the principles of the constitution and encouraged excessive centralization. In addition, the document pointed out the need to modify the Organic Law of Municipal Government in order to restore the municipality as a 'primary and autonomous political unit'; achieve a division of powers at the municipal level of government; and to create the office of mayor, elected by secret ballot and by universal, direct suffrage.

Two documents related exclusively to decentralization were proposed in 1987 (COPRE 1987a, 1987b). The first outlined a brief diagnosis of the situation facing federal bodies, that is, the states, the Federal District, and Federal Territories established in the 1961 Constitution, and recognized that in practice, they had lost their autonomy, since their constituent communities did not participate decisively in the choice of governing officials.[3] Moreover, these authorities lacked real power, since they had lost faculties in favor of the central government and did not have the institutional capacity to raise resources necessary to permit self-administration.

This first document analyzed the existing centralization of public services and concluded that Venezuela maintained a fictitious federal structure. The federal units did not provide services to residents—that was being done by the central government. Nevertheless, they spent the resources allocated to them in reproducing this federal structure, which generated bureaucratic employment of little utility that impeded efficient administration and lent itself to clientelist practices.

In response to this general diagnosis, the Commission first recommended the restoration of the federal and municipal entities as the ideal units for channeling a coherent process of decentralization. By doing so, COPRE rejected other models of regionalization which had shaped national planning policies, proposing instead a return to the territorial division envisioned in the constitution. It noted that the suprastatist approaches that had been developed in the area of planning only sought to decentralize administration but never had the purpose of transferring political power.

In addition, COPRE recommended a series of complementary reforms, some of which were already present in the 1986 document, including: strengthening the

[3] Governors were designated by the President, while deputies to the Legislative Assemblies of each federal unit were elected by direct, secret, and universal suffrage through a system of closed lists. Each voter cast only one vote, which in addition to the slate for legislative assembly deputies, included the slates for the Senate, the Chamber of Deputies, and the Municipal Council. Thus, voters expressed a preference for a party, and the parties chose who would serve.

decision-making powers of state and municipal governments; direct election of governors and mayors; electoral system reform enabling regional and local officials to be chosen by their constituents, rather than by political parties; and reforms in the administration of federal entities to guarantee a professionalized civil service (entrance exams, job security for efficient functionaries, adequate salaries and guarantee of employment rights, and judicial access).

COPRE did not recommend increasing the economic role of regional state administrations, but suggested instead that mechanisms be established to redistribute available resources. For example, COPRE called for a restructuring of local tax systems in order to improve collection. COPRE argued that if political and administrative reforms were implemented, they would generate the sense of local identity and commitment of local authorities and their constituents necessary to bring about improvement in regional governance.

Some of these proposals stimulated strong opposition from President Lusinchi and the AD. The traditional leadership of the governing party saw, correctly, that the reforms had the potential to change the rules of the political game, and thus the prevailing distribution of power. In contrast, these same proposals obtained a great deal of support from opposition parties, and especially from interest groups of all types, including neighborhood associations, the media, and professionals, all of whom saw in reform the possibility of opening spaces for political expression and action. Causa R could be included among these groups, although at this point it was just one of many microscopic (except for the MAS) groups on the left of the Venezuelan political spectrum.

The result of this confrontation was a broad debate and significant tensions, as the governing party used a strategy of delay in an effort to sink the reforms. Nevertheless, during the electoral campaign of 1988, the government was forced to make concessions. Moreover, the Caracazo of February 1989 further pressured the government of Carlos Andrés Pérez to keep some of its earlier promises. The period between 1988 and the first year of the Pérez administration witnessed the approval of the Law of Election and Recall of State Governors (1988 and 1989), the Law on the Time Periods of the State Authorities (1989), the Organic Law of Decentralization, Delimitation, and Transfer of Policy Responsibilities (1989), and the New Organic Law of Municipal Government (1988 and 1989). These measures opened new possibilities for changing the functioning of the state and the political system.

2. The Origins of Causa R and its Trajectory until Implementation of the Decentralization Laws

The original nucleus of the political organization, officially registered in the 1970s as the Causa Radical, consisted of a small group that split from the Venezuelan

Communist Party (PCV) in 1970 and that did not join the majority of party dissidents in founding the Movement Toward Socialism (MAS) in January 1971.

The late 1960s and early 1970s were a period of great social effervescence in Venezuela. The first government of Rafael Caldera (1969–74) faced significant mobilizations of students and workers. By now efforts to reach power and to bring about 'revolution' through armed struggle had been defeated, and as a result the government took the initiative of granting an amnesty to guerrillas in a so-called pacification policy. Meanwhile, the political parties involved in the armed struggle, the PCV and the Movement of the Revolutionary Left (MIR), were torn by internal disputes, a logical outcome of the failure of their sociopolitical project (López-Maya *et al.* 1989).

The most important offshoot of the PCV gave rise to the MAS, which would soon become the third most important actor in the Venezuelan party system. The ideological positions of the MAS were derived both from a fierce criticism of the conception of the party which had characterized the PCV—and which was widely blamed for the failure of the armed struggle—and from the ideas of the Venezuelan student movement, which had been influenced by its European counterpart and by the 1960s 'New Left' (Ellner 1988: 43 *et seq.*). The ideas of democracy and socialism became the new focus for debate on the left during this period. While the MAS did not obtain sufficient votes during the 1970s and 1980s to be able to compete with the two major parties for control over the Venezuelan government, it played a relevant role in the Congress and participated in the multiple alliances and traditional negotiations of the political system.

At the founding convention of the MAS in January 1971, one of its leaders, Alfredo Maneiro, clarified his differences with his comrades. As one of the *comandantes* of the armed struggle in the eastern part of the country, Maneiro had for eighteen years been an activist in the PCV, where he rose to become a member of the Central Committee. He was also one of the protagonists of the party's internal rupture, and he had been named a member of the Central Committee of the MAS for the convention. Nonetheless, Maneiro was a reluctant participant in the meeting, disagreeing on a wide range of matters such as inclusion in the MAS of sectors of the PCV that he considered more conservative than those of himself and of Teodoro Petkoff.[4] These were the sectors of the party that had been least critical of the PCV's actions and most willing to reconcile with the past. As a result, Maneiro chose to break with the MAS, though only about ten people would leave along with him.[5]

Within this small nucleus, comprising former mid-level militants or rank-and-file activists of the PCV, Maneiro would become the undisputed leader. His papers

---

[4] Teodoro Petkoff, the founder of the MAS, is one of the best-known and most prestigious representatives of the Venezuelan left, and has been President of his party as well as its presidential candidate.

[5] Among them, Pablo Medina, José Lira, and Lucas Matheus, all of whom are today key leaders of the Causa R.

reveal his own intellectual talents and political instincts (Maneiro *et al.* 1971; Maneiro 1986). As he notes in his writings, although during 1971 informal contacts continued among the members of the group, the idea of establishing a party seemed implausible in those initial months. In his words, 'There existed nine chances out of ten that the group would lose its initial character, its confidence in itself, and would end up no longer insisting on the political principles it was based upon' (Maneiro *et al.* 1971: 9).

'VENEZUELA 83' AND CAUSA R

Even though Maneiro hesitated in establishing a political organization that would embody elements that seemed absent from either the PCV or the MAS, he quickly decided to act to ensure the continuation of ideas that he and a series of other people, most of them youth linked to popular movements, had been discussing. The result was the publication in 1971 of a collection of the group's writings in a book called *Notas negativas* (Maneiro *et al.* 1971).

This group was known as 'Venezuela 83', and it constituted the immediate antecedent to La Causa R.[6] In *Notas negativas* Maneiro analyzed the failure of the armed struggle in Venezuela, sharply criticizing both the structure and functioning of the PCV, and reflected on one of his obsessions, the role of the vanguard of the popular movement. He also discussed the problems of efficiency and the revolutionary quality of organizations which purport to represent the people. He stated that very few organizations were notable for their internal organization, their freshness, creativity, or their relations with and sensitivity to the masses (Maneiro *et al.* 1971: 29–33). The final writings of *Notas negativas* laid out the conceptual framework of what would later become Causa R.

In effect, Maneiro believed that the formation of a party should not be conceived as the beginning of a revolutionary movement, but rather the other way around, a party was the product of a revolutionary movement at a certain level of its development (Maneiro *et al.* 1971: 39). He said that it was necessary to give political content and shape to the awesome and spontaneous capacity of the masses to mobilize and to participate in the infinite and various forms of the popular movement, with the conviction that the masses themselves would resolve the question of their political leadership. Instead of departing from a given political structure, it was necessary to believe in the capacity of the popular movement to take in its own hands the task of producing a new leadership from within its own ranks. The construction of a vanguard linked to the mass movement, rooted in its practice and experience, was also, in Maneiro's view, an ideological construction (Maneiro *et al.* 1971: 39–41).

---

[6] Maneiro named it Venezuela 83 to associate it with the year (1983) in which the majority of oil contracts in the hands of transnational oil companies would revert to the Venezuelan government. Maneiro understood that this process would be crucial for Venezuelan society and argued in favor of moving up the date for the process.

These ideas should be seen in the context of the debate about forms of revolutionary struggle that took place among intellectuals and activists of the Venezuelan left during the 1960s, a debate that was, in turn, inserted into the broader context of the Latin American left. In the Venezuelan case, given the magnitude of the guerrilla defeat, but also the intellectual capacity and political diversity of its leaders, the debate generated a profound questioning of *foquista* strategies, of extrapolations from other experiences, and of the authoritarianism of Communist parties. It should be noted that the Venezuelan guerrillas were drawn for the most part from middle-class and university backgrounds, and that the PCV and its offshoots were not the only participants in the armed struggle. On the contrary, dissident factions of Acción Democrática, the so-called MIR, were also involved. Moreover, by the end of the decade, much of the membership of these groups recognized that the conditions prevailing at the time, and the military defeat they had suffered, precluded any return to a revolutionary struggle. Thus, *comandantes* such as Maneiro and Petkoff, the latter one of the founders of the MAS, strove to achieve a new articulation with the popular movement through theoretical and practical proposals adapted to the specific conditions of Venezuela and to the impossibility, in the short and medium term, of using violence as an instrument of struggle.

In keeping with these ideas, the small group that formed Venezuela 83 decided not to create an organization with a formal charter, bureaucracy, and statutes, but rather emphasized the need for a party to be in a permanent process of formation. For this they believed it necessary to dedicate all of their efforts to the construction of a type of vanguard that would ensue from the encounter between their own group, which they characterized as a product of the crisis of Marxism, and the leadership that emerged from the spontaneous movements of the masses. Maneiro often said that popular leadership was being developed constantly in everyday activities, in popular baseball games for instance, and that it was essential to seek out and interact with this kind of leadership.

During 1971 Maneiro and his group sought to evaluate what type of mass movements existed in Venezuela that could be tapped in order to create a vanguard. The three they selected were the student movement of the Central University (UCV), the workers' movement of the Orinoco Steel Works (Sidor), and the popular movement in the Catia district in Caracas. The UCV was at the moment enjoying considerable dynamism as a result of the process of university reform. Sidor had recently experienced a highly significant, albeit unsuccessful strike that had resulted in the dismissal of 514 workers. There was much discontent among workers, and an alternative labor movement was being formed outside the traditional union organizations. The community of Catia, Maneiro said, was virtually a city inside Caracas, with half a million inhabitants and its own upper, middle, and lower classes. It had a long tradition of militancy, was relatively free of the political riff-raff so widespread in other communities, and its population was more stable than the poor neighborhoods of Petare in the east of the city (Maneiro 1986: 146–52).

Although the project may have seemed far-fetched given the ragged nature of the initial group, Maneiro and his colleagues envisioned a slow, meticulous process which, over the short and medium term, might begin to have a positive impact on the political system. Thus, in 1972 Pablo Medina, one of the group's members, went to Ciudad Guayana with the task of creating an organization within Sidor.

The state-owned Orinoco Steel Works has been one of the principal industrial projects of Venezuelan democracy. Located in a sparsely populated region in the south of the country, the steel works derived a set of comparative advantages offered by the location, among them a large supply of hydroelectric power. Thanks to the dynamism generated by this industry, and later by the establishment of an aluminum industry, Guayana City became from the 1960s onwards a pole that attracted internal migrants who, over time, constituted a population without historic ties to the region and defined by its status as laborers in state industry and employees in the public sector. However, in contrast with the industrial areas of the central and coastal regions of the country, working and living conditions in Ciudad Guayana were hard, workplace safety and hygiene were poor, and the state had been disinclined to play the role of paternalist owner. The workers of Sidor endured these conditions for years before gaining a collective contract. The potential for militancy anticipated by Venezuela 83 was derived from these characteristics of the community. Thus, when Medina set out for Ciudad Guayana this was also the destination of other left organizations, although the traditional parties appeared not to have anticipated what was to result from conditions in the region.

Pablo Medina took a job as a worker on the night shift and began to publish a newspaper entitled *El Matancero*. At first the paper was clandestine, due to the authoritarian practices of local unionism, dominated by the corrupt bureaucracy associated primarily with AD (Medina 1988: 47). The first issues were written by Medina virtually on his own, with the help of a few activists from Caracas who came down on weekends.[7] However, by the end of 1972 Matancero included ten workers. A year later, an electrical worker, Andrés Velásquez, had begun to collaborate with the group. In 1974, Velásquez gave his first speech before the Portón de Sidor,[8] speaking in favor of the Matancero slate in the union elections. It was around this time that he met Alfredo Maneiro (Sesto 1992: 18).

Five years later, in 1977, Tello Benítez, another leader who had arisen, as members of the Causa R would put it, from the popular movement, gained a seat on Sutiss, the Sidor union. This initiated the rise of the 'new unionism' represented by Matancero. In addition to the honesty they exhibited in contrast to the traditional unionism, the Matanceros struggled for goals such as democratic participation of workers in union decisions that affected them, an issue that was

---

[7] Morella Barreto, interview of 25 Oct. 1993.

[8] The Portón de Sidor is the principal door through which workers enter and leave the plant. This is where the buses stop to take workers home or to bring them to the factory. At the beginning and end of each shift there is a considerable concentration of workers and employees, and for that reason it was an excellent place from which to address them. Velásquez was known as 'the leader of the Portón'.

non-existent in unionism in the region, and workplace safety and hygiene, which were ignored by other labor leaders. At the negotiating table Benítez debated with both management and with the mainstream union, while Velásquez kept the workers informed at the Portón (Sesto 1992: 47).

Two years later, in the 1979 elections, the El Matancero slate, headed by Velásquez, won control over the Sidor union. In response, following a series of conflicts, in 1981 the union was taken over by FETRAMETAL, the parent union of Sutiss, which has always been controlled by AD unions. Velásquez, Tello, Benítez, and several other workers were dismissed from their jobs, but seven years later, in 1988, the union regained its autonomy and union elections again were held. Matancero triumphed anew, and traditional unionism had lost the battle. It was during this period that the fame and expansion of the alternative unionism, which by this time encompassed some forty unions and labor organizations across the country, began to grow (Sesto 1992: 43).

The other mass movements which Venezuela 83, or Causa R, sought to influence enjoyed occasional successes, but never consolidated the organizational nucleus achieved in the case of the Matancero unionism.

In the case of the UCV, while the process of university reform was under way, the group organized around the newspaper PRAG played an important role in the Schools of Engineering and Architecture. PRAG was founded in mid-1971 by José Rosales and José Lira, and continued later by a leadership coming out of the League of Students, most notably by Edgar Yajure in Engineering and Federico Villanueva in Architecture.[9] Offering a harsh critique of the *politiquería* of the political parties and of the corruption of some parties—including the PCV and the MIR—in the University, PRAG demanded a restoration of student dignity, trampled by the government's 1969 seizure of control over the university.[10]

The incorporation of the PRAG into Causa R gave the latter a significant presence in the UCV, but introduced tensions inside the organization, stemming primarily from leadership struggles and personality differences between Maneiro and Yajure. The tensions culminated in a confrontation over whether to place more or less emphasis on theoretical and conceptual debates.[11] In September 1976, PRAG was expelled from the Causa R after Maneiro rejected the trajectory of its demands regarding goals and strategies. Among other things, PRAG favored the creation of a research center and greater attention to the training of cadres, something that Maneiro considered inconsistent with his vision of Causa R as a 'movement of movements'.[12] After publishing a few more issues of the paper, PRAG was dissolved in 1979.

Maneiro attributed the failure of Causa R to consolidate an intellectual movement such as PRAG to the negative impact that the Venezuelan oil boom after 1974 had on the country's intellectuals (Maneiro 1986: 241–7). For those who departed,

---

[9] Farruco Sesto, interview of 18 Nov. 1993.   [10] Edgar Yajure, interview of 26 Nov. 1993.
[11] Ibid.   [12] Ibid.

however, the absence of intellectuals was a result of the excessively pragmatic tendencies of the organization founded by Maneiro, a characteristic which over time would encourage an *ouvriériste* bias and a lack of clarity in its political programs.[13] In the Universidad de los Andes, BAFLE, a group similar to the PRAG, was created, but it had less impact and disappeared once its founders left the university.

In 1980 Maneiro sought again to open space to facilitate interchange and debate among Venezuelan intellectuals. Known as 'La Casa del Agua Mansa' (Maneiro 1986: 241–7), this project involved thirty to forty people and included the Agua Mansa publications, edited by Farruco Sesto. Agua Mansa was to organize, develop, and present the ideas and key characteristics of Causa R.[14] Once again problems emerged similar to those which affected the previous expansion of Causa R and PRAG. Thaelman Urguelles and Angel Cacique, among others, led one group while Sesto headed another. The debate over the role of Agua Mansa became especially heated, with Sesto seeing it as a space for promoting open discussion, and Urguelles arguing that it needed to take positions on issues facing the intellectual and artistic community. These difficulties of deriving a consensus regarding conception and leadership led to the downfall of the project.[15]

The group known first as 'Catia 83', and later as Pro-Catia, had a long and difficult beginning during the early 1970s as it attempted to launch a publication entitled *Pro-Catia*, but it eventually came to oversee a wide range of activities. Maneiro believed that newspapers were the most appropriate and democratic medium for recruiting militants, in contrast to what he called the 'convince by promising' practices of the traditional parties (Maneiro 1986: 50). The initial group that composed Catia included, among others, the Mora brothers and Denis Favier and Alberto 'the scientist' Luquen.[16] Pro-Catia supported a wide range of community activities and political initiatives, among the most noteworthy of which was the collection in 1976 of 24,000 signatures to promote a reform of the Organic Law of the Municipal Council. Pro-Catia also sought to make Council members representative of their constituencies and to establish procedures for popular recall (Medina 1993: 47). Even though more than half a million people lived in Catia, no member of the Caracas City Council had ever come from that community. In addition to political demands, Pro-Catia launched a campaign to establish popular grocery stores for the neighborhood; requested trash compactors to resolve sanitation problems; argued for the construction of a public park; and organized *pelotica de goma* tournaments in response to the lack of sufficient recreational facilities (*Resumen* 1982a). The Pro-Catia group weakened and was finally dissolved during the early 1980s, primarily because of the tension and eventual division within the Causa R which occurred in 1983 after Maneiro's death. Conflict over the presidential candidacy of Andrés Velásquez would be the principal cause.[17]

It is worth emphasizing that each of these groups or movements operated

[13] Barreto, interview of 25 Oct. 1993. [14] Sesto, interview of 18 Nov. 1993.
[15] Ibid. [16] Luis E. Lander, interview of 11 Nov. 1993.
[17] Sesto, interview of 18 Nov. 1993; Barreto, interview of 25 Oct. 1993.

relatively independently from what was known first as Venezuela 83 and, beginning in 1973, as Causa R. This identity became a mechanism for establishing linkages among them. The newspaper *Causa R* began to appear in February 1973 and increasingly served to give an identity to the organization of the same name.[18] The R was written backwards purely by accident, according to its founder, Sesto, but later it became common to assert that this was because Venezuela was a backwards (upside down) country. And though many say that the symbol had no meaning,[19] nothing was done to block its association with the concept of 'revolution'. According to Yajure, the organization lacked formal structures, and had no founding charter, not to mention any statutes, but it did have a selective mechanism for incorporating new members. As reflected in the writings of Maneiro, it was a movement of movements, or 'a sort of complex of autonomous organizations . . . distinct among themselves . . . (and with) . . . a minimum of ideological and political agreement which links it together' (Maneiro 1986: 151–2). There was a political team[20] and a National Leadership (instead of the Central Committee structure used by the PCV) formed by the leaders of the three movements, but in practice they met at most two or three times throughout the entire decade of the 1970s.[21]

THE DIVISION OF 1983

At the beginning of the 1980s the two successful Causa R movements were the alternative unionism in Sidor, which controlled one of the most important unions in the country, and Pro-Catia, which had become known for its community affairs initiatives. Nevertheless, Causa R was still a small group centered exclusively around two specific locations in the diverse landscape of Venezuelan society. In 1978, to fill a requirement of the Supreme Electoral Council (CSE), the R was assigned the meaning of radical, in the sense of 'enrooted' (Sesto 1993).[22]

From the time of the first oil boom of 1974–9 Maneiro had been reflecting upon the difficulties of political expression which plagued Venezuelan popular movements. For example, in the elections of 1973, he criticized the MAS for, as he saw it, diluting the concept of socialism in such as way as to strip it of any transformative meaning, thus ensuring that the electorate did not see it as a viable option for effecting real change. He also admitted as a mistake the abstentionist position adopted by Causa R and other leftist groups, since the population went to the polls in any event, thus demonstrating their confidence in the political system's institutional mechanisms (Maneiro 1986: 103–16). Maneiro understood early on that in Venezuela it would be necessary to seek transformation through these very mechanisms.

---

[18] Sesto, interview of 18 Nov. 1993.   [19] Ibid.; Barreto, interview of 25 Oct. 1993.
[20] Yajure, interview of 26 Nov. 1993.   [21] Barreto, interview of 25 Oct. 1993.
[22] 'Radical' in this sense of enrooted or deep is distinct from the more common use of the word in English, which alludes to 'the most distant from tradition' or 'the extreme'. Causa R never sought to be confused with extremists.

But the key theme that arose during the late 1970s and in the elections of 1983 was that Venezuelan politics was frozen. AD had lost its capacity to convey its message to the general population, and COPEI could not generate enthusiasm following the woeful government of Luis Herrera. This, according to Maneiro, was producing a phenomenon of 'electoral homelessness' for some 2 million Venezuelan voters. The time was ripe to unblock this situation by appealing to the electorate in the center of the political spectrum. In order to do this, it was necessary to produce a centrist option rather than a leftist one, since the organizations of the left lacked the capacity to mobilize the population and had reached a limit beyond which they seemed incapable of further growth (Maneiro 1986: 252–7).

Causa R began at this juncture to make overtures to such centrist individuals as Jóvito Villalba, to whom it initially offered its presidential candidacy.[23] Ultimately, the candidate nominated in July 1982 was a journalist, Jorge Olavarría, the editor of the journal *Resumen* (*Resumen* 1982*b*). Of wealthy background and essentially conservative leanings, Olavarría had played an important role in denouncing all kinds of corruption, particularly that which plagued unionism in Guayana. Olavarría defended the positions of the new unionism and his articles contributed to publicizing the movement in Matancero and the role of its leader, Andrés Velásquez. Although this alliance appeared surprising, Olavarría gave Causa R access to one of the most widely read journals of the time.

For as long as Alfredo Maneiro remained alive the popular movements of Causa R backed this nomination, apparently without conflict.[24] His unquestioned leadership and the autonomy and ideological ambiguity of the movements ensured his ability to manage any difficulties that these measures could provoke. But all this changed in November 1982, when Maneiro died suddenly at the age of 45. His death was a severe blow to the organization, for it came at a time when it seemed to have gained a degree of visibility, thanks to the candidacy of Olavarría and the resulting publicity given its activities through the journal *Resumen*. Many feared that Causa R, as a political project, would disappear as a result of Maneiro's death. There was dismay in Pro-Catia, for it was believed that many years of work were now to be lost.[25]

Olavarría thought that he could fill the void left behind by Maneiro. While it was true that he enjoyed good relations with the Pro-Catia movement, where the movie director Thaelman Urguelles had some political weight, he had conflicts with the founding leaders of the organization, especially with Pablo Medina and Lucas Matheus. Moreover, Olavarría had a domineering personality and had little in common with the workers of the Sidor.[26] Shortly before the deadline for submitting candidacies, Olavarría placed a series of conditions on the Causa R, including a demand that he be given the post of General Secretary. Urguelles was willing to support him, but others within the Directorate rejected the proposal and managed to prevail.[27] Olavarría resigned and launched his campaign through an organization known as Opina. For the Causa R, problems had only just begun.

[23] Sesto, interview of 18 Nov. 1993.   [24] Ibid.   [25] Ibid.
[26] Barreto, interview of 25 Oct. 1993.   [27] Sesto, interview of 18 Nov. 1993.

Following the strategy of seeking out the center, Urguelles and his group advocated uniting behind the candidacy of ex-president Rafael Caldera. In a plenary session of Causa R held at the Central University the candidacy was debated, and the group even released a press communiqué. For the Matancero movement, Caldera was unacceptable, since it was during his government that 514 workers had been fired from Sidor. Instead, they supported the candidacy of the president of their union, Andrés Velásquez.[28] Maneiro was no longer available to mediate the dispute.

Once Caldera's candidacy had been rejected, Urguelles together with Pro-Catia and the majority of the intellectuals who remained in the group abandoned Causa R. Thus was lost the neighborhood branch of the movement and the remnants of its intellectual constituency. This reduced the organization to those who had originally left the PCV in 1970 plus the leadership of the Matancero movement. The *ouvriériste* profile that characterized the group from this point onward was inevitable.

After the 1983 elections, Causa R appeared to be mortally wounded (Medina 1988: 61). Andrés Velásquez received some 6,000 votes for the presidency, and in what many observers believed to be the result of fraud, the party lost the governorship of Bolívar. Six months later, however, in the 1984 municipal elections, Causa R achieved second place in Bolívar. The organization then decided to concentrate on that state, basing its strategy on, and mobilizing efforts around, the workers of the iron regions in order to defeat the two-party hegemony of AD and COPEI (Medina 1988).

From this point onwards Causa R evolved slowly, attempting to strengthen itself as a local organization in the most populous townships of the state, and to extend the influence of the Matancero movement among the unions. Without Maneiro, Causa R did not try again to develop new popular movements, basing its efforts instead on Matancero unionism. At the same time, the organizational dynamic and limited breadth of the party meant that recruitment of new members was slow. This continues to be the case, for recruitment is highly selective and depends, to a large extent, on individual commitment since each prospective member is expected to be a political activist.[29] During this period, the only significant group to join the party was a small group that had split of from the Party of the Venezuelan Revolution (PRV) in 1987, led by Alí Rodríguez. Aristóbulo Istúriz, today one of the most important leaders of the Causa R, joined basically on his own in 1986, though he had founded the teachers' union SUMA and part of this union joined the Causa R.[30]

3. Causa R after 1989

Causa R played a relatively insignificant role in the elections of 1983 and 1988. While the presidential candidates of AD and COPEI split a total of 87 and 93 per cent of

---

[28] Ibid.   [29] Ibid.   [30] Ibid.

Table 5.1. Presidential elections by party, 1983–1993 (in total votes and in percentages)

Party	1983		1988		1993	
	Votes	%	Votes	%	Votes	%
Causa R	5,917	0.09	26,870	0.4	1,232,853	21.97
AD	3,680,549	55.32	3,859,180	52.8	1,304,849	23.23
COPEI	2,166,467	32.56	2,932,277	40.1	1,241,645	22.11
MAS	223,194	3.25	198,361[a]	2.7	595,042	10.59
Convergencia[b]	—	—	—	—	958,529	17.07

[a] For these elections MAS made an alliance with the Movimiento Izquierda Revolucionario (MIR), a party that later merged with MAS.

[b] Convergencia is a new party that participated for the first time in the elections of 1993, backing the candidacy of Rafael Caldera, now president.

Sources: Consejo Supremo Electoral, Dirección de Estadísticas, *Elecciones 4 de diciembre de 1983*, Caracas: Ediciones del CSE, Sept. 1984; *Elecciones 1988*, 2 Ts, Ediciones del CSE, Sept. 1990; 'Elecciones 1993. Votos Grandes', Caracas (mimeo), 1994.

the vote, respectively, in the two elections, the MAS, left alliances, and electoral movements such as those of Olavarría in 1983 or Vladimir Gessen in 1988 easily surpassed the vote of Velásquez and his party (see Tables 5.1, 5.2, and 5.4). But in Bolívar the vote for Causa R was significant. In 1983 it obtained 7.96 per cent of the vote, an increase of 178 per cent over the previous elections. In addition, six months later, in 1984, it reached 17.11 per cent in the elections for municipal councils, earning it four council posts in the municipality of Caroní and one in Heres (Yépez Salas 1993: 59). In December 1988 Causa R gained a deputy from Bolívar in the National Congress and unexpectedly added two more from the Federal District and the state of Miranda. Causa R was growing in Guayana and had made inroads in Caracas as well (see Table 5.3).[31]

Within this context two processes developed that would bring Causa R to the forefront of the political arena: the severe social and political crisis affecting Venezuela and, in close relation with it, the approval of the decentralization laws. We have already discussed the latter, but let us now turn briefly to the manifestations of the former.

DEMOCRACY IN THE BALANCE

On 27 February 1989 and for several days afterwards urban dwellers across the country, impoverished by years of economic crisis and disappointed by Pérez's

---

[31] The city of Caracas, in addition to the Federal District, extends to include several municipalities of the state of Miranda where Causa R obtained the vote that awarded it a deputy in that federal entity.

Table 5.2. Parliamentary elections by party, 1983–1993 (in total votes and in percentages)

Party	1983		1988		1993[a]	
	Votes	%	Votes	%	Votes	%
Causa R	35,304	0.54	118,700	1.7	974,190	20.68
AD	3,284,166	49.9	3,115,787	43.3	1,099,728	23.34
COPEI	1,887,226	28.68	2,238,163	31.1	1,065,512	22.62
MAS	377,795	5.74	731,179[b]	10.2	509,068	10.81
Convergencia[c]	—	—	—	—	651,918	13.84

[a] In this year, for the first time in Venezuela, the Congressional election was conducted according to a mixed system of voting for both individual candidates and for party slates. The data in this table are those of votes for deputies on the party slates.
[b] For these elections MAS made an alliance with the Movimiento Izquierda Revolucionario (MIR), a party that later merged with MAS.
[c] Convergencia is a new party that participated for the first time in the elections of 1993, backing the candidacy of Rafael Caldera, now president.

Sources: Consejo Supremo Electoral, Dirección de Estadísticas, *Elecciones 4 de diciembre de 1983*, Caracas: Ediciones del CSE, Sept. 1984; *Elecciones 1988*, 2 Ts, Ediciones del CSE, Sept. 1990; 'Elecciones 1993. Votos Grandes', Caracas (mimeo), 1994.

Table 5.3. Parliamentary groups by party, for the periods 1984–1989, 1989–1994, and 1994–1999

Party	1984–9		1989–94		1994–9	
	Deputies	Senators	Deputies	Senators	Deputies	Senators
Causa Radical	0	0	3	0	40	9
AD	113	28	97	22	55	16
COPEI	60	14	67	20	53	14
MAS	10	2	18[a]	3[a]	24	5
Convergencia[b]	—	—	—	—	26	6

[a] For these elections MAS made an alliance with the Movimiento Izquierda Revolucionario (MIR), a party that later merged with MAS.
[b] Convergencia is a new party that participated for the first time in the elections of 1993, backing the candidacy of Rafael Caldera, now president.

Sources: Consejo Supremo Electoral, Dirección de Estadísticas, *Elecciones 4 de diciembre de 1983*, Caracas: Ediciones del CSE, Sept. 1984; *Elecciones 1988*, 2 Ts, Ediciones del CSE, Sept. 1990; 'Elecciones 1993. Votos Grandes', Caracas (mimeo), 1994.

Table 5.4. Provincial election results for Andrés Velásquez, presidential candidate of Causa R, 1983–1993 (in percentages)

Province	1983	1988	1993
Amazonas	0.05	0	15.0
Anzoátegui	0.07	0.3	34.0
Apure	0.05	0.1	3.9
Aragua	0.09	0.3	31.9
Barinas	0.04	0.1	8.2
Bolívar	0.5	1.2	49.6
Carabobo	0.09	0.5	27.6
Cojedes	0.09	0.1	12.4
Delta Amacuro	0.11	0.1	11.6
Falcón	0.05	0.2	9.4
Guárico	0.05	0.1	15.8
Lara	0.07	0.2	8.5
Mérida	0.06	0.3	10.8
Miranda	0.08	0.7	30.7
Monagas	0.06	0.1	21.2
Nueva Esparta	0.07	0.2	15.2
Portuguesa	0.05	0.1	7.3
Sucre	0.07	0.2	16.9
Táchira	0.03	0.1	13.4
Trujillo	0.04	0.1	6.4
Yaracuy	0.06	0.2	6.9
Zulia	0.03	0.1	13.7
Federal District	0.11	0.7	35.0

Sources: Consejo Supremo Electoral, Dirección de Estadísticas, *Elecciones 4 de diciembre de 1983*, Caracas: Ediciones del CSE, Sept. 1984; *Elecciones 1988*, 2 Ts, Ediciones del CSE, Sept. 1990; 'Elecciones 1993. Votos Grandes', Caracas (mimeo), 1994.

inaugural address, in which he indicated the government's intention to request assistance from the International Monetary Fund, took to the streets in a looting rampage. The protests were followed by a curfew, the suspension of individual freedoms, and severe police and military repression that caused some 500 deaths. The *sacudón*, or *caracazo*, revealed the rupture in state–society relations that had occurred during the previous years. Not only did the parties and unions fail to recognize the depths of popular dissatisfaction, but they had no capacity to channel or to control the ensuing explosion (Carvallo and López-Maya 1989: 48–50).

This open manifestation of protest and discontent did not generate a reaction from the traditional parties, and did not lead the government to change its policies. It did, however, lead to implementation of decentralization measures that had remained on hold since the middle of the Lusinchi government. The persistence of the blockage of mediations, we argue, is related directly with the extreme political situation of 1992 as well as the 'political phenomenon' which Causa R has become.

During the dawn of 4 February 1992, a coup attempt was launched by middle-and lower-level officers in the army. The coup's goals were to overthrow the Pérez government, end corruption, and replace the market-oriented policies that were being implemented by alternative measures that were never clearly defined. The coup attempt received significant popular support, and for some sectors the young leaders of the uprising gained heroic status. Pérez and AD suffered an additional blow when, on the day after the military *putsch*, they called an urgent session of Congress to adopt emergency measures. Although they attempted to secure a un-animous declaration rejecting the military and giving unconditional support for the government, they were forced to modify the language of the resolution due to harsh criticism from ex-president Caldera. Caldera's position was seconded by the Causa R deputy Aristóbulo Istúriz, who held the government responsible for hav-ing brought the country to this situation. After 4 February the Pérez administra-tion went into a deep crisis from which it would never recover. Meanwhile, both Caldera and Istúriz saw their political fortunes rise.

A second coup attempt took place months later, on 27 November. This upris-ing was not as well coordinated, but clearly involved high-level military officials. Though it was said that the image of the government and of democracy emerged strengthened from this failed attempt, both the government and AD remained unable to gain the confidence of the population. Finally, in May 1993 Carlos Andrés Pérez was suspended from his post by the National Congress following a Supreme Court ruling that there were grounds to try him for embezzlement and secret diversion of funds (López-Maya 1993).

CAUSA R IN THE 1989 AND 1993 GUBERNATORIAL AND MAYORAL ELECTIONS

The first regional and municipal elections were held in December 1989, ten months after the dramatic events of the Caracazo. These elections reflected the degree of popular rejection of the AD government led by Carlos Andrés Pérez. This electoral rejection explains, in part, why the AD, which had won nineteen of Venezuela's twenty states in the national elections a year earlier, lost control of nine crucial governorships, including those of Miranda, Carabobo, and Aragua (which together with the Federal District are the principal sites of manufacturing industry), Zulia (where most of the oil industry is located), and Bolívar (headquarters of the Cor-poración Venezolana de Guayana and of the basic aluminum and iron industries).

But alongside the vote of censure cast by regional voters the first gubernatorial elections also suggested the potential significance of regional leadership, which until that time had been irrelevant in the choice of public officials. If in the past candidates were evaluated on the basis of their skill in providing favors and weaving together the coalitions needed in order to secure support from the party kingpins (*cogollos*), those barons now needed to consider the charisma and regional appeal of their candidates if they wished to compete electorally.[32] This development began to create tensions at the heart of the hegemonic parties and produced numerous confrontations between the national leadership and local party elites. In Aragua and Bolívar, the regional strength of the MAS and Causa R candidates, Carlos Tablante and Andrés Velásquez, played a major role. To a lesser degree, this also contributed to the victory of the COPEI candidate, Oswaldo Alvarez Paz, in the state of Zulia (López-Maya 1993: 259).

It is worth noting that the state of Bolívar, where Causa R had concentrated its efforts since the beginning of the decade, had always been an AD stronghold. Nonetheless, serious charges of corruption affected party leaders as well as the unions linked to them. In addition, conflicts among the regional leaders had brought AD to a point of serious crisis, and many rank-and-file members seem to have crossed over and voted for Causa R (Yépez Salas 1993: 60). This internal strife may have been sufficient to account for the narrow winning margin for Velásquez, who received 40.3 per cent of the vote compared to 36.69 per cent for the second place AD candidate. Abstention was the fourth highest in the country, reaching 55.82 per cent of the potential electorate (CSE 1990: 19–22 and 259).

In addition to the gubernatorial election of Velásquez, Causa R gained two mayoralties. Clemente Scotto won in Caroní, in the state of Bolívar, with 27,200 votes, or 33.86 per cent of the total, and Luis Lorenzo Aguilar won in Miranda, in the state of Carabobo with 975 votes, or 37.75 per cent. The latter was a small town, in which the number of votes received was less than anticipated by the Causa R leadership (Medina 1993: 48).

The triumph of Causa R in Bolívar was a surprise to the rest of country, but according to Velásquez, the AD leadership in the region learned days beforehand that they would be defeated, and undertook measures to perpetrate electoral fraud. Causa R, mindful of its past experience in Sidor, began early in the afternoon to denounce fraud, while the population of Ciudad Guayana took to the streets in support of fair elections. Velásquez recalls that after going to Radio Caroní to denounce the fraud, he was met by a throng of supporters and a caravan of vehicles, as word of what was occurring swept factories across the region and workers abandoned their posts. The next day, with the winner still unannounced, Sidor was paralyzed as a demonstration in front of the Electoral Center drew thousands of people. Velásquez flew to the Supreme Electoral Council (CSE) in Caracas to publicize what had occurred and to seek an official declaration. Upon his return, he reports, there were no fewer than 10,000 people waiting at the airport. These demonstrations were the deciding factor, for soon afterwards AD called a press conference to recognize the Causa R victory in the state. Velásquez says that people were prepared to defend the victory with their lives, and Causa R was with them (Sesto 1992: 137–9).

---

[32] In Venezuela *cogollo* refers to a small group of party and union leaders who control virtually all political decisions. The most notorious *cogollo* is that of the AD, along with that of the CTV labor organization, but the system is generalizable to the COPEI and, to a lesser degree, other parties as well.

The situation was similar in the mayoral race in Caroní. There, too, it was suspected that AD and COPEI were planning to commit fraud, and there as well people mobilized to defend the Causa R victory. Tensions were such that the votes could not be counted on site, and ballots had to be transported to the Caracas offices of the CSE to be counted. The Electoral Council in Caroní, however, awarded the victory to AD, and even swore in its candidate as mayor, while in Caracas the Causa R candidate, Clemente Scotto, was declared the winner (Sesto 1992: 142–3).

Three years later, the political crisis had grown more acute as a result of the two coup attempts. In December 1992, just eight days after the last uprising, Andrés Velásquez was re-elected governor with 63.36 per cent of all valid ballots, a total of 135,673 votes. Causa R also gained mayoralties in the three most populous cities in the state. Scotto was re-elected with 68.36 of the valid ballots. In the capital city of Ciudad Bolívar (municipality of Heres), Causa R received 47.88 per cent of the valid votes, compared to 39.84 per cent for the alliance of AD and FPI. In Piar, Amerigo Grazia of the Causa R won 45.77 per cent against the 41.55 per cent awarded to AD. Of the ten mayoralties in Bolívar, only these three have more than 60,000 eligible voters. The other seven have fewer than 25,000. AD won three of these on its own, and COPEI won the four others in alliance with other parties. In the municipalities won by Causa R abstention remained high, surpassing the average across the state: 52.71 per cent in Caroní, 49.73 per cent in Heres, and 53.85 per cent in Piar (CSE 1993).

The triumph of Causa R in Bolívar was expected, as the administrations of both the governor and mayor Scotto had received broad popular support. Nonetheless, the expansion of Causa R surpassed even its own expectations. It could be said that the organization which had for so long guarded jealously its status as different from other Venezuelan political parties now began to reap the fruits of its strategy. Determined to punish the traditional parties and political system, the urban population of Caracas, as well as that of the surrounding state of Miranda, found in abstention and the vote for Causa R two means for leaving a clear message. On 6 December, against all predictions, Causa R pulled ahead in the vote count from the municipality of Libertador. The popular neighborhoods in Caracas had tended toward Causa R.[33] Once again, rumors that fraud was about to occur mobilized hundreds of people who gathered in front of the CSE awaiting official bulletins.

On the morning of the 7th, the CSE still had not given definitive numbers, but it was made known that the AD and Causa R were running very close. Thousands of people filled Plaza Caracas, in front of the Council, to defend Istúriz's victory. At around 3.00 p.m. the President of the CSE called the two candidates in an effort to secure an agreement to respect the results, whatever they might be.[34] Claudio Fermín of AD accepted happily, but Istúriz rejected the proposal, arguing that he

---

[33] *El Nacional*, 'Aristóbulo Istúriz, Alcalde de Caracas', 7 Dec. 1992, p. A-1 (Caracas).

[34] *El Nacional*, 'Manifestación popular proclamó ante el Consejo Supremo Electoral triunfo de La Causa R', 8 Dec. 1992, p. D-1 (Caracas).

had not broken the rules and that 'the only thing that needs to be respected is the vote of the people'.

Aristóbulo Istúriz won with 34.45 per cent of the valid votes. Null ballots accounted for 3.59 per cent of the total. Even though abstention reached 62.57 per cent, the popular sectors took to the streets to celebrate the victory.

Outside the state of Bolívar and the Federal District Causa R would win only two more mayoralties, both of them quite small. These victories came in Miranda, in the state of Carabobo, where Causa R repeated its winning performance of 1989 by 30.05 per cent of the valid vote, and in Arismendi, in the state of Nueva Esparta, where its 1,823 votes accounted for 27.74 of the valid ballots. Elsewhere, Causa R received a low percentage of the vote, averaging in the single digits except in some municipalities in the state of Miranda, Cabimas in the state of Zulia, and Santos Michelena, in the state of Aragua. Yet even in these cases it did not surpass 16 per cent of the valid votes (CSE 1993).

The bipartisan arrangement that had prevailed in Venezuela since the end of the 1960s broke down in the 1993 national elections. An alliance between the MAS and dissidents from the COPEI joined with a number of small parties in forming an organization known as the 'Convergencia', which won a victory for its presidential candidate, Dr Rafael Caldera, with 30.45 per cent of the valid votes. Second place was closely contested between three candidates, with the official results placing Causa R in fourth place with 21.94 per cent of the vote. AD came in second with 23.59 per cent, and COPEI was third with 22.74 per cent. In the Congressional race Causa R came in third, displacing the MAS, and will thus enjoy a significant parliamentary presence from 1994 to 1998, with nine Senators and forty deputies, far more than the MAS had ever received in the past (See Tables 5.3 and 5.4).[35]

CHANGES IN DISCOURSE?

It is reasonable to ask whether the process of steady expansion experienced by Causa R over the last four years has been accompanied by a transformation of its objectives and discourse. An initial point stands out as especially noteworthy. During his lifetime the founding leader of the organization, Maneiro, was also its principal political thinker. This was the case not only with respect to evaluations of the Venezuelan political situation for purposes of strategy and tactics, but also in terms of conceiving the kind of organization and ideology that should characterize Causa R. Maneiro's death in 1983 thus represented a very significant loss, and it can be argued that the ensuing void has only partially been filled.

While Maneiro remained at the head of the Causa R he kept debate alive. The various newspapers founded by the group in order to embed Causa R in popular

[35] *El Nacional*, 'Cinco partidos dominan el Parlamento', 9 Jan. 1994, p. D-4; *El Universal*, 'Cifras definitivas sobre voto presidencial', 10 Feb. 1993, p. 1-1.

movements reflected Maneiro's skill at seeding and testing ideas concerning popular movements, the vanguard, and politics in general. Moreover, during the 1970s and the early 1980s PRAG and Agua Mansa also contributed to the circulation of ideas about Venezuelan reality, as well as about the organizational imperatives of a group that claimed to be pursuing 'social revolution' (Causa R 1973).

It is worth noting that the conceptual framework guiding the reflections of Venezuela 83 and the Causa R was fundamentally Marxist, though it was far from orthodox. As noted earlier, Maneiro gave special emphasis to the concepts of popular movement and the vanguard and the relationship between them. One of his constant preoccupations was how it would be possible to guarantee the efficacy and 'revolutionary quality' of the vanguard. His rejection of the PCV led him to conceive of an organization separated from the Leninist framework within which most all of the other Venezuelan parties operated. It was necessary, in his view, to create a party from below, organically linked to popular movements. Causa R would be a party in permanent construction, with an ideology forever in motion, creating and recreating itself alongside popular struggles.

After the 1973 elections and the petroleum boom that began in 1974, Maneiro's writings reveal a number of other key concepts and phrases in his discourse. For example, debate about democracy is needed, he contended, because the prevailing interpretation of the term was that of the AD, which merely entails the renewal every five years of council members, deputies, senators, and the President, and thus constitutes a minimal, purely electoral definition of democracy (Maneiro 1986: 161–9). The difference between types of democracy is developed further with regard to local politics and in relation to human rights, with Maneiro proposing 'radical' democracy as the banner of the left. The oil boom, in turn, forced modifications in the diagnosis of the Venezuelan situation and the conditions under which the popular movement would have to develop. The populist measures implemented at the time by the first government of Carlos Andrés Pérez undermined the negotiating capacity of revolutionary unions, as well as the left as a whole (Maneiro 1986: 123–9).

During these years, despite the clear effort to differentiate itself from the political organizations of the left, Maneiro did not deny his identification with Marxism or the left. In a 1981 interview with Agustín Blanco, Maneiro rejected 'leftism' but said that he was more on the left than many of those who claimed he was not. Asked whether Causa R was Marxist, Maneiro questioned whether it was necessary to have a label at all, and identified the ideology of Causa R as democratic in the sense meant by Marx when he wrote that 'when the revolutionary movement conquers power it conquers democracy'. Later he pointed out that to characterize him or Causa R as Marxist was to present them in a way meant to encourage people to associate them with parties such as the MAS or the Socialist League, neither of which Causa R wanted to be associated with. Maneiro preferred to let the people decide on the basis of the party's actions. He would agree to call Causa R Marxist only if it were accepted as the only Marxist organization in Venezuela (Maneiro 1986: 185–239).

As noted above, Causa R was built on broadly Marxist theoretical bases. Its political actions, in contrast, were shaped by constant assessments, principally by Maneiro himself, of the sociopolitical realities of Venezuela. By the end of the 1980s, the idea of the 'political center' was added, as pointed out earlier in reference to the candidacy of Jorge Olavarría.

What took place after Maneiro's death was essentially the use of these assessments, concepts, and ideas to offer new interpretations in light of new facts: the emergence of Matancero as the principal popular movement of the Causa R and the transformation of the organization into a viable option for government at the local, regional, and national levels.

In 1990, Andrés Velásquez, now governor of Bolívar, said that a fundamental idea of Causa R was that 'the workers can govern' (Sesto 1992: 122). This reference to the category of 'workers', rather than 'the working class', broadened the social sector represented by Causa R, and would remain from this point on. Pablo Medina, Secretary General and one of the founders of Causa R, has stated the point more directly. For him, Causa R is a party of workers. This is reflected in its leadership, which according to him is composed mainly of workers. For Medina, it is clear that in Venezuela the worker leadership is more advanced than that of students, and if it does not surpass intellectuals in knowledge, it does so in political skill (Medina 1988: 31 and 35).

The centrality of workers can be seen as a narrowing of Maneiro's conceptualization of Causa R. Indeed, his better-known writings include no reference to the 'ultimate subject' of this movement of movements. However, his Marxist framework and his conception of a project constructed on the basis of the action of the popular movement is not logically at odds with this manner of conceiving the organization. Indeed, we might say that this is a historical by-product of the hegemony that the Matancero movement gained within Causa R once the other movements disappeared. It is worth noting that there is also no longer any reference to the problem of the vanguard, although membership in the party continues to be conditional on one's being a political activist.

After Velásquez's gubernatorial victory in Bolívar, the demand to address the needs of governing has filled in additional elements that define, however vaguely, the concrete goals of Causa R for Venezuelan society. These elements remain without major theoretical backing or conceptual foundation, reflecting the organization's tendency toward a pragmatic and short-term vision of politics.

Velásquez's program upon taking office in 1990 can be seen as an embryonic version, on a regional level, of the sociopolitical project of Causa R for Venezuela as a whole. It includes four broad orienting principles: first, practicing democracy, not only as a means of electing officials but also of governing. Second, to end corruption. The third point involves efficiency and clarity in the provision of services, especially health, education, and personal security. The fourth aspect entails an approach to the development of the Guayana region that diverges from the vision advanced by the Venezuelan state. Instead of the strategy of mega projects in support of industry based primarily on exports of raw materials (iron, aluminum, bauxite), Causa R favored development downstream, with medium-sized and manufacturing industries transforming raw materials locally (Sesto 1992: 150–3).

In 1991, with his sights not only on re-election as governor but also on the 1993 presidential campaign, Velásquez presented what he saw as an alternative project for Venezuelan society. The outlines of the project resemble those sketched above with respect to Guayana, though opposition to 'extreme privatization' has been added to the fourth point. In addition, there is a nationalist component that was not evident in the past: 'It is (will be) a government . . . with a love for the fatherland, which in my opinion does not now exist' (Sesto 1992: 233–7).

It is important to point out that the elements of Causa R's discourse relating to the desirable model of economic development are simple, lack detail, and are taken from the opposition discourse promoted during these years by a group of COPEI dissidents, led by Dr Caldera, some independents, and the MAS. The first two of these formed a party, known as 'Convergencia', to ally with the MAS in support of Caldera's successful candidacy in the 1993 presidential elections. In comparison to the Causa R, the group assembled around the Caldera campaign has provided a more elaborated vision of a development strategy opposed to the neoliberal project of AD and COPEI.[36] Nor are the other elements of Causa R's discourse particularly original, though its emphasis on the 'worker' origin of the Causa R government, and its careful management of public resources, afford it more support than other parties among certain social sectors.

During the 1993 election campaign Causa R issued a basic document outlining its project for Venezuela. The introduction underscored the urgent need to overcome the current crisis and to bring about a 'just, balanced, tolerant, efficient, productive, and civilized' society (La Causa R 1993: 2). The project envisions two major ways of achieving this: a profound cultural transformation and a productive revolution. The former envisions a 'society formed by true citizens, who can enjoy the liberty that is their due and receive all the benefits that are offered by societal living' (La Causa R 1993: 3). It commits itself to the democratization of all aspects of social life, a profound educational reform, establishment of a State of Law through reform of the national legal system, urban reform, an anti-corruption program, and a restoration of notions of patriotism and sovereignty (La Causa R 1993).

The 'productive revolution' aims to leave behind the rentier economy and to effect a comprehensive reform of the petroleum sector, recognizing that this industry will remain the centerpiece of the Venezuelan economy but that it must be integrated into the productive economy. The reform is based on three elements, including continued membership in OPEC as long as reciprocity is maintained; development of strategic alliances needed to ensure financial support; and access to markets and technology. This means that relationships are possible with domestic as well

[36] See e.g. *Economía Hoy*, 'Respuestas al reto: Rafael Caldera', 5 Nov. 1993, pp. 17–24 (Caracas).

as international capital, and that hydrocarbons should be used primarily for manufactured products rather than energy (La Causa R 1993: 6). This petroleum policy is to be complemented by the development of the country's food production capacity and by placing greater emphasis on small and medium-sized industries, which will in turn expand the internal market. The expansion of the internal market is considered to be a necessary condition for a rational insertion of Venezuela into the external market. Other economic issues include the need to foster science and technology as engines for a productive revolution; lower the fiscal deficit through decentralization; re-employ and provide training to displaced workers; renegotiate the debt; privatize non-strategic rather than strategic industries; and implement a progressive tax reform, which would include a tax on Venezuelan capital deposited abroad.

Conclusions

Causa R has benefited more than any other Venezuelan political force from the current profound crisis of the political system and the loss of prestige of its hegemonic actors. This is the result of a combination of factors.

The first is its clear differentiation from other political organizations, both in terms of its conception of the party and in the priorities it has set out since its origin. Causa R was conceived as a political organization halfway between a movement and a party, which rejected formalism (constituent charter, statutes), organizational hierarchies, and the formation of party cadres, all of which were typical of other Venezuelan parties. A 'party in permanent formation', it functions with minimal ideological agreement and seeks its social base and orientations in the popular movements. The peculiar character of this organization can be considered the fruit of the search by its founding leader, Alfredo Maneiro, for conceptions and strategy that would go beyond the tensions inherent in the Marxist debates and praxis of the 1960s.

In addition to its distinctive conception of the party itself, Causa R also developed a political strategy of clearly distancing itself from the rest of the political groups which emerged from the armed struggle. Maneiro exhibited an almost obsessive determination not to be confused with the remainder of the 'left', which he invariably characterized as timid, mediocre, and exhibiting 'leftism'. He and subsequent leaders would decline, except on rare occasions, to ally with other parties in elections or in parliamentary affairs. In addition, its idea of ideology as a process in permanent construction brought Causa R to reject ideological strait-jackets, such as communism or socialism, granting the organization a flexibility or ambiguity that permitted it to engage even conservative figures when it seemed politically convenient.

These characteristics of Causa R ensured it a unique position once two political factors external to the organization converged. First, during the 1980s, the urban poor increasingly came to reject the traditional parties and the system they had constructed. In this context, Causa R tended to obtain high dividends, since it was easily differentiated from the hegemonic parties and the pacts that tied them together. Second, the process of political and administrative decentralization, which began to take form after 1989, created a space through which this small organization, with a clear strategy at the local and regional levels, could gain visibility. Causa R had already been working for more than ten years in the Guayana region, specifically in the union and poor-neighborhood movements, when reforms were enacted that would enable it to energize regional and municipal levels of state government. In the first gubernatorial election, aided by an internal crisis of AD in the region, it gained the first magistracy of Bolívar. From this initial victory, and from the mayoralty of Caroní it established a basis for further growth.

The fact that Causa R had a chance to win the 1993 national elections is explained by the continued legitimation crisis of the political system and the hegemonic actors, and by the gradual change in the image of Causa R, which had gone from being a small radical group on the left of the political spectrum to an organization of proven honesty and responsibility in its management of regional and municipal governments. This is especially true in the region of Guayana, since the mayoral administration in Caracas is still too recent to be evaluated.

The consolidation of Causa R will depend on the manner in which its members resolve the problems brought about by its growth. Traits that have until now been a virtue, such as having a barely formalized structure in which votes are not taken and decisions are adopted by a small political leadership tied by bonds of personal friendship, could become a defect hindering the organization's expansion. Similarly, the lack of internal mechanisms for incorporating new activists in decision-making processes carries with it a risk of a certain arbitrariness and even authoritarianism, given that differences will inevitably come up now that the party enjoys significant power in the Congress.

Another problem facing Causa R is the lack of preparedness of its militants for efficiently handling municipal and regional administration. This will become increasingly important should the rapid expansion of Causa R continue. Although it is true that no contemporary political party has sufficient personnel for these new tasks, the rejection of the academic and intellectual world by prominent members of Causa R, and their unwillingness to involve these sectors in forums in which decisions are made, could lead to problems. Honesty alone is not sufficient to govern. There will also be a need for great skill to extend scarce economic resources. This problem is evident at the national level as well, given the significant fraction of the congressional seats that the electorate has awarded to Causa R.

Until now Causa R has developed with minimal contact or negotiation with other actors in the political system. In the past this conferred enormous political benefits, but if maintained as a strategy during the period that is now opening it could prove counter-productive. In light of the importance it has achieved in the Congress,

Causa R will become one of the factions with greatest negotiating potential. This gives it an unavoidable responsibility to formulate proposals or to join other groups in formulating or approving legislation that favors popular sectors in the difficult road toward a solution to the severe economic and political crisis facing Venezuelan society. To find its own style of negotiation and compromise with other political groups is one of the most serious challenges facing Causa R.

To date, the 'popular' character of Causa R would seem beyond question. Its ideological positions, though elementary or simplistic, are based on the search for power for the representatives of the working classes as a means of advancing toward a more just and integrated society. Causa R is based on popular movements, and the political origins and activities of its principal leaders are consistent with the objective of achieving power for the people. Nevertheless, the dismissal of intellectuals, noted above, carries the risk of undermining a popular project to the degree that an excessive pragmatism may obstruct the development of analyses and strategies which could protect the interests of these sectors. Already, in the last election campaign, it was clear that although Causa R could easily mobilize these sectors, it remained a step behind groups such as Convergencia in the formulation of strategic approaches to elaborating an alternative project. As the party further expands this could become one of its greatest limitations.

The success of Causa R, like that of the PT in Brazil or the PRD at some moments in Mexico, reveals the reappearance of popular sectors demanding that they be heard in the political arena. In Venezuela this was made possible by state decentralization and the strategic focus of Causa R on working at the local level. Causa R is not a new political organization; it was already present in unions and poor neighborhoods, where it acted without violating its principles or succumbing to corruption. Finding themselves without channels of mediation with the state, poor and middle sectors reached out to the organization, which in both theory and practice had most clearly remained untainted by complicity with the existing political system. Causa R reaped the fruits of its consistency, but today, when popular sectors have given it power, a series of new challenges await it.

New regional and municipal elections took place in Venezuela on 3 December 1995. Although at the time of writing (18 December 1995) the results remain unclear due to the innumerable accusations of fraud and irregularities, it is nevertheless certain that Causa R has suffered important reverses. It lost the mayoralty of the municipality of Libertador (the seat of Caracas) and the governorship of Bolívar. However, it won for the first time the governorship of Zulia, whence independent Francisco Arias Cárdenas had launched his candidacy. He, together with Hugo Chávez, headed the unsuccessful coup of 4 February 1992. It also increased its presence in other eastern and central states, emphatically in Anzoátegui, Guárico, and Monagas.

A preliminary evaluation of the results would appear to indicate that Causa R, although it lost to AD in Caracas, was strengthened as an alternative political force in the capital. In 1992 the vote for Causa R was circumstantial in the sense that it was not a vote for Causa R as a party, but rather a protest vote against the traditional parties. This time, however, anti-party protest was repeated, though not through Causa R, but rather through an extremely high abstention rate (according to official figures, over 70 per cent). The men and women of the poor neighborhoods in Caracas simply did not vote. In any case, among the very few voters in these sectors, Istúriz, the mayor, came in second. Among many middle-class sectors, living in residential developments, the majority voted for the Causa R candidate, shortening the distance between the winning Ledezma of AD and Aristóbulo Istúriz. Curiously enough, the municipal campaign had paid the least attention to the middle-class sectors.

The results in Bolívar, independent of the fact that in the next months it may be verified that there was fraud in favor of AD, reveal a weakening of the party in its firmest base. Clumsiness on the part of the regional leadership, held by Andrés Velásquez, appears to have been the cause of the defeat. Velásquez and his followers obstructed the gubernatorial candidacy of Clemente Scotto, mayor of Caroní. The party, in an exhibition of political style from the past, violating the sensibilities of the vast majority of its bases and of the people of the state in general, ran a candidate with no appropriate background to be regional leader, believing that he would win by the party's prestige alone. The electorate responded by giving the majority vote for mayor of Caroní to Pastora Medina, Scotto's wife. However, they abstained from doing the same for the Causa R gubernatorial candidate. With this they sent an instructive message to Causa R: citizens want to elect their representatives, and will not assent to having them imposed by the party machine.

Arias's victory should be viewed from the perspective of what is, at this stage of Venezuela's social crisis, a sociopolitical constant: the electorate votes for whoever best symbolizes a rejection of the traditional system. This factor, which gave Causa R its 1992 victory in Caracas, was one of the main reasons why the poor of Caracas did not vote for Istúriz, nor for anyone else, in 1995. Although AD won the contest, it was with fewer votes than those received in previous elections. In the country's capital, the national is superimposed upon the local, and the majority of the electorate seek to punish 'the government', without differentiating among levels, for the continuing severe economic recession and deteriorating quality of life. The clearest way to send a message was through abstention. In Zulia the choice of Arias as governor could surely be interpreted as a type of protest vote against the political system.

6 | The Seven-Month Itch? Neoliberal Politics, Popular Movements, and the Left in Mexico

Kathleen Bruhn

Only six years before, the extraordinary electoral success of leftist presidential candidate Cuauhtémoc Cárdenas in July 1988 had seemed to presage an imminent sea change in Mexican politics, with momentous implications for the future of the left and for modes of popular representation. Yet in the 1994 presidential election continuity carried the day—at least on the surface. The world's longest continuously ruling party managed to keep its hold on national power, winning the presidency as well as a solid majority of Congress in an election that probably ranks among the most expensive, most scrutinized, and relatively clean elections in recent Mexican history. In a country that has experienced as much fundamental economic change and state reform in the last ten years as any other in Latin America, political change, and particularly democratization, appeared at a standstill. Despite ferment from below, including the emergence of a rebel guerrilla force in the state of Chiapas, impatience with existing opportunities for political expression had failed to result in the constitution of a broad alternative project. What are the implications of recent changes? And if no sea change has occurred, what factors have blocked the fundamental transformation of forms of popular representation in Mexico?

At its broadest level, popular representation refers to the ways in which popular preferences are shaped, expressed, and interpreted, or in other words, the organization of popular participation in social decisions. Given their complexity, patterns of popular representation elude easy classification. At an ideal-type level, one can distinguish three main *classifications* of representation (the party or electoral system, the interest group system, and the administrative system, which includes direct state–society contact), multiple *levels* of representation (local and national, but also intra- vs. inter-organizational), and multiple *types* of representation linkage (defined by characteristics like majoritarian/proportional election vs. self-representation/direct democracy, and formal/institutional vs. informal/ *ad hoc* representation). Patterns of representation may change when the dynamics of a subsystem change, when the internal characteristics of component groups in a system change, or when the type of linkage *between* systems of representation changes, particularly from informal/*ad hoc* to formal and institutional articulation—the difference between 'representation' as advocacy (reflecting the concerns of another individual or organization) and 'representation' as a mode of articulation. A party may voice popular concerns without a formal relationship to popular organizations, but an institutional relationship gives party leaders regular channels of communication as well as incentives for cooperation with popular movement leaders. In its absence, they tend to respond more to activist members and the voting population. Without an institutional relationship, popular organizations may have more flexibility, but lack a reliable mechanism for holding political representatives accountable. The formation of institutional alliances is thus a critical turning-point which changes the dynamics of popular sector representation.

What happened in Mexico in 1988 appeared to break with previous patterns of popular representation in at least two senses. First, the emergence of an electorally strong left coalition behind the independent presidential candidacy of Cuauhtémoc Cárdenas introduced a degree of party competition previously absent in Mexico's hegemonic, one-party regime—ruled for over sixty years by the dominant Partido Revolucionario Institucional (PRI). Less than a year after Cárdenas announced his resignation from the PRI and his intention to run for president, he won the most support ever officially acknowledged for an opposition candidate since the foundation of the PRI. While it is not clear that electoral fraud actually changed the outcome of the election, as Cárdenas's supporters contend, actual results were certainly closer than the official margin of 51 per cent to 31 per cent would indicate. Equally startling, his success showed that the PRI's origins in a popular revolution and its corporatist control of unions and peasant organizations did not condemn the left to permanent marginality. At a minimum, the *cardenista* threat promised to force the PRI to pay more attention to popular preferences, in the interest of staying in power. At a maximum, the *cardenistas* promised to create a new channel for the expression of popular demands, in the organization of a political party which would join a significant segment of the traditional Revolutionary left—the ex-*priistas* who followed Cárdenas out of the PRI—with the ex-communists and other leftists of the Mexican Socialist Party.

Second, the appearance of the *cardenista* movement seemed to forge new links between some self-organized social movements and national political parties, further changing patterns of popular representation. In contrast to heavily elite-based parties (*partidos cupulares*, in the succinct Spanish expression) 'representing' popular sectors largely by advocating popular causes, the left saw an opportunity in the *cardenista* movement to develop closer organizational links with popular sectors.[1]

---

[1] In discussing the organized 'popular classes' I am looking primarily (though not exclusively) at the urban popular movements in Mexico, due to the peculiarity that Mexican class-based movements remain mostly captured by the ruling PRI in its sectoral structure, and therefore are not available for institutional alliance to the left. I follow Foweraker's definition of popular movements as the demand-making organizations of the popular classes (that is, excluding entrepreneurial organizations) (see Foweraker and Craig 1990: 5–7).

In response, many popular movements that previously resisted electoral cooperation with *any* political party enthusiastically joined the national electoral alliance
backing Cárdenas. Several signed the founding documents of the FDN, or National
Democratic Front, the hastily assembled coalition of political parties that gave his
candidacy legal registry. Many ran candidates under the FDN banner. Thus, for
the first time since the 1930s, one could argue that 'all left and social movement
forces of any importance are part of the [Cárdenas] coalition' (Fox 1989: 60). In
the afterglow of this union, Cárdenas announced the formation of a new political
party to act as the 'expression of the [organized] plurality and at the same time
of the immense citizen mass [which is] still unorganized . . . to gather together
and extend the great experience of self-organization and defense of citizen dignity
. . . [and] to be an instrument of society, and not just of its members or leaders'
(Cárdenas 1988: 16, 18). It appeared that, 'finally, the foundations were set for a
party with strong ties to social movements and with the potential to articulate them
politically' (Tamayo 1990: 121).

Neither of these anticipated changes—party system change or close institutional alliance—fully materialized. On the one hand, the *cardenista* party lost
much of its electoral strength and fell prey to internal divisions between the many
heterogeneous currents that had created it. On the other hand, the unprecedented
'marriage' between left parties and independent popular movements soured soon
after its electoral consummation. Though some popular movements continued
to cooperate closely with the Partido de la Revolución Democrática (PRD), for many
movements the honeymoon ended within a year. Seven months after the election,
one of the *cardenistas*' most important popular movement allies, the Comité de
Defensa Popular of Durango, signed a *convenio de concertación* with the Salinas
government which committed it to a policy of cooperation with the state and
effectively separated it from the PRD. It was an early indication of an important
trend. Despite efforts to consolidate strong left–movement alliances, the new party
failed to attach most independent popular movements to its cause. It lost the
active, and in some cases even the passive, support of the very movements that helped
make possible its 1988 success.

This chapter examines the second of these aspects—the changing nature of representational links between popular movements and left opposition—with special emphasis on the obstacles to formal linkage. I argue that four factors tended
to push popular movements toward a more informal, *ad hoc*, and even cyclical
relationship to political parties: the institutional context of Mexican politics, the
inclusion of compensatory social policies in the neoliberal framework, the characteristics of the parties themselves (in this case, the PRD's internal structure and
its position as a *new* party built on top of pre-existing organizations), and the element of competition in party–movement relationships. The adoption of neoliberal policies helped undermine the PRI's popular support, and played an important
role at the elite level in creating the new left option. However, ideological differences with the direction of neoliberalism did not prevent many popular movements

from cementing an ongoing relationship with the neoliberal state. At most, the neoliberal orientation of the PRI government encouraged it to inhibit ties to a left political party that couched demands in explicit class terms—a behavior that might well have occurred anyway given the PRI's incentive to discourage the consolidation of *any* party that posed a significant electoral threat (like Cárdenas in 1988). Still, the existence of a left party alternative—either electoral (like the *cardenistas*) or non-electoral (like the Chiapas rebel army)—tends to improve the bargaining position of popular movements *vis-à-vis* the neoliberal state.[2] Thus, movements may see short 'affairs' with the left as strategically advantageous, even in a relatively unfavorable context for permanent articulation through left parties. This could create a cyclical rhythm, or boom-and-bust pattern, in the relationship between popular movements and political parties.

Neoliberal Policies and the 1988 Convergence

Popular movements in Mexico traditionally resisted close collaboration with political parties, for many of the same reasons that would later complicate their relationship with the PRD. One could cooperate with the PRI in exchange for the benefits that only the ruling party could provide. However, PRI-incorporated unions seemed to gradually lose their political independence, their ability to challenge government decisions against their interests, and finally their prestige and popular support. On the other hand, opposition parties could not offer much help toward immediate material goals, due to the centralization of resources in the federal (PRI) government. Moreover, independent left parties, including the Mexican Communist Party, often seemed to prioritize electoral struggles over organization of the masses and direct struggle for material goals, raising doubts about their motives in seeking popular movement commitments. The left current Linea de Masas, whose activists played a very significant role as organizational entrepreneurs in the formation of many modern popular movements, grew out of this critique of left parties as 'distanced (physically and practically) from the mass movements' (Hernández 1991: 23–4; see also Bennett 1992). While they sought the formation of a proletarian party as their ultimate goal, they tended to be skeptical of elections, and argued that a true proletarian party could only be built from the ground up, on the basis of independent popular organizations with democratic internal structures. Because of this emphasis on self-determination of the bases, these movements in practice fiercely defended their autonomy from 'outside' institutions.

[2] The rebels seized several towns in the state of Chiapas on New Year's Day, 1994, in protest against their conditions of life, official neglect and corruption, lack of democracy, and the Free Trade Agreement.

Cooperation in opposition electoral struggles seemed particularly risky and unrewarding. In the first place, many of the organizers that encouraged the formation of new urban popular movements in the 1970s were veterans of the 1968 student movement, whose violent repression led many to discard the possibility of peaceful change in Mexico. In the second place, since the PRI controlled electoral institutions, opposition parties usually lost, either cleanly or through fraud. However, the legalization of left parties in the 1977 electoral reform gave popular movements more electoral options. By the mid-1980s, electoral cooperation had become more frequent. In 1985, the National Revolutionary Coordinating Committee called for more cooperation between popular movements and parties, arguing that 'some regional organizations can challenge the PRI and win elected offices . . . The best help they can receive is from registered parties in coalition, *with the name and banner of the regional organizations*' (quoted in Tamayo 1990: 126–7; emphasis added). The idea was to allow movement candidates to campaign under (and publicize) their own organizational identity, while still enjoying the legal benefits of registered candidates, such as taking office if they won, and receiving government subsidies for their campaigns. Some alliances did occur, but 'the electoral results of this agreement were not very significant', and many popular movements that *did* try electoral gambles 'not only . . . experience[d] electoral defeats that undermined the previously recognized mobilizational capabilities of the movement, but in some cases internal weakening, division, desertion, and demobilization clearly followed electoral participation' (Tamayo 1990: 127). In successful electoral participation, one tends to find a well-established popular movement borrowing the registry of a party for a temporary and regionally limited electoral alliance.[3] However, most popular movements in the 1980s concentrated on forming horizontal alliances with each other, chiefly through National Coordinating Committees.

In this context, the massive affiliation of movements to the Cárdenas campaign seemed particularly significant. What convinced reluctant popular movements to line up so openly with an opposition electoral option? According to one hypothesis, movements reacted to the impact of the economic crisis and the rightward drift of the government by seeking new allies to defend themselves and press their demands. During De la Madrid's presidency (1982–8), Mexico experienced the worst economic crisis in its post-revolutionary history, precipitated by a sudden decline in oil prices which drastically reduced Mexico's principal source of dollars with which to pay its massive foreign debt. Mexico's heavily protected industrial sector could not compete effectively enough in international markets to pick up the slack. The ensuing financial panic led to capital flight and inflation, and significant deterioration in standards of living, with real minimum wages down

---

[3] The case of COCEI and the Mexican Communist Party is one example. In 1980, COCEI and the PCM joined in an electoral alliance in Juchitan, Oaxaca, allowing COCEI to field registered candidates. The PRI committed fraud and declared victory, but after intensive COCEI mobilization, had to schedule new elections in 1981, and for a time, COCEI governed the only left-held *municipio* in the country.

40–50 per cent and inflation over 100 per cent in some years.[4] Many blamed PRI incompetence and corruption for the economic disaster—for accumulating a massive debt in the first place, and then failing to cope with the results.

In addition, partly in response to the crisis, the Mexican government became increasingly dominated by what scholars now term 'neoliberal policies', usually including fiscal austerity (especially state budget cuts), promotion of free trade and foreign investment, and limits on the state's role in the economy (especially rejecting the state's role as capitalist employer and promoting privatization). De la Madrid's initial response, demanded by international banks and the IMF, coupled severe fiscal austerity with a package of wage and price controls and limited privatization.[5] When these measures failed to yield the expected improvement, Mexico moved toward deeper restructuring of the economy, entering GATT in 1986.

This shift helped drive popular movements into the arms of Cárdenas. In the first place, these policies changed the strategic and political environment for popular movements, leading some to consider electoral struggle as a necessary tactic to block the advance of the right. In the 1980s, popular demands seemed 'incompatible with the state's strategy for economic restructuring' (Tamayo 1990: 122). Due to severe budget constraints, the government was unable to increase social spending to compensate for market losses and the effects of inflation. According to some calculations, social spending fell an average of 6.2 per cent per year between 1983 and 1988 (Lustig 1994: 82). Others find less shrinkage, but agree that 'social expenditure . . . continued to lose ground' under De la Madrid (Ward 1994: 53). Organized social movements also rejected these policies. The hard-pressed state could offer little to satisfy the movements as they became increasingly vocal about their demands.

At the same time, many movements felt isolated from other sectors of society who also had reason to resent the PRI. For some of them, electoral participation and alliance with parties became a way to reach out to these sectors, end their marginalization, and create a counterweight to the country's rightward drift. For example, the first venture into electoral politics of the Comité de Defensa Popular of Durango (the local elections of 1986) reflected their growing sense of isolation and their diagnosis that in the absence of an electoral left challenge, the unpopular policies of the PRI actually improved the electoral fortunes of the *right*— Partido Acción Nacional (PAN).[6] Said one movement leader:

In the city of Durango, we had grown a lot, but we were isolated from other sectors of the population . . . in that context, the PAN began to capitalize on the popular discontent against the PRI . . . To break the siege in which the state had put us, to win over or

[4] According to Lustig, total wage income fell a cumulative 40 per cent between 1983 and 1988 while the real minimum wage fell 48.5 per cent (see Lustig 1992: 68–9). For other representative estimates, see Weintraub (1993: 13) and Collier (1992: 128).

[5] At this point, the primary goal appears to have been cutting the budget by eliminating or shutting down unprofitable enterprises subsidized by state ownership (see Gentleman 1987: 41–62).

[6] In 1983, the PAN had won a majority of the vote in several CDP strongholds.

neutralize other sectors of the population, and to put a brake on the *panista* advance, we decided to participate in the elections. (Hernández 1988*b*: 29)

The relative success of its first venture—one state congressman and four *regidores* —reinforced the CDP's inclination to participate in elections. Leaders felt that 'the electoral struggle gave us legitimacy and greater political weight . . . The positions we won have allowed us to increase our capacity for mediation [*gestión*]'.[7] In its first electoral experience (1988), the Asamblea de Barrios took into account similar considerations, stressing:

It is important to emphasize the singularity of the current electoral process . . . we must assert our political and economic independence in favor of the people, in the face of the selling out [*entreguismo*] of the state, the antidemocracy and growing impoverishment to which they have condemned the majority of Mexicans . . . If we succeed in demonstrating that the PRI and Salinas no longer have a consensus, we will be approaching a crisis of legitimacy of the government that will open the way to change . . . In this conjuncture, that is the central problem: to isolate the PRI and the project of the PAN. (Saucedo 1988: 33–4)

However, the Asamblea's experience also suggests that neoliberal policies without Cárdenas would not have produced the same left–movement alliance. Cárdenas symbolized a high point of popular struggles, for during his father's presidency oil was nationalized and land redistributed. Perhaps more importantly, his popularity significantly improved the likelihood of electoral success. Until October 1987, when Cárdenas became an opposition candidate, organized civil society remained aloof and abstentionist. In the words of one early Cárdenas ally, 'one could not say that civil society [before October] had participation, no, it really didn't . . . It was *ready* to participate, that is something else, that was the secret . . . but that wasn't known until later.'[8] After Cárdenas became available, organizations began to flock to him. 'When we say that there is singularity in the current electoral process', added Francisco Saucedo of the Asamblea, 'it is in the sense that today more than ever conditions exist that permit [us] to translate these elections into a vast movement against the PRI and the right. It is a moment in which the worsening of the economic situation has coincided with the internal crisis in the PRI as a result of the process of *destape* of Carlos Salinas, the formation of the *Corriente Democrática*, and its virtual expulsion' (Saucedo 1988: 33).

Neoliberal policies played a very important role in creating this candidacy. Cárdenas and other PRI elites initially chose to form a dissident 'Democratic Current' in the PRI in large part because of their opposition to the De la Madrid program and their exclusion from positions with the power to influence policy. Even their demand for democratic selection of the PRI presidential candidate was connected to economic policy differences with the government. Says Cárdenas: 'we saw that it was not possible to draw a line between change in economic policies

---

[7] Hernández (1988*b*: 29). A *regidor* is approximately equivalent to a city councilman.
[8] Confidential interview by author, Apr. 1991.

and political change. That is, the economic policy that had been imposed since 82 responded to the interests of those who make political decisions. So, for us it was clear that winning, winning political power . . . was an indispensable condition for there to be a change in the orientation of economic policies."[9]

Thus, the neoliberal program and its social consequences promoted an *acercamiento* between popular sectors and the independent left, culminating in the formation of a new party intended to act as 'articulating axis' for the democratically organized population (Cuéllar 1991: 12). When the Mexican Socialist Party decided to join the *cardenistas* in the PRD, its leaders emphasized their commitment within the new party to 'a conduct that foments the organization of the people independently from the state and from parties and [that is] receptive to the state of mind, the aspirations, the requirements of the social movement' (Partido Mexicano Socialista 1989: 27). In 1988—given the popular conviction that Cárdenas won the election and the prospect of six more years of neoliberal policies—it appeared that the new party had a chance of succeeding.

Political Cycles: Obstacles in the Consolidation of a Permanent PRD–Movement Alliance

Nevertheless, despite the commitment by a broad range of movements and parties, the PRD lost many popular movement allies. Even worse, a number of important popular movements left the PRD only to cooperate with the Salinas administration—the same team that a few short months before they had denounced as usurpers. Neoliberal policies clearly did not provide a strong enough glue to hold the left coalition together, nor did they prevent a *rapprochement* between popular movements and the PRI. What then accounts for the breach between the PRD and popular movements?

Frequently, observers pointed to the behavior of the PRD itself. Many feared from the beginning that the PRD would prove 'no more than another populist trap— a new version of the PRI-run corporatist system that social movements are currently fighting' (Munck 1990: 33). Furthermore, since many top leaders of the new party cut their political eyeteeth in the PRI, there was considerable suspicion that the PRD would develop a '*priista* political culture', which would retain 'many of the traditional vices—sectarianism, authoritarianism, centralism, opportunism, and political myopia' (Tamayo 1990: 135). The popular movements often cited PRD authoritarianism as the reason for defection.

The characteristics of the PRD, especially its newness as a party, its internal structure, and its confrontational strategy, did contribute to problems between the left and popular movements. However, three other broad factors played a role:

[9] Interview by author, May 1991.

(1) institutions at the regime level; (2) the inclusion within the neoliberal program of social welfare policies designed to attract political support to the governing party; and (3) differences in strategic interests between political parties and organized popular movements.

In the first place, the attempt to consolidate an institutional alliance required more from popular movements—and a different kind of representational linkage—than the 1988 coalition. As a new movement, barely organized itself, the FDN was in no position to demand compromises or discipline from popular movements. Cárdenas represented them only as an advocate, not in a formal institutional sense. As I argue later, short-term strategic alliance gave popular movements important benefits, including the ability to use elections to strengthen their organization and the chance of electing their leaders on the coat-tails of Cárdenas. After the election, he could no longer deliver these benefits, and his new party began to ask for more significant sacrifices. Many movements distanced themselves.

Because of the Mexican institutional context, the PRD could not credibly offer many of the alternative benefits that might have made a permanent alliance more worthwhile, such as the ability to mediate, to consistently put movement leaders in office, and to satisfy substantive demands. The traditional option of many left parties—strong alliance to unions—was largely foreclosed by the official incorporation of unions in the ruling party. Though sectors of some unions, such as the teachers and petroleum workers unions, have been sympathetic to the PRD and even occasionally participated as individuals, the PRD made relatively few inroads in these unions, especially in terms of formal alliance. The specter of corporatist incorporation also frightened popular movements away from a closer relationship to political parties. Empirically, it is unlikely that the PRD will duplicate PRI forms of articulation. In the first place, the party maintains a strong commitment to individual membership and to non-corporatist linkages. In the second place, and probably more importantly, the PRD does not have the resources to cement a true corporatist alliance. It cannot offer a state monopoly, subsidies, or support in arbitration of labor disputes, and it cannot enforce alliance obligations on anyone. Even if it wished to, it could not be another PRI. Nevertheless, the institutions of corporatism limit the kind of appeals that the PRD can make, and the kind of audience that can hear them.

More fundamentally, the lack of competitive democracy made the PRD a less attractive alliance partner. The PRI used every conceivable method, including fraud and violence, to undermine the PRD. In Cárdenas's home state of Michoacán, the PRI literally stole the July 1989 local congressional elections, in such an obvious fashion that it seemed meant as an object lesson, proving that the PRD could not defend electoral victories, and therefore that a PRD vote would be wasted. Particularly vulnerable as a very new party, the PRD later developed a capacity to make such actions so costly that the PRI must think twice, and accept some PRD local governments. However, the government's clear bias against the PRD limited what it could offer potential allies. Without access to state resources, except at a local level, the party had a hard time delivering concrete benefits to PRD-allied popular movements. Even worse, cooperation with the PRD could expose a popular movement to increased hostility from the ruling party, including repression and unwillingness to listen to popular movement demands.

In addition, the PRI used its control of state authority to sow divisions between the PRD and popular movements. In one *colonia popular* in the Estado de Mexico, for example, a popular movement sought help from a local PRD committee in a dispute over water fees and supply. A PRD committee member researched and presented a petition to the PRI municipal government, and arranged a meeting between the organization and municipal authorities. At this meeting, the PRD activist did most of the talking, but failed to make any impression on municipal officials. After nearly two hours, the government mediator got up and walked to the other end of the table, where he quietly offered *colonia* members resolution of their fee complaints *on an individual basis* to those willing to break ranks and come to the municipal offices. The PRD activist protested vigorously, but his very protest caused problems; once outside, several *colonia* representatives accused him of trying to determine their tactics for them, and walked off in anger. Similar stories of obstructionism toward PRD-associated movements abound. Long-term alliance to the PRD clearly involves potential costs, and may endanger important popular movement goals.

The most famous example of how the PRI used state resources to win support and drive a wedge between the PRD and popular movements is the National Solidarity Program. Solidarity is a social spending program, created by Salinas the day of his inauguration, which offers popular movements a chance to achieve long-standing substantive demands and even administer development projects. Salinas designed Solidarity to be compatible with a neoliberal approach. In contrast to traditional populism, which involved state alliance with labor, Solidarity distributes benefits primarily on a *non*-class basis, resisting policies that distort prices. By targeting selected groups, for example, Solidarity tried to avoid general subsidies to inputs or basic consumer goods. Furthermore, particularly in its early phase, Solidarity concentrated on public works projects that in addition to improving the quality of life of residents, would also improve economic infrastructure and/or their ability to participate in market production.

Nevertheless, the inclusion of these social programs made the formation of strong popular movement/PRD alliances more difficult—on the one hand, because Solidarity tended to improve the government's popular image, and on the other, because Solidarity gave popular movements a better deal with the government than the PRD could possibly offer. Although initially Solidarity represented a relatively small percentage of overall expenditure (less than 4 per cent of programmable spending and 7.7 per cent of total social spending), by 1992 Solidarity absorbed almost half of all public investment in social development (Cornelius *et al.* 1994: 282). Thus, for the kinds of demands made by many popular movements, Solidarity was a key funding source. Moreover, Solidarity tried to involve popular movements in project administration by requiring the formation of a 'Solidarity Committee' which—in theory—proposed projects and helped administer the money. In practice, most Solidarity Committees were created from scratch for specific projects, but popular movements could and did qualify. Although movements did not have to join the PRI, or renounce criticism of the ruling party, most recognized that brazen support for the PRI's despised enemy, the PRD, did not improve the odds of getting Solidarity money. If the PRI could lure movements into neutrality, it accomplished a major goal.

Particularly in the first year of its existence, the PRD's insistence on non-negotiation forced popular movements to make this choice. Again, because of the concentration of resources in the federal government, most popular movements end up bargaining with the government at some point, even if self-help and mobilization also play a role in their strategy. Yet in the months after the 1988 election, Cárdenas committed his supporters to intransigent confrontation with the 'usurper' Salinas, who had 'robbed' Cárdenas of his rightful victory. Originally only a rejection of deals to accept the official voting results (especially for the presidency), the policy extended in practice to any collaboration with the Salinas government which might tend to legitimate it. This was functional in *party* terms, as an early basis for unity and identity, but essentially cut off movements from access to Solidarity funds.

The first important movement to break with the PRD over this issue was the Comité de Defensa Popular of Durango (CDP), only seven months after the election. The Convenio de Concertación it signed in February 1989 amounted to a contract with the Salinas government, according to which the government provided money for basic services and public works projects, proposed and administered by the movement itself, and in addition, money to fund CDP-run small businesses, an important potential source of independent funding for the movement. As a movement, the CDP got a chance to achieve community development goals and form connections in the administration for future benefits. Through such contracts, movement leaders could at one stroke relieve pressures on the movement from below (member demands) and above (government hostility and repression). Nevertheless, the PRD saw the decision as treason, and publicly criticized the CDP for 'selling out' to Salinas. Moreover, party leaders felt betrayed by the fact that the CDP did not consult them before announcing the deal. Their perception that the Convenio drew the CDP toward alliance with the PRI influenced the PRD's crude handling of negotiations over candidacies for the local July 1989 elections, which culminated in the CDP's decision to break finally with the PRD and form its own regional party.[10]

The PRD lost a number of popular movements in such conflicts over Solidarity money, and must accept some responsibility for these losses. Particularly during 1989, the PRD and the *cardenista* leadership tended to take the loyalty of the popular

[10] Under Mexican law, parties can register at a state or national level. The government rushed through the CDP's state registry, delighted to take popular support from the PRD. On the CDP-Durango, see Haber (1994: 255–79).

movements for granted, imagining that the movements cared as much as the party about electing Cárdenas. Had PRD leaders realized how contingent their support was, they might have been more understanding, and salvaged at least limited cooperation. Instead, showing little sympathy for the popular movements' desire to negotiate, the PRD requested unconditional support to bring down Salinas. Still, even after the party softened its position and accepted more popular movement negotiations, its overall stance of confrontation with the PRI and its disadvantage in competing with the PRI as a service provider tended to limit the potential for alliances.

Ironically, a third source of problems resulted from the PRD's attempts to *avoid* authoritarianism and a corporatist '*priista* political culture'. In early meetings of the Comité Nacional Promotor del PRD, a strong constituency argued in favor of a semi-corporatist, dual representation system. The working group on Social Movements at these meetings concluded that 'it is necessary to understand that the PRD has two legs of political action. These are, on the one hand, the territorial organization, and on the other, the sectoral organization.'[11] While entire unions would not join the PRD, members could have representation in the party leadership according to their economic activity. Thus, there would be a Peasant Council, Union Council, Student Council, etc., to 'coordinate and direct activity . . . in each sector'. By the second round of discussions, this proposal had been dropped, due precisely to concern that it would be perceived as corporatist. Instead, party statutes specified that its linkage to popular movements would operate 'through those militants of the party that at the same time participate in movements'.[12] The resulting pattern of informal, personal linkage tended to favor the movements' institutional autonomy, but discouraged coordinated decision-making. It failed to provide popular movements with a way to hold PRD leaders accountable or to guarantee fair representation on leadership and candidate lists. Overlapping membership could be quite haphazard. Its success depended ultimately on the will of PRD leaders to include and listen to popular movement leaders—and this varied considerably. Even when PRD leaders tried to recruit popular movement leaders, the size of a movement's representation rarely reflected the size or importance of the movement.

Moreover, in conflicts between movement and party, dual members had to choose between loyalties. Party statutes provided little guidance about the obligations of party or movement to resolve these conflicts. According to early statutes, 'members of movements and social organizations that militate in the party have a duty to promote its political line', but this political line, 'the policy of the party in social organizations will be determined by its members in each one of them . . .

---

[11] 'Resoluciones de la Mesa de Movimientos Sociales', *La Unidad*, 26 Feb. 1989 (Mexico, DF: Partido Mexicano Socialista), 8.

[12] *Documentos básicos (proyectos)*, 34. Later versions of the statutes dropped even this minimal provision. Except for a vague mention of 'party affiliates and *comités de base* in the social movements', the 1990 statutes did not specify a means of linkage.

[and] the members of the party will respect the decisions that are democratically adopted in the social organizations of which they form part'.[13] In concrete disputes, dual members tended to take positions favoring their primary loyalty, usually the first organization joined. For example, one local PRD committee debated the 'obligation' of a PRD-allied union of street vendors in the 1991 electoral campaign. Several party activists argued that the union had *no* obligation to participate *as an organization*, but that union members should participate as individuals in their districts of residence. The union leader on the committee accepted a duty to participate, but argued that union members should all participate in one district regardless of residence because a union member was the alternative (*suplente*) to the candidate for Congress in that district.[14] This solution discharged the union's 'obligation' to the party through support for a candidate that, if elected, would give them a useful contact in government.

Similarly, PRD methods of candidate selection—though designed to ensure internal party democracy—essentially gave the power of decision to party activists and often deprived movement leaders of a sense of effective voice. Primary elections afforded movements a chance to compete on equal terms for PRD candidacies, usually for majority seats (such as senators, congressmen elected by plurality, and mayors). In order to stimulate popular movement participation, PRD statutes did not require that aspirants join the party. However, there were three problems with this method of attracting movement interest. First, it forced movements to compete not only with party activists, but also with other movements. Within this competition, smaller movements could easily lose primaries. Second, due in part to expense and logistical problems, the PRD held primary elections in less than half of Mexico's 300 electoral districts in 1991 and none at all in 1994 (although in the latter case, the reason was a party decision to reserve half its candidacies for 'external' candidates—i.e. non-party members). Third, even if a movement placed a candidate through the primary, he still had to beat the PRI in the general election. In 1991, the PRD lost every majority district. Instead, all its congressmen reached office through its proportional representation list, elaborated at a party convention which over-represented active party members.[15] PRD activists, in no mood to hand out precious seats to militants in other movements, fought bitterly for those sure seats, pushing aside movement leaders. Identified leaders of popular movements got only four of the top 25 slots in 1991, and only two in 1994.[16]

[13] *Documentos básicos (proyectos)*, 34. Again, statutory responsibilities became *more* vague over time rather than less. Later versions suggested convoking conferences to resolve differences between party and movement; in the meantime, the party would 'respect equally the different positions found [*sic*] in the [Basic Documents]'. *Documentos básicos 1990*, 48.

[14] Personal observation of meeting, May 1991.

[15] The Mexican Congress is composed of 300 plurality seats (winner-take-all districts) and 200 proportional representation seats, apportioned on the basis of a party's percentage of the vote. Delegates to conventions were chosen at open caucuses, but party activists predominated, mostly due to interest.

[16] Parties present five lists, one for each region, with the top candidates on a list most likely to get a place. The 'top 25' refers to the top five names in each of the five party lists. Candidates that belonged to left parties before 1988 got 12 slots, or 48 per cent. Source: Caballero (1991: 3).

Pure party activists took over 60 per cent of the top congressional list positions. Movements did somewhat better on the top 50 slots in 1994 (eight candidates, most of which reached Congress), and much better in the party's list for the Federal District's local congress (the Asamblea de Representantes), composed almost entirely of popular movement candidates.[17] According to the PRD president in the Federal District, this reflected a deliberate decision to 'compensate the organizations of the [urban popular movement], the majority of which had been left out of the nominations for congressmen' (Ballinas and Urrutia 1994: 52). Yet most successful popular movements had strong connections already within the PRD within the Federal District, which gave them an advantage in negotiating places.

Conflicts over candidacies proved the final straw that led to complete breach between the CDP of Durango and the PRD. The main dispute arose over the proportional representation list for the July 1989 local elections. CDP leaders felt cheated of their rightful share of candidacies. They argued that left votes in Durango came from CDP supporters; therefore, the CDP—and not left party activists—should get the lion's share of candidacies. In this instance, the political party should accept junior status in the alliance, and allow the CDP to determine who would take the top slots. When the PRD balked at this, the CDP pursued an independent party registration, which the state pushed through with alacrity—and which outpolled the PRD two to one.

Alliances that assign candidacies to popular movements through party–movement negotiations may have a better chance of survival than alliances that allocate candidacies based on intra-party politics. In a negotiation process, the movement can place people it trusts in positions of authority, without having to subject them to uncertain 'popular primaries' in which anyone may participate, or to competition with ambitious party activists. Negotiation may reduce the risks for popular movements who worry about co-optation of 'representatives' that they do not themselves choose. However, sporadic PRD attempts to negotiate an electoral alliance frequently undermine the original goal of democratic primaries and raise fears of corporatist manipulation. If the assignment of candidacies to popular movements sounds strikingly like the sectoral quotas used within the PRI, the irony has not escaped either popular movements or the PRD founders.

Such calculations may help explain why even the tiny Trotskyist Partido Revolucionario de los Trabajadores (PRT) ran more candidates from urban popular movements in Mexico City in 1991 than the much more formidable PRD (Hernández Montiel 1991: 39). The PRT could offer candidates little hope of electoral success, even through proportional representation. In fact, it got less than the 1.5 per cent of the vote required to qualify for proportional representation, and seated no congressmen. However, as a party virtually without militants, the PRT was not in a position to impose conditions on popular movements, and happily accepted secondary status in candidacies. Some popular movements who broke

[17] Calculations by author, based on confidential interviews with scholars and PRD members. Nine of the fifty remained unidentified or unconfirmed.

with the PRD (including the CDP-Durango) later created the Partido del Trabajo in 1991 as essentially a federation of regional popular movements, in which the movements retained the ability to choose candidates in their region. Again, though the party's national electoral weakness left it unable at first to win registry or seat candidates, the CDP-Durango and other movements still preferred it to the PRD.

To some extent, these problems suggest potential conflicts between popular movement goals. At the level of institutional design, for example, what structures would *both* guarantee movement autonomy *and* ensure party accountability and responsiveness? Direct participation in PRD leadership could promote communication and party responsiveness. But incorporation (or co-optation?) of popular movement leaders might also give party activists a way to exact their pound of flesh, to use the movement's bases and mobilization capacity to support party policy and electoral goals. Direct participation can trap movements in the intransigent opposition.

These tensions over movement obligations and party responsiveness, while in some ways particular to the PRD, also suggest an underlying tension between what one might call a 'movement logic' and a 'party logic'. There is an intrinsically competitive element in relationships between organizations that attempt to draw upon the same resources for different purposes. This factor affects the relationship between party and popular movement in two principal ways. First, to the degree that parties and movements retain separate organizations, their bureaucratic drives lead to competition over scarce resources. As separate organizations, they develop internal rules of advancement (so that advancement in one organization does not automatically lead to advancement in the other) and maintain separate budgets and programs. Thus, activists pursue their personal ambitions according to different rules, creating divided loyalties and disputed turf. Questions about personal power and authority easily turn into questions about the responsibilities and authority of one organization versus the other. For example, in cases of overlapping membership, a popular movement leader with considerable authority in his own movement must accept the will of the majority in the PRD committee to which he belongs. Yet the principle of one-person–one-vote is frequently difficult to accept when a popular movement leader brings an unequal (and greater) level of support to the party. The equivocal status of the leader leads to conflict between the organizations over who makes binding decisions and by what decision-making principle.

In addition, party and movement compete for the limited attention and energy of essentially the same constituents. Leaders may channel scarce resources into one organization in order to reinforce their position, or use the resources of one organization for power struggles in the other. A movement leader can use his party connections to enhance his prestige, and a party leader can enlist movement support in internal party battles. For 'dual leaders', the scarce resources over which parties and movements compete clearly include their own time and energy. Among those who have made serious commitments to both movement and party, this is one of the chief sources of conflict between their roles as party activist and movement activist. As they gain more influential positions in the party, they often have to withdraw to some extent from intensive movement activism (though they continue to participate), or complain about exhausting workdays. Those who remain more active in their movement tend to miss party meetings and end up somewhat marginalized. Finally, organizations tend to try to enhance their own power and control over their environment. The relative size of national parties versus local popular movements may make it hard for the latter to control their environment while in close association with a larger organization whose actions—even in the best and most democratic circumstances—cannot be controlled by each small associated organization. If a small organization does not derive significant resources from its association with the party, there is less reason to accept this trade-off.

Despite these conflicts, alliance might work if both organizations pursued identical goals. On the surface, this appears feasible. Left parties like the PRD passionately declare support for popular movement struggles. Movements often support party goals of democracy and the creation of a strong left party. However, in practice, their *priorities* do not match. While political parties tend to prioritize electoral success and national regime change, most popular movements put substantive goals and local struggles first. As a result, the tactics that a political party adopts to achieve its goals may actually undermine the popular movement's attempt to achieve *its* goals.

The problem of intransigence versus negotiation is one example of this dilemma. Popular movements have a long tradition of bargaining with the state to resolve their primary problems. They may use confrontational actions, strikes, and mobilization to get the attention of the state or extract concessions, but at some point, bargaining and negotiation usually play a role. In the aftermath of 1988, despite all the rhetoric about providing a vehicle for popular movements, the primary goal for the political party was to establish itself as an independent electoral force and if possible to bring about the inauguration of Cárdenas. The party leadership judged that it could best accomplish these goals by confrontation and nonnegotiation, aimed at distinguishing the PRD from other parties and maximizing its blackmail potential. Alternative strategies would not necessarily have improved articulation of popular movement goals. For example, the *cardenistas* might have bargained with the state over electoral rules in exchange for tacit acceptance of Salinas. They might well have been reluctant to add to their agenda the material demands of the popular movements at least at that stage.

More commonly, the conflict between electoral and popular movement goals manifests itself in choices about the allocation of scarce resources, including energy and time. Popular movements that become involved in elections often fear—with reason—that the excitement of elections will divert the attention of their leaders from the movement's original goals, and worst of all, to little practical effect. Unlike mobilization for popular demands, elections cannot take place at a strategically chosen time, but must follow externally determined rules. In addition, the competitive dynamic of elections encourages ever greater expenditures of time and money. However, if leaders continue to mobilize for original movement goals as well, party and movement risk exhaustion. So choices are made which affect the position of both organizations.

The problems afflicting the Unión de Campesinos Democráticos (UCD) illustrate one extreme of movement subordination to the PRD. The UCD grew primarily out of PRD frustration with their lack of progress in PRI-affiliated unions. In 1989, without explicitly renouncing work inside PRI unions, Cárdenas called for the formation of a new independent peasant union. Its first national convention convened in April 1990. Although the UCD worked with some independent peasant organizers, it is primarily a PRD-built organization. Its early membership and leadership came from PRD activists. The convention elected as its first 'national' president[18] a young *michoacano* with little experience in peasant organization, but considerable political experience as the state president of the PRI during the (PRI) governorship of Cárdenas. Membership on local PRD/UCD committees often overlaps nearly 100 per cent. The PRD and the UCD use common resources. In two of seven interview communities in Michoacán, they shared an office. The entourages of PRD candidates in 1991 traveled in UCD trucks. As one member of a PRD *comité municipal* (also a member of the local UCD committee) put it, the UCD is 'almost . . . a branch [*dependencia*] of the party'.[19]

Because of its political identification with the PRD, the UCD struggled against heavy state pressure, yet there was no reconsideration of the alliance and little strategic mobility. Peasant organization constantly takes second place to mobilization for electoral purposes. Even worse, political rivalries in the PRD infected the UCD from the beginning. As of 1992, *michoacanos* reported to no fewer than three 'national leaderships' of the UCD, each claiming authority to speak for the entire organization. Two leaderships were connected to the rivalry between the two PRD senators from Michoacán (1988–91), Senator Cristóbal Arias and Senator Roberto Robles Garnica. The third leadership represented the remnants of previous independent peasant organizing in Michoacán, and rejected both other leaderships as 'outsiders', party hacks who exploit the peasants for electoral gain.[20] In sum, the UCD's thorough subordination to the needs of the PRD severely undermined its effectiveness and even its existence as a popular organization.

Though less severe, the effects on other organizations closely associated with the PRD made themselves felt. Activists in the Asamblea de Barrios reported constant government harassment and attempts to 'ban' the Asamblea from extending its presence into the urbanized areas surrounding Mexico City in the state of Mexico. Party divisions also contributed to a 1993 split in the Asamblea that resulted in two rival leaderships—one led by an activist inclined toward a different party current

---

[18] The UCD does not really exist as a 'national' organization. The biggest response to Cárdenas's call came from the adjoining states of Michoacán, Guerrero, and Guanajuato. Other major peasant areas like Chiapas and Oaxaca had little UCD activity.

[19] Confidential interview AR, July 1991.   [20] Confidential interview DD, July 1992.

than the current preferred by the other three top leaders. While government pressure and division might well have occurred in the absence of the Asamblea–PRD alliance, party problems contributed to strains on the Asamblea.[21]

At the other extreme, political parties that continually subordinate their electoral needs to the demands of popular movements may fail to consolidate themselves as electoral competitors, leaving the movements once again without a party voice. The Partido del Trabajo initially experienced such problems partly as a result of its dependence on movements. Created in 1991 by several regional popular movements, the Partido del Trabajo is a highly decentralized organization, 'a federation of various parties and organizations', that is 'far from being a national party' (Hernández 1991: 22, 26). It lacks a presence in many areas, a program, a party structure, and an intellectual base. Without a party structure or a unifying national candidate, the PT failed to win the 1.5 per cent of the national vote required for registry in 1991. In 1994, the party did get enough votes to keep its registry, thanks in part to increasingly close affiliation with the government. The PT's lavish campaign created strong suspicions that the state was secretly (and illegally) funding its activities, and its presidential candidate Cecilia Soto—not herself a major movement leader—was widely believed to be the personal selection of the president.[22] Achieving registry at this price put in question the party's ability to act as a genuinely independent voice of civil society.

In the case of the PRD, attempts to include popular movement leaders sometimes undermined party unity and consolidation. Even some movement leaders recognize this; Marco Rascón, a top leader of the Asamblea de Barrios, admitted that the terms of the party–social movement relationship have distorted the organic development of the party and inhibited the consolidation of a party structure (still mostly built around pockets of movement organization in the Federal District) (Ballinas and Urrutia 1994: 51). The candidacy issue again illustrates a key aspect of the problem. In order to remain 'open to civil society', party policy officially allowed anyone to enter PRD primaries. In a number of cases, this resulted in candidates relatively hostile to the PRD. One such candidate in the Estado de Mexico had

---

[21] The Asamblea has tended since its foundation to get involved in confrontations with the government, which naturally exposed it to pressures from the regime. Further, the division in the Asamblea reflected their origins in political currents that pre-date the formation of the PRD. The leader who split—Francisco Saucedo—had always been associated with a different political current than the other three.

[22] According to Mexican law, government subsidies of party campaigns are proportional to their vote in the last election. The PT's ability to run a campaign that outshone the PRD—which had won eight times the PT's vote in 1991—in quantity and quality of propaganda therefore mystified observers. Cecilia Soto's explanation that the party had saved its money did not convince anybody. She belonged to the parastatal party PARM until one day before her nomination as the PT candidate, and her biography reveals more political activism (in Congress, and even as a Lyndon LaRouche supporter) than movement activism. The PT's recovery of registry after 1991 also appeared due to government intervention. The PT sought and won 'definitive' registry—a status which requires holding assemblies in half the Mexican states, with a minimum number of attendees ratified by notaries. Many observers questioned whether the PT had actually fulfilled the requirements, but state institutions approved its application.

previously supported the party of abstention, urging supporters not to vote for anyone (including the PRD) in the November 1990 local elections. Even after his selection as a congressional candidate for 1991, he refused to join the PRD *or* to sign an agreement publicly supporting the basic PRD platform. His campaign managers said he would 'coordinate' with the PRD bench if he won, but that he would not 'take orders' from the party.[23] He did not ask for PRD help in organizing the campaign, or encourage PRD participation. Moreover, he frequently failed to inform the local PRD of campaign events. Instead of working with the candidate to win, local activists worked to prevent him from defecting before the election. Only a few days before the deadline to register candidates with the electoral authorities, the candidate's alternate resigned, citing his concern over 'the [candidate's] lack of identity' with the PRD.[24] When the local PRD committee scheduled an emergency meeting to choose a replacement, the candidate did not show up. He ultimately refused to accept the committee's suggestions. At the last minute, the PRD registered his (non-PRD) nominee in order to have a candidate. The struggle divided PRD supporters and contributed to the party's defeat in the district.

However, a bench full of such congressmen would not necessarily be an improvement. It would make it even more difficult for the PRD to coordinate actions, provide effective leadership, build a common ideological proposal, or foster an image of the party as a credible alternative government. Without these qualities, its national presence and support will undoubtedly suffer. Relaying the demands of dozens of popular movements does not *ipso facto* give a party a broad, consistent ideological perspective to offer the electorate. Rather, people may perceive it as simply the tool of small groups, and the party's very usefulness to popular movements may drive away voters outside the popular movements—in Mexico, the vast majority. The party may also suffer from divisions among competing popular movements. Popular movements need parties that will prioritize popular movement needs, and yet still be effective enough electorally to survive and give them the institutional position to pursue their goals. This is difficult to achieve.

Political Cycles and Collective Action Problems in the Left–Movement Relationship

Despite obstacles that discourage the formation of permanent institutional alliances, popular movements may benefit from strategic, conjunctural alliances. A strong left party can improve the bargaining leverage of local popular movements. There can be little doubt that the emergence of Cárdenas as a serious threat influenced Salinas's decision to implement a major social spending program after years of

---

[23] Confidential interview P, May 1991.   [24] Personal observation of meeting, May 1991.

stagnation and cuts in social spending. The ability of popular movements to get access to Solidarity money owes at least something to the PRI's aim of dividing them from the *cardenistas*. The government's eagerness to support the Partido del Trabajo also owes something to its desire to split the Cárdenas vote. At best, then, elections offer a chance to put movement leaders in positions of state authority; at worst, elections may become a strategic option for attracting state attention, convincing the state of the mobilization capacity of the movement, and getting favorable terms for negotiation.

Indeed, some popular movements viewed 1988 in such strategic terms, including the CDP-Durango, whose defection was taken as a sign of popular movement disillusionment with Cárdenas. The CDP formed an electoral alliance with the Partido Mexicano Socialista (PMS) for 1988. CDP leader Marcos Cruz stated baldly that 'the alliance with the PMS is a conjunctural alliance. We are not convinced that it is the most suitable unitary project of the left. That means, obviously, that we have no intention of participating organically in it, although we will [particip- ate] with its parliamentary bench . . . Our strategic project continues to be the construction of autonomous organizations of masses. Under this optic we will par- ticipate in elections' (Hernández 1988*b*: 30). A number of smaller organizations expressed similar views:

[we got involved] through a group of the Asamblea de Barrios, who see that tactically the personality of Cuauhtémoc Cárdenas is important for the movement . . . it permitted us to think about winning in the majority districts. Besides, the popular leaders of represent- ative organizations could get a place in the Chamber of Deputies and push from there to resolve the demands of the population. [*Unión de Cuartos de Azotea e Inquilinos del DF*]

The object was to use the electoral space to fix [our] influence, consolidate [our] work, and seek new spaces for organization and popular struggle. [*Unión de Vecinos de la Colonia Guerrero*] (Palomo 1988: 9–10)

Thus, in discussing the purpose of participation, most popular movements did not emphasize the creation or strengthening of a political party. Rather, they tended to perceive electoral participation as a way of putting their members in office, and interpreted the results in terms of their *own* organizational strength. In one study of ten small *colonia* groups, nine participated on behalf of their own candidates nominated through different political parties; the tenth participated on behalf of another group's candidates (Palomo 1988: 9–10). Afterwards, CDP leader Gonzalo Yáñez argued that: 'For us, electoral participation was very im- portant . . . in the heat of the campaign, we grew significantly. We could push the struggle against the contamination of our water at a higher level; we were linked closely with more than thirty peasant groups . . . establishing consolidated rural bases . . . and if that weren't enough, we could equip ourselves with certain infra- structure for our permanent functions . . . a small press, and a computer center' (Hernández 1988*a*: 28). Such movements—to the extent that any party could attract them—preferred a federated party project, essentially a legal fiction through which each movement could nominate its candidates. This was in fact the kind of party the CDP later helped create. The PMS and the ex-*priistas* had in mind something quite different.

Nevertheless, in 1993, on the suggestion of Cárdenas, the PRD voted to reserve 50 per cent of its candidacies in 1994 for such conjunctural alliances with 'popular sectors'. Under these circumstances, movements expressed some interest in participating in the 1994 electoral campaign, on behalf of Cárdenas and of their own candidates. However, particularly at the national level (congressional candidacies), the more successful movements had established relationships to internal PRD currents, or even participated themselves in the national leadership of the PRD (for example, Asamblea de Barrios leader Marco Rascón). Said one observer, 'the balance that had to be guaranteed internally eliminated the possibility of offering candidacies to more organizations of the alliance [the group of organizations that supported the candidacy of Cárdenas]'; or, in the words of Marco Rascón, 'the dynamic of the party itself exceeded its commitments, and therefore, to avoid splits, [we] opted for reaching consensus inside' (Ballinas and Urrutia 1994: 52). The policy did attract some additional participants, including defectors from various other political parties. However, these alliances are no more likely to result in permanent institutional relationships than in 1988. There is even reason to question whether all those elected by the PRD (especially the dissident *panistas* on its slate) will cooperate consistently with the PRD bench.

Thus, over time one might see a deterioration in the cyclical pattern of attachment which popular movements might ideally prefer, to maximize their power through strategic maneuvering in and out of the left's orbit. In the first place, the left may have trouble sustaining itself as a threat in the intervals between its *encuentros* with popular movements. Popular movement defections do hurt the PRD, damaging its image and depriving it of organizational and voting support. However, as the PRD develops a support base that enables it to survive on its own, popular movements tend to lose influence. This in itself poses problems for party responsiveness to popular movements. A less dependent PRD has less incentive to pay attention to popular movements, and may feel little obligation to those who have 'betrayed' them.

Therefore, the continued loyalty of some popular movements to the PRD becomes crucial. Not only does it appear a surprising outcome, given the obstacles this chapter has already discussed, but their support helped the PRD keep some credentials as a popularly based party, and survive several lean years. In its alliance with these movements, the PRD somehow overcame the collective action problem that affects its relationship with popular movements in general: the fact that while it may be to the collective advantage to have a strong left party as a threat, individual movements may gain more by defecting.

To understand why movements remain allied to the PRD, it seems appropriate to examine the case of the Asamblea de Barrios and (to a lesser extent) the Unión de Colonias Populares (UCP), two of the most important movements that continued to cooperate relatively closely with the PRD. While a complete analysis must await more information, preliminary information suggests three key reasons for support: (1) greater ideological and tactical affinity with the PRD; (2) strategic motivations arising from the movements' location in Mexico City; and (3) selective incentives available to leaders of these movements.

Socioeconomic and demand differences do not entirely explain outcomes, but may give the Asamblea greater tactical flexibility. The Asamblea de Barrios formed as a coordinating committee of urban popular movements in Mexico City in April 1987, to alter the terms of struggle of the older National Coordinating Committee of Urban Popular movements (CONAMUP) and the Coordinating Committee of Earthquake Victims (CUD). The demands of the Asamblea have tended to reflect more overtly political concerns and awareness of larger struggles.[25] The Asamblea also stressed the concerns of relatively better-off residents of the city center—such as rent control—in addition to the service and infrastructure gaps on which CONAMUP focuses. Of the initial members of the AB, 63.5 per cent were renters, higher than in CONAMUP *colonias populares* (Ramírez Sáiz 1991–2: 115). Since renter concerns do not fit well into Solidarity programs, Solidarity funding may tempt Asamblea organizations less.[26] Nevertheless, the social bases of the UCP look more similar to those of CONAMUP. Furthermore, CONAMUP organizations defend renter concerns in addition to the *colonia popular* agenda.

Tactical preferences look more promising as an explanation. The CONAMUP emphasizes negotiation with the government and non-electoral activity. It maintained non-affiliation, and a number of its member organizations broke with the PRD over its confrontational stance. Its dominant current, associated with the Linea de Masas, has long been skeptical of electoralism. Other organizations believe the PRD is neither confrontational enough, nor radical enough, to bring about real change. The PRD-allied Asamblea de Barrios, in contrast, encourages non-violent confrontation and electoral participation. The Asamblea openly argues that 'concertation'—the negotiation of cooperative agreements with the state—can demobilize, divide, depoliticize, and disarticulate popular movements. Confrontation, on the other hand, produces opposite effects; such actions should therefore occupy a privileged place in the tactics of popular movements. Furthermore, Asamblea leaders favored the broadest possible alliances with other social sectors—an objective facilitated by alliance with a national political party. Without a national party, said one, the 'weight of regionalisms' would have increased, and democratic forces would have been scattered.[27] They argue that electoral participation is vital for achieving real progress in popular struggles, that it reinforces the movement's

---

[25] Ramírez Sáiz (1991–2: 103–29). On the Asamblea de Barrios, see also Cuellar (1993).
[26] Indeed, World Bank restrictions on some funds that went into Solidarity cut out a major Asamblea expenditure—the purchase of land (unlike other popular movements, the Asamblea tends to buy land rather than invading it). In part as a result of this restriction, and in part as a result of government hostility, Asamblea activists reported 'very little' access to Solidarity. Confidential interviews, Sept. 1994.   [27] Confidential interview, Sept. 1994.

territorial presence, and that it transforms simple mediators into 'more transcendent' figures.[28] These perspectives coincide nicely with those of the dominant tendency of the PRD.

However, these similarities do not fully explain continuing alliance with the PRD. In the first place, these organizations are far from monolithic. All experience internal divisions over tactical questions, including electoral participation and confrontation/negotiation. Many organizations now in the Asamblea signed a Convenio de Concertación para la Reconstrucción in 1986 while members of the Coordinating Committee of Earthquake Victims. Similarly, UCP organizations accept government money and aid. The line between 'negotiation' and 'confrontation' blurs quickly; indeed, both tactics may represent different moments of one process. In the second place, it is difficult to establish the direction of causality. The Asamblea has little prior history against which to measure its current preferences. It coalesced less than a year before the 1988 electoral struggle. The tactical preferences of its leaders were probably influenced by this experience, in which confrontation and electoral participation did strengthen popular movements. Their continued contact and close cooperation with the PRD reinforced these tactical positions. The UCP has a longer pre-PRD history. One of the first coordinating groups, it pre-dates the CONAMUP by two years. Yet from the beginning, the UCP openly argued in favor of electoral participation, and in spite of harsh criticism from the dominant leadership of CONAMUP. Nevertheless, not all organizations that used confrontational tactics or participated in elections remained allied to the PRD. Other factors must play a role.

A second hypothesis suggests that regional location affects alliance potential, due to wide variations in the local strength of the PRD. In Nuevo León, for example, as in much of northern Mexico, the PRD practically does not exist. There is naturally less incentive for the Frente Popular Tierra y Libertad of Monterrey to go out of its way to stick with a party that can give them no local support, mediation assistance, or opportunities to place members in government positions through elections. In contrast, because of its strength in Mexico City, the PRD can offer movements there an important capacity for mobilization, logistical support, considerable organization, and—most importantly—the opportunity to elect representatives. Both the UCP and the Asamblea de Barrios are basically Mexico City organizations. Although Asamblea leaders complain about the party's slow (or null) response to their requests for mobilizational support, and its tendency to expect a contingent of Asamblea supporters whenever an Asamblea leader is invited to some event, they clearly appreciate the advantages of getting one of their members into government. Even the ability to use official letterhead paper for petitions helps, said one.[29]

Furthermore, because the PRD itself is not a unified organization, movements may fare better or worse depending on the quality, priorities, and judgments of

---

[28] Confidential interviews, Sept. 1994.   [29] Confidential interview, Sept. 1994.

local PRD leaders. Some go out of their way to defer to popular movements; others try to dominate and manipulate them. At the micro level, this affects movement attitudes toward the party. The proximity of Mexico City movement leaders to influential national PRD activists may enhance their sense of centrality. Not only do they tend to have more regular, open access to top PRD leaders,[30] but their presence in an area of great PRD interest (the capital) enhances their importance to party leaders. The case of Tabasco tends to confirm the importance of this factor. Tabasco's state president, Andrés Manuel López Obrador, is widely acknowledged for his attention to popular movement struggles and his capacity to lend party support to their demands. He has also achieved greater integration with popular movements (even making some headway in the PRI petroleum workers union), and—probably not coincidentally—greater electoral improvement than virtually any other state.

Yet ultimately, such success depends heavily on political will, personal style, and the availability of suitable popular movement allies. The type of access and influence given to (or won by) popular movements within the party is an aspect of selective incentives that may prove the most important factor in explaining popular movement participation in left parties. Mancur Olson has shown that such selective incentives operate on the individual level to improve the chances for successful collective action and group commitments (Olson 1971). Incentives like leadership positions and candidacies can attract popular movement leaders on several grounds. Such positions may enhance a leader's prestige within his own movements; they may also provide some security against betrayal (though not against co-optation). When a movement member occupies the party's legislative seat, supporters have a chance to hold him accountable within the framework of the movement as well as the party, though Mexico's constitutional ban against re-election prevents voters from either punishing or rewarding elected representatives. Furthermore, in the PRD, movement leaders with close political and personal ties in the party had a better chance of getting positions. This may well account for the reproduction of patterns of affiliation. For the present, all three factors—tactical and ideological preferences, regional location, and selective incentives—seem necessary to an explanation of popular movement loyalty to the PRD.

Explaining the Left–Movement Dynamic

None of these factors, however, has much to do with neoliberal policies. Indeed, much of this analysis has focused on strategic incentives as shaped by institutional arrangements, and not on the particular policies adopted by a neoliberal

---

[30] Indeed, several became important figures in the national leadership. One of the Asamblea's top four leaders (Marco Rascón) was president of the PRD in the Federal District, and is now on the National Executive Committee. This helps considerably in a party that operates to a great extent on personal ties.

government. Neoliberal policies may discourage states from taking sides with popular sectors against business interests, upon which the success of the free-market strategy ultimately depends, but do not preclude the adoption of socially oriented policies designed to bolster the legitimacy of the government. Such policies—far from contradicting the neoliberal project—may stabilize it by giving the neoliberal coalition popular support it would not otherwise attract. Yet it is the organization of an effective anti-neoliberal coalition that appears most significant in sparking such policy changes, not the neoliberal approach *per se* or even the existence of discontent. This is by no means automatic, though one cannot conclude from this that neoliberal policies have no impact on the relationship between popular movements and the left. Neoliberal policies played a major role in bringing about the formation of the PRD in 1988–9, sharpening elite divisions and popular discontent, and driving opponents together in a broad coalition to block neoliberalism. This in turn created a different strategic environment for popular movements —including those that chose not to formalize an alliance with the PRD. Nevertheless, the theoretical question remains: what can we generalize from these events about the impact of neoliberal policies on left–movement articulation? With more specification of the facilitating conditions in 1988, I think Mexican events suggest three major hypotheses:

1. The impact of neoliberal policies depends on their short-term economic effects.

The package of 'neoliberal policies' does not have a uniform and predictable economic impact. Although it reduces the parsimony of the analysis, it seems necessary to specify the economic impact of 'neoliberal programs' on popular classes and government finances. The rejection of neoliberal policies in 1988 resulted largely from the social impact of the crisis and the perception that PRI policies worsened the situation by exposing fragile Mexican companies to international competition and by cutting back social services. A neoliberal approach may leave popular classes unprotected from the effects of the market, but the market does not always have as devastating an impact as it did in the 1980s in Mexico. The severity of the crisis drove popular movements and elites to take unaccustomed risks in 1988, risks they were not willing to continue to take when the economic and political environment changed. Furthermore, the level of scarcity in government finances varies by country and time period. These two points affect the effort *needed* to win back popular support and the effort that the government can *finance*. For example, while the Mexican government began privatization in the mid-1980s, it did not sell off more profitable companies until 1990–1. Proceeds from these sales helped support a dramatic expansion of Solidarity that otherwise seemed unlikely. Likewise, debt relief won by the Mexican government in 1989 contributed to inflation control and relieved pressure on the federal budget.

2. Neoliberal governments discriminate against appeals made on a class basis. This tends to undermine linkages between left parties and popular organizations.

Responsiveness to popular class appeals could result in confrontations with capital which neoliberal governments are unwilling to risk, given their dependence on private capital as the engine of economic growth. Neoliberal governments want to avoid policies that change factor prices from market values, and in any case have usually not been able to afford large-scale subsidies under fiscal austerity. However, a Solidarity-type program can select targets based on non-class criteria (like poverty, or support for the opposition), and provide public benefits that do not seriously distort prices. Because left parties tend to make broad appeals that evoke class demands, affiliation can hurt popular movements that might otherwise maneuver in the gray space of non-class-based politics. If they oppose neoliberalism, left parties also attract government hostility. These factors encourage popular movements to avoid close linkage.

3. Neoliberal policies tend to weaken the bargaining position of popular sectors. However, a strong electoral left can mitigate this trend. Therefore, one may see strategic electoral alliances between popular movements and the left.

Under neoliberal governments, social sectors—often with greater needs— pursue fewer state resources. Shrinking state budgets left popular movements and other social sectors out in the cold for much of the 1980s. However, the existence of a credible left threat to the neoliberal project encouraged the state to pay more attention (and devote more resources!) to these sectors and movements. Thus the paradox: a strong left party alternative may improve bargaining leverage to get resources out of the state, but individual movements can only take maximum advantage of their bargaining leverage by abandoning the left party. They may therefore try to move toward the left when this could bolster the left's status as an electoral threat, and away from the left during inter-election periods. This strategy involves risks of miscalculation which may weaken the movement back toward the left party—i.e. the left party may be too far gone by the time movements decide to renew the alliance, or the left may no longer be willing to accept them. Thus, like a pendulum that loses its momentum, each swing back toward the left may carry fewer movements, until a new crisis gives an additional push.

Nevertheless, the analysis as a whole suggests that the institutional context and the general party system have a far greater impact, and even shape the effect of neoliberal economic policies on patterns of left–movement articulation. A system of relatively strong parties, in which most unions are already captured, offers different opportunities to left parties to change patterns of popular representation than systems in which parties are traditionally weak and ephemeral. In Mexico, the PRD could claim some of the credit for improvement in PRI responsiveness (albeit limited to social spending programs) and for demonstrating the potential of left–party alliances. However, because of the context in which it emerged and its own characteristics, patterns of articulation did not change as dramatically as PRD founders anticipated.

7 | The Politics of Identity Reconstruction: Indians and Democracy in Ecuador[1]

Melina Selverston

Introduction

The indigenous movement in Ecuador has emerged in recent years as one of the most important social movements in the country. In the context of the shift from developmentalist to neoliberal economic models, the indigenous movement is providing a political voice for one of the most excluded sectors of Ecuadorian society. In this chapter I will demonstrate how, by demanding participation for the indigenous sector, leaders of the movement are challenging the lack of democratic participation in the national political system. Concurrently, by questioning the economic issues which affect them, such as land tenure, the movement challenges the neoliberal framework of economic reform in the country. Within that context, by defining themselves as a social group excluded from the country's economic and political development, the indigenous movement may provide the opportunity to disclose structural inequalities in the political system and to propose alternatives to those structures.

Politics in Ecuador today, as in much of Latin America, is largely defined by state-led economic reform focused on the privatization of national industries, liberalization of market restrictions, and technological advancement in industry, particularly the export sector. As many analysts have noted, these reforms tend to affect dramatically the poorer sectors of society who benefited from job security or price controls, leading, in many cases, to social unrest. In Ecuador, these policies were implemented through President Sixto Durán Ballén's 'Modernization Law'.

[1] This research was supported by a grant from the Organization of American States, and FLACSO-Ecuador provided institutional support. I am indebted to indigenous activists and friends in Ecuador who are too many to name. In particular, I thank Luís Macas, Fabián and Humberto Muenala, and the CONAIE leadership and staff. A special thanks to Mario, Efraín, and Rosita for their constant help. Thanks to Jorge León for inspiring conversation. Doug Chalmers and Monique Segarra gave useful comments on earlier drafts.

One of the most important economic sectors in Ecuador to be affected by privatization, agriculture, also directly affects the indigenous subsistence economy based on small-scale agricultural production in the highlands. In the following pages I will briefly examine both the indigenous political response to modernization of agricultural production, and the political struggle for bilingual indigenous education in the country. Through analyzing these two cases I will suggest some ways in which the indigenous movement has affected the political process.

In both cases, I argue, the focus of the demands by indigenous leaders is participation. Indigenous leaders are demanding that their perspectives be taken into account in the development plans for their lands and environment. The centrality of 'participation' as a demand is a result of the context of exclusion in which the indigenous movement developed.

Indians have gained few positions and count on few allies within the state, but they have succeeded in winning a political space for themselves in both national and local politics. They have brought their issues firmly onto the political agenda. This has been achieved partly through demonstrations of organizational capability, such as a monumental indigenous uprising that dramatically affected commerce in the country for a week in 1990 and, partly, as will be demonstrated below, through influencing society's general understanding about Indians.[2]

Indigenous intellectuals, I argue, have successfully permeated Ecuadorian society with an 'indigenous ideology' that has influenced the way the dominant mestizo culture perceives Indians, as well as the way that Indians think about themselves. One of the most effective ways in which the 'ideology' has been spread is through bilingual literacy campaigns and education. The process of teaching society, both native and non-native, that the indigenous language was legitimate allowed bilingual education workers to inform the public about the reality of the indigenous condition. At the time of the 1990 uprising, one statistical study shows, 'there was a national consensus: most Indians live in sub-human conditions and it is the responsibility of all of Ecuadorian society to resolve this situation' (Nieto 1993: 61).

The indigenous population of Ecuador resides mostly in the rural highlands, where it constitutes a majority of the population, and in the Amazon region, where the people live in dispersed communities. There are small indigenous communities in the coastal region as well. There is no accurate count of the indigenous population because ethnic identity is inconsistent, the strong effort towards acculturation continues, and because, as a recent statistical survey notes, there is 'an absence of statistical data collected with the express goal of measuring the ethnic variable' (Zamosc 1993: 5). The largest indigenous group are the Quichua, who predominate in the highlands. In the Amazon there are more Quichua as well as the Shuar-Achuar, Secoya, Siona, Huaorani, Cofan, and in the coast there are Tsachila, Chachi, and Awa communities.

[2] For an analysis of the uprising see Selverston (1993).

Throughout the chapter I will refer to the most prominent indigenous organization at the national level, the Confederation of Indigenous Nationalities of Ecuador, CONAIE. According to the Ministry of Education, CONAIE represents 70 per cent of the indigenous population, which is about 40 per cent of the total national population. CONAIE was formed in 1986 to unite indigenous federations of each province. The motor behind the 1990 Uprising, CONAIE quickly became the national and international representative of Ecuador's indigenous people and the political center of the indigenous movement.

In this chapter I argue that the indigenous movement in Ecuador is challenging the meaning of citizenship and democratic participation through the framework of its distinct identity. This analysis complements a growing body of literature concerning identity-based movements in Latin America, but is an attempt to carry the discussion further into the actual political ramifications of these movements. How do they affect the distribution of power and the structures of the political system? Is identity an effective way for civil society to organize? In the case of the indigenous organizations, I argue that in their struggle for what appear to be sectarian concerns they are actually one of the strongest influences towards the opening of the democratic system in Ecuador.

The chapter will begin with a discussion of the history of exclusion to provide context for the two cases. This is followed by a discussion of what I refer to as the modern indigenous ideology, including reference to the 'class vs. ethnicity' debate, and the actual precepts of the ideology.

With this background established, the chapter presents two cases of indigenous political intervention, first in the struggle for bilingual bicultural education, and second in the response to plans for economic reforms in the agricultural sector. Finally, the case-studies are followed by a brief comparative analysis and some conclusions.

A Context of Exclusion

Exclusion of indigenous peoples in Ecuador is cultural, economic, and political. It is cultural in the sense that a colonialist mentality of Spanish domination of indigenous peoples laid the framework for the development of a European-style nation-state that required economic and political integration and projects of forced cultural assimilation. Indigenous models of societal organization were considered inferior to the European ones, as were the people, and the resulting relationship was one of cultural domination. This history still influences political authorities in the country to the extent that the governor of one province recently said in an interview 'the reason Ecuador is so poor is that we have too many Indians'.[3]

Colonial relations of production also led to the economic exclusion of indigenous

---

[3] Interview, Loja province, 1993.

peoples. The indigenous population in the highlands was not given a reprieve from semi-feudal agrarian structures, such as the *encomienda*, and *Huasipungo*, the Ecuadorian form of land tenure, until the agrarian reform in the 1960s and 1970s. Large landholdings, however, still dominate the highland economy and land shortage due to demographic pressures continues to place immense economic and social pressure on local communities. Small farmers still control only 30 per cent of cultivable land (Charvet 1991: 239).

In the Amazon, agrarian reform had a different impact on indigenous communities. The 1964 Agrarian Reform law included 'as a national urgent priority the colonization of the Amazon region'.[4] In response to demographic pressures in the highlands, the government gave land titles to colonists who cleared and produced on land that was considered vacant. Vacant land was defined as that which has 'remained uncultivated for more than ten consecutive years'.[5] Unfortunately much of the colonized land was indigenous territory, part of its complex system of 'foresting', or living with the land in an ecologically sound manner without permanent clearcutting. Thus, while some Indians in the highlands gained land titles through agrarian reform, the net result for indigenous groups in the Amazon was a loss of territory.

Economic and cultural exclusion reinforced the political exclusion of indigenous people that prevails in Ecuador. Currently, there is only one indigenous member of Congress, a bilingual educator from the Amazon who was once a member of CONAIE. At the provincial level indigenous participation as elected representatives is practically non-existent. This low level of participation has become a central issue of the modern indigenous platform. Indigenous leaders claim that the current system is a foreign one which fails to respect indigenous cultures or acknowledge their existence. A Shuar intellectual explained: 'The Constitution and the Laws do not represent our aspirations, nor are they meant to. They are laws of an unjust society, a different society, culture, politics, and structure that do not correspond to our reality.'[6] Another local leader made a similar observation when asked what he wanted from the state: 'That they consider that we are also a part of the state and we have rights just like everyone else, which we are now demanding.'[7] Indigenous activists argue that the Ecuadorian nation-state is not 'theirs', and until it is they have a right to challenge its legitimacy.

As many analysts have noted, the nation-state is a relatively new construct that, in many cases, does not correspond to the culture and society it means to represent.[8] The building of a single nation-state, these authors point out, has become a goal of modern development. In the 'third world' it is considered a necessary step towards democracy.[9] However, in many cases, the process of nation-building in

---

[4] 'Ley de Colonización de la Región Amazónica', 89.
[5] 'Ley de Tierras Baldías y Colonización', 89.
[6] Interview with Karakras, 1991.　　[7] Interview, leader from Bolívar province, 1991.
[8] For examples, see Warren (1993), Gellner (1983), Anderson (1983), Smith (1989).
[9] For example, see Rustow (1970).

Latin America created a political system based on exclusion rather than inclusion. In Ecuador, the tension between the demands of the nation-state and the reality of political exclusion based on ethnicity has been expressed in a myriad of ways.

In Ecuador, illiterate persons, a group that included most of the indigenous population, were allowed to vote for the first time in the post–military regime 1979 elections. Although they were legally freed from service tenure in 1964, they were not yet free of their impoverished condition in the agricultural sector, as is further discussed below. The nation-building project that has included teaching Spanish to the indigenous population in an attempt at cultural integration has been contradicted by the socioeconomic separation of the indigenous population, I argue. The modern indigenous movement is now capitalizing on its context of exclusion to strengthen its identity as an indigenous people.

Finding a Voice: The Development of an Indian Ideology

The fact that a university student, an indigenous intellectual in Quito, a bilingual schoolteacher in the countryside, and an indigenous peasant all respond in the same way to a question about their indigenous identity suggests that they share a similar political ideology. By ideology I mean 'the ideas and beliefs that symbolize the conditions and life-experience of a specific, socially significant group or class'.[10] The above-mentioned individuals live in very different contexts and have diverse material needs, but they share the experience of marginalization because they are Indians. When asked, for example, what the main issue of the 1990 Uprising was, they all answered, 'dignity'. The shared ideology, or understanding of their condition, is the result of the evolution of modern organizing, political debate, and the process of bilingual education. Out of the land struggles in the countryside during the 1970s and 1980s, an indigenous movement emerged that differentiated itself from the traditional left in Ecuador.

CLASS AND ETHNICITY

The story of the modern indigenous organizations in Ecuador can be told in terms of the theoretical and practical struggle between class-based and ethnic-based movements.[11] Many indigenous organizations, particularly in the highlands, were

[10] This definition is taken from Geuss (1981). For a wonderful discussion of meaning and debates about ideology see Eagleton (1991). Modern discussion of ideology considers that the subordinate classes can develop an ideology that can challenge that of the dominant class. Thus, ideology is linked to social transformation. (See the work of Marcuse for example.)

[11] For a class-based perspective of this process see Ibarra (1987). There is less written from the ethnic perspective, but Sánchez Parga (1990) provides a solid example.

shaped by a leftist ideology based on the *campesino* struggle for land and by left-ist parties' struggle for political power. Using an organizing ideology based on class struggle, however, appeared in many ways to contradict the goals of the indigenous communities.

Classic Marxist-Leninist theory, for example, calls for the unification of the oppressed classes under a vanguard party. In rural Ecuador, however, there exists vehement discrimination against indigenous groups by the Hispanic population, making unity amongst them extremely difficult. Luís Macas, president of CONAIE, pointed out that: 'A mestizo worker and an Indian are both exploited, but the worker has a higher social status, so he has the privilege of insulting the Indian.'[12] Similarly, many of the perspectives of indigenous and mestizo workers differed significantly. For example, Ibarra argues that the leftist intellectuals of the period saw the Ecuadorian state as a tool of capitalist development, while intellectuals who focused on ethnicity, often young indigenous scholars and anthropologists, were likely to see the state as defending a dominant culture rather than a dominant economic class.[13]

These types of differences became evident not only in discourse but in the actual organizational process. Mass strikes that increase the power of workers in a labor dispute are not necessarily appropriate in a land struggle. Although indigenous communities supported workers' strikes during the 1970s, they found that they did not receive the same type of solidarity from labor in their land struggles.[14] It became evident that the indigenous leaders needed to develop their own strategies, although they retained many strategic elements from the traditional left, such as confrontational tactics (Zamosc 1994: 282). Moreover, there is no evidence that indigenous organizations in Ecuador have ever been involved in armed subversion, and it is often inaccurate to categorize indigenous groups as 'the left' since their ideology differs and they generally try to distinguish their position from leftist parties' positions.[15]

In the 1970s, while the workers' movement was at its height and the first Indians were attending college, the left had a more direct influence on indigenous communities. In order to launch indigenous candidates, mostly in provincial or cantonal elections, indigenous organizations affiliated with parties such as the Socialist party, or the Broad Leftist Front (FADI).[16] This linkage increasingly became important in the 1979 elections, when many indigenous communities, freed from voting restrictions, voted for the first time. Young indigenous intellectuals, especially in the highlands, were influenced by the left, as were other youth in the country:

[12] Interview, Luís Macas, 1991.
[13] 'Dominant culture' is an anthropological term referring to the cultural group that controls the sources of authority in a society, and thus influences cultural reproduction, often imposing cultural values (Ibarra 1987). [14] Interview, María Pacca, 1991.
[15] In fact, some current indigenous leaders were involved in an armed movement in Colombia in the past, and some past members of the Ecuadorian subversive organization 'Alfaro Vive, Carajo', who at the time were critical of the movement, are now working closely with indigenous issues.
[16] See Ayala-Mora (1989) for descriptions of parties in Ecuador.

Maybe we weren't members, but we were sympathizers, helpers of the Socialist movement, what with everything that was happening with Allende in Chile . . . We were the ones who translated what they wanted to say in the indigenous communities, and when we began to talk about our own proposals, like indigenous education, they started to get angry.[17]

Throughout the tenuous alliance there was debate among Indians about the efficacy of workers' organizations and leftist parties to resolve the specific problems of the indigenous population. For example, in one of the first land takeovers, in Chimborazo province in 1988, FADI supporters began to produce on an hacienda. However, after a month they were dislocated by indigenous supporters of the MPD (Democratic Popular Movement) who had an allegiance to the landowner. According to one participant, the dispute between the leftist political parties led to division among the indigenous communities themselves.[18]

When indigenous intellectuals began to discuss bilingual education and to challenge the Marxist discourse that cultural differences would disappear with the revolution, it was perceived as a threat to some established Indian groups that were formed with a class-based ideology, such as the Indian Federation of Ecuador (FEI), which was formed by the Communist Party in 1944. 'There was not a strong identification with Indian-ness (*lo indígena*) in the Sierra, although their roots were all indigenous identity . . . Any other movement that wanted to emerge, in this case the indigenous movement, was considered racist, separatist, and divisionist.'[19] As the traditional left began to lose power in Ecuador, in the 1980s, older class-based organizations, such as Ecuarunari, the largest indigenous federation representing the highlands, began to adopt more of the indigenous 'identity-based' ideology that was developing in the countryside and among intellectuals.

THE IDENTITY-BASED IDEOLOGY

The indigenous movement in Ecuador can be said to have shifted from class-based to identity-based, but it was never divorced from the struggle for land. Land is usually at the center of any indigenous movement because it is an integral part of cultural reproduction as well as an economic necessity. It is the issue of land that brought together the two divergent perspectives of the indigenous movement of the early 1980s, according to leaders of the movement: 'There were two visions: the indigenist cultural vision, focused on bilingual education, and the class vision, focused on land conflicts. The two merged when we realized that we could not have our culture without land.'[20]

The vision that has emerged is still constantly changing, but can be seen as the framework of the ideology upon which today's indigenous movement is based. In order to present an overview of what the ideology encompasses, I will refer to the

---

[17]   Interview, Muenala, 1993.   [18]   Interview, Miguel Lluco.
[19]   Interview with Ampam Karakras, 1991.   [20]   Interview with Miguel Angel Carlosama, 1991.

political platform of the prominent Confederation of Indigenous Nationalities of Ecuador, CONAIE.

The CONAIE platform has expanded to include not only the resolution of land conflicts, but also specific political demands of the Ecuadorian state. In general, the movement asks for the rights of indigenous people to be treated as 'equal but different'. Analyst Jorge León has categorized the demands of the indigenous movement into three areas: ethnic, class, and citizenship (León, 51). Following this general typology, I will summarize the CONAIE platform in terms of culture, economy, and political policy.[21]

In the arena of culture, the work of CONAIE revolves primarily around educational issues, because that is where the government directly intervenes in cultural reproduction. The main demand is for bilingual, intercultural education, that there be guaranteed funding for the program, and that it be administered by Indians. Recently, CONAIE has included a stipulation that the Spanish-speaking population be required to study an indigenous language.

In the area of economics, the demand of the Confederation is that there be funding for and brevity in the resolution of land conflicts. This is an important issue, given the inefficiencies in the land redistribution program. For example, the government's Agrarian Reform Institute, INRAC,[22] may rule in favor of a community and against a landowner in a conflict, but fail to provide the necessary funds for the community to buy the lands in a timely manner. In some cases this situation lasts many years and leads to violent conflicts.[23] Another constant demand emanating directly from the highland communities is for price controls on agricultural necessities, such as fertilizers. Other economic issues include the establishment of funds for indigenous development, and some level of profit-sharing for the indigenous communities of the Amazon from the state-owned petroleum industry based within their territory.

The most controversial and publicized policy demand by CONAIE is that the Constitution be changed to recognize Ecuador as a plurinational, pluricultural state. This proposal is extremely important because it would grant indigenous communities specific rights as 'different' citizens, as specified by the UN Human Rights Commission, according to their needs as 'peoples' with cultures. The CONAIE definition is as follows:

Plurinational State—Is the organization of government that represents the joint political, economic, and social power of the peoples and nationalities of a country: that is, the Plurinational State is formed when various peoples and nationalities unite under the same government, directed by a Constitution. This is distinct from the present Uninational State that only represents the dominant sectors. (CONAIE 1994: 52)

---

[21] For a brief outline of CONAIE demands see the Plurinational Mandate, Annex I. For a much more detailed version see the 'Political Project' of CONAIE, which can be obtained directly from the organization.   [22] Instituto Nacional de Reforma Agraria y Colonización.
[23] In the recent case of Yuracruz, for example, international pressure finally led to the expulsion of a hired 'security company' that had raped, tortured, and killed members of the indigenous association that INRAC had granted title to over seven years previously.

Based on my interviews with members of the Ecuadorian state and the Ecuadorian mestizo elite, it appears that government representatives are threatened by the concept of a plurinational state because it challenges their legitimacy as part of the dominant culture, and they argue against it on the grounds that it would divide an already small 'nation'. For example, the social scientist and ex-President, Osvaldo Hurtado (1979–84), gave the following comment on the issue: 'to speak of an Ecuador of many nationalities would not help the objectives that all Ecuadorians should strive towards: constructing, bit by bit, a unified nation' (Hurtado 1993: 33).

Although the level of autonomy under discussion varies among communities, the proposal at present is not to divide Ecuador. Instead CONAIE is striving to push the government to reflect the diversity of society and create a more inclusive, participatory system. CONAIE President Luís Macas explains: 'Little by little, the indigenous movement has qualitatively developed its struggle, its proposals. Before it was a struggle for survival, for land, for defense and recuperation of territories. Today it is a political proposal, and it is a proposal for all of society' (Macas 1991: 132).

Interestingly, while there are indigenous groups and individuals who oppose CONAIE, their 'ideologies' are surprisingly similar. Alberto Andrango is a leader of the National Federation of Campesinos (FENOC), a *campesino*/indigenous organization affiliated with a workers' union and which has a strong following only in its home canton of Cotocachi. FENOC is considered to be class-based, and has criticized CONAIE for being too 'culturalist', yet when asked about the objectives in forming the organization, Andrango replied: 'Against discrimination . . . the first point was respect for indigenous people.'[24] Similarly, José Quimbo, President Durán's adviser on indigenous affairs, is engaged in a bitter political rivalry with CONAIE, but when asked about his objectives, he claims that just by being in the National Palace he is winning respect for indigenous people by the ruling elite.[25] Both José Quimbo and Alberto Andrango agree with CONAIE that Ecuador is a plurinational country despite that concept's association with CONAIE.

Based on interviews throughout the country, it seems clear that the basic ideology that CONAIE has been promoting has generally been incorporated by indigenous communities as well as by other sympathetic sectors of society. This is not to say that there is no longer a discrepancy between the language of intellectual leaders and the needs expressed in local communities. Rather, the general conceptions of the conditions and goals of indigenous peoples are, to a large part, shared conceptions. Indigenous communities and intellectual leaders define themselves as 'nationalities'[26] that deserve respect and the same rights as mestizos, without having to give up their cultures.

[24] Interview with Andrango, 1991.   [25] Interview with Quimbo, 1993.
[26] According to Ileana Almeida, the term 'nationalities' seems to have been imported by anthropologists who studied the case of nationalities in the ex-Soviet Union (herself included). It refers to an ethnic group with a territorial component, something like a 'tribe' but without the negative (savage) connotations.

The political vision based in indigenous culture and identity is directly linked to the movement for bilingual education which will be described in more detail below. The movement for bilingual education taught pride in indigenous culture and at the same time created a generation of leaders throughout the country who shared that perspective. The movement was led by young indigenous intellectuals based primarily in Quito, who sparked a bilingual education project that was designed to promote native languages. Since colonial times, bilingual education was considered a method of teaching indigenous children Spanish and thus integrating them into the dominant mestizo culture. The new generation of leaders turned this notion on its head and used bilingual education to encourage cultural pride in their communities. They urged indigenous communities to fight back against the discrimination that made them ashamed to be Indians. The issue of discrimination had resounded in these communities, and by placing the issue of discrimination at the forefront, indigenous organizing flourished.

Politics of Identity: Bilingual Intercultural Education

According to most sources, including my own research, indigenous leaders in Ecuador today overwhelmingly received their political formation during the first bilingual literacy campaigns in the 1970s and early 1980s. The individuals trained in these programs became the conveyors of the new indigenous ideology. They also became political actors because of their involvement in the empowerment of their communities and their demands for changes in the national educational system. The political battles in the arena of national education policy climaxed in 1989 with an accord between CONAIE and the Ministry of Education and Culture that established the National Directorate of Indigenous Bilingual Intercultural Education (DINEIB), which oversees bilingual schools throughout the country.

The bilingual education movement has its roots in the radio literacy programs run by evangelical church groups in the Amazon, particularly the Summer Institute of Linguistics (SIL), and the progressive evangelical church of Monsignor Proaño in the highlands.[27] Because of rural geographic isolation and continuing illiteracy, radio is a major form of communication and news among the indigenous population. The radio programs taught Indians basic literacy using their own languages although the goal of the project was integration into the Spanish/mestizo culture. In contrast, an innovative literacy project by the Center for the Investigation of Indigenous Education (CIEI), at the Catholic University, trained indigenous people

[27] Proaño, known as the 'Bishop of the Indians', was a liberation theologist who was dedicated to work with the indigenous communities during his tenure, 1954–84. See Gavilanes del Castillo for more information. The Summer Institute of Linguistics has worked in the Amazon jungle for decades, controlling education, transportation, and territory in many parts of the jungle.

to teach Quichua literacy in the communities in order to retain rather than erad-
icate indigenous languages.

The CIEI program was innovative not only in that it intended to promote,
rather than diminish Quichua usage. It also represented a dramatic change in
government policy towards the language. The CIEI was supported by an agreement
with the Ministry of Education during the Roldós/Hurtado administration
(1979–84). The project, although led by a mestiza woman, was staffed almost fully
by indigenous students, many of whom are national leaders today, including Luís
Macas and José Quimbo, Director of the Office of Indigenous Affairs to President
Durán, to name just two.

The main projects of the CIEI were to train community educators to teach literacy in indigenous communities and to develop a curriculum for bilingual, bicultural education. It reflected a political decision by the Ecuadorian political center
to begin with adult literacy: 'We needed our adults to be an example to our children, so first we had to win them back.'[28] Workshops were held to train literate indigenous adults, delegated by their community organizations, to be instructors.
Over 1,000 educators, armed with CIEI didactic materials, returned to their communities during the period 1980–4. The choice to involve adults from the beginning enabled the program to achieve its other objective: the strengthening of
cultural identity.

Beyond the goal of promoting literacy, the content of the instruction materials
was structured to encourage students to resolve the problems facing them. In one
book, for instance, they were asked where they should go to complain if they did
not have electricity or potable water in their community. When they did not know
the answer, it was discussed, and in that way they were encouraged to take action
that previously they would have been too shy or ignorant to take.[29] Along with the
practical lessons in literacy, and local political processes, the students also learned
to value their language, and with it, their culture. In a country where, only a decade
before, schoolchildren were forced to cut their braids and speak Spanish, this constituted a significant change.

Perhaps the most remarkable evidence of the changing attitudes about the
Quichua language came in 1980 when the President elect, Jaime Roldós, gave part
of his acceptance speech in Quichua, recognizing the indigenous vote's contribution to his victory, and promising to defend their rights. The director of the CIEI
wrote: 'it was the first time a state authority addressed the population in a language
other than Spanish.' In practice, the action represents the fruit of years of work on
regaining the value of indigenous languages and cultures, in terms of both the dominant groups and the dominated. There is a new consciousness, although still passive, about the importance and value of the other languages spoken in the country
(Yañez Cossio 1991: 88). The importance of bilingual education was becoming
clearer among several indigenous organizations, including, for example, the

---

[28] Interview with Humberto Muenala, 1993.   [29] Interview with Tránsito Chela, 1993.

CONAIE member organization from the highlands, Ecuarunari, whose Marxist leadership had caused it to be suspicious of 'bourgeois' Indian intellectuals.

The CIEI, besides training instructors, oversaw the opening of 300 rural bilingual education schools with trained instructors and contributed to the reduction of illiteracy in the country from 25.7 per cent in 1979 to 12.6 per cent in 1984. Despite their successes, indigenous organizations claimed that the CIEI prevented their direct control over bilingual education. The fact that it was directed by a mestiza further delegitimized the center from their perspective. A direct agreement between CONAIE and the Ministry of Education and Culture was reached at the end of 1988 during the government of Rodrigo Borja. This contract instituted the National Directorate of Bilingual Intercultural Education (DINEIB), which, although administered by the Ministry, would be staffed by CONAIE.

The establishment of DINEIB was a triumph for the indigenous movement after many years of political struggle that ranged from lobbying politicians to occupying the Ministry of Education. Beyond the direct gains of having the government grant legitimacy to bilingual education and to CONAIE, there was a broader political impact, I argue: the agreement made a dent in the clientelism that greatly impedes democratic systems in Ecuador, especially in the countryside. Clientelist relations were directly affected by the shift in control over teachers in indigenous areas created by the establishment of the DINEIB.

The schoolteacher is often one of the most important influences in an indigenous community, and also one of the few steady jobs in the countryside. Prior to the establishment of DINEIB, the task of assigning teaching positions was the responsibility of national congressional representatives from each province, and their party representatives. With the establishment of DINEIB, the task was delegated to the indigenous organizations affiliated with CONAIE. The first Director of the DINEIB, Luís Monteluisa, reported:

I saw in Napo province, for instance, that the provincial Deputy (Representative to Congress) named 80 per cent of the teachers, the provincial Director of Education named 10 per cent, and the Party director the other 10 per cent. All of this power passed directly to the indigenous leaders.[30]

Congressional representatives strongly opposed President Borja's proposition to relinquish this important local power to the Indians. 'Some people didn't even realize it,' recalled Monteluisa, 'but others knew what it meant to administer education: there is power there.'[31] Although public figures rarely expressed their disapproval in public for political reasons, President Borja's party, the Democratic Left, secretly threatened to boycott him if he went through with the agreement. It took political acumen and pressure, but Borja did uphold his agreement with CONAIE, institutionalizing its influence throughout the country.[32]

DINEIB has been racked with political and economic difficulties since its

---

[30] Interview with Luís Monteluisa, 1993.   [31] Interview with Luís Monteluisa, 1993.
[32] Interview with Alfonso Calderón, 1993.

creation in 1988. In some cases clientelism has not been eradicated but simply transferred to a different social sector. In their haste to establish control, the regional indigenous organizations (members of CONAIE) did not always choose the most technically effective candidate for administrative positions, but rather the one most loyal to the organization. Similarly, since many of the teachers are also organization activists, they are allowed to miss an unacceptable amount of schooldays in order to attend assemblies, protests, etc.[33] While these problems, through a process of self-criticism, are being addressed, the politicized nature of the bilingual education process appears to be undermining its successful implementation. Despite a proliferation of literacy and education programs, the use of the Quichua language continues to drop at a dramatic rate (Zamosc 1994: 8–9).

The National Directorate of Bilingual Education is now a permanent institution within the Ministry of Education and Culture. The indigenous organizations consider it to be among their most important political triumphs. When President Durán (1992–present), early in his administration, attempted to dismantle CONAIE control of the Directorate he was met with mass protest and public criticism. In a press release regarding the changes, CONAIE stated that 'the Ecuadorian government is putting in serious danger the rights of the indigenous peoples of the country'.[34] The dramatic dismantling was halted, but negotiations continued within the Ministry to modify the bilingual education system.

DINEIB is not only a public affirmation of the continued existence of indigenous cultures, it is a concrete political space that assures the continued promotion of an indigenous ideology with the communities and at the national level. In their struggle to defend the survival of their culture, the indigenous people have also contributed to the democratization of the educational system by promoting the participation of local communities in choosing their teachers, who are important political actors in the countryside.

The story of bilingual intercultural education in Ecuador demonstrates that the indigenous movement, by organizing to defend its culture, is affecting the political system.[35] This trend can be further demonstrated by examining the issue of Agrarian production in the 'modernization' program of President Durán.

Agrarian Development and the Indigenous Voice

As Ecuador is predominantly an agrarian society, one of the priorities for national development is the modernization of the agricultural sector. While mechanized production of sugar cane and bananas for export exists in the coastal region, the majority of agricultural production in the highlands is traditional crop production

---

[33] Observations based on my field research and informational interviews.
[34] 'Indígenas Aclaran Situación de Educación Bilingüe', CONAIE archives, 23 Dec. 1992.
[35] This argument is developed more extensively in Selverston 1994.

for national consumption. The plan for 'modernizing' the agricultural sector has been the subject of controversy and social unrest in Ecuador. The indigenous sector has demanded to be included in the formulation of those plans.

Rural land tenure in Ecuador has been regulated by the Institute of Agrarian Reform and Colonization, IERAC, since its foundation through the 1964 agrarian reform law. The agrarian law was the first large-scale attempt to abolish the semifeudal-feudal agrarian system and to alter the unequal distribution of land in the countryside. The main effect was the transformation of the poor, mostly indigenous rural population, from indentured servants into rural laborers. In an attempt to strengthen the agrarian reform process, a second agrarian reform law was implemented by the populist military ruler General Rodríguez Lara in 1973. Included in the law was article 30, which provided for the expropriation of lands that were not sufficiently productive and became a basis for indigenous takeovers of large landholdings.[36]

The overall goal of the original agrarian reform laws was the redistribution of land tenancy and the abolition of semifeudal-feudal agricultural practices to promote small independent farms and modern capitalist relations in the countryside. In recent years new proposals for agrarian reform have emerged that correspond to the neo-liberal economic framework which is influencing development policies throughout Latin America today. The new agrarian project promotes modernization of agricultural practices in general, and export agriculture industry more specifically. The indigenous movement engaged in a struggle against these reforms in Ecuador in order to defend certain legal protections granted by the original agrarian reform laws.

The indigenous response to agrarian modernization plans began after President Durán presented a proposal for an agrarian development law to Congress in 1993. Favoring agribusiness, the proposal called for the removal of government intervention in land and agricultural products markets and for the sale of small plots. The proposal fit within President Durán's policy of privatization in order to 'modernize' the country and to quell inflation by increasing free market influences on the economy. CONAIE immediately protested the proposal, arguing that it represented the interests of only a small sector of society, and that it directly assaulted the life-style of the rural, indigenous population.

A main issue of concern for indigenous groups is changes in land tenure policy. The Ecuadorian constitution (at present) acknowledges four types of landholdings: private, public, mixed, and communal. The Agrarian Development Law proposal, CONAIE feared, would recognize only private property, disavowing the communal land ownership important to many indigenous communities. CONAIE declared the proposal unconstitutional, and took an unexpected step: CONAIE united with other rural organizations, including some historic adversaries, such as FENOC, and created an alternative agrarian law proposal.

---

[36] The indigenous groups call these takeovers 'land *recuperations*' while the dominant Spanish society refers to them as 'land *invasions*'. This is an interesting comment on discourse when one considers the use of the term 'invasion' by the Spanish about the Indians.

The alternative proposal was developed through a series of consultations, congresses, and workshops so that, theoretically, it would represent the proposals not only of CONAIE's intellectuals, but of indigenous people and *campesinos* throughout the country. The actual investigation and elaboration of the document was carried out by a committee called the Agrarian Coordinator, made up of representatives of the various participating indigenous organizations and led by CONAIE's legal advisers.

The alternative law focused on three principal issues: (1) production for internal consumption instead of export; (2) participation in decision-making at different levels of the political system; and (3) fair distribution of land. Moreover, the alternative law demanded the respect of communal landholding traditions, the preservation of indigenous territories, and the protection of the environment, as agricultural production increasingly incorporates modern technology. The proposal suggests that to increase production small farmers need incentives such as credits, rather than investing all of their small plots into agribusiness.[37]

On 9 June 1993, the Committee led a peaceful march of hundreds of indigenous leaders and their supporters to the National Congress to present their proposal. The President of the Congress, Carlos Vallejo, denied the Commission admittance, and instead called upon heavily armed police to guard the Congress. The event became violent, and the marchers were tear-gassed and beaten with billy clubs. The President of CONAIE, Luís Macas, was beaten over the head with a club, which caused an uproar when shown on television news that evening.

The indigenous leaders called for an 'Uprising' in response to police repression and the government's refusal to consider their point of view in its debate over national agricultural development. The short-lived Uprising of June 1993 closed sections of the Pan-American highway for a few days, and three Indians allegedly were killed during the protests. The protests coincided with the Soccer World Cup Qualifier that was being hosted by Ecuador that year. The indigenous leaders decided to take advantage of the international press to gain coverage for their cause. However, this strategy may have backfired, as the government and the national media, in general, accused the indigenous organizers of attempting to undermine the World Cup and promote a negative image of Ecuador, a country that is otherwise considered an 'island of peace' in the Andes and a haven for tourism. Thus, although unrest was quickly stabilized, the agrarian law was temporarily shelved.

Although the 1993 agrarian law protests may have been short-lived, they brought the debate about the agrarian law forcefully into the public sphere. Debate over the new law was postponed as members of Congress and the public questioned its validity. The Agrarian Coordinator Committee finally had its proposal submitted to Congress to be studied and debated. The proposal was, in fact, never introduced to the floor for debate but filed in the Agriculture Commission of Congress.

---

[37] 'Integral Agrarian Reform Project', published by CONAIE for the public.

A year later, without official discussions between government and indigenous groups, the 'Agrarian Development Law' was presented to Congress by the Social Christian Party, and signed into law by the Executive on 13 June 1994. The 'new' law adhered to the same basic principles as the 1993 law, with some language added to address indigenous and ecological issues.

As with the previous law, indigenous organizations claimed that the Agrarian Development Law was geared towards developing the export agriculture industry at the cost of small farmers. Article 15, for example, gives a five-year, 50 per cent tax break to new agro-industry businesses. The bias towards agro-industry in the law, indigenous groups claimed, directly challenged indigenous rights to small farms, credits, and even the communal way of life: 'The indigenous people cannot accept a law that promotes the re-concentration of land in the same hands as always and that prohibits indigenous communities access to land so that we, with no place to grow, will have to leave to die of hunger and misery in the cities.'[38]

In the Amazon, indigenous groups feared that the new law would promote further colonization of the rainforest. Although the law mentions ecological protection as a secondary point in some articles, they find that it is neither adequately elaborated nor specific in regard to monitoring measures.[39] For example, in article 36, after describing how the new law will help ethnic groups in the Amazon incorporate new technology (a policy that is questioned by CONAIE), the article reads, 'The actions, methods and instruments used should preserve the ecological system.' In both the Amazon and the Highlands, the general reaction to the new law was that the agrarian reform of the past was being replaced without consulting indigenous smallholders.

On 14 June, the day after the law was enacted, an unprecedented mobilization of the indigenous people of Ecuador began. During the mobilization, three indigenous activists were killed, and many more hospitalized, primarily from gunshot wounds. The number of detentions is still unknown. CONAIE, together with the two other national federations, the National Ecuadorian Federation of Campesino and Indigenous Organizations (FENOC-I) and the Evangelical Federation of Indigenous Ecuadorians (FEINE), called upon their member communities to protest the Agrarian Development Law.

The indigenous communities demanded that the law be overturned on the basis of its unconstitutionality. The new law was passed without the fifteen days of debate required by article 65 of the Constitution. The indigenous organizations had repeatedly called for national debate concerning agrarian reform. They claimed that the government was attempting to bypass that debate by putting the law through so quickly.

To protest the Agrarian Development Law hundreds of thousands of Indians closed strategic points on the Pan-American highway, preventing transportation of agricultural products to the cities, and refusing to bring their own produce to

---

[38] CONAIE press release, 14 June 1994.   [39] Interview with Leonardo Viteri, OPIP.

market. In some towns government buildings were taken over, and up to 30,000 indigenous protesters at a time filled the city streets in marches. In the Amazon, along with effective road blocks, three oil wells were taken over by indigenous communities and oil production was halted for days.

On 22 June the President passed a 'mobilization decree' giving the armed forces free rein to do whatever necessary to halt the protests.[40] (See Annex II for a partial list of repressive actions.) On 23 June the Tribunal of Constitutional Guarantees officially upheld the indigenous organizations' petition that the law was unconstitutional, and it sent the case to the Supreme Court. The President declared the pronouncement of the Tribunal invalid, but agreed to meet with the indigenous leadership to try to resolve the dispute.

As a result of the dialogue between the indigenous leadership and President Durán, a Commission was formed that included disparate members of society affected by the law, including indigenous and *campesino* representatives, members of the dairy farmers' association, a historically conservative and anti-indigenous group, members of government ministries, and the President himself. The main topics of discussion were water rights, land tenancy, and agricultural credits. Finally, after weeks of debate the working commission unanimously approved amendments in the Agrarian Development Law to incorporate many of the indigenous demands.

The events surrounding the Alternative Agrarian Law demonstrate the way that the indigenous movement is bringing into the public forum the continued exclusion of civil society from political decision-making in Ecuador. At the same time, CONAIE is providing a vehicle for sectors of civil society to present their interests to the government. If CONAIE did not exist, it is conceivable that the original Agrarian Law might have passed unnoticed by the small landholders in the countryside directly affected by it, because they are generally ill-informed of the nature of policy processes. CONAIE's attempts to intervene directly in the political system by proposing an alternative law to Congress and petitioning the Tribunal of Constitutional Guarantees were not directly effective. United with the mass demonstration of strength through the protests, however, CONAIE was able to bring its position to the negotiating table of the President. CONAIE argued that it was not only the issue of landholding that was at stake, but the very survival of indigenous cultures themselves, cultures which are centered on land relations and the cycles of agricultural production.

Indigenous Rights and Democratization

The story of the indigenous response to modernization of the agrarian sector and the story of the struggle for bilingual education both illustrate my argument: in

---

[40] The 'mobilization decree' is short of a state of emergency, which would call for stronger measures such as control of the press.

demanding participation in the political process surrounding issues which affect them, indigenous leaders are in fact challenging the lack of democratic participation in the political system as a whole. To discuss the cases comparatively I will refer to the questions I asked in the introduction: how does the indigenous movement affect the distribution of power and the structures of the political system? Is identity an effective way for civil society to organize?

In regard to the question concerning the distribution of power, both cases suggest that the indigenous movement, while mobilizing around sectarian issues, did indeed affect political structures. The creation of a bilingual education system not only challenged the hegemony of Hispanic culture but, as described above, it broke the practice by political party representatives of naming teachers in return for political favors such as money and votes. Beyond undermining clientelist relations, the indigenous movement was able to institutionalize indigenous participation in the Ministry of Education through the creation of the Directorate for Bilingual Intercultural Education.

The Agrarian Law battle did not lead to the institutionalization of indigenous participation in the Ministry of Agriculture, but it did lead to their participation in the Presidential Commission, where they were able to significantly alter the law in their favor. Moreover, the movement challenged the unofficial authority of the 'unholy alliance' of capitalist agricultural producers and the urban commercial elites that has traditionally controlled power and economic relations in rural Ecuador.[41] The large agricultural producers, particularly the Association of Dairy Farmers, were contributing authors to the original Agrarian Law. By protesting the law, the indigenous sector challenged the authority of the 'unholy alliance' to define agricultural policy for the entire country. The struggle against the Agrarian Law is an example of how the indigenous movement has widened the democratic arena through their demands to participate in defining policies which would affect them.

The second question refers to the effectiveness of political organizing based on identity, in this case, ethnic identification. Again, both cases suggest the effectiveness of identity-based organizing, within the context of continued exclusion. Indigenous communities have directly been excluded from economic and political power in Ecuador, and thus question their very citizenship in the nation, as described above. As Indians, then, their basic complaint with the Ecuadorian state is that they should be included, in other words, that they be given the opportunity to participate in the government. However, the very exclusion which has isolated the indigenous activists from the national politics has galvanized them into an organizational sector, and unites them in their desire for some sort of participation. Inherently, I argue, their political demands are centered around democratic participation.

---

[41] The term 'unholy alliance' originally referred to the alliance between hacienda owners and the Catholic Church. That alliance was replaced by the modern one with the growth of capitalism and agrarian reform (Korovkin 1993: 12).

This struggle for participation in the educational system was finally considered legitimate because the movement represented a large sector of society which was seeking to strengthen its identity. The indirect result was the political opening within the education system. The agrarian question, while intrinsically a material question of land rights, appeared to have more legitimacy because of the link between indigenous culture and the land, and was unified because of the identity factor. The underlying indigenous call for inclusion resulted in the strong mobilizations demanding indigenous land rights.

Conclusions

It was my concern in this chapter to bring to light some of the political ramifications of the discussions about social movements in Latin America. I argue that identity-based movements, although organized around the interests of a specific sector, can successfully lead to broader democratic openings in the system as a whole. Because they are often developed in response to a context of exclusion from economic and political power, identity-based movements are usually centered around demands for access to power, or political participation. Political participation, as many theorists have suggested, is central to democratic reform.

In the case of Ecuador, the indigenous population has largely been excluded since the Spanish conquest, but despite attempts at mass acculturation, a large percentage of the rural population has maintained a distinct identity. Modern circumstances have led to the development of a unique indigenous ideology which forms the essence of the modern indigenous movement. That movement, with CONAIE at the forefront, has spread a new concept of indigenous identity. Beyond the development of an ideology, the indigenous movement has made concrete changes in the political system as exemplified in the two cases described here: bilingual education and privatization of the agricultural sector.

This chapter presents only one aspect of the very complex situation of indigenous politics in Ecuador. More research is needed at both a micro and a macro level of analysis. At the micro level there is room for study regarding alliances and disputes within the indigenous movements and with other sectors of Ecuadorian society. At the macro level there is important information to be analyzed regarding the increasing international influence on the movement, including international development assistance (from the World Bank, AID, etc.) and the human rights community. Most important, it remains to be clearly discussed what is unique about the indigenous movement that has made it so successful in relation to other identity-based movements. For example, why has the women's movement in Ecuador had such limited success as compared to the indigenous movement?

Scholars of social movements are often criticized for their optimism and I certainly accept that criticism. By no means do I intend to present the case of the indigenous movement in Ecuador as uniformly positive. The movement suffers from political conflicts between 'traditional' and 'modern' practices that restrain its development. Moreover, while Ecuador is peaceful in comparison to its neighboring countries, neither is it a stable democracy according to most analysts.[42] Still, it is clear that the intervention of indigenous communities into national politics is a radical break from the not too distant past of 'submissive' Indians. That radical break can be understood in terms of the development of a modern indigenous movement challenging their exclusion from political society.

ANNEX I. **Demands presented to President Sixto Durán when he took office, to initiate dialogue: Indigenous Plurinational Mandate – CONAIE**

This mandate contemplates the principal necessities of the indigenous people of Ecuador, which we present to the Ecuadorian state, as an urgent proposal to be implemented through compensatory measures in the face of the recent economic measures.

1. Juridical Policy

1.1. Constitutional recognition of the Plurinational and Pluricultural character of the Ecuadorian state.

   1.2. Ratification of Agreement 169 of the OIT, concerning Indigenous and Tribal Peoples.

   1.3. Reform of the Municipal Regulations Law, referring to the Non-Payment of Rural Property Taxes.

   1.4. Participation in the 1 per cent of the cost-per-barrel of oil exploited in the territories of the indigenous peoples.

   1.5. Amnesty for prisoners and penal defendants who have been sentenced as a result of the fight for land or in defense of land.

   1.6. Revision of the signed agreements between Religious Missions and the Government that refer to indigenous peoples.

   1.7. The Government, the National Congress, and the Supreme Court of Justice must express their lack of accord with the commemorations of the quincentenary, and ask an indemnity for damages of the Spanish government and the European Economic Community, which should be used for the benefit of the indigenous people and popular sector.

2. Economy and Production

2.1. Creation of a fund in the amount of ten billion sucres annually for the solution of land conflicts.

   2.2. Delimitation and legalization of the ancestral territories of the indigenous peoples within parks and natural reserves throughout the country.

---

[42] See for instance Hurtado (1985), Corkill and Cubitt (1988).

2.3. Creation of a Special Indigenous Fund for Integrated Development Programs.

2.4. Freezing of the prices of necessary industrial products as well as of machinery and fertilizers.

3. Education and Culture

3.1. Continuation of the Bilingual and Intercultural Education Program, properly financed and with respect to the administrative, technical, and financial autonomy of the National Directorate of Bilingual and Intercultural Education.

3.2. Respect for and continuation of the Agreement signed by CONAIE and the Ministry of Education, as well as for other cultural programs, infrastructural projects, etc.

3.3. Establishment of scholarships to support the training of indigenous students.

3.4. We declare that the Bilingual and Intercultural Education Program be directed towards all of Ecuadorian society. The government proposal should not be limited to learning the Quichua language alone, but should include the study of the different Peoples that constitute Ecuador.

ANNEX II. **Examples of violence incited by the anti-mobilization actions in 1994, listed by province**

1. Cotopaxi: The indigenous radio station is invaded by the military, equipment destroyed, two vehicles and radio equipment are taken, and the radio announcer, Alma Montoya, is arrested.

2. Tungurahua: Marco Manabanda and Lorenzo Masaquiza are both shot and killed, and the indigenous radio station is shot at and closed down.

3. Chimborazo: A violent military parachute operation leaves two critically injured and many others wounded, and 500 indigenous are violently forced out of a convent. In Achupallas, the military used bombs to force out protesters, leaving many wounded and asphyxiated. Two indigenous radio stations are invaded by the military and shut down as well as the offices of the indigenous organization.

4. Cañar: Gangs led by the Social Christian Party provoke looting and burning of the indigenous organizations' offices, killing Manuel Jesus Yupa and wounding 35 more. Racism is encouraged by the Party and local government. The indigenous radio station is closed.

5. Sucumbios (Amazon): Military actions in Limoncocha leave David Andi shot and critically wounded, others injured, and 2 others possibly killed.

ANNEX III. **Interviews cited**

Luís Macas, Saraguro-Quiche, President, CONAIE, 1991, 1993.
Ampam Karakras, Shuar, Director of Finances, CONAIE, 1991.
Alberto Andrango, Quiche, FENOC-I, 1991.

Leonardo Viteri, Quichua-Amazon, OPIP, 1991, 1993.
Humberto Muenala, Quichua, Otavalo, Proyecto EBI, 1991, 1993.
Federation of Cabildos of Bolívar, 1991, 1993.
Miguel Angel Carlosama, Quichua, Federación de Indígenas de Imbabura, 1991.
Alfonso Calderón, assessor to President Borja for Indigenous Affairs, 1993.
Luís Monteluisa, Quichua, first Director of DINEIB, 1993.
María Pacca, Movimiento Indígena de Chimborazo, 1991.
Miguel Lluco, Quichua, Ecuarunari, 1991.
Ileana Almeida, Anthropologist, 1991.
Tránsito Chela, Quichua, DINEIB, 1993.
José Quimbo, Quichua, Asesoria Indígena de la Presidencia, 1993.

ANNEX IV. Documents

'Ley de Colonización de la Región Amazónica', *Leyes Reforma Agraria*, Corporación de
    Estudios y Publicaciones, Apr. 1993, Quito.
'Ley de Tierras Baldías y Colonización', *Leyes Reforma Agraria*, Corporación de Estudios
    y Publicaciones, Apr. 1993, Quito.

8 The Evolution of the Brazilian Environmental Movement and Its Political Roles

Kathryn Hochstetler

This volume is premised upon the notion that while vital new forms of associational life emerged among the Latin American popular classes in recent years, the region also experienced a steady decay of popular organization throughout the economically 'lost decade' of the 1980s, especially as democratic transitions became party politics. Such contradictory views have several sources. First, it should by now be clear that there is a tremendous variety in the recent popular mobilizations in Latin America. These movements have both attempted and achieved different levels of political participation. Whatever general conclusions may be drawn, they must rest on this acknowledged diversity. Second, and more problematically, different observers approach the same organizations and mobilizations with different theoretical or political agendas. Their different perspectives may cause them to exaggerate some features of current popular political participation, while missing others altogether. In this chapter, I focus on one specific lens: the expectations which observers bring concerning what political role(s) social movements play. I use the experiences of the Brazilian environmental movement to highlight the contradictory conclusions which such different role expectations can produce about the same empirical movements. While such theoretical or political blinders do not necessarily produce incorrect portrayals of social movements, it is important to understand the ways in which they are systematically incomplete, and the ways in which those omissions may produce overly optimistic or pessimistic appraisals of popular participation.

There are many definitions of popular movements. By virtually all of them, Brazilian environmentalists do not comprise a popular movement. Participants in the Brazilian environmental movement, like those in environmental movements across the globe, are disproportionately well educated and middle class in their social origins. Teachers, scientists, bureaucrats, and their fellow professionals make up many Brazilian environmental groups. Similarly, environmentalists' focus on what have been called post-industrial values and aims seems to have little relevance to the impoverished popular sectors, who still have unrealized hopes for what their inclusion in industrial society could bring.

Nevertheless, with regard to popular political representation, the argument that the substantive agenda of environmentalists is irrelevant to popular sectors is grossly overstated. When ecologically unsound agricultural practices bring desertification; when deforestation decimates the habitats of plant and animal species *and* those of human social groupings; when poor sanitation practices kill fish, rivers, and people, the links between environmental concerns and basic human survival are clear. Sustained economic production, a key to the eventual economic inclusion of the popular classes, is not possible with a destroyed and contaminated resource base. Most Brazilian environmentalists explicitly acknowledge that their project as environmentalists in a developing country requires a two-part effort. In the words of Green Party founder Fernando Gabeira, the special challenge of environmentalists in Latin America is to take on *poliséria*, a combination of the Portuguese words for pollution and misery (Gabeira 1987: 172). Instead of defending the romantic environmentalism of untouchable natural resources, they ask questions like the following: for whose benefit will irreplaceable resources be used? How can they be used to balance the needs of present and future generations? In the Amazon region, rubber tappers, peasants, and indigenous groups have already founded a well-known collective struggle based on the convergence between their social justice concerns and environmentalism (Landim 1993: 218–29).

Self-described environmentalists, who are concentrated in the industrialized south of Brazil, are also increasingly developing such links to popular organizations. Social movement 'spillover' between the two movement communities has been promoted by all four of the routes of movement–movement transmission recently identified by Meyer and Whittier: 'organizational coalitions, overlapping social movement communities, shared personnel, and changes in the external environment achieved by one movement that then shape subsequent movements' (Meyer and Whittier 1994: 278). Such ties have been irregular, but crucial to the environmental movement's development and increasing sensitivity to popular concerns. In fact, environmentalists' interactions with popular movements—especially in such organizational coalitions as the mobilizations for the Constituent Assembly and Earth Summit—have shaped the characteristic mix of political roles which the Brazilian environmental movement plays at the national level. Alliances between multiple social sectors and organizations can be a crucial political laboratory for all sides, promoting creative new participatory strategies as well as new aims. Needless to say, larger cross-sectoral coalitions carry more weight in political arenas. Coalitions between popular actors and other non-governmental political actors may prove to be one of the most important new elements in the developing patterns of interactions between popular actors and political institutions in Latin America in the 1990s. Environmental movements are one potential non-governmental alliance partner for popular movements.

With regard to the theoretical representations of popular movements and their political participation, popular movements are studied through many of the same analytic lenses as other social movements. In this chapter, I seek to explain the nature and political roles of the Brazilian environmental movement—and how it can be simultaneously invisible, important, or threatening in the views of those who observe it. The concepts I develop here to understand this specific movement and its development can be extended to popular movements as well. Several examples will illustrate the wide range of perceptions of the Brazilian environmental movement, from dangerous to irrelevant.

In 1990, the Brazilian Superior War College issued a document citing environmentalists—with drug traffickers and indigenous peoples—as one of several potential threats to Brazil's national security in the Amazon region (Escola Superior de Guerra 1990). From the other end of the political spectrum, an intellectual of the leftist Workers' Party used the party publication *Teoria e Prática* to tell 'our green friends' that environmental issues were too important to be left to them (Benjamin 1990: 6–21). A recent study of Brazil's environmental bureaucracy made almost no mention of the environmental movement, and environmentalists found no entrance there even after one of their own pioneers, José Lutzenberger, became the National Secretary of the Environment.[1] Similarly, self-described grassroots environmental groups in Brazil have been left almost wholly outside international funding networks for both grassroots and environmental organizations, which might be expected to embrace them.[2]

In order to understand such disparate perceptions of the same organizations and mobilizations, I begin by drawing on recent collective action theories to discuss the potential political roles of social movements. Political roles can be defined by social movement aims—the kinds of impacts they hope to have on politics—as well as by the actual functions social movements play. In this chapter, I present four potential political roles of social movements: representation, state transformation, cultural politics, and the 'informal polity'. The first two roles directly engage the state institutions charged with governing society, while the second two are political without directly entering the conventional political arena. Each of the four roles is associated with a characteristic set of tactics, although similar tactics can be used to play different roles. In addition, each political role carries its own definitions of success and failure.

The exercise of identifying potential political roles is theoretically important because both political allies and opponents *and* academic observers look to find social movements in particular political roles. Yet specific social movement networks may be absent or irrelevant in some of these roles, while very important in

---

[1] Guimarães (1991). Environmentalists' sense of exclusion was documented by UPAN, an environmental group in Rio Grande do Sul. See 'Manifesto: Por uma Política Ambiental Verdadeira' (1991) and 'Movimento Ecológico Gaúcho Toma Posição' (1990) and accompanying articles.
[2] Mafra (1993). Mafra begins his analysis with a similar list of the divergent responses to the Brazilian environmental movement.

others. Since social movement networks often unevenly occupy the range of roles theoretically open to them, they appear as absent to fully present to different observers. Consequently, the paradox of the contradictory views of the same social movements can be unraveled by asking in which political role(s) the observer sought the movement. The second part of this chapter illustrates this argument through a brief survey of the Brazilian environmental movement. This is followed by a discussion of the ways that different theoretical and 'real life' searches for social movements in particular roles can produce contradictory and even misleading conclusions about the nature and importance of social movements in general, as well as about individual social movement networks.

Potential Political Roles of Social Movements

Social movements—groups of citizens gathered to pursue more or less shared aims—participate in an astonishing array of political activities.[3] Their political activities can be categorized in at least two ways: by the tactical forms of their participation and by their political roles. Tactics are the observable action forms, while political roles necessarily include the meanings given to those actions by the social movement itself and by the standards of the external political system. The political roles of a social movement can be analyzed from either vantage point, from the kind(s) of impact which social movements try to have on politics or from the kind(s) of impact which social movements do have on politics. Many discussions of social movements begin with their political tactics, singling out protest and mass mobilization as the most characteristic or even defining political activities of social movements.[4] Nonetheless, the same social movement organizations commonly pursue a wide repertoire of political participation strategies, which includes both institutional and non-institutional tactics. During the three years that Brazilian environmentalists mobilized for the Constituent Assembly, for example, the same individuals and groups staged protest parades at the doors of the National Congress, collected tens of thousands of signatures for popular amendments, gave testimony as environmental experts, used interest group tactics like lobbying individual representatives, and tried to reframe the legislation as fundamental to the survival of

---

[3] This definition of social movements purposefully is rendered as inclusive as possible, in order to be a noun form of the similarly general 'collective action'. While the social movement label is often reserved for any of a number of more specific empirical referents, e.g. class-based movements, non-class-based movements, spontaneous eruptions, defiance of systemic limits, and so on, I want to remain able to ask when collective action takes one of these forms or another.

[4] Several recent collections on Latin American social movements make this assumption. Susan Eckstein's edited volume, *Power and Popular Protest: Latin American Social Movements* (1989) makes the equation of social movements and protest in its title—as does the introductory essay ('Introduction: Theory and Protest in Latin America Today') of Arturo Escobar and Sonia Alvarez's edited volume, *The Making of Social Movements in Latin America* (1992).

the human species. Even if we accept the use of protest or mobilization tactics as a defining characteristic of social movements, their other participatory strategies also help define them as political actors. And social movements do not necessarily lose their unique character in their non-protest activities. They have shown remarkable creativity in their use of conventional political mechanisms and institutions, as is illustrated by the anti-party Green Parties all over the globe, including in Brazil. In conclusion, focusing only on protest and mass mobilization misses a good deal of the political participation of social movements. In addition, acknowledging the different relations, meanings, and kinds of political roles embodied in current forms of collective action avoids such sterile debates as whether 'new social movements' are truly new—some are, sometimes, in some ways.[5] The question is how, when, and why.

I begin to answer these questions by outlining the different kinds of impacts that social movements can have on the political system, or their potential political roles. The four potential political roles—representation, state transformation, cultural politics, and informal polity—each include a specified role in the political system (and an implicit definition of the political system), a characteristic set of tactics, and a set of standards for success. All four political roles assume that social movements are active participants in politics, and not merely by-products of, or simple responses to, macro-level changes in the polity or society. Although I illustrate and discuss these political roles with reference to the experiences of Latin American social movements, social movements in other Western-style representative democracies should play a similar range of roles, although the distribution of social movements' activities across the roles will differ.

The four roles are distinguished on two dimensions, their aims and their location, as summarized in Table 8.1. By substantive aims, I mean that a primary goal of the social movement's political participation is to provide concrete goods and services, especially those related to its specific agenda, e.g. the environment or workers' rights, without directly challenging existing political institutions and relations. Transformative aims are more abstract, and involve efforts to change forms of social and political organization and collective understandings. The location dimension describes where the political participation takes place: in confrontation with the formal political arena or not. In locating actual mobilizations within this four-part framework, two different analytical questions may be relevant. First, how does the social movement understand its own aims and political location? Second, in the terms of the conventional political arena, how do the social movements' aims and tactics appear? For example, in understanding the political impact of the Brazilian Green Party's 1989 presidential campaign, it is necessary to know both that the Green Party considered this an important and successful opportunity to redefine politics as including sexual and everyday politics (cultural politics) *and* that presidential candidate Gabeira received only 0.17 per cent of the

---

[5] On this debate, see also Melucci (1989: 40–5).

Table 8.1. Potential political roles of social movements

Aims	Location	
	Formal political arena	Informal political arena
Substantive	Representation	Informal polity
Transformative	State transformation	Cultural politics

vote (representation role). This two-part questioning is especially important because the same tactics may be used for different aims and the same aims may be pursued with different tactics. In actual mobilizations, the four potential political roles are therefore inevitably overlapping, but they can be distinguished here analytically.

REPRESENTATION

The first political role is a part of most conceptions of political participation: citizens act to influence government decision-makers as they formulate and implement policies related to the citizens' substantive interests and values. Environmental movements seek to influence environmental policies, women's movements seek to influence policies which have an impact on women, and so on. In this role, social movements become 'another form of representation used by those who claim to speak on behalf of some excluded group or ignored interest'. Like other forms of representation such as political parties, social movements can serve as intermediaries between individual citizens and the government.

The political role of representation is played in a largely given political context, defined by the existing institutions and actors of the formal political system. Government decision-makers are the main target of this form of political participation. Their responses therefore define the degree of social movement success in playing the representation role. Following Gamson, there are two basic components of social movement success (Gamson 1990). The first is when decision-makers accept the social movement as an interlocutor for an identifiable and important political constituency. The constituency may be defined in various ways, including in geographical, interest, or identity terms. Second, the social movement might gain public-policy victories on issues of lesser and greater importance to it. A crucial piece of this second component of success is that the policy is effectively budgeted and implemented. In many Latin American countries, this step is often omitted, as legislation frequently outruns execution of laws.

Social movements are most clearly distinguished from other agents of representation by their tactics. Political parties and interest groups not only address institutional actors, as do social movements playing the representation role. They also commonly follow institutionalized procedures for gaining access to decision-makers. In this regard, political parties typically occupy one pole of the institutionalization continuum, while social movements tend to cluster near the other pole of uninstitutionalized participatory tactics. The protest-oriented social movements in Susan Eckstein's edited volume, for example, adopted unorthodox tactics such as publicly wearing white handkerchiefs or launching urban riots in order to voice institutionally unrepresented demands like the release of political prisoners or the repudiation of economic structural adjustment policies (Eckstein 1989).

Such direct representation, which relies on large numbers of loosely organized people and eschews institutionalized access points, is a hallmark of the representation tactics of social movements. Nonetheless, such tactics typically compose only one piece of many social movement networks' representation strategies. More institutionalized participation of various forms often supports and politically interprets the direct mass mobilizations. Activists write and call their representatives; they give expert testimony; they take jobs in relevant bureaucracies; and so on. Extended mobilizations, like the multiple preparations for the Earth Summit conference, require more organization. In addition, they also often offer special institutionalized opportunities to participants in mobilized social movement networks. Environmental activists in Brazil, for example, accepted a position on Brazil's official delegation to the Earth Summit—a position which did not preclude other more oppositional forms of participation in the conference. The Green parties, where one institution of representation (the social movement) takes on the form of another (the party), are a particularly vivid example of the kinds of hybrids of institutionalized and uninstitutionalized tactics which social movements can use. A central issue thus becomes the relationship of social movements to other parts of the representative system.

In summary, the political role of representation includes social movements' attempts to influence primarily governmental decision-makers on policies and legislation related to their interests and values. Success is measured by the responses of those decision-makers, and ultimately revealed in effective legislation and policies which match the social movements' substantive objectives. Direct representation through protest and mass mobilization is a characteristic tactic often used by social movements, but they also use more institutionalized participatory strategies which may engage other institutions of representation.

STATE TRANSFORMATION

State transformation, the second political role of social movements, figures prominently in studies of Latin American social movements. In this role, social movements target the organization and nature of the state and its political institutions directly. Like the East European social movements, the story of recent Latin American social movements is intricately bound up with concrete processes of large-scale political regime transformation. New social movements—both new kinds and new manifestations of more traditional social movements—multiplied across Latin America, contemporary with a continent-wide transition from military to civilian political regimes. Analysts saw the wave of new social movements in the 1970s and 1980s as both a cause and a consequence of the political transition.[6] The social movements' protests delegitimated the state and its claims to effective governance, while the retreating military regimes gave them new spaces to play a representative role. Even after the formal regime transitions, however, social movements' demands for political transformation continue, especially on issues of state–society relations. In the 'second transition' of democratic consolidation,[7] they demand increased accountability and responsiveness from decision-makers and a devolution of power from the state to society.

In addition to their transformative role *vis-à-vis* formal political institutions, Latin American social movements have also sought transformation in the state as it is more broadly defined. A conception of the state as institutionalized relations of domination which go far beyond the conventional political sphere has been compelling in Latin America (e.g. Cardoso in Collier 1979: 33–57), and social movements have also aimed for state transformation at this level. Most commonly, this translates into a demand for transformation of the existing economic model, although social movements have also singled out for transformation patriarchy and other relations of domination which sustain the state. Such demands clearly involve important elements of a cultural political role as well.

Both the tactics and standards of success for the political role of state transformation are clearest in the case of formal transition processes from authoritarian political regimes to more representative and participatory ones. Authoritarian political regimes are in part defined by their politically exclusionary nature. Typically, authoritarian governments close institutional mediations between state and society and attempt to exercise unilateral control over collective decision-making processes. In these circumstances, where most institutionalized participatory channels are blocked, protest is a logical tactical choice for social movements. Protest mobilizations, which seek to directly contact state decision-makers, can continue to happen even without institutional intermediaries like parties. While the heavy-handed repression of opposition makes long-term organization difficult in authoritarian regimes, the characteristic spontaneity and minimal organization of protest mobilizations allow social movements to slip through military controls. Mass mobilization also robs the military of a clearly delimited target. These

---

[6] Many, many examples could be cited. Several works which trace the relationship between social movements and regime transformation in Brazil include Alvarez (1990); Alves (1985); Boschi (1987); Sader (1991); and Stepan (1989).

[7] This label is developed in Mainwaring *et al.* (1992).

characteristics of protest mobilizations make them a particularly effective choice in periods of transition. Mass protests, with up to a million people in the streets of Brazil and elsewhere, in fact dramatized civil society's growing opposition to the military's political control in Latin America. A multitude of social movement networks joined together in protest mobilizations, as they focused on their common goal of regime transformation instead of other tactics and aims. These focused oppositional protests have equally apparent standards of success. Popular elections of civilian presidents and new legislative bodies, constituent assemblies, and the creation of new institutionalized mediations between state and society mark clearly successful transformations of the political regime *from* authoritarian rule.

When representative fora for public demands exist, however limited, the participatory strategies of social movements diversify. On the one hand, protest continues because many transformative demands cannot be easily channeled through existing institutional mediations between state and society. Even where participatory opportunities formally exist, some participants in social movements may still doubt the willingness and capacity of political actors to change themselves and the mechanisms which have brought them to a position of power. On the other hand, political reorganization is sometimes on the formal political agenda. Constituent assemblies, where participants self-consciously set out to write new rules of the game, offer institutionalized opportunities to transform politics. Formal state reform processes also establish institutionalized routes for changing political institutions and rules. Even routine elections can help establish the groundwork for transformative politics. In such cases, social movements can also pursue their transformative aims with the institutional participatory strategies they use for representing their substantive interests and values. The balance of protest and institutional participation in the state transformation role of social movements depends on the nature of the existing political regime, the nature of the transformative demands of the social movements, and the degree of fit between the two. When more kinds of participatory opportunities are available, or when participants in social movements are philosophically or strategically divided, multiple participatory tactics may coexist.

Finally, while formal political liberalization has been an important aim of recent social movements in Latin America, the concept of a 'second transition' suggests that a formal transition to civilian constitutional democracy is an incomplete standard for successful political transformation. Additional political transformations are not only possible, but also actively demanded by many social movements. Where social movements have emerged and made transformative demands in a context of constitutional democracy, as in Venezuela and Mexico, this point is clear. In any case, however, success in the transformative role is principally measured by changes in macro-level institutions and structures which are external to the social movement itself.

In summary, the state-transformation-seeking political participation by social movements targets the institutions, organization, and social relations of the state itself for transformation. In the paradigmatic examples of the 1980s in Latin America and elsewhere, social movements used protest mobilizations to pressure political actors into initiating a formal institutional transition from authoritarian to more participatory and representative political regimes. Where representative mediations between state and society exist, social movements' transformative tactics may include either protest or more institutional strategies; without them, social movements usually turn to protest tactics. Success in this political role is seen in changes in the state itself, whether formal political liberalization or other possible forms of state transformation.

CULTURAL POLITICS

In the third political role of social movements, cultural politics, the focus on state institutions is replaced with the starting-point of 'people's self-understanding, with giving an account of people as agents whose practices are shaped by their self-understanding' (Escobar in Escobar and Alvarez 1992: 63). Understandings, and self-understandings in particular, define the political realm instead of formal governing institutions. In other words, the view of politics as a single institutionalized space where social actors might represent interests or decide to change institutional forms is replaced by a much more diffuse image of politics as present in all aspects of social life.[8] Outside of the formal political sphere, social movements experiment with new questions, new answers, renaming reality, and so on. The politics of everyday life becomes what Melucci calls 'laboratories of experience [which] . . . are displayed publicly only within particular conjunctures' (Melucci 1989: 208). Everyday interactions and alternative utopias may reconstitute the meanings of everyday practices, reproducing or creating new collective identities.

In terms of the standards of the first two political roles (political effectiveness in influencing or transforming the formal political sphere), the playing of cultural politics often has few evident results. In fact, the notions of standards and tactics themselves are different for this political role. Success is not defined in terms of concrete outcomes in the formal political arena, but in changes in the social movement participants themselves and in their collective understandings. Such new collective identities may, in fact, eventually alter the existing institutions and policies of the state as participants in the social movements assert their presence in new ways, but this impact is not seen as more important than the impact on the participants and everyday life. The process of participation may be an end in itself, as the experiences produce new symbols, identities, and needs. Creating a sense of solidarity may also be an important project of cultural politics.

Similarly, the word 'tactics' is itself misleading as a category for thinking about

---

[8] For examples of this approach in the Latin American context, see the selections in Scherer-Warren and Krischke (1987) and Slater (1985).

the cultural political role; its instrumental implications are inappropriate. The action referents of cultural politics take many forms, although cultural politics are most often played out in everyday lifestyles and interactions or in public spaces of communication and information. Universities and the media are two prominent examples of public loci of cultural politics. More rarely, the cultural political role can be played through apparently traditional forms of political action. For example, the intended political role of the Brazilian Green Party can be understood better as an expressive exercise of cultural politics than by the standards of party politics, despite its very traditional legal party form.

In summary, the cultural political role differs dramatically from the first two political roles in its tactics and standards. These differences are based on its different conception of politics, which moves from politics as embodied in formal macro-level institutions and structures to the politics of everyday life. The importance or 'success' of cultural political participation is seen in the production of new symbols and identities, while the 'tactics' or action forms include personal lifestyle choices and participation in public communication and information fora.

INFORMAL POLITY

Finally, social movements may play a fourth political role, the 'informal polity' role.[9] Despite recurring calls for neoliberalism and rolling back the state, in the 1990s governments worldwide are still held responsible for a daunting array of tasks. Governments have taken on many tasks like national security, health care, and mundane services like garbage collection, in addition to their legislative, regulatory, and judicial functions. On the other hand, in countries like Brazil where unyielding fiscal crises and repeated corruption scandals have greatly scaled back the effective scope of the national government, the gap between the state's tasks and its capacities has widened dramatically. In many developing countries, and in some policy sectors of developed countries as well, the informal polity fills part of the gap left by the inadequacies of the formal political system. Social movements can be an important part of such an informal polity, directly providing collective political goods and services for their communities which the government is not providing. In addition, they may play this role to compete with an overly intrusive state, providing non-coercive alternatives. Unlike the cultural political role which highlights the production of new ideas, in the informal political role social movements help produce concrete goods and services.

Several examples will illustrate the range of activities of the informal polity. One

---

[9] I borrow this label from the related concept of the informal economy, which is discussed, among other places, in the work of Hernando de Soto (1989). The informal polity is distinguished from the informal economy by the different nature of the goods and services they provide. The informal polity provides goods and services which are either *collective* or which are commonly provided by the welfare state.

striking example is the Peruvian rural justice groups (*rondas campesinas*) who 'evolved into an entire alternative justice system with open community assemblies to resolve problems ranging from wife-beating to land disputes' (Starn in Escobar and Alvarez 1992: 90). Their success at resolving conflicts has led to an estimated 90 per cent drop in the case load of one Peruvian state's office court system (Starn in Escobar and Alvarez 1992: 108). A very different example is the increasing practice of preservation by purchase, where tracts of land are bought for environmental conservation. Here, environmental groups like Conservation International and its Latin American associates draw on the authority of the market-place rather than the state to provide a collective good. Somewhere between these two examples are the numerous activities of oversight and enforcement by social movements, which give teeth to legislation passed on paper but not yet translated into budgets or practices. One of my interviews with an environmental activist in Canoas, Rio Grande do Sul, was interrupted by a panicked visitor who warned that someone was clearing a green area downtown. We rushed to the site, and he persuaded the site foreman that the job had to be stopped until a certain permit was acquired. In one final example of the informal polity, women's groups have provided such health services as safe abortions, a service not only unprovided but illegal in many Latin American countries. These examples show the ways that social movements may enforce legislation, privately provide collective goods like environmental protection, and substitute for ineffective state institutions—all tasks which might belong to the government.

Both the standards and the tactics of the informal polity role are defined by the collective need that the social movement is meeting. Here, the political space is defined by collective needs or by the government's own claimed or assigned policy scope. The aim of this kind of participation is directly to meet the collective needs of a community, so success includes the community's use and valorization of the goods and services provided. Both the definition of collective needs and the collective assessment of success or failure are socially constructed.

In terms of tactics, the only ones which are excluded analytically are those which call on the formal polity to meet the community needs. Tactics actually used for providing these goods and services vary widely, as illustrated by the examples given. Local grassroots social movements are relatively well equipped with resources like time, human numbers, and simple presence; these resources are particularly well suited for such functions as oversight and enforcement. International funds have also multiplied the tactics available to Latin American social movements. Southern social movements are increasingly becoming the preferred conduit for funds coming from outside the country for such purposes as environmental conservation. This has always been the case for northern non-governmental organizations, but is increasingly true for governmental organizations as well, as Segarra's chapter shows.

These four potential political roles of social movements are ideal types, and can be more easily distinguished analytically than in actual mobilizations. In the same mobilizations, social movements frequently play several of these ideal-typical political roles. The roles themselves are interrelated. Representative participation, for example, may itself be transformative of the state and relations of domination when historically excluded popular groups are involved.[10] Similarly, the capacity of such historically excluded groups to participate depends on their reconceptualization of their political role possibilities, a part of cultural politics. The capacity to imagine new identities and new utopias is also clearly linked to state transformation. Finally, political representation and informal politics may be seen as alternative possibilities for achieving collective substantive interests. This brief summary does not exhaust the possible political roles of social movements, singly or in relation to each other, but it should help to establish that there are many political spaces where social movements might be found. Where and if social movements are found as political actors depends in part on where they are sought.

The Evolution of the Brazilian Environmental Movement

Environmental ideas and activism have a long history in Brazil.[11] The current generation of environmental activism dates back to the early 1970s, when environmental organizations formed from Rio Grande do Sul (AGAPAN) to São Paulo (MAPE) to Belém (SOPREN). Throughout this chapter, I have spoken of 'the Brazilian environmental movement' as though it were a unified and homogeneous entity. This is patently untrue. Like other social movements, the Brazilian environmental movement has many facets and divisions. For example, there are significant regional variations, with many differences between environmentalists in the industrialized south and their counterparts in the Amazon and northeastern regions. In addition, environmentalists' participation in local politics takes characteristic forms which differ substantially from their participation in national politics. In terms of both aims and strategies, 'the Brazilian environmental movement' looks different depending on whether the observer uses a regional, local, or national lens. Each of these lenses also imposes a false unity on a movement which is further split in non-geographic ways, e.g. on basic conceptual disagreements about the meaning of environmentalism. The following discussion of Brazilian environmentalism highlights three empirical cuts into the complexity of the Brazilian environmental movement. First, a turn to ecopolitics in the 1980s[12] developed in

[10] For example, Joe Foweraker argues that the new autonomous political participation of urban grassroots groups in Mexico is itself transformative of Mexico's historical patterns of state–society relations (see Foweraker in Foweraker and Craig 1990).

[11] José Augosto Pádua has documented this history in an effort to show that environmentalism is indigenous to Brazil, and not an import from outside (see Pádua 1991: 135–61).

[12] Eduardo Viola writes of a transition from a predominately environmentalist or conservationist stance in the 1970s to a predominately ecopolitical stance in the 1980s (see Viola 1987).

a series of national-level encounters. For the first time, something like a 'Brazilian', i.e. national, movement appeared. In successive national-level mobilizations, Brazilian environmentalists negotiated—literally and figuratively—an identifiable repertoire of characteristic collective strategies and aims. In particular, they began to de-emphasize the political role of representation in favor of other forms of collective participation. Simultaneously, however, local organizing continued in different forms. While some environmentalists and some environmental groups emerged as important participants in national politics, scores of small, locally based environmental groups concentrated their energies on playing a representation role in local politics. The second empirical cut I take here looks, therefore, at these local participation forms. Finally, I briefly discuss the nature of environmental mobilization in one region, the Amazon. Environmental organizing there has followed very different timetables and models than in other regions of Brazil.

NATIONAL MOBILIZATIONS

When the current generation of Brazilian environmental organizations began to form in the early 1970s, they did so in the shadow of a military government which was just beginning a decade-long promise of political opening. Like other social movements at the time, environmentalists often put their unique agenda second to the broader political agenda of regime transformation. They joined in broad anti-military coalitions with both popular and elite opposition groups. Participants from all of these sectors, including the environmental movement, found that direct mobilizations for political transformation produced new understandings of their political role as social movements. They increasingly recognized their own role as democratizers and transformers of a political system marked by the exclusion of all but a limited elite. They also began to emphasize the ways that their policy agenda depended on economic transformation. Later national environmental mobilizations reflected these lessons.

Unlike many other Brazilian social movements, the environmental movement began a successful sustained effort in the mid-1980s to reinsert its unique environmental agenda into the larger processes of political consolidation and reconstruction. The prospect of an upcoming Constituent Assembly was the single most important factor impelling the national organization of the environmental movement and its subsequent national political participation.[13] National discussions were initially promoted in 1984 and 1985 by a group of Rio activists who wanted to form a Green Party. Although environmentalists eventually decided to accept

[13] See Hochstetler (1994, chs. 2 and 3). This account of the Constituent Assembly and other organizing in the 1980s is based on interviews in 1990 and 1991 with Congressman Feldmann, two coordinators of and other participants in the environmental movement's Interstate Coordination of Ecologists for the Constituent Assembly (CIEC), and leaders of the Green Party (PV), in addition to documents from those offices. Maria Helena Antuniassi generously shared transcripts of interviews she had conducted in the mid-1980s with environmentalists in São Paulo.

the Green Party (Partido Verde—PV) as only one party voice among many to represent them, the discussions about party formation were expanded into larger debates about their participation in politics in general. After much discussion, environmentalists chose to participate in the constitution-writing process. The Constituent Assembly mobilizations lasted from 1985 to 1988 and were second only to the Earth Summit mobilizations in terms of the number and variety of Brazilian environmentalists who participated.

Environmentalists pursued two different kinds of aims in the new constitution. On the one hand, they sought some specific environmental clauses, such as the prohibition of all nuclear production, demarcation of natural areas to be protected, indigenous rights, and so on. In this representation role, they achieved a chapter on the environment, although they lost some of their most cherished provisions. The Constituents reacted most strongly against environmentalists' proposed restrictions on nuclear production, while accepting general principles of conservation. Environmentalist Congressman Fábio Feldmann, the only successful candidate on the environmental movement's national 'Green Lists' of candidates for the Constituent Assembly, spearheaded this effort. Environmentalists used an array of institutional and non-institutional participatory tactics, from confrontational demonstrations and popular amendments to Feldmann's insider bargaining.

Environmentalists also pursued a second set of transformative aims, setting their environmental mobilization in the context of a larger mobilization to transform the state by expanding civil rights (including the right to a healthy environment) and citizens' participatory opportunities. For example, environmentalists led by Congressman Feldmann fought to retain language which gave both the state and citizens responsibilities toward the environment. They argued that a constitutional responsibility toward the environment would also give citizens the right to participate in environmental decision-making, a participatory channel they wanted to create. In order to promote state transformation for more citizen participation, environmentalists joined informally with popular organizations and their supporters in the Plenary Pro-Popular Participation in the Constituent Assembly. The Plenary monitored and proposed participatory channels for popular sectors in the Constituent Assembly itself and in the new constitution's provisions. Many environmentalists used the Plenary as a key source of information and supported its efforts in turn.

Following the Constituent Assembly mobilization, environmentalists returned to local and regional activism, while maintaining national coordination primarily through a series of national conferences which grew out of the earlier mobilization. The ENEAAs (National Encounters of Autonomous Environmental Organizations) also provided a starting-point for the next major national mobilization, for the Earth Summit. After the United Nations selected Rio de Janeiro as the location for its 1992 global summit on environment and development, Brazilian environmentalists began two years of their own preparation as non-governmental hosts. While they did not ignore the official conference and the opportunities it presented to play a representation role on a global scale, they spent much of their time creating an alternative set of political opportunities. They sponsored the Global Forum, a citizens' summit of social movements and non-governmental organizations (NGOs). The Forum attracted 30,000 participants to its meetings, which were concurrent with the official summit. The attention and resources devoted to the United Nations conference became a conduit for the global articulation of citizens' groups with each other. At the gathering, many participants concentrated on the informal political roles of cultural politics and the informal polity. The Global Forum eventually produced about thirty 'people's treaties', which committed the citizens' groups to develop their own alternative developmental and environmental practices, rather than merely hoping to influence and oversee governmental actions. The NGOs pledged to promote new understandings of both 'development' and 'environment', in support of their new practices.

Non-governmental participants from across the globe split their attention and participation between the official and unofficial conferences. One rough measure of the relative importance national environmental movements gave to one conference or the other can be seen in the ratio of the number of environmentalists who registered for the Global Forum to those who registered for official consultative status, which allowed them to lobby the official conference. The Brazilian non-governmental participants had the highest ratio, with almost thirty-six organizations attending the Global Forum for every one which applied to observe the official conference. In comparison, the United States had only six participants in the NGO conference for every one participant in the United Nations conference.[14] Brazilian participants were emphasizing the second of the two tracks of their Constituent Assembly participation, focusing on transformative and informal politics while eschewing the formal representation opportunities. As they had done earlier, they used the conference preparations as an opportunity to build additional concrete ties to other sectors, inviting popular groups, unions, churches, professional associations, and the scientific community to join them in their preparations for the Earth Summit. In the years since the Constituent Assembly mobilization, the network of environmentalists who participated in collective national-level mobilizations had already become cynical about the capacity of governments to legislate environmental protection. They increasingly believed that only broad-based mobilized groups of citizens could promote the necessary changes. The political role of representation appeared ineffective, even when successful on its own terms. Symbolic and informal politics appeared as the more appropriate foundation for the necessary political and economic transformations.

---

[14] These ratios were calculated on the basis of the lists of registered participants found in *Who is Who at the Earth Summit* (1992). The lists were of individual registrants, not groups.

LOCAL ENVIRONMENTAL ORGANIZING

A different image of Brazilian environmentalists emerges at local levels of political organization. By definition, it is difficult to generalize about local organizing, since it responds to local conditions and opportunity structures. Nonetheless, grassroots, locally based environmental groups across Brazil face some common challenges and opportunities.[15] In this section I use the experiences of one well-known and perennially interesting environmental group to discuss these commonalities. AGAPAN, the Gaucho (of Rio Grande do Sul) Association for Protection of the Natural Environment, is too big, long-lived, and visible to be truly representative of local environmental organizing in Brazil. On the other hand, it exemplifies some of the most promising characteristics of grassroots environmental organizing in Brazil while remaining subject to some of those common challenges, writ large.

Long recognized as a pioneer in the modern environmental movement (AGAPAN was founded in 1971), its continuing prominence was underlined when then-president Fernando Collor selected founder José Lutzenberger to be his National Secretary of the Environment in 1989. From the point of view of the organization, it is even more important that AGAPAN survived Lutzenberger's spin-off into environmental celebrity. AGAPAN is an unusually 'deep' volunteer-based organization, with numerous active members who bring special skills and resources to the organization. Lutzenberger himself began his work career as a technical adviser on fertilizers, and his successor was a chemist who chaired the committee which wrote the national pesticide law eventually passed in 1989. They and other members made AGAPAN a powerful force on one of its trademark issues, pesticide control. AGAPAN has historically encouraged its members' direct political participation as environmental experts, mobilized citizens, and even elected politicians. Member Caio Lustosa of the PMDB was one of the first three environmental legislators elected in 1982. Two second-generation members, Giovani Gregol and Gert Schinke, successfully ran for city council positions in 1988 with AGAPAN's support. Both are members of the Workers' Party (PT). AGAPAN members see their own support as crucial for the continued political success of the

---

[15] During a four-month period in 1990, I attended state-wide conferences of environmental groups in Rio Grande do Sul, Rio de Janeiro, Santa Catarina, and São Paulo states, as well as a number of sub-state level gatherings in Rio de Janeiro and São Paulo. Each of these meetings gathered representatives of 20–50 grassroots environmental groups, many of which lacked any other regular mechanisms for integration and communication with environmentalists outside of their specific localities. In each state, however, several groups and/or individuals were active in larger regional or national environmental networks. These were most commonly from the state capitals or large cities, and they tended to dominate the agenda and course of the meetings. These individuals and groups were one source of common themes across the states—all discussed the Earth Summit, for example—but similar experiences also provided commonality. In the short organizational reports which typically began the conferences, participants repeatedly raised the common dilemmas and participatory strategies I discuss here. AGAPAN gave me full access to its archives for a ten-day period in 1990. This account is also based on interviews with six members of the organization.

two, and Gregol and Schinke repay the support by giving AGAPAN 10 per cent of their incomes. By one account, an additional eight members worked in municipal secretariats in 1990. In general, members expressed satisfaction with their inside channels to political power, with the proviso that members have organic connections to the movement, and are activists both before and during their political positions. Such members provide information, infrastructure, and access for AGAPAN as a whole. Although AGAPAN contains an unusual number of members who are direct participants in local and national politics, many Brazilian grassroots environmental groups cultivate ties with local bureaucrats and politicians who help them play a representation political role more successfully.

Many of AGAPAN's activities fall into the category of representative politics. AGAPAN is clearly accepted as an important voice on environmental issues, and holds seats on a number of government commissions as an NGO consultant. The organization has won a number of substantive legislative battles, including legislation controlling pesticides, nuclear waste and production, and chlorofluorocarbons. The line between representative and transformative and cultural politics is hard to draw, however, at least from AGAPAN's point of view. To take pesticides as an example, AGAPAN's members vehemently deny that the issue can be resolved with simple legislation on the 'correct' use of pesticides, a misconception Lutzenberger characterized as 'part of the ideological dogma which sustains the powers who are dismantling social structures and destroying the environment'.[16] Instead, AGAPAN seeks to back up its legislative successes with a larger transformative and cultural political agenda which addresses at least the politics of technology, the developmentalist foundation of the state, dependence on multinationals, agrarian reform, the distortions of a consumer society, and ultimately a new model of civilization.

Consequently, as a supplement to its more immediate agenda on pesticides, AGAPAN has also pursued this second agenda in both rhetoric and action. The struggle for agrarian reform, for example, has become a piece of AGAPAN's agenda and one axis of its connection to popular groups. As early as 1985, AGAPAN laid out a two-track strategy of building ties with the rural unions and landless (*sem terra*) movement, and pressuring the national environmental bureaucracy to contribute to an ecologically sound agrarian reform. In 1988, AGAPAN sponsored a round table with the CUT trade union, teachers' unions, the landless movement, and other groups to discuss how to further 'ecologize' those movements while advancing AGAPAN's *trabalho de base*, or grassroots organizing. City councilor Gregol articulated a philosophy which connected these issues in a 1990 interview:

Our political parties, our projects of social transformation, have to reflect the Brazilian reality. There is a restricted set of options in Brazil since we have no middle class. There are only two classes which could be hegemonic, the rich and the poor, the vast working

---

[16] Interview with José Lutzenberger, 'O modesto trabalho de refazer o mundo', *Isto É*, 30 Jan. 1980, p. 44.

majority. [Gregol includes the small middle class with the poor, since they work.] Any political project has to choose which side it is on.

Gregol went on to explain that environmental problems hurt the poor most, and so the environmental movement must be on their side.[17] This includes supporting issues like agrarian reform, which AGAPAN also supports since smaller-scale production tends to be more ecologically sound. Such strongly expressed views have led many to label AGAPAN as 'ecosocialist', a label some members deny. They say they are anti-capitalist, without necessarily embracing class struggle and socialism. Whatever the label, AGAPAN is clearly an organization which links more substantive demands to a broader political project. This broader political project is a potential foundation for new alliances with popular organizations. Many other organizations in Rio Grande do Sul share this focus. At the fractious 11th State Conference of Ecological Groups, held in September 1990, all participants agreed that environmentalists should broaden the base of the environmental movement through new popular coalitions, although they disagreed on how this should be done. This consensus is higher in Rio Grande do Sul than in most other regions. Many locally based environmental groups in fact restrict their focus to representation aims on narrowly defined substantive issues—the correct use of pesticides without the new model of civilization. Their alliances with popular movements are then more tactical rather than transformative in their motivation. In general, it is the volunteer organizations with more participation in regional and national environmental fora who articulate broader conceptions of environmental problems and solutions, while the more locally based grassroots groups and the environmental foundations highlight more local and scientific causes. National mobilizations apparently do not aggregate all dimensions of Brazilian environmental activism. Instead, they transform the subset of participating organizations and their characteristic political roles through the experience of participation.

Despite AGAPAN's organizational vitality and expansive agenda, it shares many of the dilemmas which dog grassroots environmental organizing in Brazil. All such organizations share problems of financing their activities. In recent years, AGAPAN has been heavily dependent on the contributions from its two member-politicians, which pay for its rent, telephone, and part-time receptionist (the only employee). AGAPAN has been seriously divided internally about accepting money from other sources, like businesses or international groups. They want to retain their independence of action and image, but need more funds to carry out even everyday activities and mobilizations. AGAPAN, like other grassroots organizations, is both tantalized by and fearful of the prospects of professionalization. And, like them, it lacks the funds to do so.

A second dilemma comes from AGAPAN's many political ties, which are both a channel for AGAPAN into the state and also potentially a device for political control over the organization. Here, AGAPAN magnifies the dilemmas of common

---

[17] Interview with Giovani Gregol, Porto Alegre, 6 June 1990.

grassroots organizations because of the exceptional prominence of its members. The 11th State Conference mentioned above was dramatically polarized from the first vote on voting rules to the last vote on adjourning the meeting. The source of the polarization was a deep division over whether they should criticize Lutzenberger (then National Secretary of the Environment) personally as a whitewasher of a flawed national environmental policy, or whether they should only criticize the policy. Those who favored targeting Lutzenberger spoke of the need to rescue the political independence and radical nature of the movement, while those against argued that attacking Lutzenberger only weakened their only reliable voice in the administration. These two positions dramatize the potential gains and losses of direct political participation. Similarly, AGAPAN's two PT councilors have alienated some former members and some potential political allies, since their presence persistently identifies AGAPAN with the PT. Many grassroots groups try to dodge this issue by building ties with bureaucrats, and then creating temporary coalitions for specific legislative efforts. The small scale of local politics makes perceptions of independence difficult to maintain, however. Both of these dilemmas capture what many local environmental groups see as their principal challenge—acquiring adequate resources for their environmental agenda, without sacrificing their ability to autonomously decide what their agenda (and solutions) should be.

ENVIRONMENTAL MOBILIZING IN THE AMAZON

Turning to the third empirical cut into the Brazilian environmental movement, a regional one, the real puzzle is the apparent absence of the self-identified environmental movement from the most important Brazilian environmental issue in the eyes of most non-Brazilians: the Amazon. While all other regions of Brazil can claim dozens and even hundreds of environmental organizations, they have only appeared in the Amazon region itself in the very late 1980s, and have not been well integrated into the national mobilizations.[18] This observation does not mean that there has been no regional environmental mobilization on environmental issues. Indigenous and rubber tapper groups have joined with other peoples of the forest to protect their lands and ways of life; they have given stunning testimony on the need to preserve the Amazon in international fora like the World Bank; and they have pioneered creative tactics (e.g. the *empates*, where communities physically and peacefully block destruction of the forest) and aims (e.g. the extractive reserves, which promote communal ownership of land and preserve both

---

[18] There are some exceptions to the temporal generalization, like SOPREN. These few examples have mostly acted in isolation from other environmental groups, largely for reasons of distance and expense in interacting with other parts of the country. The relative isolation from other regions of Brazil continues to exist. This was exemplified in 1991, when environmentalists who were gathered in a national preparatory forum for the Earth Summit released a statement repudiating a Pilot Plan for the Amazon—which a small group of regional environmentalists had helped to shape.

the forest and traditional forest-based livelihoods) in both local and national political confrontations.[19] From the standpoint of environmental politics, it does not matter much that these groups do not describe themselves as environmentalists. They acknowledge certain congruences in their aims with those of environmentalists, and have formed successful coalitions on that foundation. From the standpoint of the more sociological network analysis here, it does matter. These non-environmental actors are much more systematically integrated into international environmental networks than into their own national environmental movement. There are some extremely important exceptions to this generalization, such as the Institute for Amazonian Studies (IEA), a Brazilian organization which facilitated the initial contacts between the Amazonian popular groups and international environmentalists. The various national fora and gatherings of self-described environmentalists, however, have discussed only tangentially the Amazon. The last broad sustained mobilization on the Amazon that included substantial numbers of Brazilian environmentalists took place in 1978 and 1979, well before the Amazon was a global household word. These networking (or non-networking) facts would be a mere curiosity except for the political implications for both sides. The prominence of their international allies made the forest peoples vulnerable to a backlash of claims that the Amazon was being 'internationalized' in the late 1980s. A broader domestic base outside the region—which a mobilized environmental movement could have supported—would have made these claims less credible. From the other side, environmentalists have so far missed a clear opportunity to build their commitment to the intersection of environmental and survival concerns, through political support of the forest groups.

When questioned, many Brazilian environmentalists replied that they *had* mobilized on issues related to the Amazon. However, they locate the causes of and solutions to the disappearance of the Amazon not in specific policies, but in a whole set of political and economic structures. Brazilian environmentalists tend to focus on the Amazon's integration into Brazilian national systems of production and power. Their approach de-emphasizes the Amazon's uniqueness as a Brazilian environmental heritage and concern, or as an irreplaceable link in such global collective goods as climate and biodiversity. According to them, the same forces of international and national capitalism at work in the Amazon's grandiose and destructive projects like Grande Carajás are those which produced Cubatão, a São Paulo city which was globally renowned for its industrial pollution. The small-scale agricultural producers of the Amazon, who contribute their share to the Amazon's depletion, are the unacknowledged offspring of unequal patterns of arable land distribution in other regions of Brazil, and were displaced by the same large-scale commercial agricultural producers who have made pesticide and herbicide pollution a major concern for southern environmentalists. The

---

[19]   These mobilizations have been followed and documented better than any other facet of Brazilian environmental politics (see Hecht and Cockburn 1990; Hurrell 1992: 398–429; Mendes 1989; and Place 1993).

same military government which initiated the accelerated occupation of the Amazon in the 1970s for security reasons also tried to build a major nuclear program and institutionalized political exclusion and centralization—two additional rallying points for Brazilian environmentalists. Consequently, neither the forest peoples nor international environmentalists have found a national self-described environmental movement partner for their policy mobilizations because Brazilian environmentalists have understood the Amazon as a problem requiring political transformation, and not isolated policies. Whether this stance will continue is not clear. During the Earth Summit mobilizations, representatives of the Amazonian rural unions and indigenous groups were a vital part of the Brazilian preparations, along with self-described environmentalists from all over the country. Such contacts may reduce the strategic distance between the groups.

In summary, at the national level during the 1980s the Brazilian environmental movement has increasingly played transformative and symbolic political roles. At the local level, representative/policy roles predominated, but all roles were played to various degrees by individual organizations. Finally, most 'mobilizing' on the Amazon by Brazilian self-described environmentalists has involved transformative and cultural political roles rather than representation-oriented participation. These observations form the basis for an initial evaluation of the partial purview of other observers of these movements.

Images of Social Movements and their Political Roles

This chapter began with the paradox of simultaneous and very different interpretations of popular movements. Understanding the different potential political roles of social movements resolves this paradox. Both academic and non-academic observers look to find social movements in different political roles. As a corollary, they downplay or even omit discussions of social movements in other political roles. The old metaphor of the blind people examining an elephant and—in its trunk, its tail, its ears, and its body—discovering incompatible images of the elephant comes to mind. Both academics and potential political allies of social movements tend to construct similarly partial views of the same social movements because they search for them in limited political roles. Since popular movements have occupied unevenly the range of roles theoretically open to them, they variously appear to different observers as absent to fully present. In this section, I illustrate this point in two different ways. First, I identify two other sets of actors in Brazilian environmental politics—international environmentalists and the Brazilian military—and show how their very different expectations of Brazilian environmentalists have produced their disparate conclusions about its importance. Second, I examine two prominent approaches to the study of social movements—resource mobilization and new social movements approaches—and show

how their respective political role emphases would lead them to make nearly opposite evaluations of the political importance of the Brazilian environmental movement. Finally, I briefly discuss how these observations apply to popular movements as well.

International environmentalists and the Brazilian military have drawn nearly opposite conclusions about the national Brazilian environmental movement, which can be easily traced to their political role expectations of the movement. From the point of view of international environmentalists, the Brazilian environmental movement has been largely invisible. International environmentalists have looked for Brazilian allies most often on environmental policy issues. Even more specifically, they have looked for mobilizing partners on policies regarding the Amazon. They have found domestic partners in indigenous and rural union activists, who did not historically think of themselves as environmentalists. With a few exceptions, self-described environmentalists have not joined these mobilizations. Their absence is less a matter of differing ultimate aims from the international environmentalists than it is a difference on political strategy. While international environmentalists looked in vain for allies among Brazilian environmentalists in a representation role, Brazilian environmentalists were stressing transformative politics as an approach to the same empirical referent, the Amazon. The result is that the Brazilian environmental movement vanishes as a partner for the kind of political participation which international environmentalists want.

The Brazilian military, on the other hand, has looked for the environmental movement as a symbolic and transformative actor, and found what it feared. The Brazilian armed forces have largely justified their own overweening political role on symbolic grounds, and are themselves masters of symbolic politics. Even in Brazil's independence struggle, the Brazilian armed forces did not engage in physical defense against an external foe, and they have rarely played this classic concrete role of a military. 'Order and progress', the 1960s fight against an internal enemy, the original acceleration of the settling of the Amazon in order to occupy this foreign land within Brazilian borders—all of these are examples of the Brazilian military's own performance of symbolic politics. It is small wonder that it takes the symbolic and transformative aims of the environmental movement seriously. The environmental movement aims to threaten the military's cherished conceptions of development, security, and so on, and the military feels threatened. Its own interpretations of these concepts are, after all, the basis of its claims to a prominent political role. Whereas the more limited policy mobilizations of the 1970s in Brazil largely were tolerated by a military then in power, the symbolic and transformative mobilizations of the 1980s are far less acceptable to the military.

There have been very few studies of the Brazilian environmental movement, and fewer yet which consider them through the lens of social movements theories. Nonetheless, the two dominant paradigms of social movements—resource mobilization and new social movements—make certain assumptions about political roles which would produce contradictory conclusions about the Brazilian environmental movement. Like the Brazilian military and international environmentalists, they would find only pieces of the 'elephant'.

Resource mobilization theories and the related political opportunity approaches highlight the formal political arena and the roles for social movements there. These theorists have provided excellent and detailed images of the points of contact between the formal political arena and less institutionalized forms of collective action like social movement organizations, especially as the social movements seek to influence government policies (the representation role). Because these approaches typically do not distinguish the kinds of demands social movements make on the formal political system—substantive or transformative—they also provide some framework for thinking about the state transformation political role. Resource mobilization theorists tend to de-emphasize the informal political arenas, however. In particular, these theorists commonly have underemphasized the cultural political role.[20] The instrumental and utilitarian foundations of the resource mobilization approach and its offshoots took grievances, preferences, and values as given, rather than as socially constructed. If they did consider the process of constructing meanings, identities, and utopias, these were most commonly seen as by-products of the other political roles, rather than as important political practices in their own right. Such an approach would not find the Brazilian environmental movement to be very successful. Brazilian environmentalists gained a chapter on the environment in the 1988 Constitution only at the expense of many of the clauses they themselves considered most important. In addition, they have eschewed evident opportunities to play an important representational role, notably on the Amazon. Although Brazilian environmentalists collectively have pursued important transformative aims, these have produced few concrete changes in the formal political sphere.

New social movements theorists, on the other hand, focus most of their attention on the cultural political role and its accompanying state transformation role. This emphasis is in part the product of an effort to avoid the political reductionism of other social movements theories, where only the measurable impact on formal political institutions is highlighted. Nonetheless, some go far in the opposite direction, even restricting the label 'social movement' to conflicts over fundamental social relations of power or to transformative aims.[21] In this way, new social movements theorists often disregard the more substantive and concrete political roles which many social movement organizations play. Such roles may be denigrated as 'interest group' politics, implying that working within existing political institutions is a band-aid approach to deeper problems and not worthy of

---

[20] This gap is beginning to be filled. One early attempt, which identified this same gap and tried to fill it with a social psychology of collective action, was the collection of essays in Morris and Mueller (1992).

[21] For examples, see Touraine (1981) and Melucci (1989). Melucci does emphasize that observable actions and their impact on political institutions are legitimate objects of inquiry, but not at the expense of the cultural dimension.

collective action. In this view, Brazilian transformative coalition building—however successful or unsuccessful in measurable results—embodies important new political understandings and relations.

In very similar ways, different observers draw contradictory conclusions about popular movements. At least since Marx, many scholars and activists have expected popular movements to play a transformative political role. At the workplace and the voting box, popular actors were to fight for transformation of economic and political structures. They also expected popular movements to engage in cultural politics, transforming their own and their fellow workers' consciousness. This approach has tended to de-emphasize or even denigrate the efforts of popular organizations and individuals to pursue their most immediate substantive needs through collaboration with the welfare state (representation politics) or community organizing (informal polity). In this view, as revolutionary movements have declined across the continent since the 1970s (although not in all countries!), popular movements appear to be declining as important political actors. At the other extreme, the Catholic Church, northern aid organizations, and some academic observers have sometimes decried the 'co-optation' of ecclesiastic base communities, soup kitchens, and so on when they turn from their original purposes to more transformative aims. In their view, the informal political and simple representation roles are more authentic popular political roles than transformative mobilizations which challenge the military, the church hierarchy, or the political status quo. For observers between the two extremes, it is still worth remembering that it is both theoretically and politically limiting to assume that popular movements *will* play specific political roles. Popular movements need to remain creative and experimental in their political participation in order to assure their continued survival and vitality in political systems which still, too often, exclude them.

9 The Authoritarian Alternative: 'Anti-Politics' in the Popular Sectors of Lima

Aldo Panfichi[1]

'In Peru everything is possible', Peruvians say when we are asked about the multiple paradoxes of our history. These paradoxes include: that the country's most popular governments have been authoritarian; that the democratic left, the largest in Latin America, virtually disappeared in a few years; and that current President Alberto Fujimori completed a successful five-year term and was re-elected in 1995 by a majority of poor voters, despite the harsh economic policies his government has applied and the persistence of widespread hunger and misery.

The objective of this chapter is to analyze the processes behind these paradoxes, especially the factors that explain the re-emergence of authoritarian political leadership in Peru in the 1990s, in a context of economic crisis, political violence, and lack of alternatives. It is particularly concerned with explaining why a broad sector of the urban population of Lima identifies with or feels represented by authoritarian and personalistic leaders. The central argument is that the articulation of three factors, in a specific historical moment, favors the emergence and popular support of this type of leadership.

First, the dramatic worsening of an economic crisis which began in 1974 led by the end of the 1980s to the general impoverishment of society, and to an unprecedented collective sense of insecurity and despair throughout the country. This economic crisis was the final expression of the collapse of a development model based on import-substitution industrialization and the unrestricted defense of the internal market. Second, democratic institutions, especially political parties, were unable to represent the interests of the majority and resolve concrete social problems. These problems were exacerbated by the indiscriminate violence of Sendero Luminoso (SL) and the Movimiento Revolucionario Tupac Amaru (MRTA). The Peruvian case is relevant in that *all* political parties, including the Marxist and democratic left ones, have experienced failure in local and national government.

[1] The author is grateful to Cynthia Sanborn, Felipe Portocarrero, Joanna Drzewieniecki, Carlos Franco, Guillermo Rochabrún, and Romeo Grompone for their valuable comments on this chapter. The editors would like to thank Judy Rein for her translation of the essay.

The convergence of these processes generated a serious destructuring of the social order, which opened space for a third factor: the emergence of personalistic and authoritarian leaders, from social sectors marginal to the political system, who offer hope for a better future. The initial construction of these leaderships is facilitated by the existence of common life experiences shared by the leader and the masses which create elements of identification between them. This identification later becomes conditional political support when the leader proves his effectiveness with concrete achievements related to the greatest perceived needs of the population.

This chapter is based on a larger research project on survival networks and political identity among the popular sectors of Lima between 1980 and 1995. The project combines a 'macro' analysis of the recent transformations of Peruvian economy and society, with field research in two poor Lima neighborhoods. Interviews with neighborhood residents, as well as a review of various quantitative and qualitative sources, suggest the importance of the three factors outlined above in explaining the popular support afforded to leaders such as Alberto Fujimori.

An Unresolved Economic Crisis

A primary factor in the resurgence of authoritarian political leadership in contemporary Peru is the failure of democratic governments throughout the 1980s to resolve the economic crisis inherited from the previous military regime. This persistent governmental incapacity had its greatest expression in the economic débâcle of Alan García's government (1985–90), which produced a collective sense of insecurity and despair without precedent in Peru's history.

The economic crisis that began in 1974 played an important role in the political exhaustion of the reformist military regime and the search for a negotiated transition to democracy (1978–80). In effect, after several years during which economic growth averaged 5 per cent per year, the military regime was unable to continue its anti-oligarchic and redistributive reforms because of the eruption of the economic crisis and the exacerbation of powerful social tensions.[2] This situation threatened the institutional stability of the armed forces, leading to the replacement of General Velasco in the government leadership in 1975 and, soon after, the pursuit of a negotiated transition to democracy.

The transition to democracy in Peru was different from other Latin American experiences at that time. As Cynthia Sanborn observes, this transition had as its point of departure a reformist regime in crisis (1991). The regime had suspended important political liberties, but had implemented structural reforms with a socialist orientation (McClintock and Lowenthal 1983; Stepan 1978). These included a

---

[2] The economic crisis was triggered when the military regime was left without financial resources due to the falling prices of Peruvian exports and the refusal of international lenders to provide new loans. Without fresh money, the military government could not continue its social and political reforms, nor maintain the arms race with Pinochet's Chile.

radical agrarian reform, the nationalization of large industries, and worker participation in the profits and ownership of companies. The reforms eliminated the material bases of oligarchic domination and facilitated the creation of unprecedented forms of social organization and democratization.

For this reason, the transition to democracy was characterized by extensive social struggles and intense debate over how to preserve the social gains achieved under the military, how to resolve the economic crisis, and which social sectors ought to be most affected by austerity measures. The Marxist left and APRA (Partido Aprista Peruano) played an active role in this debate, since together the two groups constituted nearly two-thirds of the Constituent Assembly elected to direct the transition.

The re-establishment of democracy in 1980 sparked considerable expectations for immediate political and economic improvements. These expectations are explained in part by the active role that social movements played in the regime change. It was expected that the demands of these social movements would be addressed by the new government. Furthermore, the electorate participating in the transition was larger, younger, and more politicized than in the previous election in 1963, and thus almost without any experience of the functioning of democracy. Demographic growth, the extension of public education, and legal reforms such as the right of illiterates to vote and compulsory voting for those 18 and older, expanded the electorate from 2 million in 1963 to almost 5 million in 1980. In the latter election, 60 per cent of the voters were less than 35 years old and voted for the first time to elect a President (Tuesta 1994). The electorate was also much more politicized and conscious of its rights, given the impact of the Velasco reformist experience and the redistributive expectations that it unleashed.

Fernando Belaunde won the 1980 elections, becoming President for the second time. Belaunde, an older populist caudillo, had been ousted from power in 1968 by a group of military officers headed by Velasco Alvarado. His victory was interpreted as a rejection of the military and a new embrace of a centrist option. Nevertheless, immediately after the victory, Belaunde established an alliance with the rightist Partido Popular Cristiano (PPC), through which he obtained absolute control of the executive and legislative branches of government.

In the electoral campaign Belaunde promised to solve the economic and social problems that were the legacy of the military regime, especially the economic crisis with its consequence of an enormous foreign debt and a significant drop in wages. His principal promise was that in five years his government would create a million new jobs and would promote fair wages for all. Nonetheless, it was not long before people realized that these promises were merely rhetoric. In reality, the Belaunde government implemented an economic policy that contradicted his electoral promises. In exchange for new loans from international banks, Belaunde, surrounded by a group of intimate friends and relatives, decided to implement a semi-liberal economic program based on easy credit for the export mining and agriculture sectors, elimination of subsidies for basic needs, maintenance of protectionist measures for certain national industries, and a partial roll-back of labor rights for workers.

Beginning in 1983 the economic situation worsened dramatically. The combination of inefficiency and corruption in government administration, falling export prices, and pressure from international lenders for payment of the foreign debt made the situation very difficult. At the end of the Belaunde government the situation was much worse than at the beginning. Between 1980 and 1985 the foreign debt grew from $8.7 to $12.7 billion. Wages lost 40 per cent of purchasing power; inflation went from 60.8 per cent to 158.3 per cent; and the currency devaluation from 30.4 per cent to 244 per cent (*Perú en números* 1992). Obviously, the electoral promise of a million jobs remained a distant memory.

Despite popular dissatisfaction with the Belaunde government, the 1985 elections continued to arouse interest and expectation. The principal political parties (Acción Popular, the Partido Popular Cristiano, APRA, and Izquierda Unida) enjoyed substantial support. Opinion polls in 1986 revealed that 76 per cent of Lima residents sympathized with a political party and only 16 per cent declared themselves independent. A few years later this trend was totally reversed. In April 1993, only 12 per cent of Lima residents declared any party sympathy, while 86 per cent claimed to be independent (Torres 1993).

The 1985 elections were also characterized by a consensus among citizens to support continued democracy while emphasizing changes in the economic situation and greater social justice. This consensus facilitated the re-emergence of nationalist political alternatives with a clear social-democratic profile. The victory of APRA with Alan García and the consolidation of Izquierda Unida as the second political force in the country confirmed this situation (Sanborn 1991).

Alan García was the president who generated the greatest expectations at the beginning of his term. In August 1985, one month after the installation of his government, polls revealed that 90 per cent of Lima residents approved of his leadership (Torres 1993). García, a charismatic leader and dynamic orator, criss-crossed the country announcing that a new era of progress and justice had begun in Peru. In this new era government would be for the poor majority and not for the rich as in the past. Thus, the goals of the government were to control inflation, stimulate economic growth, and reduce poverty. In this way, the material bases of injustice would end and the country would embark, finally, on a period of progress and development.

With these objectives, García sought an alliance with the country's most powerful private economic groups, to protect the internal market so that they could invest in an import-substitution industrialization process. In addition, García declared his intention to limit payment on the foreign debt to 10 per cent of the value of exports in order to use these resources for financing politically expedient measures. He froze prices on basic goods, reduced charges for public services to below cost, indiscriminately expanded subsidies, and offered direct public credit, at times with zero interest. These policies, which Dornbusch describes as typical

of Latin American economic populism, paid insufficient attention to risks of inflation, excessive growth of the fiscal deficit, and the new restrictions imposed by the
globalization of the world economy (Dornbusch and Edwards 1991).

García's strategy soon proved to be mistaken. Domestic big business did not re-
invest its profits, but, as had often been done in the past, private profits were deposited in foreign banks. The unrestricted defense of the internal market in the
context of globalization of the international economy ultimately favored the shady
dealings of the President's friends and cronies. Furthermore, limiting payments
on the foreign debt brought the state in conflict with international lenders, to the
point that Peru was declared ineligible for new international credit. Faced with this
situation, and determined to maintain his popularity at all cost, García pursued
a disastrous economic strategy. Faced with a shortage of funds, the APRA government printed money without effective backing, took control of exchange operations, and finally, tried to nationalize the banks. The successive errors provoked a
virtual catastrophe. In 1990 annual inflation reached the record rate of 7,649 per
cent; currency devaluation was at 4,597 per cent, and 75 per cent of the work-force
was unemployed or underemployed. Furthermore, between 1985 and 1990, the
foreign debt grew from $12.7 billion to $19.8 billion and wages lost 60 per cent of
their purchasing power (*Peru Statistics* 1993).

This catastrophe was the greatest decline within the medium-term trend of
deterioration in the Peruvian economy beginning in the mid-1970s. The electoral
promises made by Belaunde (1980–5) and García (1985–90) to control the crisis
and improve the living conditions of the majority were refuted by reality. Worst
of all was that the economic collapse occurred in conjunction with the sustained
growth of subversive violence and generalized corruption at all levels of government. The simultaneity of these processes tremendously affected popular confidence
in the handling of government by the so-called 'political class'. Also, as Julio Cotler
indicates, it would contribute to the development in the 1990s of an entirely new
political scenario marked by the emergence of new actors, the exhaustion of others,
and the redefinition of the meaning of the political (Cotler 1994). The latter point
is examined in the next section.

The Delegitimization of Politics

A second factor that explains the resurgence of authoritarian leadership is the
belief of the majority of the population that political parties do not represent their
interests, much less that these organizations are competent to govern.[3] The rejection
of parties is a product of the continuity of oligarchic and clientelistic characteristics

---

[3] Since 1989, besides Fujimori, 'independents' have won the majority of mayoralties in the principal cities of the country. The outgoing mayor of Lima, Ricardo Belmont, was a popular television
celebrity who was elected in 1989 and 1992. His well-known slogan was 'works and not words'.

in the structure and functioning of these organizations, which in a new historical context are seen as unable to provide for the common good through government action. Parties in power had become client networks entangled in struggles over the use of public funds for partisan benefit. As the economic crisis deepened, this inefficient and ethically questionable behavior increasingly distanced political parties from the interests and needs of the majority.

Historically, Peruvian political parties, with the exception of APRA, have had little institutional development and weak insertion in society (Cotler 1978). Parties that have come to power generally have been electoral movements based on particular segments of the population, organized around a political *caudillo*, and seeking access to state benefits. After the close of electoral campaigns, the organizational dynamism of parties declined notably or rested on local leaders holding public office. There never has existed the will to organize the population or to construct permanent political institutions that channel their interests and aspirations. This was the case of Augusto B. Leguía's Partido Civil, Sánchez Cerro's Unión Revolucionaria, General Manuel Odría's Unión Nacional, and Fernando Belaunde's Acción Popular, among others (López 1991; Cotler 1978).

Most political parties, regardless of their ideology, have developed oligarchic and clientelistic forms of organization. A closed group of white educated men, many of whom are linked by family and friendship ties, unite around a central leader. This self-proclaimed leadership makes the important decisions without consulting the so-called base of support, with whom they are linked clientelistically through prebends and benefits that are acquired through access to public administration. The structure of the organization does not facilitate channels of incorporation and participation of sectors other than the original bases of support.

The reformist military experience (1968–80) affected the activity of the parties even though, as we shall see below, it maintained the bases of the traditional ways of doing politics. In effect, the military regime developed structural reforms with significant democratizing impact, but it also sought to construct a corporatist model of society, distributing prebends from the state in exchange for political support. The aim was to restrict the emergence of autonomous political groups and control their capacity to make demands (Dietz 1980). Parties were excluded from any role in political intermediation. They were reproached, just as Fujimori has done throughout his term, for failing to have carried out promised reforms. Without the possibility of accessing public spending and, therefore, of satisfying demands, political parties fell into inactivity. Only APRA maintained a degree of activism, organizing annual demonstrations in which it claimed intellectual paternity of the reforms. In addition, youth in the party attempted to take advantage of any conflict to maintain the effectiveness of the organization in the streets.[4]

---

[4] On 5 Feb. 1975, after a police strike was repressed by the army, looting and acts of violence against public buildings erupted in Lima. Eighty-six people died, 137 stores were destroyed, and the losses were more than $6 million. APRA and Bandera Roja (later Sendero Luminoso) militants tried to give political direction to this popular explosion (see Panfichi 1983).

Nevertheless, during these years new political alternatives arose. Countless small Marxist political parties were organized and gained influence in social sectors mobilized in favor of reforms. These parties, with radical discourses and confrontational practices, fueled an unprecedented process of popular organization. Numerous unions, peasant communities, neighborhood associations, women's groups, and student organizations burst upon the political scene with demands of autonomy, improved living conditions, and greater democracy. The unprecedented encounter between these organizations and the Marxist left gave shape to social movements which played a fundamental role in the transition to democracy. Large national strikes in 1977, 1978, and 1979 compelled the military to seek a negotiated retreat. At the end of the military regime, everything seemed to indicate that great changes in the political representation of the poor were becoming reality.[5]

The transition to democracy led to renewed popular interest in political parties. These organizations were thought to be the best instrument to channel popular demands and to overcome the economic crisis. Interest in parties was expressed in the establishment of a more or less stable pattern of voting between 1980 and 1986.[6] The greatest surprise was the speed with which some parties were able to rekindle citizen expectations, especially since some of them had been inactive for years. There has been no convincing explanation for this phenomenon.

Frances Hagopian (1993) nonetheless offers an interesting analytical path. She suggests determining whether the military regime dismantles or restructures the social mediation networks between state and society, and how this legacy influences the problems of consolidation of democracy. In Peru, as noted above, military reformism did not modify the clientelistic practices of intermediation between state and society. Rather, the initial revitalization of the most established parties appears to have rested on the expectations of the very sectors that maintained these practices. Other social sectors, especially those who were mobilized by the reforms, including the working class, the poor peasantry, teachers, and students, placed their hopes for political representation on the left.

Unfortunately, subsequent events demonstrated that the re-establishment of democracy did not entail organization of a party system that would represent the new social correlations and that, in addition, would serve as a support for the institutional functioning of democracy. The linkages between social movements and parties were weak and lacking articulation. Furthermore, the parties maintained traditional forms of operation that reinforced clientelistic relations with specific social groups, without transcending those narrow confines. Resources

[5] The alliance of interests among popular organizations and the Marxist left led some analysts to posit a militant image of urban squatters, who appeared to definitively surmount former clientelistic practices with radical demands and confrontational practices (see Degregori *et al.* 1986; Stokes 1991*b*).

[6] Between 1980 and 1986 the country appeared to divide itself in three electoral blocks, the right (AP-PPC), the center (APRA), and the left (IU) (Tuesta 1994).

distributed through partisan networks were concentrated in a few sectors, while the economic crisis weakened the functioning of the popular organizations and exacerbated poverty.

Nonetheless, after the reformist experience under Velasco, the population was not the same as before. Not only was it much larger, but it was also more demanding of its rulers and conscious of its rights. Thus, as people perceived themselves to be excluded from state benefits in the context of extreme need, many became impatient and accused politicians of 'not helping the most needy, only their own people'.[7] Thus, the old clientelist networks lost effectiveness, 'liberating' the population from its previous political sympathies and producing an electorate much freer to seek other options. During the 1980s, with the successive failures of left and right parties, the space for independent forces had been opened up.

The left, which was the new political force, is the most illustrative case. As Sanborn (1991) indicates, the incorporation of the left into democracy was not the product of political repression or ideological conviction but a pragmatic response to the possibilities of electoral success. Popular expectations of the left were high. It had in its favor the prestige of having stimulated popular organization and an egalitarian political discourse. It was also thought that the left would provide a greater number of people access to state benefits and administer government more ethically than traditional politicians. Nonetheless, the subsequent behavior of the left would reveal that it was not so different from more traditional political parties.

Leaders on the left, with few exceptions, were university students and upper- and middle-class intellectuals. They were young whites and mestizos from coastal cities, with an extremely ideological and confrontational discourse. The popular masses, in contrast, were poor workers and peasants, Indians and mestizos with strong roots in rural Andean society. The links that the leadership of the left sought to forge with the people were generally utilitarian. Parties competed among themselves to 'capture' popular leaders for electoral purposes. Rarely did these popular leaders rise to the directorship of the parties, a task reserved for a closed group of enlightened leaders. The justification for such elitism could be found in the aristocratic attitude of those who felt naturally called to govern or rule. The leadership of the political parties in the country has not been able to escape this attitude (Nugent 1993).

The creation of the United Left alliance (IU) was also the result of electoral calculations rather than the product of ideological or programmatic agreements. After the electoral disasters of 1979 and 1980, when the left ran divided, the parties decided to form Izquierda Unida. Yet, IU never had an organization of its own, nor did it open channels of incorporation to the mobilized masses. The majority of these parties, fearful of losing bureaucratic control of the leadership,

[7] In our work in poor neighborhoods it is common to observe how access to certain political client networks is a factor of differentiation and conflict within the population. In an old neighborhood in the center of Lima, the few young people with salaried employment in the state obtained their positions through family political 'contacts'.

maintained their own party structures, fighting among themselves for quotas in the central leadership and on the list of candidates for parliament, mayoralties, and city councils. This struggle would lead to the political paralysis of Izquierda Unida, and later, to its splintering into several regroupings.

After the transition to democracy, the behavior of all the political parties, whether in the government or in opposition, has emphasized their own interest to the detriment of the general interest. The institutional weakness of the political system has facilitated this behavior by impeding the organization of a 'public' sphere where the 'common welfare' is the purpose of politics. In the government, the norm has been to capture the state without opening spaces for political negotiation or consensus-building. Parliamentary minorities have always been browbeaten into following the instructions of the party 'chiefs'. Promises of serving the 'common good' have been quickly cast aside, and public resources used to the benefit of client networks, the badly labeled 'base of support'. As Passer notes, neither Acción Popular with Belaunde nor the APRA of García was able to generate benefits beyond the sphere of its own followers (Pásara 1993). The left that gained control of many local, regional, and municipal governments also failed in this manner.

In the opposition, political strategy was also determined by narrow group interests. The idea was to use the material needs of the people to foment the greatest possible discrediting of the government, without considering the feasibility of the demands. All government initiatives were rejected out of hand. To do otherwise was understood as a renunciation of the future political expectations of the leaders. This was the nature of García's opposition to Belaunde and the left's opposition to García (Pásara 1993). With the economic débâcle and the political violence of the end of the 1980s, the effectiveness of the political system was put into question. The needs were more pressing than ever but the behavior of the political class did not change. The perception of the uselessness of the parties for generating benefits and solving difficult situations then became generalized. The conditions for the rise of another type of political leadership were set.

The Authoritarian Alternative

In 1989 and 1990, the combination of economic catastrophe and political crisis created the daily perception of loss of known forms of reproduction of the social order. Hyperinflation made any economic planning useless, devaluation crushed the currency, and wage labor was no longer a viable alternative. Furthermore, party politics lost legitimacy as it was considered a corrupt and ineffective practice. And social organizations of a corporative nature were no longer the principal forms of popular sector association.

This situation, aggravated by the Sendero Luminoso terrorist offensive, unraveled the social organizations that had arisen in the previous decade and heavily impacted people's basic beliefs. Changes occurred unexpectedly and the referents of times past lost their previous effectiveness. Without known criteria to structure the future, the population was increasingly overtaken by uncertainty and fear.[8]

Given these conditions, we need to consider a third factor: the emergence of personalistic leaders from social sectors marginal to the political system, who offer strong solutions to the predicaments engendered by the general crisis of society. These leaders break rules and undermine institutions that interfere with their exercise of authority, placing themselves above civil society. Their legitimacy is based initially on relationships of identification between themselves and the masses, and not on mechanisms of democratic representation. To achieve this identification, leaders must possess personal qualities that have a real correlation with the life experiences of the population. But there also must be elements within the political culture that validate this type of leadership as well as some immediate inclination to follow leaders who offer order and security. This is a complex and highly problematic relationship. It arises from frustration and lack of alternatives, and evolves into conditional political support only if the leader gives proof of his effectiveness with concrete achievements linked to the greatest felt needs of the population.

This is the case of President Alberto Fujimori. His popularity is inscribed in a long-standing tradition in the political culture of the country: the belief that a strong and decisive man can, from the state, make significant changes in a rigid and exclusionary society. The extension of state benefits to the poor and marginalized population is particularly central. These expectations have a certain degree of validity in concrete historical experiences. Military coup leaders of humble origins, such as Manuel Odría (1948–56) and Juan Velasco Alvarado (1968–75), have carried out the most important social reforms in the twentieth century (Collier 1979; Bourricaud 1970). Nevertheless, the mere existence of this tradition does not accurately explain the rise and popularity of Fujimori. We must look at how relationships of identity are generated between the leader and the masses within a specific historical context, and how this relationship, in the course of the subsequent political process, is converted into conditional political support.

The general elections of 1990 took place in a context of political disenchantment: economic deprivation continued, politicians were enormously discredited, violence seemed to demolish all manner of peaceful coexistence, and all signs indicated an impending triumph for the candidate of the right, Mario Vargas Llosa. Yet, in only six weeks Alberto Fujimori, an unknown *nisei* (Peruvian of Japanese descent) with almost no publicity, went from 1 per cent of voters' preferences to 24.6 per cent of the votes in the first round of voting on 8 April. Two months later, in the second round, Fujimori won the Presidency with 62.4 per cent of the vote.

Fujimori's sweeping victory represents the biggest electoral surprise in the polit-

[8] During those years, in several parts of the country a series of fantastic stories and popular religious ceremonies appeared that reflect this context well. Crowds gathered around apparitions of crying virgins; preachers performed miracles in large stadiums; and '*pichtacos*' were rumored to steal children to sell them to 'gringos' abroad (see Panfichi 1993).

ical history of the country. His votes came from the poor and excluded sectors of society: youths unemployed because of the crisis, peasants from the poorest provinces, migrants to popular neighborhoods in Lima, street vendors and informal sector workers, workers in cottage industries, and other impoverished middle sectors (Grompone 1991*b*; Castillo 1991). The strongly polarized electoral behavior of the different districts of Lima is one example of this outcome. As seen in Table 9.1, Alberto Fujimori of the independent movement Cambio 90 obtained his strongest support in the capital from among the residents of the poor districts that surround the city. In these districts, Fujimori received between 35 per cent and 50 per cent of the votes in the first round, and up to 75 per cent of the votes in the second. The division of the left into two candidacies (IS and IU) was another factor that contributed to the frustration of many leftist sympathizers, who preferred to vote for Fujimori this time in order to head off a right-wing victory. The opposite occurred with Vargas Llosa, who obtained his greatest support in the middle- and upper-class districts. This support remained in the second round, but was not sufficient due to the numerical weight of the poor that determined the victory of Fujimori in 1990. These poor sectors, characterized by the precariousness of their occupations and existence, facing the need to elect a president in the context of considerable deficiencies and lack of alternatives, projected onto Fujimori their demands for justice, hope, and order.[9]

The initial identification with Fujimori was based on two considerations. First, it was a rejection of Vargas Llosa and the traditional politicians that surrounded him. This rejection, which had a clear class and ethnic connotation, was the initial force that mobilized voters to seek within a few weeks an alternative who was 'different' from the elites but 'close' to them. Second, within this search, a recognition of closeness is developed—the 'us' of the leader and the masses—which is based on the recognition of similar life experiences (Valentín 1993).

The existence of this recognition entails a break with the traditional patterns of legitimacy of the classic Latin American populist leaders. In effect, in earlier periods these leaders needed to appear to be wise, extraordinary men with vibrant oratory. Currently, it would seem that the basic condition is that they must resemble the common people. Upon this empathy people construct other imaginary attributes that make the leader the 'best' to handle difficult situations. In the case of Fujimori, his *nisei* background allowed him to benefit from the values of honor, work, and technology associated with this ethnicity in the popular imagination. As in many parts of the contemporary world, ethnicity emerges as an important

---

[9] Why did popular sectors identify with Fujimori and not with some other unknown candidate? Two explanations have been offered. For Grompone (1991*b*), Fujimori with his slogan 'honor, technology, and work' best captured the desire of the poor to tap into the benefits of modernity. Valentín (1993) prefers an argument based on the emotions: in the midst of uncertainties people identified with Fujimori because he is *nisei* (hard-working and honorable), poor (lacking publicity), and did not make false promises (he spoke little). He also represented the new and modern in the face of the traditional and known.

Table 9.1. Presidential election 1990: voting by districts in Lima (%)

	First round						Second round	
	IS	IU	C-90	PA	FREDEMO	Other	C-90	FREDEMO
Upper-class districts								
La Molina	3.5	4.8	18.2	8.7	63.4	1.4	32.1	67.9
Magdalena	3.5	3.8	21.5	12.3	58.2	0.7	34.8	65.2
Miraflores	2.7	3.2	13.8	8.8	70.9	0.6	24.0	76.0
San Isidro	2.1	2.6	9.9	7.1	77.7	0.6	17.8	82.2
San Borja	2.4	3.6	13.6	8.5	71.3	0.6	24.5	75.5
Middle-class districts								
Barranco	3.3	4.2	25.9	12.9	52.9	0.8	38.8	61.2
Breña	3.9	5.5	28.3	17.3	44.3	0.7	47.1	52.9
Jesus María	3.4	5.1	18.3	12.3	60.3	0.6	33.1	66.9
La Victoria	4.0	5.4	35.8	14.3	39.2	1.3	52.6	47.4
Lince	3.2	4.3	20.7	13.2	57.9	0.7	35.3	64.7
Pueblo Libre	3.4	4.5	18.1	12.3	61.2	0.5	31.8	68.2
Rimac	4.5	5.7	35.4	15.1	38.3	1.0	53.5	46.5
San Luis	3.7	6.1	36.4	11.8	40.6	1.4	51.4	48.6
San Miguel	3.3	4.1	24.1	13.1	54.9	0.5	37.6	62.4
Surco	3.2	3.6	21.6	9.9	60.6	1.1	33.7	66.3
Surquillo	4.4	4.9	32.0	14.9	42.9	0.9	48.5	51.5
Lower-class districts								
Ate	4.4	7.8	44.2	11.5	30.3	1.8	63.3	36.7
Carabayllo	6.8	8.9	39.1	18.7	23.5	3.0	70.5	29.5
Comas	7.7	8.5	43.6	17.3	21.1	1.8	72.0	28.0
Chorrillos	4.3	4.6	39.0	12.4	37.7	2.0	52.8	47.2
El Agustino	5.9	8.1	49.7	12.1	22.0	2.2	70.2	29.8
Independencia	10.1	8.3	46.3	14.7	19.1	1.5	73.3	26.7
Los Olivos	5.1	6.6	35.4	14.7	37.4	0.8	55.4	44.6
Lurigancho	2.6	6.3	49.0	11.5	29.4	1.2	63.7	36.3
San Juan L.	5.4	8.6	46.0	13.4	24.8	1.8	67.3	32.7
San Juan M.	6.3	6.0	42.2	14.9	28.8	1.8	62.5	37.5
San Martín	5.8	6.7	40.9	15.5	30.1	1.0	62.0	38.0
Villa María	7.1	7.1	45.8	15.4	22.6	2.0	68.6	31.4
Villa Salvador	6.2	9.5	47.2	17.5	16.9	2.7	75.1	24.9

Abbreviations: Izquierda Socialista (IS); Izquierda Unida (IU); Cambio 90 (C-90); Partido Aprista Peruano (PAP); Frente Democrático (FREDEMO)

Source: *Jurado Nacional de Elecciones* 1990.

political criterion when ideological or partisan arguments are no longer able to create loyalties.

There are two important experiences in the initial identification between Fujimori and his electorate: migration and ethnic discrimination. According to Franco (1991), for many poor Peruvians migration has been the central decision of their lives. Migration is not only a physical move from the country to the city but also the uncertain experience of immigration to another country, from the rural, poor, backward, and indigenous Peru to urban, modern, *limeño* and creole Peru. For migrants this has been a successful process facilitated by the modernizing attempts of the state and society between 1940 and 1980; but with the current crisis it is increasingly a more difficult prospect. Migrants transformed into squatters in Lima have altered the face of the city. They have created institutions where it was not permitted. They have constructed their own neighborhoods with collective effort beyond the limits of the modern city. And they have created a vigorous informal urban economy. All of this is accompanied by an active cultural presence that is noticeable in the streets, plazas, and mass media (Portocarrero 1993*b*; Franco 1991; Matos Mar 1984; Altamirano 1988).

President Fujimori's personal history is similar to that of these migrants.[10] His parents were poor Japanese immigrants who arrived in Peru to work as peons on a coastal plantation and shortly afterwards moved to the capital to work as caretakers in a public school in the La Victoria district. In the city, they started small business activities that allowed them to educate their children in public schools and universities. Alberto Fujimori, like many children of immigrants, adopted the myth of education as a means of personal progress. He went to the state university, received a degree in agricultural engineering, and then became an educator, thus following a path of social achievement similar to the personal experience of many migrants.

The other common experience is ethnic discrimination and racism. This experience results from Peruvian elites' adhesion to cultural criteria of social exclusion that are colonial in origin: in other words, the belief that 'the best' comes from developed countries, that Indians and blacks are inferior to whites, and that the road to progress demands the adoption of the cultural universe of Western societies.[11] Discrimination against Indians and blacks also extended to Asians. Between 1910 and 1930 several societies opposed to Asian immigration organized in Lima to 'avoid the degeneration of the race' (Morimoto 1979). The Japanese arrived in Peru beginning at the end of the nineteenth century to work as agricultural laborers. After decades of hard work and patient saving, these migrants freed their children from semi-servile work, and moved to the cities where they set up small family businesses largely located in popular neighborhoods.

Nonetheless, in 1939 World War II broke out and shortly afterwards Japan became involved. In Peru, which was allied with the United States, dozens of small businesses belonging to families of Japanese origin were attacked and destroyed by mobs (Jochamowitz 1993). Sectors of the dominant elite encouraged these

---

[10] See Jochamowitz (1993). For a comparative analysis of the personal and political trajectories of Alberto Fujimori and Abimael Guzmán, see Panfichi and Francis (1993).

[11] In a study on the desires and fantasies of different social groups in Lima, G. Portocarrero found in upper-class youth the following lament: 'It is a shame that Perú was discovered by the Spanish. If it had been the English the Indians would have been eliminated and Perú today would be a great and prosperous country like the United States' (1993*a*: 176).

demonstrations out of a desire to demonstrate their allegiance to the allies. Years of family labor were lost and many Peruvians of Japanese origin were deported to concentration camps in California. The Fujimori family did not experience any direct attacks, but as a result of the general hostility they did lose the first family business—a tire repair shop. They were also terrified witnesses to the attacks on their community and the indifference of the authorities toward preventing them.[12] These experiences, similar to those lived for centuries by the black and Indian majorities of the country, created a sphere of identification and closeness among these ethnic groups, at the same time that it separated them from the white Peruvian upper class (Macera 1992).

Of course, the United Left presidential candidate, Alfonso Barrantes Lingan, also represented similar personal traits, in that he was a *cholo*, a migrant of humble origins, and a popular labor lawyer. However, by 1990 Barrantes was seen by the voters as part of the political elite, and in fact a fairly close friend of Alan García and the APRA. In this sense, for many the former Mayor of Lima (1983–6) was another 'traditional' politician. Furthermore, his candidacy was damaged by the division of the left into two opposing candidacies and multiple warring voices, which discredited the entire left sector.

In fact, in addition to Fujimori's own personal traits, popular identification with his candidacy was fueled by popular hostility towards the entire existing system of political representation, including the parties of the left. This is a characteristic of all modern democracies, but it reaches extreme levels in Peru. For example, a survey of political attitudes in ten poor districts of Lima conducted three months after Fujimori's first government began revealed almost unanimous negative views toward politicians.[13] Ninety-four per cent of those interviewed said that they were in agreement that 'the people are always deceived by politicians'. The same percentage said that 'politicians always end up arranging things among themselves', and 89 per cent agreed that 'the politicians and the wealthy are always in collusion'.[14]

This widespread rejection of political parties has been based on the principle of effectiveness and has always been accompanied by a strong ethical condemnation: politicians are 'demagogues' and incapable of constructing the forms of consensus that ensure good government. In the public view, they only want to reach state power to appropriate gains for their own benefit. Parties have been perceived as instruments of social differentiation, with a real gap between their discourse

[12]   A detailed version of the incidents and abuses suffered by the Peruvian-Japanese community and, to a lesser extent, the Fujimori family, can be found in the fascinating book by Luis Jochamowitz (1993).

[13]   This survey was carried out by Jorge Parodi and Walter Twanama of CEDYS between 19 Oct. and 12 Nov. 1990. The districts chosen were Carabayllo, Comas, El Agustino, Independencia, San Juan de Lurigancho, San Martin de Porras, Chorrillos, San Juan de Miraflores, Villa el Salvador, and Villa María del Triunfo.

[14]   Similar results were found in the survey 'Youths and the Constituent Congress', taken by *Alternativa-Tarea* in November 1992 of young people in the popular neighborhoods of Cercado, Comas, Independencia, San Juan de Lurigancho, San Martin de Porras, Rimac, and Villa María del Triunfo. See Pineda *et al.* (1993). Interviews done by the author in Barrios Altos, Comas, and Independencia also confirm this perception.

and practice. Nevertheless, a further element intensifies the popular rejection of parties—the feelings of injustice and resentment that the popular sector has towards the upper classes. These feelings are also directed at the parties, given the class and ethnic make-up of their leadership and their oligarchic practices with respect to their so-called bases of support.

According to the Parodi–Twanama (1993) study, 85 per cent of those inter-viewed considered their situation unjust or very unjust in comparison with that of upper-class neighborhoods, a rate which increases as socioeconomic status declines.[15] The opinion of the rich is also very negative. In the same study inter-viewees were asked to select two words from a series of adjectives that best described the rich. The results: 'exploiters', 64 per cent; 'selfish', 54 per cent; 'look down on the people', 33 per cent; 'hard-working', 22 per cent; 'polite', 15 per cent; and 'kind', 1 per cent. These figures are more pronounced among poorer respondents. The same opinion is repeated in domestic workers' testimonies about their employers (Sindicato de Trabajadoras del Hogar 1983), or among poor *pobladores* who voted for Fujimori (Valentín 1993).[16]

Fujimori's popularity was, and continues to be, reinforced by the President's continuous attacks on the parties and other institutions of representative demo-cracy. With these attacks Fujimori has sought to de-institutionalize the norms of political coexistence and personalize the expectations of the masses onto himself. Nonetheless, he could only transform this initial identification into firmer polit-ical support once he had obtained concrete achievements related to the needs and hopes of the population. This effectiveness has been a crucial factor in the legit-imization of his leadership, added to the fact that his government has not seemed to be associated with problems of corruption and immorality.

The formidable political impact of lowered inflation and new growth, the cap-ture of Shining Path leader Abimael Guzmán and virtual halt of terrorist activity, and the revival of foreign investment is difficult to evaluate.[17] For many Peruvians, these achievements have made Fujimori the 'strong hand' necessary to establish

---

[15] The CEDYS survey divides the population in two sectors according to income and housing characteristics (middle and lower sector). With these criteria, 18 per cent of those interviewed cor-responded to the middle sector (family income above $150 and housing with basic services) and 82 per cent belonged to the lower sector (family income less than $150 and housing without services). The lower sector was subdivided into three levels: A: 27 per cent, B: 59 per cent, C: 14 per cent. See Parodi (1993: 21–3).

[16] One of these squatters said: 'I am from the lower class . . . there are great differences between classes . . . the upper class hired my daughter and do you know how they have kept her? . . . [S]emi-slave, like a *chola* in every sense of the word, and this is discrimination. She was born a *chola*. If they were nicer, more human, but no, they try to get every last bit out of her . . . her payments is where they take the most . . .' (Valentín 1993: 103).

[17] Inflation had declined from 7,650 per cent in 1990 to 10.2 per cent in 1995. In June 1992 the top leader of the MRTA, Victor Polay, was captured. Three months later Abimael Guzmán fell. Since then, most of the members of the central committees of MRTA and Sendero Luminoso have been detained. In 1993, after several years, the Peruvian economy grew 6.8 per cent, followed by a remarkable 13 per cent in 1994 and 7.3 per cent in 1995. Meanwhile, foreign investment increased notably from 1993 onward. This is a significant amount but still modest if we consider that between 1986 and 1987 alone the economy of the country contracted between 23 per cent and 14 per cent.

order and put an end to the previous violence and uncertainty. Public opinion polls have reinforced this view and shown that expectations for the future are great. According to Apoyo SA, for example, in June 1994 57 per cent of Lima residents believed that the country was progressing. Furthermore, 60 per cent said that Peru would be a better place to live in the coming years. The expectations of prosperity are in any case individual, reflecting the breakdown of forms of association that accompanies application of a liberal economic program.

The effectiveness demonstrated by Fujimori over 1990–5 lent a certain credibility to his promises and fueled the hopes that the situation was going to improve 'little by little'. Between October 1990 and May 1995, the approval ratings for his administration were above 60 per cent, rising to 81 per cent after the *autogolpe* of April 1992 and to 74 per cent with the capture of Guzmán in October 1992. Even in November 1993, after a constitutional referendum in which the Fujimori 'YES' vote obtained a very narrow victory, the approval of the President was 67 per cent. It is worth noting that approval of Fujimori by that date was high in all social sectors.[18]

The new Constitution in 1993, in turn, strengthened even further the power of the Executive at the expense of other representative political institutions. The size, authority, and representativity of the Parliament were all seriously reduced, while some of the basic social and political rights that citizens had enjoyed for years were eliminated. The authority of cabinet ministers was also reduced to such an extreme that today they are considered mere secretaries to the President. The resources, design, and implementation of anti-poverty programs has also been concentrated in the Executive. The concentration of power and its arbitrary use is a long-standing characteristic of Peruvian politics. In this sense, the Fujimori administration was not very different from its predecessors (Panfichi and Sanborn 1995).

The 1995 Re-election and Beyond

In 1995 President Fujimori was re-elected for a second five-year term with 64.4 per cent of the national vote, followed distantly by Javier Pérez de Cuéllar with 21.8 per cent of the votes. As seen in Table 9.2, the results in Lima confirm this overwhelming victory, which was not really a surprise given the continuous public support which the President received during his first term. But in contrast to 1990, when Fujimori benefited from a context of social polarization, this time he obtained significant electoral support from all social strata. In other words, not only among the poor but also the middle and upper classes. This citizen 'consensus' around

---

[18] The figures noted come from monthly surveys of 32 districts in Lima done by Apoyo SA, the most prestigious of the Peruvian companies in the field. The reliability of these surveys is estimated at 95 per cent. The sample divides the population in four sectors according to income, education, and housing criteria. The author is grateful to Apoyo SA for permission to use this information.

Table 9.2. Presidential election 1995: voting by districts in Lima (%)

	C90-NM	UPP	AP	PAP	CODE	OBRAS	IU	Others
Upper-class districts								
La Molina	65.3	24.9	1.0	1.3	1.9	5.4	0.1	0.1
Magdalena	57.8	29.8	1.0	2.5	1.9	6.1	0.2	0.7
Miraflores	63.7	26.9	0.9	1.6	1.5	4.9	0.1	0.4
San Isidro	64.8	26.8	0.8	1.3	1.3	4.5	0.1	0.4
San Borja	60.5	29.4	0.8	1.4	1.5	5.8	0.1	0.5
Middle-class districts								
Barranco	60.0	27.3	0.8	2.7	2.2	6.2	0.3	0.5
Breña	55.1	30.1	0.9	3.9	2.4	6.8	0.3	0.5
Jesus María	54.4	34.0	0.8	2.3	1.9	5.9	0.2	0.5
La Victoria	62.2	23.7	0.7	2.7	2.4	7.2	0.3	0.8
Lince	56.6	30.9	0.8	2.6	2.0	6.4	0.3	0.4
Pueblo Libre	56.5	32.3	0.8	2.4	1.8	5.7	0.2	0.3
Rimac	58.2	26.8	0.8	3.2	3.0	6.8	0.3	0.9
San Luis	65.9	21.1	1.2	2.0	2.2	6.4	0.2	1.0
San Miguel	56.9	31.1	0.8	2.5	2.0	6.1	0.2	0.4
Surco	63.7	25.7	0.8	1.6	1.8	5.6	0.1	0.7
Surquillo	61.6	24.6	0.7	2.8	2.5	6.8	0.2	0.8
Lower-class districts								
Ate	69.0	18.1	0.6	1.9	3.4	5.1	0.3	1.6
Carabayllo	66.5	21.1	0.8	2.9	3.2	2.9	0.3	2.3
Comas	66.6	20.3	0.6	2.6	3.8	4.2	0.4	1.5
Chorrillos	67.5	19.2	0.7	1.9	3.2	5.6	0.2	1.7
El Agustino	67.1	16.8	0.7	2.3	3.4	7.5	0.4	1.8
Independencia	66.3	19.3	0.6	2.4	4.1	5.5	0.4	1.4
Los Olivos	62.4	23.3	0.8	2.3	3.6	6.9	0.2	0.5
Lurigancho	62.7	25.8	1.5	2.5	3.0	2.8	0.6	1.1
San Juan L.	67.4	18.1	0.7	2.0	3.9	6.0	0.3	1.6
San Juan M.	67.6	17.5	0.7	2.2	3.2	7.0	0.3	1.5
San Martín	62.6	22.6	0.7	2.8	3.4	6.8	0.3	0.8
Villa María	71.1	13.9	0.9	2.4	3.4	6.3	0.3	1.7
Villa Salvador	70.0	14.6	0.7	2.5	3.8	6.4	0.3	1.7

Abbreviations: Cambio 90-Nueva Mayoria (C90-NM); Unión por el Perú (UPP); Acción Popular (AP); Partido Aprista Peruano (PAP); Coordinadora Democrática (CODE); Izquierda Unida (IU)

Source: *Perú Elecciones Generales 1995: Resultados del Jurado Nacional de Elección.*

Fujimori cannot be explained by emotional factors or cultural identification, as in 1990, but instead by the demonstration of concrete achievements that overcome a situation of crisis and raise hopes for future prosperity.

The elections of 1995 also appear to signal the social and even legal demise of all the 'traditional' political parties, including those of the left. At the national level, the APRA obtained 4.1 per cent of the votes, Acción Popular 1.6 per cent, and the Izquierda Unida just 0.6 per cent. In Lima, where more than half of the Peruvian poor reside, the average vote for known political parties was even lower. It is important to note here that it was other independent 'movements', such as the UPP, OBRAS, and CODE, that received the second place preferences of the electorate.

Nonetheless, it would be an error to explain approval of Fujimori in terms of a supposedly authoritarian political culture in Peru. On the contrary, this has been a calculated, pragmatic option subject to Fujimori's continued capacity to 'prove' his effectiveness. In effect, behind the pendulum of dictators and democracies that characterize the political history of the country, the constant factor in popular behavior has been the incessant drive towards material progress and genuinely representative political leadership. Given this long-term tendency, popular loyalties in different historical conjunctures have not been defined by firm ideological commitments, but by pragmatic calculation of the costs and benefits of supporting one or another leader. For this reason, political loyalties have not been stable, but mediating and provisional, subject to a permanent evaluation as a function of concrete achievements.

As Franco (1991) observes, the poor of Lima have participated in the conservative populism of Odría, the modernizing pronouncements of Belaunde, and the populist illusion of García. Also, as Grompone (1991a) notes, they have searched outside the traditional political class for other identities and representations. Fujimori is the latest in a series of wagers in this direction. A prior one occurred in 1979, when the Marxist left headed by Hugo Blanco, an ex-guerrilla dressed in sandals and a cord tied around his waist, surprisingly received 29 per cent of the vote. Later, in 1983, Barrantes was the first Marxist mayor elected by popular vote in a Latin American capital. Blanco and Barrantes, says Degregori, came from 'outside' of the traditional political structure, they were *cholos*, provincials, Marxists with a poor and Andean social base. Nonetheless, both leaders failed when they integrated into the democratic system without transforming the left into a political force that was representative of the popular sectors.

The popular pragmatism from which Fujimori has benefited combines several strategies—individual, clientelistic, associative, or confrontational. The guiding principle has been to obtain resources and improved life conditions, and only later the recognition of civil and political rights. Needs and not ideology determine the strategies to take. Fujimori understands this well. Thus, with the legitimacy of achievements obtained, he has fed hopes for a better future at the same time that, in the short run, he has developed a clientelistic politics of gifts and donations.[19]

---

[19] Fujimori's politics of donations has clear popular approval. Carmen Rosa Balbi obtained a very revealing testimony from a professor at La Cantuta University. The President arrived there with computers as a present. Until very recently, Sendero Luminoso had influence in La Cantuta, and eight students and a professor had been kidnapped and disappeared there. 'We all expected the announcement of the closing of the University . . . but it was not like that. Fujimori's presence had a great impact and made students and instructors happy; people said that despite everything, the "*chino*" had thought of us' (1993: 55).

Still, popular support for Fujimori has depended entirely on his ability to continue proving his effectiveness. By 1994, surveys taken in Lima demonstrated changes in public perceptions of the most important problems of the country. Inflation and terrorism, the principal targets of Fujimori, had declined in public importance, and the central concerns became the lack of work, lack of food, and poverty.[20] The ability to satisfy these new demands will determine the destiny of Fujimori's second administration.

Conclusions

Our principal conclusion is that to understand the re-emergence of popularly supported authoritarian political leaders in some Latin American democracies it is necessary to consider the way in which three central factors are articulated. The first factor is a deterioration in the economic and material situation, to levels rarely experienced by the society as a whole. A second factor is that the majority of the population believes that the system of political representation, especially political parties, does not represent their interests or needs. The delegitimization of party politics is, in turn, rooted in the specific institutional traditions of political systems.

In countries that do not have a tradition of strong democratic institutions, the combination of economic crisis and disillusion with political parties produces a profound sense of loss of familiar forms of reproduction of the social order. The changes occur in an unpredictable way and the referents of the past lose their previous effectiveness. Without known criteria to structure the future, the population is overwhelmed by uncertainty and fear.

Given these conditions we should note a third factor—the emergence of personalistic leaders who offer hopes and firm solutions to the problems caused by the general crisis of society. In some cases, such as Fujimori of Peru and Fernando Collor de Mello of Brazil, these leaders come from outside the established political system. In others, like Carlos Menem of Argentina, the leader arises from within a party, although later also governs in a personalistic manner.

The legitimacy of these leaders is constructed in a process of interaction with society that includes at least two differentiated moments. Initially, it is based on the relationship of identification between the leader and the masses. For this, the leader must possess personal qualities that have a real correlation to the historical and daily life experiences of the population. But elements also must exist in the political culture of the population that validate this type of leadership. This identification relationship is problematic. It arises out of frustration and the lack of alternatives, and is a gamble for hope. Nonetheless, the leader soon must demonstrate

---

[20] According to Apoyo SA, in July 1994, 48 per cent of the population believed unemployment to be one of the most important problems of the country, followed by poverty with 34 per cent and hunger with 27 per cent. Further down was terrorism at 15 per cent and inflation at 10 per cent.

concrete 'achievements' related to the greatest felt needs of the population so that this relationship is transformed into political support.

We should not think that there is a natural propensity towards authoritarianism in the urban popular sectors, or that there is a mechanical relationship between material poverty and political choices. On the contrary, the support that these leaders receive is conditional. It is subject to the capacity they have to continue 'proving' their effectiveness before the ever greater demands of their supporters. This can generate a circular process: the more success a leader has in proving his effectiveness, the greater his tendency to concentrate personal power; yet the demands of the population also will be increasingly greater (Lindholm 1990). Thus, a vortex is created which, in most cases, ends up consuming the leader himself. The task is to determine at what point the virtuous circle turns into a vicious circle.

PART III. The Stubbornness of Violence

10 | The Quetzal is Red: Military States, Popular Movements, and Political Violence in Guatemala

Deborah J. Yashar[1]

The Guatemalan state historically has excelled at repression. The state has used coercion to regulate and extract labor from rural and largely indigenous communities, to delimit the spaces for the development of civil society, and to threaten, disappear, and/or assassinate those suspected of subversion. The professionalization of the military in the past few decades has increased the state's capacity to penetrate rural and urban areas while increasing the military's political capacity to dominate the state apparatus itself. By the mid-1980s, military officers had assumed prominent decision-making powers in most if not all branches of the state. In the process, they developed professional and economic interests that have become integrally tied to the maintenance of a coercive state that deploys violence to restrict civil and political society and foster a politics of public silence.

Yet states, however repressive, neither are monolithic nor can they be totalizing. For individual and collective voices can be and have been expressed in the interstices of state power—both because of and in spite of state efforts to control the growth of civil society and civic participation. Hence, just as we read of widescale repression in Guatemala, we also learn of popular resistance, illustrated by the now renowned case of Nobel laureate Rigoberta Menchú Tum but initiated and experienced just as intensely and painfully by thousands of other Guatemalans. Faced with ongoing efforts by the state to quash political organizing, popular associations have emerged to claim the right to citizenship, material well-being, and human dignity. One of the fundamental axes of contemporary Guatemalan politics, therefore, is this violent confrontation between the state and organized popular sectors, who view one another as antagonists. This confrontation has continued despite a formal transition from authoritarian rule in 1986.

Yet in the ironic twist that accompanies almost all political action, I suggest that the military and the popular movement have (re)created since 1986 the very

[1] I thank John Gershman, Deborah Levenson-Estrada, Kay Warren, and the editors of this volume for their constructive criticism on an earlier version of this chapter.

conditions that they seek to transcend. In the military's effort to deny official political space for 'left' voices, it has in fact generated the very types and intensity of protest politics—popular sector organizing at the margins of, and in opposition to, the state—that it had attempted to displace. In other words, in the effort to deny political participation, it has politicized and radicalized an agenda emanating from the popular sectors, forcing them to express these demands through protest in the streets. Similarly, popular movements have been forced by the very violence that they confront to create hidden arenas for organizing, thereby replicating, perhaps unavoidably, the non-democratic practice of privatizing discourse, communication, strategizing, and decision-making—which inhibits accountability, transparency, and democratic exchange.

It is against this backdrop of confrontation, violence, and protest that Guatemala's 1944 'October Revolution' and ensuing ten years of democratic rule have become a vivid and contested national symbol. Guatemala officially celebrates the October 1944 overthrow of Ubico's thirteen-year dictatorship. Both the military and popular movements highlight the courageous, spontaneous mobilization of Guatemalan society that toppled the dictatorial regime. Yet, they have disagreed, at times violently, over the normative consequences of the popular mobilization and socioeconomic reforms that followed in the ensuing decade (1944–54). While spokespersons for the contemporary popular movement refer to the decade ushered in by the October Revolution as a historic example of democracy in practice and a symbolic vision of what can be, spokespersons for the military and its allies refer to the same period as democracy gone awry, as ascending communism, and as an example of what must never happen again. I suggest, however, that both the military and popular sectors have overemphasized and, therefore, misinterpreted the role played and spaces created by popular mobilization in Guatemala's history, with serious implications for how the different sides portray the transition to and functioning of a future democratic polity.

While more than four decades have passed since the overthrow of the October Revolution, the contested normative legacy of popular organizing continues to divide contemporary political discourse—providing a focal point and language for competing visions of Guatemala. Conflicting interpretations of the mid-twentieth-century democratic period serve as a historical reference for bitter struggles over the appropriate boundaries for popular mobilization, political participation, and policy agendas. This binary vision of a just society has informed the cycle of political violence and popular protest that has marked Guatemala's history in the past few decades and which continues despite a formal transition to civilian rule in 1986. Political violence and popular protest appear to have locked state and society into a cycle of irreconcilable goals, political confrontation, and escalating distrust, as popular sectors seek to reclaim the public space that the military attempts to monitor and constrain.

This chapter analyzes the 1986 political transition in Guatemala against the backdrop of the 1944 October Revolution that initiated the short-lived decade of political democracy and against the 1993 multi-class mobilization that did not. It focuses on the conditions under which popular movements contribute to democratic change—of national regimes and within the movements themselves. To do so, it adopts a comparative historical approach. First, this chapter compares historical and contemporary transition moments in Guatemala to discern the conditions under which transition coalitions construct institutions and spaces for popular participation. Second, it compares the types of popular movements that have emerged following these transitions in order to analyze how popular sectors confronted with violence struggle to ensure their participation and democratic rights. The record in Guatemala suggests that the contemporary politics of protest under conditions of violence can create significant spaces for voicing opposition but ultimately cannot lead to a democratization of polity and society so long as these movements remain at the margins of a violent state. From this perspective, military and popular discourse regarding the power of popular movements to effect democratic change belies historical and comparative analysis.[2] Similarly, it highlights that without fundamental state reform as part of the transition process, democratic prospects remain slim. In the absence of state reform, Guatemalan state and society have remained locked in an antagonistic and zero-sum relationship where the emergence of civil society itself has triggered military repression.

Overview: Redefining Institutions and Reclaiming Public Spaces

Prior to the 1944 and 1986 transitions, the Guatemalan state attempted to collapse public and private boundaries to inhibit the expression and growth of civil society and to assert a more pervasive if not absolute role for the state in people's daily lives; in the 1930s this became the prerogative of one man while by the 1980s this had become the prerogative of the military as an institution. Through military penetration of the cities and countryside and the development of civilian and military intelligence networks, both authoritarian regimes attempted to define away public spaces for autonomous organizing and expression while controlling non-public activity.[3] The state then and now has repressed public organizations and expression by collectivities and individuals and, in the process, has created a 'climate of fear' whereby individuals often sense that they are being observed, that someone

---

[2] As discussed below, I am not arguing that political organizing is unimportant for democratic changes; indeed, it is essential. Rather, I am arguing that it cannot be singled out and emphasized as the cause of change without analyzing state capacity and the interaction with other social actors.

[3] Non-public activity cannot exactly be called private in so far as the Guatemalan state does not respect the argument that civilians have jurisdiction over their actions within this allegedly private sphere. Garretón (1992: 18), writing about the Southern Cone, notes: 'When the state is omnipresent and the society is underground or submerged (when society actually *is* an underground), the struggle against fear tends to be individual and atomized . . .'.

is listening to their speech, and that their actions are being judged. This sense of a pervasive and predatory intelligence network has been captured by the metonymical expression *orejas*, which refers to spies that infiltrate organizations and report on what is said and done. Corradi, referring largely to the dictatorships of the Southern Cone, states,

Especially when the public/private distinction has collapsed, a system may develop that combines the worst features of both assaults on personal integrity. As we shall see, terrorism, state terror, and various intermediate or combined forms of both may succeed in establishing true 'cultures of fear'. In such instances, the blurring of boundaries between a private and public sphere takes on the form of a perverse dialectic. On the one hand, the private sphere becomes vulnerable to sudden, brutal and arbitrary intrusions on the part of authorities. On the other hand, the authorities cease to operate in a true public fashion. Punishment becomes secretive, unavowed, in what amounts to the privatization of state coercion. (Corradi 1992: 272)

Repressive states often attempt to collapse the public and private for society, while privatizing power within the state, shielding state actors and actions from public scrutiny and accountability. The institutional and technological capacities of the contemporary Guatemalan military have provided the means for a tighter, and often more extreme and thorough, form of social control than five decades prior. Nonetheless, it has been exceedingly difficult during the length of Guatemala's authoritarian history for popular organizations to organize independently of the state while the state operated independently of social, political, or economic accountability.[4]

Guatemala's 1944 and 1986 transitions ostensibly re-established the boundary between public and private, to allow for a functioning democracy coincident with the growth of civil and political society. Both transition moments were characterized by the holding of a constituent assembly, the election of a civilian president, and the discursive embrace of democracy. It is commonly agreed, however, that while the former initiated a process of democratization, the latter initiated a controlled political liberalization characterized by continued military control and political violence.

Why did the 1944 transition initiate a democratic opening while the 1986 transition initiated a more restricted political liberalization? I suggest that the opportunity to effect democratic change in Guatemala has appeared only when popular

[4] State–elite relations differed in the 1930s and 1980s pre-democratic transition periods. The thirteen-year Ubico dictatorship (1931–44) prevented the organization of all expressions of civil society, including the elite. By contrast, the 1980s military governments prior to 1986 inhibited the expression of all popular organizations suspected of subversion, but did not inhibit the growth of economic elite organizations, which, in fact, grew and tended to support the military regime. O'Donnell's (1977) discussion of privatizing corporatism and Evans's (1992) discussion of embedded autonomy are quite suggestive here. By the 1970s and 1980s, the Guatemalan military as a professionalized institution had become independent and dominant within the state apparatus, asserting autonomous goals and interests. Nonetheless, the military maintained alliances with the economic elite, which continued to possess channels of influence within the state.

mobilization has occurred in tandem with a public division within the economic elite and the military, as in 1944.[5] Popular movements for their part have tended to spearhead the public outcry to overthrow authoritarian rule, often attempting to create both the organizational base and the discourse for change; in the absence of popular mobilization, domestically generated democratic change will not occur.[6] Yet, to understand why popular movements have met more often with repression than with democratic change, one must analyze the state and the conditions under which it has chosen primarily to deploy force and/or to refrain from violence. My reading of Guatemalan history suggests that when part of the Guatemalan elite has withdrawn its support from the state this withdrawal has tended to reveal and exacerbate latent divisions within the military, weakening both the rationale and the capacity of the state to clamp down effectively on public spaces. These are rare moments when the lines of allegiance and purpose are blurred publicly. They offer the possibility to form new political alliances and, in the best of circumstances, to push for democratic changes. On the other hand, a division within the military in the absence of popular mobilization (or aftermath of demobilization) creates the conditions for a potential political liberalization but, in the absence of popular mobilization and state reform, does not lead to democratization; as with the 1986 transition, it tends towards a change *in* rather than *of* regime. Conversely, popular mobilization in the absence of this division has resulted in violence, as illustrated by the late 1970s and early 1980s. And, finally, the absence of both popular mobilization and of a division has resulted in a relative status quo. These four scenarios outlined in Table 10.1 are ideal types and are not meant to define or explain all causes or situations; binary typing obviously obscures the textured combination of varied resources, strategies, goals, and overlapping histories. Nonetheless, these combined categories do provide a heuristic device for thinking about the conditions under which popular mobilization has contributed to democracy in Guatemala.

As elaborated below, popular mobilization and a division within both the elite and the military precipitated the 1944 October Revolution. The 1944 transition reformed the state, founded a democratic regime, and encouraged the growth of civil society; with the acquisition of political and social rights, the civic associations that emerged tended to focus on material demands in the workplace. The

---

[5] See Yashar (forthcoming, chs. 1 and 3) for an elaboration of this argument. This argument differs somewhat from the influential argument developed by O'Donnell and Schmitter (1986). They claim that one needs the resurgence of civil society for a transition from authoritarian rule. They argue that this resurgence places pressure on the state to call for elections after which it is advantageous for the newly constituted civil society to become less vocal and oppositional—to decrease the likelihood of a coup. I agree that the resurgence of civil society articulates the call for democratic change; however, I disagree with the argument that the subsequent quiescence of popular movements is advantageous for the founding of democracy. Indeed, the case of Guatemala highlights the fact that their exclusion from the process can further reinforce the power bases that undergirded the prior regime while ensuring limited formal spaces for popular participation in the new regime.

[6] I am limiting my discussion to domestically generated changes, excluding internationally imposed democracy.

Table 10.1. Potential moments of regime change in Guatemala

		Publicly stated division within elite and military	
		Yes	No
Popular mobilization and demands for citizenship	Yes	Democratizing moment; possibilities to reform state and reconstitute power relations; exemplified by Oct. 1944.	Repression as in the 1970s–1980s.
	No	Potential for transition from one authoritarian regime to another; part of military maintains control over state apparatus as with the 1984–6 political transition or coups.	Political and social constraints on civil society; exemplified by Ubico dictatorship.

1984–6 transition, by contrast, was engineered by an internally divided military, a constituted and institutionalized power that set out to liberalize its apparent control of the civilian regime in the face of a demobilized civil society. The military did so without guaranteeing a reform of the state or respect for the newly defined constitutional rights for individuals or for collectivities; under these conditions, the popular movements that emerged following the 1986 transition appeared more heterodox, demanding not only material changes, but the politically prior respect for constitutional rights which, in practice, are denied. Let us look at each of these transitions and their consequences for popular organizing and representation.

1944: October Revolution, Reconstituting Democratic Institutions, and Citizenship[7]

In May and June of 1944, a handful of university students demanded university-wide reforms. These seemingly harmless public demands constituted one of the first times that any sector of the Guatemalan population had voiced dissent against the dictator, General Jorge Ubico y Castañeda, who for thirteen years had sought to atomize society and silence public expression.[8] Ubico had banned the formation of any civic associations. While primarily fearful of working-class and communist

[7] The discussion of the period 1944–54 draws from Yashar (forthcoming).
[8] See Grieb (1979) for the most thorough discussion of the Ubico dictatorship. Also see Gleijeses (1989) and Handy (1984).

conspiracies, he also remained suspicious of middle-class and elite organizations. Demands by the clandestinely reorganized student association, Asociación de Estudiantes Universitarios (AEU), posed, therefore, a challenge to the regime and its effort to maintain a disarticulated society. Ubico y Castañeda's initially flexible response to these demands and subsequent suspension of social guarantees precipitated multi-class and city-wide mobilizations described by their participants as the spontaneous birth of urban civil society. This mobilization occurred against the backdrop of what a student leader of the time and later democratic reformer described as: 'The dry rot of fear and of servility [that had] infested everything'.[9]

This popular mobilization and Ubico's response made manifest the latent opposition that had been developing within the oligarchy. During his regime, the oligarchy was forced to dissolve its agrarian peak association, AGA; its regional power was further diminished as Ubico centralized control in the rural areas.[10] In a striking move, 311 members of the Guatemalan elite issued and signed a public document that criticized Ubico for having suspended these social guarantees. The suspension of guarantees, and the oligarchy's criticism of the dictator's move, had presented an excuse to demonstrate declining oligarchic support for the dictator and his policies—for the dictator had disregarded constitutional provisions and civil rights throughout his thirteen-year rule.

While the popular mobilization created the demands for political inclusion and citizenship rights, the elite-expressed, public opposition to the regime weakened the social foundations of the regime. Together, these developments constituted a challenge from without, resulting in Ubico's unexpected resignation. However, within five months of his resignation, it became apparent that political liberalization would be short-lived as Ubico and his proxy continued to control the state apparatus and used the coercive branch to control the growth of independent power bases expressed in the newspapers, political parties, and civic associations. It is within this context that military officers broke with the regime—signaling a weakening of the state itself. Ubico had initiated the professionalization of military training while maintaining a military institution dependent on patron–client relations and corruption. In the process, Ubico had alienated young officers who opposed the corrupt administration and confronted limited spaces for professional advancement. They joined the multi-class opposition. And in October 1944, they overthrew the regime.

This transition by collapse created an unprecedented opportunity for the re-constitution and institutionalization of political power within Guatemala. The

[9] Galich (1977: 39). All translations by author, unless otherwise indicated.
[10] The Guatemalan oligarchy had developed an agro-export economy that revolved around the production and sale of coffee. However, throughout the Liberal period (1870s–1940s) it remained extremely dependent on the state. With the Liberal reforms, the state facilitated the concentration of lands while ensuring the delivery of rural labor to the coffee plantations. The oligarchy became increasingly dependent on the state during the Ubico regime. See Grieb 1979; McCreery 1976, 1983, and 1990; Yashar (forthcoming); and Williams (1994).

prior regime had rested on the disarticulation of society and the centralization of power with the dictator, creating an almost complete absence of horizontal associations within society and the almost complete absence of horizontal communication within the state.[11] Under these conditions, the 1944 overthrow presented the opportunity for the growth of civil society, the reconfiguration of state institutions, and the creation of a democratic regime with inclusionary principles.[12] The regime-founding coalition that emerged included representatives from all sectors of *ladino* society, including the working class, students, professionals, and military men. Within the first few months, the revolutionary junta served as a transition team and called a constituent assembly, which expanded the terms of suffrage, prepared for new elections, created the space for the formation of political parties and civic associations (including unions), and issued sixty-seven decrees to undermine coercive state practices and to extend individual and collective rights (Silvert 1969: 29; Handy 1985: 94). These changes prepared the terrain for the 1944 elections that brought to power President Juan José Arévalo, who subsequently oversaw the 1950 elections that brought to power President Jacobo Arbenz Gúzman. Most dramatically, the transition coalition initiated a substantial demilitarization process which undermined the coercive and centralized control characteristic of the prior authoritarian period. The reform coalition made a concerted effort to professionalize and depoliticize the military. These institutional changes originally created the conditions for civilians to embrace democratic rule and political participation.[13]

Popular and middle sectors assumed dominant public positions in the legislature and oversaw significant social legislation that came to include labor codes, security reforms, and ultimately the highly disputed land reform. Moreover, the multi-class governing coalition expanded the discourse and practice of citizenship to include civilian, political, and social rights.[14] These changes allowed for the expansion of suffrage rights, delineated the terms of freedom of association and expression, and created the basis for an incipient welfare state that would provide a modicum of social welfare.

With a reformed state and supportive governing coalition, there was an unpre-

---

[11] See Migdal (1988), who discusses this phenomenon, which often takes place in 'weak states'.

[12] The absence of organizations created the opportunity for reconstituting power and reforming the state. However, as I have developed elsewhere, the shallow basis on which civil society subsequently emerged and the failure to develop more vital political parties proved detrimental to the maintenance of political democracy.

[13] These 1944–5 institutional changes to the Guatemalan military unexpectedly created an autonomous and political military, part of which participated in the 1954 coup.

[14] T. H. Marshall (1963) has written perhaps the most influential discussion of citizenship that includes (*a*) civil rights—freedom of expression and organization; (*b*) political rights—the vote; and (*c*) social rights—a right to a certain standard of living. While he has been criticized duly for, among other things, his evolutionary image of the extension of citizenship rights, his discussion clearly addressed the older debate about the tension between political equality and economic inequality in the 'modern age' of political democracy and capitalism. With the implementation of neoliberal reforms in the 1980s and the exacerbation of economic poverty, the state has retreated from social entitlement policies, thereby retreating from the social rights that he identified as the third element of citizenship.

cedented growth of civic associations over the next decade, particularly those which mobilized along class-based lines. In 1944, organizing began with an incipient labor movement among teachers and railroad workers. Although the labor movement developed along fragmented lines in the initial years, by 1951 a largely united labor movement had emerged with the Confederación General de Trabajadores Guatemaltecos (CGTG). At the height of organizing, the labor movement claimed an estimated 100,000 members in 500 unions (Cardoza y Aragón 1955: 98; Bishop 1959: 137–48).[15] Although President Arévalo placed limits on rural organizing, the labor movement began to organize the peasantry. The peasant federation Confederación Nacional de Campesinos Guatemaltecos (CNCG) was founded in May 1950. During the second civilian administration, President Arbenz supported the rural mobilization as part of his developmental plans and as a political base of support. The revision of the 1947 labor code and the legislation of the 1952 land reform created the legal framework and the political impetus for a more active rural organizing effort by both the CNCG and CGTG. By the end of the reform period, the peasant federation had mobilized unions throughout the country, between 200,000 and 240,000 *campesinos*, 37 per cent of the economically active rural population (Cardoza y Aragón 1955; Schneider 1958; López Larrave 1976; Figueroa y Ibarra 1980; Handy 1985: 229; García Añoveros 1987: 139).

The development of civil society during the October Revolution occurred primarily along class lines and only secondarily along ethnic and gendered lines. Hence, while many indigenous men participated, particularly, in the CNCG, they did so as rural workers and/or peasants. Indeed, the reform administration adopted an ambivalent policy towards Indians, praising their historical legacy yet hoping for their assimilation. Similarly, the reform period also witnessed the mobilization of women in party auxiliaries and within the labor movement, particularly the teachers' union. Nonetheless, in both cases, participation occurred for material reasons in order to improve work standards, access to land, etc.[16]

The unions were able not only to gain a voice within the workplace, but also within the formal political realm. Thirteen labor leaders were elected to the Congress between 1945 and 1954 (Gutiérrez 1964: 39–40).[17] Moreover, the reform administrations of Arévalo and Arbenz came to rely increasingly on organized labor as

[15] According to the official CGTG paper, the CGTG claimed twelve legal federations with six federations whose juridical status was pending; it had 380 member unions with 78 unions still waiting for their juridical status, with a total of 104,392 union members (*Unidad Organo Central de la CGTG*, year 2, No. 11, 31 Aug. 1953); also see *Tribuna Popular*, 21 Aug. 1953. José Alberto Cardoza, national deputy and member of the executive board of the CGTG, stated that the CGTG claimed 521 unions, 440 of which had juridical personality, totalling 110,000 members (*El Imparcial*, 14 Dec. 1953).

[16] See Yashar (forthcoming, ch. 5) for a discussion of the primarily class-based nature of these organizations. While the reform coalition saw these organizations along class lines, the opposition saw them as a material threat reinforced by fear of an Indian uprising.

[17] The Hermeroteca at the Guatemalan National Archives houses a fascinating collection of political paraphernalia from these years. The *hojas sueltas* from 1944 and 1945 include the political platforms and campaign material from many of the parties that first emerged in these years. An excellent discussion of the political parties from these years and their ties to the popular movements is included in Jim Handy's (1985) dissertation on this period.

an electoral and social support base, just as they came to advance the 'interests' of this same group within policy-making circles.[18] Similarly, political parties primarily dominated by middle sectors formed alliances with unions and civic associations; the latter advocated entitlement, regulatory, and redistributive reforms legislation that advanced popular sector access to newly formed state institutions, their bargaining power within the workplace, and their right to organize. Some political party leaders dominated key union positions and oftentimes seemed to gain electoral advantages through popular mobilization. Yet despite electoral fronts at national election time and right before the 1954 coup, the reform parties tended to give way to internal bickering that hindered the development of strong political parties linked ideologically and/or sectorally with an emerging civil society. The weakness of these reform political parties was mirrored by their conservative counterparts, which made minimal efforts to develop political parties at all.[19] In the absence of a political society in which the reform and counter-reform factions could compete, conflict was expressed in increasingly zero-sum terms.

With the support of the United States the counter-reform movement overthrew the democratic government in 1954. Over the course of the next three decades, the counter-reform government dismantled many state institutions, repressed popular organizations, and reversed social reforms. By the 1980s, the military had come to dominate the state and to penetrate public spaces in a way that promoted a politics of silence and subterfuge.[20]

1986: Political Liberalization, Continued Violence, and Underground Citizenship

In the mid-1980s, the military that had both participated in the 1944 overthrow of Ubico and the 1954 overthrow of the subsequent democratic regime participated in a round of political liberalization. General Mejía Victores oversaw a trans-

[18] Arévalo developed a somewhat ambivalent position towards organizing, particularly among rural workers. Hence, if the social reform legislation during Arévalo's term opened up the arena for urban labor organizing, it was both prohibitive, and at times repressive, towards the rural sectors. The first reform administration at times adopted coercive measures against rural organizing. The army often used violence to put down strikes in rural areas. It was only at the end of his administration that Arévalo reformed the restrictive labor rules for organizing in the countryside. See Gutiérrez Alvarez (1985: 98–101) and Handy (1985: 214).

[19] Monteforte Toledo (1965: 317), a moderate reform politician and sociologist, argued that the opposition had committed to organizing in accord with the following principles: 'a) to operate through civic, Catholic, regional and trade unions; b) to reduce their definition exclusively to "anti-communism"; c) to discredit and negate constructive programs advanced by the government; d) to incite military coups; and e) to consume the left's power in unimportant skirmishes.'

[20] Between 1954 and 1986, military men dominated the executive office through violence, fraudulent elections, and/or coups. The only exception to this pattern was in 1966, when the civilian Méndez Montenegro took office in what many hoped was a political opening. However, it became apparent shortly thereafter that he had little latitude to maneuver and that indeed the military still made the

ition to civilian rule. Two reasons are generally put forth: (1) that the country needed to gain access to foreign direct investment, foreign aid, and foreign exchange and, therefore, set out to present a better international image; and (2) that having largely disarticulated the popular movement and defeated the guerrilla movement that had re-emerged in the 1970s and 1980s, part of the military concluded that it was time to adopt a strategy of low-intensity conflict. In either or both cases, Mejía Victores' more moderate faction of the military initiated a transition process that culminated in a 1984–5 Constituent Assembly and 1985 and 1990 elections to transfer political rule to civilians.[21] Civilians assumed office following both elections, with Christian Democrat Marco Vinicio Cerezo Arévalo taking office with 60 per cent of the vote cast in 1986 and Jorge Serrano Elías of the recently constituted Movimiento de Acción Solidaria (MAS) party taking office in 1991 with 67 per cent of the vote (Trudeau 1993: 71, 150). These developments symbolically announced the retreat of the military from political decision-making and raised hopes that Guatemala, like the rest of the hemisphere, might be experiencing a transition to political democracy.

Yet, the 1986 transition did not and could not repeat the experiences of the 1944 transition. First, the transition took place with a disarticulated society that did not participate either in generating the demands for transition or in defining the new rules for the post-military period (see Table 10.1). Following a decade of brutal repression that left an estimated 50,000–75,000 dead, 35,000–40,000 disappeared, 1 million internally and externally displaced, the previously strong popular movement was seriously debilitated; many chose to leave the movements, either disillusioned or fearful for their lives (Manz 1988: 7, 30). Others chose to remain with the popular movement as various organizations went underground. And others still joined the guerrillas who by the mid-1980s had taken a serious blow from which they have never recovered. In short, by the mid-1980s the military largely had succeeded in constraining public expression of popular dissent. In this context, the power of decision-making was not reconstituted but remained firmly entrenched in a military that, public statements notwithstanding, continued to assume the right to define the parameters of political rule, policy-making, and public space for political participation. Second, the military had come to occupy a different position within the state and *vis-à-vis* society than it had in 1944. In 1944 the military was fragmented, corrupt, and beholden to General Ubico; by 1984, the military had become a professionalized institution that had not only come to occupy the state, as had so many other Latin American militaries, but had also come to penetrate the countryside with an organized military presence in even the most remote areas of the country. While individuals within the military certainly

significant political decisions in the country. The 1986–90 presidency was in practice quite similar to the administration of Méndez Montenegro in so far as the military retained veto power over the presidency, and in so far as the civilian administration served initially to legitimate the military.

[21] See the publication by the Guatemala-based news organization *Inforpress Centroamericana* entitled *Guatemala: Elections 1985* for an analysis of the 1985 elections.

benefited from this situation, it seems more significant within this context to highlight that the Guatemalan military's very *raison d'être* as an institution had become to strengthen and continue its control over state and society.

Under these conditions—of a disarticulated popular sector and a division within the militarized state—a political liberalization did occur. The civilian administrations established a human rights prosecutor (elected by the Congress), human rights offices in many of the ministries, forums for national dialogue, and a training program to improve the functioning of the legal system—the latter of which was later dismantled.[22] But this political liberalization was a limited transition; the military provided only a modicum of additional latitude for civilian rule, freedom of expression, and freedom of association.[23] As human rights organizations have documented, these reforms remained ineffective and, in some cases, even increased military control over the rural areas—i.e. with the creation of the Inter-Institutional Council which placed the army's chief of staff as head of development programs, the foundation of multi-force policing organizations such as SIPROCI, and the maintenance of development poles, model villages, and civil defense patrols. And, in October 1988, the military formed ESTNA (The Center for Strategic Studies of National Stability).[24] Hence, despite the transition to civilian rule, the military maintained a strong veto power over politics and, despite a momentary lull between 1985 and 1987, repression increased noticeably after 1988.[25] Roberto Lemus, a Guatemalan judge, stated when living in the USA that: '[the indigenous population] definitely does not trust the civilian institutions. In fact, they are afraid of them, and they know that these institutions are based on violence and money.'[26]

The legacy of repression, particularly after the 1954 coup and in the early 1980s, had led many organizations to go underground. In a March 1990 interview with two national peasant leaders from the Comité de Unidad Campesina (CUC), one of the leaders spoke about the repression of the early 1980s and said: 'It was important

---

[22]   See Amnesty International (1993: 2), Lawyers Committee for Human Rights (1990: 2–3, 25), Minnesota Lawyers International Human Rights Committee (1990: iii). The Guatemalan government established a law program through AID with Harvard Law School. However, Harvard canceled the program at the end of December when it became apparent that the government had no intention and little will to prosecute men in the military, police, or influential social groups (Minnesota Lawyers 1990: 22).

[23]   In a summer 1990 interview with Ernesto Capuano, a Guatemalan lawyer and mid-twentieth-century reformer now living in Mexico, he stated that the 1986 Constitution was a beautiful legal document. He lamented, however, the great discrepancy that exists between the written document and its implementation.

[24]   The military indicated its intent to remain an integral part of government programs, as stated at an August 1987 conference with the business community and the press entitled 'Años de Lucha por la libertad'. For human rights organization reports see, for example, Minnesota Lawyers International Human Rights Committee (1990) and Washington Office on Latin America (1989). Also see Jonas (1991: 165–6) and Trudeau (1993: 65–8).

[25]   *Inforpress Centroamericana*, gathering information from other news sources, provides some of the most reliable information on this matter. The Archbishop also formed a human rights office based in the National Cathedral that documents human rights abuses, recalling a similar role assumed by the Chilean Church during the Pinochet dictatorship.

[26]   See *Report on Guatemala*, 13, Issue 2, Summer 1992, Interview with Roberto Lemus, p. 3.

to arrive at a new level of organization in order to avoid appearing publicly. This was not a question of clandestinity but of protecting life. Clandestinity is different than hiding yourself. . . . With all of the ashes and shootings, our comrades had to hide themselves, hide with all their heart.' The repression has remained a constant reminder of the military's antagonism to autonomous civic organizing. Consequently, the 1986 transition did not generate an immediate growth of civil society, as in 1944, but in fact led to rather tentative and furtive efforts to reconstitute political parties and civic associations.

The political parties that have emerged in Guatemala have lacked institutional integrity, constituencies, and freedom of ideological expression.[27] These feeble ties with society are, in part, a legacy of the historic absence of political party competition in Guatemala. But they are also a response to a pattern of political powerlessness; political parties in Guatemala have not had freedom of expression, have not had power to pass and implement legislation, and ultimately have known that the parameters of decision-making rest outside of the legislature and executive. The Christian Democrats have been the one partial exception to this pattern. A programmatic party with, relatively speaking, strong rural ties, it successfully put forth presidential candidate Marco Vinicio Cerezo Arévalo. During his administration (1986–91), the party seemed to strengthen clientelist ties in the countryside, taking advantage of the 8 per cent of the budget committed to rural areas—money that CD mayors used effectively to sustain support in areas under their jurisdiction; in 1985, the Christian Democrats won 148 out of 267 municipal elections, and in 1988, they won 140 out of 226 municipal elections (Trudeau 1993: 72–3). However, with rampant corruption in the party, the ineffectiveness of the Cerezo administration, and the embarrassment generated by rumors of drug ties by Cerezo's vice-president, the party seems to have fallen apart and joined the ranks of the other parties characterized in the public record by greed and opportunism. The CD's decline in political capital was illustrated by the 1990 municipal elections, where they won in only 86 out of 300 localities (Trudeau 1993: 147). The failure of this party to maintain its political integrity has only reinforced beliefs about corruption in the party system and the powerlessness of the parties to effect any change other than the deposits in their bank accounts. As one peasant leader of the CUC stated in an interview, June 1990: 'We don't believe anymore in politics which is full of deceit, lies, and [unfulfilled] promises. We don't place our trust anymore in elections.' The rise in electoral abstentionism illustrates this point; in the 1990 presidential elections, turnout was 53 per cent (Trudeau 1993: 147).

Disenchantment with political parties and the closing of political space has been informed by ongoing political violence. Indeed, the cycle of violence largely has undermined political parties as a meaningful form of expression. The armed

---

[27] I do not claim that 'true' political parties 'really' represent, channel, and express societal interests. This is a naïve vision of political parties and representation. However, I do wish to underscore the point that political parties in Guatemala lack any semblance of representation or accountability.

forces have monitored political parties; parties of the left rarely emerge and, when they do, are often victims of violence; and society has been largely distrustful of this formal political process. The political murders since 1989 of party leaders such as Social Democrats Hector Oqueli, Gilda Flores, and Dinora Pérez, Christian Democrat Danielo Rodrigo, and Unión del Centro Nacional (UCN) two-time presidential candidate and newspaper owner, Jorge Carpio, effectively have illus-trated the limited spaces for participating meaningfully and safely in and through political parties and elections. The 85 per cent abstention rate in the January 1994 plebiscite for constitutional reforms is yet another dramatic example of the dis-credited formal political process that has evolved since 1986 (see *Inforpress*, 3 Feb. 1994). In theory, political society serves as a space for competition between state and society. In its absence, the Guatemalan state and organized popular sectors in society have remained locked in conflict.

Against this backdrop, civic organizations began to (re-)emerge tentatively in 1986. In a series of interviews during the course of 1989–90 and December 1992, a constant rejoinder was the general need to overcome the fear of organizing and to break the silence.[28] A peasant leader commented: 'At the end of 1986, we had a lot of work to do . . . It was not easy, and it took a lot of effort to find the path to convince men, women, the elderly, Catholics, and evangelicals to join once again the struggle and to begin to break the fear and the terror embedded in the people.' A union leader stated: 'After the strong repression at the beginning of the 1980s, it has taken a great deal to rebuild the popular movement; we are still in a process of rebuilding.' On two separate occasions, two widow leaders referred to the fact that one of their major successes was overcoming fear and fright: 'Having over-come this fear has allowed us the chance to know our constitutional rights.' And a representative of the Communities in Resistance said: 'We broke the silence.'

The comments by popular movement organizers recall those of the 1940s leaders. In both cases, leaders speak of the need to break the silence that the prior authoritarian regime had attempted to impose on them. They have attempted to reclaim a right to a public voice and a public space. In the first few years of the 1980s transition, a new popular movement emerged that seemed to revolve primarily around class-based demands. Civic associations (re-)emerged, for example, amongst university students in the AEU, peasants in the CUC,[29] and the trade union movement in the Unión Sindical de Trabajadores de Guatemala (UNSITRAGUA).[30]

[28] *Quebrando el silencio*, the title of a 1993 book edited by Santiago Bastos and Manuela Camus, echoes the language used by people I interviewed.

[29] This peasant organization began organizing in the early 1970s and formally was founded on 15 Apr. 1978. It incurred devastating repression, most vividly remembered by the 31 Jan. 1980 massacre at the Spanish embassy but more pervasively experienced throughout the countryside. The organ-ization went underground in the early 1980s and re-emerged after the 1986 transition.

[30] UNSITRAGUA emerged 8 Feb. 1985. A union leader from UNSITRAGUA indicated that by the end of 1992 the federation had 46 affiliated unions and an estimated 20,000 members out of an eco-nomically active work-force of 3.5 million. He estimated that out of Guatemala's total work-force, 5–7 per cent are unionized. He also claimed that 30 per cent of the organized work-force are women (interviews, Mar. 1990 and Dec. 1992, Guatemala City).

These material demands have become all the more salient with the increasing immiseration in Guatemala. ECLAC (1991: 65) reported that of the 183 million poor people in Latin America, Guatemala had the highest proportion of national poverty (two-thirds of households with 30 per cent indigence) followed by Peru (around one-half of households with 20 per cent indigence).[31]

The re-emergence of these unions was striking, given the history of repression. However, perhaps more striking than the re-emergence of organizing among these sectors was the fact that organizing assumed a seemingly more heterodox cast. First, organizations emerged that were an outgrowth of and direct response to the violence. Hence, organizing emerged among widows of the violence (Coordinadora Nacional de Viudas de Guatemala—CONAVIGUA);[32] men organizing against the forced participation in civil defense patrols (Comunidades Étnicas Runujel Junam—CERJ); families organizing to reclaim civil rights denied when they were displaced by the violence (CONDEG—Council of Displaced Guatemalans); and communities that had fled to the mountains demanding that the state recognize their legal existence and rights and stop bombing them (CPRs—Comunidades de Población en Resistencia). To take an example, CONAVIGUA led a campaign demanding the exhumation of clandestine cemeteries following the massacres of villages in the early 1980s. The exhumations that have taken place have been a physical reminder of the past and have generated increased demands to work against the impunity that the military has achieved. The Catholic Church also established in January 1990 a human rights office to document abuses and to extend legal assistance.

These organizations are all a living legacy of the violence and military regime and a constant reminder of the military's continued dominance of the regime.[33] They join GAM, formed in June 1984, which began organizing on behalf of the disappeared. However, they differ from Grupo de Apoyo Mutuo (GAM) and organizations such as Las Madres de la Plaza de Mayo in Argentina in so far as the former organizations are not acting *on behalf of* victims but *as* victims. Hence, while the now more traditional class-based organizations have called for material changes, often posing a challenge to economic elites organized in the peak association CACIF (Comité Coordinador de Asociaciones Agrícolas, Industriales y Financieras), the latter round of organizing has taken place around questions of human and civil rights, military impunity, and dignity, posing an apparent challenge to the military's penetration of the state and society. It is important to keep in mind, however, that these organizations tend to work together; many of the leaders have worked with previous organizations and often have family members working

---

[31] An ECLAC document reported that, as of 1986, 73 per cent of the Guatemalan population lived in poverty while 49 per cent lived in extreme poverty. These figures were obviously higher in the rural areas, as noted in tables included in the ECLAC report (1991: 53–5). More recent figures have been even higher.

[32] CONAVIGUA held its first assembly Sept. 1988. In a Mar. 1990 interview with Rosalina Tuyuc, Tuyuc estimated that the violence had left around 50,000 to 60,000 widows.

[33] See essays in Carmack (1988) and Warren (1993) for a discussion of the ways in which some indigenous communities have experienced and interpreted the violence in Guatemala.

in the sister organizations. They have joined together in national campaigns and federations such as the Unidad de Acción Sindical y Popular (UASP) and the Movimiento Nacional por la Paz. According to a leader of the UASP, speaking in March 1990, they have rallied around four themes: 'the struggle for social justice, respect for human rights, peace, and authentic democracy. Everyone sees these themes from their own perspective and with their particular interests.'[34]

The heterodox nature of the emerging society also is reflected in the increasing salience of ethnic- and gender-based demands.[35] The traditional 'popular'- (i.e. class-)based organizations began to refer more explicitly to ethnicity and gender. For example, the peasant organization CUC historically has declared that it unites peasants regardless of ethnic background. However, its members are largely indigenous, as is the case with CONAVIGUA and CERJ. In the early 1990s, these organizations more actively began to denounce ethnic discrimination. They have participated in the formation of new popular organizations, most notably Majawil Q'ij, to organize the historic 1992 conference for '500 Years of Indigenous, Black, and Popular Resistance' that was held in Quetzaltenango, Guatemala. Mayan nationalist groups have also emerged, including the Academia de Lenguas Mayas (ALMG), Cakchiquel Center for Integral Development (COCADI), and Council of Maya Organizations (COMG) (C. Smith 1992). The mass base of these last three organizations seems to be considerably smaller and more middle-class than that of the popular organizations—which at times has created tensions on all sides about more authentic representation and debates over whose interests are being promoted by the respective organizations.

Women's organizations have also emerged not only within unions but also articulating more explicitly feminist and/or gendered concerns. CONAVIGUA is again an important example and has attempted to mobilize and educate largely indigenous women who have been widowed by the violence. Grupo Femenino Pro-Mejoramiento Familiar (GRUFEPROMEFAM) started off as an organization for the wives of union leaders that turned into a union dedicated to consciousness-raising and organizing among women workers. And Tierra Viva, a small non-governmental organization dedicated to feminism, addresses issues of sexual assault, health, and women's rights.[36] These organizations have articulated an agenda addressing women's issues and have organized, separately and in coalition, around International Women's Day and workshops. And, with the increasing feminization of the work-force in the rising number of *maquilas*, predominantly male unions have started, if with ambivalence, to act on the realization that they need to begin addressing concerns raised by and for women.[37]

---

[34] These united fronts, however, occasionally have given way to internal divisions, as in the fall of 1993 (see *Central American Report*, 27 Aug. 1993).

[35] As discussed earlier, indigenous men and *ladina* women did organize civic associations during the 1944–54 reform period. But they tended to organize within associations dedicated to class rather than ethnic and/or gender-based concerns.

[36] Based on series of interviews 1989–90 and Dec. 1992 with members of GRUFEPROMEFAM and Tierra Viva.   [37] Based on Dec. 1992 interviews with leaders in UNSITRAGUA and UITA.

In short, these organizations have assumed an increasingly diversified, vocal, and public presence since the 1986 transition—although they have not achieved the same strength or militancy that they had in the late 1970s. This diversification of civil society has not garnered, however, adequate spaces for interest representation within politics.[38] Many of these organizations do not have juridical personality, either because the state has denied them such status and/or because they fear that providing the state with a list of members could result in further repression. A CUC leader declared in a March 1990 interview:

> Most of the organizations in the popular movement do not have a juridical personality. But we are legal. Our ties with the popular sectors provide us with this legality. Who are the legal ones? Those who rob the workers, the workers that are demanding social justice without repression?

Moreover, continuing repression has made it extremely difficult to trust that the public spaces that they have acquired will continue to be respected.[39] The repression that has continued under the civilian regimes of Cerezo and Serrano has forced these organizations to maintain a semi-public existence for fear that a more public and open organization might lead to infiltration and betrayal. While fear of infiltration is a universal concern, in Guatemala it has assumed a particularly extreme form—with infiltration seen as a pattern that is expected and with particularly high stakes often ending in torture and murder. Cases such as the village massacres in Aguacate in 1988 and the disappearance of over a dozen students in August/September 1989 are particularly vivid reminders of what can happen to people (suspected of) participating in these organizations. This fear has forced these organizations to hold closed meetings, to limit the lines of communication, and to speak in cloaked language. This is a natural survival technique; however, it has also inhibited democratic practice within these organizations and created an impasse between these organizations and the unorganized majority. Similarly, it has increased state suspicion of these organizations, irrespective of the fact that the state created the impetus for these hidden forms of communication and organization.

Consequently, these organizations have engaged in a politics of protest rather than participation. Violence has become a living memory, indeed a painful optic

---

[38] The state has made various proposals for national dialogues and *concertación*. For example, a number of task forces were formed with the transition that included popular sector representation. These state fora, however, have elicited great suspicion by many activists who have seen these initiatives as efforts at co-optation and pacification that simultaneously provide a means for the military to identify 'troublemakers'. In 1990, the Guatemalan government allowed representatives from the popular movement to attend one meeting between the government and URNG; it was the fifth round of meetings that invited different social sectors. Yet, there has been little follow-through on the proposals that have emanated from these varied meetings and, as of this writing, the dialogue as a whole is stalled.

[39] Amnesty International (1993: 2) reported that: 'Although the overall number of extrajudicial executions and "disappearances" has decreased in 1992, and progress was made initiating criminal proceedings against selected individuals . . . [there was a] marked increase in other human rights abuses—in particular serious death threats, harassment and other serious acts of intimidation.' In December 1992 interviews popular movement activists made similar observations.

for viewing the past, present, and future. Having lost any traces of faith that might have accompanied the 1986 transition, these organizations have reinforced an antagonistic relationship with the militarized state that the military initiated through its use of violence. As Rosalina Tuyuc stated in a March 1990 interview: 'the civilian government is only cultivating despair/hopelessness . . . we had placed our faith in it . . . But the only thing that we have found is deceit, hunger, and despair. . . . Not a single political party can solve this situation.' And with this increasing polarization, popular organizations hark back to 'better times' for popular organizing and participation during the reform period of 1944–54. By the early 1990s, state and society remained locked in a cycle of repression, protest, and escalating distrust.

1993: Anti-Coup Mobilization, Suspended Regime Change, and Continuing Demands for Citizenship

Guatemalan President Jorge Serrano tried to appropriate political power on 25 May 1993 and rule by decree, claiming the need to break the political paralysis that had developed. This coup attempt followed a month of particularly heated debates and demonstrations over structural adjustment plans, including a rise in electricity rates, efforts to privatize energy production and other state enterprises, and a decline in social services. Recalling Fujimori in Peru, Serrano attempted to suspend the Congress, Supreme Court, and Court of Constitutionality as well as to arrest key political figures, including the human rights ombudsman Ramiro de León Carpio. While Serrano was the spokesperson, it is generally assumed that segments of the military participated in this coup attempt. Ex-Minister Hector Gramajo declared to a Mexican paper that 'this coup could have not have taken place without the consent of the military or without the use of military resources placed at the disposition of Serrano' (quoted in *Inforpress*, 8 June 1993, p. 13). Even if the 1986–93 civilian governments had remained subordinate to the military, it appeared that segments of the military had found the existing situation—political paralysis in the legislature, political bickering between political parties, and the rise of popular movement protest—problematic and unbearable. As in 1954, part of the military decided that it was time to close the political and social spaces that had accompanied the political transition of 1986.

Against this backdrop, a multi-sectoral opposition led by the already existing popular movement and unorganized sectors quite courageously took to the streets, gathered in the national cathedral (diagonal from the National Palace), and voiced their opposition.[40] They formed the Foro Multi-Sectorial Social (FMS), which served

[40] The Catholic Church hierarchy and some members of the Protestant churches also voiced their protest. At the end of May, a condemnation was read in churches throughout the country (see *Report on Guatemala*, 14, Issue 2 (June 1993), 3). This opposition to the coup contrasted starkly with the position that the Church adopted in 1954, when it used national pulpits to stir up opposition to the democratic regime.

as a coordinating body to mobilize against the coup. And indeed, after a series of dramatic mobilizations, Serrano stepped down. This widespread protest led many reporters to conclude that popular mobilization had undermined the coup attempt.[41]

The prior historical comparison, however, has highlighted that while popular mobilization does articulate a force for change, that in and of itself does not bring about reform without divisions within the elite and military.[42] And indeed, what seems to have undermined Serrano's coup attempt was popular mobilization coincident with a publicly articulated division within the elite. As in 1944, segments of the economic elite in May 1993 broke ranks and voiced their public opposition to Serrano's authoritarian actions for fear of losing the trading status accorded by the Generalized System of Preferences (GSP); the United States had announced the suspension of economic assistance and GSP status and threatened to use votes to obtain sanctions with the World Bank and International Monetary Fund; the EEC responded in a similar fashion. Mario Granal y Fernández, President of CACIF, the peak association of economic elites in agriculture, commerce, industry, and finance, declared: 'If measures are not taken very quickly to resolve this crisis, the cost to Guatemala would simply be too high' (*New York Times*, 1 June 1993). Fearful of the consequences of economic sanctions, Guatemala's industrial export elite joined one of the emerging multi-class opposition coalitions, a move that exacerbated latent divisions within the military, part of which withdrew support from Serrano, who shortly thereafter was forced to step down. In a surprising turn of events, the legislature, presumably constrained and/or guided by competing positions within the military, selected Ramiro de León Carpio as president for the remaining two and a half years. He was sworn in on 6 June 1993.

In many ways, the rise in popular mobilization, elite division over authoritarian measures by the regime, and the resignation of the political executive describes both the events of May/June 1944 and May/June 1993. In both cases, while the political leader was forced to step down, the organization of coercive power within and by the state apparatus remained in place.[43] Yet, while the 1993 coup attempt was overturned, it did not precipitate democratic change. De León Carpio did not assume the political space, resources, and, perhaps, will to reconstitute political power within the state. While it appears that he attempted to reshuffle power within the military in favor of its relatively more moderate branch, he reversed his position regarding military penetration of the countryside and supported the civilian defense patrols that he had previously criticized as human rights ombudsman.[44]

---

[41] Foreign governments also placed significant foreign pressure on the Guatemalan military. Nonetheless, it is difficult to argue that United States pressure forced this retreat given that the Guatemalan military had ignored this type of pressure in the past, most notably during the Carter administration.

[42] Aguilera Peralta, a Guatemalan social scientist, also agreed that the popular sectors played an important role but not the only one in undermining the success of the coup. See interview in *Report on Guatemala*, 14, Issue 6 (Fall 1993), 13.

[43] Indeed, in both cases, a prominent newspaper owner and editor was killed: Alejandro Córdova of *El Imparcial* (1944) and Jorge Carpio of *El Gráfico* (1993).

[44] See *Inforpress*, 8 June 1993, p. 12; 26 Aug. 1993, p. 6.

Moreover, he called for new elections to replace members of Congress and the Supreme Court, ironically attempting to achieve what Serrano had failed to do through the *Serranazo*. Most politicians refused to resign in a series of embarrassing exchanges that demonstrated de León Carpio's tenuous political power, the political opportunism of the congressional leaders, and the ongoing political paralysis in the country.[45] Popular protest, similarly, increased. By October 1993, popular movements voiced their disgust for the integrity of the political parties and began calling for an electoral reform including the right of civic associations to field candidates for Congress and governorships (*Central American Report*, 1 Oct. 1993).

With this analysis, various Mayan, labor, and grassroots organizations forged an electoral alliance in the months just prior to the 12 November 1995 presidential, legislative, and municipal elections.[46] The broad left front, entitled Frente Democrático Nueva Guatemala (FDNG), represented a significant change of strategy, as political leaders experienced in organizing and protest outside of the state campaigned to gain a political voice from within. Voter turnout was 46 per cent, less than past presidential elections but higher than past mid-year elections.[47] To no one's surprise, the FDNG did not emerge as the dominant political force—losing the presidential race and most legislative seats.[48] But to the surprise of many, this new left political front garnered six legislative seats out of eighty.[49] The new legislators include Rosalina Tuyuc of CONAVIGUA, Amílcar Méndez of CERJ, and Nineth Montenegro de García, all popular sector leaders in Guatemala's protest movements. With the formation and moderate electoral success of the FDNG, Guatemala's heterodox popular sectors have chosen to develop political spaces not just at the margins of the state but also within it.

It would be premature to draw any conclusions about the emergence, participation, and support base of the FDNG. Whether the FDNG will be able to sustain a voice within Guatemala's traditionally corrupt and stalemated party system remains to be seen. Whether the FDNG will provide a forum for more transparent and democratic practices within the left is also an open question. What is certain, however, is that political violence has remained an ongoing component of Guatemalan politics. 1995 did not lead to a decline in political violence overall. The Director of the United Nations Mission for the Verification of Human Rights and

---

[45] See *Inforpress*, 2 Sept. 1993, p. 1; 30 Sept. 1993; 25 Nov. 1993; 9 Dec. 1993; and *Central American Report*, 3 Sept. 1993, pp. 257–8; 10 Sept. 1993; 1 Oct. 1993; 15 Oct. 1993; 19 Nov. 1993.

[46] For a discussion of the election, see reports in *Central American Report, Cerigua, Notisur, Noticias de Guatemala*, and *Latin American Regional Reports*.

[47] Guatemala's guerrilla front, the URNG, historically had denounced Guatemalan elections as a sham and called on Guatemalans to boycott elections. However, the URNG declared a unilateral ceasefire in the two weeks prior to the 1995 elections and encouraged Guatemalans to turn out for the vote.

[48] No presidential candidate in the 1995 election garnered a majority vote, forcing a run-off scheduled for 7 Jan. 1996.

[49] At the time of writing, there is a discrepancy in the various news reports, all of which claim to have reported the final results from Guatemala's Supreme Electoral Tribunal (TSE).

of Compliance with the Commitments of the Comprehensive Agreement on Human Rights in Guatemala (MINUGUA) reported: 'The society has continued to suffer from the climate of generalized violence and public uncertainty, as demonstrated by the high rate of abduction and violent deaths and by the proliferation of firearms.'[50] As the MINUGUA report lays out, the military continues to act with impunity. Guatemala's legal system and police force provide limited protection to Guatemala's citizenry.

Without a reform of the militarized state, and an end to military impunity, Guatemala will remain mired in this situation of suspended regime change. Historical analysis suggests that without a publicly expressed division within the military and the elite over authoritarian practices to accompany the rise in popular mobilization, state reform cannot happen. It is within this cycle of violence and protest that the sharply divergent understanding of the October 1944 overthrow of authoritarian rule remains vivid. Jorge Toriello, the only surviving member of the triumvirate that followed the 1944 October Revolution and a conservative democrat, commented on the political paralysis: 'What Guatemala really needs is a[nother] revolution like the October Revolution . . . This revolution, which would be supported by all the people, is necessary immediately because the prevailing insecurity and the vice of the new tyrants is insufferable.'[51]

Conclusion

A number of authors who write about democratization have agreed with the argument that: 'successful transitions to democracy are necessarily conservatizing, because only institutional arrangements that make radical social and economic changes difficult provide the security that induces actors to play by democratic rules of the game. For democracy to be established, it must protect to some degree the interests of the forces capable of subverting it, above all capitalists and the armed forces.'[52] Aspirations or exasperations aside, this is probably true for capitalist democracies. However, the question remains, what does it mean to say 'to some degree' and who defines those parameters?

The comparative overview in this essay suggests that democratic change, defined even in its limited form, is impossible so long as power remains beholden to

---

[50] Reported in United Nations Document A/50/482, 12 Oct. 1995, Annex, English version, p. 3. Third Report of the Director of the United Nations Mission for the Verification of Human Rights and of Compliance with the Commitments of the Comprehensive Agreements on Human Rights in Guatemala (MINUGUA).

[51] Jorge Toriello Garrido, quoted in *Central America Report*, 22 Oct. 1993, p. 319. Toriello was a member of the triumvirate that oversaw the 1944–8 transition to political democracy in Guatemala.

[52] Cited in Mainwaring *et al.* (1992: 13) in their introduction summary of Przeworski's argument in the same volume.

the priorities of the military with the public support of a united elite.[53] Hence the dilemma confronted by democratic reformers. The institutions of the state that need to be reformed for new democratic institutions to function and have deeper meaning are the very ones that maintain a gun in one hand and cash in the other; for the military in alliance with the oligarchy have historically assured that power remains privatized and that the power of decision derives from institutions that are not accountable. It is within this context that we need to move beyond discussions of democratization that focus either on democratic institution-building at the macro level or social movements operating at the micro level to a more integrated analysis that returns to discussions of the ways in which state–society relations are constructed. So long as state and society are viewed as de-linked and antagonistic entities, the military will continue to resort to repression and popular organizations will continue to organize in hidden spaces but express demands as protest. In the absence of more transparent institutions and organizations which allow for the development of a public sphere, the most minimal conception of citizenship proves meaningless. In this inauspicious contemporary situation, democratic prospects appear slim. In his discussion of Latin America's new democracies, O'Donnell (1993c) referred to patterns of low-intensity citizenship experienced throughout the region. In Guatemala, even this form of citizenship has remained a distant dream against the practice of low-intensity conflict.

[53] Given the constraints of this chapter, I have focused largely on the military rather than the Guatemalan elite and its relationship to the state. Nonetheless, it is accepted commonly that the Guatemalan elite has relied historically on the state to regulate, often coercively, urban and rural labor. This dependence created the political opportunity and conditions for the military to dominate the Guatemalan state.

11 | Popular Responses to State-Sponsored Violence in Brazil

Paulo Sérgio Pinheiro

In 1989, the first president to be democratically elected in Brazil after twenty years of authoritarian rule was accused of corruption. A parliamentary investigation into the affairs of the President and a subsequent criminal investigation led to popular protests throughout the country in 1992, in which protesters filled the streets, urging their congressmen to vote for the President's impeachment and to vote against pardon. This process finally concluded in September 1992 with the impeachment of President Fernando Collor on charges of corruption.

In early 1994, a special commission of the federal Congress presented the final report of its three-month-long investigation—sessions were transmitted by radio and television—on what became known as 'the Federal Budget mafia' scandal, centering on a group of congressmen who had pocketed more than 100 million dollars from the federal budget in 190 checking accounts dispersed in twenty-seven banks. The federal Congress promoted its own 'clean hands' investigation, proposing the expulsion of eighteen of its members and indicting two dozen.[1]

All participants in these investigations—the government, political society, the judiciary, and civil society—strictly adhered to the rules of the game. Linz and Stepan have recognized that 'what was impressive about the impeachment proceedings is that in the midst of the multiple crises of democracy, every major component of Brazilian politics carried out their fundamental democratic tasks' (Linz and Stepan forthcoming: 263, 264).

Almost simultaneously, while the impeachment and the parliamentary corruption investigations were being carried out, government agents directly participated in gross human rights violations—such as the October 1992 Carandiru massacre of 111 prisoners by the São Paulo military police; the July 1993 killings of street children near the Candelária church by the Rio military police; and extra-judicial killings by *justiceiros* and police forces. These contrasting events show that the government has not succeeded in changing many of the arbitrary practices of its institutions or in imposing the restrictions expected of the state's monopoly on legal violence. Brazil thus illustrates the problems that new democracies face

---

[1] See James Brooke, 'Scandals Shaking Faith of Brazil in Democracy', *New York Times*, 4 Jan. 1994.

in bridging the growing gap between the state's political gains and its persistent violations of economic, social, and civil rights. These conflicting practices show the challenges that developing countries face in establishing connections among the heterogeneous spheres of power—democratic values continue to coexist with authoritarian ones.

The fundamental contradiction that this chapter addresses is whether basic political and civil rights can be protected adequately in countries where 'structural violations' of economic, social, and cultural rights seem to be a permanent feature of society (Stavenhagen 1990; Pinheiro *et al.* 1993: 25). It seeks to explain why democratic consolidation, despite constitutional freedoms which have been granted and competitive elections which have been held during the last ten years, still faces so many obstacles. The chapter argues that one of the main difficulties is the continuation of authoritarian practices in a society now under a democratic political framework.

After examining the main aspects of this continuity and the characteristics of socially rooted authoritarianism, the chapter discusses two closely interconnected and mutually reinforcing phenomena that pose, in our view, the most serious threats to the consolidation of democracy in Brazil. The first is the failure of democracy to integrate large segments of the population as full-fledged citizens into the development process and consequently into the decision-making process. The second is the failure to achieve pacification of society through the universal application of the rule of law and the legal control of violence. The chapter focuses on these phenomena by examining the question of corruption and the persistence of illegal violence against the most disadvantaged groups. It also evaluates the role that impunity, accountability, and transparency play at the present juncture in Brazil. Despite this grim picture, the chapter also examines how a free and active civil society developed in specific sectors, exemplified by the activities of NGOs in Brazil—especially those involved in human rights. The chapter discusses the strategies of human rights NGOs concerning the effective enforcement of the rule of law and the struggle against violence. Finally, we discuss the democratic framework that can gradually create conditions for civilian governments to make transparency a requirement for addressing gross human rights violations.

1. Democratic Consolidation and Authoritarian Continuity

The end of authoritarian regimes and the return to constitutionalism through political transitions proved insufficient to guarantee access to democracy for large segments of the population in developing countries. This is because democracy is more than writing a constitution and introducing an electoral system.

If political democracy could be defined, as Kenneth Bollen proposes, 'as the extent to which political power of the elites is minimized and that of the non-elites is maximized', then the present situation of democratic regimes in developing countries is extremely precarious. For, as Bollen indicates, 'it is the relative balance of power between elites and non-elites that determines the degree of political democracy. Where the non-elites have little control over the elites, political democracy is low. When the elites are accountable to the non-elites, political democracy is higher' (Bollen 1991: 5).

The main prerequisites which enable non-elites to control elites—popular sovereignty through free and competitive elections, alternation in government, separation of powers, independence of the judiciary, control of the military—may become real in any stage of economic development. Even if these characteristics often are found more easily in richer countries, some changes in the political process can reform political institutions in any polity. But contemporary history has demonstrated that the pacification of violence, with few exceptions, has become a reality only in more economically and socially developed societies (Pinheiro *et al.* 1993: 201–2).

Needless to say, the control of violence has represented a challenge to Western countries where democracy has flourished and become deeply rooted. With the establishment of the modern state and its rational politico-administrative apparatus, these countries largely have achieved 'the monopoly of violence', and ensured the pacification of social conflicts through the universal applications of laws (Weber 1963, Bobbio 1984). This process was not achieved without intense social struggle and confrontation. The break with the past occurred when the state succeeded in ensuring the basic principles of human rights, political pluralism, the social contract, and political representation.

Many Latin American countries were not entirely successful in ensuring one of the basic cornerstones of democracy: the legal control of violence. The return to civilian rule carried the hope that the human rights victories achieved by political opponents under military rule would now be extended automatically to all citizens, especially the most destitute and vulnerable groups. While the most egregious forms of human rights violations by the military regime were eliminated under civilian rule, the long-awaited democracies did not succeed in playing their role as guardian of public order and protector of the fundamental rights of all citizens. The pacification of society through the rule of law is still precarious in many countries.

In many of these new democracies, as Guillermo O'Donnell has pointed out, the installation of a democratically elected government does not necessarily open the avenues for institutionalized forms of democracy. In many emerging democracies without a democratic tradition, that 'second transition'—after the 'first transition' from authoritarian rule—is immobilized by the many negative legacies of the authoritarian past (O'Donnell 1994: 56).

If we can consider the linking of authoritarian practices with a democratic regime as constituting a new system of government—unable to realize all the prerequisites of the formality of democracy—then perhaps we can understand the dynamics of the present system. Tentatively, if we refer to the presence of corruption or gross human rights violations, we can conclude that the authoritarian regime (1964–85) and the civilian democratic government (1985 to the present) are expressions of the same system of government as a whole. One of the explanations for this continuity is that social forms of authoritarianism have survived well beyond political democratization (O'Donnell and Schmitter 1986, Pinheiro forthcoming). This authoritarianism is not only socially rooted in macropolitical institutions, but also in the micro-physics of power (as defined by Michel Foucault).

Within that system there persists a clientelistic political style that is 'normal in an oligarchic republic, founded in a predominantly rural society, with a very limited expansion of capitalist relations and with a very limited mobilization and organization of the popular classes'. But that political style is profoundly inadequate for an eminently urban society, where capitalist relations are fully hegemonic and where a civil society is present. The perpetuation of the ruling class after the authoritarian regime, as O'Donnell has observed, indicates a very high level of continuity of authoritarian practices in Brazil, even when compared to other successful democratizations since World War II. In Brazilian society, as in many new democracies, there are profound authoritarian strands that pervade not only politics but society. Implanting democratic institutions following political transitions was much more difficult than had been expected previously: 'The combination of extreme inequality and very authoritarian patterns of social relations poses great difficulties in creating a more solid and open democracy . . . In Brazil, just to name one country, the lower classes are treated as inferiors, as subcitizens. With those kinds of inequalities and social authoritarianism a democracy is difficult' (O'Donnell 1993e).

The institutional changes made to the Brazilian government structure after the return to democracy were never accompanied by economic and social changes for the majority of the population. There is a dramatic inequality between rich and poor people, a profound and historical gap that continues to widen and still divides Brazilian society. The lack of democratic controls on the ruling classes has been combined traditionally with denial of human rights for the poor. This combination reinforces a strong social hierarchy, where rights and the rule of law are an illusory reference for sheer domination. As a consequence, only a few sectors of society which have access to economic and social conditions of survival do, in fact, benefit from effective control over the means of violence in the social interactions of daily life.

2. Citizen Representation and Lack of Accountability

Brazil experiences the incredible paradox of strictly defined constitutional guarantees combined with very weak citizenship. To understand this contrast, it is worth considering that political institutions for citizen representation are very problematic and that most of their limitations, defined under the authoritarian regime, were maintained by the 1988 Constitution.

Most striking among those institutions is the over-representation of the less populated states in comparison with the most populated one: the state of São Paulo today has only sixty congressmen (11.9 per cent among the total members of Congress representing 20,774,991 people, approximately 21.9 per cent of the 94 million voters).[2] In comparison, the state of Roraima elects eight congressmen (1.6 per cent of the total in Congress) when its voters total 119,399 voters, or 0.1 per cent of all voters in the country. The states of the Brazilian federation that are over-represented are the northern and north-eastern states, those with the worst social indicators and where elements of social authoritarianism are most visible, especially through the continuous presence of oligarchic politicians who have remained in power since 1964. These states also have the largest concentrations of illiteracy—46 per cent in the north-eastern states and 35 per cent in the northern states.[3] In the states of these two regions, rates of illiteracy are much greater than in other states: Sergipe, 23.30 per cent; Alagoas, 23.22 per cent; Maranhão, 21.68 per cent; Paraíba, 21.64 per cent; compared to São Paulo, 3.07 per cent, or Rio de Janeiro, 3.09 per cent.

It is precisely in the northern and north-eastern states where free access to information is most limited and where local politicians control the media—television and radio—by concessions from the state and the press. Eight private groups control the country's television in a situation of virtual oligopoly. Many concessions are divided among members of the same family to escape the provision in the law that forbids individual ownership of more than ten television concessions. Most of the power of politicians from the oligarchy in those states of the north and north-east is based on control of the media in their states. The families of former presidents Sarney and Collor each have one television concession, and five and three radio stations, respectively, in their states, Maranhão and Alagoas; former Bahian governor Antonio Carlos Magalhães, Congressman Inocêncio de Oliveira of Pernambuco, former President of the Chamber of Representatives, as well as several former governors, ministers, and senators from those regions also own television concessions, radio stations, and very often local newspapers.[4]

These limitations in the system of representation have direct consequences for citizen participation because this clientelism systematically builds strong obstacles to human development in the region and to the possibilities for organizing the participation of civil society. Underdevelopment in those two regions is not a result of fatality or of pathology. It is the concrete consequence of the maintenance of social authoritarianism through the complex interplay of control over political (representation, media access, judicial institutions, police) and economic

---

[2] 'Câmara nunca seguiu porporcionalidade', *Folha de S. Paulo*, 31 Aug. 1994: Especial-2.
[3] 'Taxa de analfabetismo diminui para 20%', *Folha de S. Paulo*, 4 Aug. 1994, p. 3-2.
[4] See 'Coronelismo agora é eletrónico', *Jornal do Brasil*, 7 Sept. 1994.

resources (privatization of state budgets through corruption) in the hands of those oligarchies—as the investigation concerning the 'congressional Mafia' has demonstrated. Poverty, illiteracy, and epidemics are by-products of the continued presence of traditional and authoritarian elites in the consolidation of democracy. Such elites, so far unchallenged by civil society, have enjoyed recourse to illegal controls and many times to terror; the absence of transparency, the absence of accountability, and impunity are the pillars of traditional economic and political domination in the north and north-east region.

One of the most characteristic flaws of democratic states like Brazil which have difficulties in implementing the rule of law is the absence of 'accountability', the principle which requires that political representatives and public officers be made to answer for their actions. In modern political practice, as Juan Linz and Alfred Stepan have observed, accountability requires that 'all financial records . . . be routinely subject to inspection, and that it is the obligation of the officials who use public funds to follow transparent procedures . . . Bureaucrats and officials who treat state resources as their "patrimony" are held accountable and can be put in jail' (Linz and Stepan 1994: 262).

Political oligarchies, through their control of the electronic media, make transparency impossible and create obstacles to strengthening institutions crucial to the enforcement of constitutional guarantees and to making the ruling class and public officers accountable to the citizens. The judiciary is not subjected to any kind of external control by administrative proceedings or expenses. State public prosecutors have had their competence broadened by the new constitution and in practice try to make their prerogatives real, but in many states they are submitted to serious limitations. Civilian police posts, as we will see, do not exist in the poorest states, and police commissioners, who preside over every criminal investigation, are completely dominated by the Executive. This incapacity of the state to make public officers accountable and to strengthen the political institutions most exposed to corruption is a phenomenon which affects both new and consolidated democracies. The extremely fragile consolidation of democratic institutions, lacking in effective accountability, assures virtual impunity, especially for crimes committed by the ruling classes and by organized crime.

The absence of serious mobilization dramatically restricts the weight that popular mobilization could have on changing the foundations of political power. Certain elites, especially in the most underdeveloped states, clearly perceive that if citizenship and democratic participation become a reality, this will inevitably lead to demands for economic change, which is long overdue (Cammack 1993: 189).

To be fair, it is necessary to recognize that in the south-eastern states, like Rio de Janeiro or São Paulo, even though the rate of illiteracy is smaller and there is greater transparency and a higher degree of independence enjoyed by the judiciary, violent crime—as the homicide rate indicates—as well as illegal violence and impunity nonetheless are high. Despite the relative weakness of clientelism, corruption helps to establish a very active collusion between crime and state agents.

Thus, despite democratic governance and the clear definition of constitutional guarantees, we must recognize that in Brazil there is democracy without citizenship. Here, as in several other Latin American societies, 'the blocking of participation outside elections by local elites and state security forces forces the prevalence of clientelism, and elite resistance to the building of strong and autonomous association by the poor themselves' (Cammack 1993: 189).

Besides these political aspects, it must also be remembered that most Latin American countries have reached democracy with stark inequities in development and relatively poor social indicators. Notwithstanding democratization, both trends worsened during the so-called 'lost decade' of the 1980s. According to the UNDP Human Development Report, Brazil, which has the worst income disparity (among the countries of more than 10 million inhabitants) in the world, experienced an increase in the ratio of the income of the richest 20 per cent to that of the poorest 20 per cent from 26 to 1 in 1991 to 32 to 1 in 1993.[5]

Latin American specialists consider structural violations of economic and social rights a permanent feature of these societies and question the feasibility of protecting the fundamental political and civil rights of the population without undertaking profound changes in these structures. The exclusion of important segments of the population from economic progress and political participation, leaving them with little hope to better their lives, means that countries in transition will only be able to achieve 'imperfect' or 'restricted' forms of democracy (Stavenhagen 1990: 48–50).

Structural violations of human rights that are rooted in the economic and social structure of a country are as destructive to democratic principles as the better-known civil and political violations; yet they are much more difficult to combat than the latter, in the sense that the state alone cannot be responsible for solving them. Society as a whole has to be mobilized to put an end to these secular distortions (Stavenhagen 1990: 48–50).

3. Lack of Accountability in a Culture of Corruption

On many fronts, including gross human rights violations, violence, and corruption, the Brazilian experience offers an example of continuity in—rather than rupture with—past authoritarian practices.

If we can consider the linking of authoritarian practices with a democratic regime as constituting a new system of government then perhaps we can understand the dynamics of the present system. Perhaps in the realm of corruption if we could consider the authoritarian regime (1964–85) and the civilian and

---

[5] According to the World Bank, 51.3 per cent of national income is concentrated in the hands of 10 per cent of the population; the 20 per cent poorest get 2.1 per cent. Daniela Falcão, 'Brasil é o primeiro em desigualdade social', *Folha de S. Paulo*, 28 July 1995, p. 1-5.

democratic governments (1985 to the present) as a single system then we would be able to understand the endemic corruption that characterizes many new polities, such as the present one in Brazil. The Brazilian corruption scandals may be of particular interest for the analysis of transition processes where in fact there is evidence of continuity rather than of rupture.

Democratization, meaning free and competitive elections and constitutional guarantees, is not sufficient to overcome what Gunnar Myrdal called twenty-five years ago in *Asian Drama* 'the soft state': the state that failed to supersede personal, family, ethnic, and tribal loyalties (Woollacott 1993: 6). Many elected presidents or democratically appointed officers do not perceive the boundaries between state finances and private expenses. Even in democratic regimes many officers continue receiving bribes or regular commissions, or take money directly from public funds.

Corruption may also be interpreted as an absence of efficient political institutions. Public officials, as Samuel Huntington noted some time ago, have no autonomy and tend to subordinate their institutional roles to external demands. In many societies, the use of public positions for personal enrichment is accepted as normal. In many countries, like Italy and Brazil, several public institutions, especially those which are supposed to be above influence like the parliament, are extremely susceptible to untoward practices.

In the face of a weak state, political institutions, especially the parliament, are those most exposed to corruption. It is a phenomenon that is cross-cultural and which affects new and consolidated democracies alike. Many congressmen worldwide continue to be available to be bought. Alan Doig, in his work on corruption in contemporary British politics, considered government Ministers (and Cabinet Ministers also) 'the most marketable and vulnerable commodity'. Quite recently, in an opinion editorial which appeared in the *International Herald Tribune*, historian Arthur Schlesinger Jr. quoted Mark Twain as having considered congressmen 'the only distinctly natural criminal class'. Brazilian and Italian congressmen are competing to affirm the truth of these assessments which link political representatives and corruption.

For twenty years, the Brazilian parliament did not have a say in the preparation of the federal budget. When, after the return to democracy, the Congress regained control of the budget, decisions became subject to control through collusion between members of the congressional budget commission and half a dozen executive officers. The Congress, as a whole, has also developed a very particularistic approach to the preparation of the budget, a large percentage of the budget being allocated directly to private organizations nominated by each congressman. In fact, one aspect of the scandal was the discovery that an apparently favorite way of stealing from the federal budget was to channel grants to those charitable foundations controlled by members of Congress. In response to these disclosures, the government ruled in December 1993 that 3,200 'non-profit' groups were no longer eligible for subsidies (Brooke 1994).

Beyond state and political institutions, however, to understand corruption we must take into account that this is also a dimension of a political culture characterized by an insufficient acknowledgment of the difference between the public spirit, *l'esprit public*, and private interests. In many societies there is a generalized compulsion to take private advantage from a given situation, especially from public resources. This is particularly so in those countries where public resources are so scarce. On the other hand, the belief that all those who are in government or in the parliament are corrupt functions as an excuse for the majority of the population to disrespect the law, to evade taxes, and to carry out administrative irregularities.[6] In many societies the very notion of 'conflict of interest' does not exist.

The enormous difficulties encountered in trying to clean up a country after an investigation by the Congress (as in Brazil) or by the Judiciary (as in Italy) indicate that the phenomenon of corruption is quite pervasive and profound in society. This skepticism was recently echoed by Umberto Eco: 'Nowadays 95 per cent of the people are enraged and shout "Thief!" at the MPs walking down the street. But what were they doing before? Running some kind of Committee of Public Health? Let's not go along with this idea of a country with a clean bill of health in revolt against a High Dome of corruption. Confronted by an examination of conscience, we find a country which is, for the most part, corrupt.' There is no real guarantee that allows us to conclude that the 'clean hands movement' in Brazil, Italy, or other parts of the world has become consolidated in the sense of achieving effective cultural reform. It would be extremely misleading to suppose that the present campaigns against corruption announce the end of generalized practices of corruption accepted and even practiced by all the population.

In any case, these new and unexpected developments in the fight against the impunity of corruption practices have produced a new civic awareness and may contribute to strengthening democratic values. In December 1993, in a national survey taken by the daily *Folha de S. Paulo*, 54 per cent of Brazilians agreed that 'democracy is always better than any other form of government'—the highest percentage registered in the ten times the question has been asked since September 1989. This was the year after the numerous public demonstrations for impeachment, the reawakening of investigative journalism, and the parliament's investigation of corruption. Transparency makes a difference.

4. Endemic Violence and Gross Human Rights Violations

After nearly ten years of restored democracy, Brazil has yet to find a solution to endemic violence and gross human rights violations. Violence in Brazil emerges in a setting of extreme economic and social inequalities, of huge income gaps inside as well as outside Brazil's borders.

---

[6] Quoted by Ed Vulliamy, 'A Culture of Corruption', *Guardian Weekly*, 25 Apr. 1995.

Crime as a whole became more violent in the 1980s; the murder rate in recent years has risen dramatically in Rio de Janeiro and São Paulo. Prominent among the assaults on life in Brazilian cities are traffic accidents and deaths, causing us to recognize a category of violence meted out by 'educated' people. The state, in most cases, is not directly responsible for committing these abuses; its responsibility lies in the failure to control the arbitrary practices of its own repressive apparatus.

The failure to control violence is illustrated by: (1) the continued use of torture against suspects in most police precincts throughout the country; (2) the ill-treatment of inmates in prisons and in closed institutions;[7] (3) extra-judicial killings by police-linked death squads; (4) the murder of street children and adolescents by *justiceiros* and other non-identified groups; (5) widespread rural violence. The majority of these cases have a common denominator of impunity. The failure to enforce the law not only affects the equality of citizens before the law, but also makes it more difficult for governments to strengthen their legitimacy and perpetuates the illegal circle of violence (Pinheiro *et al.* 1993: 10).

The victims are no longer a small minority of educated, mostly white, middle-class political opponents. Under democratic rule, the principal targets of arbitrary rule and of human rights abuses are the most defenseless groups—the poor, prison and closed-institution inmates, rural workers and trade-union activists, racially discriminated minorities, destitute children and adolescents.

Violence is widespread in rural areas of Brazil, where, José de Souza Martins indicates, at least 90,000 people were at some time enslaved during the last twenty-five years (Foreword to Sutton 1994: 8). Generally, people are 'hired' to work and are brought to the work site, after which they are informed that they are indebted for their transportation and food during transport. The workers are not paid wages and are threatened with death if they attempt to escape.

Many visible manifestations of this endemic violence also are present in urban areas. Between 1980 and 1990, the rural population decreased from 23 million to 15 million, with an average 1 million people leaving the countryside every year (Sutton 1994: 24). The urban population in Brazil grew from 67.5 per cent of the total population in 1980 to 75 per cent in 1990. This was the consequence of massive migrations during the last three decades from the rural to the urban sector. Large parts of populations in Brazilian cities live in miserable conditions of urban marginality, similar to those of the least developed countries in Asia and Africa (Jaguaribe *et al.* 1989: 17 and 31).

There is a strong correlation between the places where the poor live and violence. Shootings, stabbings, and traffic accidents kill more in the poor periphery of São Paulo than all the types of cancer. The further we go from the central regions of the city to the periphery, where there are large concentrations of poor (mostly

[7] At present, some 126,000 prisoners are held in jails built to hold 51,000. The rate of incarceration is moderate by international standards, but Brazil has one of the highest levels of lethal violence by the police in the world.

living in shantytowns—*favelas*),[8] the more we see a clear reduction in mortality rates due to cardiovascular disease and cancer and an increase in 'external' causes of death (violence, homicide). There is a clear link between living conditions and violence and mortality rates which indicates an epidemic of violence—violence being a significant part of social deprivation (Sen 1993: 46).

This violence is not a new phenomenon in Brazil; rather, it is the continuation of a long tradition of authoritarianism that was hidden behind the political violence of the military regime and the restrictions imposed through censorship. The formal configuration of democracy opened space for repressed contradictions and unresolved social, cultural, and other conflicts to come to the surface.

5. The Failure of the State to Control Illegal Violence

This aggravation of gross human rights violations occurs despite the existence of what we could call a 'bill of rights'—one of the most far-reaching in Brazilian history—written into the 1988 Constitution (especially the 77 provisions in article 5, chapter 1 on individual and collective rights). The new Constitution brought enormous progress in the area of protection of fundamental individual rights. Violations which traditionally have plagued Brazilian society, such as torture and racial discrimination, are treated as crimes; the rights to life, liberty, and security of the person have been reinforced. The formal recognition of these rights, however, has not been sufficient to put an end to a wide range of violations.

Let us look in more detail at the situation of legal institutions. The reform of the judicial system, the most crucial institution for enforcing the rule of law, has not accompanied political and legal changes introduced in the text of laws by the new democracies. The judicial system has both a precarious structure and an insufficient staff. The lack of judges in rural areas, the slow pace of legal processes, and the differential access of the rich and the poor to justice are but a few examples of the poor performance of this institution.

Brazil, as Alfred Stepan has recently observed, is a country with great problems concerning the normative and institutional presence of the state. Many studies have revealed that the overriding number of Brazil's citizens do not believe that the state has attempted or will ever attempt to enforce laws on all its citizens equally and impartially. In particular, most citizens think that the justice system fundamentally exists to protect the powerful (Stepan 1993: *passim*).

Reform of the judicial system has been slow in coming to Brazil's new democratic administrations. Today there are fewer than 6,000 judges in the country, as

---

[8] Indeed, a large percentage of housing in the principal cities is in the form of *favelas*: 42.3 per cent in Recife; 12.4 per cent in Rio de Janeiro; 10 per cent in Belo Horizonte; 6.5 per cent in Porto Alegre; and 5 per cent in São Paulo. In the latter city (8 million pop.), 61.7 per cent live in shantytowns, slums, and squats, cit. P. S. Pinheiro, 'Survivre dans les favelas de São Paulo', *Esprit*, June 1994, p. 30.

evidenced by the data published by the National Judiciary Data Bank of the Supreme Court (1991). In the northern and north-eastern states—which are politically over-represented in the Congress, where the accountability of public officials is practically non-existent, and where social and economic conditions are worse and impunity is more evident—the ratio of judges to people is smaller than in the southern states.[9]

This pattern is duplicated in other public posts crucial to the rule of law, such as the public prosecutors' offices in each state. Many cities in areas of intense rural conflicts have no judge or public prosecutor. In most states in the north and north-east there is no police career track—police commissioners, who preside over every criminal investigation, are political appointees of state governors and the requirement that they must have a law degree is not always respected. In the state of Bahia, for instance, 60 per cent of police commissioners have been appointed by the governor. The result is that police investigations, decisive in the struggle against crime and impunity, are extremely fragile.

Evidently this failure of the democratic regime is not limited to the more underdeveloped states; the federal police, an essential instrument for investigation of crimes involving corruption, contraband, and human rights violations, number less than 5,000 agents, the great majority of whom are concentrated in Brasília and in the biggest state capitals.[10]

The police and the legal system are virtually absent concerning the detection and prosecution of rural violence against the poor. According to the Comissão Pastoral da Terra, from 1964 to 1992 there were 1,730 killings of peasants, rural workers, trade union leaders, and lawyers as well as of religious people serving in advisory capacities in rural and labor conflicts; just thirty of these cases had been brought to trial by 1992 and only eighteen of these resulted in convictions (Sutton 1994: 24).

In the state of Pará, where more rural workers and their leaders have been killed than in any other state, only one gunman was convicted of murder in 1993 and no landowner has ever been convicted for paying for the killings, as oftentimes has been the case. In a rare case where a landowner was convicted and jailed for murder, Darli Alves and his son Darci (the killers of rubber-tapper leader Chico Mendes) escaped from the Acre state prison on 15 February 1993; many human rights groups have charged that the escape was aided by authorities. A federal manhunt failed to find them and they remain at large (US State Department 1994: *passim*).

As a result, many violent and organized crimes and most gross human rights violations—such as those allegedly committed by state agents—are never prosecuted. Moreover, rigorous and respected legal precepts regulating arrest, right to

---

[9]   In the state of São Paulo, there is one judge for 20,228 people; in Pernambuco state in the northeast, one judge for 40,228 people. See Pinheiro (1993: 10). By comparison, Germany has one judge for 3,448 people and Italy one judge for 7,962. Sadek and Bastos (1994: 39).

[10]   In the port of Santos, the biggest in the country, with 15 km, there are only two agents. Brazilian borders are almost completely unprotected—in most outposts there are on average two agents.

counsel, interrogation, and imprisonment are unknown to the poor segments of the population on the periphery of metropolitan areas.

In the majority of the states police investigations are extremely precarious. Disrespect for civil rights is the rule in relations between police and the poor. Public opinion holds that the police cannot be trusted. A study of the state civilian police (Paixão 1982), which is responsible for investigations in the large cities of Brazil, showed that members of the civilian police see themselves as 'purifiers of the society', justifying their routine use of illegal methods of investigation: torture and ill-treatment of suspects, especially those who are not able to defend their civil rights. The study also underlined the precarious character of the formal mechanism of investigation, the rule of law, 'which is often considered by police agents as an obstacle rather than an effective guarantee of social control' (Pinheiro 1992 and 1993).

The state military police, under the control of the governors of each of the twenty-six states of the Brazilian federation and in charge of patrolling and crime prevention, have been reported to commit some of the most blatant human rights violations in the form of summary execution of suspects (Americas Watch 1993*a*, Chavigny 1990). The military police view these deaths as a way of protecting society against 'marginal' elements, and they are rarely punished.

The 1988 Constitution has preserved a separate system of criminal justice set up under the dictatorship—the *justiça militar*—for the discipline of the military police. Crimes committed on duty by the military police come under the jurisdiction of special military police courts set up by the military police in each state (not by the armed forces). But, in fact, military justice is not designed to work well for acts of violence committed by the police; it works much more efficiently for cases that present a threat to the organization, such as corruption and breaches of discipline, than for violence against citizens (Americas Watch 1993*b*: *passim*; US Department of State 1994: *passim*).

6. The Role of Civil Society and NGOs' Strategies

If we turn to the organized sectors of civil society, namely the human rights movements and non-governmental organizations (NGOs), we find that during military rule they were quite successful in denouncing political rights violations but did not engage in defending those who were demanding their social and economic rights. Even in the case of persecuted trade union leaders, human rights activists primarily focused on the political aspects of the persecution. Social and economic rights usually were disassociated from political and civil rights and treated as part of the country's economic policy.

The new juridical framework opened up space for new movements and organizations among women, blacks, indigenous people, rural workers, and others. These emerging movements have introduced a dynamism and a capacity for innovation in the system that have challenged the limitations of weak political parties and trade unions, as well as the more narrow concerns of national interest groups (Stavenhagen 1990). Yet, despite their vitality, the activities of these groups are still fragmented and localized. They can complement but not substitute for political society.

It is interesting to note that the same groups that fought arbitrary rule in Brazil and in other Latin American countries have, over the past two years, begun to act in defense of the poor and other disadvantaged groups. The most famous initiative is, undoubtedly, the 'Campanha da Cidadania contra a Fome e pela Vida' (Citizens' Campaign against Hunger and for Life), launched by the well-known Brazilian sociologist and activist Herbert de Souza ('Betinho'). This nationwide campaign is mobilizing the enthusiasm of significant segments of the population and receiving support from several authorities. The concrete results are still modest compared to the gigantic needs; however, this is a reflection of the country's 'malaise' in relation to the rising social crisis.

Although all protagonists—state, civil society, political parties—agree that something should be done, no government in the region has committed itself seriously to changing the balance of power in favor of the most vulnerable minority in all societies, the poor. Although they represent the majority, the poor are 'institutionally excluded and systematically discriminated against' in societies governed by laws that are not enforced and markets that exclude them (UN 1991). Most Latin American countries are far from possessing the ideal distribution of power resources between competing groups to foster the democratization process. Yet, as Vanhanen explains, economic and intellectual resources are important means of power, 'as long as the struggle for power remains more or less peaceful'. When competing groups resort to violence, it becomes the most important power resource (Vanhanen 1990: 51). In the next section, we shall analyze how this violence takes an endemic form that is perpetuated by public institutions and society.

7. Civil Society vs. the State: Fighting Illegal Violence

The persistence of illegal violence among the poor after the return to democracy is a crucial obstacle to the emergence of civil society—considered as the institutional framework of a modern world 'stabilized by fundamental rights' (Cohen and Arato 1992: 442). The situation is most devastating for those rights that secure socialization, which are crucial to the building of solidarity (Pinheiro 1992: 5).

Despite these obstacles and the failure of state institutions to enforce the rule of law, it is important to note that civilian rule and the 'formality' of democracy (using Agnes Heller's term), even with all its limitations, have opened the possibility of accountability. Many important changes have occurred in civil society and in the democratic structure of the state.

The struggle against the military dictatorship has contributed to the awareness of civic and social rights. In marked contrast to the situation evident in the 1970s or 1980s, there is a widespread network of non-governmental human rights organizations, both urban and rural, as well as neighborhood and professional associations and environmental and indigenous groups.

NGOs have proliferated at a tremendous rate since the political opening. Research carried out in 1988 showed that there were 1,208 NGOs (spread over 378 cities), 85 per cent of them created in the last fifteen years, and about 100 focused exclusively on human rights. According to recent estimates, that number has more than doubled in the last few years.

The south-eastern region contains 53 per cent of these organizations, the majority of which have programs with a national focus, are research institutions, or defend indigenous peoples' rights. The second-largest concentration of NGOs is in the north-east at 27 per cent. These NGOs have developed a number of activities, such as organizing assistance to grassroots movements and popular groups, primarily linked with rural and urban labor unions; education and communications; and assistance to vulnerable and destitute groups (Garrison 1993: 5).

Considering their size and resources, the contribution of NGOs is notable, as recognized by Miguel Darcy de Oliveira, who writes: 'The NGOs' contribution was great, because they were able to speak legitimately today in Brazil of a civil society. In their function as micromultimediators, they explored the unsuspected space of social articulation—places of privilege, themes, actors and powers that circulate at the base of society' (Oliveira 1992: 173).

During the military regime, human rights activists had succeeded, in spite of their small number and the repressive measures taken against them, in building a powerful regional and international network. Moreover, they deserved credit for the elimination of the most brutal forms of political persecution. Their struggle was courageous, well targeted, and succeeded in winning the support of national and international public opinion.

Today under civilian rule, although working conditions are more secure, activists are faced with the more difficult task of defending the rights of the poor and the vulnerable groups. In comparison to the small groups of political opponents, the new victims are more difficult to identify, as they do not constitute a homogeneous group and their number is much higher. Moreover, public opinion in general has not been mobilized in the same way in defense of their cause, and the middle class that gave its support to democratization does not take action to end these new manifestations of human rights abuses.

An additional element that we need in order to understand the Brazilian case is the difficulty poor people encounter in recognizing their own rights within human rights. This is combined with a high level of acceptance of the illegal practices of state agents on the part of the population at large, even among the poor, who despite being the preferential victims of this violence see this acquiescence as a way of distancing themselves from 'marginal elements' and criminals (Pinheiro *et al.* 1993; Caldeira 1992). On the other hand, the overriding majority of Brazilians do not believe in the impartiality of the justice and police system. For this reason, they often take justice into their own hands, in the form of vigilante actions or lynchings, thereby reinforcing illegality and violence.

To sum up, the poor continue to be the preferential target of human rights violations, in Brazil as well as in other new democracies. The failure of governments to respect their own laws not only perpetuates human rights abuses, but also jeopardizes their legitimacy, and makes it more difficult for them to obtain the necessary support from the population to undertake structural reforms for more equitable development.

On the other hand, in the present juncture of recession, unemployment, and social injustice rebellions against inequity often take the form of endemic violence, rather than organized movements to demand civil rights. Increased marginalization and the lack of future prospects for the most deprived segments of the population, especially the chronically unemployed and the young, make them turn to violence and illegal activities.

All of these phenomena show the survival in modern Brazil—and in other developing countries—of asymmetric power relations, which combined with a low trust in institutions of law enforcement put their democratic achievements at risk. With the increasing use of violence as a means of resolving power conflicts, democracy is not 'the only game in town'.

During the past decade, denunciations of gross human rights violations committed against unprotected populations have multiplied. Demands for formal legal protection have been formulated by movements for the defense of human rights, many of them published through national dailies and the electronic media. The 1988 Constitution abolished all forms of censorship. The press and broadcast media routinely discuss controversial social and political issues and engage in investigative reporting. The Brazilian government imposes no formal obstacles to human rights monitoring, and many local organizations have promoted actively the rights of the rural and urban poor, street children, women, indigenous communities, prison inmates, and other victims of human rights abuses.

Most radio and television stations are privately owned; however, the government, through Congress and with the limitations we have already pointed out, controls licensing authority. Newspapers, which are also privately owned, vigorously report and comment on government performance and human rights violations (US Dept. of State 1994). The NGOs have access to the press and the electronic media to present their work and express their criticisms throughout the day on radio and during prime-time television. Thanks to these denunciations, the failure to put an end to violence during the new democratic phase is now visible (USP 1993: 82).

The cases we have already mentioned here—police killings, the killing of street children, the massacre of the Casa de Detenção at Carandiru, the 1993 massacres of Candelária and Vigário Geral in Rio de Janeiro, to cite only a few—were the targets of NGO investigations and reports. These cases also served to renew networking with international organizations that had been so intense during the period of military dictatorship. In 1987, Americas Watch published the first report related to human rights in Brazil, *Police Abuse in Brazil* (1987), soon followed by another report published by Amnesty International. Since then, Americas Watch (now Human Rights Watch/Americas) alone has published twelve reports and newsletters regarding various types of gross human rights violations in Brazil. This international dimension of the activities of Brazilian NGOs constitutes an important instrument of pressure and influence on government policies.

Brazilian NGOs actively investigate allegations of human rights violations and often initiate legal proceedings. In 1992, the Center for the Study of Violence along with Americas Watch and seven other Latin American NGOs established a corporate law office in Washington, the Center for the Study of Justice and International Law, CEJIL, to present cases to the Interamerican Commission. By the time of this writing CEJIL had presented several formal complaints concerning human rights violation in Brazil:

- Mass killings, São Lucas Police Precinct (#0301)—filed directly by Americas Watch; arising from prison events of February 1988 in the São Lucas police precinct in São Paulo, where eighteen inmates died when they and many others were forced into a small cell. The government claims that domestic remedies have not been exhausted. On 29 September 1993, one of the police officers involved in the killings is convicted and sentenced to 516 years in prison. This sentence is one of the largest handed down in Brazil. More convictions are expected to follow.
- Slave labor, the Fazenda São Luiz. A petition is filed by CEJIL and Americas Watch with the Interamerican Commission on 13 September 1992, seeking condemnation of the Brazilian government for failing to protect its citizens from conditions amounting to slave labor. The petition is temporarily rejected by the Secretariat of the Commission for failure to exhaust internal remedies. CEJIL will file a brief, arguing that no internal remedies remain to be exhausted.
- Slave labor/freedom of association, João Canuto. On 23 September 1992, CEJIL, Father Ricardo Rezende from the Comissão Pastoral da Terra, and Americas Watch file a petition with the Interamerican Commission arising from the murder of João Canuto for his active involvement in seeking to put an end to slave labor through a rural workers' union. Although Mr Canuto received death threats, the government did nothing to protect him. The Secretariat of the Commission temporarily rejects the petition for failure to exhaust remedies. CEJIL will file a brief contending that domestic remedies are exhausted.
- Prison massacre, Comissão Teotônio Vilela. On 21 October 1992, CEJIL and the Comissão Teotônio Vilela file a petition with the Interamerican Commission seeking the condemnation of Brazil for killing 111 prisoners while responding to a disturbance at the Carandiru Prison. The petition is rejected temporarily

by the Secretariat due to the non-exhaustion of domestic remedies. CEJIL will file a brief addressing the exhaustion issue.

As regards human rights, the role of the state is to respect, protect, and promote their effective realization. This foundation of the state is Janus-faced: on the one hand, as bearer of the monopoly of legal violence, the state has to observe the limitations placed on its powers and actions; on the other hand, as guardian of the public order, it must be the protector and provider of all liberties (UNDP, Pinheiro 1993: 31).

This influence of NGOs in demanding that the state be a guarantor of rights was especially felt after Brazil adhered to the principal instruments of human rights protection adopted by the international community. Until 1985, Brazil was an outlaw country in the system of international human rights protection. Only after the end of the military dictatorship did the new civilian government, after 1985, decide to sign and actively promote the ratification of the most important human rights instruments, such as the American Convention; the International Covenant on Economic, Social, and Cultural Rights; the International Covenant on Civil and Political Rights; and the Convention against Torture, among several others.

There was a substantial shift in government policy toward human rights: the Brazilian government today acknowledges human rights charges and tries to practice a policy of transparency toward the international community. The federal government has taken on some public responsibility in the fight against impunity. In 1994, the Brazilian government submitted its first report to the International Covenant on Civil and Political Rights.[11] The new administration of President Fernando Henrique Cardoso also has launched several initiatives in the area of human rights. A law proposing the recognition of the death of disappeared citizens during the military dictatorship and the granting of indemnities to their families was prepared by José Gregori, former president of the Justice and Peace Commission (and now the cabinet chief of the Ministry of Justice), submitted by the government, and approved by the National Congress. A commission for the ascertainment of these facts was initiated in December 1995. In September 1995, President Cardoso created a National Prize for Human Rights, and the highest award went to one of the most outspoken critics of the military regime, Cardinal Arns of São Paulo. Never before in recent history has the Justice Ministry pushed so actively to promote human rights. The preparation of a National Plan of Action for Human Rights, following a recommendation of the Vienna Declaration of Human Rights in 1993, was launched in October 1995 by Justice Minister Nelson Jobim, with the participation of NGOs and under the supervision of the Center for the Study of Violence at the University of São Paulo.

---

[11] See Brasil Ministério das Relações Exteriores, *Relatório inicial relativo ao Pacto Internacional dos Direitos Civis e Políticos de 1986/Ministério das Relações Exteriores, Fundação Alexandre de Gusmão e Núcleo de Estudos da Violência da Universidade de São Paulo* (Brasília: Funag, 1994), 176 pp. There is an official English translation in mimeo.

The Federal Ministry of Justice, the Federal Attorney General's Office (Procuradoria Geral da República), and senior Rio de Janeiro state government officials attempted to deal with two recent massacres 'with speed and vigor', recognized Americas Watch (1993*b*), and took initial steps during 1993 to put an end to impunity. The federal government has promoted investigations through the Federal Council for Human Rights and the Federal Police, publishing reports about the incidents and acting at the state level as well. In the Candelária killing, four men, including three military policemen, were arrested and indicted for homicide in early August. A subsequent investigation into the killing revealed a network of organized crime within the police force and resulted in the arrest and indictment of thirty-three men—twenty-eight of them military policemen—accused of being part of a death squad. Several top figures in the civilian police were indicted on charges of corruption and organized crime.

Concluding Remarks

After over a decade of democratic transition, Brazil is probably one of the most eloquent examples in the region of the persistence of illegal endemic violence and high levels of human rights violations, with extremely limited accountability for past or present abuses. This contrasts paradoxically with the rising commitment to democratization on the part of the state and society, a good record with respect to the functioning of the formal aspects of democracy, and a highly sophisticated media.

Despite all these continuities and obstacles, we may conclude that we are not facing in Brazil an entirely crystallized situation. A high level of political liberties coexists with problems in the area of civil liberties; *Freedom House*, on a scale of 1 to 7, gave Brazil grades of 3 and 4, respectively, in 1993. As we have seen, thanks to the interplay between civil society and government, some progress has been made in terms of accountability and the fight against impunity, even while gross human rights violations persist.

To consolidate democracy, economic growth—although imperative—will not be sufficient to change power relations in countries where structural imbalances are deeply rooted in social relations. Priority attention will have to be given to the distribution of economic growth and of resources (in the widest sense as defined by Vanhanen). This means that countries which have adopted a democratic political system of free elections and political freedoms will have to undertake measures of economic equality and human rights (both civil and political and social and economic rights) in order effectively to consolidate democracy.

Such a structural change in power relations, as we have seen, will not be achieved without pain and resistance; yet, without such an effort, democracy will continue to be restricted to a ruling minority. No easy solution can be devised. Changes will have to be introduced through social pacts among all protagonists—the state, the political system, and several sectors of civil society. Violence and human rights violations, which are not restricted to Brazil or to developing countries, must also be considered in the international context.

The struggle is not limited only to human rights entities. All organized groups have social and economic equality as an objective in their programs. New actors are claiming their social, economic, and cultural rights: women, racial minorities, rural workers, indigenous peoples, and others. Their claims are formulated mostly in terms of collective rights, as the defense of individual rights is no longer sufficient. Moreover, in the case of the human rights violations we have discussed here, the role of civil society is vital, as the state cannot bring about solutions on its own (Stavenhagen 1990, Poppovic and Adorno n.d.). Today more than ever, an alliance is needed between state and society, between human rights and other groups. The main priority must be the eradication of the most unsustainable forms of social injustice and exclusion, on the one hand, as well as, on the other, the restoration of human rights, by breaking the vicious circle of 'institutional vacuum', social violence, and the persistence of impunity. Without a mobilization of all forces and massive popular participation, democracy will remain in jeopardy.

12 | Political Violence and the Grassroots in Lima, Peru

Jo-Marie Burt[1]

One summer morning in early 1988, several hundred workers gathered in Lima's Plaza Dos de Mayo to participate in a general strike called by Peru's largest trade union confederation, the General Confederation of Peruvian Workers (CGTP), to protest government austerity programs and spiraling inflation. The political impact of the strike was minimal, especially in comparison to the dramatic general strikes that a decade before helped bring down the military regime of General Francisco Morales Bermudez (1975–80);[2] after several years of economic recession, factory closings, and anti-labor legislation, trade unionism in Peru had lost much of its political clout.[3] It was the presence of several dozen members of the Maoist guerrilla organization, the Communist Party of Peru (PCP-SL), better known as Sendero Luminoso or Shining Path, at the CGTP strike, and their violent attempts to radicalize the protest measures, that made this strike memorable.[4] Shining Path members disrupted the gathering with shouts of 'Long live the popular war!' and 'Long live President Gonzalo!' (the *nom de guerre* of Shining Path leader Abimael Guzmán) and harsh criticisms of the CGTP and their allies in the electoral coalition, United Left (IU), for their 'revisionist' politics (López Ricci 1988). Later in the day, they tossed a handful of dynamite sticks at the CGTP locale, generating panic amongst the protesters and causing the crowd to disperse.

These events marked a notable turning-point in Shining Path's overall strategy

[1] I am grateful for the generous support of the Inter-American Foundation, the Institute for the Study of World Politics, the United States Institute of Peace, the Aspen Institute, and the North-South Center at the University of Miami, which allowed me to carry out extended field work in Lima between 1992 and 1994, and make a follow-up visit in 1995. I would like to thank my adviser, Douglas Chalmers, and Margaret Crahan, Deborah Levenson, Kay Warren, Carlos Iván Degregori, and the editors of this volume for their valuable comments on an earlier draft of this chapter. My thanks also to Nena Delpino, Luis Pásara, Nelson Manrique, José López Ricci, Carlos Reyna, Carmen Rosa Balbi, and Steve Stern.
[2] For a comprehensive review of this period, see Cotler (1986) and Lynch (1992).
[3] For a good overview of the political crisis of trade unionism, see Balbi (forthcoming).
[4] This was the first time since the Maoist guerrillas declared their 'revolutionary' war on the Peruvian state in 1980 that they made a public appearance at a national strike called by the CGTP. In fact, Shining Path had consistently denounced such measures as 'trade union consciousness' and openly refused to participate in the eight national strikes called by the CGTP since the late 1970s.

for seizing state power. Since it declared its 'prolonged popular war' against the Peruvian state in 1980, the Maoist organization had focused its military and political activities on Peru's rural hinterlands. But given the long-term process of urbanization in Latin American countries like Peru, winning a foothold in the city was a key objective for the Maoists (Guzmán 1988). Until 1988, Shining Path's visible activities in Lima were limited to armed attacks and sabotage of economic infrastructure and symbols of government authority, although evidence now suggests that there were important levels of underground organizing going on, especially in public universities (McCormick 1992).[5] The CGTP strike was one of the first indications of open activity by Shining Path in Lima. It also marked the first time that the Maoists supported a national strike called by the CGTP and attempted to influence its outcome, indicating what would later become evident as an open push to radicalize the labor movement and other popular struggles as part of their logic of furthering the cause of the 'popular war'. Strategically, Lima was no longer important just for its symbolic and propaganda value; Lima itself had become a central objective in the Maoists' plan to seize state power.

It did not seem coincidental that Shining Path began to focus on organizing in Lima at this precise moment.[6] 1988 marked the beginning of a period of intense labor agitation and political instability. The collapse of Alan García's (1985–90) heterodox economic program plunged the economy into a prolonged recession and hyperinflation that drastically cut living standards. The combination of a drastic fiscal crisis with growing government corruption and ineptitude led to a severe weakening of the government's legitimacy and fed widespread popular unrest. Around this time, Shining Path began publishing its own newspaper, *El Diario*, which published harsh invectives against the Maoists' enemies, ranging from the 'fascistoid' government and the 'genocidal' Armed Forces to the 'parliamentary cretins' of the United Left. More importantly, the newspaper openly began to champion popular causes such as land invasions and protest marches, claiming that this growing 'combativeness' reflected the 'advancement' of their cause.[7] Subsequent incursions by Shining Path into other organized protests in Lima in the

[5] The first important increase in Shining Path military activity in Lima occurred between 1984 and 1986, when their actions in the city nearly doubled. However, the number of actions dropped after that, probably as a result of the prison massacres in June 1986 in which over 200 Shining Path cadres were killed. Military activities began to pick up again in 1989 and 1990, and they nearly doubled in Lima between 1990 and 1991 (armed activities in the rest of the country diminished only slightly). In 1990, it carried out 903 armed attacks in rural areas and 395 in Lima, while in 1991 it carried out 826 and 789 attacks, respectively. Statistics from DESCO's DataBase on Political Violence.

[6] Studies of Shining Path's urban activities have been limited. Accounts by local journalists and human rights organizations have provided the most nuanced information about Shining Path's urban activities. See especially articles in *QueHacer*, DESCO's bi-monthly publication, and *ideéle*, a monthly magazine produced by the Institute of Legal Defense. Scholarly accounts have been more limited. Gordon McCormick (1992) presents a well-laid-out overview of Shining Path's strategic objectives in Lima, and Michael Smith (1992) offers an informative look at Shining Path's urban activities in Ate-Vitarte, a strategically located popular district in Lima.

[7] Shining Path often boasted leadership of these popular protests, although most were autonomous and often spontaneous reactions to local conditions and needs.

months following the CGTP strike revealed the organization's new emphasis on urban politics; generating chaos and provoking state repression was a key tactic designed to 'deepen the contradictions' and hasten the final 'revolutionary moment' which was, according to Shining Path strategists, clearly in the making.[8]

The decision to step up its urban activities after 1988 evidently reflected Shining Path's belief that the growing crisis of governability could turn into a full-blown crisis of the entire political system; it was necessary to prepare the terrain for that inevitable moment, when the masses would rise spontaneously against their 'bureaucratic-capitalist oppressors'. Shining Path's urban presence was not negligible at this point; they had been engaged in sabotage activities as well as clandestine political work in universities, high schools, factories, and some shanty-towns since the early 1980s. But this was a new ball game altogether: in May 1991 *El Diario* announced that Shining Path had reached the stage of 'strategic parity', which ostensibly permitted them to fight on more or less equal terms with state security forces despite the superior man- and fighting-power of the latter. This was the crucial second stage of their 'prolonged popular war', the linchpin to the third and final phase of urban insurrection, the 'strategic counter-offensive', which would bring ultimate victory.[9] To reach 'strategic parity', it was necessary to win political, if not territorial, control over key populations.[10] In Lima, the natural scenario for this battle was the vast *barriadas*, or shantytowns, that ring the capital, home to well over half of the capital city's population, and whose situation of economic deprivation made them—as far as Shining Path was concerned—a captive audience to their call for revolutionary change. It was in these *barriadas*, Shining Path argued, the 'decisive battle' would be fought (*El Diario*, January 1992).

Few observers considered that Shining Path posed a serious threat in Lima, where they were outgunned vastly by state security forces and where, it was presumed,

---

[8] Just a few weeks after the CGTP strike, Shining Path members infiltrated a student protest marking the first anniversary of state intervention in the previously autonomous national universities, provoking confrontations with police and resulting in the death of one student. A few days later, the Maoists infiltrated a protest march by residents of Huaycan, a poor shantytown in Ate-Vitarte, who were demanding government action in providing basic services. Two dynamite sticks exploded, generating panic and chaos. In the confusion, a police tank ran over two Huaycan residents, one of whom died as a result. *Resúmen Semanal*, 11: 455, Lima: DESCO, 29 Jan.–18 Feb. 1988.

[9] The central committee had met in early 1991 to evaluate the development of the armed struggle. The committee decided that the 'open popular committees' established in the countryside had been consolidated, establishing the crucial groundwork to erect the 'People's Republic of Peru'. After a decade of military struggle, the central committee declared, the organization had maintained the military and political initiative, and the enemy was increasingly on the defensive. The experience gained by the 'Popular Guerrilla Army' meant that the party was now ready to move from the initial phase of 'strategic defense' to the second phase of the prolonged popular war, 'strategic parity'.

[10] This kind of all-out political and military struggle for political and territorial control over civilian populations was not common in Latin America, and certainly there were no comparable guerrilla organizations that acted with the brutality of the Shining Path. Thus, the literature about the use and effect of terror has centered primarily on state terror (Corradi *et al.* 1992). The situation in Peru was in some ways more similar to circumstances in some African and Asian countries, such as Mozambique and Sri Lanka, in which aggressive guerrilla movements fought to establish control over civilian populations. See the essays in Nordstrom and Martin (1992).

their attempts to extend their influence would not go unchallenged. Shining Path had developed in remote regions of the country like Ayacucho, where the state's reach was tenuous, political parties were largely absent, and civil society was weak. Lima was not only the center of government. Its political space was also populated by a broad spectrum of political and social groups. Parties ranged from the center-right Popular Action (AP) and Popular Christian Party (PPC), to the populist American Popular Revolutionary Alliance (APRA) party and to the left-wing coalition United Left (IU). Social organizations included neighborhood associations, soup kitchens, women's clubs, and the non-governmental development organizations (NGDOs) that supported them. Even more significantly, it was believed that, unlike in places like Ayacucho where organizational alternatives were weak, in the capital the IU represented a viable alternative for social change. Poor people in Lima were engaged broadly in community organizations that often identified with the ideals of social change promoted by the IU. Indeed, throughout the 1980s the IU had gained widespread influence in Lima's poorest neighborhoods. At the municipal level, the left had won control of many popular districts, especially between 1983 and 1989.[11] The links forged with grassroots groups, including neighborhood committees, soup kitchens, and other local groups, during the struggle against the military in the late 1970s, and the struggle for social justice within the framework of democratic rule in the 1980s, represented a viable alternative for democratic and non-violent social change that provided poor people with an alternative to the desperation and frustration that underlie Shining Path's political violence.

Yet, by 1991 Shining Path had made important inroads in Lima, both in terms of its rising organizational influence in specific districts in the city and its growing military presence. By late 1991 and the first half of 1992, Lima was a city under siege. Successive Shining Path offensives rocked the capital during this period, and the scope and intensity of Shining Path's military operations increased dramatically. Already familiar acts of sabotage against banks, government buildings, and basic infrastructure were overwhelmed by potent car-bombs, 'armed strikes', and political assassinations. But these armed actions were only the most obvious evidence of the Maoists' urban presence. There was also growing evidence of Shining Path inroads into Lima's immense *barriadas*.[12] What surprised many

[11]   The United Left was influential in muncipal-level government in Lima throughout the 1980s, particularly in the poorest districts of popular extraction. In 1980, IU won 9 out of 39 municipal districts; in 1983, when Alfonso Barrantes of IU won the mayorship of Lima, IU won 22 out of 41 districts. In 1986, IU lost ground to APRA, which was riding on the tailcoat of Alan García's presidential victory in 1985, losing control of 11 districts. Reflecting a larger crisis of the political party system, as well as its own shortcomings, the IU won only 7 out of 40 districts in 1989, and in the wake of the coalition's division, became a marginal political force. In 1993 no left-wing group won a single one of the municipalities in Lima, which were dominated by so-called 'independents'. See Tuesta (1994).

[12]   In 1992, the Institute of Legal Defense, a leading human rights organization in Peru, noted ominously: 'Shining Path has grown in the popular *barriadas* of Lima not only in relation to the number of attacks and armed actions; they have also managed to construct a vast social base. The [neoliberal] economic policies that have pushed a high percentage of the families that live in the shantytowns into a situation of extreme misery has helped Shining Path's plans' (IDL 1992: 211).

observers, however, was Shining Path's growing influence in *barriadas* like Villa El Salvador, where the IU–popular organization matrix was most developed and vast organizational networks brought community residents together to resolve their common problems of land tenure, infrastructural development, joblessness, and hunger. Shining Path specifically sought to penetrate areas like Villa El Salvador that symbolized the 'revisionism' of the mainstream left parties. Gaining influence in these areas would permit Shining Path to 'unmask' the 'revisionism' of the IU and prove that it offered the only truly 'revolutionary' alternative for social change.

By early 1992, alarmed observers noted that Shining Path appeared to be on the verge of taking state power. After winning the presidential elections in 1990, Alberto Fujimori could boast important achievements on the economic front by taming hyperinflation and gaining renewed access to international credits. However, he had had little success on the counter-insurgency front. The rhythm of Shining Path's advances in the city seemed unstoppable, and government forces seemed too paralyzed to respond. The growing possibility of a Shining Path victory provoked great consternation in the United States: at a US congressional hearing on the impending crisis in Peru in March 1992, then Assistant Secretary of State for Inter-American Affairs Bernard Aronson warned congressional leaders that the US government must be prepared to take determined action in Peru to prevent Shining Path's rise to power, which he argued would result in the twentieth century's 'third genocide'.[13] Not even President Fujimori's dissolution of Congress and suspension of the Constitution in April of that year—in part because the opposition overturned a series of draconian decrees granting the military vast powers to combat the subversive threat—seemed to detain Shining Path's relentless advance. A wave of bombings in Lima in the months after the 'Fujicoup' culminated in an 'armed strike' that virtually paralyzed Lima. It was only with the spectacular capture of Abimael Guzmán and other top leaders in September 1992, which forced the insurgents on the defensive and gave the military the upper hand for the first time in the course of over a decade of internal war, that Shining Path's spell effectively was broken.[14]

Shining Path's activities have waned since, although they have not disappeared, and a split has emerged between the leadership that remains at large and Guzmán and others who are behind prison doors over whether—and how—to continue the 'popular war' (Burt and López Ricci 1994). While Shining Path activity continues in specific local and regional contexts, there is a general consensus that the group no longer represents a significant challenge to the Peruvian state, at least in the medium term (Pedraglio 1995). The population in general has sought to put this particularly difficult period of Peru's recent history behind them. For scholars,

[13] Statement of Bernard W. Aronson, Assistant Secretary of State for Inter-American Affairs before the Subcommittee on Western Hemisphere Affairs, House Committee on Foreign Affairs, 12 Mar. 1992.

[14] The capture was the result of the persistent intelligence work of a small police unit, National Direction against Terrorism (DINCOTE). For an evaluation of Shining Path after Guzmán's capture, see Burt and López Ricci (1994).

however, this should not signal the end of studies of Shining Path. It should, rather, stimulate new scholarship to explore many still unanswered questions about the nature of the Shining Path insurgency. As the politically charged context of studies of Shining Path attenuates, perhaps scholars can begin more exhaustive, objective studies of an organization that remains in many ways enigmatic.

The emergence of Shining Path has been widely examined both from an organizational as well as an ideological perspective (Degregori 1986*a*, 1990, 1992; Gorriti 1990; Harding 1988; Granados 1987; McClintock 1984, 1989; Palmer 1986, 1992). The dynamics of Shining Path's expansion into areas beyond its original and principal zone of influence in the central-south highlands, however, have not been sufficiently explored, particularly in terms of the interactions between Shining Path and local populations.[15] An examination of Shining Path's capacity to expand into Lima and surrounding areas—as well as into other parts of the country in the late 1980s and early 1990s—reveals important lessons not only about the strengths and weaknesses of the organization itself; it also tells a fascinating story about the nature of Peruvian society and the cleavages and fissure points that fed Shining Path's violence. How can we account for Shining Path's capacity to expand into new areas, particularly Lima's *barriadas*? What kind of actions did they carry out—not only on a military level, but at the level of political action and interaction with the local population—that facilitated their move into these areas? What was the nature of popular responses to Shining Path's activities?

This essay will start with a brief description of Lima's *barriadas* and the importance of controlling these areas for Shining Path. It will then describe the kinds of activities realized by Shining Path in these areas, and attempt to draw out the reactions and responses of the urban poor to these military and political actions. Terror was a central element of Shining Path's activities in Lima's shantytowns. Shining Path routinely intimidated and threatened community organizers, especially at the leadership level, in an attempt to undermine existing grassroots organizations, particularly those with links to the IU. These organizations were part of the experiment of *autogestión*, or 'self-management', promoted by the 'revisionist left', which, according to Shining Path, was functional to the capitalist system of domination they were seeking to overthrow. Over 100 community leaders were killed in Lima's shantytowns between 1989 and 1992, including female leaders of the milk program and community soup kitchens. Hundreds of other leaders quit their positions, and some fled into exile to avoid the fate of leaders like María Elena Moyano, who was killed brutally in February 1992 by a Shining Path hit squad. Terror and intimidation were key tools used by Shining Path to instill fear and neutralize resistance in Lima's shantytowns.

---

[15]   Only a handful of studies have attempted this task. Manrique (1989) has examined Shining Path's push into the central highlands (Junin) and the Huallaga Valley, and Rénique (1993) looks at the changing dynamics of Shining Path activities in Puno and the changing responses of the *campesino* movement. Gonzales (1992) examines Shining Path's move into the coca-growing Upper Huallaga Valley. McCormick (1992) and M. Smith (1992) provide an overview of Shining Path in Lima.

At the same time that Shining Path used these coercive tactics, it also engaged in other activities that sought to build support among the urban poor. The dramatic and brutal nature of Shining Path's terrorist activities overshadowed the less spectacular, more day-to-day politics in which they engaged in Lima's shantytowns. If the use of terrorism and intimidation was the stick that Shining Path used to gain inroads in Lima's shantytowns, the provision of certain material and symbolic goods (or incentives) was the carrot.[16] I will focus on these aspects of Shining Path's urban activities in this chapter, not because they are more important than their terrorist activities but because they are less well known—and crucial to understanding Shining Path's ability to operate in Lima's shantytowns. These goods, I will argue below, generated currents of sympathy among some sectors of the urban poor. In combination with its strong-arm tactics, this facilitated Shining Path's urban activities, allowing it to move in Lima's shantytowns in classic Maoist fashion—like 'fish in water'—and providing a crucial platform to launch its offensives in late 1991 and 1992.[17]

Discussing Shining Path as a political organization that obtained some degree of popular sympathy or support is not an easy—or a savory—proposition. Indeed, as Nelson Manrique (1989) pointed out several years ago, academics making such an assertion were often accused of being complicit with this organization. Shining Path has resorted to terrorist methods in pursuit of its political objectives, including armed attacks and murders of civilians often caught in the crossfire of a war not of their making. Denouncing Shining Path's authoritarianism, their often brutal disregard for human life, and their contempt for any organization not made in their own image has had a rightfully important place in academic discourse about Shining Path. At the same time, it is important to examine the *political* nature of Shining Path's activities, and their attempts to build support on the ground. Terrorism was one element of Shining Path's activities, but it also engaged in a series of different tactics—ranging from imposing social order, to creating alternative modes of imparting justice, to exploiting the contradictions in left-wing strategies—that were attempts to construct a social support base.[18] This was an

---

[16] Migdal (1974) discusses the way guerrilla organizations use selective incentives (the carrot) and selective sanctions (the stick) in building a local support base.

[17] It is illustrating to cite an editorial from *Expreso*, an important conservative newspaper, from 5 July 1992. After extolling Fujimori's attempts to regain state control over Sendero's strongholds in the universities, the prisons, and key rural areas in the aftermath of the 5 April coup, the editorial goes on to criticize his failure to address Shining Path's growth in the *barriadas*: 'But there is a fourth front that Fujimori does not mention frequently: that of the "young towns" (*barriadas*), where Shining Path's advancement is consistent and the government has done very little to support the population in order to oppose this advancement. We worry more about the armed attacks that the subversives carry out in the commercial and financial centers of the city, in San Isidro. But that is the spectacular part, the psychological terror. What is truly worrisome is the organizing activity, which is daily and subterranean, that the Shining Path subversives carry out in the peripheral human settlements of Lima.'

[18] Such an endeavor requires some rethinking of the 'terrorist' label that has been routinely applied to Shining Path. This label is meant to distinguish Shining Path—given its particularly brutal nature—from other guerrilla organizations in Latin America's recent history. As Gustavo Gorriti, a Peruvian

intimate part of Shining Path's larger political objective: taking state power. Sufficient time has passed to reassess Shining Path from a political perspective, and examine more closely the appeals they made to different segments of Peruvian society and carry out careful empirical studies to understand the responses and reactions of these different groups. The point here is not to downplay Shining Path's use of violence and terror, nor to underestimate the role terror played in paralyzing resistance efforts; it is rather to understand how a group that was so violent, so authoritarian, so brutal, could obtain some degree of sympathy, and even support, from segments of the urban poor.[19]

A NOTE ON METHODOLOGY

The nature of the enterprise proposed in this chapter is interpretive; aside from a handful of public opinion polls specifically asking people about their opinion of Shining Path and their activities,[20] there is no hard data to draw from to obtain a representative sample of the attitudes and responses of the urban poor to the Shining Path. Yet, given the importance of Lima for Shining Path after 1988 and the particular importance of the *barriadas* within that larger strategic shift to the city, our lack of understanding of the relationship between Shining Path and the urban poor represents a glaring gap in the growing body of work on that organization.

In order to glean an understanding of popular responses and reactions to the Shining Path and its activities in Lima's *barriadas*, I carried out a series of extended, semi-structured interviews in four popular districts in Lima in which Shining Path had established an active presence: San Juan de Lurigancho, Ate-Vitarte, El Agustino, and Villa El Salvador. Within each district, I first interviewed at least five informed observers who had several years' experience working in the

journalist who covered the Maoists for the Lima weekly *Caretas*, noted several years ago: 'In reality, guerrilla and terrorist are not really antonyms, and they can be—in fact they are in most cases—complementary. During the war of Algeria, the FLN utilized terrorist tactics. In South Vietnam, at the beginning of the insurrection, the Viet Cong systematically liquidated local village authorities, with slogans similar to those used by Shining Path since late 1981 such as "*batir e[l campo]*" ["shake the countryside to its foundations"]. . . . Terrorist or guerrilla organization? It seems clear that Shining Path is a guerrilla organization that utilizes terrorist actions, which are part of a much broader universive of insurrectional resources which are carefully planned and divided into progressive stages, and whose objective is the taking of [state] power, and to never let it go' (Gorriti 1987).

[19]   Manrique (1989) raises similar questions about Shining Path in the central highlands.

[20]   A public opinion poll carried out in June 1991 in Metropolitan Lima found that 17 per cent overall considered that subversion was justified, and when asked their reaction to a terrorist attack, 11 per cent said they would 'understand' it, while 16 per cent stated they would be indifferent to it. The polls produced an important degree of surprise among intellectual circles, who did not believe that Sendero could obtain such significant levels of support. More startling was the clear class-based nature of the responses: while only 2 per cent of the highest socioeconomic level (A) considered subversion justified, 23 per cent considered it so within the lowest socioeconomic level (D); and while none within level A held a favorable opinion of Abimael Guzmán, 17 per cent within level D openly expressed their favorable opinion of him. Poll material gathered by Apoyo, SA, June 1991.

area and with local organizations, including NGDO workers, Catholic Church activists, local schoolteachers, and municipal government workers. I then interviewed at least a dozen local residents within each district, chosen from specific *barriadas* with significant Shining Path presence.[21] I participated in dozens of workshops and informal meetings organized by different Lima-based NGDOs with the local groups they work with in the shantytowns during the two years I was engaged in field work in Lima.[22] I also organized a number of focus groups with the assistance of a local public opinion consulting firm, which permitted a more representative survey of popular attitudes, especially among sectors who were not actively involved in community organizations (who are usually more difficult to interview). This combination of interviews, workshops, and focus groups offers a revealing glimpse of the complex and often contradictory nature of popular attitudes toward Shining Path in areas in which the guerrilla organization had some degree of influence and activity.

Shining Path and Lima's *Barriadas*

Just fifty years ago, Peru was a predominantly rural and agricultural society. In 1940, 65 per cent of the total population lived in rural areas. The growing difficulties of rural life, coupled with the opportunities for employment and better social services in the capital, fed waves of rural migration to urban centers, especially Lima. Today, Peru is highly urbanized: 70 per cent of its inhabitants are city dwellers, and 30 per cent live in Lima. Lima's growth has been spectacular: a city of 500,000 in 1940, Lima today has 6.4 million inhabitants.[23]

Rising unmet demands for low-cost housing led many rural migrants and urban slum dwellers to organize massive land invasions on the city's outskirts, where they built precarious dwellings and struggled to obtain basic services. Successive governments since the 1950s adopted a *laissez-faire* attitude toward the *barriadas*, often permitting squatters to remain on the land to prevent pent-up demands for housing from becoming a political problem, but not developing social policies to

[21] I did more extensive interviewing in Villa El Salvador, where my previous research experience permitted me greater access to local residents. Informants were chosen from two basic 'types' of shantytown residents: those with leadership experience in some community organization (such as neighborhood associations, soup kitchens, women's club, or the glass of milk committees); and those who either participated in such organizations (usually soup kitchens and milk committees) as rank-and-file members, or who had no organizational affiliation of this type. For security reasons the names of those interviewed must remain anonymous.

[22] Given the security situation in Peru, and Shining Path's attacks on several rural and urban NGOs, I prefer not to name these organizations. I would like to express my gratitude to them for making time for my incessant questions, their sharing of their insights, and their invitations to participate in their workshops.

[23] Urbanization is a result of various factors, including the declining opportunities, both in terms of life chances and basic services, in the countryside, and perceived growing opportunities in the city. Political violence was also an important factor in rural migrations in the 1980s and early 1990s.

improve the living conditions of these settlements.[24] These areas, known traditionally as *barriadas* and more recently as *pueblos jóvenes* or 'young towns', generally lack basic infrastructure (water, electricity, sewage, public transport, health and educational facilities, etc.); as an alternative, community residents have mobilized to demand basic services from the government and pooled local resources to provide some services themselves on a self-help basis.[25] The growth of Lima's *barriadas* has been dramatic. In 1961, 316,426 people lived in the *barriadas*, about 17 per cent of the overall population. By 1981, nearly a third of Lima's population lived in *barriadas* (1.5 million). Estimates a decade later suggest that between 3 to 3.5 million Limeños live in *barriadas*—about half of the capital's total population.[26]

Underlying this process of rapid urbanization was a development model based on import-substitution industrialization which tended to concentrate the economy in urban centers, especially Lima. That model entered into crisis in Peru, as in other parts of Latin America, in the 1970s. The 1980s witnessed various attempts to implement structural adjustment programs and alternative heterodox programs whose eventual failure led to the collapse of the Peruvian economy by 1988.[27] Negative growth rates and dramatic levels of hyperinflation reduced living standards to 1960s levels and severely undermined the government's capacity to provide elemental public services,[28] including the provision of basic levels of social order and security. In Lima, crime and common delinquency rose sharply, particularly in the *pueblos jóvenes*.[29] The problem was not only the incapacity of the police to provide basic security to Lima's citizens. The police also had become notorious both for the routine bribes they extracted from the citizenry and their increasing involvement in more violent crimes, including outright theft, kidnapping, arbitrary brutality, and rape.[30] Neoliberal restructuring in 1990 and 1991 exacerbated these conditions.[31] The stabilization program implemented in August 1990, just weeks after Fujimori was inaugurated, devastated living standards. Price increases and cuts in social expenditures[32] nearly doubled the number of Peruvians

---

[24]   The one, brief exception was Velasco's attempt to actively promote self-help efforts in Lima's *barriadas* as a way of obtaining local support for his reformists experiment. See Driant (1991).

[25]   For a discussion of *barriada* development, see Riofrío (1978) and Driant (1991). For a discussion of self-help organizing in Lima, see Burt and Espejo (1995).

[26]   Census information provided by Driant (1991).

[27]   For an excellent discussion of these policies, see González de Olarte and Samamé (1991).

[28]   'The problems of Lima today are linked to the exhaustion of its capacity to reproduce itself as a city and as a market. The exaggerated dimensions of the city make it nearly impossible to provide basic infrastructure, and it borders on collapse. This is reflected in the rationing of water and electricity, for example, which at the most critical point reached 66 per cent in 1992' (Olivera and Ballón 1993).

[29]   'Sicósis en Lima: Delincuencia', *Caretas*, 25 Mar. 1991, pp. 39–45.

[30]   A reflection of the deep institutional crisis of the state's security apparatus were the open confrontations between members of the police and the army. See 'El vacío interior', *Caretas*, 3 Feb. 1991, pp. 6–14.

[31]   Otárola Peñaranda (1994); *Caretas*, 21 Apr. 1994, pp. 33–6; *Expreso*, 9 Jan. 1994, pp. 20–1.

[32]   An official document of the Ministerio de la Presidencia (1993) recognizes a continual decline in social spending after 1986 in real terms. Social spending dropped from 4.61 per cent of GDP in 1980 to 1.78 in 1991 (Fernández Baca and Seinfeld 1993). The education sector lost three-fourths of its value between 1986 and 1990, and the situation was similar in the health sector.

living in conditions of critical poverty—from 6 to 11 million overnight, fully half of the country's population.[33] In Metropolitan Lima, consumption expenditures, which had already dropped by 46 per cent between 1986 and 1990, fell an *additional* 31 per cent between June 1990 and October 1991, the period when Fujimori's economic package was implemented (FONCODES 1994).

For Shining Path, this large—and growing—population of urban poor, mostly concentrated in Lima's *barriadas*, was fertile terrain to build a support base for their revolution, converting Lima's *barriadas* into a key political objective. But Lima's *barriadas* were central to Shining Path's overall plans for strategic reasons as well: in geopolitical terms, Shining Path conceived the *barriadas* as the chokepoints—the 'iron belts of misery'—from which the enemy forces would be encircled.[34] Shining Path had been building up its presence in the departments surrounding Lima, including Junín to the east, and the Norte Chico and the Sur Chico regions located to the north and south of the capital and within the department of Lima (McCormick 1992). Controlling Lima's *barriadas* was the next crucial step in building a circle around Lima, and establishing control over travel routes to the north and south via the Panamerican Highway, and to the east along the Central Highway, the principal route to Lima's breadbasket and source of crucial supplies (water, electricity) and export earnings (mining). Such control would give Shining Path a critical advantage by permitting it to isolate Lima from the rest of the country as well as from the immense ring of shantytowns that encircle the city. As the January 1992 edition of *El Diario* argued: 'Lima and the surrounding shantytowns are the scenario in which the final battle of the popular war will be defined.'

Much has been written about Lima's *barriadas*. Throughout the 1980s, progressive scholars focused extensively on the self-help activities of the urban poor, highlighting their ingenuity, their efforts at resolving their own problems in the face of state indifference, and the solidarity that inspired their collective activities.[35] Others noted the radical attitudes held by many *barriada* dwellers, especially *vis-à-vis* the state, and portrayed their grassroots efforts at promoting community development as part of the larger construction of a new society based on communal values and social solidarity.[36] These 'pioneers' were forging a 'new social order', a 'new way of doing politics', and a platform from which to resist elitist forms of domination. Whether defined as new social movements or the construction of a new civil society, the collective action of the urban poor was seen as a wholly positive development, one that was breaking down old forms of doing politics (clientelism, authoritarianism),

---

[33] This widely accepted estimated was corroborated by official government figures from 1994. In 1994, 54 per cent of the population, or 13 million people, lived in *critical poverty*, defined as insufficient income to cover a basic food basket for a family of five, while 23 per cent of the critically poor suffer *extreme poverty*, defined as insufficient income to cover minimum nutritional requirements for a family of five. Figures are taken from a recent study commissioned by the Fondo de Compensación y Desarrollo Social (FONCODES), the government-sponsored social emergency fund which was founded a full year after the initial adjustment measures were applied, in Aug. 1991. See FONCODES (1994).   [34] Quotation from Guzmán interview (1988).

[35] See the rich empirical study by Degregori *et al.* (1986).

[36] The most paradigmatic studies of this kind are Ballón (1986) and Tovar (1986*b*).

and ushering in a new era of more democratic and participatory politics from below. The important electoral victories of the United Left at the municipal level in the mid-1980s, especially in the poorer districts of Lima, fed this enthusiasm about the democratizing potential at the grassroots.[37] Many left-wing leaders actively sought to promote grassroots organizing from their position in municipal government, as a means of furthering the leftist agenda and building popular support on the ground.[38]

When Shining Path made its orphaned appearance at the CGTP strike in 1988, it was presumed that this group of rural bandits lacked the political savvy to win a foothold in the more sophisticated environment of urban politics, where the labor movement as well as grassroots *barriada* organizations had been active for over a decade. Shining Path first established its presence in the most remote parts of the country, where the relative absence of state actors and other political entities made their insertion more viable (Degregori 1986, 1990). The collapse of the old oligarchic order had not been replaced by new relations of authority in these areas, and Shining Path ably took advantage of the political vacuum existing in these historically marginal and poverty-stricken areas. The organization was able to establish a presence in the Andean highland departments of Ayacucho, Huancavelica, and Apurimac because they were the most remote, neglected areas of the country, with little organizational life—the 'weakest link' in state–society relations. Its authoritarian leadership style was capable of being reproduced in these areas precisely because the absence of modern, democratizing forces meant that traditional relationships of authoritarian domination were commonly accepted by the population[39] (Degregori 1986; Manrique 1989).

The analysis derived from this explanation of the origin of Shining Path suggested that in those parts of the country not characterized by a political vacuum—where, in other words, the state administered, parties organized, and grassroots groups mobilized—Shining Path would prove less effective. Some variants of this line of argument suggested that in those areas where left parties and social organizations were well organized, Shining Path would not be able to develop; the democratic practices of grassroots organizations, the strong sense of identity generated by the empowering experience of *autogestión* promoted by the left, and the identification of the urban popular sectors with the left as evidenced in

[37] Alfonso Barrantes won the mayorship of Lima in 1983 on the IU ticket, and the left carried nearly half of Lima's districts. Barrantes came in a close second to Alan García in the 1985 presidential elections. The IU held its own in the 1986 municipal elections, though enthusiasm for APRA cost the left a handful of municipalities. The left's electoral sway began its decline in 1989, and virtually disappeared after 1990 with the splintering of the IU into several small parties.

[38] Such was the case with the municipal milk program, which organized thousands of women into local 'glass of milk committees' to distribute the nutritional supplement program to children under 13 years of age and lactating mothers. Left-wing leaders such as Michel Azcueta, elected mayor of Villa El Salvador, a prominent shantytown in Lima, also used their position in local municipal government to promote grassroots organizations (Tuesta 1989a).

[39] Moore (1966) notes that revolutionary movements often end up resembling the very society that they seek to destroy.

electoral processes throughout the 1980s together would act as a barrier to Shining Path's overtures (IDS 1989). Specific experiences of intense grassroots organizing, in which the left, NGDOs, and often the progressive Catholic Church united to form virtual 'popular fronts', would contain Shining Path's advance in important regional and local contexts. The active and well-organized peasant movement in Puno, the innovative experience of autonomous *rondas campesinas*, or peasant defense patrols, in Cajamarca, and the self-managing community of Villa El Salvador were highlighted as examples of solid popular organizing that effectively would counter Shining Path's attempts to woo the urban and rural poor. This argument seemed particularly valid for Lima, where social organizations were widespread, a wide range of political parties was active, and government and security forces outgunned Shining Path, together forming a seemingly more solid social bulwark against Shining Path's advances.

However, Shining Path not only expanded its presence into Lima; it also sought quite methodically—and with relative success—to establish influence in precisely those areas in Lima where the legal left had been strongest.[40] The explanations for Shining Path's initial success in Ayacucho were not good predictors of Shining Path's possibilities for success in other areas, suggesting that convincing explanations of the organization's *emergence* may not necessarily be useful in understanding subsequent processes of *expansion*.[41] Specifically, their capacity to compete on a political terrain with other actors was underestimated greatly, and the capacity of the left and the popular movements to resist them was overestimated.[42] Ironically, the most sustained resistance efforts were mobilized from peasant communities in remote areas of Junín and Ayacucho—where civil society was supposedly weakest, and where the state and political parties were virtually absent—which began to resent Shining Path's incursions and often sought out the military as an ally to defend themselves against them[43] (Starn 1991, 1992; Coronel 1992; Del Pino 1992).

---

[40]   This move into Lima, however, did imply significant security risks, as revealed by the 1988 capture of Osmán Morote, Shining Path's second in command, and the 1992 capture of Abimael Guzmán and other important members of the Central Committee, the Lima Metropolitan Committee, and Socorro Popular, an important support group for Shining Path's activities in Lima.

[41]   A key difference in organizational terms is that Shining Path was already well established by the time it made its main push into Lima, having survived the three principal dilemmas for new guerrilla movements as outlined by Manrique (1989): surviving the critical phase of state repression; obtaining secure supplies of resources and weapons (primarily through the coca trade); and constructing a social base, particularly to replace captured or killed cadre. It thus made this push to Lima from a very different position than when it initiated its activities in Ayacucho, having survived the crucial phase of repression (1983–4) and consolidated its organizational structure.

[42]   Evidently other factors came into play, such as the deepening of Peru's economic crisis and sustained hyperinflation after 1988, which will be examined further below.

[43]   In the early 1980s, the military sought to conscript peasants in arbitrary fashion into the counterinsurgency effort by forming civil defense patrols. By the late 1980s, however, many peasant communities in the south and central highlands began to organize autonomously to defend their communities from Sendero's incursions. Unfortunately I cannot develop this issue further in this chapter, but it would be fascinating to compare and contrast changing responses to Sendero in rural and urban contexts.

Why was the 'social bulwark' unable to resist Shining Path's advances? Why were social scientists and political analysts alike taken off-guard by their effective penetration into organizations and communities that were left-wing strongholds in Lima?

By the time Shining Path began to focus more centrally on Lima after 1988, Peru's overall political, social, and economic situation had deteriorated dramatically. The initial success of García's heterodox experiment, spearheaded by a demand-led recovery of the economy between 1986 and 1987, collapsed under the weight of foreign exchange constraints and looming government deficits by 1988. Spiraling inflation—1,722 per cent in 1988 and 2,775 per cent in 1989—forced a sharp decline in real wages and a 25 per cent contraction of the economy between 1988 and 1990 (Pastor and Wise 1992). This provoked massive labor unrest and seriously weakened the government's fledgling legitimacy. The process of state decomposition that followed the economic fiasco, and the consequent decline of public services and drying-up of social programs, caused major discontent. Political violence was growing and expanding into new areas, adding to the sensation of a situation gone out of control.

Popular support for APRA eroded quickly. For a short time, it seemed possible that the IU—APRA's principal competitor for support among the lower classes—would pick up votes from disaffected *apristas* in the 1989 municipal elections and presidential elections the following year. However, long-standing tensions between moderates and radicals within the coalition culminated in the division of the IU in early 1989, deflating the left's electoral chances.[44] The division of the left fed the growing perception that representative institutions were incapable of resolving the political and economic crisis. Political parties across the ideological spectrum increasingly became seen as vehicles of personalistic power and patronage, and parliament became seen as an ineffective body that spent hours debating irrelevant points while the country veered toward instability and chaos. The political expression of this growing disaffection was the election of independent candidates who played up their status as 'outsiders': Ricardo Belmont won the 1989 municipal elections, while Alberto Fujimori defeated novelist Mario Vargas Llosa for president in 1990.[45]

This combination of a devastating economic crisis and the collapse of traditional mediating mechanisms between state and society formed the background against which Shining Path stepped up its organizing activities in Lima after 1988. The exacerbation of the economic crisis fed feelings of frustration and desperation

[44] Disagreements over the presidential candidacy of Alfonso Barrantes, an independent and former mayor of Lima, sparked the division. For moderates, a Barrantes candidacy would attract support amongst centrist and independent voters and carry the IU to the presidential palace. Radical parties within the IU had long-standing qualms about Barrantes's centrism, and they specifically opposed his proposal of a broad-based front to save Peru's fledgling democratic institutions from the onslaught of the economic crisis and Shining Path's violence. Other more long-standing conflicts underlie the split, however, including personal rivalries, different visions about political democracy, strategies for achieving social change, and attitudes *vis-à-vis* Shining Path (Pásara 1992).

[45] This disaffection was also reflected in Apr. 1992, when Fujimori closed Congress and suspended the Constitution, which won wide popular support.

amongst important segments of the urban poor. Hyperinflation was especially devastating to the poor, who often had few available cushions in times of crisis. This was particularly true for newer migrants. Whereas governments from the time of Odría sought to obtain the support of the urban poor via specific social programs and clientelistic handouts (Collier 1976), the fiscal crisis after 1988 eroded the government's capacity to respond to growing demands for housing and infrastructure.[46] The growing incapacity of the state to mediate popular demands and to provide even basic public services, including public order, left the poor with few resources to negotiate the crisis. The closing, or collapse, of traditional mechanisms of interest representation, such as political parties and trade unions, meant that poor people had fewer options in seeking redress for their grievances. This combination of factors provides important contextual variables that help explain why Shining Path's push into the cities was more successful than was predicted originally. Growing frustration and discontent among important sectors of Lima's urban population gave Shining Path a crucial 'window of opportunity' to organize in Lima.

However, these contextual factors cannot be considered both the necessary *and* sufficient causes of successful Shining Path organizing in the city; if this were so, it could be argued that given the depth and multi-dimensionality of Peru's political, social, and economic crises, support for radical alternatives like Shining Path should have been far more extensive than it actually was. More importantly, structural variables may stimulate or feed insurgent movements, but it is crucial to examine the mediating political variables at play. Examining how relationships between political organizations and potential constituents are constructed, mediated, and negotiated, and how the 'goods and services' offered by political organizations—what Migdal (1974) calls 'exchange relationships'—mediate those relationships, is crucial in understanding the evolution of insurgency movements. In constructing a social base, guerrilla groups seek to mobilize support, simultaneously delivering certain goods or benefits to local populations and imposing symbolic and material sanctions. In terms of benefits offered, local populations offer or withdraw support according to a rational calculation of their own interests (Popkin 1979).[47] Shining Path was adept at playing on the growing social

---

[46] Driant (1991) offers an excellent description of the process of consolidation of older land invasions, as squatters slowly build up their homes from cane matting to brick and concrete, basic services such as water and electricity are obtained, and other local infrastructure develops, and contrasts it to new land invasions, largely after 1984, that often encountered greater difficulty in obtaining government assistance to develop their local communities.

[47] In his rational-choice-inspired model, Popkin (1979) argues that the free-rider problem is overcome by the revolutionary group's (*a*) proving their trustworthiness and (*b*) effectively delivering desired goods to their potential constituents. He argues that a self-abnegating leadership is more likely to win trust, and initial organization based on delivering desired goods in a short time is likely to win further confidence. This model is helpful in providing a framework with which to approach a study of the exchange relationships between guerrilla movements and their potential allies (peasants as well as the urban poor), though it does not go very far in helping explain how the revolutionary group came into existence—and themselves overcame the free-rider problem—in the first instance.

conflicts that began to unravel in Lima as these multi-dimensional crises deepened, and the state seemed too paralyzed to respond. The deepening of Peru's economic and political crisis after 1988 was the raw material for Shining Path's organizing attempts in Lima. Below, I shall explore how the organization attempted to use this raw material—the growing crisis of the state, of mediating institutions, of the economy—to generate sympathy and build alliances with local populations, and thereby establish a foothold in Lima's *barriadas*.

Shining Path operated at different levels within Lima's shantytowns to take advantage of the growing crisis of the state for its own organizing purposes. At one level, they sought to take advantage of the situation of increasing crime, disorder, and public insecurity within the *barriadas* as an easy way of building local support. Similar to their tactics in rural areas, Shining Path played upon the state's incapacity to provide basic security to its citizens, and their actions of intimidating and sometimes physically eliminating thieves, delinquents, and drug addicts won them a great deal of sympathy. At the local level, Shining Path attempted to construct an image of itself as a harsh but fair imparter of justice in a country in which justice was routinely bought and sold, and where conflict resolution mechanisms at the grassroots were sorely lacking. It 'punished' local authorities, vendors, and community leaders who it claimed were corrupt, and in many instances successfully manipulated in its favor popular outrage at such petty acts of corruption. This broadly paralleled Shining Path's attempts to build sympathy and support in rural areas, where they focused on conflicts revolving around land ownership in the aftermath of the agrarian reform, and played on popular resentment against merchants, state-run cooperatives, and local state authorities (Favre 1984; Berg 1992; Isbell 1992). At a more political level, they tried to demonstrate the futility of peaceful strategies for social change—an attempt both to discredit the left-wing parties that continued to organize and were its chief rival on the ground and to radicalize popular struggles. Shining Path also used intimidation and fear as a way of demobilizing real and potential opponents to their larger ends, including 'selective assassinations' of those who stood in their way. They used both carrot and stick in their urban strategy as a way of mobilizing sympathy by providing certain goods, and at the same time neutralizing resistance through intimidation and violence. I will explore each of these levels of Shining Path's intercursion into Lima's *barriadas* to illustrate popular responses to their activities.

Before elaborating on my empirical findings, it is important to lay out some definitional clarifications. As Berg (1986–7, 1992) has suggested, it is crucial to delineate the distinct levels of support that may exist for an insurgent movement. 'Sympathy', defined as a positive view toward some aspect of the organization's actions or goals, is distinguished from 'support'. Berg divides support into two categories: 'active support'—participating in acts of commission—is quite different from 'passive support'—not snitching to police, lending safe haven, etc. Sympathy with Shining Path does not necessarily imply acceptance or even understanding of the organization's ideology or its strategic objectives; it can be generated by small, local-level actions that are deemed desirable or acceptable by the local population (Berg 1986–7, 1992). Passive support is a misleading term, however. Behavior that looks like passive support may in fact hinge more on fear of reprisals than on a favorable view of an organization, or a more complex combination of both elements. This ambiguity was a recurring theme in my interviews and discussions with *barriada* residents and informed observers.

Imposing Order

The fiscal and administrative crisis of the Peruvian state after 1988 had direct consequences for residents of Lima's *barriadas*. In addition to the precipitous decline in living standards due to economic recession and hyperinflation, benefits and resources from the state were largely cut off as social programs were shut down and clientelistic networks faltered. Public order also became a growing problem in the *barriadas*. In part because of growing poverty, crime and delinquency rose dramatically there; it is often easier for thieves to operate in poor communities than in wealthy areas, where residents have the resources to pay for private guards and high electric fences. Drug addiction has also become a growing problem in Lima's *barriadas*, especially among young people. The state security apparatus grew increasingly ineffective in protecting citizens. More alarming, however, was the growing involvement of police officers in criminal activity, including assaults and robberies, exacerbating the population's traditional mistrust of the police.[48] In October 1991, the Lima daily *La República* published a manual on 'How to Defend Yourself against the Police'.

In the face of the incapacity of the national police to provide protection and security, municipal governments in Lima's wealthier districts had the resources to create *serenazgo*, a local anti-crime force. Municipalities in poorer neighborhoods lacked the resources to implement such local forces, and sometimes the residents themselves established local patrols, known as *rondas*, to dissuade criminals and thieves.[49] However, as crime became more pervasive and violent, these unarmed patrols proved inadequate to the task.

Regarding this growing situation of crime and insecurity, most of my informants expressed a common sentiment: the police are ineffective in dealing with crime, and in many instances they themselves are in cahoots with the criminals. This

---

[48] Bribery was common amongst the police forces, but this more violent and criminal activity was qualitatively different. Coupled with human rights abuses committed by police and army forces, the image of these forces deteriorated sharply. While the army's prestige increased after the capture of Guzmán, the image of the national police continues to be dismal. Proposals about how to improve the police force are still in debate in Peru. See IDL (1995).

[49] These patrols often were established at the initial stage of a land invasion, to protect the community (which was relatively small) from thieves as well as eviction by the police. As invasions became established settlements, these patrols tended to disappear.

sentiment has been widely corroborated in numerous public opinion polls. In the annual polls carried out by Apoyo, since 1987 the two principal institutions in charge of providing justice and order—the judicial system and the police—have received consistently low marks in terms of their efficacy.[50] In a 1989 poll, 60 per cent stated that they did not trust the police, and 43 per cent said that they felt fear (as opposed to security) when they saw a police officer; 49 per cent said that if they had the resources they would purchase a weapon for defense purposes (Bedoya 1989). An August 1993 poll showed that 45 per cent had been the victims of a robbery in the previous twelve months. Only 39 per cent of the victims denounced the crime to the police. Of those 59 per cent who did not report the crime, 40 per cent said that the police 'don't do anything'; 16 per cent said it would be 'a waste of time'.[51]

Shining Path maneuvered this situation to its advantage in many *barriadas* by providing a much-needed good—public order—at a time when the state was increasingly incapable of fulfilling its function as provider of public order and security. They recognized the growing problems of violence, crime, and insecurity manifested by a state in crisis, and in many shantytowns, Shining Path offered people a greater sense of protection and security by adopting harsh measures—including extra-judicial executions—to control crime. Shining Path first warned thieves and delinquents to change their ways, then physically beat them if they failed to heed. Those who refused to reform were often killed as a final resort. Some informants also reported that Shining Path publicly berated and sometimes physically beat wife-beaters, and adulterers were also publicly scorned. In Villa El Salvador, local residents had formed a crime-watch patrol to dissuade criminals. Shining Path visited the leaders of the *rondas*, telling them to stop the patrols because they would take care of the crime problem. A couple that I interviewed who participated in the *rondas* said that most people felt relief, because crime would be stopped and they would not have to maintain their all-night watch.[52]

The majority of my informants expressed varying degrees of sympathy with Shining Path's punishment and even physical elimination of thieves, delinquents, and drug addicts, who were widely considered 'social deviants' and threats to the larger community. One resident of a *barriada* in San Juan de Lurigancho stated her agreement with Shining Path's policy of punishing thieves in her neighborhood: 'I think it's a good thing, because it helps get rid of the thieves and the drug addicts,

---

[50]   Refers to public opinion polls taken annually by Apoyo SA, and published in *Debate* ('Encuesta anual sobre el poder en el Perú'), reviewed between 1987 and 1994.

[51]   *Imasen Confidencial*, Lima, Aug. 1993.

[52]   The *rondas* established in Huaycán were probably the best known during this period, but the peculiar situation they faced made them unrepresentative of other experiences. The *rondas* were reactivated in Huaycán as crime grew in the settlement during 1990 and 1991. Shortly after the 1992 coup, Fujimori visited the *rondas* in Huaycán and delivered a speech praising the *rondas* as the 'first line of defense' against Shining Path in the *barriadas*. While leaders of the communities and the *rondas* tried to distance themselves from the government, the military presence in the district made this extremely difficult. As a result, the *rondas* became 'traitors' for Shining Path, which has killed three *ronda* leaders and threatened many others.

who harm the community.' State authorities could not be counted on to do the job: 'The [police] don't even come around here, and even if you go to them to denounce a robbery, they won't come up this far.' One woman who expressed her approval of such activities explained her reasoning: 'we are completely unprotected here, you see, the nearest police station is far away [a fifteen-minute bus ride]. People do whatever they want here . . . With [Shining Path], crime has gone down, they leave us alone now.' By threatening and sometimes killing delinquents, Shining Path imposed social order at a micro level, giving the local population a greater sense of security. A community activist from a *barriada* in Ate-Vitarte noted a dramatic rise in crime and delinquency in his neighborhood, including robberies, assaults, and rape, after 1993, when after the capture of Guzmán Shining Path was forced to retreat, and their vigilante activity decreased significantly. 'Shining Path combated [crime],' he said. 'They definitely killed several delinquents. They were a kind of counterweight to [criminal] activity. . . . In one way or another, they stopped these criminal activities from manifesting themselves so aggressively, as they do today.'

This sense of security and social order was one key 'good' delivered by Shining Path that generated an important degree of sympathy. Most of my informants saw the democratic mechanisms that are supposed to ensure order and provide justice as dysfunctional. The police did not protect citizens or provide order, and were more often seen as delinquents themselves. The court system was seen as riddled with corruption and inaccessible to poor people. In this context, popular notions of justice, in which residents impose sanctions on their own without relying on the court system or police intervention, have flourished. This has been the case in the countryside as well, notably in the north, where peasants have organized patrols, or *rondas campesinas*, to protect their communities from cattle thieves and other related problems (Starn 1992). As Starn has noted, these *rondas* are effective in providing security to the community, but their methods are often not democratic and they resort to physical beatings, and sometimes lynchings, to punish the aggressor and teach a lesson to other potential thieves.

Support for the physical punishment or extra-judicial execution of individuals who have been caught *in flagrante delicto* may seem extreme. However, popular notions of justice may be quite different from Western systems of justice based on the development of a court system and the rule of law, as the *rondas campesinas* suggest. A brief look at a related issue may help make the point. In Peru, lynchings of thieves caught in the act are not uncommon in both rural areas and in Lima's shantytowns. In the context of a state that is ineffective in providing order and justice, lynchings are accepted widely. A 1993 public opinion poll found that nearly half the population in Lima—and over 60 per cent amongst the poorest—approved of lynchings.[53] Such acts are seen as a way of punishing wrongdoers and symbolically dissuading future thieves through the threat of physical punishment, and

[53] *Imasen Confidencial*, Lima, Aug. 1993.

possibly death, if they are caught in the act. A follow-up poll carried out in December 1994 by the same company revealed nearly identical findings.[54] This is not a unique phenomenon in Peru; lynchings have been reported in recent years in Venezuela and Brazil,[55] and the killing, death-squad style, of criminals and 'undesirables' in El Salvador is widely popular (Tracy 1995). Democratic institutions appear dysfunctional; few mechanisms exist at the local level to resolve conflicts. Shining Path often filled this gap at a local level, playing upon the state's growing incapacity in the shantytowns to provide order and justice. By engaging in activities that were imbued with popular notions of justice, they obtained an important degree of sympathy amongst shantytown dwellers.[56]

Shining Path and Grassroots Organizations

Lima's *barriadas* were, as described amply in numerous studies, the center of intense organizing activities by left-wing party activists and local community leaders throughout the 1980s. Many of the social organizations active in *barriada* life, such as neighborhood associations, soup kitchens, women's clubs, 'glass of milk' committees, and youth groups, emerged as collective efforts to meet the concrete needs of the local population. Neighborhood associations usually were formed during the initial period of preparing a land invasion, and continued to be active after securing the land in promoting community improvement projects and pressuring the government and cajoling state bureaucrats for basic services. Communal soup kitchens began to form in the late 1970s due to the growing economic crisis and the inability of some families to meet their basic nutritional needs; Catholic Church activists were key in bringing families together and helping provide them with organization tools as well as basic supplies.[57] The 'glass of milk' was a municipal program developed during the left-wing Barrantes administration, and actively promoted the formation of grassroots organizations, known as milk committees, to distribute the milk at the community level. Lima's *barriadas* became the site of some fascinating experiments in grassroots and community organizing, and many people benefited materially as well as personally (in terms of securing greater participation, gaining organizing and administrative skills, etc.) from their participation in these movements.

[54] *Imasen Confidencial*, Lima, Dec. 1994.

[55] In a *barriada* in Caracas, residents killed one young man and almost burned another alive after they accidentally shot a 6-year-old girl. This was the sixth lynching registered in 1995. InterPress World News Service, 27 Nov. 1995. For Brazil, see Paulo Sérgio Pinheiro's chapter in this volume.

[56] It is ironic that Fujimori's authoritarian project draws on similar sentiments of the inefficacy of democratic and representative institutions and a desperate desire for law and order.

[57] Although much of the literature on the soup kitchen movement portrays these as spontaneous expressions of social solidarity, the role of external actors, including the church and NGOs, has been key in the formation of most soup kitchens. The state, as well as some political parties, has also mobilized soup kitchens in clientelistic fashion as a way of obtaining local support.

While community soup kitchens and milk committees proliferated as the economic crisis worsened after 1988, the neighborhood councils tended to dissipate once initial goals (obtaining land titles, water, electricity) were realized.[58] While new settlements have emerged on the periphery of districts like Villa El Salvador and San Juan de Lurigancho, they rarely encounter solidarity in the older, more established parts of the district to obtain basic necessities. State assistance was not forthcoming, and municipal governments, also suffering a budget crunch, were unable to fill the gap. Moreover, the deepening economic crisis after 1988 and Fujimori's structural adjustment measures in 1990 undermined the resource base of many organizations, especially the soup kitchens, deepening their dependency on external donations and exhausting their members. 'The enthusiasm that existed before is no longer the same,' said one leader who has been active in the soup kitchens since 1979. 'It is necessity that forces us to participate . . . It used to be like a service to the community . . . [but now] there is much sadness, resentment, and bitterness.' The soup kitchens provide important benefits for some families, but others cannot even afford the low cost of a daily ration.

This context of growing deprivation exacerbated the tensions and conflicts that were part and parcel of these social organizations.[59] Scholars and activists alike often understated these more complex and difficult aspects of the social organizations, while their positive features were highlighted—they fomented grassroots participation; women were increasingly involved in the public sphere; they represented a democratizing potential at the grassroots (Ballón 1986; Tovar 1986a, 1986b). Not only did problems of leadership styles (*caudillismo*), ideological differences, and power struggles exist; there was also a great deal of conflict about the way resources were administered and controlled (Delpino 1991). Corruption was a real and growing problem in organizations like the soup kitchens and the milk committees, which received donations from NGOs, religious organizations, and especially in the case of the milk committees, the government. The fragile institutionality of these organizations meant that few mechanisms existed to resolve problems and conflicts, including arbitrary decision-making, *caudillismo*, and petty corruption (Delpino 1991). These tensions grew as resources became more scarce. The closing of government channels of benefit and patronage to the sectors, particularly in the last years of the García administration and the first two years of the Fujimori administration, further undermined the capacity of grassroots leaders to deliver

[58] For a brief overview of the evolution of grassroots organizing in one popular district, see Burt and Espejo (1995).

[59] In addition to my dissertation research, this discussion is based on my own personal experiences living in two *barriadas* in Lima between 1987 and 1988 and in 1989 (Villa El Salvador and Ciudad de Dios respectively), as well as extensive interviews carried out in 1990 of activists in neighborhood associations, soup kitchens, and milk committees in six different *barriadas* before and after the 'Fujishock'. I owe a great deal to the women I interviewed over the years, especially to Teresa L., who has also become a dear friend. I also learned a great deal during a four-month study of development non-governmental organizations and from the insights of my research partner, Nena Delpino, who has written one of the best critical analyses of women's organizations in Lima. See Delpino (1991).

desired goods to the rank and file. Because leaders were increasingly judged by the rank and file according to their ability to obtain needed resources (Parodi and Twanama 1993), as resources dried up the legitimacy of these leaders increasingly was undermined (López Ricci 1993).

Shining Path played on these internal conflicts within the organizations and the growing problem of scarcity. One of their primary objectives was to further undermine the legitimacy of grassroots leaders, many of whom were associated with the left-wing parties that had split from the IU—for Shining Path, the 'revisionist left' that had to be eliminated. The division of the IU in 1989 favored Shining Path's activities in Lima's *barriadas*, as the splintering of the left into several smaller parties undermined popular confidence in the left as well as local community activists affiliated with it. Shining Path initiated intense propaganda campaigns in *El Diario* and within the *barriadas*, accusing left-wing grassroots leaders of corruption and selling out the 'revolution', in an attempt to deepen the growing wedge between leaders and the rank and file. This was part of the Maoist tactic of 'deepening the contradictions' to advance their cause. Shining Path sought to manipulate popular sentiments of mistrust and anger over corruption, playing on rank-and-file suspicions of leaders who—by virtue of their very positions as leaders—were perceived as likely to engage in some form of corruption; 'everybody does it', from government officials to grassroots leaders, has become popular wisdom.

Between 1989 and 1992, Shining Path killed over 100 community leaders and local political activists, including about two dozen women from the soup kitchens and milk committees, and hundreds of others received death threats. This assassination of unarmed civilians was deplored by many Peruvians from different social sectors and internationally, especially in the case of María Elena Moyano, a well-known community activist and the left-wing vice-mayor of Villa El Salvador, who became a vociferous critic of Shining Path.[60] Part of Shining Path's goals in killing Moyano and leaders like her was to eliminate local left-wing leaders and neutralize any attempts at resistance. Accusations of corruption were a way to justify the killings to the population at large. Some of my informants expressed their repudiation of this kind of 'sanction', but many others had much more ambiguous attitudes. 'Por algo será'—'they must have done something to deserve it'—was a common-heard phrase when people discussed these cases.[61] As one of Moyano's

---

[60] See, for example, the extensive coverage of the brutal assassination of María Elena Moyano in *Caretas*, 20 Feb. 1992. Moyano became highly critical of Shining Path after the organization intensified its activities in Villa El Salvador. However, she herself admitted that before 1990 she did not vocally criticize them because she saw them as 'part of the people' even though she disagreed with their methods. (Interview with Moyano in *La República*, 19 Sept. 1991.) This reflects the ambiguity of some sectors of the left *vis-à-vis* Shining Path, which ultimately played into Shining Path's hands. See Pásara (1992).

[61] In a workshop held in late 1994 with popular leaders from soup kitchens and milk committees throughout Lima, the participants expressed their concern with this persistent problem of corruption. They believed that only by creating more transparent mechanisms to administer resources could they regain their social legitimacy. This was a crucial step in undermining the widely held belief that 'everybody steals', so ably manipulated by Shining Path.

close friends told me, 'in these trying times, people believe that everyone steals—everyone, including grassroots leaders like María Elena'.

A member of a milk committee in a poor shantytown in San Juan de Lurigancho recalled that Shining Path had killed a leader of the milk program in her neighborhood in 1991. She said that it was justified, since it was well known that she was hoarding some of the milk and reselling it for profit. In Villa El Salvador, one soup kitchen leader stated that she believed the Women's Federation (FEPOMUVES) was attacked by Shining Path because they stored their food in warehouses, which inherently gives rise to suspicion that the food is being sold for profit.[62] In contrast, the church-run soup kitchens in which she participated had not been targeted by Shining Path because they do *not* store their food, suggesting that corruption was not a widespread problem: 'our food supplies are immediately handed out to the members [of the soup kitchen], we don't store them . . . That's why we haven't had any problems [with Shining Path]. There are other organizations that sell their food donations, and Shining Path is against that.' It was also notable that many leaders suggested that they had attempted to show the rank and file that they were honest administrators of the resources. The effect of these assassinations—Shining Path called them 'exemplary sanctions'—was to inhibit petty corruption to some extent and to garner important levels of sympathy.

Indeed, at the *barriada* level, many accepted the accusations of corruption as true, whether or not proof existed, and viewed these assassinations as the 'just deserts' of individuals who had used their positions of leadership to enrich themselves. Interviews with informed observers who worked in the shantytowns corroborated this attitude amongst many *barriada* residents. While it is difficult if not impossible to prove or disprove the allegations of corruption in specific cases, the existence of corruption amongst some leaders led to a growing perception that all leaders with access to resources would seek some personal benefit. In a context of extreme poverty that feeds mistrust and suspicion of leaders and those with access to benefits and power, rumors of corruption often *became* reality.[63] As economic conditions worsen, tolerance for corruption seems to decline, and drastic measures are often seen as justified. As was the case with Moyano, Shining Path consciously tried to exacerbate this inherent suspicion and mistrust to undermine local leaders, creating 'truth by rumor'. The actual reality of corruption mattered less than people's belief that corruption is more than likely and, moreover, deserving of harsh punishment. Like a self-fulfilling prophecy, leaders killed by Shining Path were a posteriori accused of corruption, and many perceived the 'sanction' as therefore 'justified'. This was a convenient tactic for Shining Path, who eliminated several left-wing leaders in this way.

---

[62] On 11 Sept. 1991 a warehouse storing foodstuffs administered by the FEPOMUVES was destroyed. All reports indicate the bombing was the work of Sendero (*La República*, 12 Sept. 1991). However, the official mouthpiece *El Diario* denied authorship, and argued that the leaders of the organization themselves blew up the warehouse to avoid detection of corruption by an impending audit.

[63] This draws on the concepts elaborated by sociologist Thomas Luckman (1980) about the social construction of reality.

While Shining Path's anti-corruption activities were most extensive at the local level, it occasionally targeted national figures who were engaged in corruption and who were widely unpopular. Such was the case of Felipe Salaverry, head of the Social Security Institute under the García administration, who was killed by Shining Path in 1989. Most of my informants expressed repudiation of Salaverry, and their sympathy with Shining Path's sanction. A quote gathered by López Ricci (1993) is illustrative both of the ambiguous nature of popular attitudes toward violence, and of the popular rage against corruption that Shining Path's actions were able to channel:

There are innocent [people] who die and that is very bad, but there are also people who deserve to die and that is the truth. One reaches the point of recognizing this. Look at what happened to the man who was president of the Social Security Office [Felipe Salaverry]. [Shining Path] killed him and everybody said 'he deserved it' ('está bien muerto') because he was an undesirable man who closed the doors to everyone, and President [García] supported him. In my opinion, he reaped what he sowed.

Providing Other 'Goods'

Greater public security and punishing and inhibiting corruption were not the only 'goods' that Shining Path sought to provide to *barriada* residents. Informants also attested to Shining Path's attempts to assure fair market prices and prohibit speculation and hoarding in some shantytowns. Not all my interviewees were aware of this kind of activity in their neighborhoods, but those who were held a generally favorable attitude. One informant described Shining Path's warnings to a local merchant who was overcharging for her merchandise: 'they took some of her merchandise, and warned her to lower her prices, that it wasn't fair to the poor people in the neighborhood to charge such high prices. Everybody was glad, because that woman was really abusive with her prices.' Playing upon people's sense of injustice when prices were too high for them to afford, Shining Path sought to enforce price controls. This sometimes meant warnings, as in the case just described. It also meant, however, assassinations—'exemplary punishments' in Shining Path lingo—of vendors who refused to abide by these price controls. A priest who worked in a *barriada* described Shining Path's harsh attempts to dissuade vendors from raising their prices in the market-place. 'They have a policy of controlling the prices of the vendors, who sometimes can be abusive or speculative. For example, there were a number of assassinations of people who had stalls in the Sarita Colonia market-place in Bayóvar. The news spread quickly: they kill one vendor, then everybody in Canto Grande knows about it. It acts as a kind of a warning.'

Shining Path also focused on more tangible 'goods' for the urban poor. For example, in some areas it seized on the problem of the tenuous legal situation of squatters, particularly in newer squatter settlements in outlying areas of popular districts like Villa El Salvador and San Juan de Lurigancho. Its mode of operation was different in each case, but in the cases I examined the underlying dynamic was the same: to use the unresolved problem of land tenure for squatters to agitate against the government and rally support. In Pachacamac, a rapidly growing settlement within Villa El Salvador, hundreds of young people had invaded unoccupied houses in 1987 and 1988 that had been constructed during the Belaunde government. After two years of failed attempts to obtain legal title to the houses, the squatters had grown increasingly impatient with the municipal government, which in turn depended on the Housing Ministry to issue the titles. Shining Path maneuvered ably around this issue of growing contention, and even mobilized public rallies against the municipal government.

Land tenure was also a problem in Raucana, but the origins of this settlement in Ate-Vitarte were quite different. Raucana began as a land invasion in July 1990. Police violently evicted the squatters, killing one man. After the dust settled and the squatters resettled on the land, Shining Path began intensive political work in the settlement. A year later the police returned to evict the squatters, this time with a judicial order. The squatters—under the lead of Shining Path cadres—blocked the central highway and engaged in violent confrontations with the police to prevent their eviction. The owner of the land received death threats and a car-bomb was exploded in front of a factory he owned, leading to the withdrawal of the eviction notice. The lesson was clear: heavy-handed measures are an alternative way of obtaining desired goals (Burt and Panfichi 1992: 25).

However, in both the cases discussed above, Shining Path's interaction with squatters demanding legal land titles was focused more on confronting the state than actually resolving the problem of land tenure. In Pachacamac, the issue of land tenure was used to delegitimize the left-wing municipal government, and to demonstrate the futility of peaceful mechanisms in obtaining local demands. Shining Path did help the squatters establish their settlement in Raucana, and this helped consolidate pro-Shining Path sentiment in the *barriada*. However, Shining Path was aware that its open activity and confrontation with the police would provoke a response from the government—and, in its logic of all-out confrontation, it was expecting that response to be violent and repressive. Provoking the security forces was a way of 'deepening the contradictions' and hastening the 'revolutionary moment'. However, the army reacted in quite a different manner in Raucana. It occupied the settlement, but, rather than engaging in indiscriminate repression, it started handing out food and medicines. This new civic-action approach, designed to win the 'hearts and minds' of the local population, was accompanied by selective repression, and the arrest of several suspected Shining Path activists. These civic action campaigns became more widespread in 1992 and 1993 in Lima's *barriadas*.

That Shining Path was intent on demonstrating the futility of peaceful means of social change was clear from my interviews with community leaders. The closing of government and other channels as means of obtaining resources and other desired goods played into Shining Path's hands, and helped undermine the legitimacy of community leaders, as discussed above. An extensive quote from a leader from El Agustino is worth highlighting. First, the leader discusses Shining Path's arguments against peaceful forms of organizing:

We were organizing a protest march to the government palace to demand solutions to a series of problems in the *barriadas*, including land titles, legal recognition of new squatter settlements, problems of water, electricity . . . We were in Bocanegra, discussing the plans with the local organizations . . . Then some leaders linked to Shining Path intervened, publicly saying that a peaceful march would not get us anywhere, that it wouldn't resolve any problems, and that if we did organize a march it should be confrontational. They said the kind of march that we were trying to organize—a peaceful march, where the leaders try to talk to the mayor of Lima, to give him our list of demands, or to go to the government palace—was futile.

He noted that he and his associates argued against this position, and the march was eventually carried out.

We mobilized a mass protest to the center of Lima, we put together delegations to go to the government palace, but no one would receive us. We wanted to give them our memorial of demands, but in the municipality of Lima, [mayor] Belmont refused to see us . . . It was difficult for the leaders to return [to the community] because we had to tell them that nothing had happened. . . . The spaces of democratic struggle for our demands were closing up . . . This hurt the possibilities of maintaining the organizations. In the end, the organizations are [seen as] useless because they don't resolve the problems [of the community]. I think there has been a systematic shutting out of the people's organizations [by the government], though there are some vices to be criticized in these organizations.

Shining Path sought to agitate around other unpopular measures at the local level. In Villa El Salvador, for example, Shining Path led a campaign with its allies in the district's centralized neighborhood organization, the Self-Managing Urban Community of Villa El Salvador (CUAVES), against the municipal property tax in 1991. The tax was a heavy burden for most of the district's residents, whose real incomes had bottomed out after the combined effects of hyperinflation and neoliberal austerity. As a result, the campaign against the tax won a great deal of sympathy amongst the *barriada*'s residents (Burt 1995). This caused a dramatic impact on public opinion in Peru, since CUAVES was a key symbol of the popular movement and of left-wing organizing in the *barriadas*.

The establishment of political alliances, such as those described with the CUAVES, was another important element of Shining Path organizing in the *barriadas*. I cannot fully develop this argument in this chapter, but a brief example will help illustrate the point.[64] Shining Path used two key tactics in building alliances at the local level in Villa El Salvador: first, their cadres attempted to infiltrate some organizations and/or recruit local leaders to their cause, especially at the intermediary level

[64] For a more developed version of this argument, see Burt (1995).

of organization; and second, the Maoists established tactical alliances with disaffected groups when it believed such alliances could advance its cause. In the latter case, the principle 'the enemy of my enemy is my friend' was operative, as Shining Path actively sought out disaffected groups and constructed alliances to further their own cause. This was the case in Villa El Salvador, where radical political groups within the CUAVES long-opposed to the left-wing municipal government joined Shining Path in a number of campaigns, including those centered on land titles in Pachacamac and the municipal tax, to delegitimize their common enemy. An earlier stage of low-key organizing locally in Villa El Salvador as early as 1986 facilitated Shining Path's position in CUAVES. For example, Shining Path cadres had joined land invasions on the periphery of Villa El Salvador, and many became active in the local neighborhood councils. The presidents of these councils formed the rank and file of the CUAVES, and were charged with overseeing the community's development. Through infiltration of several of these councils Shining Path was able to exert influence in the CUAVES. Other local activists became more sympathetic to Shining Path's viewpoints, especially as the economic crisis deepened and means of peaceful social change seemed increasingly futile. Shining Path built up sympathy by playing on the harsh conditions in which people lived, and the drying up of resources from the state and other actors. This was especially the case with young people, as the testimony of a nun who noted Shining Path's often successful attempts to recruit young people from the shantytown where she worked in San Juan de Lurigancho suggests: 'Well, it's because what they [Shining Path] say is true, and you can't refute it because it's the truth: the poverty, the lack of jobs. These young people finish high school, and where do they have to go? They can't get admitted to the university, it's impossible.'

Concluding Remarks

In Lima's shantytowns, marked by the absence of state services, extreme poverty, growing crime and insecurity, and weak local institutions to mediate conflict, Shining Path's use of intimidation and violence became seen as an effective means of restoring social order and imparting justice. The failure of the police and justice system to protect poor Peruvian citizens and provide for their material security provided the Shining Path with the raw material to win local sympathy by imposing social order and punishing wrongdoers. Such activities garnered local sympathy when they were perceived as contributing to a larger, socially desired good. As institutional mechanisms of providing order and justice waned, popular codes of justice and morality became more widespread. Authoritarian methods and even physical violence were not rejected unilaterally by the urban poor, but evaluated according to the target, the motive, and the social desirability—and utility— of the act: Did it achieve a specific—if not necessarily tangible—social good? Did it punish someone who 'deserved' to be punished for transgressing group norms or because of some real (or, oftentimes, imagined) wrongdoing? Did it serve to inhibit future instances of such wrongdoing? Subaltern groups were not inherently disposed to accept violence, as some have suggested (Manrique 1989), but nor were they completely opposed to violent acts, as others have claimed (Degregori 1991*a*, 1991*b*).

My findings broadly parallel those of recent studies of Shining Path's rural activities in highlighting those elements of Shining Path's activities that generated important currents of sympathy amongst subaltern groups during their peak in the late 1980s and early 1990s. In the countryside, the Maoists initially generated a great deal of sympathy and to a lesser degree passive support by killing hated landowners and merchants; distributing goods like cattle, sheep, and land; rallying against state-run cooperatives that had become widely repudiated by peasants; and punishing cattle thieves (Berg 1987, 1992; Isbell 1992; Manrique 1989). In his discussion of Shining Path's activities in Andahuaylas, Berg (1992) argues that peasants generally were sympathetic to Shining Path's assassinations of wealthy peasants, abusive merchants, and cooperative functionaries. These individuals were seen as having distanced themselves from a moral economy based on reciprocity and mutual obligations, and they had become viewed widely as abusive (Berg 1992). Such sympathy did not become revolutionary sentiment or active support for Shining Path or its war. It did, however, allow the Maoists important room to maneuver in the countryside. Sympathy often became *de facto* passive support. The peasants' long-standing mistrust of the police and army also worked in Shining Path's favor. In Lima, they were similarly able to marshal important levels of sympathy amongst the urban poor by playing on popular resentment against abusive authorities and real or perceived corruption, by providing greater levels of security, and in some cases by championing local popular causes.

At the same time, however, both Berg and Isbell note a crucial weakening in Shining Path's peasant base when they failed to protect their peasant allies from military repression in 1983–4, and when they attempted to close down local and regional markets, which are crucial to peasant subsistence. Later studies of developments in Junín revealed a similar phenomenon; after the initial 'honeymoon' between Shining Path and local peasant communities—when the former were widely applauded for attacking hated landowners and state co-ops, distributing land, and punishing thieves (Manrique 1989)—concrete divergences began to appear between Shining Path's objectives and timing and those of the local peasants, eventually giving rise to the formation of civil defense patrols to protect peasant communities against Shining Path's incursions (Starn 1991). This suggests an ongoing and dynamic reappraisal on the part of the rural poor to Shining Path's varied repertoire of actions.[65] I believe that the ambiguity evident in my interviews in Lima's *barriadas* is related to a similar phenomenon in urban areas. In other words,

[65] This would form the basis for the proliferation of peasant *rondas*, or civil defense patrols, in many parts of Ayacucho, but especially in the highest altitudes where dependence on markets was greatest (Favre 1984; Coronel 1992; Del Pino 1992).

popular support or sympathy for a given group hinges on ongoing subaltern appraisals of that group's capacity to deliver certain desired goods. When that group delivers, sympathy is forthcoming. Diverging from local concerns and interests may result in the undermining of that support, and may become, as was the case in many parts of the countryside, active resistance.

What this ultimately suggests is that Shining Path's success in organizing amongst the urban poor hinged on their delivery of socially desired goods, which reflects a complex and dynamic pattern of political behavior amongst Peru's subaltern groups that challenges more static views. It highlights a pragmatic understanding of politics, which focuses on constantly negotiating the terrain of politics with external actors, whether they are guerrilla groups like Shining Path, right-wing populists, or state agencies seeking to co-opt the poor. Subaltern groups in Peru are not the simple receptors of clientelist or populist—or guerrilla—actions. Rather, they are constantly negotiating and renegotiating the terms of their relationships with outside actors. This was true not only for Shining Path, but also for popular relations with the García administration, with the IU, and even today with Fujimori. What Stern (1987) has termed 'adaptive resistance' seems a particularly useful concept in this regard, as it recognizes the ongoing struggle at the grassroots level to negotiate goods and services that outside actors offer, without glossing over the attempts to keep those outside actors at arm's length and preserve local spaces for action and decision-making.

I have tried to highlight those elements that were uncovered during my interviews and discussions with *barriada* residents that generated currents of sympathy for Shining Path activity in Lima's shantytowns. These elements, I believe, are crucial for understanding their ability to operate in Lima's shantytowns between 1989 and 1992, the height of their urban activity. However, this examination of the nature of Shining Path's exchange relationships with the urban poor also suggests the limits of their organizing abilities in the shantytowns. Generating sympathy was less difficult than building longer-term bases of support. Shining Path eschewed the latter—in part because of its dogmatic belief in the ability of its 'self-generated' organisms and the 'contamination' of those grassroots groups that participated in the electoral process and sought change through local organizing. This was an inherent limitation to their capacity to develop more sustained levels of popular support. Moreover, it helps to understand why the sympathy that Shining Path had generated dissipated so quickly after the capture of Guzmán. As the group was forced to retreat, its capacity to deliver desired goods waned. The sympathy it generated waned in tandem. When the military gained the upper hand—and moreover, began its civic action campaigns, designed precisely to return a sense of security to the *barriadas* and deliver foods and medicines to win local support—passive acceptance of the army was evident in many *barriadas*. Shining Path did not channel sympathy into any structured way of building longer-term support. Perhaps it was not interested in such channels. Perhaps its own authoritarian and dogmatic logic prevented it from conceiving of the importance of such long-term support.

PART IV. Dilemmas of a Social Democratic Project

13 | Rethinking Economic Alternatives: Left Parties and the Articulation of Popular Demands in Chile and Peru

Kenneth M. Roberts

Few political actors have been as profoundly challenged by Latin America's wave of neoliberalism as left-wing parties and political movements. The neoliberal ascendance in the 1980s combined with the debt crisis and the collapse of empirical socialist models to wreak havoc with the left's traditional conceptions of state-led development. After long emphasizing the role of the state as investor, producer, protector, and redistributive agent, the left was placed on the defensive when fiscal crises generated pressure to reduce the size and scope of the developmentalist state.

How have left parties responded to these challenges, and how have they adapted their economic and political projects to the exigencies of an era dominated by neoliberalism? In recent years, the Latin American left has demonstrated a fertile capacity for self-critical reassessment and 'renovation', at least in the spheres of politics and ideology. Experience with military coups, authoritarian repression, and redemocratization encouraged leftist intellectual and political leaders to reconsider the costs, benefits, and risks of revolutionary strategies, while simultaneously embracing democratic institutions and reformist options that many previously disparaged. Indeed, the 'revaluation' of political democracy spawned an avalanche of literature and a widespread reconceptualization of socialism as the gradual 'deepening' or extension of democratic practices into new domains of social interaction.[1]

However, 'new thinking' in the sphere of economics tended to lag behind in this process of ideological redefinition. It generally received less attention than the question of democracy, and fell considerably short of a new consensus on the main features—or even the rough outlines—of a progressive alternative to neoliberalism. While some pioneers linked the renovation of political thought to a critique of state-centric socialism from the start (Petkoff 1976), more generalized reassessment of economic principles was considerably delayed.

---

[1] The revaluation of democracy is analyzed in Barros (1986), Lechner (1988), and Garretón (1987).

Although the preoccupation with democratic transitions was understandable in the 1980s, the relative neglect of economic issues occurred at the precise moment that Latin America plunged into its deepest economic crisis in half a century. As such, this neglect undermined the capacity of the left to pose a viable and compelling alternative to neoliberal structural adjustments. Nevertheless, as inequalities were exacerbated and living standards fell across the region, and as the collapse of the Soviet bloc obliterated bureaucratic collectivism as a development alternative, the Latin American left eventually began a more systematic reassessment of economic strategies (Flisfisch 1991).

One of the most prevalent responses—and one which paralleled the political orientation of the aforementioned process of ideological renovation—was to propose some type of social democratic reformism combining market competition with state regulation and redistribution (Castañeda 1993b; Bresser Pereira *et al.* 1993; Vellinga 1993). Is social democracy, then, the left's most viable alternative to neoliberalism in contemporary Latin America? If so, what forms will it take in the Latin American context, and what opportunities and constraints does it face? This study addresses these questions, first, through an analysis of the different tendencies that can be found within the increasingly heterogeneous political space of the Latin American left. It then examines the social democratic option, arguing that it may have feasibility advantages over other alternatives, since it has the potential to garner multi-class political support and neutralize business opposition. Nevertheless, the social democratic option faces serious constraints of its own in Latin America. These constraints are predominantly structural in nature, taking two basic forms: (1) the internationalization of economic competition and capital markets, and (2) the structural weakness of labor and the fragmentation of civil society in the social sphere. While these constraints may not preclude social democratic experiments in Latin America, they will inevitably shape their prospects and content, giving local variants of 'social democracy' distinctive features which are likely to diverge from classical European models.

The prospects for social democracy are analyzed through case-studies of the left in Peru and Chile, allowing a comparison of political dynamics before and after neoliberal adjustments. In Peru, the left was a serious contender for political power during the national crisis of the 1980s, before the neoliberal adjustment of President Fujimori. In Chile, the Socialist Party returned to political importance in the 1990s in the aftermath of the military regime's neoliberal revolution. The comparison suggests that neoliberal transformation may help consolidate a social democratic option within the left, yet limit the possibilities for social democratic reforms on the national political stage.

This emphasis on structural conditions represents a sharp departure from the predominant theoretical trends in the study of Latin American politics. While the classic literature on authoritarianism in the 1970s highlighted structural factors (O'Donnell 1973; Collier 1979), more recent scholarship on democratization has largely ignored them, while emphasizing the 'possibilism' of statesmanship and elite accommodation (O'Donnell and Schmitter 1986; Higley and Gunther 1992). Although political voluntarism may expand the boundaries of *lo posible*, this study suggests that reformist boundaries in contemporary Latin America are more narrow and confining than those which prevailed during the era of social democratic ascendance in Western Europe. As such, caution should be exercised when transplanting the social democratic label to the progressive and reformist alternatives that are identifiable on the Latin American horizon.

Change and Continuity in the Latin American Left

Social democracy does not have the deep historical roots in Latin America that it possesses in Western Europe. As Aricó has noted, progressive political space in Latin America has traditionally been dominated by various strains of Leninism or populism (Aricó in Calderón *et al.* 1992). Although social democratic forces have developed rapidly in the region since the 1970s, it is probably premature to claim that they have established a hegemonic position within the left; instead, they have been a major contributor to the growing heterogeneity of the Latin American left.[2]

Within this pluralism, four principal tendencies can be identified. The first is a fundamentalist orientation which holds fast to one of several variants of Marxist-Leninist orthodoxy, including a commitment to the revolutionary conquest of state power as a precondition for the collectivization of property and production. This orientation rejects the winds of ideological renovation which have influenced the left in recent years, and manifests high levels of continuity with historical identities and political objectives. The most significant and extreme example of this tendency is the Maoist fundamentalism of Sendero Luminoso in Peru.

A second orientation could be characterized as a form of class-based oppositional populism. The hallmark of this orientation is the encouragement of confrontational forms of popular mobilization tied to the immediate particularistic demands of subaltern groups. This mobilization is economistic and particularistic rather than ideological, and is primarily a tactic of political opposition, with little capacity to be transformed into a national-level governing alternative. In some cases, this orientation is found among parties—such as the Chilean Communist Party—which have had their ideological moorings shaken by the collapse of communism, but have been unable to reconstruct political identities around new transformative projects. Instead, they 'bunker down' among core social constituencies —organized labor, urban popular sectors, the peasantry, etc.—while emphasizing class conflict and immediate redistributive demands. In the process, these parties retreat from the teleological visions of socialism which prevailed in the past.

A third orientation leads to a radical democratic project. While retaining a critique

---

[2] This heterogeneity is discussed by Cavarozzi in Vellinga (1993).

of capitalist inequalities, it does not attribute social domination exclusively to capitalist relations of production or class divisions. Instead, it identifies class exploitation as one of the multiple forms of social, economic, political, or cultural domination. The radical democratic project thus enjoins the struggle to transform capitalism with struggles against patriarchy, racial and ethnic discrimination, environmental degradation, and other forms of exploitation or subjugation. This orientation emphasizes the role of grassroots organizations as popular democratic subjects and agents of social and economic transformation. The primary locus of political initiative thus shifts from the state to civil society, where base-level protagonism extends the democratic norms of equality and popular sovereignty from the political sphere to the terrain of social, economic, and cultural relations. The traditional notion of socialism as an alternative mode of production may thus be diluted or reconceptualized as the extension or deepening of democracy. This orientation was highly influential in the Brazilian Workers' Party (PT) during its formative years, and found considerable resonance in less orthodox sectors of the Peruvian left in the 1980s.

The fourth orientation has a social democratic character, and although it shares important features in common with the radical democratic approach, it also manifests subtle distinctions. Its primary political objectives are to transform the left from an oppositional force into a serious and viable governing alternative within the framework of pluralistic democracy, and to use state power as an instrument for social and economic reform. The social democratic orientation stresses an activist state which can 'govern' market behavior through regulatory, industrial, and lending policies, and redistribute income through taxation and social policies. In general, it aims to modify capitalist development to allow for more equitable and sustainable patterns of growth. It also seeks to ameliorate class conflict by incorporating organized labor into institutionalized channels for political representation and social concertation. Generally wary of confrontational forms of social mobilization, the social democratic approach opts for technocratic pragmatism over ideology, and multi-class, catch-all electoral movements over class-based forms of organization. Expressions of this orientation can be found in sectors of the Chilean Socialist Party, although the party's contemporary positions fall short of the reformist and redistributive standards of traditional social democracy, as will be discussed below. The leadership of the Brazilian PT may also be moving in a social democratic direction as the party competes for political power at the national level.

Clearly, the third and fourth orientations are both manifestations of the new emphasis on political democracy within the left, and the distinctions between them can be easily blurred, especially in parties that are internally heterogeneous. Both correspond to an era when the teleological certainty of socialism has faded from view, and more open-ended political and economic alternatives have replaced predetermined socialist models (Garretón 1987: 32–3). While the third orientation maintains a vision of grassroots empowerment and radical social transformation, it is inherently difficult to translate into alternative political and economic institutions at the national level. As Claus Offe has argued, dispersed and decentralized grassroots movements rarely exhibit a comprehensive vision or the institutional design for an alternative social order, much less an integrative, national-level transformative strategy.[3]

In contrast, the social democratic option sacrifices radical change on the altar of political realism, moderating its objectives—and ideals[4]—in order to ameliorate opposition and enhance its viability as a governing alternative. But if the moderation and pragmatism of the social democratic option enhance its political feasibility, they do not necessarily enable it to escape the structural constraints which differentiate the contemporary Latin American context from that of Western Europe when social democracy rose to prominence during the Great Depression and the early post-war era. Any future social democratic option in Latin America will be shaped by these constraints, and forced to develop innovative strategies to overcome (or at least ameliorate) them.

Economic and Social Constraints to Social Democracy

Perhaps the most fundamental constraint upon a social democratic project in Latin America—or anywhere else, for that matter—is the increasing internationalization of capital markets and productive activities. As Przeworski has demonstrated, there is an inherent contradiction between the process by which capital is accumulated and reproduced on an international level, and the domestic process by which social democratic forms of class compromise are constructed (Przeworski 1981). Even in the European context where social democracy developed and thrived, it came under increasing pressure in the 1970s as national economies became more thoroughly intertwined. The enhanced competition of a global market-place can undermine social welfare provisions which impose higher taxes or labor costs on firms without clearly increasing productivity (Pfaller *et al.* 1991). Corporate downsizing may thus be complemented by pressures for welfare downsizing as governments and firms try to cut the costs of extra-economic objectives.

The effects of international competition are compounded by the growing international mobility of capital. Disinvestment has always been a weapon of capitalists confronted with unfavorable government policies, but this 'exit' option has been considerably eased with the transnationalization and liberalization of capital markets, which facilitate capital flight and overseas investment (Goodman and Pauly 1993). As patterns of investment and financial speculation become increasingly

---

[3] Offe (1990). A detailed analysis of some of these difficulties in the Peruvian case can be found in Pásara *et al.* (1991).

[4] For an argument that the left must modify its political ideals to become more realistic and 'responsible', see Flisfisch (1987).

transnational, capitalists have ever greater leverage to force national governments to adopt pro-business policies and to punish those which do not.[5] In short, increased international capital flows exacerbate the structural dependence of the state on capital, modify the power balance between labor and capital, and thus complicate or skew efforts to institutionalize class compromise within the domestic polity.

This problem is especially acute in the context of dependent capitalism in Latin America, where important components of private capital are in the hands of highly mobile transnational corporations or domestic firms with deep ties to foreign capital. Even in Europe, the internationalization of capital markets has undercut traditional sovereign tools of national economic management which were effectively used by social democratic governments in the past. As the early French experience under Mitterrand showed, countries whose fiscal, monetary, or exchange rate policies diverge from international norms are either forced into line or plunged into crisis by currency speculation, capital flight, and liquidity pressures.[6] In the nations under investigation here—Chile and Peru—the plight of Salvador Allende and Alan García provide ample evidence of the domestic and international economic pressures which can suffocate the plans of reformist governments that transgress international norms.

These economic pressures pose a fundamental political constraint upon any left-wing project which leaves important production and investment decisions in private hands; in order to be economically (and, therefore, politically) viable, the planning, regulatory, and redistributive policies of the state will have to be not only compatible but functional to the process of capital accumulation in the private sector. This is not a novel constraint, nor is it unique to Latin America; social democracy has never been imposed against the interests of capital, as it has always relied upon some type of compromise or partnership with capitalists. The point is that this political constraint has been aggravated in the contemporary period by an internationalized economic order in which the behavior of capitalists is less and less bound by purely domestic class relations and power balances. No matter how strong a political majority a social democratic option musters, it cannot compel capitalists to fulfill their entrepreneurial function in the domestic economy. It is no small irony, then, that Latin American leftists have embraced the social democratic option at a time when it is on the political defensive in its European homeland. While European socialist and social democratic parties have continued to have electoral success in some contexts, they have generally done so by rearranging their political constituencies, articulating new communitarian and libertarian concerns, and prioritizing market efficiency over the traditional emphases on class-based

---

[5] As Jeffry A. Frieden (1991) notes, capital mobility is never absolute, as there is considerable variance between different sectors of business and finance. However, the general trends have tended to enhance the structural economic power of capital and lead to more pro-business public policies internationally.

[6] For a discussion of policy implications for European social democracy, see Scharpf (1991) and Moses (1994).

redistributive policies and the Keynesian welfare state (Kitschelt 1994). If the social democratic policy orientation is no longer what it was in most of Western Europe, it is even less likely that Latin American societies will be able to approach traditional social democratic standards for redistributive reform and market governance.

Given the exit option of capitalists and their structural advantages over labor, scholars have argued that social democracy in Latin America requires either that capital secure a hegemonic position (Cammack in Vellinga 1993), or that it be incorporated into an East Asian–style partnership with the state to promote an export-oriented industrial policy (Castañeda 1993b). It may be true, as Cammack suggests, that only a powerful capitalist class will be secure enough in its economic and political position to view redistributive reforms as an asset to hegemony rather than an intrinsic threat to the social order. The problem, of course, is that a capitalist class which is too dominant may perceive no need for redistributive reforms, and be capable of vetoing them when they are demanded by others. Clearly, then, social democracy requires a powerful labor or popular movement as well to generate political pressure for redistribution; the dilemma is that popular forces must be strong enough to create a balance of power conducive to class compromise, without so threatening capital as to encourage the exit option or its ultimate recourse to coercive methods of domination. The historical record provides few, if any, enduring examples of this delicate balance of forces in the Latin American context.

This issue highlights the second broad structural constraint to social democracy in the Latin American context—the relative weakness of organized labor and the social fragmentation of the popular sectors. If the industrial proletariat in Western Europe never achieved the majoritarian status that early Marxists anticipated (Przeworski 1985, ch. 1), it nevertheless comprised a far higher percentage of the population (over 40 per cent of the work-force in most of northern Europe during the heyday of social democracy) than it ever has in Latin America. European social democracy emerged within a proletarian subculture, and its success was closely tied to the political strength of large, centrally organized working-class movements with organic linkages to the partisan left. These structural and organizational features were also central to the establishment of neocorporatist patterns of interest intermediation, with their characteristic forms of tripartite bargaining and institutionalized class compromise (Korpi 1983). Not surprisingly, structural changes in the European economy which have increased social heterogeneity and diminished the relative weight of the working class have coincided with a weakening of social democracy in some of its traditional European bastions.[7]

In the Latin American context, the industrial proletariat remains a small minority within the working population. Even in relatively developed Chile, employment

---

[7] This issue is discussed in Merkel (1992). Kitschelt (1994) argues persuasively that the relative decline of the traditional working class need not spell the electoral demise of social democracy, so long as parties can adapt their program and discourse to accommodate the interests and concerns of more heterogeneous white-collar and professional sectors. This entails, however, a significant shift in the traditional economic policy orientation of social democracy.

in mining and industry comprised less than 19 per cent of the work-force in 1989 (Díaz 1989: 30). The corresponding figure in Peru was only 13 per cent (*Perú: Compendio Estadístico* 1992: 574). Unionization rates are also far lower than in European social democratic societies; even with the structural shift toward less unionized service sectors, Germany retained unionization rates over 38 per cent in the early 1990s, while Sweden boasted more than 80 per cent. In Peru, the 1980s economic crisis reduced unionization levels from 18 per cent of the work-force to only 12 per cent in 1991. In Chile, unionization levels fell from the very high 32.3 per cent achieved under Allende to only 8.5 per cent in 1985 under Pinochet, before recuperating partially to 15.4 per cent under the new democratic regime in 1991.[8]

Furthermore, labor movements in Latin America are often fragmented rather than united in centralized and broadly representative peak associations. Although lower-class or 'popular sectors' represent a social majority in most Latin American societies, their structural heterogeneity militates against class-conscious collective action in highly segmented labor markets. Workers in formal industries—often a relatively privileged sector—may have few apparent interests in common with workers in the informal sector, who generally pursue individualist strategies for survival and lack the workplace socialization experiences that are conducive to collective action. The provision of integrative political direction to such fragmented working- and lower-class sectors is a *sine qua non* for the transformation of the popular social majority into a political majority capable of sustaining a social democratic project. This involves a complex process of interest articulation and identity construction across diverse social sectors; although overarching labor federations or national popular movement centrals may help aggregate interests in civil society and channel them into the political arena, party organizations find it difficult to effectively represent such heterogeneous interests, and rarely come close to capturing the power potential which inheres in their numerical majority.

How, then, have social democratic projects been shaped by these constraints in Latin America? As the following case-studies suggest, left parties have responded in very different ways to the challenges they face. In Chile, a social democratic option triumphed within the left during a period of democratic transition, but has struggled to devise an alternative to the neoliberal economic model inherited from the military regime of Gen. Augusto Pinochet. In contrast, Peru's legal left fragmented under the pressure of trying to craft a progressive response to a deepening national crisis in the 1980s. Trapped between the violent fundamentalist insurgency of the Sendero Luminoso guerrilla movement and a profound fiscal crisis of a populist-developmentalist state, Peru's legal left was unable to construct a viable social democratic (or any type of socialist) option; indeed, the self-destruction of the democratic left cleaned the slate for the eventual imposition of neoliberalism

---

[8] Data for Germany, Sweden, and Peru are taken from the US Department of Labor series *Foreign Labor Trends*. Chilean data is taken from Patricio Frías (1989), and the statistical annex in *Economía y trabajo en Chile 1993–1994* (1994: 229).

under the autocratic direction of Alberto Fujimori. It is to this political defeat that we will first turn.

The Peruvian Crisis and the Dissolution of the Leftist Alternative

Peru provides a sobering case-study of the capacity of the left to respond to the debt crisis, economic recession, and hyperinflation with a viable alternative to neoliberal shock programs. In the 1980s Peru combined an exceptionally severe economic crisis and a brutal guerrilla insurgency with a democratic left that was among the strongest in the region. The ultimate failure of the Izquierda Unida (IU) electoral coalition to capitalize politically on the economic crisis by constructing a governmental alternative is instructive for an understanding of the challenges faced by reformist options in contemporary Latin America.

Throughout most of the 1980s, the Peruvian left seemed to have greater potential to gain governmental power through elections than any other in the region. The partisan left rode a groundswell of popular mobilization in the 1960s and 1970s into political prominence, and actually benefited from the military regime of Gen. Juan Velasco Alvarado, whose economic reforms between 1968 and 1975 were accompanied by new organizational efforts among workers, *campesinos*, and urban popular sectors.

Whereas the left in neighboring countries was decimated by repressive military dictatorships, Peru's left-wing parties expanded their bases as the Velasco regime failed to consolidate corporatist controls over the popular organizations it helped to mobilize (Stephens 1983: 57–93; Stepan 1978). Although highly fragmented between competing Leninist, Maoist, Trotskyist, Guevarist, and socialist tendencies, the partisan left helped coordinate a series of general strikes and popular protests in 1977–8 which rocked the more conservative military regime of Gen. Francisco Morales Bermúdez. After a gradual transition to civilian rule in 1980, six parties founded the IU, which captured the mayorship of Lima for its coalition president, Alfonso Barrantes, in 1983. The IU quickly consolidated a position as the second largest electoral force in the nation after APRA; it consistently earned between a quarter and a third of the vote in municipal and national elections, and swept dozens of mayorships in the impoverished Andean highlands and sprawling urban popular communities.[9] The IU received strong support from Peru's largest labor confederation, the Confederación General de Trabajadores del Peru (CGTP), as well as from peasant associations and community organizations in urban lower-class districts. A deepening economic crisis and spiraling political violence under the administrations of the conservative Fernando Belaunde Terry from 1980 to 1985

[9]   The IU's base of support in urban lower-class communities is analyzed in Tuesta (1989b).

and the populist Aprista Alan García from 1985 to 1990 made the IU the early front-runner for the 1990 elections.[10]

However, the coalition was unable to resolve its own internal disputes or craft a compelling political and economic alternative. From the outset the political viability of the IU was undermined by its heterogeneity and by the lack of internal consensus over basic objectives and strategies. The factionalism of the IU reflected competing international loyalties and ideological identities, as well as basic disagreements over the compatibility between revolutionary ideals and institutionalized democratic participation. The coherence of the IU was also undermined by intra-alliance competition, which was exacerbated by the tendency for individual parties to be organized in a sectarian manner around the leadership of a prominent personality.

The coalition's radical wing was anchored by the two organizations with the most electoral appeal and the deepest roots in popular movements, the new-left Partido Unificado Mariateguista (PUM) and the Maoist alliance UNIR. The radical wing generally adopted an instrumentalist approach to the IU's participation in the fragile new democratic regime, seeing it as an arena in which to accumulate forces for an eventual process of revolutionary transformation.[11] The IU's more moderate sectors lined up behind the leadership of Barrantes, who believed the necessary social and economic reforms could be achieved within the institutional framework of the democratic regime. Although it was very weak organizationally, the moderate tendency had the potential support of political independents who were attracted by the personal appeal of Barrantes.

Beyond ideological differences, the dominant parties in the IU clashed with Barrantes over a number of tactical issues, including his political flirtations with APRA and his unwillingness to adopt a staunch opposition line to the Belaunde and García administrations. Most important, perhaps, was their rejection of his personalistic leadership style, which they considered too independent of the IU's constituent parties and popular organizations. The PUM, in particular, feared that Barrantes embodied a new expression of populism which prioritized electoral victories and governmental office over the long-term objective of building base-level organizations as the foundation for a revolutionary project.[12]

[10]   For example, in a public opinion poll conducted in March 1988, Barrantes was the preferred presidential candidate of 36 per cent of the respondents, followed by the conservative novelist Mario Vargas Llosa with 25 per cent and APRA leader Luís Alva Castro with 22 per cent. See 'Informe de Opinión de APOYO S.A.', published in *Debate*, 9/49 (Mar.–Apr. 1988), 10.

[11]   The PUM, created through a 1984 merger of new left groups with their roots in the Guevarist movements of the 1960s and progressive Christianity, contained internal tendencies with very different orientations. While much of the party's intelligentsia favored a strategy of 'deepening' Peru's democratic regime, the majoritarian tendency insisted on the revolutionary construction of alternative organs of popular power. Although these differences led to a division of the party in 1988, the PUM remained the single most powerful force within Peru's legal left.

[12]   For an early statement of the PUM's criticisms, see 'Los Resultados del 14 de Abril y el Reajuste de la Táctica', Second Plenary Session of the Central Committee, May 1985, pp. 8–17.

After several years of internecine conflict, Barrantes and his followers provoked a rupture of the IU following the coalition's first congress in 1989,[13] forcing the left to run two separate tickets in the 1989 municipal and 1990 national elections. Meanwhile, García's populist-heterodox economic program collapsed after two years of euphoric but unsustainable expansion, causing the economy to shrink more than 25 per cent and inflation to reach four-digit levels the last three years of his administration.[14] The political right—considered moribund after Belaunde's disastrous administration and an abysmal electoral performance in 1985—was rejuvenated under the new leadership of Mario Vargas Llosa, who pledged a severe neoliberal shock program to stabilize the economy.

In theory, the social costs attendant to Vargas Llosa's promised shock therapy and his open alliance with traditional political and economic elites should have given impetus to a progressive alternative. The IU, in fact, under the direction of a programmatic task force led by the highly respected economist Javier Iguíñiz, made a serious effort to devise an economic project that would be an alternative both to neoliberalism and to the erratic populism of APRA. The centerpiece of this program was a strategy to stabilize the economy and control inflation without a deep recession or a reduction of living standards, as shock therapy would entail. Indeed, the IU proposed a selective reactivation of the economy, centered on the domestic agricultural sector and basic consumer goods industries, in harmony with anti-inflationary objectives.

For the IU, Peru's economic crisis was not attributable to excessive state intervention, as neoliberal critics alleged. Instead, it was indicative of a state which had been captured by private interests and weakened in its capacity to pursue collective national objectives (Iguíñiz 1991: 18–24). Therefore, in contrast to neoliberalism, the IU's prescription was not to privatize economic activity but to deprivatize the state and restore its public character. This involved, first and foremost, tax reform to correct the Peruvian state's notorious inability to extract resources from the private sector, thus addressing the fiscal crisis through revenue gains rather than painful cuts in public services or the inflationary printing of money. It also called for state subsidies and credits to be withdrawn from favored private monopolies and redirected to small and medium-sized producers in domestic agriculture and consumer goods industries. Wage indexation and subsidies for the popular organizations of the urban poor would help to sustain aggregate demand for economic reactivation while maintaining popular consumption levels. The IU also promised to protect job security, establish workers' right to participate in enterprise management, defend the property rights of indigenous communities, and transfer the

---

[13] With support from two small parties in the IU, Barrantes tried to isolate the PUM and UNIR by polarizing the coalition and drawing to his side the 'neutral' sectors led by the Communist Party and independent left Christians. However, the neutral sectors rejected these divisionist tactics, and remained with the PUM and UNIR in a truncated IU through the 1990 elections.

[14] The economic crisis and policy swings are analyzed in Pastor Jr. and Wise (1992).

management of public enterprises to regional governments in order to democrat-ize and decentralize economic power.[15]

The strategy of the pro-Barrantes sector of the left, grouped together in the Izquierda Socialista (IS), included many of the same features, including reforms to eliminate tax exemptions and government subsidies for the private sector. However, the gradualist approach to economic stabilization advocated by the IS was distinguished by two major emphases (Gamero 1990: 9–12). First, the center-piece of its anti-inflation plan was a 'national accord' between labor, capital, and the state to create a consensus on wages and prices. This accommodative stance was designed to elicit the cooperation of the private sector as well as organized labor in a national strategy for economic reactivation. Second, Barrantes's campaign—in keeping with his populist image—gave high priority to a 1.6 billion dollar pro-gram to provide a basic food 'basket' to the neediest sectors of Peruvian society, including milk for young children and expectant mothers, school lunches, and direct assistance to community soup kitchens. Although the IS pledged a 'tax shock' on the elite as an alternative to neoliberal shock treatment, Barrantes's commitment to an anti-inflationary program was called into question by assertions that tough measures would have to be delayed until after economic recuperation.[16]

Clearly, neither the IU nor the IS envisioned the type of socialist project attempted by the Allende government in Chile in the early 1970s, with radical changes in prop-erty structures and state–market relations. Both coalitions proposed reformist programs that would maintain a substantial state role within an essentially mixed economy. Even the more radical IU tried to reassure skeptics that it was opposed neither to private property nor to foreign investment, so long as they operated under clearly defined rules and were oriented toward productive rather than speculative activities.[17] Nevertheless, the essence of the IU program was to dramatically shift the burdens of economic adjustment from subaltern sectors to the middle and upper classes, while democratizing political and economic structures by incorporating base-level organizations into decision-making procedures and promoting pop-ular, self-managed institutions.[18] Such a project would have posed patent chal-lenges to the traditional dominance of propertied sectors, whose collaboration was essential, given their control over financial and investment resources that a bankrupt state and poverty-stricken popular organizations could hardly hope to match.

In short, the IU could not escape the structural dependence of the Peruvian state on capital, making the economic viability of its project heavily contingent upon the cooperation of the private sector. Leaders of the IU argued that a strong state

[15] The IU's economic program is detailed in Comisión Nacional de Plan de Gobierno, *Plan de Gobierno de Izquierda Unida 1990–1995: Plan de Acción Inmediata* (1990).

[16] *Resúmen Semanal*, 23–9 Mar. 1990, p. 5.

[17] See *Resúmen Semanal*, 25 Jan.–3 Feb. 1990, p. 11.

[18] The IU's emphasis upon base-level protagonism and self-managed political and economic structures was a major factor distinguishing its project from that of European social democracy, whose statist and bureaucratic orientations precipitated a backlash from 'left libertarian' movements advocating participatory democracy and decentralization. On these distinctions, see Kitschelt (1988).

establishing clearly defined rules of the game could earn the confidence of capital even while pursuing a redistributive agenda. In particular, they believed they could induce the private sector to cooperate by establishing the state as its protector against the insecurities of market competition and economic contraction that would accompany a neoliberal shock (Iguíñiz 1991: 19–20). As such, they hoped that economic self-interest could induce capitalists to participate in a national project for economic reactivation under the leadership of political forces identified with the popular sectors.

However plausible these hopes might have been in theory, in practice most Peruvian capitalists threw their political support to Vargas Llosa, despite the potential risks of the market-place. Indeed, neither the IU nor the IS came close to being able to test the economic viability of their plans; both coalitions received crushing blows in the 1990 elections, as voters delivered their verdict on the political viability of a divided left. Barrantes—the erstwhile front-runner—finished in fifth place in the presidential race with a dismal 4 per cent of the vote after being the central protagonist in the left's division, while IU candidate Henry Pease did little better with 7 per cent. Although the electorate soundly rejected Vargas Llosa's neoliberal project, for an alternative they turned not to the left but to an independent and ill-defined political novice, Alberto Fujimori, little knowing that he would impose a neoliberal shock of his own upon taking office. The IU subsequently unraveled, and by 1993 the left had even lost most of the municipal governments that it held during the 1980s.

Ultimately, the Peruvian left was defeated not so much by the inevitability of neoliberalism—which a substantial majority of the electorate clearly rejected in 1990—as by its own inability to construct political foundations for an alternative project. Indeed, the profound crisis of the Peruvian social order, far from strengthening the left, undermined its prospects in two fundamental ways.[19] First, it exerted a polarizing effect upon the IU and weakened its political coherence, as the coalition's radical and moderate wings adopted very different responses to the economic crisis and the challenge of Sendero Luminoso. Barrantes and the moderates, fearing social disintegration and civil war, believed it was necessary to buttress the democratic regime—whatever its limitations—through a national accord involving multilateral social and political pacts. Their de-emphasis of radical social and economic change corresponded with their belief that consensual politics were required to dampen social conflict and overcome the national crisis.

In contrast, the PUM and other radical sectors interpreted the deepening crisis as visible evidence of the regime's failure and exhaustion. Attempts to salvage the regime or seek ephemeral power within it were doomed to failure;[20] the only viable strategy, they believed, was to construct new organs of popular power from

---

[19] A more thorough analysis of the impact of the crisis can be found in the author's 'Economic Crisis and the Demise of the Legal Left in Peru', forthcoming in *Comparative Politics*.

[20] See the interview with PUM leader Javier Diez Canseco in *The Peru Report*, 3/5 (May 1989), B3–4.

below as the foundation for a revolutionary alternative both to representative democracy and to the sectarian militarism of Sendero Luminoso. The Senderista insurgency merely compounded this polarization in the legal left; if it drove the moderates toward the political center to distinguish themselves from the insurgents, it also exerted a radicalizing effect by competing at the base level with popular organizations linked to groups like the PUM. Given Sendero's relentless advance in the 1980s, the PUM feared that the legal left's adherence to the crumbling façade of institutional politics would cause it to relinquish revolutionary terrain entirely to the minions of Abimael Guzmán. This 'fundamentalist backlash' from radical sectors of the IU strengthened as Barrantes and his followers laid the groundwork for the political compromises that would be necessary to attain institutional power.[21] Believing these institutions to be an empty shell, far removed from the real loci of political and economic power in Peruvian society, the radicals feared the left would be destroyed if it took office behind a personalist figure who lacked the organizational force required for a genuine transformative project.

In short, the crisis in Peru was such that it polarized the legal left and made it difficult for a coherent social democratic project to congeal within the IU. It encouraged the IU's dominant parties and sectors of its popular bases to explore revolutionary alternatives to established institutions. More moderate tendencies were left suspended in mid-air, without the organic backing of political parties or their affiliated social movements. Even the IS, whose ideological orientation was ostensibly closer to that of social democracy, had its project heavily tinged with the populist style and *asistencialismo* of Barrantes.

The economic crisis also hurt the left's prospects by eroding the structural conditions for class-based collective action and political identities in Peru, thus weakening and fragmenting the social base of the IU. The surge of the political left in Peru in the 1970s coincided with the strengthening of the labor movement, which had organic ties to the partisan left. Organized labor served as the backbone and socializing agent for a dense network of popular movements.[22] Its political strength peaked in the late 1970s when unions led the protest movement against the military regime, but then steadily declined as the Peruvian economy lurched from one recession to another in the 1980s. The process of deindustrialization and huge cuts in public sector employment produced a dramatic informalization of the workforce, which reached 57 per cent in 1992 (Sulmont Samain 1994: 11). The industrial work-force alone in Lima shrank from 744,000 in 1976 to 430,100 in 1989 (Wilkie and Contreras 1992: 373). While inflation devastated real wages, union militancy and representativeness were undermined by the explosive growth in the number of underemployed, informal, and temporary contract workers, whose individualistic survival strategies complicated class-based identities and collective

---

[21] The idea of a fundamentalist backlash induced by political institutionalization is discussed in Offe (1990).

[22] For an analysis of the impact of union exposure on political militancy in shantytown communities, see Stokes (1991*b*).

action (Balbi 1989). Although community organizations remained active, they also adopted localized survival strategies that were difficult to coordinate into a national-level political project.

The atomization of social life in Peru severely complicated the political project of the IU, which relied heavily upon class and community-based collective action. Given its own internal polarization, the IU was hardly capable of reintegrating such a fragmented social fabric or providing political direction to increasingly heterogeneous popular interests. Instead, social atomization was transposed to the political realm, where the electorate opted for the individualistic mediation of new, independent personalist figures—such as Fujimori and Lima mayor Ricardo Belmont —over the collective mediation of political parties.[23] By 1992, when Fujimori suspended Peru's constitutional regime, not only the left but the entire party system had lost its capacity for political representation, as voters turned *en masse* to independent candidates. The once-formidable left had been decimated, forced to begin a process of political recomposition over the base of an alienated and atomized social constituency.

The nature of the Peruvian crisis, then, exacerbated the pre-existing cleavages within the IU, which blocked the construction of a viable left-wing political alternative. In such a context, a social democratic option was unable to consolidate a hegemonic position within the IU. In contrast, the Pinochet military dictatorship in Chile produced patterns of political and economic change which encouraged the predominance of a social democratic option within the left. However, as shown below, there continue to be significant structural constraints to the success of such an option on the national stage.

The Neoliberal Road to Social Democracy? The Case of Chile

As Chile returned to democratic rule in 1989–90, it became clear that dramatic changes had occurred within the Chilean left in the sixteen years since a military coup ended Salvador Allende's brief experiment in democratic socialism. The Socialist Party (PSCh) to which Allende belonged had anchored the radical wing of the governing Popular Unity coalition from 1970 to 1973, rejecting compromises with the political opposition and insisting that armed struggle was inevitable on the road to socialism. In contrast, the Communist Party (PCCh) backed the more moderate position of Allende, who was willing to negotiate compromises with Christian Democratic opponents while upholding the possibility of a peaceful, democratic transition to socialism in the Chilean context.[24]

However, two fundamental changes occurred within the Chilean left under military rule from 1973 to 1990. First, the Socialist and Communist parties reversed

---

[23] Changing voting patterns are dissected in Cameron (1991*b*).
[24] An overview of the Chilean left can be found in Faundez (1988).

political positions. The Socialists engaged in a self-critical process of ideological renovation which culminated in a patently social democratic orientation, as well as an alliance with the centrist Christian Democrats which made the PSCh a pillar of Chile's democratic transition.[25] Political change in the Communist Party was diametrically opposed, leading to a new emphasis on the role of force in political affairs and to support for armed struggle against the military dictatorship.[26] These divergent paths produced a rupture of the political alliance which had elected Allende to the presidency and united the PSCh and PCCh since the 1950s.

Second, the power balance between the two linchpins of the left shifted in favor of the Socialist camp as Chile moved toward a democratic transition in the late 1980s.[27] The Socialists and their offspring, the Partido por la Democracia (PPD),[28] became central actors in the multi-party Concertación coalition which formed Chile's new democratic government. After absorbing several smaller parties of the Christian left, the PSCh and PPD combined for 24 per cent of the vote in the 1993 national elections, earning a quarter of the congressional seats and strong representation in the cabinet. The PSCh–PPD bloc is increasingly capable of challenging the Christian Democrats for leadership of the Concertación. The Communist Party, on the other hand, paid a high price for having insisted that armed rebellion rather than electoral mobilization was the most viable strategy for toppling the dictatorship. The PCCh was left on the margins of the new political order, excluded from the Concertación and shut out of Congress by an unrepresentative electoral system bequeathed by the military regime. The PCCh established a new alliance with a number of very small, radical left groups, which has received between 5 and 7 per cent of the vote in recent municipal and congressional elections.

The economic programs of the PSCh and PCCh reflect their respective alliance options and their differential access to governmental responsibilities. Long a loyal adherent to Soviet ideological orthodoxy, the Communist Party in the post-perestroika era was ill prepared to put forward a national-level political and economic alternative, especially in the wake of the party's strategic defeat during the democratic transition. However, with its deep roots in the labor movement and shantytown organizations, the PCCh has been able to play the type of oppositional populist role outlined above. After initially declaring a policy of 'constructive

[25] The process of ideological renovation in the PSCh is discussed in Walker (1990).

[26] Patterns of change in the PCCh under the military dictatorship are discussed in Varas (1988).

[27] Prior to the late 1980s, the PCCh had been dominant in the left-wing opposition to Pinochet, since its organizational cohesion enabled it to withstand repression and organize resistance more effectively. In contrast, political and ideological divisions led to the rupture and fragmentation of the PSCh in 1979, forcing a difficult recomposition in the late 1980s.

[28] The PPD was created as an 'instrumental' party in 1987 at the initiative of moderate Socialists led by Ricardo Lagos to circumvent the legal proscription of traditional left parties. With its image of modernity and non-ideological pragmatism, the PPD attracted political independents and quickly occupied the center-left political space. It increasingly established its own identity and asserted its autonomy from the PSCh in the early 1990s, although the two parties maintained an electoral pact and jointly sponsored Lagos's candidacy for the presidency in the 1993 primary of the Concertación coalition.

independence' toward the new democratic government in 1990, the party moved quickly to an opposition stance, criticizing the Concertación for continuing the neoliberal policies of Pinochet. Completely shut out of national political institutions, the PCCh devoted its energies to social protest, articulating the sectoral demands of labor, student, human rights, and shantytown organizations. The party encouraged labor strikes and other forms of confrontational mobilization, and condemned the political and institutional constraints which inhered in Chile's 'pacted' democratic transition. Its support for economistic demands has been related less to a global vision of an alternative order than to a political strategy to enable the party to maintain a core social constituency in a period of adversity and ideological uncertainty.

In contrast, the Socialist Party oriented its program explicitly toward governmental responsibilities, prioritizing political stability, social consensus, and macroeconomic equilibrium. Although the PSCh remains internally heterogeneous, the process of ideological renovation in the party hierarchy has given it a notable social democratic hue, in sharp departure from the Marxist-Leninist positions which dominated the party in the 1960s and 1970s. Among the most significant changes are an unswerving commitment to representative democracy, the belief that a majoritarian, center-left political coalition is essential to sustain any process of social and economic reform, and a willingness to eschew socialist economic transformation in favor of a growth-with-equity strategy of capitalist development.

This new, growth-with-equity strategy reflected with the context in which the PSCh assumed governmental responsibilities in the early 1990s in partnership with the Christian Democrats. The Pinochet regime had been the trailblazer in Latin America's neoliberal revolution, privatizing industries and public services, slashing tariffs, and exposing both labor and capital to the vagaries of a competitive marketplace. After a speculative boom in the 1970s ended in financial collapse and a deep recession in 1982–3, the Chilean economy rebounded after 1984, with growth sustained by a primary product export boom and a process of reindustrialization. But if the new democratic regime inherited Latin America's most dynamic economy, it also inherited an economic model with two basic Achilles' heels: it had sharply exacerbated social inequalities, leaving over 40 per cent of the population below the poverty line (*Dimensión y características de la pobreza según CASEN 1990*, 7), and it remained highly dependent upon agricultural and raw material exports, which were vulnerable to international market fluctuations, contingent upon natural comparative advantages, and not clearly linked to an integrated process of industrialization.

The new government, then, faced the challenge of sustaining this economic dynamism while distributing its benefits more widely. In response, the PSCh—anxious to demonstrate a capacity for governance after the economic chaos of the Allende years—has tried to craft a post-neoliberal economic project capable of synthesizing the often contradictory objectives of growth and equity. The centerpiece of this project is a reconceptualization of the developmental role of the state, one which is distinct both from the minimalist, subsidiary conception of the state under neoliberalism and the suffocating statism of classical socialism.[29]

As part of this reconceptualization, the PSCh has accepted much of the economic restructuring of the Pinochet era as a *fait accompli*—and even, perhaps, as a necessary reorientation of Chile's development trajectory. The party program does not anticipate a reversal of the privatizations carried out under Pinochet; indeed, not only are private property and entrepreneurship accepted as the principal engines of economic growth, but the property structure in general has been deproblematized as a public policy issue. Likewise, the party has accepted the low tariff levels adopted under Pinochet and the openness of the Chilean economy both to foreign competition and to foreign investment. The party has supported the export orientation of the economy as a stimulus to productivity and growth, and ratified the essential role of market mechanisms for an efficient allocation of goods and services.

In short, contrary to its socialist project of twenty years ago, the PSCh no longer views the state as a major producer, entrepreneur, or planner of economic activity; instead, these functions are relegated primarily to the private sector operating in a competitive market-place.[30] Likewise, the economic nationalism of the past has yielded to strong support for international integration. However, the project of the PSCh differs from that of neoliberalism in important respects, particularly in the role that it assigns to the state as regulator of the market, agent of social integration, and strategic promoter of private economic activity in new spheres of production. The new vision rejects the assumption that free markets and natural comparative advantages in the production of primary commodities are adequate to sustain long-term development. It proposes a strong, efficient state to regulate the market in the public interest by correcting externalities and oligopolistic distortions, while trying to level the playing field to facilitate integration into the marketplace by previously excluded sectors. Likewise, it reserves a powerful role for the state in promoting technological innovation and labor capacitation so as to facilitate a shift toward higher value added lines of production, especially in export activities. The state is also expected to facilitate social concertation between labor and capital, institutionalizing forms of class compromise that allow for a genuinely national development model.

The call for the state to promote a 'second phase' of export development based upon agroindustrial activities and raw materials processing is indicative of this

---

[29] Information for the analysis which follows has been drawn, in part, from party documents, including the *Propuesta programática de los Socialistas para el Segundo Gobierno de la Concertación de Partidos por la Democracia* (Sept. 1992). Information was also obtained through an interview by the author with Alvaro Díaz, a member of the Economic Commission of the PSCh and an adviser to the Ministry of Economy, Santiago, 13 Aug. 1993.

[30] This does not mean, of course, that the state plays no role in these areas, only that it is subordinate to the private sector. Even the Pinochet regime did not privatize the copper industry, for example, which remains Chile's largest earner of foreign exchange, and the Concertación has likewise resisted calls from the business community to extend privatization to this sector of the economy.

strategic vision. Rather than rely upon natural—and often unstable—comparative advantages in the international market-place, the state promotes the development of specialized niches of production where 'acquired' comparative advantages based upon higher productivity prevail. The state can also promote domestic economic integration through backward and forward linkages, using its resources and regulatory power to modify incentive structures where market signals alone are incapable of inducing the desired private behavior.

For the PSCh, this new type of developmentalist state is essential for a growth-oriented strategy that moves beyond primary commodity production to generate an integrated industrial economy. The party does not perceive equity objectives as being incongruent with this growth orientation; indeed, it sees growth and equity as being not only compatible but mutually reinforcing. The party's strategy for alleviating poverty in Chile relies more heavily upon the employment-generating effects of economic growth than governmental redistribution of income or assets. In fact, the party has consciously downplayed traditional welfare-type transfer payments and emphasized targeted social investments to provide the poor with greater access to education, worker training, and other benefits that can facilitate their integration into the market economy. Such investments in human capital development are designed to equalize opportunities and enhance the autonomous capabilities of the poor to improve living standards. Moreover, they are seen as beneficial for labor productivity and long-term economic growth, particularly growth that is oriented toward more technologically advanced, higher value added lines of production.

Clearly, this new vision is a far cry from the state socialist project of the Allende era and the textbook neoliberalism of Pinochet's Chicago Boys. It also diverges sharply from the state capitalist model of development adopted by Chile and other Latin American nations from the 1930s until the 1970s, which emphasized import-substitution industrialization, high tariff protections, and public enterprises. It bears most resemblance, perhaps, to the forms of strategic capitalism practiced in various European and East Asian societies that have successfully used the state to mediate between domestic and international markets and help carve out specialized niches for highly competitive international economic integration (Katzenstein 1985; Wade 1990). Indeed, the program of the PSCh largely conforms to the trends in policy orientation that Garrett and Lange have identified within the European left; given the constraints on national policy autonomy posed by international economic integration, the left-wing alternative is identified not so much by fiscal and monetary policies, which tend to converge across nations and partisan divisions, but rather by supply-side policies in the labor market and industrial sphere which enhance competitiveness on quality (rather than price) indicators (Garrett and Lange 1991: 539–64).

But does the project of the PSCh warrant the social democratic label? Although possessing clear similarities, it would appear to have several subtle but significant shades of difference from classical European social democracy. First, it is not as consciously redistributive, as it places less emphasis on direct subsidies and transfer payments to eliminate poverty than on a new, more inclusive model of accumulation that would distribute its rewards more broadly. Second, the social benefits that are extended by the state tend to be targeted and selective, rather than founded upon the universal rights of social citizenship that are integral to social democracy.[31] Third, more than an agent of redistribution or social welfare, the state is envisioned primarily as a strategic actor with two fundamental objectives—that of promoting economic growth through technological advancement, and that of facilitating social concertation and integration. Fourth, this project rests upon a more diffuse social constituency than that of European social democracy, which very gradually evolved from working-class to catch-all parties. This final difference is attributable to several factors: the structural heterogeneity of the Chilean work-force, relatively low levels of unionization, and the fragmented political loyalties of Chilean workers, whose central labor federation uneasily aggregates Socialist, Communist, and Christian Democratic workers.

Given the absence of a politically loyal labor movement, the PSCh has developed a catch-all, electoralist orientation and a technocratic style that is designed to appeal to the middle class, somewhat reminiscent of Felipe González and the Spanish Socialists. Unlike the Spanish Socialist Party in the 1980s, however, the Chilean Socialist Party does not face a vacuum in the political center waiting to be filled. Indeed, the presence of the Christian Democratic Party places limits to the growth of the Socialist/PPD bloc, and makes it likely that the Socialists' access to government will continue to be contingent upon their participation in a broad coalition of forces. The content and success of their social democratic project—if it can be called that—is thus subject to the vicissitudes of their alliance with the political center, and therefore to the programmatic leanings of the Christian Democrats themselves.

In addition to this basic political constraint, the project of the PSCh is inevitably shaped by the structural balance between labor and capital in Chile, which shifted dramatically in favor of capital under Pinochet. After the imposition of a neoliberal model which entailed early deindustrialization, political repression of organized labor, and a labor code designed to enforce market principles rather than collective rights, labor clearly lacks the 'structural weight' (Jilberto in Vellinga 1993) required to balance the interests of capital in the political process. Therefore, one of the stated objectives of the Concertación government was to encourage unionization and modify the labor code to create a balance of forces that would be more conducive to institutionalized forms of class compromise. However, after a growth spurt at the outset of the democratization process, the rate of unionization declined in 1992 and 1993, remaining less than half the pre-1973 rate.[32] By mid-1994 the

---

[31] On the distinctions between targeted benefits and universal rights to social citizenship, see Esping-Andersen (1990). On social citizenship in general, see Marshall (1965).

[32] The unionization rate reached its post-transition peak in 1991 at 15.4 per cent, then declined to 13.7 per cent by 1993; see *Economía y trabajo en Chile 1993–1994*, 229.

central labor federation had become increasingly vocal in its criticism of the government's tepid reforms (and implementation) of the labor code.[33]

On the other side of the ledger, the private sector accounts for three-quarters of all investment in Chile today—compared to half of direct investment and a quarter of indirect investment in 1970 (Guardia 1993: 40)—and its economic centrality has been magnified by widespread privatizations and low levels of taxes and public employment. Consequently, the structural weight of capital—even in the absence of coherent partisan representation in the political sphere—has encouraged the PSCh to make its project palatable to business interests. Indeed, the party has actively cultivated support among small and medium-sized entrepreneurs, and proposed a form of strategic collaboration with capital that is aimed at submerging the political animosities of the recent past.

In many respects, the structural weight of capital—and the decisive triumph of capitalism under Pinochet—probably contributed to the consolidation of a project resembling social democracy within the Chilean left. Certainly, this social democratic hegemony within the left cannot be attributed solely to structural economic factors; the dynamics of self-criticism, political learning, and ideological debate in the PSCh after the 1973 coup had a political logic of their own, and exile experiences in Europe had a powerful impact as well. However, in conjunction with the institutional constraints of Chile's democratic transition, the economic boom after the mid-1980s undermined the revolutionary option of the Communist Party and shifted the internal balance of power toward the more moderate sectors within the Socialist Party, who spoke of modifying rather than abolishing capitalism. Although the neoliberal model was highly inegalitarian, its dynamism encouraged Socialist leaders to explore reformist options that would modify its distributive impact while safeguarding its vibrancy. Likewise, the neoliberal model established an extreme reference point which probably made a social democratic alternative more palatable within the left, even if it fell short of traditional revolutionary objectives.

The contrast with Peru could hardly be more striking—in the political terrain (where the Peruvian left had never experienced a comparable process of political defeat and military repression like the Chilean left after 1973) as well as the economic. The Peruvian economic crisis not only helped sustain the insurgency of Sendero Luminoso—the only sector of the left which ended the 1980s stronger than it was at the beginning of the decade—but also encouraged the more radical tendencies within the IU to hold fast to revolutionary objectives, under the assumption that Peru had entered a 'pre-revolutionary situation'. As such, the more moderate elements in the IU were unable to commit the bulk of the legal left to a reformist project that would attempt to resolve the crisis through a broad national accord within existing political institutions.

---

[33] In July 1994, the main labor federation sponsored its first protest march under the new democratic regime. The march created tension within the Concertación, as the PSCh—wary of ceding space to more radical sectors of the labor movement—offered public support to the workers, despite its presence in the government.

But if the dynamism of Chilean capitalism helped consolidate a social democratic orientation within the left, did it create structural conditions for its advance in national politics? In some ways, the answer is positive; since the mid-1980s, Chile has witnessed a steady expansion of industrial production, the salaried workforce, real wages, and (until 1992) unionization. It could even be argued that rapid growth has the potential to establish 'material bases for consent' (Przeworski 1985), allowing both high profit levels and steady gains in real wages. Indeed, Chile's rapid economic growth enabled the new government to quickly reduce poverty from over 40 per cent to 32.7 per cent (Ruíz-Tagle 1993*b*: 642) by expanding employment, raising wages, and enhancing social programs without sharp increases in taxes or the burden of public spending on the overall economy.[34]

However, Chile remains a considerable distance from social democracy. Her international economic integration has not only limited the space for domestic policy innovation, but strongly reinforced the internal dominance of Chilean capital. This dominance, furthermore, is not fully consensual; while being reproduced within the new democratic regime, it still relies partially upon the authoritarian enclaves bequeathed by the military dictatorship.[35] There is, then, a structural imbalance between labor and capital, rather than the type of rough equilibrium that would allow more redistributive policies or more institutionalized forms of class compromise. This correlation of forces has not been seriously challenged by the Concertación, despite its center-left orientation. Wary of killing the goose that can—they hope—lay the golden egg, both the Socialists and Christian Democrats have been very cautious in their relations with capital, reassuring businessmen that new social policies complement rather than undermine the market economy. As such, both parties have staunchly resisted the 'populist temptation' of rapidly increasing social spending beyond the rate of growth of the economy itself. In blunt terms, they are addressing poverty through a trickle-down of the benefits of growth more than a redistributive program; consequently, while poverty rates have sharply fallen, indices of income inequality have been almost unchanged under the democratic government.[36]

Capital has thus shown that it can tolerate a center-left government, so long as it does not have a strong redistributive orientation, much less an intent to alter the basic model of accumulation in the Chilean economy. Given the structural constraints discussed above, the cautiousness of the new government is hardly surprising; whether it is inevitable is another question, one that may depend as much

---

[34] For an insightful analysis of the democratic government's social policies, see Weyland (1997).

[35] These include, among others, a bloc of senators designated by Pinochet who prevent the Concertación from establishing a legislative majority; a highly disproportional electoral system which over-represents the right and completely excludes the Communist Party; and a constitutional provision which prevents the President from removing military commanders.

[36] Although more than 800,000 persons were lifted above the poverty line between 1990 and 1992, the percentage of the national income captured by the poorest 40 per cent of the population only increased from 13 to 13.3 per cent, while that of the wealthiest quintile stayed flat at 55.1 per cent (see Ruíz-Tagle 1993*b*: 642–3).

upon the political will of the Concertación as its skill in pushing the limits of reform without alienating the private sector. Ultimately, movement towards social democracy will be contingent upon the ability of reformers to use the political power of democratic majorities to temper the structural imbalances that exist in civil society. To date, this process is still at a rudimentary stage.

Toward a Latin American Model of Social Democracy?

The Latin American left has long been noted for its tendency to borrow ideas and political models from Europe. A number of factors have recently converged to make social democracy an attractive import: the political offensive of European social democracy in Latin America after the mid-1970s, the ties of solidarity developed during years of exile in Western Europe by many Latin American leftists, and the collapse of the Soviet model of socialism. But as this analysis suggests, social democracy may not be any more exportable to Latin America than revolution was. Latin American societies have different political backgrounds and socioeconomic structures than the European societies where social democracy developed. Perhaps most important, they occupy a subordinate position in an international economic order whose growing integration systematically restricts national latitude for reformist or redistributive policies.

In short, the classical European models of social democracy may not 'travel' easily from one time period or socioeconomic context to another. It should thus be expected that Latin American variants of 'social democracy' will not replicate European models, and may even warrant a different label. Shaped by indigenous conditions, they will likely rest upon more heterogeneous sociopolitical coalitions, adopt different economic policies, and redefine the developmental role of the state. Given the structural constraints, they are likely to be less organically bound to labor, more conciliatory towards capital, and more inclined toward growth-oriented policies of social integration than a redistributive welfare state. Their social base will necessarily be diffuse and pluralistic, reflecting the social heterogeneity of popular sectors in Latin America. The social majority comprised by these popular sectors creates the potential for electoral success, but in the economic or policy-making arena, the requisite alliances with capital are likely to significantly constrain reformist options. Therefore, it seems reasonable to expect that the electoral prospects for social democratic coalitions in Latin America are brighter than the prospects for social democratic policy reforms. Likewise, where social democratic parties do have electoral success, contradictions are highly likely to emerge between their electoral and economic coalitions, given the conflicting interests at stake.

Clearly, local variants of social democratic strategies do not promise a direct and immediate solution to poverty and inequality in Latin America. At best, they offer gradual, tentative, and partial solutions, falling far short of more radical demands for social transformation and popular empowerment. They are highly unlikely to transcend capitalism, although they might succeed in replacing the atomistic and exclusive capitalism of neoliberalism with a more integrative, 'organized' model of capitalist development. Their most obvious advantage is their potential viability, rooted in conscious efforts to forge compromise and build consensual solutions that will address popular needs without provoking elite hostility.

What must be asked, however, is whether institutionalized forms of class compromise are possible in a region with such egregious structural inequalities. In this sense, neoliberalism has raised high barriers indeed to any social democratic project in Latin America. By exacerbating social inequalities, it has narrowed the scope of common interests and enhanced zero-sum perspectives. It has also made popular sectors more socially heterogeneous, organizationally weak, and politically fragmented, thus undermining their capacity to balance the interests of capital and sustain a social democratic project. If social democracy is to succeed in Latin America, it will only do so with a political formula which reintegrates the social fabric and reconstructs a sense of national purpose that is capable of transcending the existing social divisions. In Europe, generalized affluence and the historical development of the welfare state have created levels of economic security which diminish the political centrality of traditional redistributive issues, enabling contemporary leftists to reconfigure the social democratic agenda. In Latin America, by contrast, class-based redistributive issues are likely to be a central axis of political conflicts and popular mobilization for the foreseeable future; the challenge for the left is to find programmatic means to address such issues and generate popular support within the reformist constraints of the new international economic order.

14 | Market-Oriented Development Strategies and State–Society Relations in New Democracies: Lessons from Contemporary Chile and Spain

Eric Hershberg[1]

1. Introduction: The Context of Political and Economic Transition

Across Latin America and other regions of the semi-periphery, political and economic transformations are disrupting traditional modes of political representation, redefining patterns of conflict, and creating opportunities for the articulation of societal interests that have long been excluded from the political arena. The trend away from state-centered strategies of economic development coincides with efforts to inaugurate and consolidate liberal democratic systems of government in countries that have experienced varying degrees of authoritarianism in recent decades. The changes under way are sufficiently complex as to resist simple normative evaluation, yet there can be no doubt that they entail substantial risks as well as potential opportunities for democratic representation. Neither the economic nor the political changes have been fully consolidated, and the tensions between the two processes ensure that the years to come will witness occasional interruptions in the momentum toward reform (Whitehead 1993; Nelson 1994). Nonetheless, the combination of market-oriented economic policies and electorally based political systems is likely to persist in more countries than not.

Although there is little consensus about the patterns of state–society linkages that are apt to emerge in the new context, the demise of what Cavarozzi (1992*b*)

[1] The author is grateful to a number of scholars for insightful comments on an earlier version of this chapter, and especially acknowledges feedback from Luiz Carlos Bresser Pereira, José Joaquín Brunner, Doug Chalmers, Scott Martin, Eduardo Silva, Bill Smith, and Laurence Whitehead. Of course, they do not necessarily share all of the conclusions of the chapter, and any remaining errors of omission or commission are the sole responsibility of the author.

has labeled the 'state-centered matrix' of Latin American politics is clearly more than a transitory phenomenon. Strategies of Import Substitution Industrialization (ISI) practiced widely in the region until the 1980s, and the political alliances behind the populist modes of representation which often accompanied ISI, corresponded to a particular phase of capitalist accumulation that was common in late-developing economies during the post-war period. This era is now behind us, as advances in communications and transport technologies have fostered the emergence of a globalized system of production and exchange, one result of which has been a diminishing capacity of individual states to ensure the survival of traditional industrial sectors and to control flows of capital (Gereffi and Korneciewicz 1993; Goodman and Pauly 1993). The fiscal crisis of the state that accompanied the debt crisis of the 1980s, as well as these more fundamental shifts in the global economy, preclude the isolation from international competition which is a *sine qua non* of a development model based on ongoing protection and subsidies for a wide range of domestically oriented industries.

These trends make it extremely difficult if not impossible to recreate today the constellation of domestic political interests that engendered the developmentalist coalitions of the past, whether populist or leftist in orientation (Vilas 1992; Carr and Ellner 1993). Military regimes across much of the region succeeded in their efforts to fragment alliances that had emerged during earlier democratic interludes to challenge the established order (Hagopian 1993; Schamis 1991). Deindustrialization has further weakened pivotal actors in the traditional redistributive coalition, particularly trade unions, which are in retreat across virtually all of Latin America, and the most dynamic segments of the bourgeoisie are oriented increasingly toward production for export rather than for domestic consumption (Silva 1993). Largely as a result, international competitiveness has supplanted the expansion of domestic purchasing power as the central aim of economic policy-makers, thus placing a premium on wage suppression and undermining the traditional basis for populist alliances in the region.[2]

These circumstances compel a fundamental rethinking on the part of actors across the political spectrum, but they pose a particularly daunting challenge for the left, which traditionally advocated state intervention to preserve popular sector incomes and to promote redistribution of wealth.[3] Previous democratic openings provided

[2] The inward orientation of populist economic policies provided simultaneous justification for domestic redistribution and for state support for domestic industry. Today, in contrast, the interests of capitalists and the state are based more unequivocally on wage suppression. In theory this need not be the case. Export-based strategies could aim to maximize competitiveness not by suppressing wages but by maximizing value added, a goal which might better be served through increasing skill levels of workers and investing in productivity-enhancing technologies. Mindful of the experience of some sectors in the East Asian NICs, Latin American commentators have acknowledged such an option. To date, however, wages continue to be perceived as the key variable to price competitiveness in most countries and economic sectors.
[3] The exhaustion (economic and thus political) of the developmentalist model is one of two factors that explain the degree of disarray that characterizes the contemporary Latin American left. The other is the profound crisis of socialism and the absence of any plausible revolutionary alternative to

occasions for populist and leftist governments to deploy the powers of the state to stimulate growth and to direct its fruits to their constituents. This option can no longer be pursued by traditional means, however, as evidenced by the failure of the heterodox economic policies pursued by several transitional governments in Latin America during the 1980s (Kaufman and Stallings 1991).

Of course, the demise of the state-centered matrix also opens political spaces that were closed off during previous democratic experiments. As Vilas (1992) has argued, Latin American populism was in many respects conservative, galvanizing mass support for statist economic policies that were calculated to favor domestic capital and privileged fractions of the urban working and middle sectors. Regardless of their intended effects—which varied widely from one case to another—the distributional impact of these alliances was often highly regressive, as the benefits of state largesse accrued to sectors that were politically important rather than to those in greatest need (Dornbusch and Edwards 1991; Sheehan 1987). Moreover, the top-down, corporatist character of interest representation and the hierarchical structure of political parties tended to be highly exclusionary, impeding autonomous participation and constraining the emergence of new popular sector actors even when populist leaders governed under democratic political regimes.

It is important nonetheless to recall that ISI frequently generated substantial improvements in conditions for urban working and middle classes, and that the more radical populist leaders occasionally sought to establish broader popular coalitions for redistributive reform (Collier and Collier 1991; Sheehan 1987). This record, and these aspirations, contrast sharply with the results of the exclusionary military dictatorships of the 1970s and 1980s, which failed to restore growth to previous levels and presided over a further skewing of income distribution. The record also contrasts with that of the newly established democratic regimes in the region. Indeed, while in a few countries the recent (albeit brief) experience with market-oriented economic development strategies has begun to stimulate economic growth, the benefits of renewed expansion continue to elude vast segments of the population. Despite their shortcomings, policies dismissed today as populist were arguably no more inequitable than those prevalent in the region today.[4]

Perhaps even more troubling, though by no means unrelated, is the accumulating evidence of disjuncture between the formally democratic character of many governments in Latin America and the continuing sociopolitical marginalization

capitalism. Castañeda (1993*b*) provides an insightful analysis of these issues in the context of the end of the Cold War.

[4] This is arguably the case even if one accepts the view, long prevalent on the right but increasingly held among scholarly analysts, that populism delivers only short-term rewards and inevitably inflicts long-term damage, the costs of which (esp. hyperinflation) are borne disproportionately by the very social sectors which were supposed to benefit from redistribution (see for example Dornbusch and Edwards 1991). It is ironic, of course, that 'populist' leaders across Latin America (e.g. Menem, Fujimori, Andrés Pérez) have been at the forefront of efforts to impose radical market-oriented reforms during the 1990s.

of vast segments of the population (Castañeda 1993*b*; O'Donnell 1993*c*). This trend is particularly striking in light of widespread expectations just a few years ago that the emergence and proliferation of 'new social movements' portended an unprecedented era of popular participation and grassroots democracy in the region (Escobar and Alvarez 1992). Growing activism around such issues as human rights, community empowerment, and the rights of ethnic minorities and women appeared particularly timely in a context in which 'capturing' the state was no longer the central goal of popular mobilizations. But notwithstanding their important role in undermining authoritarian regimes and in articulating aspirations for social justice, these movements have had little success in translating their demands into tangible reforms.

Nor have new democratic regimes in the region evolved mechanisms for ensuring more participatory approaches to policy-making. On the contrary, a number of recent case-studies note the degree to which even the most innovative public policy initiatives have tended to reflect a technocratic style of governance, in which any role reserved for grassroots actors is limited to the implementation of policies which they have no role in defining (Garretón 1994*b*). Oppenheim (1993: 234) succinctly expresses the consensus among observers of contemporary Latin American politics when she writes, with regard to Chile, that

. . . despite the hopes of grass roots groups, no new style of participator-grassroots politics has emerged (under representative democracy). Instead, the political culture of elite politics, which survived the dictatorship, characterizes the political dynamic. The Aylwin government's policies were decided behind closed doors, certainly not in consultation with the masses.

Perhaps as a result, the 'resurrection of civil society' (O'Donnell and Schmitter 1986) witnessed at the outset of democratic openings has tended to be a short-lived phenomenon, succeeded by an equally dramatic generalization of political apathy and distrust. Numerous scholars have acknowledged the significance of this phenomenon for societies in which the survival of democracy appears to be in jeopardy (Malloy and Conaghan 1994; Montesinos 1993). But while regime survival is clearly an important criterion for the success of a democratic transition, so too are concerns about the quality of democracy—measured not solely by the role played by political parties and other representative institutions but also by their capacity to articulate the perspectives of competing interests in the political arena. Once again, this is of particular relevance for analyses of left politics in post-transitional contexts; despite the significance of the left's 'revalorization' of liberal democracy as an end in itself (Barros 1986; Castañeda 1993*b*), the goals of equity and participation that have motivated progressive movements in the past remain central challenges for social and political activism today. The persistence of democratic regimes may not hinge on their fulfillment of these aspirations, but this does not diminish their salience as central objectives of any progressive agenda for democratization in Latin America and beyond.

Economic and political transitions have not done away with the crisis of representation which has long characterized Latin American polities. To the contrary, transitions have often coincided with a widening gap between popular sector demands and policy agendas pursued by state elites. It has become commonplace to note the irony of the recent trend, in which leaders are elected on the basis of promises not to impose neoliberal reforms, but enact precisely these measures once they come into office. Studies of the politics of market-oriented economic reform, particularly in its initial stages, suggest that a significant degree of autonomy from popular demands is often a central determinant of success (Kaufman and Haggard forthcoming; Nelson 1994; Maravall 1993). Yet the costs of such policy-making styles are not to be underestimated; the proliferation of what O'Donnell (1993c) has termed 'deconsolidated' democracies, in which *decretismo* supplants negotiation as the approach taken by the executive *vis-à-vis* both other political elites and the citizenry as a whole, suggests that analysis of emerging patterns of political representation is of more than academic significance (Whitehead 1992).

This is the context in which one must situate considerations of how political society and civil society might coalesce in support of a viable development model rooted in democratic deliberation and social inclusion. What successful experiences can be drawn upon to promote equitable distribution and to create spaces for broader political participation? How if at all can the preservation of these spaces be reconciled with the imperatives of continuing economic liberalization? Stated differently, is political alienation destined to remain a pervasive feature of the political landscape of contemporary Latin America?

2. Spain and Chile as Potential Models of Success

Observers searching for successful models for managing and consolidating political and economic transitions, and for maintaining popular support in the process, have devoted considerable attention to recent experiences in Spain and Chile. As Laurence Whitehead has noted (Whitehead 1994: 10) with reference to the comparative politics literature on democratic transition, 'Spain . . . quite frequently appears as the exemplary case compared to which others are implicitly measured, and in general found wanting.' Analyzing the experience of more than a decade of socialist government in that Southern European country, José María Maravall has argued forcefully that market-oriented economic reforms were successful because the state intervened to compensate losers and enacted measures to enhance social rights and to establish new mechanisms for popular participation (Maravall 1993). According to this view, during the 1980s and early 1990s Spain exemplified a 'social democratic approach' to economic reform. It is thus hardly surprising that observers of Latin American political economy commonly cite Spain as a model for successful reform in democracy, albeit one that for a multitude of reasons may be difficult to replicate in a Latin American context (Smith *et al.* 1994*a*: 6–7; Vergara 1994: 255; Przeworski 1991*b*).[5]

The Chilean development model also has attracted growing interest among observers of Latin American political economy, particularly now that the success-ful transition to democracy has confirmed that it is possible to maintain market-oriented reforms in an environment of political competition. A leading architect of the contemporary Chilean model, Alejandro Foxley, has labeled that country's project as an 'alternative development model for the 1990s', characterized by greater emphasis on distributive equity and on negotiation with social actors (Foxley 1992). A fellow Latin American 'technopol', Fernando Henrique Cardoso, recently asserted that the experience of Chile during the 1990s demonstrates the feasibil-ity of combining growth, equity, and democracy in the region. These sentiments are widely echoed in the scholarly literature (e.g. Montesinos 1993; for a skeptical view, see Smith *et al.* 1994*a*).

Numerous factors account for the breadth of enthusiasm toward these two experiences of transition. Not only have democratic regimes been consolidated in both countries, but freely elected leaders committed to market-oriented economic development have secured continued electoral support for their policies. Especially striking has been the ability of socialist parties with a noteworthy tradition of sup-port for statist intervention to spearhead efforts to enact and maintain market-oriented reforms in both countries. In Spain, the rewards have included successful integration in the European Community and significant economic growth from 1986 to 1992. In Chile, the policies of the democratic government have sustained annual growth rates averaging 7 per cent without upsetting macroeconomic stability, a particularly noteworthy achievement given the generally dismal per-formance of neighboring countries during the initial years of democracy.

Given these accomplishments, and their stark contrast with experiences in neighboring countries, it is only natural for aspiring reformers elsewhere in Latin America (and beyond) to seek ways of replicating the Spanish and Chilean experi-ences. And when supporters of the governments in both countries contend that these unusual achievements have coincided with successful strategies for enhan-cing social equity in a competitive market economy, and for empowering auto-nomous social actors to participate in the public sphere, replicating the Spanish and Chilean experiences quite naturally becomes synonymous with the achievement of success.

The remainder of this chapter considers patterns of political and economic change in contemporary Spain and Chile in light of the transformations alluded to above. We are particularly interested in exploring the impact of the transitions on distribution and on the capacity of popular sector participation to shape the

---

[5] Obviously, Spain emerged from the Franco dictatorship with less income inequality, sounder macroeconomic indicators, and a more promising location in the international political economy than has been the case for any of the new democracies in Latin America.

contours of state policy. The analysis pays especially close attention to the relationship between the state and organized labor. To be sure, unions neither exhaust nor mirror the universe of popular sector organizations in either country, but it is widely acknowledged that their influence in both Spain and Chile goes well beyond the ranks of their affiliates. More importantly, a focus on unions is appropriate given the concern of this volume with the prospects in Latin America for the emergence of one or another form of social democracy, a movement which, despite its diffuse and varied characteristics, has historically been built on the basis of alliances between the state, political parties, and organized labor.

The chapter aims to answer a number of critical questions. To what degree do the Spanish and Chilean experiences afford room for optimism concerning the prospects for popular sector representation in semi-peripheral economies under conditions of political competition? What factors account for the electoral success of democratic governments that have carried out painful adjustment policies in these countries? How central is the popular sector to the constellation of interests providing the essential political support for the emerging development model? By reviewing these two experiences in some detail, the chapter seeks to clarify the prospects for combining economic adjustment with the construction of political alliances that might facilitate the elaboration of enduring linkages between political and civil society and, ultimately, generate more equitable and democratic polities across the troubled landscape of Latin America.

3. Political and Economic Transition in Spain and Chile

Though separated by more than a decade, the political transitions in Spain and Chile both involved negotiated reform of the authoritarian order imposed by military dictatorships, rather than a sharp rupture with the institutional framework underlying the authoritarian order. This characteristic of the transitions can be understood both as cause and as consequence of the persistence of 'authoritarian enclaves' (Garretón 1992) for some years after the formal transfer of power to elected civilian leaders. Rooted in the failure of the political opposition in either country to overthrow or force the collapse of the dictatorships, the negotiated character of political change meant that many features of long-standing dictatorships would not be reversed in the short term. The continued power of powers that be, together with the central role played by relatively conservative sectors in initial democratic governments, strongly discouraged wholesale purges of the authoritarian state or dramatic changes in economic policy. Cognizant of these constraints, and determined not to repeat the costly miscalculations of previous democratic elites, leaders of the center-left endorsed gradual change so as to avoid the risk of authoritarian reversal. The imperative of consolidation thus took precedence over

Table 14.1. Distribution of income and poverty in Spain and Chile

	Lowest 20%	Highest 20%	Ratio	Per capita income ($US)
Chile	4.2	60.4	14.3	1,310
Spain	6.9	40.0	5.8	6,010

Source: Larrain (1991: 282), based on data from the World Bank Development Reports of 1989 (on income distribution) and 1987 (on per capita income).

satisfaction of long-suppressed popular demands for social and economic democratization, particularly for redistribution.[6]

SPAIN

Economic matters were by no means absent from the agenda of the transitional governments in either country, of course, though here the preoccupations were inevitably quite different. Whereas the debate in Spain centered around ensuring macroeconomic stability and creating conditions which might favor accession to the European Community, in Chile the fundamental challenge was to grapple with severe and widespread poverty. A comparison of income distribution in the two countries reminds us of the profound differences between stratification levels in relatively developed countries of Western Europe and the peripheral societies of Latin America (see Table 14.1).

In Spain, the patchwork center-right coalition assembled by Prime Minister Adolfo Suárez on the eve of the first democratic elections faced a stagflationist crisis more severe than that which affected much of the advanced capitalist world following the 1973 oil shock. By early 1978 inflation had soared to nearly 30 per cent, while unemployment and the public deficit threatened to career out of control. The economic problem was complicated by the explosion after Franco's death of long-suppressed popular demands for redistribution. Throughout 1976 and 1977, mobilizations by organized labor and other opposition groups generated a climate of considerable unrest, and a proliferation of strikes resulted in significant real increases in wages (Maravall 1982).

The government's response came in the form of the Pactos de Moncloa, the July 1978 tripartite accords between the state, employers, and the political parties with tacit support from their affiliated unions. The accords mandated wage

---

[6] Kaufman (1986) and Kaufman and Haggard (forthcoming) argue that regime consolidation is facilitated when the center-right plays a leading role during the transitional phase of democratization. The Spanish and Chilean cases lend powerful support to this hypothesis, but we suggest below that they also highlight the costs of this model. For a contrary view, see Maravall (1993: esp. 119–21).

restraint and a curtailment of strike activity in exchange for a vague commitment to enact fiscal reform and to further democratize the state apparatus. These measures prevented further deterioration of macroeconomic indicators and, more importantly, underscored the commitment of the left leadership to the success of Suárez's program of political reform and economic stability. This and subsequent wage accords enabled the transitional governments of the center-right to 'muddle through' the remaining four years of their tenure, but failed to address the structural obstacles to bringing the deficit-plagued Spanish economy into position to compete successfully in the global market. Nonetheless, this period witnessed significant improvements in distributive equity. Public expenditure rose from 24.9 per cent of GDP in 1975 to 38 per cent in 1982, largely as a result of higher spending for social security, health, and education, while real wages increased on average by 3 per cent a year during the same period (Maravall 1993: 89).

The weakness of center-right minority cabinets after 1979 ensured that implementation of more profound economic reforms would come about only following the appointment of a more powerful administration. This came about in October 1982 with the landslide victory of the Spanish Socialist Workers Party (PSOE) under the youthful leadership of Felipe González, following a campaign highlighted by Socialist promises of job creation, Spanish withdrawal from NATO, and a vague commitment to espouse 'change'.[7]

The ensuing years witnessed a profound transformation of the Spanish economy. The market-oriented reforms launched by the Socialists included substantial privatization of state enterprises, restructuring of uncompetitive industries, deregulation of a wide range of markets in goods and services, trade liberalization, and encouragement of foreign direct investment.[8] In contrast to the strategy of the French Socialists following Mitterrand's inauguration in 1981, González's government sought from the outset to contain inflationary pressures by limiting the growth of public spending and the public deficit and by adhering to strict monetary policies (Fernández-Ordoñez and Servén 1992; Maravall 1993).

The social impact of these transformations was painful and far-reaching. While the rate of inflation and the public deficit inched toward West European norms, unemployment skyrocketed to more than one in five workers, and the percentage of national income accruing to wage-earners declined notably during the first five years of Socialist rule. Nonetheless, emboldened by the clear electoral mandate of 1982, and by the depth of popular sentiment in favor of 'modernization', the

---

[7] I have argued elsewhere (Hershberg 1989) that the UCD period involved two overlapping but analytically distinguishable phases. During the first phase, from 1977 to 1979, the logic of political transition was prevalent, whereas during the second phase, from 1979 to 1982, a logic of consolidation shaped political interaction. The PSOE victory of 1982 signaled the consolidation of democracy and opened the way for broader reforms of the state and of the economy.

[8] Economic opening began during the dictatorship, as the Franco regime had gradually abandoned its predominantly statist approach to the economy following the rise to power of the Opus Dei technocrats and enactment of the 1958 Stabilization Plan. These tentative reforms paled in comparison to the radical measures imposed by the PSOE governments in the 1980s, however.

government succeeded in implementing much of its program despite initial reticence (and, later, militant opposition) from organized labor and other constituencies that had supplied much of the PSOE vote.[9]

The return of rapid economic growth from 1986 to 1992, a period characterized by some observers as one of 'supply-side socialism', led to renewed confidence in the future and a sense (particularly among financial circles at home and abroad) that yet another 'Spanish miracle' was under way. Foreign investment increased fivefold during this period, as investors sought to take advantage of opportunities afforded by Spanish accession to the EEC in 1992. The (often speculative) boom of the late 1980s generated significant improvements in both employment and wages, and new hires in the public sector surpassed 300,000 between 1985 and 1989, equaling the number of public sector jobs created over the entire previous decade (OECD 1993: 69). Not only did the percentage of GDP accruing to the public sector resume the upward trajectory that had been interrupted during the first phase of Socialist government, but this occurred without the increase in debt which had accompanied state expansion under the UCD.

Having strengthened the fiscal health of the public sector, the government was able to implement a number of measures designed to modernize the state and to expand welfare programs, which remained woefully underdeveloped by West European standards. These measures lent a degree of credibility to claims that the short-term costs of adjustment were to be offset through government compensation to losers and the institutionalization of social citizenship rights.[10] Indeed, in 1985 the welfare system was reformed in a manner that reflected the principle of universal entitlement, and the following year witnessed a reform of the national health care system and the introduction of universal coverage. The underfunded national pension system was reinforced as well during these years, and minimum benefits were increased to levels equivalent to the minimum wage.

These welfare state reforms constitute an important component of what one would anticipate from a social democratic development strategy, yet it would be a serious mistake to conclude that the Spanish experience embodied the sort of democratic class compromise envisioned in the literature on social democracy (Przeworski 1985). The reforms were in no way the outcome of negotiation involving collective actors linked to the popular sector, nor were they accompanied by efforts to evolve new mechanisms for political participation. On the contrary, the government's insistence on defining on its own terms the debate concerning economic reform, and on imposing its will from above, discouraged the emergence

---

[9] The government's stance should not have surprised as many observers as it did, as González himself had stated publicly in 1981 that 'the PSOE has to carry out a bourgeois revolution . . . since the bourgeoisie has yet to achieve one' (Gillespie 1989). As the Prime Minister put it on another occasion, the Spanish authorities had the courage to implement an IMF stabilization package before the IMF demanded it (Maravall 1993: 95).

[10] Maravall (1993) bases his defense of the Spanish Socialists' model on the claim that measures to strengthen the welfare state compensated sectors of the population which had been adversely affected by liberalization.

of an enduring dialogue between relatively autonomous popular sector organizations and the state. The result, especially in light of the hostilities between the government and labor, was to undermine prospects for the emergence and consolidation of a social democratic alternative in Spain.

This is crucial to understanding why the noteworthy achievements of the PSOE in expanding the distributive capacity of the state failed to restore popular sector enthusiasm for the government. Nowhere was this more evident than in the confrontation between the government and the principal labor unions, which were arguably the most credible representatives of the working class as a whole. By the end of the 1980s, relations between the Spanish state and labor had deteriorated to the point where leaders of the Socialist union, the UGT, joined with the Communist-based Workers' Commissions (CCOO) in denouncing the regressive character of government policy and implicitly endorsing the United Left (IU), an otherwise weak electoral coalition that had emerged from the remnants of the virtually defunct Spanish Communist Party (PCE). The popular appeal of the unions' position was confirmed by the success of the December 1988 General Strike, which the unions convened in an effort to force withdrawal of the most recent of a procession of government measures to deregulate labor markets, to enable employers to hire temporary workers and to subsidize low-wage private sector apprenticeships for unemployed youth.

The potential for serious tension between the government and organized labor was apparent soon after the Socialists took office. Although during the final three years of its tenure the UCD had negotiated with unions and employers to bring about an extensive if incomplete restructuring of inefficient industries, the centrists had not imposed restructuring in cases where consensus could not be reached among the affected parties. Moreover, as noted above, important steps were taken to redress the 'social debt' that had accumulated under the dictatorship.

In contrast, the Socialists were determined to proceed unilaterally if necessary with a more ambitious program to close down uncompetitive enterprises and to compensate affected workers and communities with temporary subsidies and extensive retraining programs. In the event, workers proved unwilling to negotiate issues the resolution of which had been determined in advance by state technocrats. Restructuring by decree produced 'more strikes, more hours lost to strikes, and more participants in strikes between 1983 and 1988 than in any other five-year period since the Civil War' (Wozniak 1991). This trend has continued unabated, as since 1988 Spain is understood to have experienced the highest level of labor conflict in all of Western Europe. That the PSOE dramatically increased funding for retraining does not negate the fact that it did so to cushion the impact of a restructuring imposed through coercion.

The government's autonomy from demands of its popular sector constituents transcended matters of economic policy, as evidenced in a particularly striking way by the reversal of the Socialist Party's long-standing opposition to continued Spanish membership in NATO. Neutralist and anti-militarist sentiment was deeply rooted in Spanish public opinion, particularly on the left, and González's pledge to hold a prompt referendum to determine Spain's relationship to the Atlantic alliance was among the more popular planks of the PSOE campaign platform. Upon taking office, however, the government shifted its position strongly in favor of continued Spanish participation in NATO. Unable to avoid a referendum altogether, it resorted first to delay and then, to the consternation of a broad-based popular movement that had formed to press for a 'no' vote, to manipulation of the question to be placed before the electorate. With opinion polls predicting majority support for Spanish exit from the alliance, González tipped the referendum in the government's favor by suggesting on the eve of the balloting that he would resign and force a political crisis if his position did not prevail.

A similar pattern occurred repeatedly throughout the 1980s and has persisted into the early 1990s, as the government has managed to impose highly controversial reforms across a number of policy areas in spite of resistance from organized sectors of civil society.[11] In each instance, the government's position was strengthened by the absence of plausible alternatives to the Socialists in the political party system. By 1981, Suárez's center-right alliance had splintered beyond repair; the rightist Popular Alliance (AP) led by Manuel Fraga, a former minister under Franco, remained unpalatable to all but around 30 per cent of the electorate during the first half of the decade, and its credibility increased only marginally under a new generation of conservative leaders; and the Eurocommunist left, undermined by internal disputes and by its failure to develop a coherent vision for the role of the left in a consolidated democracy, could at most count on 10 per cent of the vote (Hershberg 1991a, 1991b). At the same time, regionally based parties steadily increased their share of the vote in national elections, thereby further limiting prospects for alternatives to the Socialists to generate governing majorities. This fragmented system of parties lent credibility to Socialist claims that only they could fill a serious vacuum in the political system. While the PSOE never regained all of the 10 million votes it garnered in 1982, the absence of credible alternatives was to remain a key trump card for the PSOE throughout the 1980s and early 1990s, as an electoral system that rewarded large parties with a disproportionate number of seats in the Cortes afforded González's party repeated, if diminishing, majorities following parliamentary elections in 1986 and 1989, and a workable plurality following balloting in 1993.

As the sole political party with a plausible capacity to govern, the PSOE leadership had little incentive to seek active support from organized actors in the popular sector or to promote linkages between civil society and the state. Indeed, ever since the 1979 Extraordinary Party Congress, in which González had engineered a shift in the PSOE platform in the direction of social democracy, the leadership

---

[11] Examples include the peace movement, compulsory military service, and conscientious objection; students and the reform of secondary and higher education; peasant movements and agrarian policies, particularly over the absence of agrarian reform; human rights groups and 'anti-terrorist' legislation, etc.

had been more concerned with ensuring governability than with increasing popular participation. Party membership averaged little more than 100,000 people throughout the 1980s, and one leading authority on contemporary Spanish politics has estimated that fully one-third of these individuals held government posts (Gunther 1986).[12] Although public opinion data showed that the desire for a redistribution of wealth and enhanced political participation were the two major factors contributing to electoral support for the Spanish left (Maravall 1982), the PSOE appealed to voters on the basis of González's charisma and its commitment to 'change' rather than through appeals to specific programmatic objectives. In effect, the PSOE has played the role that Kircheimer (1966) ascribed to the catch-all party, which, 'via its electoral role . . . produces that limited amount of popular participation and integration required from the popular masses for the functioning of official political institutions'. These trends were unlikely to be reversed by the efforts of dissidents within the PSOE, as internal party democracy had diminished since the 1979 Party Congress, during which the pro-González faction had imposed rules that excluded minority factions from decision-making posts (Gillespie 1989).

Widespread disillusion with government performance, impatience with rampant corruption, and the emergence of a new generation of conservative politicians at the helm of the AP nearly produced a transfer of power following parliamentary elections in 1993. Continued distrust of the right and González's formidable personal appeal enabled the PSOE to maintain its plurality, however, and against virtually all predictions by the pundits, to again form a government without having to enter into formal coalition with other parties.

Despite González's acknowledgments both during and after the campaign that public confidence in the government had fallen dramatically and that the authorities had failed to maintain a constructive dialogue between the state and social agents, the past fifteen months have witnessed a further deterioration in the political as well as the economic climate in Spain. The recession sweeping Western Europe has taken an especially savage toll on the Spanish economy since 1992. Unemployment, which had fallen to around 15 per cent of the work-force by the beginning of the 1990s, soared once again to more than 24 per cent during the first quarter of 1994 (*The Economist* 1994). Despite modest improvement during the summer, prospects for overcoming the ongoing crisis of employment seem exceedingly remote. The resulting hardships have been exacerbated by government cutbacks in social spending, and less than two-thirds of the jobless continue to receive state subsidies.

The climate of pervasive distrust between the government and labor was reflected in the unions' decision to break off talks designed to yield a tripartite social pact to respond to the crisis and to organize instead a January 1994 nationwide strike

---

[12] Alfonso Guerra, González's erstwhile second in command and the leading architect of the PSOE's rise to hegemony, once quipped that he would gladly trade 10,000 card-carrying party members for ten minutes of television advertising.

against González's economic policies. Despite surveys showing public opinion to be divided roughly equally concerning the strike, the Madrid daily *El País* reported that the draconian labor market reform drafted by the government received the support of 90 per cent of the Cortes. Implementation of the measures in the context of virulent opposition from the entire labor movement and from activists across a wide range of popular organizations, testifies to the distance that continues to separate popular sector organizations and the state following more than a decade of Socialist rule. Indeed, the successful enactment of market-oriented economic reforms has undermined further the relative power of labor and other popular sector actors which in the past constituted the core constituency of the center-left in Spain and elsewhere.

CHILE

In crucial respects the democratic government in Chile inherited a more promising economic environment upon taking office in early 1990 than that which confronted its Spanish counterparts a dozen years earlier. The center-left coalition headed by President Patricio Aylwin, a Christian Democrat, inherited macroeconomic indicators that were the envy of Latin America. Inflation was modest by regional standards, and GDP growth had averaged nearly 7 per cent during the final two years of the dictatorship. Moreover, the radical liberalization of trade and labor markets, opening to foreign investment, and wholesale privatization had been carried out already by the military government. This authoritarian restructuring had exacted a dreadful toll on the popular sector, but it had improved significantly Chile's international competitiveness and paved the way for continued export-led expansion in the 1990s.

Throughout the 1989 campaign and in its actions upon taking office the Aylwin government sought to reassure economic actors at home and abroad of its commitment to preserving the basic contours of the neoliberal development model inherited from the dictatorship. In part this reflected the enduring influence of key elements of the authoritarian coalition, including the military, and constraints resulting from the authoritarian 1980 Constitution, which provided (among other things) for the appointment by Pinochet of a third of the Senate. It stemmed as well from recognition that the dictatorship had institutionalized an economic order in which control over the productive apparatus was wielded by a private sector that was willing and able to undermine democracy if it appeared to challenge their interests (Silva 1992). It was not surprising that many Chileans believed that prospects for regime consolidation hinged on the new administration's economic policy, for as Montesinos (1993) has noted, 'the ideological polarization of the last decades in Chile had centered around property rights, the economic role of the state, and the structure of economic power'. Thus, government moderation was facilitated by the willingness of most of the major labor unions and other popular sector organizations to accept modest gains in order to ensure the survival of the new regime.[13]

Liberalized trade, disciplined fiscal and monetary policies, and a continued preoccupation with competitiveness thus remained the keystones of government economic policy. But if on the surface the economic agenda advanced by the Concertación during the 1989 campaign differed little from that of Pinochet's candidate, former Finance Minister Hernan Buchi, the new government placed greater emphasis on social equity and on the improvement of labor relations. These concerns reflected overwhelming public support for efforts to repay the 'social debt', manifested by the impoverished condition of the nearly 40 per cent of the population which had shouldered the costs of adjustment yet remained marginalized from the fruits of the recent economic expansion.

Considerable obstacles stood in the way of even modest reforms, however. In the first place, Pinochet himself remained as Commander in Chief of the Armed Forces, and in keeping with the 1980 Constitution a third of the seats in the Senate were reserved for officials designated by the old regime.[14] Combined with an electoral system biased in favor of rightist parties, this meant that the Concertación would often be unable to garner the two-thirds majority needed to amend authoritarian features of the 1980 Constitution. As a result, allies of the dictatorship retained disproportionate influence in the judicial as well as the legislative branches of government.

In addition, the new government inherited a state apparatus that had been transformed during the previous two decades in ways that limited severely the prospects for state intervention to promote equity and to provide broader avenues for popular participation. A series of measures taken by the dictatorship on the eve of the transition removed crucial areas of public policy from the control of elected leaders (Nef 1992). For example, Pinochet's government shifted responsibility for financing and implementing policy across several domains from the central government to the much weaker regions, and insulated the central bank from democratic pressures. State capacity had declined in other respects as well. A highly regressive tax code generated less revenue than at the close of the previous democratic period. Hundreds of firms had been privatized, depriving the state of another potentially key source of revenue. And whereas from 1964 to 1973 public employment had increased by almost 6 per cent annually, it had declined at an equal rate during the first decade of military rule and had not picked up significantly during the late 1980s. Whereas in 1975 there were 26 public employees for every 1,000 inhabitants, the ratio stood at 10 per thousand by 1989 (Garretón and

---

[13] Although the Concertación includes the Socialists, in many other respects it is analogous to the UCD governments in Spain during the late 1970s. Both centrist governments benefited from the commitment of popular sector leaders not to push for reforms that could imperil conservative support for maintaining the new order.

[14] As one senior Chilean official reports having been told by the Spanish king, 'the difference between your transition and ours is that Pinochet did not die' (author interview, 1991).

Espinoza 1992). These figures are suggestive of the degree to which the dictatorship had been successful in its efforts to deprive future governments of mechanisms for allocating resources to satisfy social demands.[15] Taken together, these factors inevitably constrained government efforts to resolve many of the social needs that had accumulated over time. However, as we shall argue below, the depth of the reforms was also limited by the unwillingness of the government itself to depart from the economic orthodoxy inherited from the previous regime.

Immediately upon taking office in 1989 the Aylwin administration sought a modest tax increase to make additional resources available for targeted social spending, and a reform of the labor code that would preserve flexibility in the labor market while restoring basic rights that had been denied workers during the dictatorship. The need to negotiate with the right-wing parties in the Congress in order to pass legislation in these areas limited the scope of reform, particularly with regard to taxation. The outcome of that debate yielded an increase in the levy on corporate profits from 10 per cent to 15 per cent and a hike in the value-added tax, from 16 per cent to 18 per cent. As a condition for securing legislative passage of the increases, the resulting $600 million in new revenues, equivalent to 2 per cent of GNP, was restricted to support for poverty alleviation programs (Muñoz and Celedón 1993).

The impact of these measures was felt immediately. The minimum wage paid to more than half a million Chilean workers rose by 44 per cent in 1990 and 27 per cent in 1991, and had increased 24 per cent in real terms by the end of 1992. Similarly, there was a real increase of 61 per cent in aid to low-income families, and spending on health, education, and housing rose by 7, 23, and 39 per cent, respectively over initial projections. These government accomplishments were supplemented by policies designed to engage the private sector in programs to train 100,000 unemployed young people and to provide training and credit to enable the poor to establish small enterprises (Muñoz and Celedón 1993). Combined with unexpectedly robust economic growth and low inflation, a noteworthy influx of foreign capital, and high levels of domestic private investment, these measures helped to produce a significant decline in the number of Chilean families living in extreme poverty (*New York Times*, 4 Apr. 1993).

Despite these impressive gains, more than 10 per cent of workers in Santiago were still earning less than the minimum wage in 1991. Real minimum wages in that year remained 29 per cent lower than they had been in 1978 and 6 per cent lower than in 1974 (Epstein 1993). And while social spending rose 20 per cent from 1989 to 1991, it was still only 7 per cent higher than it had been in 1985 (ibid.,

---

[15] Declining levels of state employment may in some instances signal more efficient and less expensive delivery of services, and in effect may enable the state to do more with fewer resources. I am grateful to José Joaquín Brunner (personal communication, June 1994) for reminding me of the complexities of this particular indicator. Halpern and Bousquet (1992: 106) provide public opinion data indicating that a majority of Chileans do not believe that there is an excess of public employment, and that this sentiment is particularly broad among the working and middle classes.

citing MIDEPLAN, 1992). It is striking to note that, despite the dramatic growth of the past several years, per capita social spending has yet to regain 1970 levels, and at least a third of the population continues to suffer levels of poverty characterized by international agencies as 'extreme'.

Perhaps more significantly, the new government had in no way challenged what Vergara (1994) has aptly labeled the 'dualistic' nature of welfare state programs imposed during the Pinochet period. In practical terms, this meant that access to health, education, pensions, and other programs associated with the modern welfare state is determined by the actions of the individual citizen in the market, rather than through membership in the political community. Those with sufficient resources can purchase services of the highest quality through the private sector, leaving the poor and middle sectors to depend on underfunded public services (Vergara 1994). Benefits provided directly by the state, if they are provided at all, are allocated according to a logic of charity rather than of entitlement.

The reliance on targeted benefits, as opposed to universal entitlements, underscores the degree to which the emerging political-economic framework is 'social liberal' rather than 'social democratic' in nature. Whereas a social liberal model deploys public subsidies to provide a temporary safety net for individuals disadvantaged by the market, or to increase the capacity of individuals to become inserted more favorably in market processes, a social democratic approach conceives of such benefits as entitlements due to all citizens. The social democratic welfare state seeks to ensure equity of conditions for all citizens, regardless of their position *vis-à-vis* the market. Moreover, social democratic experiences in Europe suggest that, when the components of universal entitlements reflect the outcome of bargaining among organized socioeconomic actors, the state has the capacity to reinforce the importance of organized labor as a representative actor (Esping-Andersen 1990).

Labor reform was a second key aspect of the government's agenda to promote equity and to overcome the dictatorship's legacy of political exclusion of the popular sector. The government sought to elicit consensus from unions and employers around a framework that would enable economic actors to negotiate on an equal footing without intervention by the authorities. While the administration sought to overcome the repressive features of the previous legislation, which curtailed the rights of workers to organize and to bargain collectively, it was equally determined to maintain employer flexibility in the hiring and firing of workers and to prevent a revival of the 'confrontational, ideologically driven, and rigidifying' patterns of labor mobilization that were said to have characterized earlier democratic periods (Muñoz and Celedón 1993).

Unable to secure agreement from the key Concertación-allied labor federation, the CUT, or from the employers' associations, the government turned over to the Congress the task of devising specific features to implement a broad framework accord (Acuerdo Marco) signed in April 1990 by the CUT, the government, and the employers. This statement of principles had advocated the persistence of an open economy, and stressed the importance of investments in human capital and the desirability of cooperative rather than confrontational labor relations. It offered few details, however, particularly on how improvements in health, education, and welfare were to be achieved (Epstein 1993).[16]

Negotiations concerning the labor reform failed to achieve many of the basic objectives of the union movement. While workers can no longer be dismissed without cause and the right of unions to attempt to negotiate on a sectoral basis is now acknowledged, business retains enormous flexibility in dismissing redundant workers and is not obligated to bargain collectively beyond the plant level. This outcome is attributable only in part to the obstacles imposed by the substantial bloc of conservative votes in the Congress. Indeed, it was the government itself that insisted on allowing many key issues to be decided solely on the basis of negotiations between labor and employers, basing its position on the rather disingenuous contention that a democratic system of labor relations was one in which autonomous actors reached accords without formal intervention by the state on behalf of one or the other party. Thus, government influence on the private sector depends primarily on persuasion, as mechanisms to compel equitable negotiations are absent.[17]

This extension of the logic of the market to industrial relations is rejected by a significant portion of the labor movement, particularly that which is not affiliated with the government-linked CUT (Ruíz-Tagle 1993a). The long-term consequences of this tension between the government and important sectors of the labor movement remain unclear. However, the 47 per cent rise in union membership between 1987 and 1991, from 10.5 to 15.4 per cent of the employed population, reflects a pattern that is rare if not unprecedented in contemporary Latin America.[18] Moreover, considerable evidence from public opinion polls suggests that unions enjoy far greater credibility within the popular sector than would be apparent from the percentage of the working population which actually belongs to unions (Angell 1991). A steady increase over the past two years in strike activity, across a wide range of economic sectors, suggests that the prospects for labor opposition's becoming more vocal should not be underestimated. Open opposition to the CUT leadership during the official May Day rally in 1994, and the union's subsequent decision to withdraw from negotiations with the government designed to reach an accord on the minimum wage, provide further indications that rank-and-file impatience is taking a toll on the Concertación's relations with labor.

Whatever tensions may exist have not been reflected in the results of local and national elections held since the onset of the transition. The December 1993 elections for President and Congress awarded more than 55 per cent of the vote

[16] A similar lack of specificity rendered the Moncloa Pacts ineffective in this regard.
[17] That business has consistently rejected efforts to conduct negotiations beyond the plant level indicates the consequences of this situation (Epstein 1993; Garretón and Espinoza 1992).
[18] It appears, however, that since 1991 the percentages seem to have remained steady. I am grateful to Rafael Agacina for sharing current data that indicate these trends.

to the Concertación candidate, Eduardo Frei, and produced impressive results for parties in the governing coalition.[19] Such overwhelming electoral support for an incumbent government has been absent virtually everywhere in Latin America in recent years, though there is also no precedent in the region for a transitional regime managing to move steadily toward consolidation while presiding over annual growth rates averaging over 7 per cent.[20]

Nonetheless, confidence in the sustainability of the government's honeymoon with the electorate should be tempered by the possibility that, like in Spain throughout the 1980s, the party system offers no obvious alternative to which dissatisfied voters could turn to express impatience with the pace of reform. Differences within the Concertación itself have been suppressed by the desire of the leaders of each of its constituent elements not to be seen as undermining the unity of the coalition that has smoothly guided the Chilean polity through the difficult process of transition.[21] This has reinforced perceptions of stability, which is undoubtedly a central concern of a popular sector electorate preoccupied above all with avoiding a return to military rule, but it has not stimulated debate about alternative policy options. The circumscribed character of the political debate is reflected inadvertently by the words of Enrique Correa, a Socialist Party leader and prominent government minister who, commenting on misgivings about the current economic model, asserts that 'there is much criticism of pragmatism and realism, but the truth is that the only thing opposed to realism is madness' (Montesinos 1993).

Though spokespersons for the Concertación commonly assert that their reliance on the market reflects a consensus in Chilean society as well as among the political class, there is considerable reason to treat these assertions with skepticism. As Garretón and Espinoza note (1992), 'various recent public opinion polls demonstrate the persistence of a basically statist climate, despite propaganda to the contrary by the military regime and neoliberal policies'. Echoing this view, Halpern and Bousquet (1992: 114) conclude on the basis of numerous opinion polls that '[w]hereas the State is undergoing profound crisis across much of the world, a crisis that is reinforced by a public discourse that delegitimizes its action . . . Chilean public opinion shows signs of not following in that direction.' Indeed, surveys have found that a majority of Chileans opposed the further privatizations advocated

---

[19] Frei's Christian Democrats, the Socialists, and the Party for Democracy (PPD) all performed well in the elections. The percentage of the vote received by groups to the left of the Concertación remained in single digits.

[20] It remains too early to tell whether Argentina may provide a similar example following elections scheduled for the spring of 1995. In Mexico an incumbent party was returned to power (once again) at elections held in August 1994, after presiding over an ambitious project of market-oriented restructuring. Yet most observers would agree that a democratic transition has yet to occur in that country, which differs from Chile as well, in that growth rates have remained sluggish.

[21] The ability of the coalition to manage potential conflicts was especially apparent in its solution to the debate between Socialists and Christian Democrats over who should replace Aylwin as the candidate for President in the most recent elections.

in recent years by Finance Minister Foxley, and instead favored a return of the state to spheres of the economy from which it had been removed during the dictatorship (Halpern and Bousquet 1992).[22] Similarly, surveys indicating strong public sentiment in support of free trade and economic integration with the United States also reveal public support for protection of domestic industries and the jobs associated with them (Halpern and Bousquet 1991).

That these ambivalent sentiments are particularly widespread among low-income Chileans does not augur well for the capacity of governing parties to articulate demands emanating from the popular sector. Equally discouraging has been the weakening and in some instances the disappearance from the public sphere of key actors in the opposition to the military regime. This development can be interpreted as a signal of widespread satisfaction, but a more plausible explanation is that it reflects disillusion and withdrawal from politics of activists who were at the forefront of efforts to bring about democracy (Garretón and Espinoza 1992). Indeed, while the government's commitment to preserving harmonious relations with economic elites has facilitated regime consolidation, even the most sympathetic analysts acknowledge that it has also 'impeded the realization of social objectives when these involve elements of conflict that hinder consensus' (Muñoz and Celedón 1993). This has been evident not only in the debates concerning fiscal policy and labor reform, but also in tensions over the refusal of the democratic government to challenge the market-oriented policies in health, education, and housing inherited from the Pinochet era.[23]

It is surely premature to assess how deep these apparent disjunctures may be or to predict whether they are likely to persist or grow deeper over time. It is also too early to tell with any certainty whether there may be space within the existing configuration of parties and party coalitions for the representation of demands by popular sector actors that remain disadvantaged despite efforts to place a more human face on the neoliberal economic model. Several observers have noted that Chilean socialists confront a particularly difficult dilemma in this regard. Having cast their lot with the Concertación, they are destined to share equal responsibility for the shortcomings of the development model as well as for its successes. Moreover, in contrast to the situation that existed in Spain a dozen years ago, the chances of the Socialists stepping in to fill a vacuum in the center of the Chilean political spectrum are exceedingly remote, as the Christian Democrats remain the senior partner in the Concertación and benefit from a tradition of partisan identification that predates the onset of military rule (Santesmases 1988).

The increasingly blurred character of distinctions between 'renovated' Chilean socialism and its Christian Democratic coalition partners is underscored by the

[22] Halpern and Bousquet report (1992: 107–8) that 52.6 per cent of respondents across all social classes opposed further privatization of state industries. Among the lower and middle classes the percentage was higher, 55.7 per cent and 52.9 per cent, respectively.

[23] I am referring here to the consequences of welfare state mechanisms predicated on extreme need rather than on entitlement by virtue of citizenship.

words of Enrique Correa, who describes a left suited to the contemporary situation as one that is

... moderate, democratic, that trusts in the rules of the market ... that does not believe any longer in statism and centralism, that believes in a state more and more regulatory and in an economy more and more private ..., and who anticipates ... competition between Christian Democrats and Socialists to determine who, within the coalition, embodies modernity with greater strength and vigor. (Montesinos 1993)

4. Democracy and the Market in Spain and Chile: A New Social Compact?

A review of the Spanish and Chilean experiences of political and economic transition suggests noteworthy parallels between the two cases. To be sure, in Spain the most painful phase of economic restructuring took place under the PSOE, once the political order had already largely been consolidated, while in Chile the Concertación inherited an economy that had fully incorporated market mechanisms but faced the challenge of re-establishing democracy despite deeply entrenched authoritarian enclaves operating in a constitutional framework designed by the dictatorship.[24] Nevertheless, the similarities are significant: governments in both countries confronted the inevitable tension between a commitment on the one hand to maintain market-oriented economic policies and, on the other hand, a need to address demands for distribution and for strengthening mechanisms for popular participation.

The Spanish and Chilean experiences demonstrate clearly that it is possible to pursue market-oriented economic policies and, indeed, to successfully undertake or maintain economic restructuring, without jeopardizing the consolidation of democratic rule. Moreover, they show that, contrary to long-standing conventional wisdom, political parties associated with simultaneous processes of political and economic liberalization can be re-elected. But what more can be made of the experiences of these two countries, particularly in light of the questions posed at the outset of this chapter?

Optimistic interpretations of the two experiences hold that the most painful period of adjustment has passed and that democratic governments have enhanced their legitimacy by cushioning the effects of market processes on the most vulnerable sectors of society (Muñoz and Celedón 1993; Maravall 1993). Evidence

---

[24] A key difference, but one that is beyond the scope of this relatively brief paper, concerns the international context in which the two countries underwent reforms (Stallings 1994). Both the political and economic transitions in Spain were assisted enormously by the country's proximity to Western Europe and by the tangible assistance provided by the EEC to both processes of reform. In contrast, Chile was surrounded by crisis-ridden economies with fragile democracies, and could not expect the United States to offer assistance analogous to that provided to Spain.

for this proposition is provided by the combination of strong economic growth and anti-poverty programs in Chile, by the expansion of state entitlements and the protracted boom of the late 1980s and early 1990s in Spain, and by the repeated electoral successes of both the Concertación and the PSOE. According to this optimistic reading, having established the basis for sustained growth and having reinforced democratic institutions, distributive concerns can perhaps take on greater emphasis in the future, as policy-makers build on their achievements and become more adept at enacting regulations to attenuate adverse market outcomes without undermining investor confidence.[25]

Thus, as noted earlier in this chapter, it has been widely suggested both that the Spanish experience offers a model to which reformers across Latin America might wish to turn, and that the Chilean transition raises the possibility for the emergence of a new, democratic consensus on economic matters in the region. Encompassing party-affiliated technocrats and the rank-and-file constituencies of center and left political parties, the apparent success of the Concertación is said to open the potential for class compromises akin to those of the Keynesian accord of post-war Western Europe (Montesinos 1993).

In contrast, Epstein (1993) analyzes the nature of negotiations between the state and social actors in contemporary Chile and concludes that notions of concertation and of shared interests constitute no more than a 'foundational myth' designed to legitimize the new political order. In his words,

[L]egitimizing myths . . . [facilitate] the political acceptance of a distribution of economic privilege only marginally different from what existed with the previous dictatorship, but without the need for the open use of force now incompatible with democracy.

According to this view, elections between competing elites who share a consensus on the desirability of the development model imposed by the military are little more than a mechanism for the legitimation of continuing structural inequalities.[26]

In a rather more tentative vein, Silva (1993) reminds us that the shift from ISI to internationally oriented economic policies in Latin America reflected the interests of the social coalitions to which state elites—democratic or authoritarian—turned for support. That this coalition has not changed dramatically with political reform is underscored by the priority elected policy-makers have assigned to ensuring continuing support from these dynamic sectors of Chilean business. Of course, governments have little alternative but to satisfy these groups. As Przeworski has shown (1985), in market-oriented economies in which state capacity to influence investment is limited to gentle persuasion and the structuring of economic

[25] This would be consistent with the optimistic scenario that was at least implicit in much of the regime transitions literature of the 1980s: if actors focus first on ensuring the survival of democracy, even at the risk of postponing resolution of other grievances, it could be hoped that the resulting consolidated democracy could eventually address social and economic demands.

[26] A similar if not even more unequivocally critical view is outlined in considerable detail in Petras and Leiva (1994).

incentives, severe rifts between the state and the private sector can have devastating consequences. Stated more bluntly, capitalist economy governments, elected or otherwise, enjoy limited capacity to satisfy popular sector demands when these conflict sharply with the perceived interests of private economic elites.

This is more true than ever in the contemporary era, when inward-oriented development models of the past no longer appear to be feasible. While it is not inconceivable that exchanges between popular movements and their political representatives could generate consensus around state policies to confront this dilemma, our analysis of experiences in Chile and Spain points to innumerable factors that suggest that this has not yet occurred. Elites advocating strict adherence to market-oriented policies have won elections in which no credible alternatives were available. Nor has the room for debate and for the expression of dissenting views been sufficiently broad within the relevant political parties to permit any definitive conclusions about the 'fit' between rank-and-file demands and state policies. And when the subject of negotiation has involved policies considered central to the logic of market-oriented reform, particularly the deregulation of labor markets, the question at hand has only been whether the policy will be portrayed as a product of consensual negotiations or acknowledged as the outcome of technocratic decree.

It is fully understandable that 'pragmatic' policy-makers have found themselves ('are left'?) with no alternative but to impose their will on recalcitrant sectors of society when opposition can only be interpreted as evidence of 'madness', rather than as an expression of legitimate aspirations or fears. Nonetheless, that this climate continues to characterize much of the interaction between state and society following successful transition suggests that the task of forging representative polities under contemporary conditions poses unprecedented challenges and difficulties for the left, in Latin America and beyond.

15 | Putting Conservatism to Good Use? Long Crisis and Vetoed Alternatives in Uruguay

Fernando Filgueira and Jorge Papadópulos[1]

Introduction

Looking back on the last two decades of neoliberal reform in the Southern Cone of Latin America, Uruguay appears as a country highly resistant to change. While Chile experienced a veritable market revolution during the Pinochet dictatorship, and Argentina continues in this direction under the Menem administration, Uruguay appears to preserve many of the characteristics that once earned it the title of Latin America's first 'welfare state' (Pendle 1952).

Yet if the welfare state label was already somewhat exaggerated during the 1950s, today it is clearly unrealistic. The quality of services provided by the Uruguayan welfare state, the real value of pensions, and other monetary benefits have shown marked signs of deterioration over the last four decades. Similarly, the role of the state as an employer, a provider of wages, goods, and services, and a market regulator has been diminished and attacked.

Nevertheless, these transformations have been gradual and have affected the middle and working classes differently from transformations in countries where the neoliberal model has taken hold. The deterioration in the quality of life has generally followed a relatively egalitarian pattern (see Appendix, Tables 15.2 and 15.3) and has not segregated sectors that eke out minimal living standards from those completely excluded from the growth model and its benefits (see Appendix, Table 15.1). Critical to this outcome has been the political logic guiding resource allocation, which has endured despite attempts to replace it with market principles.

Beginning with the onset of the military dictatorship, noteworthy changes in matters of finance and trade have taken place. Among these are the opening of the economy and the deregulation of financial markets. Yet these transformations have

[1] Research support for this chapter was provided to Fernando Filgueira by the Social Science Research Council and to Jorge Papadópulos by the Inter-American Foundation. The editors would like to thank Alexandra Cordero and Eric Hershberg for their translation of this chapter.

not been accompanied by the erosion of social citizenship, the reduction of the role of the state in the production of goods and services, and diminished protection of the middle-class and popular sectors.

Uruguay has experienced the dismantling of the public sector and the growing predominance of the market on the discursive level as well as in certain concrete measures. But these transformations have been weak, uneven, and tenuous. Moreover, they have been defeated politically in critical moments and at key points in the policy-making process. Thus, Uruguay has not replaced its integrated socio-political order with a segmented one, typical of the so-called 'dual' societies.[2]

The persistence of elements peculiar to the developmentalist model, which are evident in the state, public policy, and the social structure, is even more surprising if we observe the situation elsewhere in the region. As noted above, neoliberal models have been predominant in the Southern Cone. The cases of Mexico, Peru, Bolivia, and Venezuela allow us to extend this characterization to much of the rest of Latin America. Most academics explain this homogeneity by contending that the end of the 1980s witnessed the last of the ECLA-influenced models of developmentalist growth. For some, neoliberal processes of stabilization and structural adjustment are a more or less inevitable outcome of restructuring induced by transformations in the world market and by the conditionalities imposed by international financial institutions (Stallings 1992; Brock *et al.* 1989). For others, the problem is more nuanced. The timing, coherence, and degree of change depend on factors that cannot be reduced to economic or international aspects (Nelson 1990). Few see any possibility that these models might not be implemented. According to these interpretations, the demise of the developmentalist state and the international context limit these countries' choices in public policy matters.

Scientific enquiries generally posit questions about why certain things happen. In certain cases, a counterfactual question such as the one that inspires this chapter is justified. Thus, this chapter examines the reasons why *certain things did not occur*. In particular, we offer a tentative explanation of Uruguay's capacity to resist the adoption of neoliberal policies and a neoliberal model of internal regulation. This enquiry offers bases for comparative analyses which can help to clarify processes of transformation across the region.

Uruguay possesses attributes that make it an ideal test case. The independent variable is the same in Uruguay as in the rest of the countries of the region: the country essentially exhausted its ECLA model of development towards the end of the 1970s. Similarly, like other countries in the region, Uruguay has witnessed internationalization of its economy and has been exposed to the incremental penalties that this new context levies on countries with high inflation, fiscal deficits, and other signs of irrational economies. Finally, it has experienced modifications in its

---

[2] The idea of segmented or dual societies has been used extensively. Vilmar Faria has taken enormous poetic licence in using an expression in reference to Brazil: Belíndia. With that he attempts to express that in the country, the Belgian and Indian realities coexist.

relations with creditors and multilateral agencies: conditionality, tightened credit, and interest rates (Kaimowitz 1992).

Uruguay, however, does not share the dependent variable with the rest of the region: Uruguay has had no effective process of neoliberal transformation. Thus, an explanatory model based on the exhaustion of the previous model, external shocks, and conditionalities, is insufficient.

A wide range of scholars from various perspectives (Haggard and Kaufman 1992; Bresser Pereira *et al.* 1993; Kahler 1992) also have made this observation. We argue, however, that their analyses fail to seek explanations in the political sphere. These scholars recognize that international pressures affect processes of policy reform, but suggest that this occurs only through intervening variables that are political in nature. Among those who favor such an approach, some opt for explanations based on notions of regime type (authoritarian vs. democratic). According to Waterbury (1992), reforms consolidate only in settings that correspond to the authoritarian models of Chile and Turkey.[3] However, this explanation loses much of its credibility in light of the recent Argentine experience where reforms have been carried out and sustained by a popularly elected government. Haggard and Kaufman (1992) find the argument about the advantage of military regimes over democratic ones plausible, but contend that it must be further developed. In particular, they point out that institutionalized democracies with 'catch-all' parties may be more capable of transformation and structural adjustment than other democracies.

Uruguay remains a test case for either of these political hypotheses. The country did not undergo a neoliberal transformation during its dictatorship. As for the democratic period, Uruguay is, as O'Donnell (1992c) points out aptly, a highly institutionalized system. It is also a country with two strong 'catch-all' parties. Here again, the dependent variable does not correspond to what one would expect in light of prevailing explanatory models.

This does not imply that explanations that look to the sphere of politics are invalid. Rather, analyses must consider a broader range of political dimensions. In particular, social structure helps to define, albeit in mediated fashion, the map of interests and the potential forms of demand aggregation, and thus helps to impede or favor processes of neoliberal transformation.

To specify the factors which facilitate or complicate neoliberal transformations, we will analyze three areas of public policy: social security, labor relations, and privatization of state enterprises initiatives. For each area, we consider its historical development, recent reform initiatives, political conflict over alternative policies, the actors involved, and the final result of the process. The three areas comprise institutions that were key axes of the developmentalist state and that persist despite the end of that overall development model. For this very reason, they now confront strong transformative pressures.

[3] Here also it is important to point out the now classic work of O'Donnell (1973) on the bureaucratic-authoritarian state.

A New Actor in the Distributive Struggle: Associations of Retirees and Pensioners and Social Security Reform

Nine years after the return of democracy, seven different attempts have been made to reform the social security system in Uruguay. The only successful reform reinforced the old developmentalist and interventionist scheme that had characterized the system in the past. This reform emerged as a popular initiative and was approved by plebiscite. The other six attempts began in the executive branch of government and reflected an approach to reform consistent with the dominant stabilization and adjustment in the region. These initiatives were all defeated.

In the following pages we show: (1) how the emergence and consolidation of a new actor in the political arena, the associations of retirees and pensioners, was possible; (2) how the use of pre-existing institutional mechanisms allowed this new actor to incorporate its demands into the decision-making system; and (3) how the structure of a political system hindered by clientelist pressures and the absence of techno-bureaucratic isolation contributed to the failure of attempts to reform the social security system.

The Uruguayan social security system is one of the oldest and most developed in the region (Mesa-Lago 1978, 1985). The percentage of public spending devoted to social security (16 per cent of GNP in 1991), program development, population coverage (approximately 640,000 people in 1991, of a total of 3 million inhabitants), and quality of benefits support this assertion. Still, evidence reveals that these policies have deteriorated since the 1970s.

The overall crisis began to converge with the crisis of the social security system itself, as it became a scarce good subject to distributive struggles among diverse societal groups. Some of the indicators of the deterioration of the social security system include: reduction of the ratio of contributors to beneficiaries,[4] administrative irrationality, reduction of the cost and quality of benefits (between 1966 and 1985 there was a drop of approximately 50 per cent in the value of disability, ageing, and welfare (IVS) benefits), growth in the deficit of real contributions[5], and a corresponding growth in public contributions (2 per cent of GNP).

Hyperpoliticization was both a cause and consequence of this situation. The

---

[4] 80 per cent of social spending corresponds to disability, old age, and survivors' benefits (IVS), or to retirement pensions. The remaining 20 per cent corresponds to unemployment insurance, health insurance, family allowances, and maternity programs. The IVS system is tripartite, that is, it is financed by contributions from workers, employers, and the state. What began as a system of capitalization, for reasons that no longer matter, degenerated into a system of intergenerational distribution. For these reasons, financial and actuarial health of the system is, to a great extent, a function of the ratio of contributors to beneficiaries. At 1.9 contributors per beneficiary, this ratio is one of the lowest in Latin America.

[5] 'Genuine contributions' are considered to be those made by workers and employers. The evasion of contributions to the system is approximately 42 per cent.

process from which this system emerged and was developed generated conditions that made it particularly vulnerable to political penetration.[6]

In 1967, a constitutional reform was approved that attempted to make public policy-making less politicized and more technical. This reform, among other measures,[7] stripped the power of Parliament to introduce policies on matters of social security and public finance. These powers were transferred exclusively to the Executive branch. In addition, this reform created a central social security agency, Bank of Social Security (BPS), whose goal was rationalizing administration.

The Constitution mandates that the BPS be administered by a directorate consisting of representatives of the Executive branch, workers, the private sector, and pensioners. The new concentration of power in the Executive blocked avenues of access for demands relating to social security. Nevertheless, the new corporatist structure of the system's administration opened new points of access for particularistic interests. At the same time, it offered potential channels of representation to system beneficiaries, who had not previously played a central role in the distributive battle. The technocratic logic of planning that guided the new constitution was overcome by the corporatist and clientelist logic that dominated the administration of the BPS.

The law regulating the incorporation of social sectors into the system was not approved by Parliament until 1992. Nevertheless, from 1967 to 1973 (the year of the *coup d'état*), and from 1985 to 1992 (from the democratic opening to regulation), the mere anticipation of corporatist administration constituted an additional demand on the democratic governments.

The return to democracy in 1985 entailed the complete restoration of the political system and the Constitution of 1967. This recreated the BPS and its institutional framework. The accumulated deterioration brought about by the structural characteristics of the system and the measures adopted by the dictatorship had raised the deficit[8] and produced a very significant decline in the quality and level of benefits.

The conditionalities imposed by international lending agencies and the policies of adjustment attempted by the Sanguinetti administration led to benefit cuts as a means of reducing the fiscal deficit (Saldain 1987). This led the average value of benefits to fall even further in 1985. During the first year of the democratic

---

[6] A careful review of the legislation and its objectives shows that through social security the state sought to make more attractive certain occupations considered vital to its own institutionalization, including educational, military, and public sector occupations.

[7] An Office of Planning and Budget (OPP), dependent on the President, was created with ministerial standing but with no political responsibility before Parliament. The Office, like the rest of the measures of a centralizing nature, was shaped by a dual logic: one of governability and the other developmentalist. The former aimed to reduce the points of conflict in the political system; the latter was guided by a logic of centralized planning.

[8] Aside from fiscal measures, the system facilitated evasion and delay by eliminating controls and taxability. In this way, it sought to stimulate employment as it permitted hiring without worker contributions and enrollment in the DGSS.

government, the opposition political parties, committed to a strategy of governability and negotiated compromise, chose not to create obstacles to these policies.[9] Nor were trade unions, preoccupied by the issue of wage recuperation, intensely opposed to this adjustment. Thus, direct beneficiaries of the social security system, retirees and pensioners, were left without representation. This void, together with the existence of potential spaces, the retirement of a large number of older trade unionists, and the political opportunities sensed by some political leaders, provided the resources needed for the creation of a multiplicity of organizations of retirees.

In July 1985 the Plenary of Associations of Retirees and Pensioners of Uruguay, encompassing thirteen of the most important associations of retirees in Uruguay, was created. These organizations arose from trade union circles (Plenary of Retired People and Pensioners of the PIT-CNT), or as expressions of the political parties (National Vanguard Association, an organization founded under the Secretariat of Social Issues of the National Party). In addition, various associations that previously had a social or recreational function (National Union of Affiliates—UNA —to the Social Security and General Confederation in Defense of Beneficiaries— CGRCP) were reconstituted with a more political agenda. Initially, all these organizations came together around a central demand: the recuperation of the real value of pensions. This 'single issue' demand allowed these associations to act independently of political parties. The party identification of the leaders did not prevent them from opposing the positions of their parties. This applied equally to organizations led by sympathizers of the Colorado Party during the Sanguinetti administration and those led by Nationalists during the administration of President Lacalle.

These organizations systematically opposed attempts to reform social security. They forged a political coalition with diverse fractions of all the political parties and the trade union movement, and achieved a partial recovery of the real value lost from benefits.[10] In 1987, this coalition blocked a proposal to reform the system inspired by recommendations of the World Bank. It also succeeded in establishing that no retirement benefit could be lower than the nationwide minimal wage by the end of 1990.

In 1989, along with national elections, the organizations of retired persons called for a plebiscite on a constitutional reform that would incorporate an automatic indexation of benefits. The article proposed that the level of benefits be indexed to the average index of salaries.[11] This reform was submitted to a plebiscite

[9]   During the first year of government, the political opposition attempted not to complicate the task of the new administration or to inflict severe setbacks in what was considered to be a key year for democratic stabilization.

[10]   It is important to emphasize that this coalition encompassed diverse factions of all the political parties. These parties did not want to abandon a central actor in electoral disputes. In this way, social security was removed from the sphere of partisanship.

[11]   The value of benefits would be readjusted each time the salaries of the functionaries of the central government were increased, which occurred, by law, four times per year.

coinciding with the national elections of November 1989 and was supported by 82 per cent of the voters.[12]

Three phenomena together explain the result of the plebiscite. First, those represented by the organizations of retired persons and pensioners are more than one-quarter of the electorate. While the political parties may have opposed reform, they did not campaign against it because the reform was submitted to a plebiscite simultaneously with the election of the President and the members of the legislature. Second, throughout the five years of the Sanguinetti administration, the organizations of retirees and pensioners played their representative role very effectively, gaining near unconditional support from the majority of pensioners. Third, the parties lacked a comprehensive proposal for dealing with the crisis of the social security system. Therefore, pensioners and the majority of the population opted for a short-term solution that in the future might produce negative effects, but in the short term met the needs of this population.

The success of the plebiscite had three consequences. First, benefits improved substantially. Second, attempts to adjust the system to the general orientation of the government's macroeconomic policies failed. Third, beneficiaries of the IVS system linked the growth of their benefits to variations in the average wage index. Thus, this produced an alliance between beneficiaries of the IVS system and workers active in the labor force.

In 1992 Parliament mandated the corporate integration of the BPS, which enabled organizations of retirees, the trade union movement, and business associations to have an institutional channel through which to make demands on the system. This marked the close of a period during which new forms of representation became institutionalized and acquired spaces for negotiation with more traditional representative organizations. Earlier, in 1991, the National Organization of Retirees and Pensioners of Uruguay (ONJP) was founded, encompassing 120 different local, neighborhood, functional, and political organizations. In an election carried on among all the retirees and pensioners, the ONJP managed to elect its president as a member of the BPS Directorate.

Following the constitutional reform, critics of the social security system could no longer base their criticisms on the level of benefits as a tool for adjustment (Saldain 1993). Structural reform of the system, or a new constitutional reform, became the only possible mechanisms for carrying out an adjustment strategy.[13]

As short-term measures, the only viable strategies were to raise the retirement

---

[12] In Uruguay there exists considerable legislation regulating mechanisms of direct democracy. Since 1985, there have been three plebiscites in the country. Those plebiscites have aimed to reform pre-existing legislation (i.e. amnesty for the military and privatization of public enterprises) or constitutional reforms like those we are addressing. Mechanisms of direct democracy have been used with relative frequency throughout this century. Nevertheless, the will of the voters has never before been so distanced from that of their representatives. This may indicate some degree of loss of representativeness of the parties and the emergence of corporate identities strongly rooted in society.

[13] Lacurcia (1990) and Mesa-Lago (1993) discuss three major alternatives presented by the system, as well as their advantages and disadvantages.

age, change the calculation of the basic retirement income, make the requirements for retirement more stringent, or enact a combination of all three. During the administration of President Lacalle (1991–5), the Executive submitted to Parliament four proposals that contained these modifications. Three were rejected, and the fourth is being considered at this writing (January 1994) with no probability of being approved.

A fifth project was more thorough and sought to change the overall structure of the system.[14] This project, by the form in which it was elaborated and negotiated, introduced novel forms of 'policy-making'. Nevertheless, these elements coexisted with old styles of doing politics, which finally came to predominate, thereby blocking approval of the project.[15]

In July of 1991, President Lacalle assembled the leaders of all the political forces to hear the president of the BPS offer a diagnosis of the system crisis. Following debates and other meetings held in the Ministry of Labor and Social Security, all parties decided to delegate study of the topic to a technical commission designated by the political representatives and representatives of the social organizations. This commission constituted a 'political group' which came to be known as 'multipartisan', and a 'technical group', coordinated by the president of the BPS, which functioned intermittently for almost a year and a half (until December of 1992).

As a result of this effort three reports were completed and forwarded to the political group. The third and last report summarized the technical consensus reached up to that moment. In April, the Executive delivered the final project to the Legislature for consideration. After three months of debate the project was rejected by Parliament, garnering support only from the National Party and a minority faction of the Colorado Party.

Two aspects of this process should be highlighted: the first was the attempt by the Executive to depoliticize the reform. Even though it was multi-party in nature and included technical representatives from the trade unions and the retirement associations, the establishment of a setting for technical debate of social security reform was unprecedented in Uruguay. The Executive branch sought to bestow technocratic legitimacy on the reform project by betting on a technical agreement, which eventually was achieved. Second, once the project was transferred to the decision-making bodies around Parliament, the bottlenecks in the system intervened once again.

Technical rationality could not be imposed successfully over political logic. The project was opposed not only by the left—stemming from a perceived lack

---

[14] The project proposed to increase retirement ages, to impose stricter requirements for retirement, and to change the calculation of the basic retirement incomes, reducing the value of initial benefit. Nevertheless, the most novel aspect is that a 'mix' of intergenerational distribution capitalization was proposed. The latter would not be administered by the private sector, as in the Chilean case, but by the social security institutes themselves.

[15] This section is based on a personal communication of Rodolfo Saldain, president of the BPS, to the authors.

of social solidarity of a system of capitalization—but also by important factions in the traditional parties. Two factors contributed to this opposition. First, the proposed system sought, among other things, to make the administrative steps of the system transparent.[16] This transparency threatened to destroy the institutional bases for alliance among the 'hidden professionals of politics' (Panebianco 1988) and political leaders. Second, the associations of retirees and pensioners opposed the reform and threatened to punish at the polls any political parties that endorsed it.

In sum, some control—though precarious—over spending was attained during the first democratic administration, but a radical transformation of the social security system was not achieved. The second administration took over in a new context. The stabilization policy carried out by the previous government contributed to the emergence and consolidation of new actors in the distributive battle: pensioners and retirees. All attempts to blaze a path from the minimal stabilization attained during the initial three years of the Sanguinetti administration toward structural adjustment of social security collided with these new actors, with the political parties and their clientelist logic, and with the impossibility of isolating and transferring power to the team of technical experts.

Labor Relations and the Trade Union Movement: Adaptation and Resistance to Change

There are three levels on which to approach the question of neoliberal transformations in the area of labor: (1) elements of private law specific to labor legislation; (2) modes of capital–labor negotiation; and (3) the power, degree of unification, and forms of pressure within the trade union movement. Each of these merits detailed consideration. This chapter lacks an adequate treatment of the first level, but we can note that there have been no significant changes in the provisions of Uruguayan law involving labor protection, which by regional standards are considered especially advanced. This is not to imply that procedures for hiring and dismissing workers have not become more flexible. Nor does it mean that managers have not extended piecework systems or informalized capital–labor relations. In some cases these developments have been aided by weak or compliant trade unions. In any event, this chapter focuses in greater detail on collective bargaining as a form of representation, and the action of the trade union movement as a whole.

The Uruguayan Trade Union Movement (MSU) traces its origins to the turn of the century. Throughout the twentieth century the movement assumed characteristics that were unusual for Latin America. Autonomous of the state and of enterprises, with a strong leftist identity and with high legitimacy in public

[16] The bureaucratic framework of the system is such that the steps leading to the granting of pensions frequently get blocked. The relations between politicians and functionaries facilitate 'unblocking', and this constitutes the favor that the politician offers the citizen.

opinion, the MSU became the representative of urban wage labor and an important actor in the political system as a whole[17] (D'Elia 1984; Rodríguez 1986).

By the end of the 1940s the country's primary products (meat, leather, and wool) enjoyed a highly favorable position in international markets. Surpluses helped finance the development of protected import substitution industries and the expansion of the state apparatus. In the 1960s, Uruguay began to lose its advantageous insertion in the international market. Opportunities for continued public sector expansion and financing a protected domestic industrial base decreased (Rial 1988).

This economic model permitted the development of a robust labor movement that successfully increased affiliation rates, secured laws for worker protection, and defended collective wage levels. Due to characteristics of Uruguay's dominant types of production,[18] trade unionism both began as and has remained an essentially urban phenomenon, structured around protected industries and the state. This trade unionism simultaneously maintained a class discourse and resorted repeatedly to the strike weapon. The survival of private sector industry owed more to state subsidies than to market processes. The persistence of the state as an employer depended, in turn, more on clientelist and electoral logics than on the efficiency and profitability of its services (Filgueira 1990).

In sum, where trade unions existed, politics rather than markets provided the central sphere of regulation, and where market requirements prevailed, there were no trade unions. The market appeared only weakly as a means of regulating capital–labor or state–labor conflicts at the urban level.

With the crisis that began towards the end of the 1950s and exploded in the 1960s, economic abundance came to an end. The crisis had such a deep effect on the economic standing of the working-class and middle sectors that trade union conflict increased and white- and blue-collar sectors united into one central workers' organization (1964–6).

Behind the outward signs of crisis a more profound process of transformation was unfolding. In the future, trade unions and the market would not be separated as they had been in the past. Gradually, key areas of the national economy and the arenas of trade union activity began to overlap. At the same time, the state's relative abundance of resources diminished, causing increased international dependence in financial matters (see Table 15.5).

External debt highlights the situation of scarcity which the country continues to experience. In turn, the non-traditional export sector grew because of the

---

[17] There is no reliable data on trade union affiliation rates, which vary in the formal sector between 20 and 50 per cent. It should be noted, however, that strikes, whether by enterprise or sector, benefit from a high level of union discipline. In other words, beyond formal levels of affiliation, it may be said that the MSU effectively represents the urban formal sector workers.

[18] The main source of the country's revenue came from the exportation of primary goods. For this reason, a dominant form of production based on a structure of land ownership and a low level of manpower utilization contributed to the absence of trade unions and other corporate forms in rural society (Filgueira 1990).

dynamism of industrial and urban activities. These industries, unlike their predecessors, did not rely on protected markets. On the contrary, they fully competed
in the international market.

These transformations posed serious challenges and threats to several characteristics of the trade union movement. Entrepreneurs began to favor a new,
less centralized and less politicized kind of trade unionism. In addition, business
and government pressed to change the logic of collective action in the trade union
movement, unleashing strategies that emphasized company, rather than class,
unionism.

The difference between the strategies put forth by the first and second democratic administrations illustrates the increased emphasis on company unionism.
The first administration (that of President Sanguinetti) reorganized the rules
of the game inherited from the old system of capital–labor intermediation: this
involved a tripartite framework negotiated by sector, which implies the granting
of public status to the trade union movement (Offe 1988).

Nevertheless, this model presented some innovations with respect to that which
existed before the dictatorship. First, through the maintenance of certain norms
of 1966 and of the dictatorship, the government retained the right to set limits
on wage increases in order to control income policies. This measure, however, had
the unanticipated effect of reinforcing the organizational unity of the MSU. Since
wage ceilings were debated between the government and the trade union movement as a whole, rather than by individual sectors, the MSU was compelled to adopt
a unified strategy. To counteract this effect, in certain cases the government permitted the signing of bilateral agreements exceeding wage ceilings. In this manner, the government allowed some unions to engage in forms of negotiation
outside the centralized framework, thereby offering space for 'free-riders'. Third,
in conflicts with the public sector unions, the government resorted to the use of
decree. In these cases, the Executive would designate certain public services as
essential, enabling the Executive to use discretionary state power to break up
strikes and labor conflicts.

The final outcome of these strategies is ambiguous. At the public sector level,
there has been a clear recomposition of the MSU. Nevertheless, segmentation
between export, domestic, and state sectors grew. This weakened the structural bases
of trade union unity, and in some cases was expressed in the levels of aggregation
of capital–labor negotiation. Regarding economic stabilization, the result was reasonably positive: a controlled increase in private sector wages combined with the
use of the minimum and public sector wages as an instrument of adjustment. The
power and demands of the MSU were controlled and channeled, but there was no
substantial modification of the structure of representation and aggregation of
trade union interests. These were simply weakened (Filgueira 1991).

The Lacalle administration adopted a strategy quite different from that of its predecessor. It considered it necessary to radically modify Uruguayan trade unions.
To do this, the government announced plans to implement three complementary

measures: regulation of the right to strike; regulation of trade union activity (elections and decision-making criteria); and a period of wage bargaining during which wages would be fixed by decree, after which the state could distance itself from negotiations. Through these initiatives the government sought to pave the way for a bilateral, deregulated system.

Only one of these measures ultimately prospered: the state's retreat from capital–labor negotiations. Two elements explain this result. First, two general strikes during the first year of the administration and an increase in labor tensions were a harbinger of the levels of conflict which the government would need to confront as it pressed on with its initiatives.[19] Second, the fact that business and unions declared publicly that they had arrived at wage agreements above the levels authorized by decree convinced the government that it was not possible to negate by decree the respective powers of capital and labor. Either the government would involve itself in the negotiations, or it would have to accept bilateral agreements (Filgueira 1991).

In sum, the MSU, which regained its legal status with the process of democratic opening, soon demonstrated the persistence of some of its historical characteristics. Beyond these continuities, transformations, brought on by the economic context and by government initiatives, left an imprint on the unionism of the 1980s. Among these, the three most important concern the forms of representation, action, and aggregation of workers' interests.

First, the transformations in the area of collective bargaining should be evaluated.[20] Historically, collective bargaining was characterized by two defining features: negotiation took place at the industrial sector level, and wage-related issues were central. Regarding the latter, unions invariably sought to link compensation to indices of inflation. The outcome of these negotiations almost always depended more on the balance of political power between labor and capital than on previously established economic criteria, such as the productivity or profitability of the enterprise.

Given the structural transformations noted above and the rhetorical and political pressures that sought to moderate the styles of negotiation of the trade unions, one could expect important changes in this area. Among these are the decentralization of bargaining at the firm level and, given the sectoral restructuring of Uruguay's export economy, the prevalence of agreements based on productivity. One might also expect trade unions to seek agreements governing technical change and labor peace (see Table 15.6).

[19] In a country that seeks to become a financial safe haven, declarations made by leaders of the bank unions that to intervene into union life was akin to violating a financial secret, constituted a veiled threat of action which the trade union was prepared to carry out in order to halt the Executive.

[20] This and the following point are based to a large degree on a series of works by Francisco Pucci (1992a, 1992b, 1992c), who has made the most important contributions to clarifying recent trends. The authors are grateful to Pucci not only for his contribution of information and studies, but also for his willingness to comment upon and to reflect on our efforts to understand recent transformations in the trade union arena.

Although we lack historical time series, in each instance the expected patterns encompass less than half of all cases (with the exception of labor peace) and in many instances less than a quarter of the total cases (see Table 15.6). In particular, agreements related to technical change and enterprise level accords are of only marginal significance. With respect to the criteria for wage negotiations, today only slightly more than a third choose to negotiate on criteria of productivity instead of seeking wage adjustments in keeping with inflation and the cost of living.

In sum, contrary to what might be expected, the MSU largely maintains centralized criteria and traditional agendas in the mediation and defense of workers' corporate interests. Nevertheless, a certain moderation may be noted in matters of 'trade union peace'. Similarly, distinguishing firms on the basis of their percentage of exports, Pucci (1992a, 1992c) generally confirms the hypotheses outlined above. In enterprises with the highest percentage of export production, agreements addressing technical change and productivity reach 45.5 per cent in both cases (against 32 per cent and 24 per cent, respectively). Analyzed on the basis of sector or enterprise, the difference is less dramatic, but significant (the average is 12.7 per cent for all enterprises, while among firms with a high proportion of export production 18.2 per cent negotiate at the firm level). It is likely, then, that in so far as the growth model's structural tendencies persist, we will witness a gradual transformation of the forms of trade union mediation towards levels that are less aggregative and tied more to market criteria than to the political capacity of the labor movement. Nevertheless, for the moment it appears that the MSU continues to maintain a relationship with capital more consistent with the protected model than with the neoliberal export model.

A second aspect refers to the repertoire of collective action available to organized workers to push their demands. For the MSU, the strike historically has been the most important means of pressure in its collective action repertoire.[21] Given its leftist ideological framework and the low levels of social differentiation among subordinate sectors, the solidaristic and political component of the MSU has been evident in its use of the strike and the general strike on various occasions.

The importance of the MSU's identity and the absence of significant social differentiation are revealed in the high cost paid by sectors that attempted— or appeared—to split from the MSU, as well as in the absence of forces that do not belong to the country's historic left. The MSU has become part of a true party system, linked to the left, in which corporatist aspects and political capital constantly intermingle. Solidaristic and general strikes often respond to party loyalties disseminated widely throughout the trade union structure. Another factor that foments broad intersectoral or national support has been the peculiar social structure evident since the 1950s, in which blue- and white-collar workers, skilled

---

[21] In order of hierarchy and frequency, strikes on the level of firm and sector are predominant. This is followed by the general strike, attempts to influence public opinion, and finally, boycotts. A strategy of informal pressure, especially at the level of the public sector unions, is to use long-standing clientelist structures to lobby the national state, departmental governments, and parliament.

and unskilled, public and private sector all possessed—and to some extent still possess—more interests in common than in conflict.

Nevertheless, the transformations noted above would lead us to expect a reduction in the percentage of conflicts based on solidarity as well as of conflicts of an openly political nature. The requirements of an export economy that is highly competitive on the international level should also militate towards a reduction of the total number of conflicts (see Table 15.7).

In fact, the trend between 1985 and 1987 reveals this. Later, in those years for which information is available (1992–3), the number of conflicts becomes relatively stable. The increase in conflicts is registered in disputes involving wages. In keeping with the structural changes, this trend would not be predicted. Except for 1987, when the government strongly attacked public sector strikes, diminishing temporarily their percentage of the total, there is a clear tendency for public sector conflict to increase and to represent a higher percentage of all labor conflict. This is the sector where the transformation of trade unions would not be compensated by benefits derived from sectoral growth and dynamism. Similarly, conflicts over employment show a constant increase consistent with an economy that is being restructured and becoming more flexible, and that consequently offers less job security. The increase in conflict among public sector workers indicates the resistance of the MSU to adjustment measures and to cuts in the size of the public sector and in social spending. The relative reduction of conflicts in the private sector shows that the MSU successfully adapted to the new productive and competitive context.

Finally, we turn to analyze the effects of structural and political pressures on the unity and power of the trade unions. Trade union unity was achieved during the mid-1970s, in part by overcoming partisan splits due to the hegemony of the Communist Party, and because of the relative deterioration in the condition of white-collar sectors, which brought their agenda closer to that of blue-collar trade unions (Rial 1988).

The 1973 *coup d'état* froze trade union structures, which were resuscitated virtually unchanged in 1985. By the same token, and even more clearly than before the coup, Communist sectors maintained political hegemony inside the MSU, albeit in competition with other political parties of the Uruguayan left. The penetration of parties and the influence of these organizations were more an incentive for unity than a source of division. There exist unions that could strengthen their negotiating capacity outside of the union federation. Nevertheless, the political presence of the organized left in the union movement discourages the emergence of these 'free-riders' (Filgueira 1991). The decision of any single union to secede from the national federation could only be reached by a vote of the political sectors possessing a majority in the central union. A political sector that adopted this position in a given sector would be strongly punished in others. In this context, the balance of costs and benefits exerts pressure toward syndical unity, even in the case of those unions with relative advantages in individual negotiation.

The débâcle of the Communist Party is, in this sense, a key factor for understanding the weakening of labor unity.[22] Union leaders recognize that partisan competition is making room for competition inside the labor movement; the costs of 'free-riding' have diminished.

In sum, the reduction of party influence within the MSU and new segmentations characterizing the map of labor point to a weakening of labor unity, though without public expression. Moreover, trade union leaders widely perceive a reduction in the overall power of the MSU and especially of its structures at a more aggregated level. MSU leaders point out that, unless they take radical steps, their organization could cease to function at the central level.[23]

The Misfortunes of Privatization: The State and Party System

State penetration of Uruguayan society was (as in the two cases analyzed previously) the result of a peculiar model of development. An agro-export model with a weakly developed internal market supplied the resources that the state utilized in the industrialization process. Beginning in the late nineteenth century the state began playing a powerful role in the promotion of industry. This was achieved through two different routes. On the one hand, it fostered the birth of new private enterprises through significant protectionist measures and a wide range of tax exemptions. On the other hand, it created industrial and commercial entities operating under the auspices of the state.

The 1918 Constitution introduced an important change in the system of government which was incorporated into the administration of public enterprises. The so-called 'coparticipation policy' stipulated that the minority party would play a limited role in the nomination of enterprise directors (Finch 1980). If statist proposals in economic matters emerged from the Colorado Party, the creation of 'decentralized enterprises' or 'autonomous entities' received full support from the opposition National Party, which opposed state monopolies and defended economic liberalism. Nevertheless, the National Party accepted coparticipation and defended the institutional framework proposed for public enterprises. This strategy permitted the National Party to obtain two types of benefits. First, it stripped the Executive of economic powers (Frega and Trochon 1991). Second, it secured public resources to sustain clientelist politics like those practiced by the Colorados. From the outset, therefore, public enterprises were administered mostly by politicians, not technicians. From that moment onward, the state and its enterprises became both an engine of economic growth and a prebendary resource managed by political parties.

Not only was the management of public enterprise conducted according to a logic of 'coparticipation', but the appointment of functionaries was also based on

[22] Information based on reports by qualified informants of internal party debates regarding union unity. Some union leaders have told their parties privately that if it is necessary to sacrifice labor unity in order to achieve certain corporate advances, this should be accepted (interviews by the authors, Jan. 1993).
[23] Rental for the central headquarters, photocopy paper, and other minimal items used for daily operation are in jeopardy due to a lack of resources.

this logic of political distribution. A 1931 standard legally established that functionaries would be designated on the basis of proportional representation. Directors of public enterprises were free to appoint functionaries based on political criteria and in proportion to the distribution of positions in the National Council of Administration.[24] In this manner, a mixture of technical and political logic constituted the foundational matrix of public enterprises in Uruguay.

Given the relative weakness of domestic private capital, the activities carried out by the state did not aim to be competitive with those of the private sector, yet the positions of the latter in the face of state intervention were contradictory. As noted above, during much of the twentieth century the predominant economic activities were linked to agricultural exports and the internal market remained weak. Thus, governments during the initial two decades of the century tried to provide the basic infrastructure for the development of the national industry. State monopolies were constituted around monetary emission; production and generation of energy; telecommunications; insurance; railroad and trolley transportation; and port services. Domestic business and the state itself sought forms of 'intersection' (Frega and Trochon 1991) which they pursued through a variety of cooperative arrangements.

Nevertheless, beyond these attempts at 'intersection', the private sector maintained a dual attitude toward state intervention. It saw that the capacity of the state to absorb labor power constituted an important mechanism for the reduction of tensions generated by a market facing difficulties generating new jobs. But at the same time, it viewed the state as a competitor and a source of burdensome taxes. In addition, business feared the increased power that political elites acquired through clientelist politics.

Public enterprises, moreover, were criticized as inefficient. During their first decades in operation, however, these very enterprises were 'efficient'. That is, their balance sheets showed profits, they increased their capital, they distributed a portion of earnings as general income, they reduced tariffs and raw materials prices, and they extended credit to private enterprises and provided services. As in the case of social security, however, with the passage of time their explicit achievements were undermined by implicit goals. As noted earlier, while the most dynamic sector of the economy by its nature generated few jobs, the growth of industry was slow and had little capacity to generate significant opportunities for upward mobility. In this context, electoral competition, the institutional framework of public enterprises, and the widespread use of the state as a prebendary resource, encouraged a growth of public sector employment higher than in neighboring countries (see Table 15.8).

By the mid-1950s one might have predicted that the exhaustion of the development model would limit the expansion of the state and of public enterprises. The opposite, however, occurred. Political parties used the public administration and state enterprises to employ workers that remained unabsorbed by the private sector.

---

[24] The Constitution of 1918 created a collegial Executive, the National Council of Government, composed of nine members, six representing the majority party and three from the party with the second greatest number of votes.

At this point the significance of understanding the peculiar nature of the clientelist system practiced by Uruguayan political parties is clear. Originally established as top-down prebendary systems of control and legitimation, closely fought elections and electoral legislation that encouraged fragmentation enabled intermediate and lower-level party leaders to acquire substantial power. Thus, the Uruguayan clientelist system has functioned over the past four decades less as a mechanism of domination and more as an instrument of popular incorporation and political competition (see Table 15.9).

As can be seen, during the period under consideration the growth of public sector employment outpaced that in both the EAP and the private sector. This trend was stronger until the beginning of the authoritarian government, when the dissolution of representative mechanisms (trade unions and political parties), mass dismissals of functionaries on ideological grounds, and the relative growth of informal sector employment stripped the sector of its dynamism. Nevertheless, the growth of state employment was higher in public enterprises than in other sectors (see Table 15.10).

Also, the growth of public sector employment was achieved at the expense of a reduction of variations in pay scales. While data on the spectrum of wages in public enterprises is not available, information on the central government constitutes a good substitute for assessing those remunerations. Nor do we have current figures, but there is no reason to believe that the tendency evident during the years for which we do have information has changed (see Table 15.11).

The relative growth of personnel in public enterprise is the result of the institutional framework and of the 'patchwork politics' and 'tension absorption' (Filgueira 1970) practiced by various governments. Nevertheless, this patchwork politics subsequently would generate two types of dysfunction. First, the growth of the public sector and of a large, dependent middle class, together with shrinking pay differentials and gradual wage reductions, would increase the reservoir of unsatisfied demands directed towards the state. Second, mechanisms of negative retribution, functional growth beyond technical demands, and the hyperpoliticization of public enterprise would cause public enterprise to function irrationally. Third, arguably, this process generated structural opportunities for an alliance of impoverished sectors of the dependent middle-class sectors and 'blue-collar' workers. In this sense it inadvertently contributed to the establishment of the National Central of Workers (CNT).

The military dictatorship (1973–85), despite its neoliberal rhetoric, made no attempt to modify the property regime governing public enterprises. This would become a key issue on the political agenda of the first and second democratic administrations (1985–94). The Sanguinetti administration sought to achieve four priority objectives: to control social spending, eliminate hiring of additional state employees, close deficit-ridden public enterprises, and transfer some healthy public enterprises to the private sector or to public–private partnerships. The first two objectives were achieved to some degree. The first goal was accomplished through repeated presidential vetoes of budgetary items, some of these of dubious constitutionality from the opposition's perspective.[25] The second was achieved through enactment of a civil service law which limited opportunities for creating new public sector jobs. The third objective was partially reached, but not without significant trade union conflict in the affected enterprises, particularly the state railway, which eliminated passenger service.[26] The government made virtually no progress toward its fourth objective. It failed to achieve even a parliamentary debate for its proposals to reform the public gasoline, alcohol, and port enterprises or the state airline, PLUNA. Union opposition contributed to this failure, as did resistance from the political parties, whose leaders and representatives rejected what they saw as an attack on their basis for engaging clients.

The Uruguayan state has provided a basis for clientelism through its ability to offer jobs, but more importantly, it has been an instrument for the political parties to engage citizens who are not and will never be employed in the public sector. The state functionary who gets a job through clientelist networks becomes a 'hidden professional of politics', reproducing the clientelist system by controlling the various instruments through which the state makes itself present throughout society. The functionary can help a retiring worker to get a pension, obtain a permit to open a private service, or accelerate construction of a neighborhood sewer system. Control over these functions enables the parties to penetrate society more deeply than does their capacity to offer public employment. Politicians fear privatization not only because they would no longer control access to jobs, but because they would lose their hidden political apparatus: the state functionary.

Sanguinetti attempted to take these constraints into account in elaborating policies of neoliberal transformation, but he was punished for his efforts nonetheless. And he was punished by his own party, which toward the end of his administration forced a primary election to select a candidate to represent the Colorados in the upcoming presidential contest. The candidate selected by Sanguinetti (Tarigo) confronted a Colorado leader (Batlle) who advocated an even more neoliberal transformation. The interesting point is that even though Batlle advocated a radical neoliberal state, his electoral support was found in the old clientelist party apparatus. Meanwhile, Tarigo's support was reduced to a strong pro-Sanguinetti faction in Parliament which had maintained a heroic (and perhaps suicidal) discipline in support of repeated presidential vetoes. Needless to say, Batlle triumphed by a considerable margin.

This context of intraparty conflict facilitated the triumph of the National Party in the national elections of 1989. Lacalle, the new president, also espoused

---

[25] A total of twenty-one vetoes during this period testifies to this point. Most of these were on budgetary adjustments. Of the remainder, many sought to reduce indexing of passive benefits. Finally, the use of decrees to set wages at the state level also contributed to this control over public spending (Filgueira 1990); Report on vetoes interposed by the Executive Power of Parliament, 1985–9. Montevideo, mimeo.

[26] It may be noted at this point that none of the passenger service employees of the railway industry were left without state jobs, as they were reassigned to other functions.

a neoliberal discourse and, distancing himself from his predecessor, called for profound transformations supported by large parliamentary majorities.

Among the most daring proposals was a Law of Privatization of Public Enterprises. This law included most of the important state enterprises and, significantly, gave the Executive broad authorization to carry out subsequent privatizations. After prolonged negotiations the government gained support from a majority of Colorado legislators and a minority of its own, which secured passage of the law in Parliament.

Soon after the measure was passed, an opposition front comprising the left, fractions of the traditional political parties, and the MSU came together to seek a referendum to overturn some of the key provisions of the law (in fact the most important ones). The process for obtaining a referendum is complex and the details of the process need not concern us in this chapter. One extremely important point, however, merits attention. The majority of the Colorados, led by ex-president Sanguinetti, in the end supported the referendum for the partial repeal of the law, even though they had voted for the law in Parliament.

A simplistic explanation for this shift is that it represented electoralist demagogy. Nevertheless, the issue is not whether Sanguinetti acted out of convenience or conviction but rather the factors which led to his decision to support the referendum. The sectors that supported the partial repeal were only a minority of the electorate. It was the middle-level leaders of his own party who exerted pressure on the top of the sector.[27] To this was added survey data showing that an ample sector of the public, though not a clear majority, supported the referendum. In 1993, 70 per cent of the voters repealed the critical articles of the Law of State Enterprises, thus burying the privatization project as a whole.

The size of the public sector, a party system based on a wide range of clientelist relations, and a union movement with some capacity for resistance to a large extent succeeded in blocking privatization initiatives. More importantly, however, like the case of the struggle over social security reform, an institutional framework facilitating appeals to direct democracy once again overturned a neoliberal initiative of popularly elected leaders. This is no great paradox. Citizens continue to identify strongly with leaders who advocate policies they do not share. This is because these same leaders belong to a system in which the citizens have institutional and informational channels through which they may become incorporated into the processes of public policy formulation.

Conclusion

This section is divided into a main section and an appendix. First we will evaluate the most important findings concerning the three policy areas analyzed in this chapter. We then venture into an area which is not addressed in the preceding pages:

---

[27] Interviews with members of the Batllist Forum, the sector led by ex-president Sanguinetti.

how have economic and social indicators evolved in the regionally anomalous case of Uruguay? The text of the appendix does not analyze the data presented in the tables (we trust that they speak for themselves), but reflects instead on their implications for the paradigms and assumptions which have shaped academic approaches to the study of economic and political transformations in the region.

Transformations in the international context and in the sphere of production within national economies impose powerful pressures to implement orthodox models of stabilization and adjustment. The new export model, external conditionality, and the need to control inflation and the deficit all influenced the discourse and proposals of government and business elites.

The form in which these pressures were processed and resolved depended, however, on factors other than those mentioned above. The degree and historical patterns of incorporation and representation of the middle and popular sectors limited the abilities of these elites to carry out structural reforms in Uruguay.

Analysis of the three areas showed the relevance of the social matrix operating on two basic levels.

1. The absolute level of popular sector incorporation into the development model and its benefits. Elements such as the percentage of state employment, coverage of social protection systems, and labor protection are central, since they indicate the relative number of people who would be affected by the proposed changes. In Uruguay, all these indicators suggest comparatively high levels of incorporation compared to the rest of the region.

2. The level of segmentation and stratification, and the degree to which the popular and middle sectors attained these rights, benefits, and protection. Social security systems based on equal distribution rather than individual capitalization tend to generate strategies of aggregation rather than atomization. At the same time, the deterioration of social welfare systems produced two effects. First, it reduced the relative distance between benefit levels. Second, it lowered the real value of these benefits as a whole. These two factors created structural bases for a potential alliance among all system beneficiaries. Something similar occurred in the case of public enterprises, as indicated by the flattening of the wage pyramid and the use of public sector wages as an instrument for reducing the fiscal deficit. In synthetic terms, these two areas appear to confirm the more general hypothesis of Goodin *et al.* (1987): the middle sectors consist not only of those in universalized systems who take advantage of resources that should go to poorer sectors; the middle sectors are also those with more power resources to defend a system that in practice does not differentiate between popular and middle-class sectors. In the case of labor, the predictable effect of productive transformation on the structure of interest aggregation has been attenuated by the intermingling of corporatist and partisan logics, and by the MSU's identity cast in terms of solidarity and the left.

If Uruguay's social matrix suggests high resistance to change, that is also true for Argentina. Nevertheless, Argentina is capable of carrying out a neoliberal transformation, whereas Uruguay is not. To understand this, the political sphere must be incorporated into the explanatory framework. Thus, when we refer in this chapter to the dimensions of incorporation and political representation, we are concerned with more than regime type alone. While in normative terms it may be prudent not to demand more from democracy than fulfillment of its minimal requirements (freedom of expression, association, and free elections), in analytical terms additional tools are needed to evaluate the participatory and representational components of policy-making processes (Acuña 1992; Panizza 1993). As Malloy (1991a, 1991b) points out, after the re-emergence of democratic regimes in Latin America, the problem of 'governance' consists of more than a redistribution of power understood in terms of 'access to office'. The latter is a problem of personnel, but not of power.

How does the structuring of public space help or hinder a given government to carry out reforms consistent with its political will? This is the crucial element to evaluate in order to comprehend adequately the nature of policy-making processes, their 'veto points', their degree of insularity, and the possible coalitions upon which they may be based.

Three key elements operated in the political sphere to block many attempts at transformation:

1. Institutional framework or formal rules of the game. These rules define potential degrees of permeability to popular sector demands and preferences. The most important findings point to the easy access to plebiscite, and a system of labor–capital regulation that explicitly grants public status to workers' organizations. These are combined with a very low level of state regulation of trade unions. These elements favored opposition strategies and augmented the capacity of popular sectors to veto strategies of adjustment and stabilization. A regulation for privatizing public enterprises would have been possible had representative democracy been the only channel for the expression of interests. Nevertheless, the existence of referendums in the Uruguayan political system favored the formation of extra-parliamentary and supra-partisan coalitions, and allowed these to appeal directly to citizens on the basis of specific policy preferences. In the case of social security, the institutional framework also favored consolidation of new social actors, which secured recognition for forms of corporate representation which had been envisioned but never implemented.

2. Techno-administrative capacities and characteristics of the state. Technical-political and technical-administrative elites make up an exceedingly low proportion of Uruguayan state elites. As we have noted in the cases of public enterprise and social security administration, personnel selection criteria are political and corporatist, not technical. At the same time, party penetration of the state leads to a situation in which the only possible strategies for 'embeddedness' pass through political parties, which plainly limits 'autonomy', the other key attribute called for by Evans (1992).

3. Cultures and styles of politics and leadership. These are rooted in long-standing practices and are transformed only with great difficulty. The extension of clientelist structures, styles of negotiation and consensus, and the absence of a populist past with a delegative type of legitimacy (O'Donnell 1991) make an extremely dense

network of political exchange necessary for decision-making processes. In these contexts, it becomes extremely difficult to reach models of 'exclusionary policy making' (Vacs 1993). It is important to emphasize that these are not marginal attributes of types of political practice and decision-making. On the contrary, they define on an informal but by no means insignificant level the boundaries of legitimate political practice. What is more, they are true political economies of exchange whose logics regulate the forms of acquisition and transmission of power in society.

The client–patron system in Uruguay can be defined as a system of redistribution of political goods sustained by the material and regulatory resources of the state. The agent for regulating distribution of these goods is the party system. Here it is important to distinguish between two different types of leadership that tend to be confused through the use of the term 'caudillo' to describe both of them. The Uruguayan political caudillo typical of the system described above is a notoriously long way from the old (Perón, Vargas) or new versions of Latin American caudillismo (Menem, Fujimori, Collor de Melo). The latter approximate the charismatic Weberian model (low institutionalization, absence of a governing elite, typical of situations of anomie, etc.). In the Uruguayan case, we find deeply rooted processes involving the routinization of charisma or, more strictly, of structuration of a system of 'remunerative legitimacy' (Real de Azúa 1989). This type of legitimacy reflects neither the rational-legal nor the pure charismatic type. It combines the personalized dimension of the latter and the structured and extended dimension of the former.

In sum, our review of the political sphere underscores the need to distinguish between personnel selection and the decision-making process. Following Eisenstad (1966), one must distinguish between the legitimacy of the governing elite and the legitimacy of its concrete actions. Uruguayan experience argues strongly against the fusion of these two levels of legitimacy or the assumption that the former leads automatically to the latter.

On one hand, the forms of 'remunerative legitimacy' (clientelism) notoriously limit the autonomy of leaders to distance themselves from the interests of those they represent. At the same time, as we argued in the case of public enterprises, by privatizing or closing areas of the public sector, these leaders would be giving up the resources through which they maintain the system of 'remunerative legitimacy'.

On the other hand, the possibility of appealing to forms of direct democracy permits the governed to give weight to the distinction between the legitimacy of the elite and the legitimacy of their actions whenever the elites manage to break the clientelist pact. This is just as much the case with regard to social security as it is with regard to the law of public enterprise privatization.

The central hypothesis that emerges from this work is that the degrees and models of incorporation determine the ability of countries to implement neoliberal processes of transformation in the face of international pressures and productive transformations. In other words, the prospects for implementing these models of adjustment are directly proportional to the historic degrees of sociopolitical

exclusion of the popular sectors. Uruguay has a state penetrated by party structures and a society that has enjoyed abundant protection and benefits from the state.
Systems such as Peronism represent cases with high levels of social incorporation,
but low levels of political incorporation.[28] Systems such as the Chilean one that
emerges from the Pinochet dictatorship represent cases with low levels of social incorporation but medium to high political incorporation. In both cases, it is possible to
carry out, maintain, and consolidate neoliberal strategies. The problem arises when
both dimensions are in the high category and the types of incorporation respond
to machine parties with a broad clientelist base that is not dominated by elites.[29]

Appendix

Academics tend to confuse what is desirable with what is possible. More worrisome still is
that we confuse resignation with the inevitable, or in other words, we assume that what we
perceive to be inevitable really is inevitable.

Even among those who oppose the new neoliberal models there is a widespread sense
that the room for maneuver is very narrow. This is based to a large measure on the discourse
of economics which has achieved considerable sway over the social sciences as a whole.
Uruguay is, in this sense, an important case, because it points out that regardless of the accuracy of economic discourse on matters of what 'should' be done, the latter may not occur.
This affirmation is not as trivial as it seems. It implies that there may exist paths other than
those suggested by economic constraints. The capacity to pursue them or not depends in
some measure on the construction of paradigms that reclaim the centrality of the political
and social dimensions.

The logical form in which this chapter is structured is illustrative. It presents Uruguay
as an empirical and theoretical outlier. Uruguay is a case in search of a theory. Today it
is only an anomaly. And perhaps despite the veiled optimism of the authors, tomorrow might
hold out the demise of its stubborn resistance and its adjustment to the regional norm. Even
worse, perhaps we are witnessing the tragedy of an immobilist society, fated to social and
economic débâcle. But perhaps we shall be surprised to find ourselves before the creation
of a new road to economic and social restructuring.

---

[28] Strictly speaking, the Peronist case is not one of low political incorporation if we compare it with
its country's past, or with other Latin American countries. Here, political incorporation takes on fundamental importance. The main actors that in Argentina carried out the incorporation of the popular sectors to social citizenship was the state and the corporate structures attached to the state. In
Uruguay the agents of incorporation were the political parties and the autonomous corporations of
the state.

[29] Haggard and Kaufman (1992) point out, as we noted earlier, the ability of 'catch-all' parties
to administer and transform national economies according to the requirements of fiscal discipline
and structural adjustment. The examples offered by the authors are those of Venezuela, Colombia,
and Costa Rica. It is important to point out that these are to a large extent cases of 'elite dominated
patronage machines'; Uruguay, as shown throughout the chapter, was not. While the concept appears
oxymoronic, Uruguay may be characterized as a case of 'democratized patronage machines' to the
extent that popular sectors possess an important share of power, in which the left holds power and
manifests a degree of mobilization that far exceeds the status of 'junior partners' (the second condition required by Haggard and Kaufman, 1992, for catch-all party systems that seek to carry out adjustment politics).

Table 15.1. Urban households in conditions of poverty or indigence for selected countries, 1980–1990 (% of total population)

| | Argentina | | | Uruguay | | | Venezuela | | | Mexico | | Chile | |
	1980	1986	1990	1981	1986	1989	1981	1986	1990	1984	1990	1987	1990
Poverty	7	12	25	9	14	10	18	25	33	23	30	37	34
Indigence	2	3	7	2	3	2	5	8	11	6	8	13	11

Source: CEPAL, Panorama Social de América Latina, 1993.

Table 15.2. Changes in the distribution of urban household income comparing relative distances between the poorest 40% and the richest 10%: nationwide data for selected countries (%)

	Part of national income received by the poorest 40%	Part of national income received by the richest 10%	Distance between the extremes	General inequality between 1980 and 1990[a]
Argentina 1980	18.2	29.8	11.8	Grew
1986	16.2	34.5	18.3	
Uruguay 1981	17.7	31.2	13.5	Fell
1989	18.9	31.2	12.3	
Venezuela 1981	20.2	21.8	1.6	Grew
1990	16.8	28.4	11.6	
Mexico 1987	14.9	33.2	18.3	Grew
1990	12.3	41.1	28.8	
Chile 1987	14.5	30.1	15.6	Grew
1988	12.6	33.4	20.8	

[a] In terms of the Gini Index for 1980 and 1990. The only two countries that CEPAL considers today as characterized by low inequality are Costa Rica and Uruguay.

Source: CEPAL, Panorama Social de América Latina, 1993.

Table 15.3. Percentage variations of average revenues of urban households by income quartile (1 = 25% poorest, 4 = 25% richest), for selected countries

	C1	C2	C3	C4
Uruguay 1981–90	3	−10	−10	−9
Chile 1978–88	−10	0	1	18
Argentina 1980–6	−11	−15	−13	2
Mexico 1987–90	−0.5	6	3	39
Venezuela 1981–90	−38	−34	−31	−14

Source: CEPAL, Panorama Social de América Latina, 1993.

Table 15.4. Average variation in selected indicators, 1980–1991, and fiscal deficit in 1980 and 1991 (%)

	Argentina	Uruguay	Venezuela	Mexico	Chile
GDP per capita	−1.5	−0.5	−1.3	−0.5	1.6
Inflation	416.9	64.4	21.2	66.5	20.5
Rate of investment	−6.9	−5.9	−3.9	−1.9	5.1
Fiscal deficit in 1980	−3.6	0.0	0.0	−3.1	5.6
Fiscal deficit in 1991	−0.5	0.4	4.5	0.8	s/d

Source: World Bank, World Development Report, 1993.

Table 15.5. Structure of exports and external debts, 1970–1985

	1970	1975	1980	1985
Traditional exports (% of GDP)	72	51	40	35
Non-traditional exports (% of GDP)	28	49	60	65
External debt[a]	564	1,135	2,137	4,900

[a] in millions of current dollars

Sources: Couriel 1988; Saráchaga and Vera 1989.

Table 15.6. Type of labor–management agreements, 1991 (%)

	Productivity	Technical change	Union peace	Labor accord at level of enterprise
Yes	32	24	52.7	12.7
No	48	54	24	68
N/C	2.7	5.3	6	5.3
N/A	17.4	16.7	16.7	14

Source: Pucci 1992*a*, based on figures from an industry survey carried out in 1991 (reflects 150 based on a total of 589 concerns).

Table 15.7. Total conflicts distinguished by principal cause and by public and private sector (%)

	1985	1986	1987	1992[a]	1993[a]
Totals	367	262	215	216	218
Private	53.1	50.0	67.9	43.5	39.5
Public	46.9	50.0	32.1	56.5	60.5
	100.0	100.0	100.0	100.0	100.0
Salarial	71.9	58.4	50.6	60.2	73.0
Job	6.3	11.8	19.5	17.8	21.0
Political	4.1	7.3	0.9	s/d	s/d
Solidarity	3.3	2.7	2.3	s/d	s/d
Others	14.4	19.8	26.5	22.0	6.0

[a] The years 1992 and 1993 include percentages only for the first nine months. Because figures for these years are based on direct recordings of conflicts whereas those for 1985, 1986, and 1987 are calculated on the base of press archives, the number of conflicts is under-represented for the first three years. The category 'others' for 1992 and 1993 contains, in both, political conflicts and ones arising out of solidarity.

Source: Filgueira 1990 and SERPAJ, Report 1993.

Table 15.8. Total state employment and public enterprises employment in relation to population, selected countries, 1985 (%)

Countries	Total	Enterprises
Uruguay	8.1	6.2
Brazil	3.5	s/d
Argentina	5.7	4.8
Chile	2.5	1.8

Note: Public employment is underestimated since certain state activities are excluded.
Source: Marshal 1990.

Table 15.9. Size of public employment; index of relative growth

	1963	1975	1985
Public employment	100	122	125
EAP	100	108	116
Private sector wage-earners	100	103	116

Source: Fortuna 1990.

Table 15.10. Public sector employment in percentages, 1955–1984

	1955	1961	1969	1980	1984
Central and local Government	66.6	65.3	64.2	57.4	56.3
Public enterprise	33.4	34.7	35.8	42.6	43.7
Total	100	100	100	100	100

Source: Davrieux 1987.

Table 15.11. Differences between maximum and minimum wages in the central government

Rank	1961	1965	1969
Administrative	6	3.4	2.1
Specialized Technician	6	3.4	2.1
Secondary and Service	2.3	1.2	0.7
Professional Technician A	2	2.1	1.7
Professional Technician	2.2	2.1	1.7

Source: Filgueira 1970.

PART V. Reconstructing Representation

16 | The Difficult Transition from Clientelism to Citizenship: Lessons from Mexico

Jonathan Fox[1]

Electoral competition is necessary but not sufficient for the consolidation of democratic regimes; not all elections are free and fair, nor do they necessarily lead to actual civilian rule or respect for political rights. If there is more to democracy than elections, then there is more to democratization than the transition to elections. But in spite of the rich literature on the emergence of electoral competition, the dynamics of political transitions toward respect for *other* fundamental democratic rights are still not well understood.

This study differs from most analyses of the relationship between social movements and democratization. Rather than focus on movement struggles for material gains or the contested notion of the post-transition 'quality' of democracy, this chapter focuses on the dynamics through which certain understudied *minimum* conditions for political democracy are constructed.[2]

Political democracy is defined here in classic terms: free and fair electoral contestation for governing offices based on universal suffrage, guaranteed freedoms of association and expression, and effective civilian control over the military.[3] Most

[1] This chapter is a revised version of an article originally published in *World Politics*, 46/2, 151–84 (Jan. 1994; © Johns Hopkins University Press, and reprinted here with permission). It has not been updated. For a more detailed version of the empirical case material, see the author's 'Targeting the Poorest: The Role of Mexico's National Indigenous Institute in the National Solidarity Program', in Cornelius *et al.* (1994). Field research for this project was partially funded by a grant from the Howard Heinz Endowment. I am very grateful to Josefina Aranda, Lucio García, Miguel Tejero, and many other local NGO and indigenous leaders for generously sharing their analyses of development policy in Oaxaca. Thanks also to Scott Martin for very thoughtful editorial comments on an earlier version.

[2] The widespread post-transition problems of institutional weakness and under-representation of certain societal groups are often conflated with the lack of political democracy itself. Under-representation and persistent authoritarianism are certainly closely related—indeed, they are mutually reinforcing—but they are analytically distinct processes. Contrast urban Brazil and Guatemala, for example. If upon closer examination many electoral transitions turn out to fall short of fundamental minimum conditions for political democracy, then what many excluded groups see as limitations of democracy may turn out to be more the result of the *lack* of democracy in the first place.

[3] In Karl's terms, this is a middle-range definition of democracy, in that it falls in between the narrow Schumpeterian range of contestation needed for strictly intra-elite competition and approaches

analyses of democratization acknowledge that these are *all* necessary criteria, but then proceed to examine only electoral competition.[4] This study develops a framework for explaining progress towards *another* necessary condition for democratization: respect for associational autonomy. The right to associational autonomy allows citizens to organize in defense of their own interests and identities without fear of external intervention or punishment. In this definition, autonomy refers to an actor's capacity to set goals and strategies. Whether relatively autonomous societal actors actually have the power to achieve their goals is a different matter. Autonomy and capacity are distinct.[5]

Most analysis of the emergence of electoral competition concentrates quite appropriately on high politics, on the pacts which define the rules of contestation and the founding elections which shape much of national politics. But analysis of the effective extension of the full range of citizenship rights *throughout* a society involves studying how most people are actually represented and governed—before, during, and after the historic turning-points of high politics. In this process, intermediate associations are crucial complements to political parties because they are potentially more responsive to the inherent diversity of societal interests. Increasingly, political scientists are stressing the Tocquevillian idea that democratic governance depends on the density of associational life in civil society. This growing consensus on the impact of civil society on the state does not imply shared explanations of how civil societies become dense and powerful—some are more 'historically determinist', whereas others grant more of a role for contingency and political action.[6] However, rather than attempt here to explain the empowerment of autonomous organizations in civil society—which often both pre-dates and encourages electoral competition—this study focuses on the empirically related but analytically distinct question of how states begin to accept the *right* of citizens to pursue their goals autonomously.

which depend on particular socioeconomic or participatory outcomes. See Karl (1990). NB: in the definition proposed in the original version of this article, accountability through the rule of law was included as a minimum defining characteristic. In light of the revelations of decades of persistent lack of accountability in consolidated democracies such as Italy and Japan, perhaps the rule of law is better understood as a possible outcome rather than a defining characteristic of the democratic process.

[4] Democratization is defined here as the process of movement towards these conditions, while the consolidation of a democratic regime requires fulfilling all of them. Regimes can therefore be in transition to democracy—further along than liberalization—but still fall short of a democratic threshold. For further discussion, see Mainwaring *et al.* (1992).

[5] On associational autonomy as a democratic right, see Dahl (1982). On the difference between autonomy and capacity, see Fox (1992c). Note that autonomy is inherently relational, and is therefore a matter of degree. An actor's autonomy can also vary across issue areas and in different institutional contexts; a group may have more autonomy to pursue some goals than others.

[6] See, for example, Cohen and Rogers (1992) on the USA, Putnam (1993) on Italy, Fox and Hernández (1992) on Mexico, and Lawson and Merkl (1988) on broader problems of party representation. This chapter treats intermediate associations as broadly representative, though not necessarily democratic. On the problem of internal democracy within such organizations, see Fox (1992b). Note also that intermediate associations in developing countries often do not appear as formal organizations; they may be kinship or religiously based community associations, for example, as in many African or Middle Eastern societies.

As authoritarian regimes give way to electoral competition, the degree to which the full range of citizenship rights becomes respected varies quite widely both across and within national political systems.[7] For example, a wide range of political systems, including many which hold regular elections, oblige poor people to sacrifice their political rights in order to gain access to distributive programs. Such conditionality blocks the exercise of citizenship rights, and therefore undermines the consolidation of political democracy. Associational autonomy is an especially vital right for the poorest members of society for two main reasons. First, they are usually the most vulnerable to state-sanctioned coercion should they express discontent. Second, their survival needs make them especially vulnerable to clientelistic incentives. Together, these threats and inducements inhibit autonomous interest articulation and collective action.[8] These relations of domination can be broadly understood in terms of clientelism, a relationship which requires political subordination in exchange for material rewards.

How, then, do subordinated people make the transition from clients to citizens? This study analyzes how less-than-democratic regimes come to respect autonomous, representative societal organizations as legitimate interlocutors. It will draw on the Mexican experience to focus on one important indicator of this transition; the study will explain the process through which poor people gain access to whatever material resources the state has to offer without having to give up their right to articulate their interests autonomously.[9]

It is undeniably risky to use the concept of political clientelism to frame the study of the construction of the right to associational autonomy. Analysts have found elements of clientelism in an extraordinarily wide range of hierarchical power relations. When the term's usage becomes so broad, however, as to encompass almost any reciprocal exchange between actors of unequal power, it becomes very difficult to distinguish what is specific to clientelism from the more general category of political bargaining. But since the core notion of clientelism captures the exchange of political rights for social benefits, it is worth trying to sharpen its boundaries.

Clientelism is certainly a form of bargaining, so it inherently involves some degree of autonomy between the parties, yet to have a distinct meaning it must also involve significantly unequal constraints on that autonomy. For the purposes of this argument, the working definition of political clientelism will be deliberately narrow, to highlight the process of transition from clientelistic to other kinds of unequal exchanges that permit somewhat greater associational autonomy. The focus here will be on specifically *authoritarian* clientelism, where imbalanced bargaining relations require the enduring political subordination of clients and are

---

[7] The rights of political citizenship in a democracy include guaranteed basic civil and political freedoms, majority rule with minority rights, the equitable administration of justice, as well as respect for associational autonomy.   [8] See Collier and Collier (1977).

[9] Another key indicator of the achievement of the right to associational autonomy would be the establishment of a guaranteed secret ballot, which would permit voters to make political choices without fear of retribution.

reinforced by the threat of coercion. Such subordination can take forms ranging from vote-buying by political machines, as under semi-competitive electoral regimes, or a strict prohibition on collective action, as under most military regimes, to controlled mass mobilization, as in communist or authoritarian populist systems.[10] Note that this definition of authoritarian clientelism refers to a 'subnational' set of power relations, not necessarily to the regime as a whole. As will be suggested below, however, the persistence of authoritarian enclaves under ostensibly democratic regimes raises questions about whether they indeed meet the conventional minimum conditions for political democracy.

The nature of the linkage between the micro-politics of clientelism and the macro-politics of regime change is problematic, perhaps in part because the literature on political clientelism virtually stopped over a decade ago, long before the flowering of analysis of regime change.[11] Only a handful of analysts of regime change explore how the persistence of machine politics affects the nature of transitions, and those that do focus more on clientelism among political elites than on how clientelism can deny citizens fundamental political rights.[12]

Political Conflict and the Erosion of Clientelism: An Analytical Framework

Most studies of clientelism show how the relationship works rather than explain how it changes. In contrast, one group of analysts show how political entrepreneurs build clientelistic systems, emphasizing the transition from patrimonial patronage to mass political machines.[13] The possible role for political action in explaining how clientelism breaks down has received less attention. Most analysts explain the erosion of clientelism in terms of gradual social changes, such as urbanization and education, or structural economic shifts, such as the commercialization of agriculture.[14] These secular trends are not sufficient, however. Political action can also either block or speed up the weakening of clientelism. Where 'traditional' patterns

[10] The appearance of subordination should not be confused with actual submission, however, see Scott (1985, 1990). Others stress the subjective importance of 'trust' in such dependent relationships, see Roniger (1990). For a view which stresses the role of coercion, see Flynn (1974). For overviews of political clientelism, see Clapham (1982); Eisenstadt and Roniger (1980); Eisenstadt and Lemarchand (1981); Gellner and Waterbury (1977); Kaufman (1974); Rouquié (1978); Schmidt *et al.* (1977); Strickon and Greenfield (1972).

[11] One important exception is the rich new set of cases collected by Roniger and Gunes-Ayata (1994).

[12] For exceptions, see Hagopian (1990); Hagopian, in Mainwaring *et al.* (1992); and O'Donnell (1988).

[13] On the construction of political machines, see Luigi Graziano, in Schmidt *et al.* (1977); Scott (1969, 1972); Shefter (1978); Steffen W. Schmidt, in Schmidt *et al.* (1977); Tarrow (1967); and Weiner (1967), among others.

[14] Anthony Hall, and James C. Scott and Benedict J. Kerkvliet, both in Schmidt *et al.* (1977), explore how clientelism can evolve from patrimonial to repressive, as the role of coercion increases.

of deference erode, for example, the political effectiveness of clientelistic controls can be bolstered by threats of violence. Note, for example, the extraordinary resilience of violent electoral machines in the backlands of Brazil, Philippines, and Colombia in the 1980s.[15] And as the Mexican case will show, political entrepreneurs can replace rigid, antiquated controls with new, more sophisticated clientelistic arrangements without necessarily moving towards democratic pluralism. But the main point here is that if political action can create (or revive) clientelism, then it can undermine it as well.[16]

To develop a framework for analyzing the transition from clientelism to respect for citizenship rights, one can draw lessons from the interactive approach to the study of the transition to competitive electoral regimes.[17] For example, many authoritarian regimes only became electorally competitive after extended periods of repeated semi-competitive contests that strengthened democrats and weakened autocrats, as in Brazil, Colombia, Philippines, and Korea in the 1980s, for example. Similarly, the right to associational autonomy is also constructed gradually and unevenly through cycles of conflict that leave nascent democratic forces with political resources to draw on in each succeeding round. In contrast to these cycles of semi-competitive electoral contests, however, the movements to broaden the political terms of access to social entitlements often unfold on extra-institutional terrain, political parties may not be the key actors, and their periodic cycles are certainly not regularly scheduled. Furthermore, the construction of the right to associational autonomy does not simply follow from national electoral change; the opening of political access to state entitlements can precede electoral competition, as in Mexico, though it is often encouraged by it.

Note that the political term of *access* to social entitlements is distinct from the *scope* or *levels* of benefits, which are sometimes referred to as 'social citizenship' rights. The argument here does not attempt to explain the determinants of the levels of material entitlements; they are logically and historically distinct from regime type in general and from the right to associational autonomy in particular. For example, democratic regimes may offer access to a narrow range of social rights without attaching political conditions (e.g. food stamps in the USA), while authoritarian regimes may offer a broad range of material entitlements in exchange for deference (as in communist and populist regimes). Analysts of the construction of rights have tended to focus either on electoral enfranchisement or on the extension of social welfare rights, but not on the political terms of access to whatever the state has to offer.[18]

---

[15] See Grzybowski (1990), Lara and Morales (1990), and Zamosc (1990).

[16] Revolutions are the most obvious examples of political processes which can sweep away clientelistic systems, but they are rarely followed by respect for associational autonomy. New webs of clientelism can emerge in their wake, especially in rural areas. See for example Oi (1985). On the tensions over associational autonomy between peasant movements and left-wing Latin American political parties which claim to represent them, see Fox (1992a).

[17] See Stepan (1985, 1988); O'Donnell and Schmitter (1986); and Przeworski (1991a).

[18] See, for example, Barbalet (1988).

The causal argument here is that the right to associational autonomy is politically constructed through iterative cycles of conflict between three key sets of actors: autonomous social movements, authoritarian elites unwilling to cede power, and reformist state managers—defined as those willing to accept increased associational autonomy.[19] The argument is based on the assumption that as long as authoritarian elites remain united, there is little room for the construction of citizenship rights. If faced with legitimacy problems, however, authoritarian political elites sometimes split over whether to respond with repression or concessions.[20] The first step in the argument, then, is that reformists, defined by their greater concern for political legitimacy and resulting preference for negotiation over coercion, may conflict with hard-line colleagues over whether and how to cede access to the state.[21] Second, if and when such cracks in the system open up, social movements often attempt to occupy them from below, demanding broader access to the state while trying to defend their capacity to articulate their own interests. Third, once triggered, these recursive cycles of bargaining between ruling hard-liners, reformist elites, and social movements can gradually increase official tolerance for autonomous social organizations, often in a 'two steps forward, one step back' pattern.[22]

Even though societal actors often fail to win their immediate demands, if they manage to conserve some degree of autonomy in the troughs between cycles of mobilization, they retain a crucial resource to deploy at the next political opportunity. This process is highly uneven within nation-states. Societal groups gain legitimacy and leverage at very different rates and in different bargaining arenas.[23]

[19]   To frame an interactive approach to state–society relations as broadly as possible, this discussion does not detail the diverse range of repertoires of action and forms of representation among poor people's movements. Note also that this argument does not attempt to account for the emergence of these three sets of actors, but rather shows how certain patterns of interaction among them can explain the construction of respect for associational autonomy. On cycles of social mobilization and reform, see Piven and Cloward (1977) and Tarrow (1989, 1994).

[20]   For the purposes of this discussion, the trigger for division within authoritarian regimes is considered here to be contingent. See Stepan (1985) and O'Donnell and Schmitter (1986). Possible causes include economic crisis, international pressures, military defeat, and the 'excessive' use of repression, as well as radical protest from below.

[21]   When reformists deliberately encourage social mobilization to offset hard-line authoritarian rulers, they can be said to be pursuing a 'sandwich strategy' for political change. See Fox (1992c). Other examples include some of the US federal government's anti-poverty and civil rights efforts in the early 1960s, Colombian agrarian reform policy in the late 1960s, and Gorbachev's glasnost policies of the late 1980s.

[22]   Note that in this argument, mass mobilization alone cannot win citizenship rights. If authoritarian elites remain united, they can simply respond with coercion rather than concessions. Even when reformists are present within the state, they can lose; cycles of bargaining may well fail to build democratic rights. If hard-liners prevail, they will both repress social movements and purge reformists from the state (as in the downward spiral which followed El Salvador's 1979 reformist coup). See Stanley (forthcoming).

[23]   In Mexico, for example, citizens' groups from the north have had much greater success at winning official respect than in the much poorer, largely indigenous southern states. Even within the south, results vary greatly across bargaining arenas; winning access to social programs is much easier than ending impunity for violent officials. Similarly, even in relatively democratic Brazil, official respect for human rights varies directly by race, class, and region of victims. For further discussion of the texture of indigenous autonomy debate, see Bermejillo (1995) and Herrera (1995).

This iterative framework suggests that the transition from clientelism to citizenship involves three simultaneous, distinct patterns of state–society relations within the same nation-state: redoubts of persistent authoritarian clientelism can coexist with new enclaves of pluralist tolerance, as well as large gray areas of 'semi-clientelism' in between. These categories are analytically distinct, though often overlapping in practice. The analytical challenge which follows is to explain the relative weights of each of these distinct 'subnational regimes'.[24]

The authoritarian and pluralistic poles of this proposed continuum from clientelism to citizenship are easily defined, but the multiplicity of political relationships 'in between' challenges analysts to develop categories more appropriate to systems in transition (especially since many regimes in transition tend to stay short of a democratic threshold). This framework suggests that the category of 'semi-clientelism' might be useful to explore those state–society relationships that fall in between authoritarian clientelism and pluralist citizenship rights. Semi-clientelist authorities attempt to condition access to state benefits on political subordination, but without the direct threat of coercion.

For the authoritarian clientelist combination of material inducements and coercive threats to be effective, elites need to appear to be able to enforce compliance. If they lack the means to oversee, discover, and punish non-compliance, then the deals they strike with their subordinates are much less enforceable. Semi-clientelist power relations induce compliance more by the threat of the withdrawal of carrots than by the use of sticks.[25] Semi-clientelism differs from authoritarian clientelism because it relies on unenforceable deals, while it differs from pluralism because state actors still attempt to violate the right to associational autonomy.[26]

The differences between these categories can be illustrated with the example of vote-buying. Vote-buying is widely considered to violate basic democratic rights. But if one is interested in understanding how the balance of power between patrons and clients can shift toward the client, then it is crucial to examine the differences between authoritarian and semi-clientelist vote-buying. There is a qualitative difference between political bosses who have the coercive capacity to require proof of compliance (such mechanisms abound), and less violent electoral inducements which 'trust' the voter to go along with the bargain. In some contexts cultural

---

[24] This study suggests that the notion of 'subnational regime' may be useful for highlighting those enclaves within a nation-state that are dominated by their own distinctive linkages between rulers and ruled. These enclaves can be either territorial, such as states and regions, or issue-specific, such as the armed forces or the central bank. The focus in the case material that follows deals with both notions, working within a relatively pluralistic issue area (rural development policy) and documenting how political outcomes then vary depending on the territorial distribution of pro-pluralism actors in both state and society.

[25] Seen from the receiving end, the differences between the withdrawal of benefits and the threat of coercion are quite significant. Both can discourage autonomous collective action, but only one is potentially permanent in its effects.

[26] The term pluralism refers here to respect for associational autonomy rather than to the political system as a whole. Access to social programs is considered pluralistic when it is not conditioned on political subordination.

norms may be sufficient to guarantee compliance, but these can change as political systems become more competitive.[27] The politics of trust is shaped by institutions. If civic mobilization and/or institutional change increase the actual secrecy of the ballot, then citizens can avoid potential reprisals associated with rejecting authoritarian vote-buyers and still vote their conscience. Ballot secrecy is one of those democratic formalities that are especially important to the weakest members of the polity, since they are the most vulnerable to reprisals for voting the wrong way.[28]

The Mexican experience is useful for exploring the transitions from clientelism to semi-clientelism and citizenship, though the political system is still largely dominated by an authoritarian corporatist brand of electoral machine politics. Mexico is a limiting case for two reasons: clientelism's deep roots and the persistent gap between electoral competition and political democracy. First, the state's hegemony has long been based on the successful clientelistic incorporation of the poor. Indeed, the deeper the roots of authoritarian clientelism, the harder it will be to uproot them. Understanding how respect for pluralism can be extended in this especially difficult case will help to shed light on the dynamics of change under less institutionalized regimes. Second, the two decades of stop-and-go political openings since Mexico's dramatic 1968 legitimacy crisis make it possible to examine the ambiguous relationship between the liberalization of associational autonomy and the prospects for electoral democratization. Mexico is perhaps the most institutionalized member of the growing but underconceptualized category of electorally competitive 'less-than-democracies' now found in Asia, Africa, and the former Soviet bloc as well as Latin America. In this context, analytical frameworks that can explain the pace and direction of change in Mexico can contribute to filling this broader conceptual gap.

The empirical discussion begins with an analysis of Mexico's repeated cycles of societal mobilization from below, openings from above, conflict and backlash

[27] Taiwan is a case where political attitudes and opportunities are changing quickly, showing how political action can undermine clientelism. Vote-buying is still pervasive in Taiwan, and traditional norms of gratitude used to be sufficient to produce compliance. In the last several years, however, partly as the result of effective civic education campaigns, increasing numbers of voters accept the money and only comply symbolically. According to a recent study by the Center for Policy Studies at Sun Yat-Sen University, 44.8 per cent of the population of Taiwan's second largest city were given money for their vote, but only 12.7 per cent of them said they would actually vote for the candidate who bribed them (Herr 1993). Reportedly, one member of the family returns the favor with a vote for the ruling party while the rest feel free to vote their preference.

[28] In Colombia, for example, an apparently small change in ballot procedures significantly weakened clientelistic bosses. Until 1990, separate ballots were cast for each party, allowing bosses to check who was going to vote for whom while they waited in line. Ballot secrecy was greatly increased after 1990, when the system changed to a single ballot. Even where individual ballots might be secret, however, if communities are united in voting for the democratic opposition, then even anonymous precinct returns still reveal their dissent to authoritarian elites. In the key 1987 congressional elections in the Philippines, for example, government military units regularly assembled farmworkers to threaten them with reprisals should their villages vote for pro-land reform candidates (author's field interviews).

within both state and society. The interactive approach presented above is then applied to an analysis of the determinants of respect for associational autonomy in the case of Mexico's indigenous peoples' terms of access to rural development programs.[29] The empirical analysis combines change over time in the course of three successive generations of targeted rural development programs with an explanation of the range of outcomes across a development policy which was especially promising in terms of increased respect for associational autonomy. In summary, the general analytical framework is applied to a limiting case within Mexico, exploring how one of the most oppressed groups in one of the most deeply rooted systems of authoritarian clientelism can gain some degree of respect for its associational autonomy *vis-à-vis* the state.[30]

Filling the Cracks in the Mexican System

Ever since the legitimacy crisis that followed the harsh repression of the 1968 student movement, Mexico's ruling political class has sought ways of accommodating change without ceding power. The result has been recurrent cycles of conflict over the terms of state–society bargaining relations. From below, political parties and organizations of civil society have pushed the state to respect associational autonomy. From above, reformists have sought to displace machine-style authoritarian brokers whose intransigence provoked opposition and unrest by creating alternative bargaining channels that bypassed parties—both official and opposition.

In Mexico, political brokers play the key role in mediating state–society relations, both inside and outside the scope of the corporatist apparatus.[31] The classic political bargain required official incorporation of social groups under state tutelage in exchange for access to social programs. Mass protest was sometimes tolerated, as long as it was strictly 'social', but if it was perceived as 'political' (i.e. questioning

---

[29] Classic individualistic ideas of citizenship can be inappropriate for non-Western social actors. For a critique of the imposition of foreign notions of citizenship on indigenous societies, see Rivera Cusicanqui (1990). In part for this reason, this study analyzes associational autonomy in terms of the state's respect for ethnic and community-based groups rather than at the level of individual members of those communities.

[30] One hypothesis suggests that physical and social distance from national centers of power can facilitate the emergence of autonomous popular organizations, despite the persistence of entrenched local clientelism. Indeed, indigenous organizations have long preserved some degree of autonomy at the community level. But the capacity to organize autonomously is different from the construction of the *right* to associational autonomy. Indeed, the main opponents of associational autonomy tend to dominate many of the local branches of the federal, state, and municipal governments, and the distance from the national media and political opposition increases their capacity to use coercion with impunity.

[31] New historical research stresses that the coverage of Mexico's well-known corporatist organizations was partial rather than complete (Jeffrey W. Rubin, in Foweraker and Craig (1990)). On rural bosses, see Bartra (1975) and Fox (1992c). On elite political clientelism, see Camp (1990: 85–107); Centeno and Maxfield (1992); Purcell and Purcell (1980); and Smith (1979).

ruling party hegemony) the usual mix of partial concessions with repression shifted towards the latter. Movements were more likely to be labeled as political if they expressed their autonomy by publicly rejecting official subordination.[32]

The pyramid of brokers managed challenges to stability for decades, but as they became increasingly ossified and provoked growing resentment, social groups sought greater autonomy. By the 1980s, ascendant technocrats who viewed the old-fashioned brokers as both expensive and politically ineffective moved social policy away from reliance on traditional patronage and generalized subsidies towards measures ostensibly more targeted directly to the poor. This targeting process deliberately favored a mix of official and non-partisan social movements. In contrast to past repression of autonomous movement leaders, this new bargaining style recognized them as legitimate interlocutors as long as they steered clear of overt political opposition.

These new targeted channels shifted the mix of clientelistic carrots and sticks faced by social movements. Where state managers replaced their traditional crude insistence on ruling party control with more subtle forms of conditioning access to the system, one can speak of emerging semi-clientelist relations. Such relationships are not pluralistic because they still strongly discouraged any questioning of the government's broader socioeconomic policies and its controversial electoral practices. While the transition from clientelism to semi-clientelism may appear to be a step in the direction of responsive government, the erosion of strict controls on voter compliance may also *increase* the incentives for state managers to rely on electoral fraud to minimize uncertainty. This may be happening in some regions of Mexico.[33]

It is important to point out that Mexico's post-revolutionary political class has a long tradition of mobilizing social groups to settle its own internal conflicts, most notably during the radical populist phase in the 1930s. What began to change in the 1970s and 1980s was that social movements gained a greater capacity to retain some degree of autonomy in the course of bargaining with the state. These small increases in tolerance for autonomy left movements a crucial political resource which, if conserved in the troughs between waves of mobilization, could permit them to take advantage of the next political opportunity.

These conflict cycles led to three distinct patterns of state–social movement interaction: continued clientelism, modernized semi-clientelism, and more pluralistic

---

[32] This 'official vs. independent' social movement dichotomy was especially pronounced in the 1970s and 1980s, as collective resistance to the state grew. By the 1990s, social movements increasingly stressed autonomy from political parties in general, since contestational 'independence' had often involved subordination to opposition parties. See Jonathan Fox and Gustavo Gordillo, in Cornelius *et al.* (1989); Foweraker and Craig (1990); and Hellman (1992).

[33] Distributing patronage through semi-clientelistic means (i.e. non-enforceable deals) can also make fraudulent electoral outcomes more politically plausible to the electorate, since even if many individuals who accepted the incentives vote their conscience anyway, they cannot be sure of how many others also did, which in turn undermines the potential for collective action in defense of clean elections.

bargaining, distributed unevenly both in geographic and social terms. With the gradual accumulation of forces in civil society, the relative weights of these patterns changed and the pluralist enclaves grew over time. The analysis that follows traces this process in Mexico's most hostile environment for the consolidation of autonomous representative organizations: the nation's poorest, largely indigenous rural regions.[34]

Openings from Above Meet Mobilization from Below

Since the early 1970s, reformist policy-makers promoted three successive cycles of rural development programs which bypassed and competed with the rest of the state apparatus. These reformists never fully controlled policy implementation, but they were sometimes sufficiently influential to open up alternative channels for access to anti-poverty programs for the rural poor, allowing them to bypass authoritarian bosses. The first cycle of reform was launched during a wave of nationalist populism in the early 1970s, in the wake of the student movement and in response to growing rural protest. The second was initiated in 1979 from above; social pressures had ebbed, but the pre-emptive goal was to create channels to contain the next wave. The third targeted reform responded to the regime's first national electoral challenge in decades, extending into urban areas and building on the policy lessons and organizations left by the previous cycles. In each cycle of distributive reform, high-level, moderate reformists tried to offset more authoritarian elites by recruiting radical reformists at lower levels to promote contained social mobilization. They attempted to create counterweights to displace more rigid elites, though not to share power with the opposition. The goal was to induce and channel conflict in the short run to make the regime more stable in the long run.

In practice, most of these distributive programs were either captured by traditional authoritarian elements or were delivered through semi-clientelistic channels, yet each also involved small but significant openings to autonomous organizations in civil society. Since this enquiry focuses on the opening of pluralistic access, the discussion concentrates on the dynamics of those exceptional programs that permitted the creation of new political space. The first two rural development reform cycles are reviewed briefly to show how mobilization from below interacted with openings from above, followed by an analysis of Mexico's most recent anti-poverty strategy, the National Solidarity Program (PRONASOL).

[34] Similar cycles of social mobilization can also be found in Mexican urban politics, but their emergence in remote rural areas as well shows that the erosion of clientelism can be encouraged by political action, and is not driven exclusively by secular socioeconomic trends such as urbanization. On urban politics and the poor, see Bennett (1992); Cornelius (1975); Eckstein (1988); Fox and Hernández (1992); and Ward (1986).

THE RURAL INVESTMENT PROGRAM (PIDER)

Mexico launched the Program for Rural Development Investments (PIDER) in 1973. After years of anti-peasant policies, rapidly growing social pressures were overwhelming the official corporatist organizations inherited from the land reform of the 1930s. Waves of radical direct action swept the countryside, and guerrilla movements emerged in the most polarized regions. Reformists gained leverage within the state and they advocated the recognition of some dissident movements to channel their mobilization. Large-scale World Bank funding for PIDER made their task easier.

PIDER claimed to target its actions directly to the rural poor, rather than powerful elites who had captured most of the benefits of previous development programs. In practice, community participation was largely nominal.[35] Where reformists controlled actual project implementation, however, they targeted investments to political hotspots as concessions to independent mass movements. The Community Access Road program, for example, created employment and increased freedom of movement in some of the poorest and most isolated regions, undermining both traditional authoritarian bosses and incipient guerrilla groups. In some areas 'PIDER Brigades' of radical organizers successfully encouraged peasant protests against regional bosses for broader distribution of credit and fertilizer.[36] However, some reformists concerned with restoring the system's legitimacy in the longer run, including a future president, concluded that they needed to open up broader channels for participation to weaken entrenched rural bosses more systematically.[37]

THE VILLAGE FOOD STORE PROGRAM (CONASUPO-COPLAMAR)[38]

The national crisis surrounding the 1976 presidential succession was followed by an emphasis on restoring investor confidence. The partial political opening of anti-poverty policy closed up. Reformers then tried to channel dissent by liberalizing electoral politics. As the oil boom revived the economy in the late 1970s, the president's concern shifted to legitimation, permitting the creation of a more open

[35] According to one PIDER official: 'If participation is stimulated too much it gets out of PIDER's control and brings political problems. It becomes a political problem for PIDER when it begins to break up or threaten commercial interests . . .', quoted in Grindle (1981: 43). See also Cernea (1983) and Lindheim (1986).

[36] In one notable case, the PIDER Brigade was so effective at encouraging autonomous mobilization that the governor expelled them from the state (Fox 1992b).

[37] Notably, Carlos Salinas de Gortari's dissertation concluded that because of the ineffectiveness and corruption of the conventional state apparatus, the regime lost the political payoff associated with increased anti-poverty spending: 'the State [must] rely on a corps of leaders of local development programs who will be attentive to the problems encountered in the delivery of development projects to targeted communities . . . They must lead, not in the hierarchic sense of demanding obedience, but in the sense of coordinating and orienting a decision-making process in which the members of affected communities participate' (Salinas de Gortari 1982: 41–2).

[38] This section draws from the more detailed discussion in Fox (1992c).

channel for delivering resources to the very poor. The National Plan for Depressed Zones and Marginal Groups (COPLAMAR), together with the National Basic Foods Company (CONASUPO), organized an extensive network of village food stores designed to weaken local monopolies over staple food marketing in remote rural areas. As with PIDER, the degree to which the CONASUPO-COPLAMAR village store program actually encouraged or tolerated autonomous mobilization varied greatly in practice, but the creation of political space was much more systematic. Radical reformist organizers deliberately encouraged the creation of democratic regional consumer organizations to challenge corrupt private and bureaucratic elites.

The program provided three key resources for community organizing. First, the offer of cheap staple foods created a material incentive for participation to ensure its delivery to the villages. Second, the program's official legitimacy limited the violent repression often directed against autonomous grassroots mobilization. The regional elites whose political and commercial monopolies were threatened did fight back and most of the reformist organizers were eventually purged, but the program survived. Third, the program opened up community access to transportation, which had been tightly controlled by rent-seeking, often violent elites. With over 3,000 trucks, the program could both stock more than 12,000 village stores and regularly bring together large numbers of otherwise dispersed local delegates to create region-wide Community Food Councils.

Elite capture of the official channels for poor people's representation is what one would expect; most Community Food Councils were at best consultative and failed to play their intended role as autonomous, 'co-responsible' partners in food distribution operations. But unlike previous populist reforms, CONASUPO-COPLAMAR did not systematically condition material benefits on political subordination. While participatory traditions had survived at the village level, especially in indigenous areas, only rarely had isolated communities been able to overcome the powerful obstacles to *region-wide* organization. Regional peasant organizations are especially important in representing the interests of the rural poor because they have the potential to combine the clout of a larger group with the responsiveness of smaller associations. Village-level groups are easily isolated by their enemies, while national peasant organizations are usually democratic only in so far as they are made up of representative regional building blocks. In areas where loyalties rarely extended beyond family and village, the warehouses and Food Councils encouraged the emergence of regional collective identities. This unusually targeted social program survived Mexico's post-1982 economic crisis; it had generated a relatively autonomous, organized constituency, which greatly raised the potential political cost to the state of reneging on its commitment to the program. By the time the rural consumer movement peaked in 1985, more than one-fourth of Community Food Councils had gained the capacity to articulate their interests autonomously, as evidenced by their willingness to join a national network to protest corrupt and authoritarian policy implementation. The Food Councils were among the first genuinely mass-based, region-wide representative organizations of any kind for between one and two million of Mexico's most impoverished rural people.[39] Thus, the Community Food Councils became a new, two-way bridge between state and social actors. From above, state reformists structured new patterns of representation within rural society. From below, these new channels became opportunities for autonomous interest articulation in some regions, which in turn left their imprint on the state. This 'objective alliance' between social movements and reformists within the government food distribution company permitted the consolidation of effective citizen's oversight mechanisms, making it the first national experience with what would later be called *concertación social*. This new bargaining relationship moved away from traditional forms of subordination to a mix of semi-clientelism and respect for autonomy.[40]

Renovating Single-Party Rule: The National Solidarity Program

After the 1982 collapse of the oil/debt boom, social spending was reduced by cutting generalized programs and clientelistic patronage while strengthening the more targeted programs.[41] By the mid-1980s, with the ruling party under unprecedented electoral pressure from the right, some federal-level reformists ceded new space in the non-electoral arena towards the left. Where autonomous social organizations were sufficiently powerful, reformists sometimes stopped requiring overt political subordination in exchange for material concessions, as in the case of Mexico City's post-earthquake housing movements. The reformists were still overshadowed, however, by the technocrats who made macroeconomic policy, the 'dinosaurs' in the corporatist sectors of the party, and the government 'alchemists' who continued to handle elections. Mexico's dominant party was then shaken by an anti-authoritarian challenge from the voters in the 1988 presidential election.

After a hotly disputed race marred by widespread fraud, President Salinas entered office declaring that the one-party system was over. He promised a new relationship between state and society, seeking to revive citizen confidence by bypassing both the partisan opposition and the traditional corporatist apparatus. The traditional bureaucratic and corporatist channels were too inefficient to buffer the social costs of austerity which had fueled the 1988 opposition. Social spending would be increased, but targeted through new, ostensibly less leaky channels that

---

[39] For the geographic distribution of autonomous Food Councils, see Fox (1992c).

[40] 'Concertación' has been translated in a variety of ways in the Mexican context, ranging from 'social dialog' to 'corporative agreements'.

[41] This shift was especially clear in the area of urban consumer food subsidies, which supported a wide range of staples until the mid-1980s. Then the government began channeling food subsidies to tortillas and milk for means-tested low-income city-dwellers.

would have the largest possible positive impact on the president's public image. Much of the new social spending was brought under the umbrella of the National Solidarity Program (PRONASOL), which claimed to shift the balance of power away from the bureaucracy and to strengthen organized citizens.[42] The impact on poverty was debated, but it worked politically; the president and Solidarity both had very high 1991 opinion poll ratings, much higher than the official party.[43]

Solidarity was clearly politically motivated in that it skillfully targeted disproportionate resources to recover areas of strong center-left electoral opposition. For example, 12 per cent of Solidarity's entire 1992 budget went to the relatively small state of Michoacán, the main base of the center-left Party of the Democratic Revolution (PRD), just before the heated gubernatorial elections.[44] One-fourth of the 2,500 Solidarity promoters nationally were deployed there. The geographical targeting of spending to swing districts does not necessarily mean that access to the program's benefits was systematically conditioned on traditional forms of subordination, however. So far, much of the debate surrounding Solidarity's political character has been based more on ideological differences than empirical evidence, but the most plausible hypothesis is that, on balance, most of the electorally targeted spending was probably delivered through semi-clientelist means. The basis for this general proposition, which will not be tested here, is that since most Solidarity programs were induced from outside the community, they lacked the official party's once-powerful capacity to monitor and punish non-compliance at the individual level. As long as fraud remains an option for the regime, however, the importance of individual compliance with clientelistic deals can be reduced.[45]

Solidarity officially targeted the urban poor, peasants, and indigenous peoples, with various programs for sewage and potable water, health, education, food distribution, electrification, street paving, housing, and soft loans for low-income rural

---

[42] Solidarity proclaimed that its 'new dynamic . . . breaks with bureaucratic atavism and administrative rigidity. Public servants increasingly share a vocation for dialog, agreement, *concertación* and direct, co-responsible work with the citizenry, which also assumes an increasingly active and leading role in the actions intended to improve their standard of living . . .' (Rojas *et al.* 1991: 23).

[43] See the *Los Angeles Times* poll, 22 Oct. 1991. For comprehensive overviews of PRONASOL politics, see Dresser (1991); Cornelius *et al.* 1994. Solidarity spending rose sharply just before the 1991 mid-term elections and was widely credited with helping to revive the official party's electoral fortunes, although its impact is difficult to disentangle from reduced inflation and the beginnings of economic growth. For journalistic accounts of direct electoral use of Solidarity funding, see Beltrán del Rio (1990a, 1990b); Correa (1990); and Gómez Leyva (1991).

[44] Golden (1992). See also Cantú (1992). In addition, the governor's election campaign expenses reportedly topped US$30 million, almost $80 per vote officially cast for the PRI (Chávez 1992). For a state-level statistical analysis of electoral targeting, see Juan Molinar and Jeffrey Weldon, in Cornelius *et al.* (1994).

[45] During the Salinas administration, most electoral manipulation appears to have occurred before election day. For example, over 100,000 likely opposition voters were allegedly 'shaved' from the registration rolls in Michoacán state elections, especially in urban PRD strongholds. See Bardacke (1992). It must also be noted that the regime still uses sticks as well as carrots; selective political violence against the left also continues with impunity. The PRD reported that 230 of its members had been killed for political reasons since 1988 (*La Jornada*, 11 May 1993). See also Americas Watch (1990, 1991b); and PRD Human Rights Commission (1992).

producers.[46] Its early accomplishments in building physical infrastructure were dramatic, delivering services to thousands of communities. At the receiving end, Solidarity usually required beneficiaries to form Local Solidarity Committees, which in turn could choose from a fixed menu of public works (e.g. electrification, paved roads, school repair).

While Solidarity's official discourse stressing participation and co-responsibility drew from earlier PIDER and village food store programs of the 1970s and 1980s, four differences were especially notable. First, Solidarity responded directly to an electoral challenge. Second, it focused on the municipality, not just federal agencies, for service delivery. Third, it concentrated on the urban poor, using lessons from rural development. Fourth, its ideological thrust was much more prominent, promoting the idea of a partnership between state and society.

Most Solidarity funding was distributed through targeted grants to state and municipal governments.[47] The actual degree of public accountability and anti-poverty targeting depended in part on whether local governments were democratically elected. Even where majority rule prevailed, however, there was no guarantee that Solidarity funding would be targeted to the poorest of the poor. Even if public works were built in poor regions, the electoral logic of high-profile bridges, highways, and basketball courts had little to do with poverty alleviation. According to one top Solidarity policy-maker, for example, less than 40 per cent of its 1991 budget should really be considered anti-poverty spending, since the rest consisted of socially untargeted public works.

Solidarity's declared emphasis on strengthening the municipality differed notably from past social policy reforms. Where opposition political parties both managed to win over the majority of voters and succeeded in getting their municipal victories recognized, federal funders appeared not to discriminate, since Solidarity spent money in almost all opposition municipalities. But many opposition mayors protested that the program bypassed them completely, linking the state and federal government directly to Local Solidarity Committees in their jurisdictions. The most notable case was Michoacán's state capital, the largest city with a PRD mayor.[48] Moreover, where democracy did not prevail at the municipal level and citizens' groups persisted in pressing charges of fraud, they could be excluded from Solidarity.

Overall, Solidarity attempted to centralize power, promoting a symbolic link

---

[46] In addition to provision of public goods, this wide range of programs also included many programs whose benefits were more divisible, and therefore more vulnerable to local elite diversion. This distinction is central to the analysis of targeting. See Tendler (1982).

[47] Solidarity spending is under discretional presidential authority, as distinct from Mexico's official revenue-sharing, which is allocated according to technical formulas (John Bailey, in Cornelius *et al.* 1994).

[48] See Cantú (1992); Kathleen Bruhn and Keith Turner, and Jonathan Fox and Julio Moguel, both in Rodríguez and Ward (1995) on the PRD, and Albarrán de Alba (1992) on the National Action Party state government in Baja California Norte. The pattern was not consistent, since some opposition municipalities of both right and left managed to bargain for control over PRONASOL resources.

between the president and the local community, often bypassing both traditional political bosses and the opposition. This provoked serious subterranean conflicts between *salinistas* at the federal level and more traditional *priista* state authorities.[49] Solidarity proclaimed the creation of over 100,000 local committees, with an estimated average of 120 members each, and they became important as counterweights to the official party apparatus. In conflict with the party's traditional corporatist sectors, the president openly encouraged the Local Solidarity Committees to build state-wide and possibly national organizations with what he called the 'new mass politics of the Mexican state'.[50]

Solidarity had a mixed record with autonomous social organizations, recognizing some while bypassing others. In some cases, Solidarity agreements permitted independent poor people's organizations to bypass hostile governors; this kind of federal alliance permitted the Popular Defense Committee (CDP) to win the mayoralty of the state capitol of Durango, displacing regional PRI elites.[51] Where hostile governors managed to deny access to autonomous social organizations, however, they used Solidarity programs to promote competing development and welfare projects and reinforced the most authoritarian elements within the ruling party (e.g. in Guerrero). In many areas the Local Solidarity Committees appeared to reflect the 'modernization' of clientelistic control, as poor people in need of basic services shifted their patrons from regional elites to federal officials.

The broader question is: what exactly was the combination of clientelist, semi-clientelist, and pluralistic policy implementation patterns embedded within Solidarity's 'new mass politics'? Because of the extraordinary heterogeneity of the programs which are carried out under Solidarity's banner, systematic generalization awaits further empirical research. The remainder of this chapter will explain the limits and possibilities for the respect for associational autonomy in a limiting case, one of the most potentially 'pro-pluralism' Solidarity programs.

Targeting the Poorest: Solidarity Bolsters the National Indigenous Institute

The National Indigenous Institute (INI) carried out some of Solidarity's most innovative development projects. Mexico's indigenous peoples represent between

---

[49] See Dresser (1991) and Fernández (1991).

[50] In this context, the president reportedly once told a long-time friend, a historic radical leader of the urban popular movement: 'You were my teacher: everywhere I go I leave a base of support.' At a meeting of 500 representatives of 5,000 urban Solidarity Committees, for example, the president called for the creation of a National Neighborhood Network outside the ruling party. See Lomas (1991*a*, 1991*b*).

[51] The CDP won the mayoralty in 1992 without allying with either the PAN or the PRD, leading some observers to suggest its access to Solidarity resources affected its approach to national politics. See Haber (1992); Paul Haber, in Cornelius *et al.* (1994).

10 and 15 per cent of the nation's population and almost one-third of the 14 million Mexicans officially considered to be in 'extreme poverty'. With Solidarity, INI's budget increased eighteen-fold during the first three years of the Salinas government.[52] Most indigenous peoples also happen to live in the rural central and southern regions which provided Salinas with his official margin of victory in the 1988 presidential elections.[53]

Before, most of INI's budget had tended to go to its own staff rather than to indigenous economic development.[54] With Solidarity funding, however, INI could transform itself from a modest service provider into an actual economic development agency.[55] But money alone was not enough; INI's capacity for innovative policy implementation also depended on the role of a reform faction left embedded within the agency since past openings. Since its founding in 1948, INI's history has been shaped by a shifting internal balance of forces among three factions: authoritarian patrons primarily identified with the ruling party and local elites, semi-clientelist opponents of local elite domination of indigenous peoples who did not support independent demand-making, and pluralists who supported autonomous self-organization for indigenous rights. The latter group, indigenous rights advocates, have long accounted for a minority of local outreach staff, but they only rarely gained input into INI policy-making. INI officials stressed that they could be 'faithful' to Solidarity principles of participation, pluralism, and transparency because most of their development funds were distributed directly, bypassing municipal and state authorities who were often openly racist.[56]

INI had nominally supported the participation of indigenous organizations since the mid-1970s, but for the first time the agency committed itself explicitly

[52] According to INI's Annual Report, its 1991 (fiscal year) budget was US$140 million. President Salinas named Arturo Warman, PIDER veteran and one of Mexico's most distinguished anthropologists, as INI director. Solidarity's overall coordinator, Carlos Rojas, had worked for INI in Veracruz.

[53] Many Mexican anthropologists see indigenous voting patterns in terms of local 'short-term considerations that have nothing to do with political programs that propose alternative models for the future. The vote is seen more as a resource for here and now, [for] finishing a road, building a school or a drinking water system; [the] small benefits which help to resolve ancestral problems which shape their daily lives' (Bonfil 1990: p. iii). Indeed, parties are not present in most indigenous regions (though this began to change after 1988). The analytical problem is to distinguish cause from effect. If opposition political parties fail to champion indigenous rights, then isolated villagers have few incentives to take the serious risks inherent in opposition collective action, especially when it so often appears non-viable. As voters, they may not lack national political preferences as much as they lack meaningful national political choices.

[54] For example, see Flores (1991); and González et al. (1987).

[55] INI's other new initiatives during the Salinas administration included a human rights program which released over 4,000 indigenous prisoners, as well as promotion of a constitutional amendment that officially recognized Mexico as a multi-cultural society for the first time. As of mid-1993, human rights groups campaigned for the freedom of several thousand indigenous people who remained in jail without due process.

[56] One top INI official also stressed that his staff was different from most Solidarity programs because they were 'usually not in any political party. It's very unusual that INI personnel are in the PRI—but they aren't in the [opposition] PRD either. They aren't people who are going to induce [i.e. manipulate] or condition.' He claimed that because they work in such remote regions, 'they will work with existing organizations—they can't invent others'.

to a pluralistic bargaining process. Now, INI was to: 'contribute to *the strengthening of indigenous organizations, increasing their autonomy and their capacity for representation and [project] management* . . . All the representative and legally constituted organizations can be subjects of these *concertación* processes, without any political or religious discrimination . . . *Public institutions will abstain from intervening in the internal decisions of the organizations with which INI has concerted actions*' (INI 1990: 41–2, emphasis added).[57]

How did INI put these policy guidelines into practice? This question is best answered by examining INI's largest economic development program, the Regional Solidarity Funds (FRS).[58] In principle, the Regional Funds went further than most Solidarity programs in developing a pluralist relationship between the state and organized citizens for two reasons. First, the state devolved *regional* development decision-making to civil society, rather than micro-managing each local project from above. Second, the interlocutors were supposed to be *systematically* made up of autonomous councils of representative organizations, in contrast to the *ad hoc* and discretionary relationships with autonomous groups which predominated elsewhere.[59] In other words, the Regional Funds were unlike any other Solidarity program because pluralistic access was officially supposed to include the entire set of representative groups in each region. Ostensibly, elected officials were not involved, and official organizations participated in the Regional Funds just like any other producer group.[60]

The Regional Funds were launched in 1990. Each INI field outreach office convened a general assembly of the formal and informal community-based social and economic organizations in its area of influence. The general assembly was to elect a Leadership Council (LC), which would actually operate the fund and evaluate project proposals submitted from the organizations of the region. Loans could last from one crop cycle to several years, and could cover a broad range of economic activities. Preference was to be given to those with region-wide multiplier effects, as opposed to projects whose benefits were concentrated in small

[57] Participation is limited to policy implementation here. INI continued to reject indigenous groups' long-standing demands for greater involvement in the policy process itself. Some of INI's most reformist policy-makers tried this in 1983, but they were quickly purged.

[58] INI's other main economic program was its support for coffee producers after the abrupt withdrawal of the Mexican Coffee Institute from the market. Two-thirds of coffee producers are indigenous, accounting for 30 per cent of national production and one-third of coffee lands (INI 1990: 17). INI's coffee program involved both pluralistic relations with autonomous producer organizations and semi-clientelist relations with INI-sponsored Local Solidarity Committees. See Luis Hernández and Fernando Celis, in Cornelius *et al.* (1994).

[59] INI described the FRSs in explicitly political terms: 'The Funds are an innovative process [to] increase the participatory role of civil society in decision-making and in the definition of policy, which reflects a change in State–Society relations. The relationship of co-responsibility established between the government and the indigenous population implies a turnaround in the role of [government] institutions to avoid reproducing paternalistic and vertical attitudes . . .' (INI 1991: 2).

[60] INI also encouraged the FRSs to go beyond economic support for production projects and become advocates for indigenous communities in the broader public investment allocation process, largely unsuccessfully.

groups. In practice, projects ranged from tiny family enterprises and corrupt clientelistic payoffs to long-term investments in group marketing that actually had region-wide development impact.

After their first two years, INI's own internal evaluations found that between one-fourth and one-third of the Regional Funds were becoming consolidated under indigenous organization control, a comparable share were failing, in part due to capture by authoritarian elites, and a plurality were still run by INI outreach staff.[61] The mixed performance was due to a variety of factors to be discussed further below, including continuing INI semi-clientelism, uneven levels of indigenous organizational development, and outright authoritarian exclusion. The most consolidated Funds emerged in regions where two factors came together: where indigenous producer groups were already well organized (a legacy of past cycles of protest and limited openings) and where INI officials were either willing or obliged to cede power over funding.

Leadership Council Consolidation: Are Adversaries Included?

Because the Regional Funds attempted to include the full range of representative economic development organizations in their regions, they were the most promising 'pro-pluralism' case within Solidarity, but to what degree did the state actually share power with civil society, as promised? The answer requires a detailed study of who was actually represented by each Leadership Council, and the extent to which those that were representative gained autonomy *vis-à-vis* INI. Administrators were to support project design, but not to intervene in the actual decision-making process. Nevertheless, the official financial procedures required that local INI directors co-sign project loan checks. This gave each director potential veto power over the decisions of the Leadership Councils, provoking serious debate between grassroots organizations and INI officials. The field study of the politics of access to the Regional Solidarity Funds focused on the southern state of Oaxaca, which accounted for twenty of the almost 100 Regional Funds nationwide in 1992.[62] INI's own Oaxaca staff used evaluation categories that paralleled the traditional clientelist, semi-clientelist, and pluralist patterns suggested above. They categorized the Leadership Councils as: (*a*) LCs whose development was blocked by the intervention of political parties, local economic or political bosses, or conflicts between local groups, (*b*) LCs which were INI-run (i.e. semi-clientelist),

---

[61]   The more consolidated Regional Funds were reportedly in Veracruz, Chiapas, and Oaxaca, while those in the Huasteca, Chihuahua, and the Yucatan peninsula did poorly. Tabasco was especially disastrous; the Governor tried to impose a corrupt crony as local INI director, provoked a mass protest movement, and then rejected any development aid that could possibly reach potential opposition sympathizers. Not coincidentally, the state PRD leader, Manuel López Obrador, had won a broad indigenous following during his tenure as local INI director in the early 1980s.

[62]   Oaxaca is one of Mexico's poorest states and at least 44 per cent of the state's population speaks one of the state's seventeen indigenous languages (Blanco Rivera 1991).

(*c*) LCs which gained autonomy from the INI, using the fund to consolidate their organizing process and pursue regional development strategies. According to INI's confidential evaluations, towards the end of their first year, of the twenty Oaxaca LCs, five were blocked or taken over by political bosses, ten were still INI-run, and five were gaining autonomy. This general pattern was confirmed by the author's direct field checks, together with a survey of independent indigenous leaders and non-governmental development experts from throughout the state. This survey also found a consensus that after the first two years of Regional Fund operations, at least six Leadership Councils had reached 'consolidation', meaning that autonomous groups played a leading role in resource allocation decisions.[63] This survey found that only three of the twenty Oaxaca Leadership Councils excluded representative indigenous organizations.

Perhaps the single most revealing indicator of relative pluralism was the presence of affiliates of the non-partisan Oaxaca State Network of Coffee Producing Organizations (CEPCO), the most consolidated autonomous grassroots economic organization in the state, including over 20,000 mainly indigenous small-scale producers.[64] In most Leadership Councils they shared power (and therefore funds) with both corporatist and other autonomous organizations, often for the first time ever. Several CEPCO members claimed to be under-represented in the Councils, but only in two cases out of ten were they excluded.[65] Overall, however, the Regional Funds program constituted a small fraction of overall Solidarity funding, even in largely indigenous rural areas.

The 'War of Position' for Pluralist Inclusion

The potential distribution of pluralistic Leadership Councils depended, fundamentally, on the varying 'thickness' of Mexico's organized indigenous civil society—in some regions richly textured, in others quite thin or still heavily structured by clientelism. This pattern was not random; the uneven map of indigenous civil society reflected the historical legacies of both past movements from below and

---

[63] These Leadership Councils were based in Jamiltepec, Miahuatlán, Huautla, Tlacolula, Guelatao, and Cuicatlán. It must be stressed that 'consolidation' does *not* imply that all or even most member groups of an LC were representative grassroots groups. Five of Oaxaca's twenty LCs were not 'test' cases because of the lack of autonomous indigenous producer organizations in those regions as of mid-1992. For details, see Jonathan Fox, in Cornelius *et al.* (1994).

[64] Most CEPCO member groups are non-partisan or operate within the PRI, although a few sympathize with the PRD. CEPCO's main activity is buying, processing, and selling coffee, setting a floor price after the state withdrew from the market in 1989 and representing about one-third of Oaxaca's small coffee producers. CEPCO's success at providing an alternative was perceived as a threat by much of the state government and the corporatist apparatus. See Moguel (1991); Moguel and Aranda (1992).

[65] A robust notion of pluralism would go beyond this inclusion/exclusion dichotomy and involve some degree of proportional representation. Funds include groups ranging in size from tiny, kinship groups to producer associations representing thousands of families, yet in most Leadership Councils each has the same vote. Some INI directors used their clientele as counterweights to keep more broadly representative groups in the minority. The Mazateca highlands Leadership Council led the

openings from above. Some regions had experienced two decades of ebb and flow of protest and mobilization, often beginning with land rights and then focusing on ethnic identity and human rights issues.[66] Most of the movements that managed to offset entrenched regional political and economic elites had previously received some kind of support, or at least tolerance, from reformist programs like PIDER or CONASUPO-COPLAMAR; each brief and partial opening of political space for new levels of region-wide collective action left the movements better able to take advantage of future cracks in the system. This 'accumulation of forces' over time was very uneven, however, and many regions still lacked autonomous groups with the bargaining power and organizational capacity needed to handle development projects. In these regions, INI officials continued to control the Regional Funds, according to both non-government development organizations and INI's own internal evaluations.

If the map of representative societal groups was uneven, so was INI's commitment to the program's pluralist principles. The directors of each of the almost 100 outreach centers were key actors, since they were responsible for convening the elections for Leadership Councils in their region. They also retained the power to co-sign the development project checks. According to high-level 'pro-pluralism' INI staff, *less than half* of the outreach directors 'understood' the goals of the Regional Funds program (i.e. were willing to relinquish their traditional discretional authority over funding).

Both state and societal actors willing to share power were distributed unevenly throughout the country, and possibilities for respect for associational autonomy were greatest where they overlapped. Where consolidated, representative organizations already existed, and INI directors were willing to devolve effective power over Regional Fund resource allocation, 'virtuous circles' of pluralistic policy implementation emerged. These nascent processes nevertheless faced two major obstacles at higher levels in the political system. The first was resistance from more authoritarian political elites, often entrenched in state governments, and the second was INI's own semi-clientelistic tendencies.

Governors are strategic authoritarian elements within the regime, in part because they can resist reform efforts in the name of federalism.[67] In states where indigenous peoples joined the electoral opposition, authoritarian elites usually blocked the Regional Funds program (e.g. Tabasco, Michoacán, Guerrero). INI may

first experiment in institutionalizing proportional representation, weighting the number of assembly delegates according to the membership of each participating organization. The INI convened this process in an apparent effort to undermine the outspoken CEPCO-affiliated leadership of the Mazateca region's LC and to strengthen the official corporatist group, but the independent coffee producers swept the elections.

[66] Recent indigenous movements have been most intense in Chiapas, Oaxaca, Hidalgo, Veracruz, and Guerrero. See Mejía Pineiros and Sarmiento (1987); Nagengast and Kearney (1990); Sarmiento (1991); and the journals *Etnias* and *Ojarasca* (formerly *México Indígena*).

[67] The rate at which presidents remove governors is an excellent indicator of the degree of intra-state conflict in Mexico. During the first three years of the Salinas administration, 9 of 31 governors had been forced to resign.

have had more room for maneuver in Oaxaca in part because the state lacked a state-wide electoral challenge. Yet the most authoritarian response to the program was in a state with virtually no electoral competition at all—Chiapas. Governors of Chiapas, one of Mexico's most socially polarized states, tend to be among the most repressive and patrimonial. Indigenous organizations in Chiapas were neverthe-less highly developed in many regions, reportedly leading to consolidation among almost half of the Regional Funds in the state (according to INI's survey). INI and indigenous producer organizations were sufficiently successful at building toler-ant relationships that the governor jailed three top INI officials on trumped-up charges of fraud. Autonomous indigenous organizations marched to defend them. As one leader put it: 'Their only crime was to work with everyone, whether or not they are sympathizers of the government . . . We demand that they respect us, now that we're learning [to carry out development projects], that they don't block our work . . . This is a political problem—they blame the INI for everything that hap-pens in Chiapas, but we want to make clear that these are our decisions.'[68]

The other main threat to pluralistic inclusion of autonomous groups was INI's political imperative to demonstrate its loyalty to the Salinas government's broader policy agenda. For example, in the brief period of public debate before the presid-ent announced his historic 1991 legalization privatization of the land reform sys-tem, INI was perceived as concerned about the possible social cost.[69] Once the constitutional reform was announced, however, INI's director closed ranks in support, calling a last-minute national meeting of 500 Regional Fund represen-tatives to meet the president as the national debate peaked. The first reaction of Oaxaca's twenty Leadership Councils was to reject the 'invitation'. They felt that, since their membership had not yet had the opportunity to discuss the proposed reform, they were in no position to go to a national meeting of *de facto* acclama-tion. Some even expressed concern for their physical safety upon their return to their communities, since they would be perceived as having supported the reform. After an extended open debate, a desperate appeal from INI's Oaxaca state dir-ector helped to swing a 14 to 6 vote in favor of their going to Mexico City. If he proved unable to deliver his ostensible social base in a major INI effort to show the agency's loyalty to this key presidential project, he risked being replaced by a less flexible director. Regardless of their vote, most fund leaders felt the INI had betrayed its promise to treat them like citizens.

This heavy-handed 'round-up' for the presidential meeting resonated with traditional clientelism, but it was actually more semi-clientelist in content. The reformist officials attempted to condition access, but indigenous leaders freely debated the strategy and tactics of their response. They faced the threat of the withdrawal of carrots, not sticks. Several months later, when INI officials asked the

---

[68] Rojas (1992). Leaders of the Chiapas funds were also involved in the successful Xi 'Nich human rights protest march to Mexico City in early 1992. On Chiapas peasant movements more generally, see Neil Harvey, in Foweraker and Craig (1990).

[69] See Pérez (1991). For a political analysis of the 1991 reform of Mexico's land tenure system, see Fox (1994c).

same state council of Regional Fund leaders to meet with the government's candidate for governor of Oaxaca, they again debated how to respond. Again, the vote was 14 to 6 to invite the official candidate, but on the condition that the state-wide council invite all other candidates for governor as well. INI proceeded to arrange the meeting, but 'forgot' to invite the opposition candidates. The indigenous leaders proceeded to meet with opposition leaders on their own; this time they used their autonomy to open new terrain for civic pluralism.

In summary, an important minority of the Regional Solidarity Funds made progress towards developing more tolerant relationships between reformist branches of the state and many of Mexico's autonomous indigenous organizations. This process also led to new degrees of power-sharing between politically and ethnically diverse indigenous organizations themselves. Nevertheless, this process lagged in much of the country because of semi-clientelism entrenched within the state, authoritarian exclusion and backlash, and the uneven degrees of consolidation among autonomous indigenous groups themselves.[70]

Towards Pluralism without Democracy?

Since the early 1970s, successive waves of rural development reform opened small but significant cracks in the system, permitting greater space for more tolerant bargaining relations between the state and society in some of Mexico's poorest regions. The openings were small because they were limited to those few regions and policy areas where reformists effectively intervened in the implementation of rural development policy. The openings were significant because they offered political and economic resources which helped the consolidation of ever-larger representative and autonomous social organizations.

Even some of society's weakest actors—indigenous smallholder movements—increased their capacity to bargain with the state while retaining important degrees of autonomy. Some chose to abstain from overt electoral challenges, mainly to avoid losing semi-clientelistic access to significant development resources. But if representative leadership remained in place, then they could choose to engage in open opposition politics if and when the political opportunity structure should change

---

[70] As of mid-1993, the future of the Regional Solidarity Funds was in doubt. The Social Development Ministry, which controls overall Solidarity funding, had frozen INI's 1992 allocations for the Regional Solidarity Funds, blaming lagging repayment rates. Repayment problems were not surprising, given problems of profitability throughout the agricultural sector, but since the government was very flexible with much larger debts from other agricultural borrowers, such as large coffee plantation owners or the buyers of privatized sugar mills, slow repayment rates alone were not an especially credible explanation for defunding the program. INI had been politically weakened by the transfer of its influential director to fill the newly created post of Agrarian Attorney General. This left INI's Regional Funds vulnerable to opposition from powerful anti-pluralist elements within the Social Development Ministry itself. Since the Secretary of Social Development wanted to win the 1994 candidacy for president, he blunted reform efforts to avoid conflict with governors.

in the future. In a gradual 'war of position', social movements and state reformists pushed back the boundaries of the politically possible, though often more through an 'objective alliance' than explicit coalitions.[71] With the National Solidarity Program, political openings from above and community organization from below further eroded classic clientelism, in urban as well as rural areas. There is little evidence, however, that pluralistic bargaining took its place, beyond unusual enclaves such as those documented here. As a result, the most plausible hypothesis is that where authoritarian clientelism did break down, semi-clientelism rather than citizenship rights usually took its place.

Yet the relationship between the distributive and electoral realms of politics remains problematic. In the electoral arena, Mexico's gradual liberalization began in the early 1970s and was largely limited to the Congress, the weakest branch of government.[72] Both the vote-counting process and the mass media remained virtually closed to the opposition. Nevertheless, by the early 1990s the regime entered an uncertain process of selective democratization, recognizing some opposition victories (usually from the right) but not others (usually from the left). The regime began to accept some electoral defeats, but more often in response to mass civic anti-fraud protests than to actual ballot results. As of 1993, most contested elections were still settled through protest and negotiation *after* the actual voting process was over, known as the 'second round'.[73]

One indicator of the ambiguous relationship between distributive and electoral politics is the uncertain relationship between the liberalization of access to distributive programs and the limited democratization in the electoral arena. Was more open access to social programs a substitute for, or in spite of the lack of, further electoral democratization? Did the relatively open distributive policies analyzed here simply constitute the exception that proves the rule of Mexican authoritarianism, in that each partial opening of social programs merely bought votes to reinforce electoral hegemony? Generalization is difficult because electoral conflict had a contradictory impact on most of Solidarity's distributive programs—all at once, it pressured reformists to encourage the legitimacy of pluralism, created an incentive for them to use the programs as a semi-clientelistic mechanism to discourage electoral opposition, and provoked an authoritarian backlash from clientelistic machine politicians. As a result, Solidarity implementation involved three scenarios which unfolded *simultaneously*: more of the same authoritarian clientelism; modernized semi-clientelism, involving attempted but unenforceable buying of political support; and pluralism, where anti-poverty resource allocation was

---

[71] Distributive reform thus became political reform, as Przeworski defines it: 'a modification of the organization of conflicts that alters the prior probabilities of realizing group interests given their resources.' See Adam Przeworski, in O'Donnell *et al.* (1986: 58).

[72] See Cornelius (1987); and Kevin Middlebrook, in O'Donnell *et al.* (1986). On electoral change in the 1980s, see Cornelius *et al.* (1989). For a comparative discussion of Mexico's transition which explores the distinction between the formal regime and the actual political system, see Camou (1992).

[73] The regime was able to manage this uncertain process largely because the most contested races—for governors and mayors—were staggered so that the ruling party faced only one or two difficult states at a time.

not conditioned on political subordination. The Regional Solidarity Fund experience showed that the trend for state action to divide into these three patterns emerged in regions both with and without electoral competition.

The clearest connection between distributive and electoral politics involves social spending in opposition voter strongholds, but the actual electoral impact of such targeting depends on the degree to which clientelistic controls have eroded on the ground. In other words, electoral impact of pork barrel-type spending on potential opposition voters depends not only on the disproportionate *amount* channeled to a given district, but also on the degree to which political control mechanisms can actually *enforce* compliance in exchange for these resources. One good indicator of the persistence of authoritarian controls is the degree of actual ballot secrecy. In the 1992 Michoacán governor's race, which coincided with massive Solidarity funding, for example, the right to ballot secrecy was violated in one-fifth of the polling places observed by an independent observer group. Ballot secrecy for indigenous people was especially vulnerable, under the pretext of literacy and language problems.[74]

Solidarity's electoral targeting certainly helped to buffer the political impact of the government's controversial macroeconomic program, weakening the opposition in the short run in some areas.[75] In the longer run, however, if the state's mechanisms for actually enforcing voter compliance continue to weaken, then more and more citizens might well both accept pork barrel funding and still vote their conscience, as Mexican voters' civic activism broadens and deepens. Opposition party leaders increasingly urged potential supporters to accept the inducements from the ruling party, especially since they were usually paid for with public funds, but to vote their conscience anyway. The prospects for this opposition response to official semi-clientelism depend largely on whether more votes can be deposited secretly and be counted fairly.

The relationship between distributive and electoral politics can be contradictory, opening in one arena while remaining closed in another. This means that Mexico's process of eroding clientelistic controls over distributive politics will not necessarily lead to electoral democratization. Indeed, it is possible that semi-clientelism's lack of guaranteed enforcement mechanisms will *increase* incentives to use electoral fraud. The prospects for clean elections are likely to reflect in part the relative strength of powerful currents within the regime that oppose further political concessions and in part the efforts of opposition parties and autonomous social actors to broaden and deepen their still uneven roots in society. The prospects

[74] On the numerous irregularities, including widespread reports of attempts to condition Solidarity funding on PRI votes, see the state election observer report by the Convergencia de Organismos Civiles por la Democracia (1992).

[75] The regime's willingness to cede legitimacy to autonomous citizens' groups while continuing to manipulate elections also sharpened divisions within the left-leaning electoral opposition. When the wounds of the 1988 electoral conflict were still fresh, the PRD harshly condemned social organizations that bargained for Solidarity funds, asserting that they were implicitly recognizing the president's legitimacy. The PRD's stance later softened, but its relationship with important social movements was damaged. See Dresser (1991) and Haber (1994).

for democratization in Mexico will thus depend on how conflict between more and less authoritarian policy currents within the state interacts with growing civic pressure from below.[76]

Conclusions

It is difficult to generalize about how national political change interacts with the process of extending effective citizenship rights to the entire population, largely because our analytical categories for 'actually existing' political systems fail to capture important gray areas.[77] Many of the authoritarian regimes around the world that have now turned to electoral politics are not necessarily in transition to more fully democratic regimes; they can stabilize far short of democracy.[78] Mexico is not the only country in the early 1990s which holds competitive elections but still falls short of a democratic threshold. El Salvador, Guatemala, Colombia, and Peru come to mind in Latin America. Asian examples include Taiwan, Thailand, Pakistan, Malaysia, the Philippines, and large regions of India; in Africa, Nigeria, Ghana, Senegal, and Kenya, among others.[79] Serbia is the most notable case of authoritarian electoral politics in Europe. Several of the former Soviet republics fall into this category as well. The point here is not to enter the important normative and analytical debates about different subtypes of democracy (e.g. presidentialist, delegative, exclusionary, etc.). Instead, the argument is that empirical democratic theory needs to deal with the implications of its own premises: if regimes fall short of *any* of the conventional minimum criteria for political democracy, then they are not democratic. This distinction matters a great deal for understanding how such regimes behave and which interests are represented under them.

The politics of social policy can tell us a great deal about non-electoral dimensions of political democratization. A wide range of regimes are now experimenting

[76] So far, two scenarios predicted by Cornelius and Craig are combining: 'modernization of authoritarianism with selective pluralism' and 'limited power sharing', along the lines of the Indian Congress Party model (Cornelius and Craig 1991: 118–19).

[77] As Pye put it, 'we need finer shades of typologies of political systems between the classical polar opposites of authoritarian and democratic. In the wake of the crisis of authoritarianism we can expect a wide variety of systems that will become part authoritarian and part free and that will fall far short of any reasonable definitions of democracy.' See Pye (1990: 13).

[78] See Karl (1990) on 'electoralism'; Schmitter and Karl (1991); Rosenberg (1991: 72–91); and Hermet *et al.* (1978). Stable electoral competition is sometimes confused with political democracy (e.g. Higley and Gunther 1992). Mexico's ruling party, for example, holds the world's record for stability; it has presided over electoral presidential successions since 1929. Some analysts fall into the opposite trap, assuming that unfair elections are politically meaningless exercises. Note, for example, the surprise military split and subsequent civic uprising following Philippine President Marcos's fraudulent 'snap' elections in 1986. See also the debate over the relevance of El Salvador's sharply constrained wartime elections of the mid-1980s in Herman and Brodhead (1984); Karl (1986).

[79] One could argue that India falls short as well, in spite of its widely acclaimed national electoral process. If authoritarian clientelism, fraud, and vote-buying are widespread in several large states, such as Bihar, then tens and possibly hundreds of millions of voters are effectively excluded from democratic politics, in turn skewing the entire national political center of gravity.

with 'demand-based' anti-poverty funds targeted to meet the challenge of making structural economic adjustment politically viable; Mexico's Solidarity program is an especially sophisticated version of this much broader trend. Bolivia's social emergency fund was the first to attract international attention in 1986, and related programs were carried out by Peru, Chile, Zambia, Senegal, Ghana, Poland, El Salvador, Guatemala, and Honduras. Like Solidarity, some of these new targeted anti-poverty programs created new political openings for social movements and non-governmental organizations, while others reinforced clientelistic partisan controls. El Salvador and Senegal used their programs as instruments of political control, at least through the late 1980s, while in Bolivia, Chile, and Zambia, transitions to electoral democracy permitted more pluralistic anti-poverty policy. Peru's program largely perpetuated semi-clientelism.[80] Across this disparate group of countries, the degree of political conditionality required for access to these new social funds is a key indicator of the transition from clientelism to citizenship.

This focus on the politics of social policy shows that the relationship between electoral competition and the erosion of authoritarian clientelism is not obvious. In other words, electoral competition can either strengthen or weaken coercive clientelism, which in turn can be either strengthened or weakened by electoral competition. Each clearly influences the other, but the direction is politically contingent. For example, if elections offer alternatives to voters, they can increase clients' leverage over vote-buying patrons and reduce the likelihood that defection will be punished with coercion (as in Taiwan and Thailand).[81] But clientelistic machines around the world have also shown that the threat of electoral competition can also create incentives for elites to sharply limit political choices. Even under ostensibly democratic regimes, the use of violence with impunity against certain groups or in certain regions can perpetuate authoritarian enclaves (as in rural areas of Brazil, Colombia, and the Philippines).[82] More generally, clientelistic bargaining relations are most imbalanced in authoritarian bastions where clients lack the exit options associated with meaningful electoral alternatives.

The persistence of authoritarian redoubts under competitive electoral systems matters for national politics.[83] The spread of seemingly small free spaces in civil society is widely recognized to weaken dictatorships, but the connection between uneven degrees of freedom at the local level and national politics is rarely considered when analyzing the prospects for democratic consolidation. The resilience of seemingly mere local authoritarian enclaves constrains national democratic consolidation because margins matter for majority rule.[84] The exclusion of potential

---

[80] On social investment funds, see Graham (1991, 1992); Carol Graham, in Cornelius *et al.* (1994). One could argue that opposition state governments in India carried out comparable programs earlier. See Kohli (1987); and Echeverrí-Gent (1992).

[81] See Herr (1993) and Shenon (1992); as well as Scott (1990).

[82] Colombia, for example, appeared to take a major step towards greater pluralism by permitting citizens to elect their mayors for the first time in 1988. But once elected, many opposition mayors were assassinated by state-sanctioned death squads. See Carroll (1991).   [83] See Fox (1994*b*).

[84] In contrast, some analysts consider elections to be democratic if they are competitive and involve 'the bulk' of the population (e.g. Huntington 1991–2: 579–616).

swing voters from access to associational autonomy and competitive elections can be enough to determine national political outcomes.

There are many examples in the Americas. Even though Chile had long been considered to be a consolidated democracy, the national political equation was skewed through the early 1960s by the disenfranchisement of the rural poor.[85] The same was true in Brazil, and the prospect of permitting the illiterates to vote contributed to the 1964 coup. Peru's largely indigenous illiterate population was also denied the vote until the return of electoral rule in 1980. Regional redoubts of exclusion persist even after such formal barriers are removed. In Brazil's 1989 presidential race, the candidate of the left took the large cities but the right won with the hinterland, where authoritarian clientelism and semi-clientelism are still pervasive.[86] In Mexico's 1988 presidential race, rural districts gave Salinas his official majority.[87] The general point that 'subnational authoritarian regimes' can tip the national political balance should not be new to analysts of the United States, where the coercive disenfranchisement of African-Americans and many poor whites in the South determined national political outcomes for most of the twentieth century.[88]

The question of how effective access to citizenship rights is extended throughout an *entire* society requires a framework which differs from most approaches to national regime change. While transitions to electorally competitive regimes are usually analyzed in terms of movement back and forth along two dimensions, the erosion of clientelism can evolve in several directions at once. Authoritarian clientelism does not necessarily erode in a linear process towards citizenship. The Mexican experience shows that sophisticated state managers rule can promote semi-clientelism as an alternative to citizenship rights, though social movements can occupy small cracks in the system and try to open them further. The result is a gradual and uneven transition which combines entrenched redoubts of authoritarianism, broad patterns of modernized semi-clientelism, and enclaves of pluralist tolerance that take on elements of citizenship. The transition from clientelism to citizenship therefore involves the simultaneous coexistence of these three different *de facto* political systems under the same formal regime. Where subnational authoritarian regimes live on within nationally competitive electoral systems, their transitions can get stuck, preventing them from crossing the threshold to democratic governance.

This conclusion suggests that the conventional notion of political democratization as a single, implicitly linear regime transition should be recast as a set of different transitions along the various key dimensions of democracy.[89] What, then, are some of the more general relationships between these different genres of transition?

[85] See Loveman (1979).

[86] See Da Silveira Cotrim (1990). On the persistent clout of the traditional political class, see Hagopian (1992).   [87] See López *et al.* (1989).

[88] The literature on the veto power of the Southern bloc in national politics is vast. See, for example, Katznelson *et al.* (1993).

[89] Because these dimensions evolve along such different paths, Schmitter suggests that it may be useful to understand democracy as a 'composite of "partial regimes," each of which [is] institutionalized around distinctive sites for the representation of social groups' (Schmitter 1992: 427).

We still lack systematic analyses of the ways in which electoral competition relates to other ostensibly minimum conditions for democracy, such as civilian control over the military, effective universal suffrage, an end to vote fraud, or ending impunity for state-sanctioned violence.[90] Such transitions may overlap, they may be mutually dependent in diverse ways, but they are logically and historically distinct.

In conclusion, this study of the transition from clientelistic subordination to citizenship rights of access to the state (and a brief glance at subsequent events)[91] suggest that the relationship between national electoral competition and the gradual process of constructing respect for associational autonomy throughout society is reciprocal. The net effect of this mutual influence, however, is politically contingent. Progress along one dimension of democratization may encourage movement along another, but obstacles in one arena can also hold back the rest of the process.

---

[90]   For a systematic analysis of degrees of civilian control over the military, see Pion-Berlin (1992). For general analyses of measurement issues, see Inkeles (1991).

[91]   Author's postscript (January 1996): the January 1994 Zapatista rebellion linked the issues of associational autonomy, political democracy, and social justice and put them at the top of Mexico's national agenda. Subsequent state-society conflicts over political change among authoritarian elites, reformist state managers, and pro-autonomy movements in civil society transformed both indigenous representation and the electoral process far beyond Chiapas.

The rebellion began with a central focus on political as well as socio-economic change. The second communiqué of the Zapatista Army of National Liberation (EZLN) was quite explicit about the rebels' view of which way the 'causal arrow' goes: 'The grave conditions of poverty of our compatriots have a common cause: the lack of liberty and democracy. We think that authentic respect for freedom and the people's democratic will are the indispensable prerequisites for the improvement of the social and economic conditions of our country's dispossessed' (11 Jan. 1994, *La Jornada*). EZLN views about autonomy emerged gradually in the two years that followed, informed by extensive dialogue with the rest of Mexico's increasingly consolidated and diverse indigenous civil society. Yet Zapatista discourse on autonomy continued to be framed more as a means to full democratic citizenship than as an end in itself. As they declared on their twelfth anniversary: 'We do not want to separate ourselves from the Mexican Nation, we want to be part of it, we want to be accepted as equals, as people with dignity, as human beings' (18 Nov. 1995, *La Jornada*).

The 1994 presidential election showed again that Mexico's uneven political transition is being driven at least as much by civic and social movements as by political parties, though their relative weight varies regionally. Opposition parties and civic movements managed to encourage a relatively 'clean' contest in some regions and cities, but in much of the country—especially in indigenous regions—they documented systematic patterns of clientelistic vote-buying and ballot secrecy violations. Persistent authoritarian electoral practices underscore the importance of dealing with all forms of voter intimidation, transcending the narrow, ballot-stuffing definition of fraud. The distinction between 'free' and 'fair' electoral processes matters. Respect for fundamental political freedoms is qualitatively distinct from also important 'level-playing-field' issues of electoral fairness, such as media access and campaign finance transparency and limits.

Space constraints prevent further discussion but, for more recent empirical analysis of the interaction between political change and rural development policy, see the author's 'Governance and Development in Rural Mexico: State Intervention and Public Accountability', *Journal of Development Studies* 32:1, (Oct. 1995); 'National Electoral Choices in Rural Mexico', in Laura Randall, ed., *The Reform of Mexican Agrarian Reform*, Armonk, NY: M. E. Sharpe, 1996; and (co-authored with Josefina Aranda), 'Decentralization and Rural Development in Mexico: Community Participation in Oaxaca's Municipal Funds Program', La Jolla, Calif.: University of California, San Diego, Center for US-Mexican Studies Contemporary Monograph Series, 1996. For further conceptual discussion, see 'How Does Civil Society Thicken? The Political Construction of Social Capital in Rural Mexico', *World Development* 24:6 (June 1996).

17 | Reconstructing the Workers' Party (PT): Lessons from North-Eastern Brazil

William Nylen[1]

Rodolfo Inácio Cascão (1992: 36–7), in a wonderfully written account of his experience as mayor in the 'democratic and popular' administration (1986–8) of Porto Alegre do Norte in the Brazilian state of Mato Grosso, laments the lack of a 'real party' that could have better supported his administration's efforts and, equally important, incorporated his and other pioneering experiments in local democratization into a national party platform.[2] Cascão's vision of what a national party can do for and with the experiences of local-level affiliates is reflected in literature on the importance of democratization at the local level to national-level democratization (Fox forthcoming; Kim and Zacek 1993; Graham 1993; UNDP 1993; Banck 1994; Reilly 1995; Nickson 1995; and Ames 1994). His vision is also relevant to a host of treatments of the state of the left in the post-Cold War era, many of which point to local democracy as an integral part of a new agenda of decentralizing and extending democracy beyond its usual national and formal-institutional definition (see for example Castañeda 1993b, esp. ch. 12; Wright 1986; Lipset 1991; Ellner 1993b; Weffort 1993; Jonas and McCaughan 1994). Most importantly for the purposes of this chapter, Cascão's vision is reflected in the efforts of one party in Brazil, the Workers' Party (PT), to build institutional bridges to PT-run local governments, and to translate its local-level experiences of governance into policy guidelines applicable to PT administrations at all levels of government.[3]

[1] I wish to thank all those in Fortaleza, Icapuí, and Quixadá who gave so generously of their time and thoughts. Space limitations prohibit me from listing all interviewees. I also want to thank Kate Bruhn, Paul Haber, Anne Hallum, Margaret Keck, Brian Kermath, Eugene Huskey, and editors of this volume, as well as students in my Senior Seminar on The Politics of Opposition at Stetson University, for helpful comments and assistance in previous drafts of this chapter.

[2] Cascão belonged to the progressive 'Popular Current' faction of the only opposition party allowed under Brazil's military regime (the MDB: Movimento Democrático Brasileiro—Brazilian Democratic Movement, later the PMDB). As Brazil's democratic opening progressed through the 1980s, the PMDB's unity, based on opposition to the military-led regime, degenerated into a loose conglomeration of personalist, clientelist, and patronage-based local political machines. Members of the Popular Current and other progressive factions were increasingly marginalized.

[3] See Jacobi (1995). Since the first municipal elections allowed by the outgoing military government in 1982, the PT emerged from each new round with a broader and more diverse geographical

This chapter illustrates and explains those efforts, and suggests that such 'party building' and 'institutional learning' are conflict-ridden processes.[4] 'Lessons' of local governance do not consist of politically and emotionally neutral techniques of 'good' vs. 'bad' administration. They emerge, instead, from the convictions and life experiences of party leaders and activists, each of whom has typically invested heavily in the interpretive lens through which he/she views the political world and his/her own role within it. When these clash, as they did repeatedly within the PT over assessments of the party's experiences in local-level governance, the results can be debilitating. Not only can a divided party squander the opportunity to profit from fruitful experience but, in the words of Anthony Wright (1986: 136), 'Parties that promise fraternity but practice fratricide deserve to have a credibility problem.' And credibility problems do not exactly enhance chances for success in electoral politics.

Nonetheless, I want to suggest that such intra-party conflict is not only inevitable, but necessary if a coherent party platform is to emerge from the fray and guide the party's strategic and programmatic choices. Out of the intra-party 'struggle for hegemony'—a euphemism, after all, for doctrinal debate and give-and-take coalitional politics—comes clarity, conviction, and leadership . . . or, of course, fratricidal fragmentation. To get the former, however, you have to risk the latter.

To research party building and institutional learning in the PT at both the national and local levels, it was necessary to test the party's institutional reach beyond the party's home base and historical stronghold in the industrial zones of the south-eastern state of São Paulo. Doing so would also allow me to counter a bias in the literature that appeared to neglect cases of PT governance outside of the industrialized and more economically developed south-east and south (see for example Keck 1992; Doimo 1990; Jacobi 1995; Castañeda 1993b: 218–35, 365–73). I chose the north-eastern state of Ceará for its geographical and cultural distance from São Paulo, and for its rich local party history.

Located just above Brazil's easternmost projection into the Atlantic Ocean,

and economic base. In 1982, the PT elected mayors in just two cities. In 1985 elections in the state capitals, the PT won in Fortaleza, Ceará. In 1988, the PT elected 32 mayors (Keck 1992: 157, also nn. 49 and 50). By 1992, that number jumped to 56. All told, by 1993, the party had governed or was governing in 72 cities ranging in size from 2,320 to 9.5 million inhabitants. Other dimensions of this diversity of experience in local governance were equally impressive. Following 1992, the PT administered municipal governments in eighteen states, as opposed to only ten during 1988–92. And while 16 (or 62 per cent) of its 1988–92 administrations were located outside of São Paulo, the corresponding figure for 1992 was 45 (or 80 per cent). In addition, while only ten (or 42 per cent) of the cities administered by the PT from 1988 to 1992 had a primarily non-industrial economic base, 33 (or 59 per cent) of those picked up in 1992 were non-industrial.

For a detailed and well-written account of the history of the PT, see Keck (1992); also Alves (1993), Azevedo (1991), and Sader (1986).

[4] While the concept of 'party building' clearly refers to the PT's efforts to construct a national party organization with an effective institutional reach beyond the highly urbanized and industrial São Paulo area, it should also include the construction of a party platform, or 'project'. In so far as this latter programmatic construction is based on interpretations of the party's own past mistakes and successes (e.g. experiences in PT-led local governance), we can speak of 'institutional learning'.

Ceará's 145,693.9 square kilometers of territory was home to 6,471,800 people in 1990.[5] As in most of the north-east of Brazil, Ceará's economy is primarily agricultural, with the state's industrial production representing less than 1 per cent of the value of national output in 1985. Land use patterns, characterized by large-scale plantation agriculture and field-pasture animal husbandry, also conform to the patterns of the region. Severe droughts in the rural interior and state-wide economic stagnation caused Ceará's urban population to jump from 41 per cent to 63 per cent of the state's total population between 1970 and 1990. Basic infrastructure throughout the state remains seriously inadequate. Of its 178 municipalities, for example, only 70 have sewer systems (62 of those only in the urban centers); and only 151 have running water (117 of those only in the urban centers).[6]

When I visited Ceará in July and August of 1993, the PT had had three very different experiences of local governance in the state: Fortaleza (the capital, 1986–8), Icapuí (1986–), and Quixadá (1993–). Open-ended interviews with party leaders, administrators, militants, and a host of 'interested parties' outside of the PT, and an extensive review of the literature covering these administrations, allow me to characterize the PT's institutional learning process in Ceará as part learning-by-doing (what Castañeda (1993b: 359) has called 'the apprenticeship of democratic rule') and part power politics (the aforementioned 'struggle for hegemony').[7] I then hypothesize and attempt to demonstrate how a growing number of PT activist/administrators throughout Brazil were not only 'learning-by-doing' in ways similar to what I observed in Ceará, but they were making a clear play at establishing hegemony within the party as a whole by codifying and institutionalizing those lessons at the national level. The self-described 'heterodox' project thus conceived will be described and illustrated below, as will the process of its formulation. First, however, we need to understand the nature of 'orthodox PT socialism' and its problems that helped give rise to the heterodox project.

Fortaleza—PT 'Orthodoxy' and the Problem of Fragmentation

In 1985, the PT in Ceará was little more than a collection of antagonistic factions when it surprised everyone, including itself, with the successful candidacy of Maria Luiza Fontenele as mayor of the capital city of Fortaleza.[8] Fortaleza was the fifth

[5] All figures are from IBGE (1991: 8, 180–1, 383–5) and IBGE (1990: 37), unless otherwise noted.

[6] In Brazil, 'municipalities' are equivalent to counties in the United States. The municipality is named for the principal town, or 'center'. Municipal 'districts' outside the center may look—and, in some cases, even function—like small towns in their own right.

[7] A list of those interviewed is included in the bibliography of the original conference paper on which this chapter is based. Olinda (1991) offers a highly competent rendering of the history of the PT in Ceará up to 1990, to which I am greatly indebted.

[8] Published sources for this section on Fortaleza include Olinda (1991) and Pinto (1992). In 1985, not even the national PT organization could be properly called an institutionalized party (see Keck 1992: 110–66).

largest city in Brazil (1,763,500 residents in 1989). Most of its population was suffering from a cruel combination of high unemployment, extremely low wages, and precarious living conditions caused by prolonged periods of draught-induced rural migration to the city that far overstretched the city's precarious infrastructure.

By all accounts and by almost any measure, the Fontenele administration was a disaster. Its problems began with unrealistic public expectations generated by Fontenele's charismatic campaign style and fiery anti-authoritarian and anti-oligarchy rhetoric. High expectations clashed with a multiplicity of harsh realities: the general economic crisis of the mid-1980s and the deliberate withholding of funds by antagonistic state and federal authorities (both of which drained the city of resources), intense opposition from the traditional political and economic elite (especially within the city council) and from the local media, the lack of preparedness (training, experience, information, etc.) of most administration officials, the lack of a real program of action beyond vague and oft-repeated revolutionary slogans, and deep and increasingly public disagreements between the administration and the state-level PT leadership.[9] Valeska Peres Pinto (1992: 19) describes the basis for this latter intra-party conflict between two increasingly defined 'camps' within the party:

One [which included Fontenele and her closest advisers] identified the administration as an instrument that should be put to the service of the general political struggle and used fundamentally as a lever to accelerate the revolutionary process. The other insisted on the necessity of combining political with administrative action, and believed in the importance of administrative gains to advance the party's political project, principally in support of the most marginalized and exploited sectors of the population.

This dispute worsened as the second camp (calling themselves 'heterodox' socialists) blamed the first for deepening Fortaleza's economic and administrative chaos. Fontenele and her increasingly isolated group of 'orthodox' supporters were finally expelled from the party in 1988.[10] In subsequent municipal elections in 1988, the

[9]   These reasons for the failure of the Fontenele administration are gleaned primarily from Pinto (1992).

[10]   Critics identified 'orthodoxy' with an essentially Leninist approach to democracy. Such an approach might be labeled a 'Trojan Horse' strategy: play by the rules of formal democracy to attain political power, then use that power to undermine democracy in the name of constructing socialism (not to be confused with Fals Borda's (1992: 310) 'Trojanism'). Such an approach is said to be necessary because legal-formal democracy is compromised by Brazil's severe social and political inequalities. These inequalities translate into informal power of such magnitude that legal-formal institutions are virtually powerless against them (as, in fact, they are supposed to be, according to the Leninist perception). The only way to attack such informal power is to go outside the legal-formal institutions of 'bourgeois democracy' to attack the roots of that power: private property and private control of the means of production. Democracy and capitalism, therefore, are two sides of the same coin. And just as capitalism is said to create the seeds of its own demise by producing the revolutionary proletarian class, democracy is seen as furthering the revolutionary cause by providing a favorable context for the creation of the revolutionary party. See Wright (1986), Castañeda (1993b), and Harris (1992).

In his analysis of the PT's historical development, Azevedo (1991) argues that the party was fundamentally split between the tenets, ultimate goals, and strategies of social democracy, on the one

fragmented and discredited PT was roundly rejected, receiving a mere 8 per cent of the popular vote.

The very magnitude of the failure of orthodoxy in Fortaleza, and the subsequent damage to the party shocked many activists into recognizing the importance of moving beyond radical anti-system rhetoric. Such arguments emphasized the need to construct a party platform or 'project' of 'good government'; one that could help future PT-led governments avoid sloganeering and self-destructive confrontationalism and actually use Brazil's existing democratic rules to improve the lives of the people with tangible policy benefits and, in the process, to improve the rules themselves.[11] As the party limped through the late 1980s and early 1990s, managing to elect only two state deputies and a few scattered city council members, a coalition of heterodox factions emerged in 1992 and 1993 to slowly isolate and marginalize remaining orthodox groups and individuals.[12]

Drawing from the long history of debates within the left over precisely this issue, orthodox critics of this emerging PT heterodoxy alleged that the party was degenerating into 'electoralism', 'bourgeois reformism', and abandonment of the party's grass roots. In the words of one militant and PT staff member, 'If we are not careful, the PT could suddenly turn itself into a party concerned merely with elections. [. . .] I'm not saying that the PT is the same as other parties, but we do need to be careful' (quoted in Olinda 1991: 110).

My research convinced me that such concerns, while important, should not be overstated. In abandoning the orthodox Leninist agenda, PT heterodoxy did not automatically abandon a transformative socialist agenda. On the contrary, by committing itself to improving formal democracy by actively promoting 'good government' and popular participation, it has returned to a socialist tradition even older than the Leninist and European Social Democratic traditions that superseded it for most of the twentieth century.[13] 'Ethical socialism', 'libertarian

hand, and those of Leninism, on the other. I would criticize this assessment on the grounds that the increasingly prominent heterodox position (to be fully defined and discussed below) differs from both Leninism and social democracy in fundamental respects.

[11] See Pinto (1992: 27); also Olinda (1991: 56–8). This 'lesson' was shared in many other parts of Brazil as well. See, for example, Keck (1992: 197–236) on the PT's administration of Diadema; also Couto and Abrucio (n.d.) on São Paulo. Other examples include Campinas and Vitória. Eder Sader (1986) was one of the first in the party to argue that the PT needed to generate a new guiding theory from the lessons of its own history.

[12] Heterodox factions included the so-called 'pessoal da igreja' (which later divided into two groups with ties to similarly named national factions: Articulação and Vertente Socialista) and the Nova Esquerda. Orthodox factions included former members of the Workers' Revolution Party, Luiza Fontenele's principal support group (formerly the Partido Revolucionário Comunista, a dissident faction of the Communist Party of Brazil, and an active opponent to the formation of the PT), and a number of small Trotskyite and Maoist groups. For a more detailed account, see Olinda (1991: 52–9).

[13] This point follows upon Wright's (1986: 18) argument that 'The world is full of socialisms. There is no unitary tradition. . . . [S]ocialism has always been distinguished by its diversity. During the long period, intensified by the Cold War, when this diversity was compressed into the two opposing blocs of official communism and official social democracy, this could be forgotten. It now reappears, along with the sort of traditions that sustained it.'

socialism', 'democratic socialism': while different in numerous particulars, all of these non-Marxist conceptualizations of socialism have in common a rejection of the competitive individualism and social inequality inherent in liberal capitalism; and all embrace 'the democratic diffusion of power in a system of socialist pluralism rooted in forms of territorial and functional devolution, in addition to effective general mechanisms to guarantee political accountability and civic freedom' (Wright 1986: 135).

I submit that this non-Marxist socialism is the essence of PT heterodoxy.[14] To illustrate its programmatic content (particularly its transformative agenda) and its development from various 'lessons' of PT local governance, I will devote the rest of this chapter to case-studies of PT heterodoxy in Ceará, and efforts to disseminate it within the party at the national level.

Icapuí—Home-Spun 'Heterodoxy'

The small fishing town of Icapuí, located on the coast of the eastern corner of Ceará, 180 kilometers from Fortaleza, is representative in many ways of small rural municipalities throughout Brazil.[15] Sixty per cent of its 13,658 residents are spread out in rural areas, with the remainder concentrated in the small urban center. Fishing directly or indirectly employs 49.5 per cent of the economically active population, 16.3 per cent (all women) produce hand-made embroidery and lace (*labirinto*), roughly 10 per cent work for the city government, while the rest of the population works in agriculture (coconut, cashew, melon, and a host of subsistence crops), commerce, and other assorted activities. Icapuí has no manufacturing industry to speak of, and its significant potential for tourism remains untapped.

Icapuí was long an ignored backwater of neighboring Aracatí. In the early 1980s, however, a group of university students and several leaders of Catholic 'Comunidades Eclesiais de Base' (CEBs: Catholic Ecclesiastic Base Communities) that had been established by a progressive local priest in the mid-1970s, jointly organized a pro-independence campaign against strong resistance from Aracatí's ruling oligarchy. They succeeded in emancipating the town in a 1984 plebiscite vote. Noteworthy in this campaign was the leadership of student-activist-turned-politician and member

---

[14] In the post-Cold War era, the left worldwide seems to have committed itself in varying ways to 'perfecting' democracy beyond legal-formal rules and institutions (e.g. elections, legislatures, etc.). Lipset (1991), for example, argues that promoting democracy is the 'new' program for the post-Cold War left. Coming from a different perspective, Escobar and Alvarez (1992) and Cardoso (1992) suggest that the post-Cold War left's focus on getting to the grassroots and stimulating a sense of agency or 'constructing identities' is part of a 'postmodern' Socialist agenda. Castañeda (1993*b*), meanwhile, wants this same focus to be seen as part of a 'post-Socialist' agenda.

[15] Published sources of information on Icapuí include: Campos (1992), Almeida (1993), Andrade and Goya (1992), and Prefeitura Municipal de Icapuí (1993).

of one of Icapuí's most prominent families, José Airton. The following year, Airton successfully ran for mayor as a favorite son candidate of the leftist 'popular faction' of the PMDB.[16] He was 29 years old when he took office in 1986.

Isolated at home by the weak but hostile local political class (which included his own family), resolutely progressive in an increasingly right-leaning party, and with all factions of the state's left focused on events in Fortaleza, Mayor Airton and his small group of fellow activists were on their own as they constructed their administration and, indeed, as they constructed the municipality of Icapuí itself. Airton tracked down and recruited friends, university colleagues, relatives, and former residents to build the necessary cadres for his governing team. Even after Airton publicly repudiated the PMDB and aligned his administration with the PT in 1988, it would be a long time before this sense of isolation, especially from the state party (then in a period of crisis, as discussed above), would begin to change.

While operating on a multiplicity of fronts with limited resources, the administration decided to prioritize public education; not just because of the extreme poverty of the existing system, but because it was determined that significant and demonstrable results could be obtained before the next elections in 1988. While required by federal law to spend 25 per cent of the municipal budget on education, actual expenditures reached 38 per cent (part of which paid for free student transportation). Teachers were paid the maximum salaries allowed by law, making them among the best paid in the state. By the end of Mayor Airton's three-year administration, the results were impressive (in spite of constant obstructionism from local elites and political opponents in the city council). Student enrollment increased from just 700 to 3,059; professors increased from 37 to 115 (and their quality improved as many took advantage of a new high school inaugurated largely to train teachers); and school buildings increased from 9 to 30.[17]

With the election in 1988 of Airton's successor, Francisco José Teixeira, the new

[16] Several crucial contextual variables present in the Icapuí case, and not exactly widespread in Brazil or the rest of Latin America, include: first, weak and divided local conservative forces—'disorganized and incompetent', in the words of Icapuí's Catholic priest, Father Lopes (interview 19 July 1993); second, a duo of state governors from the center-left PSDB who, identifying Ceará's traditional landowning oligarchy as more of a threat than the comparatively weak PT, allowed the latter to govern their cities without interference, in some cases, as we will see below in the case of Quixadá, even entering into open alliance with PT-led municipal authorities; and, finally, Title VI of the 1988 Constitution establishes strict guidelines regulating federal tax and budgetary allocations to state and municipal governments (Icapuí, for example, received fully 70 per cent of its revenues from the federal Fundo de Participação dos Municípios in 1991 (Campos 1992: 8)).

[17] Data is from Almeida (1993: 20); see also MED/UNICEF/CENPEC (1993), and Loiola (1993). So as not to give the impression that efforts to improve public education ended with Mayor Airton's administration, the number of students attending public schools continued to increase from 3,493 in 1989 to 4,160 in 1991 (virtually 100 per cent of the school-age population). In the same period, the number of professors increased from 139 to 166, and the number of schools went from 31 to 33.

Icapuí's accomplishments in public education came to the attention of UNICEF, which gave its 'Child and Peace-Education' award to the town in 1991. UNICEF also co-sponsored a 15-volume series entitled *Education and Municipal Development* in which Icapuí's experience warranted its own volume (MED/UNICEF/CENPEC 1993) as did four other PT-administered cities in Brazil.

administration launched into a new priority program focusing on public health. The Airton administration's Secretary of Health had paved the way by opening two abandoned health centers and constructing a third, setting up a dental center, acquiring a municipal ambulance, and inviting Icapuí's first resident doctor and nurse to set up shop. Teixeira's contribution came in the form of allying with former opponents in the Democratic Workers' Party (PDT) in order to oversee the construction of a proactive municipal health program that went beyond traditional curative and emergency medical services to include and even prioritize preventative and rehabilitative medicine. In conjunction with a new state-government effort to improve rural Ceará's health care, the Teixeira administration initiated or expanded existing free immunization programs for children, in-home maternity care and education, the training of local health-care agents, and the construction of health-care facilities in outlying areas. Between 1987 and 1991, 13 per cent to 20 per cent of the municipal budget was directed to health care. In four years, the number of doctors increased from one to seven, and the number of health posts grew from three to seven. By 1992, Icapuí's infant mortality rate was 50 per thousand live births, compared with 70 per thousand in the rest of the state, and 105 per thousand in the entire north-east.[18]

But 'democratic and popular government', as understood by both the Airton and Teixeira administrations, meant going beyond improving and 'universalizing' public services such as education and health care. Such 'good works' were to be complemented by efforts to decentralize public administration, to expose government decision-making to public scrutiny ('transparência'), and, critically, to stimulate popular participation in all aspects of governance.

In the field of education, for example, one party member and an active participant in both administrations reminded me of the importance of education beyond 'merely attaining literacy': 'through education the community is awakened to participate'.[19] This was understood to be true in two important senses: that the content of education would communicate the goals and ideals of the administration to the community and vice versa, while the process of carrying out the education reforms would incorporate and demonstrate the administration's commitment to promoting decentralization and 'popular participation' in policy-making and administration. As for the first of these, the administration adopted the Paulo Freire method of education, described in general terms by John Elias (1976: 9) as 'the process by which a group of people become aware of the cultural context in

---

[18] See Almeida (1993: 14). For a detailed account of Icapuí's public health-care system both before and during the PT's reign, see Andrade and Goya (1992). Andrade, recruited from the University of Ceará by Mayor Airton in 1986, was Icapuí's Secretary of Health under the Teixeira administration. In 1992, he accepted an invitation to become Secretary of Health for the PT administration in Quixadá.

[19] 15 July 1993 interview with Luiz Teixeira, Mayor's Executive Assistant. See MED/UNICEF/CENPEC (1993) for a strong focus on popular participation in the construction and operation of Icapuí's educational system.

which they live and become challenged to work actively to bring about change for the better'.[20] To lay the groundwork for popular participation in, and decentralization of, the administration's education program, Mayor Airton invited a visiting psychologist/teacher from Rio de Janeiro (and a member of the PT since 1980), Augusto Álvaro Gerônimo Gomes, to remain in Icapuí as Secretary of Education.[21] Gomes and a small group of assistants visited each of Icapuí's rural communities and urban neighborhoods, going door-to-door inviting residents to participate in community meetings to discuss the details of 'their' local school: construction/renovation, administration and staffing, curriculum, and whatever else they wished to talk about. At these meetings, residents got the chance to meet with the entire Secretariat of Education and to participate in decisions such as where schools would be built and who should be trained to teach at the school. They were then encouraged to participate regularly alongside representatives of the local school's professors, administrators, and students in school councils whose job it was to administer and oversee school performance. Each school council also voted for its representatives in the Municipal Council of Education, a body designed to discuss and vote on all budgetary allocations and planning proposals having to do with the educational system. According to Gomes, the idea was to keep decision-making concerning Icapuí's public education system out of the mayor's hands and even 'out of the Secretariat's exclusive hands': 'the public decides, the administration implements'.

Similarly, when Mayor Teixeira's Secretary of Health, Odorico Monteiro de Andrade, set out to restructure Icapuí's public health services, he included 'strengthening popular participation in health-related activities, and achieving social control by the end-users of services provided' as among his most important goals (Andrade and Goya 1992: 45, 51–3). Even before he became Secretary of Health under Teixeira, Odorico initiated a house-to-house survey of 2,275 Icapuí families. This not only gave him a valuable database of demographic, economic, health, and education statistics on which to build his municipal health system. It also gave him a 'hands on' sense of Icapuí's population and their specific health problems. Meanwhile, Odorico participated in community discussions and meetings in which local needs and resources were discussed. In July of 1989, interested community residents, health professionals, and administration officials met together in a formal Municipal Health Conference where they discussed and approved Icapuí's Municipal Health Plan. Participants also voted in the first set of officers of the Municipal Council of Health: 'Composed of 35 members, 22 of whom were representatives of local communities, 8 from government institutions, and 5 from organized entities . . .' (Andrade and Goya 1992: 75).

---

[20] Elias goes on to state that 'Freire's direct interest was in democratization. He rejected authoritarian methods in education, the social palliative of welfarism, and the stifling of political expression' (1976: 15).
[21] 19 July 1993 interview with Augusto Álvaro Gerônimo Gomes, Secretaria de Educação, Cultura e Desportos; see also Almeida (1993: 17–27).

A Digression—PT Heterodoxy and 'Popular Participation'

The 'democratic and popular' administrations of Icapuí committed themselves to providing good government in the sense of equal access to quality public services (e.g. education and health). But they were equally committed to transforming the political culture of 'paternalistic' (or 'clientelistic') relations between the government and the governed by actively promoting popular participation in processes of governance.[22] This commitment could be found among many PT-led local administrations as a defining characteristic of their mode of governance.[23] It makes sense, therefore, to take a moment to elaborate upon it further.

Keck (1992: 79) describes how the PT's early history was infused with a strong 'ethos' of popular participation 'stressing autonomy and self-organization'. This ethos was rooted in struggles against the dictatorship carried out by the 'new unions' and social movements of São Paulo's urban and industrial heartland (i.e. the party's core constituents). It 'was echoed in PT organizers' insistence that workers and the poor could not rely on elite actors to defend their interests and needed to project their own voices into politics'.

But why did this same ethos and commitment to popular participation emerge in Icapuí? Icapuí's leaders were not PT activists when they began their administration. Neither did they have any roots in urban working-class movements. Nevertheless, their political struggles for the emancipation of Icapuí and their prior roots in student politics and CEB community activism combined to give them an 'ethos' of popular participation quite comparable to that found in São Paulo.

In Icapuí, this 'ethos' is part of a broad ideological commitment to the destruction of paternalist social relations and the construction of a new political culture of governance. In Mayor Airton's words:

We believe that the participation of the community is necessary if people are to value what they are getting and what we are doing. A big problem here is individualism [defined at another point in the interview as individuals' lack of a sense of 'community consciousness' and of responsibility towards the community] and neighbor-vs.-neighbor micro-politics. Paternalism thrives on this. (Interview 18 July 1993)

Mayor Airton contrasts popular participation ('the way politics should work') with Brazil's history of 'political exclusion' ('where the people were never called upon to do anything'). The direct correlation between the tradition of exclusionary politics and Icapuí's (indeed, all of Brazil's) staggering poverty and social inequalities has

---

[22]   For the purposes of this chapter, I use the terms 'clientelism', 'paternalism', and 'patrimonialism' interchangeably.

[23]   See, for example, Moisés (1985) and Nickson (1995, ch. 8). Indeed, according to Castañeda (1993b: 365–73), local left parties and governments throughout Latin America sought to promote greater popular participation as a means to fight traditional social relations of paternalism and clientelism. These were widely seen to divide and separate the popular classes (in addition to excluding them from elite-dominated politics), thereby impeding any likelihood of horizontal solidarity and organized opposition to paternalist inequality and domination.

long been evident to Airton and his fellow Icapuí administrators and party activists.[24] Andrade and Goya (1992: 52), for example, describe Icapuí—'a small town where the relations of friendship, solidarity, and intrigue find themselves spilling over into relations with the representatives of the local government, many times coming to the point of confusing one with the other'—as a perfect case of the way traditional Brazilian social relations reproduce themselves in the realm of politics:

So it is that in a small town like Icapuí, mostly made up of needy families, and where a large part of the residents are known personally by the administration or by the city council members, the existence and permanence of a relationship of domination and consequent submission is made all the more likely. 'To owe a favor' to the mayor or 'to ask for assistance' from a city council member, are everyday events in small towns.

In short, popular participation necessarily complements the administration's basic commitment to citizens' rights of universal access to public services. As the poor and formerly excluded majority take part in processes of decision-making and policy implementation that actually end up improving and expanding their access to public services, they are able to see themselvs as agents in their own self-improvement and not mere supplicants of ultimately self-defeating 'gifts from on high'. Such recognition represents an act of citizens' 'empowerment'—spoken of in terms of 'responsibility': since one has the power to act, one is obligated to use it wisely in the continuing struggle against paternalism.[25] Providing the generative experience for citizen empowerment is the duty of a 'democratic and popular' government.

More than mere 'duty', however, left activists everywhere tend to promote citizens' empowerment because they see it as a profoundly life-altering experience, akin in many respects to a religious conversion. As such, they oftentimes urgently desire to share this experience with others. An integral part of individual members' identities, in terms of ideals and defining experiences, has been forged by mass mobilization (strikes, demonstrations, rallies, etc.) and the consequent transformation of individual consciousness that such direct confrontational politics oftentimes entails. Icapuí activists are no different in this respect. They see mobilization, or popular participation, not only as a collective action strategy necessary for the political emancipation of repressed classes or groups, but as the vehicle for an

---

[24] As an example, Andrade and Goya (1992: 41) cite the political implications of Icapuí's inadequate public services prior to 1986: 'the population in Icapuí, by necessity, had to submit themselves to a clientelistic relationship with the local politicians, which had the effect of making them dependent on favors that would guarantee their access to health services.' Similarly, Icapuí's 700 public school openings were also made available to the population by politicians and local 'important people' on the basis of clientelistic exchange rather than need or merit.

Guillermo O'Donnell (1992*a*: 49) is merely one of the more recent academic analysts of Brazilian politics to argue that 'In Brazil the principal challenge is that of overcoming its high levels of patrimonialism and elitism.'

[25] For 'the theme of empowerment' as expressed at the time of the 1982 campaign, see Keck (1992: 139–40). Empowerment (and 'praxis') are also crucial themes in liberation theology, which makes sense given the historically close relationship between the PT and Brazil's progressive Catholic church.

individual's psychological emancipation from the idea of natural sociopolitical hierarchies and/or the sense of personal impotence in breaking out of such hierarchies. Participation also offers an alternative community (the party, the neighborhood, the local school council, the Municipal Council of Health, etc.) devoid of traditional relations of domination and exploitation and fully accepting of 'popular' experience and wisdom.

There are, of course, less philosophical and more immediate reasons for combating paternalism by way of stimulating popular participation. In electoral politics, paternalism shows itself in vote-buying and populistic posturing as the new 'Savior of the people'.[26] In its more virulent forms, it translates into death threats and violence against opposing candidates, and intimidation of voters. Evidence abounds that these practices have destroyed more than one 'democratic and popular government' in Brazil.[27] Popular participation, theoretically, enables citizens to understand these traditional practices as efforts to undermine and destroy the gains made not merely 'on their behalf' by the administration (e.g. public education and health), but by their own hard work in helping the administration make those gains possible. Without participating in the struggle to realize these gains, citizens may interpret them as just another set of clientelistic favors offered 'from above' in exchange for their votes, to be weighed alongside the favors (e.g. money, jobs, home improvements, or simply absence of violence) offered by paternalist candidates. The lessons of participation (i.e. empowerment) make the immediate individual gains of paternalistic favors less likely to win out at election time against the more long-term, less tangible communal gains of improved public services and honest government. At the same time, the lessons of participation create the committed cadres necessary to sustain a future grassroots-based opposition to any paternalistic reversal and/or authoritarian backlash.[28] In short, popular participation is seen as breaking down the political culture of paternalism one citizen at a time.

Another practical concern motivating a policy of promoting popular participation stems from the desire to make sure that the government carries out policies that the citizenry actually wants. 'The community itself knows what it needs better than anybody.'[29] Getting the community to meet together and prioritize its needs, and then abiding by those priorities so that the community actually receives what it most wants, gives participants in the process an initial sense of efficacy in

[26] One administration official told me of a case of vote-buying in the 1993 election where an opposition candidate promised to buy a new house for someone who was quite popular in his neighborhood if that individual could guarantee his family's and friends' votes in exchange. The man said that would be fine, but he wanted his house now. The house was built, the election came, and the family voted as it always had: for the PT. 'I wish everyone would do that!', laughed the official. 'The local elite would carry out an income redistribution policy for us.'

[27] See, for example, Cascão (1992) and Banck (1994). The 1988 election in Icapuí included vote-buying, death threats, and smear campaigns, and ended with an unsuccessful attempt on the part of the conservative opposition to annul the election results in the courts.

[28] See, for example, the case of Chile: Portes (1971) and Schneider (1992).

[29] 16 July 1993 interview with Joyce Teixeira Bomfim da Silva, Secretaria de Ação Comunitária.

providing input into the process of governance. And that should give them greater motivation to continue their input into subsequent stages of decision-making and implementation.

Finally, strengthening the decision-making capabilities of community-based state and civil society institutions and institutionalizing the ties between them is supposed to contribute to the goal of administrative decentralization. Mayor Airton explained that such decentralization, in eliminating the excessive 'personalism' that traditionally associates effective political action with 'going straight to the top', would give the mayor and other top administration officials more time to govern in a less reactive, less piecemeal manner.

Having explained the commitment to popular participation, we must recognize that reality has tended to fall far short of the ideals just enumerated, with potentially troubling consequences. On numerous occasions and in many variations, I heard overworked and frustrated party members and leaders throughout Ceará complain about citizens 'embracing their rights without embracing their responsibilities';[30] that is, demanding public services and attention from the government without being willing to participate to help make those services happen or to protect them from conservative assault. In Icapuí, for example, the experiences of both the Municipal Council of Education and the Municipal Council of Health (discussed above) were judged 'unsatisfactory' by their respective architects.[31] In each case, initial interest gave way to a slow erosion of participation precisely on the part of community representatives. The lack of transportation to and from meetings, the lack of time not only to attend meetings but to carry out the tasks of representation—all without compensation—and the simple loss of interest following the excitement of the first meeting; all are cited as principal reasons for the basic unpopularity of popular participation. My own sense is that the obvious 'social distance' between the majority of the party/administration leadership and the general population also worked against efforts to broaden participation.[32]

At any rate, the result of such less-than-hoped-for levels of popular participation was ever-increasing workloads falling on the shoulders of already overworked

[30] 15 July 1993 interview with Francisca Alves de Sousa, Secretaria de Educação under Icapuí's Mayor Teixeira, and a teacher and 'reporter popular' (people's reporter) for the local party newsletter.

[31] 19 July 1993 interview with Augusto Álvaro Jerônimo Gomes; Andrade and Goya (1992: 75–6). Similarly, in the first ninety days of the Teixeira administration, eleven town meetings, or 'Plenárias Populares' (Popular Assemblies), took place with reasonable rates of attendance (50+). When the Administration tried to institutionalize these assemblies into a standing Municipal Council, however, interest waned, participation withered, and the experiment was abandoned. Many other PT local governments reported similar less-than-satisfying experiences with Municipal Councils and Popular Councils. See, for example, Doimo (1990), Keck (1992: 205–9), and Cardoso (1992: 293–6).

[32] In a region where 47.2 per cent of the population is illiterate, 15 (or 62.5 per cent) of the party directorate's 24 members had completed the equivalent of high school ('segunda grau') and 9 (or 37.5 per cent) had either done course work or received a degree at the university level. To further back up my point of 'social distance', Campos (1992: 8) writes that Icapuí's PT emerged from 'a segment of the local "elite"'. In her study of militants at the state level of the Ceará PT, Olinda (1991: 96) found that 66 per cent had university degrees while 34 per cent had completed the 'segunda grau' (not one had done less!).

administration officials and employees, and on the citizens who did choose to participate. These workloads served as a further disincentive for 'outsiders' to join in, and as a further impetus for administrators and party activists to complain and drag their feet, to distance themselves from the 'selfish' and 'ungrateful' masses, and even to drop out of activism and/or public administration altogether.

But one has to worry about the implications of such disappointment in what might be called the 'false consciousness' of the masses, especially where violence and patronage have traditionally been an integral part of politics. Blaming the long-suffering victims of paternalism for acting either paternalistically or apolitically can too easily lead to the morass of party vanguardism and the rejection of formal democracy from which the left, worldwide, has so recently escaped. For example, when Ceará's state party president, José Nobre Guimaraes, spoke of the frustration of the PT's experiments in popular participation, he drew the following conclusion: 'Brazil will not change from below. It will only change from above. The party in power will need to implement a shock program of honest, efficient, and public-spirited government. This will challenge the public to participate and to mobilize in defense of these gains' (interview 27 July 1993). While this 'benevolent vanguardism', if you will, is certainly a far cry from old-style Leninist vanguardism, it is an equally far cry from the PT's founding commitment to attacking the roots of paternalism through the type of citizens' empowerment that comes from hands-on popular participation in social movements and in actual governance.

Icapuí—'Home-Spun Heterodoxy' (continued)

The promise of popular participation and the threat of 'benevolent vanguardism' gives us one more reason to scrutinize Icapuí's example of having learned a different, non-vanguardist lesson: good works, combined with an understanding of the limited number of citizens willing and capable of actively participating in government, *can* translate into electoral staying power *and* continued efforts to chip away at the structures of paternalist domination.

In 1988, following three years of widely acknowledged good works in Icapuí, the PT's Teixeira won just 34 per cent of the vote against a split opposition (48 per cent divided between two conservative candidates). In 1992, the opposition unified around a single candidate, but the PT's Airton won a second term with 56 per cent of the vote against 35 per cent for his opponent.[33] In addition to this evidence of the public's recognition of the local PT's good works, Icapuí was the only town in Ceará that voted for the PT in all categories of the 1990 elections for governor and state deputies.

These results could have led the Icapuí PT to relax their tiring and 'unsatisfactory' efforts to stimulate popular participation and rest, so to speak, on their record

[33] Electoral data from 18 July 1993 interview with Mayor José Airton.

of good works. However, that was not what they chose to do. Following his election for a second term in 1992, Mayor Airton set up a Secretariat of Community Action for the purpose of stimulating the organization of autonomous neighborhood associations. Unlike the disappointing Municipal Councils of the first two administrations, these associations were to be independent from both the party and the administration. The choices of why, when, and where they might wish to participate in government decision-making would be entirely their own, based on their own evaluations of the government's 'transparent' processes of governance.

How do we explain the Icapuí PT's uncommon dedication to public service and its admittedly high-frustration (therefore, high-risk) commitment to the gradual change of citizens' values within the legal-institutional confines of democratic struggle? First and foremost, it came from the experience of local governance itself; from 'on-the-job training', or what I earlier called 'learning-by-doing'. In Mayor Airton's words:

We began with an idealistic vision that our left discourse would bring the people over to our side. Now we understand that it's a slow process, and a very difficult one. But there is no alternative. You see, I have changed a lot since I first began to be active in politics. I used to have a romantic vision of socialist society, with its image of the perfect man [or citizen]. Now I understand that man is not perfect and society can't be either. Such an understanding affects my vision of the state as well: we [the party, administration] are not perfect, so neither can our state, by itself [i.e. without popular participation], be perfect. (Interview 18 July 1993)

But while the Icapuí party had clearly learned from its own experience, the Icapuí experience must not be seen in isolation from the national PT's contemporaneous institutional learning processes. Throughout the late 1980s and early 1990s, the national party was actively debating the lessons of its experiences of local governance. This debate resulted in the formulation of a heterodox party project based on experiences, like those of Icapuí described above, from all over Brazil.

Party Building and Institutional Learning in the National PT

Discussing the PT's formative years in the early 1980s, Keck (1992: 111–16) notes 'the fragility of intraparty communication'. As early as 1982, however, when a 'unified electoral committee' was created at the national level so that the party leadership could get information about local-level PT candidates and races, party leaders clearly understood the importance of constructing a party organization with a truly national reach. By 1985, 'PT leaders began to pay attention to making party organization more effective. [. . . This] was a sign that the PT's movement-building phase might give way to greater concentration on party building' (Keck 1992: 156). While divided on issues of strategy and ultimate ends, party

activists agreed with respect to the importance of strengthening the PT as their institutional vehicle for attaining political power. There was no argument over the need
for 'party building' because all factions apparently perceived that building party
institutions was a 'neutral' process that would favor all factions equally.[34] Events
following subsequent municipal elections, like those in Fortaleza and the 1988 victories in the capital cities of São Paulo, Porto Alegre, and Vitória, enhanced this
shared sense of the urgency of party building.[35]

One result was the formation of the Secretaria Nacional de Assuntos Institucionais
(SNAI: National Secretariat of Institutional Affairs) in 1988.[36] The SNAI was intended
to act as a communications bridge between party leaders, activists, and office-holders
nationwide. Its first coordinator, Luis Dulci, decided that what the party needed
most of all was a public policy institute to provide technical assistance to PT administrations. Dulci established the Instituto Nacional de Administração e Políticas
Publicas (INAPP: National Institute of Administration and Public Policy), with
centers in São Paulo, Belo Horizonte, and Espírito Santo. The story of the INAPP
is not a happy one, however, and actually reflects the factional in-fighting in the party
that it was supposed to help resolve. INAPP's technical advisers and the municipal
administrators they were supposed to help, for example, often clashed over the content and organization of specific government programs. Many PT local governments ended up bypassing the INAPP, in some cases, going outside the party for
assistance. Ultimately, these disputes and problems led to the INAPP's dissolution
in 1992.

The SNAI, however, received a new lease on life when party fragmentation was
widely blamed for contributing to the loss of its candidate, Luis Inácio 'Lula' da
Silva, in the presidential elections of 1989. In 1990, just two years after the PT
won municipal elections in 32 cities, 12 (or 38 per cent) of those mayors had left
or been expelled from the party. Fortaleza was looking like merely the first case of

[34] Franklin Coelho, a former assistant to Jorge Bittar when Bittar headed the SNAI, stated in a
telephone interview, 1 December 1993, that 'conflict over the conception of public policies' certainly
existed within the party in the late 1980s (rooted in disagreement between party activists and party
politicians, like legislative deputies, who felt they had to represent constituents beyond those represented solely by the party). In spite of this conflict, party leaders agreed on the need 'to look for an
institutional means for the formulation of public policies'. This need spawned the creation of the SNAI.

[35] The lack of communication and the lack of a clear role distinction between the PT's party organization and its administration in the city of São Paulo, almost leading to mayor Luíza Erundina's
exiting the party, is cited by Couto and Abrucio (n.d.: 29–31) as the reason for the creation of a Political Council ('Conselho Político') of party and administration officials, the naming of an official PT
Ambassador ('Assessoria Especial') for the administration, and the creation of a 'Three-Tier Forum'
of municipal, state, and national party officials ('Fórum das Três Instâncias'). All of these occurred
in conjunction with the construction of the SNAI. Together, they illustrate the sense of urgency in the
party regarding the need to build bridges between militants in the party organization and administrators in the party-in-government. For more information see n. 36, below.

[36] Information regarding the SNAI is based entirely on data gleaned from a 22 June 1993 interview with Maria de Fátima Lavrador de Castro and Regina Toscano, SNAI staff members; and telephone interviews with Bittar's assistant, Franklin Coelho (1 Dec. 1993) and, again, with Lavrador de
Castro (5 Dec. 1993).

a developing model of PT governance.[37] Discussions about the need for party building returned to center stage.

The SNAI was resurrected and put under the leadership of Jorge Bittar, a PT city council member from the city of Rio de Janeiro and the party's unsuccessful candidate for state governor in 1990. Bittar and his small SNAI staff set out to address the problem of party fragmentation without repeating Dulci's mistake of imposing 'outside' programs on unwilling local administrators with ideas of their own. Bittar convened a 'national council of PT mayors' in late 1990 (which included Icapuí's Mayor Teixeira) to discuss the mayors' views on the 'PT style' of administration. This conference led to a series of 'sectoral seminars' where PT administrators from all over Brazil, as well as outside specialists in the specific area under discussion, would converge on one spot to discuss how PT administrations had (or should have) confronted specific issues like housing, education, health, transportation, etc. By late 1992, these seminar discussions were synthesized and compiled into a book, *O Modo Petista de Governar* ('The PT's Mode of Governance') (Bittar 1992), and a video. For the 1992 municipal elections, the SNAI organized an 'electoral work group' utilizing the book and video to provide background information for PT candidates' platforms and, if requested, to help draw up actual government programs. Following the elections, newly elected PT administrations were invited to send representatives to a new round of sectoral seminars organized by the SNAI.

---

[37] In their efforts to articulate such a model, Couto and Abrucio (n.d.) argue that factional tensions emerge when growing numbers of activists within a party strongly rooted in grassroots movement politics begin to turn their eyes towards legislative and executive office-holding as important means by which to spread their message and exercise power beyond the narrow confines of a given union, social movement, or neighborhood association. This especially holds true when party candidates actually begin to win elections:

> In a turbulent process that goes from the administrations of Diadema (1982) and Fortaleza (1985) through the collection of mayors elected in 1988, a tense relationship has set in between the party-movement and the party-institution; or, in other words, between those that are inside the institutional machinery (Executive or Parliament) and those that are only in the party's jurisdiction or inside the social movements. . . . The conflicts between PT administrations and parliamentarians with party directorates were due above all to the incapacity of the latter (whose members, for the most part, did not assume positions of responsibility in the Government) to understand the necessity that the party take up the party-institution logic. One sees a constant demand from the municipal [party] directorates that militants occupying positions in the administrations continue acting according to a party-movement logic. (Couto and Abrucio n.d.: 20, 23)

Keck (1992: 184) argues that the roots of this conflict lay in the PT's early lack of institutional autonomy from labor union leadership. The party's leaders, strongly rooted in labor union leadership, were 'attempting to act on two different institutional fronts' (i.e. the unions and the party). In so doing, however, they 'failed to identify a separate institutional arena in which the party could act on its own'. This problem has long been associated with socialist parties throughout the world. See, for example, Wright (1986, chs. 2 and 6).

Keck suggests that the PT's problem could be remedied by intra-party discussion, institutional learning, etc. leading to an eventual convergence of the two positions (an argument with which I basically concur, although I believe the process to be a much more inherently conflictual one). For an argument that the strategies are, in fact, 'contradictory by nature', see Azevedo (1991: 135–59). Azevedo suggests that the party leadership must choose either one or the other and act accordingly, or ultimately self-destruct in trying to appease both sides.

The stated objective of these and other SNAI-sponsored seminars, meetings, publications, and channels of communication was to exchange information about problems and solutions of governance among PT office-holders and administrators. It is significant, however, that the sharing of administrative expertise in the sectoral seminars was described to me by one SNAI official as 'political learning'. This reinforced my sense that the SNAI's goals went far beyond mere communication and exchange of information about the experiences of PT-led municipal administrations to include construction of a new party platform, or 'project'.

The introduction to the *Modo Petista*, for example, describes the book's main goal as the construction of a unified discourse within the party around the need 'to transform utopia and desires into plans of concrete action' (Bittar 1992: 15). The official term for this was *construção coletiva*—literally, the collective construction of general outlines for party programs and a general understanding of what those outlines meant in practice. In the words of one SNAI official:

The 'modo petista de governar' is not exactly a model in terms of a dogma or a paradigm to be rigidly applied without the possibility of change. Instead, it has been advanced in the form of general lines of public administration, emphasizing democracy and public transparency. It is not a model that *has* to be implemented. Any PT administration should be free to interpret it and to put in its own ideas. It is a model in the sense of offering general lines of direction. (Telephone interview with Maria de Fátima Lavrador, 5 December 1993)

Participants in these sectoral seminars were not ideologues, but practitioners of real-life administration. Yet they were, in fact, constructing a model of governance out of prior practical experience. In so doing, to use the term I heard so often in Ceará, they were constructing a 'heterodox' project of governance: 'to meet the needs of the people and not just PT activists'.

Bittar (1992: 11) himself argues that the seminars produced a new model of PT governance that is clearly distinguishable from the neoliberal proposals of the 'new Right' and from the populist or Leninist proposals of the 'old Left':

Following a worldwide tendency, our country lives under the great impact of neoliberal proposals which serve to inform, or better yet, to confuse large sectors of society about such questions as the necessity of the minimal State, the relationship between public and private, between State and society, and between State and social policies. The experience of the PT in its municipal governments points towards a path of democratic reform of the State and of social policies that confronts the currently fashionable neoliberal conceptions, at the same time that it challenges the lines of the authoritarian, centralizing, and populist State with which Brazilian society has historically lived. Surely the praxis developed in those municipal governments represents an important foundation of propositions for the construction of an alternative governing project for Brazil.[38]

---

[38] For the nature of neoliberalism in Brazil in the 1980s, see Nylen (1992).

'Praxis' is, indeed, the guiding concept in this 'new' model. The chapter on popular participation (Bittar 1992: 209–24), for example, begins by admonishing readers to give up doctrinal rigidity and unrealistic idealism in favor of programmatic creativity in constructing a 'new citizenship' to replace Brazil's tradition of exclusionary politics rooted in paternalistic social relations. There is a recognition that the PT's electoral gains in the late 1980s and early 1990s had more to do with a protest vote against incumbent politicians than they did with any principled support for the party itself. Far from being a bad thing (e.g. 'false consciousness'), this is interpreted as a window of opportunity for the party to construct new bases of support upon the twin pillars of 'moral reform and the recovery of the credibility of public service' and the 'lessons, hopes, and accomplishments in arenas of popular participation' (215). The chapter warns activists and administrators to lower any and all unrealistic expectations about either the 'immediate' or the 'impossible' socialization of Brazil's largely unorganized and self-interested population to accept the responsibilities of citizenship lest they fall into the traps of populism, totalitarianism, neoliberalism, or bureaucratization. It also expresses the necessity of building working alliances with other important actors (especially 'majoritarian parties' and powerful organized civil society groups) in order to avoid political gridlock and administrative stagnation, with its consequent suffering of the population.

In short, doctrinal purity is not worth these costs; but neither is abandoning basic principles. The *modo petista de governar* represents those basic principles, tested and amended by experience.

But the *construção coletiva* of a distinctive *modo petista de governar* represents only part of the lasting outcome of the SNAI's party-building efforts. Participation in SNAI events by PT activists and administrators from all corners of Brazil's vast territory resulted in the construction of informal networks of intraparty communication where practical knowledge and experience could be shared on an ongoing basis; that is, beyond the SNAI's seminars and meetings themselves. By putting party leaders, administrators, and intellectuals who shared similar concerns and experiences together in the same room, they came to see each other as something of a cohort with a collective identity beyond the seminar room.

The *modo petista de governar* represents, in essence, a clear attempt on the part of Bittar and his associates to bring the contemporary debates about socialism and democracy face to face with the practical experiences of PT municipal governance. Thus, from the context of a fractionalized party and the 'politically neutral', therefore uncontested, process of party building (e.g. creating the SNAI and convoking 'sectoral seminars'), a heterodox PT political project emerged rooted in the practice and experience of PT municipal governance throughout Brazil. In that context, the *modo petista de governar* emerged as both a practical guide and a generalized 'mind set' among an SNAI-fostered cohort who could form an important base of technical and administrative experience for contemporary and future PT administrations at all three levels of government.

Quixadá—Learning and Applying PT Heterodoxy

I made the point earlier that Icapuí administrators' on-the-job learning had to be seen in the context of the PT's generalized institutional learning processes throughout the late 1980s and early 1990s. We have just seen how numerous lessons from experiences of local-level governance, including those of Icapuí, were combined into a new party project. The PT administration of Quixadá, Ceará (elected in 1992) presents the case of a newly elected PT administration directly benefiting from prior processes of regional and national party building and institutional learning.

Located 168 kilometers south-west of Fortaleza in the central plains ('sertão') of Ceará, Quixadá was perhaps best known in the early 1990s as one of the municipalities hardest hit by the region's recurrent droughts. Of its roughly 72,300 residents in 1992, 39,785 (55 per cent) of them lived in the city center with the rest spread out over the municipality's extensive and impoverished rural areas.[39] Quixadá politics had long been dominated by an oligarchy of local landowners, industrialists, and conservative politicians who neglected even the most basic social services. The 1988 election of the candidate from the center-left PSDB indicated the public's willingness to experiment with new leadership, as well as the decline of the local oligarchy generally. With yet another brutal drought crippling Quixadá's vital agricultural economy (primarily based on cotton and livestock), combined with widely reported charges of administrative incompetence and corruption, the 1992 elections took place in an environment of extreme frustration and anxiety.

The PT's candidate, Ilário Marquez, a former state legislative deputy and a popular lawyer for the rural workers' union who had grown up in one of Quixadá's middle-class neighborhoods, won the election against a divided conservative opposition by aligning himself with a faction of the PSDB directly tied to the PSDB governor, Ciro Gomes. Mayor Marquez's executive assistant, Mônica Sousa, explained his victory in the following terms: 'The PT as a party had always been seen as radical and as an incompetent administrator. But here in Quixadá we had a great name attached to the party, Ilário. [. . .] It was not the PT that got Ilário elected. We couldn't even elect a single city council member. We are very conscious of this fact. The key was Ciro Gomes' help' (interview 29 July 1993). Marquez's election in open alliance with a party outside the small family of 'acceptable' left parties in Brazil would never have happened had not a growing number of activists in the Ceará PT (including Marquez) established the hegemony of their 'heterodox' vision within the state party's leadership. Among Quixadá party militants, strongly rooted in the rural labor movement and in the urban commercial workers' and public employees' unions, alliance with the PSDB was a difficult pill to swallow. But as the party had proven itself incapable on its own of electing candidates in previous elections, many of its members were willing to moderate their

---

[39] IBGE figures cited in 'Quixadá', *Tribuna do Ceará* [Fortaleza] (22 Apr. 1993, 20B). IBGE (1989: 14) lists Quixadá's population at 74,179.

previous hard-line stance.[40] In the words of former president of the rural workers' union and a founding member of Quixadá's PT, João Ventura, local party members had to make a difficult choice:

[W]e saw the party diluting its socialist platform, focusing on getting itself elected. This led to a certain amount of disillusionment. [. . .] Only a few people dropped out of the party, however. You see, we too were hungry to be elected. [. . .] I think the alliance, with its diluting of the PT, is bad for the future of Brazil. It is good for the present, however. People are hungry. They need to eat. The PT can respond to that. (Interview 2 August 1993)

It would be a mistake to leave the impression that 'heterodox' hegemony within the state party and within the party-in-government meant the absence of problems of party in-fighting. Upon taking office, Mayor Marquez immediately clashed with city employees over the issue of salaries and job security in the face of serious budget restraints and his assessment that there were too many civil servants for a city the size of Quixadá.[41] This clash quickly spilled over into the local party, then presided over by the president of the public employees' union. Marquez, however, was in a strong position to keep the local party leadership from initiating the familiar self-destructive process of fragmentation. Because of his alliance with the local PSDB, his highly visible personal alliance with the state's popular PSDB governor, his equally strong alliance with the leadership of the state PT, and because of the administration's successful efforts at stimulating popular participation in Quixadá's neighborhoods and rural districts (discussed below), local PT leaders outside the administration risked total political isolation were they openly to withdraw their support from Marquez.

Former opponents of Marquez and the PT spoke to me of how such compromises by former orthodox PT activists and begrudging silence from others constituted evidence of the PT's 'new political maturity'. Francisco Gladstone, for example, president of Quixadá's Landowners' Union, an organization with which Marquez had often clashed as lawyer for the Rural Workers' Union, had this to say about Marquez and his administration:

It's much easier to talk with Ilário than with anyone from a party of the right. The right is always hemming and hawing, playing politics [*politicágem*]. Within today's context [of climactic and economic crisis], our relationship with the administration is much more relaxed and open. I can sit down and talk with Ilário without all the politics getting in the way. I can talk about specific programs, ideas, etc. His Agriculture Secretary is just the same. (Interview 4 August 1993)

Similarly, the president of Quixadá's PSDB-controlled city council, Maria Irisdalva de Almeida, praised the PT administration as an example of the left's new flexibility:

[40] According to Mônica Sousa (29 July 1993 interview), prior to the 1992 elections, 25 per cent of the party's 517 registered members voted on whether or not to accept the electoral alliance with the PSDB (the required quorum was 10 per cent). The vote was unanimously in favor.

[41] This is a common complaint throughout Brazil, as evidenced in Banck (1994).

The left has no more of its old vices: where people didn't work but still received things from the government. The left now speaks of moralization, rejection of clientelism, and building up the community. To me, the left represents a style of politics opposed to the old style. And it's not just discourse. (Interview 2 August 1993)

What emerges from these comments is a broadly shared sense that the 'old style' of politics (*politicágem*, clientelism, etc.) lies at the foundation of many of Quixadá's social and political problems. This rejection of the old provided the ideological basis for the center-left coalition that swept Marquez into office. It also facilitated action on the PT's long-standing commitment to the promotion of popular participation as the best means of attacking Brazil's political cultural impediments to progressive social reform. The broadly shared perception of the sociopolitical roots of Quixadá's problems provided Marquez the opportunity to take his brand of left 'heterodoxy' beyond the limited realm of electoral alliance building. He could openly promote popular participation, for example, without being seen as constructing socialism or building the bases of revolution.

Given this opportunity, Marquez and his administration turned to the state and national party organizations for practical assistance. What they found were the lessons of past and present PT administrations available in several easily accessible formats, thanks in part to the work of the SNAI: books, videos, conference and seminar papers, party magazines, party consultants, and party-affiliated specialists 'for hire'.

Marquez turned to the *Modo Petista* book 'as a reference', but desired more specific information on actual policies of popular participation.[42] So he sent his executive assistant, Mônica Sousa, to attend a three-day seminar on 'Popular Participation in Democratic and Popular Administrations' at the Instituto Cajamar (Inca), a research and activist training center in São Paulo directly affiliated with the Central Única dos Trabalhadores (CUT) and indirectly affiliated with the PT.[43] At the seminar, co-sponsored by the PT's INAPP (discussed above) and attended almost exclusively by PT municipal administrators from various parts of Brazil, Sousa was most impressed by the former PT mayor of Diadema, José Augusto da Silva Ramos, as he described his administration's popular participation program, *Pé na Rua de Diadema* (In the Streets of Diadema). According to Sousa, Ramos described a strategy of teaching the responsibilities of citizenship by requiring communities to decide collectively upon the priorities of government policy towards their community, then giving them the opportunity to communicate their decisions directly to administration officials in their own neighborhood rather than in the intimidating confines of city hall. In this process, not only do the citizens engage in decision-making that directly affects their lives and the future of their community,

---

[42]   31 July 1993 interview with Mayor Ilário Marquez.

[43]   For a description of the program, see INAPP/Inca (1991). For a brief analysis of the Instituto Cajamar, see Olinda (1991: 70–4). Inca had concerned itself with the issue of popular participation and local governance at least as far back as June of 1988 when it sponsored a 'Seminário Internacional sobre Poder Local e Participação Local'.

but they become organized around the prioritizing exercise. Community leaders emerge and new 'bases' are constructed. These become useful both for administering the city and for building the party (the idea being that many of these newly active citizens will gravitate to the PT).

Sousa returned to Quixadá and began to draw up plans for a similar program that would eventually be called *Prefeitura Com Você* (PCV: The Administration With You). Here is how I observed the program working in its first year of operation.

The mayor's office sets up a day in which the entire administration, about eighty officials in all, comes to a previously chosen community to receive formally that community's priorities for government action for the fiscal year. Prior to the formalities, the mayor is usually received with festive presentations: dance, music, children's theater, etc. After a round of speeches explaining the PCV program and extolling the virtues of popular participation, officials attend a series of question-and-answer meetings and engage in informal conversations with residents. During the day, any and all requests for special favors are supposed to be directed to the leadership of the neighborhood association.

Some weeks before this PCV day, Sousa and about a dozen representatives from the administrative secretariats meet after normal work hours with directors of the neighborhood association as often as is necessary to describe the program: not only what each secretariat does and what it can do for the community, but the crucial fact that nothing will happen without the neighborhood association playing an active role in the process. Sousa explains that the city's resources are limited, and that the community cannot get everything it wants. She tells the association's directors that they must call a meeting of the entire community to prioritize collectively the demands of their community. Those demands will then be presented in the name of the community through its 'representative organ', the neighborhood association.

To give two different examples, in the community of São João just outside the city center, with its 2,932 residents and already existing neighborhood association, only two community meetings were necessary prior to the PCV day. Each meeting had about seventy participants, and preparations went fairly smoothly. Following the PCV day, São João's neighborhood association saw its membership increase by 10 per cent. According to its president,

People see that the association is working and doing something, so they want to join. Before, they had no faith. Now we have proven that we can get things done. People used to go to the mayor personally when they wanted something. Today he tells them to go through the neighborhood association. (Interview 2 August 1993)

By contrast, in the rural community of Custódio, where there was no pre-existing association to represent its 3,757 residents, the process of preparing for the PCV day was more difficult. Sousa held an initial open community meeting to explain the idea of the program. That was followed by two canceled meetings and a third, in which the whole process had to begin from scratch. Community interest at this third meeting, nevertheless, was high, with between seventy-five and 100 residents present throughout the two-hour meeting and about thirty signing up to join the nascent association. Interested potential leaders of the association (about ten in all) were easy to identify, as they were the ones who paid the most attention, asking the most questions and volunteering most often to answer Sousa's questions. Sousa explained that community participation through a neighborhood association was an essential part of the PT's governing program. When someone asked why the city council existed, if not to carry out this representative function, she responded that Quixadá's city council members had traditionally shirked both their representative and oversight functions in favor of engaging in clientelistic exchanges of favors in the interests of their own re-elections and in the interests of Quixadá's powerful minority of economic elites. Average citizens were reduced to begging for favors (i.e. public service), usually in exchange for promises to vote 'accordingly'. The only way to fight this, Sousa explained, was to create another set of institutions run by 'the people' themselves, as a united community.[44] Custódio's neighborhood association finally came together after several more night-time community meetings (none of which resulted in overtime pay for any of the participating administration officials). Custódio's PCV day came off on schedule.

Quixadá provides us with two examples of policies that defined its PT-led administration—*coligação* with the PSDB and the *Prefeitura Com Você* popular participation program—and that were strongly based on heterodox interpretations of other PT administrations' experiences. The Marquez administration also benefited from the unification of the state party around a flexible 'heterodox' vision of the role of the party and from the nearby Icapuí example of a successful heterodox administration. The fact that the Marquez administration was able to make use of these lessons suggests that the PT had attained a level of party building at both the state and national levels that had eluded it in the past. In effect, the party was doing exactly what non-clientelistic parties should do: learn from the past and prepare for the future.

Conclusion

The PT's experiences of local governance in Ceará have both contributed to, and benefited from, regional and national processes of party building and institutional learning. The 'lessons' of Fortaleza and Icapuí were included in discussions leading to construction of a well-defined *modo petista de governar* (PT mode of governance); and the ongoing governing programs of Icapuí and Quixadá reflect that 'heterodox' project in significant ways.

---

[44] For an analysis of the growth of neighborhood associations in Brazil in the 1980s that precisely parallels the one described here, see Cardoso (1992: 292).

It would appear that Rodolfo Cascão's belief (mentioned at the outset) was well founded: only through a party organization can the nation profit from local-level experiences of 'democratic and popular' governance. It is apparently not enough to have a significant number of party activists 'learning-by-doing' in the give-and-take world of democratic governance. Political parties' institutional self-interest in building electoral viability, in part by proving their administrative competence, is a necessary next step in turning those individuals' 'lessons' into broader efforts at party building and institutional learning.

We must be careful, however, to note that the PT is a unique political party in the Brazilian context. Its decisive commitment to oppose traditional paternalist practices and to oppose the exclusionary practices of oligarchical democracy forces it to rely on building a reputation based on 'good works', competence, and honesty. Few other national parties in Brazil would or could do the same.

We also need to be careful not to forget that institutional learning is by no means a conflict-free process. In Ceará, the state party adopted a heterodox line only after the damaging failure of Fortaleza and several years of nasty infighting. And, at the national level, while much of the impetus for party building came from a minimal consensus among competing factions that fragmentation was destroying the party, the heterodox *modo petista de governar* that emerged from the fruit of that consensus (i.e. the SNAI) never attained hegemony within the party as a whole. As if to highlight the difficulty of institutional learning actually taking place, party building had to be erroneously perceived as an apolitical process by orthodox factions who stood to lose the most from the new project's heterodox bent. And while the *modo petista de governar* certainly strengthened the heterodox groups within the party, orthodox groups remained strong within the national leadership.

It is hard for me to imagine that having seen the promise of PT heterodoxy, party leaders, activists, and office-holders would throw it all away by falling back on ideologically pure but demonstrably impractical and self-destructively divisive orthodoxy. But that is probably wishful thinking on my part. Nonetheless, the evidence suggests that the *modo petista de governar* represents an emerging new political project that reinterprets, without abandoning, the fundamental principles and goals of the PT: the destruction of paternalism and the construction of a more inclusive form of democracy than has ever been known in Brazil.

PT heterodoxy, therefore, is not 'sell-out' revisionism. I hope that I have shown that heterodox activists and administrators have in no way abandoned the idealism and transformative zeal long associated with the left. Rather they have traded one leftist agenda—Leninist and vanguardist—for another decisively non-Marxist and radical-democratic one. In describing a similar agenda for the Colombian left, Orlando Fals Borda (1992: 314) calls such individuals the true 'agents of change' in the post-Cold War era. And whatever the prospects for a more participatory kind of politics on a permanent basis, such a project is a crucial instrument to break down the old politics of paternalism.

But a warning is in order: heterodox followers run a serious risk of falling into what I called a new 'benevolent vanguardism' (or, worse, losing themselves to despair and disdain for the masses) if they do not figure out that they must fully and necessarily embrace representative democracy even as they attempt to construct a more participative democracy. The idea is to work to approximate the ideal without losing sight of necessarily having to work within the real. And the 'real', in this instance, means at least two things: first, relatively few people can be expected to sacrifice their time and energy to participate in politics on behalf of any transformative agenda, even a more 'pragmatic' one of the heterodox variety (call it a problem of collective action and 'public goods', if you must, but political activists are a rare breed); second, all effort must nevertheless be expended to provide ample opportunities and encouragement to all those who desire to participate and to those who may come to appreciate it but have never yet been given the chance. These will be the activists and the representatives of tomorrow. That they will come from the ranks of the non-elite rather than exclusively from the privileged classes will help to assure that representative democracy may, someday, live up to its name.

18 | Can a Leftist Government Make a Difference? The Frente Amplio Administration of Montevideo, 1990–1994

Peter Winn and Lilia Ferro-Clérico

In 1973, the brief history of the Uruguayan left as a major political force seemed to have come to an untimely end, foreclosed by a brutal right-wing military dictatorship that destroyed the Tupamaro guerrillas, crushed the Communist-led labor movement, and banned the Frente Amplio (Broad Front) leftist political alliance, which had won a fifth of the vote in the 1971 elections. Uruguay's military regime suspended the constitution, closed the Congress, and purged the university, converting a nation once considered South America's 'model democracy' into the country with the largest number of political prisoners per capita in the world. Most of them were leaders or activists of the left, which was persecuted and forced underground.

With the restoration of democracy in 1984–5, the left resurfaced through the Frente Amplio and tried to begin again. But first the Frente Amplio's long-time standard-bearer, Gen. Liber Seregni, was not allowed to run by the military; then, Hugo Batalla, a popular moderate, left the Frente Amplio shortly before the 1989 elections, taking his Party for the Government of the People (PGP), the Frente's strongest force, with him. This left the Communist Party as the hegemonic force within the leftist alliance, accounting for nearly half of the Frente's vote in 1989. But this orthodox Moscow-line party disintegrated after the collapse of communism in the Soviet Union, leaving the Frente polarized between 'Moderates' and 'Radicals'.

Yet, despite these successive setbacks and traumas, the Frente Amplio, an alliance of eighteen parties that runs the leftist gamut from the Tupamaros to the Socialists, is today challenging the traditional parties' dominance in Uruguay, controls the country's capital city, and has a good chance to win the next national elections.[1]

---

[1] Moreover, the left also initiated a campaign that decisively won a 1992 popular referendum against the privatization of the national telephone company that set Uruguay firmly against the

Since 1990, the Frente Amplio has governed Montevideo. This marks the first time in Uruguay that the left has controlled a local government. Moreover, its administrative debut is in the country's political, economic, and cultural capital and the home of nearly half of its citizens.

How did the Frente Amplio win control of Montevideo only two decades after the coalition's formation and less than two decades after the left's apparent destruction by the military, despite the loss of its leading moderate parties and the dominance of a Communist party on the brink of collapse? What and how did the Uruguayan left do in its first experience of local government? Or to pose the question more sharply: what difference has a leftist government made in Montevideo—and what are its implications? Can the political party left conceive, get elected on, and implement a political project for the 1990s which avoids the mistakes of the past and constitutes a viable alternative to neoliberalism's minimalist state? These are the central questions on which this chapter will focus.

Out of the Ashes: The Resurgence of the Uruguayan Left

The paradox of leftist victory being snatched out of the ashes of defeat and division is as complex as Uruguay's history and politics—and as deceptively simple as the charisma of Tabaré Vázquez, the Socialist mayor of Montevideo from 1990 to 1994.

The modern history of Uruguay began in 1904 with the inauguration of José Batlle y Ordóñez as president. Batlle, a towering figure who was one of the most progressive national leaders of his era, mobilized immigrant workers and shop-keepers into a social democratic political coalition that transformed Uruguay into the continent's first welfare state and model democracy. At the same time, Batlle's political reforms consolidated the control of Uruguay's two traditional parties, the Blancos and Colorados, which have dominated the country since the 1830s, per-haps the longest-lived two-party system in the world.

Under 'Don Pepe' and his *batllista* successors Uruguay became a 'model coun-try', a prosperous, egalitarian nation of some 2–3 million, in which the state played a leading economic role, literacy was universal, urban poverty rare, and a largely middle-class population could retire at 55 or 60 with confidence that their coun-try's and personal welfare was secure.

But the economic prosperity and social welfare of this 'epoch of *las vacas gordas*' (the fat cows) was based on a ranching economy dependent on its exports of meat and wool to Europe. When Uruguay's overseas markets shrank after the Korean War,

neoliberal trend in the region, one of several innovative uses of plebiscitary democracy in Uruguay during the past decade. For a detailed analysis of this plebiscite, see Fernando Filgueira and Jorge Papadópulos, 'Putting Conservatism to Good Use? Long Crisis and Vetoed Alternatives in Uruguay', Chapter 15 in this volume.

its economy went into a decline that deepened in the 1960s, with rising inflation and stagnant employment eroding living standards and detonating a social conflict with political ramifications. When the traditional parties, led by an unresponsive elite unwilling to make needed reforms and fixated on the distribution of a shrinking economic pie, proved incapable of meeting the deepening crisis, many Uruguayans —despite their traditional party loyalties and cultural conservatism—began to look to the left for solutions.

Although Batlle's enlightened commitment to proportional representation had preserved a spectrum of leftist parties, his advanced social policies had deprived them of a political mass base. As a result, the Socialists had remained café radicals, with greater support among intellectuals than workers, while the Communist strength in Uruguay's labor unions was not reflected in political elections. But during the 1960s, under the impact of national crisis and the Cuban revolution, radicalized Socialists formed the Tupamaro urban guerrillas and the Communist Party made a political breakthrough.

By 1971, the Tupamaros had outwitted the police, discredited the traditional political system, and were challenging a corrupt and ineffective state. By then, too, the Socialists and Communists had joined with progressive Christian Democrats and dissident Colorados and Blancos to form the Frente Amplio (Broad Front) electoral alliance, which failed to win the disputed balloting of 1971, but received an impressive one-fifth of the vote and nearly won Montevideo. It was this leftist political success, together with the rising militancy of the country's unions and the inability of the police to meet the Tupamaro threat, that led rightist Colorados and Blancos to call in the armed forces, which had not intervened in politics during this century.

The Uruguayan military who took power in 1973 proved as brutal as their Argentine and Chilean comrades-in-arms in the Southern Cone's 'dirty wars', but less deadly. Although they jailed and tortured leftist political and labor leaders, they rarely killed them. As a result, Frente Amplio and Tupamaro leaders, such as Liber Seregni and Eleuterio Fernández Huidobro, survived the military dictatorship to provide experienced political leadership when it came to an end in 1985, after a negotiated return to the barracks in which the Frente Amplio played a key role, shoring up the left's democratic credentials.

When the first elections in thirteen years were held in 1984, despite the military ban on Seregni's presidential candidacy, the Frente Amplio won roughly the same fifth of the vote it had received in 1971, and did even better in the 1989 elections. By the 1990s, voting Frente Amplio had become an Uruguayan political tradition, like voting Colorado or Blanco, with loyalties stretching back two decades, and a *frentista* identification that was more widespread than loyalty to the parties that composed it.

By then, the Frente Amplio had also benefited from the failure of Uruguay's traditional parties to resolve the country's economic and social problems. The Colorados, led by Julio María Sanguinetti, won the 1984 election, but their failures helped produce a Blanco government in 1989 under Luis Alberto Lacalle, whose efforts at neoliberal reform were no more successful in assuring growth with equity (see Filgueira and Papadópulos, this volume). The inability of the two traditional parties to solve Uruguay's chronic crisis has led to growing support for the Frente Amplio.

Although policy and leadership failures played roles in this disillusionment with the traditional parties after the restoration of democracy, at bottom it reflects a crisis of the political system. Batlle created a governable democracy by instituting the 'double simultaneous vote', in which voters cast their ballots for their favorite party faction, but their votes were counted for their party as well and accrued for the candidate of the party faction with the most votes. This measure, the *ley de lemas*, reinforced party stability and allowed Batlle to convert the support of a minority of the electorate but a plurality of his Colorado party into a national majority. Together with *coparticipación*, which co-opted the opposition Blancos by giving them a share of government posts and patronage, and proportional representation, which gave the smaller parties a stake in the system, the *ley de lemas* produced a stable, if Baroque democracy.

But the emergence of the Frente Amplio destroyed the two-party system and made minority governments all but inevitable. The result has been a crisis of governability. Uruguayans increasingly see their government as ineffective and irrelevant. One response has been a decline in political participation, seen in the decay of the urban political clubs around which Montevideo politics used to revolve (a decline that also reflects the city's transformation into an anonymous 'modern' metropolis in which television has assumed a greater political importance).[2]

A related trend has been a rise in the anti-politics and anti-party sentiments seen elsewhere in the region. This mood benefited the Frente Amplio, which had not been tainted by the exercise of failed political power, and projected an image of a fresh new start. It also benefited Dr Tabaré Vázquez, the Frente's most popular leader, a political novice whose election as mayor of Montevideo in 1989 marked the left's first access to the country's second most important elected executive post.

With Vázquez, for the first time the Frente Amplio had a candidate whose electoral appeal transcended its own ranks. Dr Vázquez is not a lawyer, like most Uruguayan politicians, but a physician in a society where doctors are respected, and a highly regarded oncologist in a nation with one of the highest cancer rates in the hemisphere. The son of a worker, he is also a Uruguayan success story in a country where education is the path to social mobility. Yet, 'Tabaré', as he is universally known, did not turn his back on his origins. He remained a neighborhood leader, who was president of his local soccer team—in a country where soccer is a passion—which won the national title the year he was elected mayor of Montevideo. Equally important were Tabaré's personal qualities. He retained a sympathetic bedside manner in politics, a warm empathy combined with a laid-back style that

---

[2] The imaginative Communist television campaign for the 1989 election is widely credited with playing a major role in the Communist—and Frente Amplio—success at the polls that year.

plays well on television and translates into an understated charisma in person. He seemed honest and open in a world of pork-barrel politicians and backroom deals. He was quick on the uptake, well-organized, and decisive. In short, Vázquez is a postmodern caudillo, a leader for the 1990s, an era in which traditional politicians are viewed with disdain in Uruguay—as elsewhere.

If many Montevideans voted for him because of their identification with the Frente Amplio and others because of their disillusionment with the traditional parties, many others voted for the Frente municipal slate because it was headed by Tabaré Vázquez. Together, these ballots, drawn from the urban poor, workers, and the middle class, swept the left into power in the nation's capital.

Montevideo in 1990

The Montevideo that the Frente Amplio inherited in 1990 was a metropolis of 1.2 million people and in many ways a microcosm of Uruguay. It was a city of faded gentility, whose spacious parks and tree-lined boulevards reflected the ideals and styles of a prosperous middle class imbued with civic pride. The decline in the national economy and in state resources was reflected in the lack of newer public spaces and the growing disrepair of parks and plazas. The deterioration was most evident in the city center, which had become tawdry and crowded with street vendors during the day, and deserted at night, with street crime previously unknown in Uruguay.

By 1990, the middle class had left the depressed city center and moved out to the beachfront communities that lined the coast, followed by the cafés, boutiques, and supermarkets that made Pocitos and Carrasco the places to live, an archipelago of fashion and prosperity on the edge of a declining metropolis. In working-class areas such as El Cerrito, the streets were lined with modest older houses whose still decent façades masked the rising unemployment, declining real wages, and slipping living standards of their residents. More visible was the spread of slums and shanty-towns on El Cerro, on the other side of the bay, and the other neighborhoods where the growing numbers of poor people eked out a living as ragpickers, lottery sellers, or street vendors, part of a rapidly expanding informal economy that filled the need for jobs left by decades of economic stagnation and the need for inexpensive goods left by neoliberal policies, with their regressive distribution of the nation's income.

The combination of economic crisis, military dictatorship, and neoliberalism had also led to a decline in social spending and urban services. The buses on which 90 per cent of Montevideans depended for transport were ancient and inadequate. Streets were no longer well maintained and garbage collection was a problem. The social safety net that had once made Uruguay a model welfare state was so frayed that the elderly homeless were now as symbolic of the state of the nation as the 60-year-old pensioners arguing about politics and soccer in the city's cafés.

For the average citizen, the burdens of this deterioration were added to the trials of dealing with a municipal bureaucracy notorious for its arrogance and inefficiency, protected by the political pull that had secured their positions and the unions that represented them. Paying your taxes or filing a form could take hours; getting services out of the centralized municipal bureaucracy could take days—or years.

Given this panorama, it is not surprising that Vázquez took office with the pledge that he had not become Intendente 'to administer a failed system, but to govern'—to implement his own program of reforms.[3] The Frente Amplio campaign platform had promised to tackle these problems, creating a municipal government that was more efficient, efficacious, and responsive, services that were both modern and affordable, and a city whose financial burdens and economic benefits were more equitably distributed. The political infratext was clear: if the Frente Amplio could turn Montevideo around in so dramatic a fashion, it would be in a position to mount a serious challenge for national power and Vázquez would become a credible presidential candidate.

The Frente Amplio in Power: Montevideo, 1990–1994

During his five years as Intendente of Montevideo, Tabaré Vázquez had to confront an array of problems inherited from the past, as well as implement the ambitious program of expanded social benefits and structural reforms he had promised in his successful election campaign. Moreover, although the Frente Amplio controlled the municipal council, its opponents controlled the national government, which in turn controlled the resources for housing, education, and health programs. The Uruguayan left was experienced at being in opposition, but had no experience at all of government, and the very different political culture that task required. It was an opportunity to project and implement a new socialist vision for the 1990s, but also a political quicksand in which the credibility of a leftist governmental alternative could disappear for a generation. It all depended on how Vázquez and the Frente Amplio dealt with the problems and opportunities they would encounter in the municipality of Montevideo.

Some of the problems Tabaré Vázquez inherited—such as the contract negotiations with the municipal workers or the clogging of downtown Montevideo with unregulated street vendors—demanded immediate solutions. These decisions, moreover, had less to do with articulating a new socialist vision than with establishing Vázquez and the Frente as a credible governmental alternative.

Both were tests of Tabaré's ability to transcend political partisanship and emerge as a successful administrator, a mayor for all Montevideans, and tests too of the Frente Amplio's ability to transmute its oppositional political culture into a political

---

[3] Tabaré Vázquez, interview of Sept. 1993.

culture of government. At bottom, they were also tests of the Frente's ability to transform a campaign platform into a program of government and to harmonize divergent interests where they had previously defended class interests. Both problems were viewed by the Frente's rivals as political traps that Vázquez's popularity was unlikely to survive.

Tabaré Vázquez did not create the inefficiency, arrogance, and immobility that characterized Montevideo municipal employees—the product of a political system built on patronage, an economic structure in which the state was the employer of last resort, labor relations in which ideological unions defended bread-and-butter interests, and a user-unfriendly workplace tradition compounded by eroding real wages. But he inherited this complex problem and a labor conflict would embarrass Vázquez politically. On the other hand, too favorable a contract would create fiscal problems for Vázquez and allow rivals to the right to argue that a Frente Amplio government was unable to defend the public interest against the class interests of its organized labor supporters.

Tabaré understood both the risks and the municipal employees. He was able to escape the trap by reducing the work day from eight to six hours, and granting a significant wage increase, but linking these salary raises to productivity increases —a difficult process, but one which gradually began to show results. Also important was the improvement in labor relations. Before, municipal labor relations were conflictual and chaotic, often ending in strikes. With the Frente Amplio in power, dialogue became the way of dealing with labor conflicts and negotiations were regularized, although union leaders complained about the technocratic bent of the Municipality executive. These changes did not solve the underlying problems of municipal services, but they were a political success.

The street vendor problem was equally complex. This problem too was an inheritance about which the Frente Amplio government of Montevideo could do little: at bottom it was a result of national neoliberal policies that had lowered real wages and raised unemployment to the point where jobs were hard to find and often paid less well than selling consumer goods on the street. As a consequence, when Vázquez took office, the main street of downtown Montevideo, Avenida 18 de Julio, was clogged with vendors, who jostled for position and customers, evoking annoyance from pedestrians and protests from established merchants whose stores they were both obscuring and underselling.

Some of these vendors were entrepreneurs and others their employees, but most were not Frente Amplio supporters. Still, the explosion of this informal economy reflected the social consequences of economic policies which the Frente Amplio had criticized and it could not just repress them. But it posed a political problem that excited emotions and could not be ignored.

Tabaré's solution was to regulate the vendors, stressing the mediating role of the state while promoting the organization of civil society. The Frente Amplio municipal government encouraged the vendors to organize themselves and then—as with the unions—entered into a dialogue with them, while resisting their extreme demands. Out of these negotiations came an accord in which the vendors agreed to limit their stands to certain areas and to a certain density within those areas. On the other side, the government legitimated their activities and turned over certain downtown markets to the vendors, even building one for this purpose. It not only solved the vendor problem, it showed Vázquez's government as willing and able to negotiate innovative solutions to seemingly intractable problems inherited from the past. Thus, it helped establish his credibility as a pragmatic mayor of 'all Montevideans', not just a representative of leftist ideologies or Frente Amplio parties.

More difficult to resolve was the issue of the *hurgadores*, unemployed poor with horsecarts who went through the garbage in search of recyclable materials to sell. This was criticized as an eyesore and an anachronism which undermined efforts to project a modern image for the city. Yet, because their own studies showed that some 10,000 poor families lived from recycling garbage, a Frente Amplio government could not put them out of business without finding them alternative sources of income, a task beyond the resources of a municipal government in Uruguay in the 1990s. Again, the solution Vázquez devised was to organize and regulate the *hurgadores* by registering them and assigning them places for going through the garbage, at the same time reducing the number of dumps and assuring that the garbage was concentrated in them, not spread around the city.

The problem of scarce resources also limited Frente Amplio efforts to expand other municipal services. Under Vázquez a record number of new street lights were installed, but many areas of Montevideo still remain dark and unsafe at night. Inadequate housing is a serious problem in Montevideo, with shantytowns expanding along with homelessness, but it is a national responsibility about which the municipality can do relatively little. Under the Frente Amplio, the Municipality has promoted housing construction by giving municipal lands and arranging loans for cooperative residential housing, or by funding the rental of machinery or contributing materials at low prices which are repaid through long-term loans. It has also given more land titles to squatters than any previous administration, and created a construction materials 'bank' to help people improve their houses. But despite this flexibility and progress, even a Frente Amplio *edil* stressed that Vázquez's campaign platform was 'too idealistic' on housing, as the resources that could solve the housing problem only exist at the national level.[4]

Health care was a similar story, despite the presence of a physician as Intendente. Under Vázquez, public vaccination plans were expanded and an eye care and clinic plan initiated, but not fully implemented. The distribution of subsidized milk tripled, yet inadequate nutrition remains a problem in too many Montevideo families.

In general, starts were made and the promise of several programs was demonstrated. But the limited resources available at the municipal level to fund ambitious

---

[4] Lilian Kechichian, interview of July 1993.

social programs, together with the social costs of national neoliberal policies, made it impossible for the Frente Amplio to fulfill its good intentions—and campaign promises—in these areas.

The exception to this rule of limited change was transportation, where Vázquez shifted the burden of subsidizing students and the elderly from other bus riders (through higher fares) to the Municipality (through direct subsidies to the bus companies), even though they absorbed a large share of the municipal budget. Bus fares were reduced as a consequence and Tabaré reaped a political dividend at the outset of his administration, but at a financial cost, which constrained his ability to fund other programs. For Vázquez it was an issue of equity: the wealthiest 10 per cent of the Montevideo population don't ride the bus, but shouldn't they pay a fair share of these bus subsidies?[5] His supporters in the Frente Amplio praised the measure as an act of income redistribution, which imposed a regulatory oversight of the bus companies, which had to prove that they had paid social security taxes in order to receive the subsidies. Critics in other parties focused on the laxness of that oversight, as a result of which, they claimed, the companies received excessive subsidies—at times despite questionable proofs of tax payments—and on the subsequent rise in bus fares. Less partisan analysts point out that the Municipality did not have the technical capacity to oversee adequately the bus companies' finances, and stressed that the measure may have been debatable economically but that it was a political success for Tabaré, because its populist message of redistribution appealed to a majority of Montevideans.[6]

A similar logic informed the new property census, the redistributive bookend at the close of his administration, which proved equally controversial. The debate revolved around the Vázquez administration's undertaking the first property census in three decades, as the first step to new tax assessments. For Tabaré and his aides, there were dual goals. One was redistributive: to make taxation more equitable. The second goal was to obtain the information to enable them to plan the development of Montevideo. The new property census revealed that the concentration of wealth in Montevideo was so great that the 37,000 most valuable homes, equal to only 10 per cent of the residences, were worth as much as the other 90 per cent of the residences combined.[7]

According to Vázquez, it was this new property census that raised the issue of tax equity. As the Frente Amplio principle is 'those who have more should pay more', he pressed the issue as one of progressive taxation.[8] When the new census—and new tax assessments—were blocked by the Colorados and Blancos in the national assembly, Tabaré called for a plebiscite on the issue, a form of direct popular participation that the Uruguayan left had invoked with great success during the 1992 anti-privatization campaign. Vázquez's aides tried to portray the conflict as one over the maintenance of such traditional Uruguayan values as solidarity and social

[5] Tabaré Vázquez, interview of Sept. 1993.   [6] Carina Perelli, interview of Aug. 1993.
[7] Ariel Bergamino, interview of July 1993.   [8] Tabaré Vázquez, interview of Sept. 1993.

justice, but to Frente Amplio opponents it was a populist political ploy. Moreover, the issue divided the Frente Amplio's working-class base from its middle-class supporters who did not want to pay higher property taxes. Tabaré proceeded with a signature-gathering campaign, but it met a lukewarm response and was stalled short of its goal when the election campaign refocused attentions in mid-1994. The census debate had elements of populism, but it helped Tabaré's credentials as a redistributive leftist, who is willing to tax the rich in order to pay for programs for the poor.

It would be an error, however, to assume that Vázquez's administration was hostile to business. In several areas, it proved ready and willing to break with the left's tradition of state services to cut deals with the private sector, over the objections of the radical wing of the Frente Amplio. Not only did Vázquez not reverse the privatization of street cleaning begun under his Colorado predecessors, he extended it until it covered a third of Montevideo. Moreover, in an imaginative move that underscored his freedom from old leftist shibboleths, Tabaré sought to solve the problem of downtown decay by getting businesses to adopt a square and assume responsibility for its renovation and upkeep. He also visited the United States, where he talked with officials of the IMF, an anathema to the Uruguayan left. This was a continuation of his pattern of seeking a dialogue with both business leaders and his political opponents, much to the annoyance of the Radicals in the Frente. Together with his dismissal of one Frente Amplio subordinate who reported to his party before he informed Vázquez and another in whose department mismanagement was discovered, these actions allowed Tabaré to demonstrate his resolve and his independence.

His show of independence caused criticisms and conflict within the Frente Amplio, but strengthened Vázquez's appeal to voters outside the Frente. It also won the grudging respect of business, who realized that he is a leftist with whom they can do business. It has even led some in the US Embassy to conclude that a Vázquez presidency would be acceptable, a far cry from the hostile US response to the prospect of a Frente Amplio victory in the past.

As a pragmatic leftist politician, Tabaré Vázquez proved remarkably adept, with an appealing style, an attractive program, and shrewd political instincts. Yet, as he is aware, this does not add up to a leftist alternative to neoliberalism. If there is a part of his program as Intendente of Montevideo that does point the way to an alternative political project, it is the decentralization plan.

Decentralization and Democracy

The Frente Amplio's redistributive measures and social programs might be laudable in their concern for social welfare and necessary in the face of neoliberal policies at the national level. In another country, they might even be applauded as revolutionary in their originality and hailed as opening a new era for the left, the state, and the people they serve. Within a Uruguayan context, however, these initiatives can best be understood as a reaffirmation and extension of *batllismo*—that uniquely Uruguayan combination of populism and social democracy, political experimentation and mixed economy, in which the state assured the welfare of its citizens through social programs, consumer subsidies, and public employment—which recent polls and plebiscites have confirmed remains the ideology of the majority of Uruguayans, irrespective of their party label. If the Frente Amplio's stewardship of Montevideo were limited to these policies, Tabaré Vázquez's term as Intendente might confirm the adage that the Uruguayan left begins with a socialist discourse but ends with a *batllista* practice.

The phased process of decentralization of municipal government that Vázquez introduced as Intendente is different. This innovative program breaks with the centralizing tradition of both socialism and *battlismo*. It is a democratic leftist project, which builds on the lessons learned from the successes of the popular movements of the last two decades and the failures of state socialism of the past seven decades in order to devise a democratic socialism for the coming decades. In many ways it is the most important initiative to emerge out of the leftist political renewal in Uruguay and its response to the neoliberal critique of the bloated and inefficient *batllista* welfare state.

Although the decentralization initiative eventually received broad political support, the thinking behind it emerged from the Socialist Party. In explaining how the Uruguayan left arrived at decentralization as the keystone to its Montevideo program, Manuel Laguarda, a leading Socialist ideologue and a strong supporter of decentralization, stressed three factors: the experience of dictatorship, the discovery of civil society, and the discrediting of state socialism. During the dictatorship, with its brutal repression and intolerance, the left began to revalue the pluralistic democracy it had criticized as 'bourgeois' and regarded as instrumental, viewing it now as a good in itself and even as 'an essential aspect of . . . socialist society'.[9]

The second revelation of those same years was the value and valor of social movements—from women's groups to neighborhood associations—first as agencies of resistance to dictatorship and grassroots mobilizations to secure the basic necessities of life, but then as a new 'popular power' through which the new socialist society could be created and its solidary values defended from the ideological assaults of neoliberal individualism. This reflected a more complex and diffuse notion of power, no longer centered in the seizure of the state, but in the growing power of the many actors within civil society whose access to state power would democratize the state, which might not wither away, but would be transformed in the process. Decentralization was where an emergent civil society and a democratized state would intersect.

---

[9] *La República* (Montevideo), 24 Sept. 1993.

This new Socialist vision reflected as well the discrediting of historic socialism, the state socialism associated with the Soviet Union. In place of the traditional Leninist focus on establishing a socialist state, what emerged was a stress on the creation of a 'socialist civil society and a societal socialism'. In this new conception, socialism was envisioned as 'the deepening of democracy and increased popular control over the state, the economy, the means of production, and the society'.[10]

Within the Uruguayan Socialist Party, the result of these reflections was the proposal for 'Democracy on New Foundations' made public in 1984. It later served as the principal source for Tabaré Vázquez's platform on decentralization in 1989, which was projected as one of the fundamental goals of his administration—to develop a local government which was a joint venture of state institutions and societal actors, who would work together to secure economic welfare, social programs, and self-management. This project was also promoted 'as a step toward a future socialist society in which democracy, pluralism, and self-management would be central features'.[11]

There were two parts to the Frente Amplio project: *desconcentración* and *descentralización*. *Desconcentración* meant a geographic relocation of some of the state bureaucracy, shifted from the municipal offices in downtown Montevideo to the local areas in order to increase their efficiency and responsiveness, as well as the control of citizens over their work. *Descentralización*, on the other hand, meant a ceding of some governmental powers to newly created local institutions, particularly the power to initiate projects. It also entailed a mix of direct democracy with representative democracy through the creation of new local institutions which would promote and facilitate popular participation, both as individuals and as organized groups, including the horizontal relations within civil society.

Decentralization would be a leftist response to the neoliberals in that it would assure both liberty and equality, promoting citizen action within the state and association in a civil society outside state control. The mediating and regulating role of the state would help secure a fair distribution of benefits, while allowing the market its own sphere. The old populist model of a paternalistic state distributing benefits to a passive citizenry would be transformed by the active role of grassroots organizations and the new local institutions in initiating and implementing policies that reflected local needs. In principle, this decentralized model of local government could be extended to the whole country, projected as a dynamic and attractive new project of a participatory democratic socialism.

The goal was not only to make government more responsive, but to use decentralization to transform the exercise of power and the management of daily life, creating a new democratic style of local government in which consultation from below replaced centralized authoritarian decision-making from above. Implicit was also the political goal of turning passive citizens, whose political participation was limited to their obligatory vote every five years, into active protagonists with

---

[10] *La República* (Montevideo), 24 Sept. 1993.   [11] Ibid.

growing power over the decisions that affect their daily lives as a community and as individuals, from where to site services and how to use parks, to planning public investments.

The Frente Amplio's control of the Montevideo government after 1989 gave it the opportunity to demonstrate the efficacy of its ideas. As a first step, the Department of Montevideo was divided into eighteen administrative zones and a Centro Comunal Zonal (CCZ) headed by an appointed coordinator was established in each as the headquarters for services within that zone. Convinced that the 12,000-person municipal government staff was unmanageable and alienated, concentrated in one enormous downtown building, some of these employees were transferred to smaller local offices, which it was believed would improve their efficiency by promoting better group work, more effective incentives, and a higher level of job satisfaction. In return for increased wages, work rules were changed to allow multifunctional work teams to be formed, altering the inflexible way in which municipal employees worked—over the objections of the Communist union leaders.

From the citizens' perspective, this decentralization meant more efficient local government, because they would not have to travel to the city center to file a paper, to secure services, or to obtain a decision. It also held out the hope of a more responsive government. It meant a citizen would not have to wait in line for hours only to confront surly 'service' from arrogant public employees for whom 'the service window [*la ventanilla*] is a center of power' and who treat citizens as 'enemies, not clients'.[12] The Centro Zonal eliminated both the need to travel and *la ventanilla*, although to make it work we had to 'submit' some employees to a 're-education', one coordinator confided. Clearly, this was a gradual process and a coordinator complained that 'at times it seemed that the public employees are our Jurassic Park: it will take 300 million years to transform them!'[13]

Inevitably, at first decentralization was a learning experience for all concerned: citizens, employees, and coordinators (who emerged as the pivotal figures of the new system of local government, orienting demands at the local level and promoting them at the municipal level). But after three years of what one coordinator termed an 'exhausting apprenticeship' and progress that varied from zone to zone, even the most embattled coordinators considered the plan to be a relative success.

Physical centers had been established within each zone; coordinators were assisted by professional staffs with training in architecture, civil engineering, gardening, vocational advising, psychology, and social work. Under them were blue-collar work teams responsible for replacing burned-out street lights, maintaining parks, and cleaning out sewers and clogged drains.

A committee structure had been established under the CCZ, open to local residents. In Carrasco, a suburban zone with sizeable numbers of both rich and poor, specialized Neighborhood Committees met monthly with the coordinator and professional staff, who also met regularly with neighborhood and social organizations and

---

[12] Arles Caruso, interview of Aug. 1993.   [13] Ibid.

also with unorganized residents. They dealt with Urban Planning, Works and Services, Culture, Hygiene and Social Services, and Communications. Their immediate functions were to aggregate the needs of the zone and translate them into concrete proposals to the coordinator, who was responsible for implementing them or securing the necessary resources from the Municipality. Some of the projects were undertaken in collaboration with the Church, NGOs, state agencies, or private enterprises.

In Carrasco, projects proposed ran the gamut from housing for shantytown dwellers to be built on municipal land and the construction of nine new streets to establishing a childcare center in a building made available by the Construction Workers' Union and health education programs on cholera prevention and oral hygiene (including children's dental check-ups in collaboration with Colgate, Palmolive). In Colón, a more rural and more socially homogeneous zone, there were also projects calculated to promote the identification of children with their zone and with rural life, as well as a decision to build roads to the best farming areas, so that producers could reach Montevideo markets, while arranging local street fairs where other farmers could sell their produce. Although few of the ambitious construction projects had been completed by 1994 and many remained at the proposal stage, there was more satisfaction than frustration with what had been accomplished. At the same time, this record and the decision-making by coordinators as to which projects to execute underscored that the local committee structure had the power to propose projects but not the authority to choose between them or to implement them. The key decisions on prioritizing projects, allocating resources, and securing budget approval remained centralized within the Department of Decentralization at the Municipality.

By 1994, it was also apparent that the structure of participation needed to be improved. In Colón, for example, local organizations were made more developmental in orientation and more democratic in structure and decision-making. Initially, the committees formed at the local level had been composed of local notables—the doctor, the teacher, the notary, the leading merchant. This discouraged broad popular participation. The solution tried was to make the committees elected and to create specialized subcommittees on everyday concerns such as roads or children, and to encourage people with an expertise or interest in this area to join them, even if they had no prior experience of local government or politics. They also tried to integrate pre-existing social organizations, such as sports clubs, and to organize autonomous cultural and social groups. Their strategy was to get the organized to get their unorganized friends and relatives to participate. Even children were encouraged to participate. Coordinators took pride in the success of their efforts. The fact that there were 50–60 people in each zone who now had the capacity to assess the local development plan and to modify it represented 'a big jump' in participation.[14]

---

[14] Arles Caruso, interview of Aug. 1993. One zone developed a Plan Arbol in consultation with its schoolchildren, who were then encouraged to do drawing and studies and to plant trees around the school, with the broader goal of getting them to identify with their zone and take pride in this identification.

Yet, in 1994, problems still remained, and the Vázquez government was ready to move on to the next phase of the decentralization plan, which would solve these problems and extend and institutionalize the project. From their experience, the coordinators concluded that there was a need for more flexibility and for different kinds of organizations than the political or social movements of the past. There was also a need to improve the coordination between zones, to avoid having 'two streets with street lights next to two streets without any street lights'.[15] But, most of all, there was a need to develop a neighborhood movement that was not just a prisoner of immediate needs, but interested and capable of thinking in terms of the development of the zone, and able to mobilize other groups in the community around these goals.

The political leaders of the Frente Amplio had also come to conclusions as to what needed to be done to improve the decentralization program, but their concerns were often different and so were the changes that they proposed. The political leaders of all the parties were worried about the decline of political participation, and looked to decentralization to reverse it. As a result, many Frente leaders and activists were disappointed in the non-partisan and non-ideological character of the new structure of grassroots participation. They had expected the unfamiliar CCZs to become the familiar mass fronts. When Frente activists arrived at a CCZ meeting and discovered there was no 'struggle plan' and that it was difficult to shape the CCZs into 'mass fronts', they concluded that these local committees were not political and *they* stopped participating in them. As one coordinator put it, many in the Frente Amplio had difficulty accepting that the CCZ was 'a place for participation, information, and cooperation, and not a place for co-optation'.[16]

This refusal of some Frente leaders to grasp—or embrace—the new modes of popular participation implicit in the first phase of the decentralization plan led them to regard the CCZs' success in securing greater citizen participation as a political failure. They rejected the coordinators' proposal for the direct election of local mayors (*alcaldes*), proposing instead that the parties should retake control of the process of decentralization. They had initially encouraged the CCZs because of the crisis of participation, but they had become afraid that the CCZs were emerging as a rival structure of participation that would deepen—not bridge—the growing divide between political parties and their mass base. In the end, it came down to a dispute over power, with the original vision of an empowerment of civil society contested by a more traditional notion of political participation linked to the political parties, both within a decentralization scheme that would diffuse power from the Municipality to the local zones. The next phase of decentralization would combine these visions in a complex system of local government that involved both Frente Amplio and opposition parties.

In order to deepen and consolidate the process of decentralization, the political parties, including the opposition parties, had to be brought into the new structure

---

[15] Ibid.   [16] María Cristiani, interview of Sept. 1993.

of local government. A Decentralization Commission, with members drawn from the Municipal Council and the Intendente's office, had been formed in 1990. This group defined the second phase of the decentralization plan, in which local institutions with political party representation would be established. Each of Montevideo's eighteen zones would have a five-member governing board (*junta*), with three from the Frente Amplio and two named by opposition parties.[17] As decentralization was supported in principle by most opposition parties, despite some criticisms they all participated.

Within the Frente Amplio, the advance of its decentralization program produced paradoxical results. On the one hand, decentralization moved closer to the Frente Amplio's goals of direct election of local authorities and grassroots participation in local government. On the other hand, the election within the Frente Amplio of its Local Board members (*Ediles Locales*) detonated the Frente's worst internal crisis of the 1990–4 era.

It was a crisis in which conflicts over the choice of local representatives intersected with growing tensions within the Frente Amplio nationally over power, structure, leadership, ideology, program, and strategy. One element was a major change in the correlation of political forces within the Frente between the 1989 general elections and the September 1993 election of Local *Ediles*. In the 1989 poll, the Uruguayan Communist Party (PCU) won roughly 40 per cent of the alliance's votes, confirming its position as the hegemonic force within the Frente. But, during the following years, the PCU fragmented into three feuding groups, two of which adopted reformist stances that were sharply critical of the old orthodox Marxist-Leninist party. It was the Socialist Party that initially filled the political and ideological vacuum left by the Communist collapse, riding the popularity of Tabaré Vázquez to a leading position in the polls and a seemingly hegemonic position within the Frente Amplio it found hard to handle. At the other end of the Frente's political spectrum, the Tupamaros and their allies consolidated a sizeable, but smaller radical grouping around the Movement for Popular Participation (MPP), which allied with what remained of the orthodox PCU, their old rivals. As a result, the Frente Amplio polarized into two antagonistic wings, popularly known as 'Moderates' and 'Radicals'. The Moderates wanted a program that would enable the Frente to attract centrist votes and ally with centrist forces. The Radicals preferred a politics of purity, arguing that there was little point in winning national elections if the Frente could not carry out a leftist program of structural change.

What brought these tensions to a head were the issues of internal structure, leadership, and power. In the light of their rising popular support in the polls, the Moderates sought to alter the Frente Amplio's structure, in which each of the

---

[17]   In the zones outside the city limits eleven Local Boards (*Juntas Locales*) were created; in the zones within the city of Montevideo, seven Special Commissions (*Comisiones Especiales*) were established. These new local authorities were identical in all but name. The different nomenclature was made necessary by the fact that the Uruguayan Constitution mandates the creation of *Juntas Locales* only outside the city limits. The 'Special Commissions' were established by municipal legislation.

Frente's seventeen parties had equal representation on departmental committees, which in turn had a dominant voice in the national structure. As a result, argued the Moderates, tiny radical parties with committed cadres dominated the Frente, although moderate groups such as the Socialists attracted more support in the polls. The Moderates wanted a new structure in which internal primaries would select the party leadership, which would then reflect the real voting power of each of the parties within the Frente. This struggle for power was lent urgency by the approach of the 1994 elections.

It was in this context of growing tensions and expectations that the Frente held its first primary election for the new Local *Ediles* on 26 September 1993. It was viewed by Moderates as a chance to demonstrate their majority support among Frente Amplio voters, but only 20,000 people voted in this unfamiliar balloting, making it a poll of cadres, in which the orthodox PCU won 37 per cent of the vote, with the moderate Socialists a distant second, with only 20 per cent of the ballots.

Within the Frente Amplio, this local primary strengthened the position of the Radicals at the National Convention held on 30–1 October 1993, which shattered the Moderates' hopes for a new Frente structure. This created a stalemate between Moderates and Radicals that was finally broken by a political compromise, which solved the immediate crisis, but not the impasse over structure, program, leadership, and strategy.

The political effect within the Frente Amplio of its first primary election for the new Local *Ediles* was immediate. The impact of this internal poll on the decentralization program will only become clear over time, but could be profound. With the orthodox PCU winning twenty *ediles* to the Socialists' eleven, there is the danger that the old Communist cadres turned novice Local *Ediles* may encourage a return to more traditional political participation along party lines, undermining the original goals of non-partisan popular participation in local government and community self-management. This risk could be compounded by a similar preference on the part of *ediles* representing the traditional parties for a local politics of clientelism, with themselves as brokers.

In addition to these political risks, the new decentralization scheme has to overcome structural tensions. As a way of institutionalizing direct popular participation, the municipal government also created Neighborhood Councils in each zone. These new institutions are deliberative bodies of 25–40 members elected by popular vote whose main tasks are to plan and propose projects for the zone, advise the Local Board and the municipal government, help organize cultural, social, and sports activities, and evaluate the actions of the municipal government. Its role was summed up by one Frente Amplio activist as forming one leg of a local government tripod: 'Together with the political "leg" (the Local Boards and Special Commissions) and the administrative "leg" (the Communal Centers), the Councils form the social "leg" of the decentralization tripod.'[18]

---

[18] Gabriel Kaplun, 'Concejos vecinales, pocos o muchos?' *Brecha* (Montevideo), 3 Dec. 1993, p. 8.

The new phase of the Frente Amplio's decentralization plan, therefore, began in 1994 with new elected decision-making bodies, the Local Boards and Special Commissions, with direct political party participation, and new deliberative bodies, the Neighborhood Councils. But it retained the old institutions: the Zone Communal Centers, the Coordinators (now Secretaries) and the various groups they formed, such as the Neighborhood Commissions. Clearly, a new period of learning and adjustment had begun, one that posed new and different problems. The most obvious stemmed from the definition of roles—on paper overlapping—that each of these institutions will play.

Given the varying mixes of parties, personalities, and residents, each zone has had to develop a *modus vivendi* among all concerned in keeping with its own characteristics. The great differences in how the zones approached these issues was clear in the perception of the old coordinators by the new *ediles*, which were not necessarily rooted in partisan differences. In one zone, the Communist President of the Local Board followed the lead of the ex-coordinator. In another zone, a Communist *edil* stressed that the ex-coordinator should be restricted to 'carrying out the orders that emerge from each session' of the Local Board, clearly confining the old coordinator to a much diminished role.[19] Although all involved seem eager to make decentralization work, it is too early to know whether these efforts will succeed or how they will alter its character.

In 1994, these processes of mutual adjustment were delayed and distorted by national and municipal elections. The 1994 presidential balloting narrowly returned former President Julio María Sanguinetti and the Colorados to power, with the second-place Blanco candidate leading Tabaré Vázquez by only 12,000 votes. Less than 2 per cent of the vote separated the three candidates. The Frente Amplio did far better than expected, taking 31 per cent of the vote, compared with 22 per cent in 1989. In Montevideo itself, the electoral result confirmed the Frente's control over the capital with a decisive 43 per cent of the vote—14 per cent more than its nearest rival. This victory made clear that the left's municipal dominance did not depend on its fielding a charismatic candidate like Tabaré Vázquez. His successor as mayor, Mariano Arana, an architect and urbanist, may be better qualified to govern a metropolis, but his vision is more technocratic, with less enthusiasm for grassroots democracy, and more concern for making Montevideo the Brussels of the new Mercosur economic community.[20]

What this all means for decentralization in its critical stage of implementation is still unclear. The Frente Amplio remains committed to decentralization, and its electoral victory in Montevideo means it will have the rest of the century to perfect it. Frente legislators have introduced bills that would strengthen the autonomy of the local boards, and Arana has reappointed Alberto Roselli, Vázquez's committed director of decentralization. Yet Arana's own priorities seem to lie

[19]   *La República* (Montevideo), 27 Oct. 1993, p. 1.
[20]   *El Observador* (Montevideo), 6 Nov. 1995.

elsewhere, and he seems more likely to focus on improving the efficiency of the new system of local governance than on deepening popular participation. Under Arana, local governments may gain decision-making power over public works contracts and the responsibility to monitor their execution, but they are unlikely to control their own budgets, a step that Roselli himself sees as necessary for the final consolidation of the new system.[21] Tensions between the local governments and the Municipality, therefore, are likely to persist. Still, recent studies show that if the ultimate success of Montevideo's experiment with decentralization remains uncertain, advances toward that goal continue to be made.[22]

If decentralization does succeed in the nation's capital, it may spread to Uruguay's other departments. What is less clear is whether decentralization will fulfill the ambitious social and political agenda with which it was launched. Less certain still is whether decentralization can emerge in Uruguay as the keystone of a leftist reform of the state, an attractive alternative to a minimalist neoliberal state, that points the way to a viable new program for a renewed Latin American left.

Conclusion: Towards a Leftist Political Alternative?

In July 1993, Tabaré Vázquez hosted a major international meeting sponsored by the Socialist International on alternatives to neoliberalism. For three days Uruguayans heard elegant and incisive critiques of neoliberalism and exhortations about the need for the Latin American left to devise them. Yet no compelling alternatives were proposed and Vázquez himself confessed that he did not have an economic strategy of his own. But, Dr Vázquez argued, 'I do have alternative principles that can guide our policies and maybe even point the way to an alternative strategy for the future.'[23]

For Uruguayan Socialists, post-Cold War socialism is about principles and values: dignity; the pursuit of happiness for all; solidarity, which embraces social justice and participatory democracy. These are the opposite of the individualism, anti-statism, and inequality that underlie neoliberalism. But they share with the neoliberals a concern for efficiency and efficacy in the public as well as the private sector, and a commitment to debureaucratize—but not necessarily to privatize. It is difficult, however, to devise a coherent program of government that will be informed by these values and also succeed in meeting the challenges and constraints of the 1990s.

The Frente Amplio is responding to an array of factors that are shaping its choices of program, policies, style, and strategy. Some of these factors are international,

---

[21] Alberto Roselli, interview March 1995; Mariano Arana, interview May 1995.
[22] *Caminando entre vecinos* (Montevideo, Instituto de Investigación y Desarrollo (IDES), July 1995); Mela Presa and Laura Escalata, interview July 1995.
[23] Tabaré Vázquez, interview of Sept. 1993.

others local; some are ideological, while others reflect pragmatic political concerns. The discrediting of the old socialist models and ideas has set off a search in Uruguay as elsewhere for a new socialism, one that is in tune with the world of the 1990s, including its rejection of state socialism as undemocratic and inefficient. This search is made both more urgent and more difficult by the global ascendancy of neoliberal ideas and the seeming success of neoliberal economic policies and reform of the state elsewhere in the region. But the Uruguayan left is also constrained in its choices by its country's situation as a small, dependent, and largely inefficient economy that is facing a process of economic integration with its far larger and more economically developed neighbors, Brazil and Argentina, in a Mercosur that might include the more competitive Chilean economy as well and eventually merge with NAFTA in a hemispheric common market.

Equally important for the Frente Amplio are Uruguayan political factors which are driving it to moderate its radicalism and move toward the center. The disillusionment with the country's traditional parties and politicians has given the left an opportunity to challenge them for political supremacy by attracting support from the urban poor, the workers, and the middle class, as well as from groups in the interior that have been unreceptive to the Frente in the past.[24] It also creates the possibility of alliances with center-left leaders and factions from the traditional parties—such as the 1994 electoral alliance (Encuentro Progresista) between Vázquez and Rodolfo Nin Novoa, a Blanco Intendente from the interior—alliances which are necessary in a tripartisan system if the Frente is to win power nationally. In order to attract this new support and make these alliances, the Frente Amplio has moderated its rhetoric and program, so that it is not perceived as Marxist. But this move toward the center has exacerbated the tensions between Moderates and Radicals within the Frente, creating problems of coalition maintenance. In addition, the left, like the other political forces in Uruguay, is faced with a crisis of participation that reflects the region's anti-party and anti-politics mood.

The search for a new socialism, the need to build broader coalitions, and the crisis of participation underlie the Frente Amplio's decentralization plan, as well as other aspects of its governance in Montevideo between 1990 and 1994. Some of the measures initiated in Montevideo by the Frente Amplio suggest the shape of a leftist response to neoliberalism and its *laissez-faire* state, one which includes a shift in budgetary priorities, the construction of a new social safety net, a more equitable sharing of the social costs of neoliberal economic policies, and an affirmation of social solidarity. Equally important has been the Frente Amplio's insistence on the active economic and social role of the state, as a regulator of the private sector

---

[24] A source of Frente Amplio optimism is that the increase in Frente Amplio support between 1989 and 1994 was across the board, part of a general trend, which included the interior of Uruguay as well, traditionally an area hostile to the left, but increasingly undergoing modernizing changes similar to those that have made Montevideo a Frente stronghold. Within Montevideo, Frente Amplio gains were biggest in working-class and lower-middle-class zones, while its greatest strength remained in the lower-class areas.

(including the informal sector), as an initiator of social programs, as a promoter of grassroots organization, and as an owner-manager of public utilities. But, it is a *reformed* state that Uruguayan socialists have supported, one that is more efficient, efficacious, and responsive, open to joint ventures with the private sector or to the privatization of state activities. In other words, it is a state that has responded to the neoliberal critique of the old *batllista* and socialist states.

The decentralization plan that Tabaré Vázquez promoted and implemented is the key to the Frente Amplio's vision of a reform of the state. Significantly, Vázquez considers decentralization his most important achievement as Intendente, arguing that it has meant an increase in both democracy and popular political participation, turning passive taxpayers into active citizens, as well as an increase in the efficiency and efficacy of local government, and a cure for the crisis of political participation that will also strengthen civil society.[25] Yet, despite some promising advances in this project, Tabaré's verdict seems premature. It is too soon to tell whether the decentralization plan will ultimately succeed in reaching these goals, or whether it will fall victim to the very crisis of the party system that it was intended to solve. In Brazil, where the left has initiated its own experiment with decentralized governance, tensions between the Workers' Party (PT) and the decentralized local governments and grassroots groups it promoted have posed serious problems.[26] In Uruguay, there is also the risk of tensions between the social, political, and administrative legs of the decentralization tripod. If decentralization does succeed in Montevideo, it may provide the Frente Amplio with a model of state reform and popular participation that can be extended to the rest of Uruguay—an alternative to *batllismo*'s centralized populism.

Less clear is whether this vision of decentralized governance with increased grassroots participation at the local level is relevant at the national level. It is possible to imagine the emergence of a consultative national council composed of representatives of these local bodies from around the country. Moreover, issues, leaders, and coalitions that emerge at the local level may well be taken up by political parties at the national level. Clearly, Uruguay, a city-state of some 3 million people—far smaller than the city of São Paulo—with a tradition of utopian political experimentation, is a best case for 'scaling up'. But this also suggests that even if decentralization does succeed in Uruguay, the difference in size may make its lessons difficult to apply to a country like Brazil.

The Frente Amplio government of Montevideo of 1990–4 symbolizes the resurgence of the Uruguayan left from the ashes left by the military government, transcending a series of obstacles along the way. It produced a charismatic leader in Tabaré Vázquez and an opportunity to demonstrate that the left can be trusted to

---

[25] Tabaré Vázquez, interview of Sept. 1993.

[26] See Pedro Jacobi, 'Extent and Limits of Local Progressive Governments in Brazil: The Workers' Party Administrations', unpublished paper presented at conference on 'The Politics of Inequality' at Columbia University, Mar. 1994, and William Nylen, 'Reconstructing the Workers' Party (PT): Lessons from North-Eastern Brazil', Chapter 17 in this volume.

govern. The decisive victory of the Frente Amplio in the 1994 Montevideo elections suggests that its governance was judged a success and that the left is now the leading political force in Uruguay's one metropolitan area. It also produced a promising decentralization plan and social programs which might succeed better with the resources available to a national Frente Amplio government. Moreover, the Frente Amplio's administration exhibited a pragmatic and innovative character that has the potential to unite a social coalition that transcends the traditional ranks of the Frente Amplio and the city limits of Montevideo. Significantly, although the Frente Amplio did not win the 1994 presidential elections, the strong showing of the Vázquez–Nin Novoa ticket suggests that Uruguay is now a fully tripartisan political system and that a Frente Amplio candidate might well be elected president in 1999.[27]

What remains to be seen is whether the initiatives implemented with success by the Frente Amplio at the local level can serve as a model for successful policies at the national level. If that proves to be the case, Uruguay may once again be viewed by its neighbors as a 'model country'.

---

[27] The identity of that Frente Amplio candidate is less certain in the wake of the 1994 elections. While Tabaré Vázquez ran well as the national standard-bearer, his Socialist Party did less well. Asamblea Uruguay, a new Frente Amplio party led by Senator Danilo Astori, an articulate economist who has attracted the support of both *frentista* independents and reformed ex-Communists, won the largest number of legislative seats and emerged as a potentially hegemonic force at the center of the Frente. With Vázquez as head of the Frente's electoral alliance and Astori as leader of its congressional delegation, the Uruguayan left has two potential presidential candidates for the 1999 elections, but also personal and political tensions to resolve if the Frente Amplio is to win national power.

19 | Targeting the Poor: The Politics of Social Policy Reforms in Mexico

Kerianne Piester

During the 1980s, economic crisis—and ensuing austerity and structural adjustment policies—provoked a dramatic rise in poverty and inequality in Latin America.[1] Despite the promise of renewed economic growth through market reforms, few believed that such growth alone could reduce poverty and inequality in the region. Fiscal constraints, the turn away from state interventionism, and the crisis of the welfare state model, meant that Latin American governments had to find new ways to provide for the most basic needs of broad sectors of their population. Confronted with the urgency of reform, many governments in the region redefined their social welfare policies to emphasize poverty alleviation and create targeted programs that relied heavily on the increased involvement of the poor and other private actors.

Mexico has witnessed this redefinition of social policy first-hand. Faced with the dilemma of learning 'to do more with less' in order to resolve increasing social demands at a time of profound political changes, the governments of Miguel de la Madrid (1982–8) and Carlos Salinas de Gortari (1988–94) created social programs specifically designed to promote poor people's participation in the resolution of social problems. More than just promises to fight poverty, these targeted social programs have built ties between the state and a growing population of poor Mexicans.

The role these programs have played in establishing links between the state and the poor raises several questions: what links do these targeted social programs create between the state and the poor? Are these links distinct from traditional forms—both corporatist and clientelist? And if so, what form do they take? How effective are these 'new' links in solving material needs and claims for citizen participation? And finally, do these links signify the emergence of a structure through which popular interests and demands are represented?

The answers to these questions are critical to understanding the relationship between welfare restructuring, political change, and the representation of the

---

[1] According to the World Bank, the percentage of the region's population living in poverty increased from 16.8 per cent in 1980 to 23 per cent in 1989. *The Economist*, 11 Dec. 1993, p. 43.

popular sectors. One hypothesis which merits exploration is that—unevenly and with the possibility of reversal—a new mode of governance is emerging that places greater emphasis on the involvement, rather than the exclusion, of people in public policy decision-making and implementation.[2] Targeted social programs that stress community participation and the participation of other private actors such as non-governmental organizations (NGOs) may be an example of such an alternative governing strategy.

Whether targeted social programs in Mexico do, in fact, reflect a new mode of governance and whether this allows for effective popular representation in the social policy arena are the focus of this chapter. Particular consideration is given to the possibility that these programs are not producing new kinds of links between the state and the poor in Mexico, but rather are sustaining the traditional clientelist and corporatist forms. Indeed, this chapter presents strong evidence that this result has occurred despite the government's stated objectives. There also is evidence, however, of new forms of linkage that allow the poor to interact with public officials without requiring the political loyalty of the former to the Partido Revolucionario Institucional (PRI). Moreover, the participation of the poor in some instances goes beyond making demands to include participation in program management and project design. And, more recently, Mexican NGOs and the state have taken steps toward the formation of policy networks that minimally will open up policy discussions to societal-based actors, including the popular sectors. By examining the kinds of interaction that occur between state and societal actors, particularly through targeted social programs, the chapter seeks to provide an analysis of the process by which the state becomes embedded, or re-embedded, within society.[3]

The chapter begins with a discussion of the factors that resulted in a shift to a poverty alleviation strategy in Mexico during the 1980s. The crisis of the traditional mechanisms for representation and control, combined with new thinking on the part of state and societal actors, are viewed as producing new but limited opportunities for the popular sectors to bargain with state officials over the use and management of state social welfare resources. Focusing on targeted social programs created during the administrations of Miguel de la Madrid and Carlos Salinas de Gortari, the chapter analyzes the links established and the outcomes achieved in reaching the targeted population and promoting their participation. This analysis is guided by the view that solutions to poverty and inequality are very likely to depend on strengthening the poor's capacity to make claims and influence social

---

[2] Current discussions of governance emphasize the necessity of coordination, cooperation, and connectedness between state and societal actors to formulate and carry out effective policies. In the area of social policy see, among others, Atkinson and Coleman 1992, Hyden 1992, Malloy 1991*b*, and Nagel 1994.

[3] While Peter Evans utilizes this term to examine how state–labor relations shape industrial policy, it is extended here to look at social policy as an important arena where embeddedness occurs (see Evans 1995).

policy-making either through their own organizations or through alternative organizations such as NGOs that may provide a voice for popular interests. In other words, the state's capacity to achieve its public policy objective of poverty alleviation will depend on the level of organization and participation of the poor (Kohli 1987, Putnam 1993).

Mexico's Institutional Crisis and the Shift to Poverty Alleviation

During the 1980s, various factors account for a shift in Mexican social policy toward an emphasis on poverty alleviation and the creation of targeted social programs for the poor. The debt crisis, austerity policies, and market reforms imposed severe costs on broad sectors of the population and profoundly undermined the living standards of the popular sectors. In this context, the question facing neoliberal reformers throughout the region concerned how to make economic restructuring politically feasible without abandoning fiscal discipline. Some governments responded to this dilemma—frequently owing to support from the World Bank—by targeting social assistance. For these governments, targeted social programs were viewed as the most effective instrument available to reduce the likelihood of mass mobilization against austerity and market reforms (Hausmann 1994, Nelson 1992). In Mexico, the creation of social programs to alleviate poverty was driven by these concerns which were intensified by the increasingly apparent crisis of the traditional institutions for representation and control.

Until the mid-1960s, Mexico's networks of patronage based on corporatist organizations and local bosses successfully incorporated and processed the demands of social groups, including the growing urban popular and middle classes, through the Confederación Nacional de Organizaciones Populares (CNOP)—the popular sector umbrella organization affiliated with the PRI. However, during the 1980s, there emerged mounting evidence of the erosion of these mechanisms which had guaranteed relatively stable one-party rule for more than fifty years. The PRI was encountering increasing political competition from opposition political parties on both the right and left which indicated that the corporatist organizations and local bosses were less capable of mobilizing support for the PRI.[4] In addition to this sign of erosion, grassroots organizing around issues like housing, health care, urban services, as well as the environment and women's issues, led to the creation of new popular organizations that were independent of the PRI and the state. From the point of view of popular sector activists and leaders, the traditional corporatist organizations were ineffective and only sought to control the popular sectors.

[4] Increased political competition came first from the right opposition party, the PAN, at the state and local levels in the mid-1980s and subsequently from the center-left party, the PRD, with the challenge mounted by Cárdenas in the 1988 presidential elections.

While corporatist organizations and local bosses have not disappeared, their ability to channel demands, secure control, and mobilize support for the PRI declined dramatically. Moreover, the fiscal constraints imposed by structural adjustment only served to exacerbate this 'crisis of representation' (Cornelius *et al.* 1989).

Nowhere was this institutional crisis more evident than in urban areas. Weakened by its heterogeneous composition, the National Confederation of Popular Organizations (CNOP) became more a structure for the domination, rather than the representation, of urban residents. This was particularly the case for the urban popular sectors which were poorly integrated and under-represented within the CNOP relative to the middle classes.[5] The proliferation of autonomous urban popular organizations centered around land tenure, housing, and urban services demands highlighted the CNOP's inability to express the needs of the growing ranks of the urban poor or negotiate for their benefit.[6] While initially the Mexican state combined tactics of repression and co-optation to address these popular organizations, the economic crisis during the 1980s made this position less tenable given the costs associated with the traditional practices of clientelism and co-optation and the declining legitimacy of the regime reflected in high rates of voter abstention in urban areas. By the late 1970s, independent popular organizations began to form coalitions to link popular urban struggles throughout Mexico and coordinate protests against the state's austerity policies (Prieto 1986: 75–94). Even though these efforts did not result in the construction of a unified mass movement or sustained popular mobilization, they did call the attention of state elites. As these elites became more aware of the crisis of traditional mechanisms, they sought new ways to build links with an increasingly independent society.

Another factor shaping the new poverty alleviation strategy was new thinking on the part of state and societal actors. Within the state, a new current of thinking among state officials, particularly those within the federal social welfare agencies, criticized the traditional role of corporatist organizations in the distribution of social welfare benefits and services. These state officials concluded that technical criteria had to replace political criteria in the provision of these benefits and services and new ways needed to be developed to make social welfare provision more cost-effective (Ward 1993). With the onset of the economic crisis, Mexico's corporatist welfare state was criticized increasingly for its corruption, politicization, and incapacity to reach the poorest sectors of the population in need of social assistance (Aspe and Sigmund 1984). In order to improve the cost-effectiveness and administration of social programs, some reform-minded state officials even advocated bypassing the corporatist organizations in favor of organizations independent of the state and the PRI—though how much political independence they were willing to risk remained a question. While it is difficult to measure how

[5] On the failed incorporation of the urban poor within the CNOP, see M. Bassols (unpublished manuscript).

[6] For a complete chronology of the Mexican urban popular movements, see Bennett 1992; Schteingart and Perló 1984: 105–25.

influential this current has become within policy-making arenas, it certainly played a role in shaping the design of new targeted social programs.

This new thinking by more reform-minded state officials was reinforced by ideas recommending the involvement of the poor and NGOs in anti-poverty projects promoted by many international actors, including international financial institutions such as the World Bank and the Inter-American Development Bank, the United Nations, and international donors and development specialists. While these international actors were not involved actively in Mexico's targeted social programs, their ideas on community participation and poverty alleviation probably influenced thinking on these issues.[7]

This period also witnessed the rise of new ideas and practices among the popular sectors and their allies, including NGOs, in Mexico. In addition to protest strategies, popular organizations added more proactive strategies to their repertoire of collective action. Working together with NGOs, these popular organizations learned ways to resolve local problems through self-managed (*autogestionarios*) projects. For these popular actors, access to public resources facilitated the development of self-managed projects in which the poor often exercised some control over their design, management, and execution. According to Martha Schteingart, this practice of self-management differs dramatically from traditional conceptions of poor people's participation, whereby the poor only contribute their labor and some resources, but lack a voice in decision-making about the projects (Schteingart 1991: 113–28). While self-managed collective projects had been limited in Mexico, during the 1980s they grew in number with the shift to targeted programs and the proliferation of non-governmental organizations. Protest and mass mobilization still remained important strategies for gaining access to state resources, but marshaling information, debating, and proposing projects—in other words, increasing proactivism—emerged as important new strategies to be utilized by social actors.

When combined, these factors shifted social policy to an emphasis on poverty alleviation. This new emphasis began to emerge during the administration of President Miguel de la Madrid (1982–8) with various targeting experiments focused primarily on poor urban neighborhoods. During his administration, the strategy included efforts to build links with independent popular organizations and even some non-governmental organizations by encouraging their participation in the implementation of targeted social programs. During the administration of President Salinas de Gortari (1988–94) poverty alleviation rapidly came to occupy a central place on the President's reform agenda. Through the National Solidarity Program (El Programa Nacional de Solidaridad, PRONASOL), the government actively sought to reshape state–society relations by building new institutional links.

---

[7] One explanation for the relative absence of NGOs from targeted social programs in Mexico compared with similar programs in other countries is the lack of involvement by international actors promoting—even conditioning their financial support on—NGO participation.

Targeting during the Miguel de la Madrid Administration

As part of an emerging strategy to confront the economic crisis, particularly the problems of inflation and the public deficit, the government of President De la Madrid drastically reduced social spending, cutting the education and health-care budgets and eliminating or diminishing subsidies for basic products and public services. The magnitude of the reduction is reflected in the social spending data. In 1981, social spending represented 17.2 per cent of total spending; by 1987, that figure had declined to 9.2 per cent (Carrasco and Provencio 1988: 95–7). Less visible, though, were the reforms in social policy introduced during the crisis to compensate for declining social spending and deteriorating living standards.

In the areas of basic foods, housing, and service sectors such as health care, new programs were created and some existing programs were reorganized to target subsidies and services to the poorest sectors of the population.[8] Two social programs, the Popular Housing Fund (FONHAPO) and the National Food Distribution Program to Popular Urban Zones (PAZPU), are important examples of targeting experiments. The analysis of these programs highlights that a few independent popular organizations did gain access to public resources to develop self-managed projects in areas where there had been a history of independent popular organizing at the community level. Support from reform-minded officials within state agencies was a necessary condition for providing this opening. However, the analysis suggests that opening from above frequently generated tensions below, particularly among independent popular organizations, concerning how to respond to state overtures. Many popular organizations feared losing their autonomy through targeted programs.

THE POPULAR HOUSING FUND (FONDO DE HABITACIONES POPULARES— FONHAPO)

Created in 1981 to finance low-income housing for citizens ineligible for support from other public housing institutions, the Popular Housing Fund (FONHAPO) introduced important innovations in public housing policy. Breaking with the existing system of assigning credits to individuals for finished public housing, FONHAPO adopted a system of collective credits to allow groups of individuals with less than a family income of double the minimum wage to develop housing projects themselves. State officials recognized that the traditional system of assigning credits to individuals through the corporatist organizations had led to inefficiencies and corruption. FONHAPO's objective of assigning collective credits to

---

[8] In terms of income level, individuals without salaried employment or families that earned less than twice the minimum wage were the sector of the population most often designated to receive targeted benefits and services through these programs.

organized beneficiaries—housing cooperatives or legally constituted organizations of *solicitantes de vivienda*—outside the corporatist institutions was meant to promote community participation and preclude the kind of clientelistic relations that plagued other housing institutions (Casanueva and Díaz 1991: 198).

In addition to this objective, the Fund was designed to provide a more integrated solution to the housing needs of poorer communities by providing credits to support the various stages of low-income housing development. FONHAPO credits allowed for the purchase of land with public services, the purchase of building materials to make improvement on existing housing or for self-built new housing, and to cover the costs of technical assistance (Casanueva and Díaz 1991: 197–9). As will be discussed further below, the success of the Fund in achieving its objectives has been limited. In the case of FONHAPO, programmatic outcomes, particularly reaching the targeted population, have depended on the type of organization that in practice received the credits.

Before evaluating how the Fund performed, it is important to recognize why these innovations were introduced into the Fund. During the 1970s, the escalation of sociopolitical conflicts centered around housing and urban services problems led to the formation of urban popular organizations and the emergence of urban popular movements. In response to increasing urban conflict, FONHAPO was created to channel the housing demands of the urban popular movements in the hopes of reducing these conflicts (Ramírez 1992: 174, 175).

In addition, many of FONHAPO's innovations in the area of low-income public housing are associated with the emergence of a housing cooperative movement in Mexico in the late 1970s. Seeking to develop an alternative to the anarchy associated with self-built housing, NGOs working on housing issues established housing cooperatives as a way to involve collectively low-income, often non-salaried workers in the resolution of their housing needs (Romero 1986: 371–407). These NGOs sought some recognition and support from the state for housing projects managed by poor Mexicans that did not have access to existing public programs (Connolly 1993: 72–7; Romero 1986). State officials instrumental in the creation of FONHAPO had worked with these cooperatives while in other housing institutions, particularly INDECO, the National Institute for Community and Popular Housing Development, and learned from their experiences. These officials recognized that the state was unable to provide for the enormous housing needs of this sector of the population, but rather could offer some financial support for beneficiary organizations to construct their own self-built housing.

By supporting the participation of the beneficiaries in developing their own housing projects with the assistance of non-governmental organizations, FONHAPO represented a more cost-effective way to increase the production and improvement of low-income housing. The state embraced the idea of promoting self-constructed housing by individuals and cooperatives through FONHAPO programs that provided sites with public services, construction materials, and remuneration for technical assistance from housing NGOs. Yet, despite the commitment of state officials to popular participation in this policy area, in practice FONHAPO has had limited success in achieving its objectives.

In its first year of operation, the Fund failed to reach the target population, nor was it able to promote community participation or housing cooperatives. In 1981–2, most FONHAPO credits were granted to the state housing institutes established to decentralize the Fund's administrative structure. These state housing institutes often fell under the control of state governors who had little interest in promoting housing projects developed by independent community organizations or housing cooperatives. According to FONHAPO, 80 per cent of the credits for this period were assigned through state housing institutes. Of the total credits assigned, 73 per cent were assigned to families with incomes greater than 1.5 times the minimum wage, and of this total, 45.2 per cent went to families with an income of more than two times the minimum wage. Moreover, the data shows that state governors preferred to promote finished housing projects through private housing contractors over projects that involved self-built housing; groups affiliated with the PRI over those affiliated with the opposition or that were independent; and beneficiaries with two times the minimum wage over those with no fixed income (Aldrete-Haas 1991: 126).

Since the first year of FONHAPO's operation coincided with elections, PRI state governors demanded access to credits, utilizing them to obtain electoral support by offering to provide housing, or the promise of housing, to segments of the electorate. The governors controlling the state housing institutes did not apply the technical criteria for selecting beneficiaries established by FONHAPO officials in Mexico City. Rather than defining a new relationship with the popular sectors, provision of FONHAPO credits at the state level reinforced patron–client relations in which access to public resources was exchanged for political support for the PRI.[9] Due to the absence of democracy at the local level—or even political competition—the decentralization of the Fund did not provide for more pluralistic access to state resources.[10] Despite these initial failures, the capacity of FONHAPO to achieve its objectives improved with the arrival of a new director willing to recognize and support the autonomous organization of program beneficiaries.

In 1983, with the arrival of a new administration, FONHAPO was reorganized to create a new subdepartment for social promotion to support the incorporation and formation of housing cooperatives and independent popular organizations and to assure their participation in the development and implementation of housing projects (Aldrete-Haas 1991: 130–1). The new administration was more willing to encourage and support the formation of housing cooperatives and to

---

[9] For a detailed discussion of the traditional form of clientelism associated with the urban popular classes, see Cornelius 1975, Jorge Montano 1976, and Eckstein 1977.

[10] Decentralization was a major initiative of the De la Madrid administration, including existing social welfare programs in health care and education and new programs. Decentralization often led to conflicts among state actors that negatively affected the implementation of these social programs. For a more complete discussion of decentralization, see Torres 1985, González 1991: 67–90; Rodríguez 1992: 127–44.

grant some credits to independent popular organizations. While the state conditioned access to the fund on the registration of popular organizations as civil associations or on their constitution as housing cooperatives, it did not formally require affiliation with the PRI or a PRI-affiliated organization. In practice, independent popular organizations, primarily those located in Mexico City which had greater contact with the central agency, were able to negotiate for housing credits with FONHAPO officials. In 1983, 23 per cent of the families that received credits earned between 0.75 and one times the minimum wage. The percentage of credits that went to independent popular groups increased from 7.8 per cent to 16.4 per cent with 10 per cent of this total granted to housing cooperatives (Aldrete-Haas 1991: 132).

Why were Fund officials willing to reach the targeted population by granting credits to independent popular organizations? The answer concerns the relationship between several FONHAPO officials and individuals active in housing NGOs. The director of the Fund during the mid-1980s, Enrique Ortiz, worked in COPEVI (Centro Operacional de Vivienda y Poblamiento, AC), a Mexican housing NGO that pioneered the formation of housing cooperatives during the 1970s.[11] Under Ortiz's direction, FONHAPO supported more housing cooperatives and independent popular organizations than at any other time. In addition, a housing NGO was contracted by the Fund to train its personnel to work more cooperatively with the target population (Connolly 1993: 74). For those popular organizations that were able to obtain credits, the Fund provided technical support for self-managed housing projects. Yet, despite these developments within the Fund, independent popular organizations and housing cooperatives were only able to capture a small percentage of the credits.

According to FONHAPO sources, from 1981 to 1986, 48 per cent of the credits were distributed to the social sector rather than state housing institutes. Of these credits, 34 per cent went to groups formally affiliated with the PRI, one credit went to groups associated with the opposition, and the rest went to groups without any political affiliation. Moreover, the value in terms of pesos assigned to PRI-affiliated groups represented 70 per cent of the total invested in the social sector (Aldrete-Haas 1991: 136). While many independent groups applied for housing credits, only a small percentage received them. Pressure from governors for credits and intra-bureaucratic conflicts within FONHAPO between officials in social development and finance resulted in the majority of credits assigned to either state institutes or PRI-affiliated organizations (Aldrete-Haas 1991: 132, 133). The only exception was the Housing Renovation Program (El Programa de Renovación Habitacional) created to rebuild housing destroyed or damaged by the earthquakes which struck Mexico City on 19 September 1985.

The Housing Renovation Program received 80 per cent of its financing from FONHAPO to provide support for new housing or to repair damaged housing for

[11] This point was brought to my attention during an interview with a member of the housing NGO, CENVI (Centro de Vivienda y Estudios Urbanos, AC), 8 May 1993, Mexico City.

families earning less than two times the minimum wage or for those that worked in the informal economy. Following a period of significant conflict with the De la Madrid government and increasing independent popular mobilization, the program was opened to the participation of various independent popular organizations. Following the earthquake, many popular neighborhood organizations united to form a common front, the CUD, to protest the government's initial response.[12] The domestic and international attention received by the *damnificados* disposed the government to negotiate with the movement of *damnificados* and resulted in the signing of the Convenio de Concertación Democrática para la Reconstrucción de Vivienda del Programa de Renovación. Despite this success, independent popular organizations were not able to secure through FONHAPO continued support for their self-managed projects during the Salinas administration. The success of this program in terms of coverage and access for independent popular organizations depended on the ability of those that needed housing to bring pressure on the state.

THE NATIONAL FOOD DISTRIBUTION PROGRAM TO URBAN POPULAR ZONES (PAZPU)

The policy of providing low-cost basic food to the urban poor experienced similar changes to those introduced in the area of low-income housing. In 1982, DICONSA, the agency responsible for guaranteeing the distribution of subsidized basic food products, was restructured and the National Food Distribution Program to Urban Popular Zones (Programa Nacional de Abasto a las Zonas Populares Urbanas—PAZPU) was created. Through this program, DICONSA administrators attempted to target more effectively food subsidies to poor urban residents by establishing CONASUPO food stores in marginal popular neighborhoods (*colonias populares*) (Appendini 1992). As in low-income housing, achieving effective targeting of limited state resources was attempted by increasing community participation in the administration of the program.

With the new program for subsidized food distribution, the state set out to establish new CONASUPO stores, referred to as CEPACs (Centros Populares de Abasto, CONSUPO), administered by committees of residents of popular neighborhoods. The committees were to provide sufficient space to install a store and assume responsibility for its administration. The program granted credits for the purchase of equipment and a commission for the management of the stores.[13] Based on the idea of coparticipation by the state and the beneficiaries, this program encouraged communities to organize to obtain a store and manage the distribution of subsidized food products.

---

[12]   See Marván and Cuevas 1987: 111–40, for a complete description of the formation of the CUD (Coordinadora de Tlaltelolco a la Coordinadora Unica de Damnificados), its demonstrations, and the process of negotiations between the CUD and the government.

[13]   The description of the way in which these stores were meant to function suggests that they were conceived of as food cooperatives (see Appendini 1992: 186, 187).

Similar to the case of FONHAPO, some independent popular organizations managed these community stores. According to a study carried out by Carlos Hoyos, by 1990 three different types of stores (CEPACs) operated in Mexico City: (1) those promoted by independent popular organizations, representing 30 per cent of the total; (2) those promoted by organizations or individuals affiliated with the PRI or by the city delegations, representing 50 per cent of the total; and (3) those promoted by individuals with no organizational base or affiliation, representing 20 per cent of the total (Coulomb and Sánchez 1992: 178, 179). Among the stores promoted by independent popular organizations, the evidence reveals a generally high level of community participation in the store's administration. In addition, several of these popular organizations received assistance, both technical and financial, from non-governmental organizations.[14] Among the other types of stores, the urban poor were unable to gain a voice in the management of the stores, nor were they able to make demands regarding the De la Madrid government's low-income food policies. The type of committee managing the store, therefore, strongly influenced the level of community participation, the state's capacity to reach the targeted population, and whether or not it served as an effective channel for popular concerns about food issues.

As the government moved to more selective forms of subsidy and even to eliminate subsidies for many products in 1985 and 1986, urban popular organizations mobilized to defend subsidies and to protest the political manipulation of subsidies. In 1986, the government began to distribute coupons, called *tortibonos*, to families with an income equal to or less than two times the minimum wage for subsidized tortillas from different centers for basic food distribution, including the CEPACs (Appendini 1992: 199). Through their management of basic food stores, some independent popular organizations established control over the assignment of these coupons, providing them with a valuable resource. The enormous demand for this subsidy by an increasingly impoverished urban population led the De la Madrid administration to negotiate agreements (*convenios*) to provide other autonomous popular organizations with access to these coupons (Coulomb and Sánchez 1992: 180). While access by popular organizations to the assignment of these coupons did not signify an end to the clientelistic distribution of this subsidy, it did indicate an important, though limited, shift away from this form of management of social benefits.

Similar to the low-income housing arena, non-governmental organizations also emerged and grew in this area of social policy during the 1980s. Though they were not as influential as the housing NGOs, the NGOs concerned with food issues were significant in terms of the assistance they offered to popular organizations. Beyond offering technical and educational assistance, they acquired international financial assistance for projects which they jointly sponsored with urban popular

---

[14] For example, El Movimiento Popular de Pueblos y Colonias del Sur located in Mexico City worked with the NGO Enlace, Comunicación y Capacitación, AC, to establish and administer several stores in popular neighborhoods in the southern part of Mexico City.

organizations.[15] In addition to the various forms of assistance provided, several NGOs concerned with popular food issues brought together popular organizations and groups to demand changes in the state's food policies (Coulomb and Sánchez 1992: 183–6).

As the analysis of both programs illustrates, innovations were introduced in the areas of low-income housing and subsidized basic foods by state officials confronted with the necessity of 'doing more with less'. Measures adopted to target social benefits to the urban poor opened up opportunities for the participation of independent popular organizations willing to negotiate with the state. Institutional openings, however, depended heavily on the support of reform-minded state administrators and the capacity of independent popular organizations to pressure the state and demonstrate their capacity to develop cost-effective projects. In many cases, the development of such projects was facilitated by non-governmental organizations that offered technical and organizational assistance. In both programs, targeting was more effective when carried out through independent popular organizations.

Overall, however, the capacity of independent popular organizations to obtain and manage state resources and projects was limited. Proximity to state reformers mattered; independent popular organizations in Mexico City were more successful at negotiating their participation in programs than elsewhere due to the growing political competition the PRI faced within Mexico City. In addition, the sociopolitical contexts in which these programs were implemented made a difference. The change in the political context after 1988 with the creation of the center-left party, the PRD, following the successful electoral challenge Cuauhtémoc Cárdenas posed to PRI hegemony, also affected policy. Beyond subsequent reductions in subsidies during the administration of Carlos Salinas, the tendency to eliminate intermediaries, particularly independent popular organizations, from the distribution of the remaining subsidies for low-income housing and subsidized food suggests the vulnerability of these types of targeted programs to political manipulation. Yet, despite the imposition of a series of anti-popular policies, some social welfare reforms adopted by the De la Madrid government opened channels for the urban poor to participate through their own organizations without affiliating with the PRI.

Targeting During the Salinas Administration: The National Solidarity Program (PRONASOL)

Throughout the administration of Carlos Salinas de Gortari, poverty alleviation occupied a central place on the national agenda and community participation

---

[15] Servicio de Desarrollo y Paz (SEDEPAC), Enlace y Capacitación, Equipo Pueblo, Centro de Estudios Ecumenicos, and Instituto Maya are among the NGOs that work in this area to develop basic foods projects, popular kitchens, and breakfasts for children (see Coulomb and Sánchez 1992: 183–6).

became an integral element of the state's social policy through the President's National Solidarity Program (PRONASOL). After taking office on 1 December 1988, Salinas aimed to re-establish the state's commitment to social justice and build popular support for his reform initiatives. At the national level, social policy was redefined to address the dramatic rise in poverty in Mexico. Salinas declared that the state's new social welfare role was to combat poverty and elevate the productive capacities of the impoverished sectors of the population (Secretaría de Desarrollo Social 1993: 4). No longer envisioned as solely the responsibility of the state, social welfare provision was envisioned as the shared responsibility of the state and society. In this new conception of the state's social welfare role, a solidaristic state that works with and assists the poor in the resolution of their needs replaces a paternalistic state.[16] According to Salinas, this required a transformation in the way the state assigned public resources and designated the beneficiaries of social policy.

The National Solidarity Program (PRONASOL), initiated at the beginning of Salinas's *sexenio* (1988–94), became the vehicle to carry out this new vision of Mexican social policy and was meant to build a new relationship between the Mexican state and society. Four new principles of social welfare provision were established to guide PRONASOL: (1) *respect* for local initiatives and community organizations; (2) *participation* of the community in all aspects of project design and management; (3) *cooperation* between federal, local, and community-based actors; and (4) *transparency* in the use of resources (Consejo Consultivo del Programa Nacional de Solidaridad 1991: 30–1). In terms of its design, PRONASOL represented more than just another targeted social program, since it proposed not only 'doing more with less', but a 'new way of doing things'. The implementation of the program reveals a more complicated picture.

ORIGIN OF THE NATIONAL SOLIDARITY PROGRAM (PRONASOL)

According to Denise Dresser and others, PRONASOL emerged to overcome the 'dilemmas of governability' facing the Salinas administration following the 1988 presidential elections (Dresser 1992: 49–57; Cornelius *et al.* 1994). More than the erosion of urban popular support for the PRI, these elections revealed the electoral force of a new opposition movement (Frente Democrático Nacional, FDN) led by Cuauhtémoc Cárdenas. While these elections were marred by fraud, the electoral results nevertheless reflected the capacity of a center-left political movement to capture the support of the urban popular sectors (Guillén 1989: 243–64). Initially, therefore, one of the purposes of PRONASOL funds was to prevent an alliance from forming between the new center-left party, the PRD, and the urban popular

[16] Salinas's own words upon assuming the presidency reflect this aim: 'El bienestar social en el Estado moderno no se identifica con el paternalismo, que suplanta esfuerzos e inhibe el carácter. Hoy la elevación del nivel de vida sólo podrá ser producto de la acción responsable y mutuamente compartida del Estado con la sociedad' (see quote Consejo Consultivo del Programa Nacional de Solidaridad 1991).

organizations, and the popular sector generally. The data reveal that the allocation of PRONASOL funds tended to support this thesis.

According to one study of PRONASOL allocation decisions during 1990, more funds were allocated to states with a combination of high levels of support for the FDN in 1988 and local elections scheduled for 1991 than to states with the poorest populations (Molinar and Weldon 1994). In addition to determining *where* funds were allocated, political criteria rather than technical criteria on poverty influenced *how* funds were distributed. During the first two years of the program, PRONASOL funds were primarily distributed through pre-existing organizations. PRONASOL officials negotiated agreements—*convenios de concertación*—with several urban popular movements over access to PRONASOL funds. Among the many agreements signed, the one negotiated with the Comité de Defensa Popular General Francisco Villa de Durango (CDP) received particular attention because it coincided with the CDP's decision to form a state-level political party (PT) rather than join the PRD (Haber 1990). This led to speculation that access to PRONASOL funds for urban popular movements had become conditioned on these movements' willingness to distance themselves from the PRD.

While negotiations with some urban popular organizations provided them with access to PRONASOL funds, the majority of these funds were distributed through the existing corporatist organizations of the PRI.[17] This combination of support for several important urban popular organizations and the existing corporatist organizations was highlighted to explain the electoral recovery of the PRI in the mid-term elections of 1991. Yet, by the end of Salinas's administration, PRONASOL was increasingly criticized as a failure with the emergence in 1994 of the Zapatista armed popular movement in the state of Chiapas. The program's association with these divergent political outcomes suggests that its political impact may vary significantly depending on its implementation at the grassroots.

PROGRAM RHETORIC VS. REALITY

Beginning in 1992, the new emphasis on the distribution of PRONASOL funds through state and municipal governments to solidarity committees (*comités de solidaridad*) raised the possibility that the intention of the Salinas administration was more than defensive and involved forging new links between the state and the poor through the institutionalization of a new grassroots structure of participation. The creation of this grassroots structure for demand-based projects distinguishes PRONASOL from the previously analyzed targeted programs in this chapter in several ways.

One of the stated objectives of the solidarity committee is to provide a space where

---

[17] In 1990, the CNOP of Durango received 75 per cent of the PRONASOL funds allocated for that state. In Oaxaca, the Confederacion Nacional Campesina Mexico (CNC) received 60 per cent of the funds (see Moguel 1992: 285).

state and municipal authorities work with beneficiaries to define, manage, and execute social welfare and public works projects. This coordination is meant to be guaranteed and promoted at the local level by a PRONASOL official, the *delegado*, who occupies an intermediate position within the program's organizational structure. At the national level, the Commission of the National Solidarity Program assisted by an Advisory Board (*Consejo Consultivo*) defines PRONASOL objectives and strategies and the Ministry of Social Development (SEDESOL) more generally manages the state's social welfare responsibilities. In this new structure, though allocation decisions of PRONASOL funds remain centrally controlled, PRONASOL was set up to perform as a decentralized structure in which decisions over project development were designed to occur at the grassroots. Conceived as a mechanism for both the representation and participation of the poor, the solidarity committee occupied an important place within this new social welfare framework for the alleviation of poverty.

While these committees are supposed to be established democratically by direct vote of the beneficiaries, existing committees vary in terms of their origin and democratic practices. In reality, four types of committees were created: (1) committees organized by the members of the community, arising where no previous organization existed; (2) committees organized by municipal presidents; (3) committees organized by existing corporatist organizations such as the CNOP or the CTM (Confederación de Trabajadores de México) affiliated with the PRI; and (4) committees organized by pre-existing independent popular organizations.[18] These distinctions are important among the committees because they strongly influence community participation, representation, and the likelihood that resources reach the target population.

In committees organized by PRI municipal presidents, for example, committee presidents are often selected, not elected, and community participation tends to be limited to the beneficiaries contributing their labor and some material resources. Where the solidarity committees have been superimposed on already existing organizations, the presence of democratic practices and the nature of community participation depends on the pre-existing organization. In the case of committees organized by corporatist organizations, clientelistic practices seem to predominate and the poor fail to obtain a voice in setting community priorities or selection of projects. Since the rules for establishing these committees are established by the state, it is difficult to view any of these committees as fully autonomous. For independent popular organizations, the requirement of participation in PRONASOL programs through a solidarity committee has been a dilemma. By meeting this organizational condition (i.e. joining or establishing a committee) these organizations risk losing both their identity and their political autonomy. However, by deciding not to meet this condition, they lose access to critical public resources.

Another significant aspect of the program's development has been the absence

---

[18] See Méndez *et al.* 1992: 60–72 for a similar typology.

—some would say the exclusion—of NGOs from its organizational structure. In contrast with other anti-poverty programs in Latin America, NGOs have not played a significant role in PRONASOL's strategy for combating poverty. The PRONASOL regional delegates serve as a kind of intermediary in the way that NGOs increasingly do in anti-poverty programs in other countries. Yet, given the politicization of the program, it seems unlikely that they act as a voice for popular concerns. Further research on intervention of these program officials locally and their incentive structure would help assess their impact on community organization and participation.

This brief analysis of PRONASOL's organizational structure reveals that PRONASOL does not represent a clear break with traditional patterns of representation and control in Mexico. While the objective of PRONASOL has been to institutionalize new links for demand-making by the poor and their participation in other aspects of project development, the imposition of the solidarity committees as a condition of participation has sustained in some places, such as Chiapas, traditional corporatist controls. However, in a few cases, where committees were formed by existing independent community organizations, PRONASOL appears to signify a way to strengthen these organizations and provide them with a channel for demand-making. PRONASOL representatives can foster this process, but again this is likely to depend on whether the incentives they face encourage enhancing program coverage, political stability, or support for the PRI. The fact that several delegates were PRI candidates for state governors suggests how these state officials may utilize the program's funds to build territorially based political machines in support of the PRI. PRONASOL does exhibit some corporatist features, such as the structuring of organizations by the state. However, it seems problematic to conclude that PRONASOL reinforces a corporatist system of interest representation.[19] Solidarity committees tend to represent territorially rather than functionally based interests and to date the state has not succeeded in organizing them into a few corporatist bodies at the national level.

Through the *pronasolization* of social policy, the Salinas administration placed limits on pluralistic access in some areas of social welfare provision where independent popular organizations had made inroads during the De la Madrid administration (Moyao 1991: 1). For example, this is evident in the area of low-income housing where several of the activities performed by FONHAPO have been taken over and transformed by PRONASOL. Under Salinas, public investment in FONHAPO decreased dramatically from 4.9 per cent in 1990 to 1.5 per cent in 1992 (*La Jornada*, 12 December 1993, pp. 16, 44). This drop eliminated some of FONHAPO's credit programs, including those for the purchase of sites with services and for technical assistance by NGOs, as well as a reduction in subsidized credits. In addition, FONHAPO credits for self-administration by popular organizations disappeared almost entirely and several credit contracts with independent

---

[19] For an alternative point of view see Ramírez 1992: 171–94.

popular organizations were suspended (Guillermo 1990). Replacing the practice of granting collective housing credits to popular organizations, the Salinas administration individualized credits for self-constructed housing and housing improvements through PRONASOL's *credito a la palabra* (Ramírez 1992: 183). For independent popular organizations, the crisis of FONHAPO accompanied by the move to individualize credits through PRONASOL eliminates access to public financing for self-managed housing projects.

The move to individualize the distribution of social benefits is also evident in the area of subsidized foods policy. In 1990, CONASUPO moved to individualize the distribution of the tortilla subsidy by granting magnetic cards to qualified citizens. This was a move to replace the distribution of the subsidy through organizations, including independent popular organizations. This change indicated the elimination of control over basic food subsidies by independent popular organizations and contributed to the demobilization of collective efforts, such as the Pact Against Hunger (Pacto Contra el Hambre), to influence the government's subsidized foods policy (Coulomb and Sánchez 1992: 181, 182).

Given the changes in targeted social programs in these two policy areas, it appears that independent popular organizations and non-governmental organizations encountered a less favorable environment during the Salinas administration than the De la Madrid administration. Faced with increased political pressures, the Salinas government tried to limit the gains of the center-left opposition party, the PRD, by building new links with the poor through PRONASOL. Yet, in many cases PRONASOL did not establish 'a new way of doing things', because the traditional corporatist organizations and local bosses were able—without interference from the PRONASOL delegate—to derail the process, capturing control over the solidarity committees. As a result, even though the government emphasized its commitment to fighting poverty through targeted social welfare projects that promoted the participation of poor communities, it was unable to accomplish this objective. In a few cases, though, prior independent organizing of the poor was a variable explaining the achievement of some of the program's objectives in some places.

State–NGO Relations and Popular Representation

As noted above, anti-poverty programs in most other Latin American countries encouraged the participation of NGOs in program design and project implementation. Mexican NGOs, however, were notably absent from participation in PRONASOL (Graham 1994). While their absence seems surprising given PRONASOL's objective of promoting local community participation, it reflects the antagonism and mistrust present in state–NGO relations. Cooperation between the state and NGOs was minimal during the Salinas administration due to the hostility in state–NGO relations. Provoked by changes in the fiscal laws regulating NGOs which allowed the state to treat NGOs as private profit-making corporations, NGOs mistrusted the Salinas government. Despite this mistrust, recent developments within the state and the NGO community suggest the possibility of greater cooperation in the future.

There are some indications of movement in the direction of greater state–NGO interaction. Rather than retreating from the state, NGOs increasingly have sought to engage the state in novel ways to bring about changes in public policy. This has not involved building a mass opposition movement—which NGOs lack the capacity to do even if they wanted to—but by organizing among themselves through the creation of networks (*redes*). During the 1990s, more than a dozen national, multi-sectoral networks were formed among Mexican NGOs and in some cases include popular sector actors (i.e. independent unions, popular neighborhood organizations, etc.). Similar to the national coordinating bodies referred to as consortia in other countries, these networks are facilitating the exchange of ideas and information among NGOs and the development of a practice of public policy advocacy.

While initially forming networks for defensive purposes, in particular to change the fiscal laws regulating NGOs like for-profit corporations, Mexican NGOs increasingly are engaged in activities to shape public policies. By providing an array of new services to NGOs as well as the popular sector actors, these networks hope to encourage the participation of an array of societal actors in public policy debates and decision-making. For example, the network organizations organize fora and campaigns on policy issues, provide information, formulate alternative public policies, establish ties with state officials and legislators of various political parties, and even hold plebiscites to mobilize public opinion. Some, though not all, of these activities, suggest the possibility of the emergence of even broader networks that involve interaction between state and societal actors focused on specific policy issues.

The formation of policy or issue networks is not only being driven by the actions of NGOs, but most recently the state has also sought improved interaction with NGOs. State officials in the social ministries have organized meetings with NGOs, created a program to fund them, and under the new administration of President Ernesto Zedillo committed themselves to building a new framework to facilitate more coordinated interaction between the state and NGOs.[20] For a variety of reasons, including the current economic crisis, it seems likely that movement in the direction of increased interaction will continue.

If this trend toward increased state–NGO interaction does continue, what is it likely to mean for popular representation? It is clearly somewhat problematic to view NGOs as representatives in the strict sense of possessing some authority

[20] In the spring of 1995, the Zedillo government consulted several NGO networks on the National Development Plan. As a result of these consultations, the new Plan recognized the need to change the fiscal laws regulating NGOs and to promote the participation of NGOs in the formulation, execution, and evaluation of public policies.

to speak for the popular sectors. Some scholars are concerned that NGOs tend to marginalize the popular sectors even further from decision-making (Arellano-López and Petras 1994). However, NGOs do offer the possibility of providing some voice for popular concerns at the national level as non-profit organizations do in many other countries, particularly where the political parties are unable to effectively perform this representational role. Moreover, as the descriptions of housing and food policy described here suggest, Mexican NGOs provide resources and training that help popular actors like neighborhood organizations develop the capabilities to play more proactive roles in the implementation, and even formulation, of social policies. The recent experience of Civic Alliance, an NGO originally formed to monitor the electoral process, which provided its expertise to hold a plebiscite in order to mobilize public opinion behind the peace process in Chiapas, illustrates how NGOs serve the popular sectors at the national as well as international level.

Conclusion: Toward an Alternative Pattern of Popular Representation in Mexico?

Analyses of targeted social programs like those discussed in this chapter tend to focus on their populist features, often missing or underplaying the processes of institution building that accompany these programs. In fact, some analyses view targeted social programs as contributing to the breakdown of institutional ties between state and society (Roberts 1995). In this chapter, the analyses of targeted social programs in Mexico show that links have been forged between the state and the poor through these programs. Frequently, the links forged worked against achieving even the limited, though still important, objective of reaching the targeted population with benefits and/or services and tended to sustain more traditional forms of control and domination. However, in a few instances, new links were built with social groups organized independent of the PRI.

As this chapter reveals, establishing effective community participation is a difficult task that is often complicated by the actions of local elites who may want to derail this process. In the Mexican case, these elites—particularly state governors —were often able to capture targeted social programs locally and prevent the emergence of new links between the state and the poor. And, unfortunately, Mexican national elites infrequently intervened to break the hold of local elites and the traditional corporatist organizations. In addition, the politicized nature of these programs created divisions among popular organizations over the issue of their participation in state-sponsored programs and contributed to the fragmentation of the urban popular movements. Despite such negative outcomes, these social programs did create incentives for popular organization centered on local issues and in some places links were built between the state and the poor that facilitated effective local participation in social welfare projects. Whether such new links—which allow for the effective expression of popular interests and concerns at the local level—will multiply is likely to depend on promoting democratic political reforms that guarantee communities the right to organize freely.

While it remains unclear whether PRONASOL will survive or whether the Zedillo government will replace it with another program, it appears that an emphasis on poverty alleviation through community participation will continue whatever name is given to the next program. Building effective community participation at the local level through targeted social programs is an important goal; however, it alone is unlikely to secure progress toward redistributive justice. Signs of increased state–NGO interaction raise the possibility of the formation of networks including both state and non-governmental actors focused on social policy issues at the national level. This development suggests an alternative link for achieving broad popular goals such as redistributive justice. As Mexican NGOs develop ways to shape public policy, research needs to continue focusing on the emerging links between NGOs and the Mexican state and the role of these links in securing popular representation.

20 | Redefining the Public/Private Mix: NGOs and the Emergency Social Investment Fund in Ecuador

Monique Segarra[1]

The apparent failure of the state-centered model of development has provoked increasing interest in the role that associations in civil society can play in both improving governance and expanding democracy. Recent work in political science argues that a civil society characterized by a dense network of associations will be able to pressure the state for better performance, increase accountability, and pluralize linkages that channel local concerns to the state (Putnam 1993; Hyden 1992; Chazen 1994). Over the past decade these assumptions, particularly those focusing on improving the effectiveness and transparency of the state, have strongly influenced the pattern of international aid. International donors, who primarily work with state institutions, are increasingly working with or through non-governmental development organizations (NGOs).[2] Moreover, international aid organizations are urging states and NGOs to work together in an effort to rationalize and coordinate public and private development efforts. The political implications of this new policy model are profound. By promoting an activist civil society as one solution to overcoming the crisis of the interventionist state, international donors are both shaping the restructuring of the state's welfare role, and altering and empowering civil society in new ways. Whether that empowerment leads to better governance and more democratic forms of participation and representation of society

[1] I would like to thank the Trickle Up Program, the Indiana University Center on Philanthropy, the Aspen Institute, and the North-South Center for their generous support that enabled me to conduct field research in Ecuador over time from 1992 to 1995, as well as comparative research trips to Bolivia and Guatemala. Katherine Hite provided valuable insights, intellectual support, and a much-needed critical perspective. Douglas Chalmers's work on the internationalization of domestic politics in Latin America has been a seminal influence. Susan Burgerman's editorial assistance is also greatly appreciated.
[2] NGOs are a diverse set of organizations ranging from neighborhood associations to professional international development institutions. In this chapter, NGOs are defined as non-profit organizations with a permanent paid staff and specific goals to promote economic or social development. Moreover, the NGO community cited in this work is national and does not include branches of internationally based NGOs such as CARE.

in national development policies, or replicates older patterns of corporatism and clientelism, is an open question.

Changes in the form and scope of the state's welfare role are of critical interest to popular sectors. Social services and social policies not only affect daily living conditions, but play an important role in the nature of the linkages between state and society. The participation of international and private domestic actors in restructuring the public welfare system raises provocative questions regarding the access, influence, and accountability popular sectors exercise in this new configuration of public and private actors. The debate over the impact of international action and pressures on restructuring the state's welfare role and its resulting form falls roughly onto a continuum. At one end is the argument that the increasing role NGOs play in public welfare is a means of privatizing social services.[3] In this process the state divests itself of many of its obligations to provide public services. Citizenship rights are minimized in this redefinition of a leaner, neoliberal state (Arellano-López and Petras 1994). Privatization also implies a depoliticization of social policy (Starr and Immergut 1987). Where once the social agenda, expressed through social services, was firmly in the public domain, management of these services is now relegated to the technical expertise of international actors, NGOs, and state planners. Social policy under conditions of restructuring the state becomes a technical problem and therefore outside of politics.

Alternatively, at the other end of the spectrum, NGOs are valued and supported for reasons that go beyond their expertise or ability to supplement dwindling state resources. NGO linkages with popular sectors and, in theory, their first-hand knowledge of the needs and interests of popular sectors endow them with a representational quality. From this perspective, incorporating private actors in welfare provision does not take social policy out of the political realm but, on the contrary, brings a new set of actors able to represent popular sector interests into the restructuring of the state's welfare system. Moreover, given the exclusionary and clientelistic manner in which social policy has typically been formulated in Latin America, it can be argued that the participation of non-traditional actors automatically extends the boundaries of policy-making. Analyzing the process of reconfiguring the welfare system in Ecuador to include international and domestic actors, this chapter asks: does the inclusion of NGOs depoliticize or expand political participation in social policy? And second, do NGOs represent or 'crowd out' the interests of popular sectors as the parameters of the welfare state are redrawn in Ecuador?

This chapter begins to address these questions by first examining the emergence of a new structure of representation in the area of social policy and social policy reform. It argues that the civil-society-focused international aid model is changing traditional patterns of representation through the construction of a new type of welfare system in Ecuador, which I term a 'welfare network'. A welfare network includes the participation of NGOs, various state agencies, and international

---

[3] For a discussion of the political implications of privatization see Feigenbaum and Henig (1994).

development actors in all stages of social services: planning, implementation, and administration of programs and projects. For example, an internationally funded Ecuadorian NGO, with accords signed with the Health Ministry, provides and manages the national system of birth control clinics.[4] Thus, varying from the traditional model of state-provided social services in Latin America, a welfare network combines private and public actors in the provision and administration of public goods. The inclusion of private actors extends and decentralizes the system of access to public goods by creating new linkage points to the state through NGOs within civil society.

However, a welfare network extends beyond the traditional boundaries of state and society by its inclusion of international actors. In Ecuador, international aid actors play a variety of crucial roles in facilitating the construction of a welfare network. They fund domestic NGOs and stimulate their professional and organizational development through training and workshops. International actors also lobby state administrators to include NGOs in national poverty alleviation programs and in the general process of state reform and decentralization. Internationally funded pilot programs proved to be critical experiential arenas for testing the possibilities and problems of state–NGO partnerships and stimulating the continuing process of constructing a welfare network. Finally, these experiences, combined with information about NGO–state interactions within Latin America, are articulated and disseminated to both the Ecuadorian NGO community and state actors through workshops, seminars, and reports. As will be shown below, this circulation of ideas and their embedding in the NGO community and among state actors is critical to creating a welfare network.[5]

All of the above actions by international agencies contribute to the process of creating informal and formal rules of the game that define and structure the respective roles of NGOs and the state. Rules are patterns of action that reflect a shared cognition over 'what has meaning and what actions are possible' (Zucker 1983: 2). Rules are institutionalized when 'certain social relationships and actions come to be taken for granted' (Powell and DiMaggio 1991). These rules, in turn, assist in the institutionalization of new practices that support the welfare network by giving them a natural status. NGOs are consulted and participate in social policy because as development organizations it is 'natural' that they do so. On an informal basis NGOs in the 1990s, along with international aid actors, routinely participate in various social ministry meetings regarding administrative and program

[4] The NGO running these clinics, the Centro Médico de Orientación y Planificación Familiar (CEMOPLAF), was originally funded by the United States Agency for International Development (USAID) as a model of low-cost reproductive and women's health clinics services in urban and peri-urban areas. Although CEMOPLAF still has ties to AID, it is now organizationally self-sufficient.

[5] Kathryn Sikkink's work on the adoption and implementation of new economic models of development in Brazil and Argentina highlights the importance of having the ideas that shape the model embedded within state institutions that are both capable of implementing policy and organizing consensus over those policies. In the case of a welfare network, those ideas must be equally embedded within the NGO community as well (see Sikkink 1991).

reform. Ecuadorian NGOs such as Fundación Esquel, Fundación Alternativa, and Fundación Ecuador are consulted by state actors on policy issues. They become part of a state planner's repertoire for gathering information and accessing expertise in the area of social policy. More formal actions reflecting the creation of new rules include accords between individual NGOs and state agencies to deliver and coordinate specific services. NGOs and NGO associations such as the Corporación Ecuatoriana de Organizaciones Privadas Sin Fines de Lucro (CEOP) assist in conducting the national health survey along with the Pan American Health Organization and the Ministry of Health. The purpose of this survey is to assess the extent and scope of private and public provision of health services. The report also makes policy recommendations regarding the reform of the public health sector.[6]

Historically, there has been an active system of international and domestic NGOs working in Latin America. What is different about the construction of a welfare network is the purposeful attempt(s), either from NGOs or the state, to coordinate, partner, or create regular patterns of information sharing. The Ecuadorian experience is typical of this transformation in Latin America. First, in the wake of the debt crisis the initial interest in NGOs by international actors stimulated a dramatic increase and change in orientation of the Ecuadorian NGO community. Prior to the 1980s, the national NGO community consisted of little more than a handful of social service providers and policy organizations focused on the issue of land reform. By 1994 registered NGOs numbered well over a thousand, and their concerns ranged from health care provision to income generation.

However, the growth of the NGO community in itself does not create a welfare network. A network is a dynamic set of relations that arises when there is a purposeful intent to interact with the state and international actors in a coordinated way. This purpose results when the circulation of the ideas underlying the new development model finds resonance with key actors in the NGO community and within the state. In Ecuador, this resonance was reflected in the first serious policy experiment to implement these new ideas about public–private collaboration in the late 1980s.[7] This activity was centered around the identification, design, and negotiation process of a major Ecuadorian poverty alleviation program, the Emergency Social Investment Fund (FISE), in which NGOs sought to gain a prominent role in program design and at the policy level. Over a three-year period, with

[6] These types of surveys can serve as potent political resources for states and NGOs. In a similar survey under way in Bolivia, NGO health associations are also participating partly in order to strengthen their position *vis-à-vis* the state. Bolivian health NGOs argue that the coverage they provide is higher than the current state estimate of NGO health coverage, which hovers around 1 to 2 per cent of national health provision.

[7] Experimentation with state–NGO collaboration is found before the FISE negotiation started at the end of the 1980s. For example the Ecuadorian government established the National Microenterprise Program (UNEPROM) in 1986 and in 1988 the National Corporation to Support Popular Economic Units (CONAUPE), both with the objective to support microenterprise development through coordinating its efforts with both private financial institutions and NGOs with expertise and access to microentrepreneurs. Since the state lacked experience in this area, it was interested in tapping the methods and knowledge of Ecuadorian NGOs working in the microenterprise area. See Stearns and Otero (1990).

the initial encouragement of the World Bank, NGOs played a role in all stages of the FISE prior to its formalization. In the end NGOs were unable to gain the institutionalized presence they sought in the fund. Yet, the FISE, which is described later in this chapter, proved to be a seminal learning experience for NGOs and crucial to the further development of the NGO community's consciousness about its potential role in national development.

This alleged 'failure' on the part of NGOs to gain entry into the FISE did not discourage key NGO actors from continuing to work to access state resources and influence state poverty programs. On the contrary, as this chapter will discuss, the strategic planning and training provided by the World Bank stimulated the development of a new type of NGO professional identity. This identity is premised on a proactive role for NGOs in national development and became embedded within a core group of Ecuadorian NGOs. In the 1990s these NGOs actively worked to organize and generate a consensus among the larger NGO community and the public over issues of state reform and alternative models of development.

If the Ecuadorian case illustrates the process of constructing a welfare network, it also shows that this process is neither smooth nor uncontested, and it is far from complete. States prove reluctant to accept partnerships with NGOs that potentially threaten a loss of power, authority, or symbolic capital accruing from social programs. NGOs, as unequal players in relation to states and international funders, fear a loss of autonomy and a subversion of their organizational goals.[8] Despite these caveats, the international and domestic trend toward rethinking the state's role in economic and social development has shown no signs of abating. Once the preserve of the state in Latin America, public services in the areas of health, education, housing, and productive services are provided now by a new mix of domestic NGOs, international agencies, and the state. NGOs are learning to be political actors as they attempt to engage the state and manage relations with, as will be seen, occasionally unpredictable international aid organizations.

How do the constructions of welfare networks affect the pattern of participation and representation in social policy? This chapter will argue that the movement toward a welfare network is broadening the pattern of political relations in Ecuador. The policies of international aid agencies to promote the growth of the NGO sector initially as a technical strategy for relieving overburdened states in fiscal crisis and for 'privatizing' state-run social programs have, in fact, generated a new set of political actors in Ecuador and widened the range of voices in social policy. As the empirical material will show, these voices meet with uneven success. However, obstacles and setbacks are incorporated into a wider process of experiential learning that contributes to the increasing political skills of NGOs as they negotiate with international funders and state agencies.

---

[8]   Deborah Brautigam discusses a similar case in The Gambia during the 1980s where NGOs, with the assistance of international funders, attempted to incorporate themselves into a national women's fund. This move was subverted by the Gambian president's interest in controlling a fund targeting women, who are an important political group within The Gambia. See Brautigam (1994).

The second question that frames this chapter, whether NGOs represent popular sector interests as the interventionist state is reformed, is more problematic. The idea of 'who represents' is intimately bound to images of political parties or elected officials. NGOs are not sanctioned by elections to represent the poor in deliberations about social policy and state reform. Yet they do 're-present' the needs and interests of popular sectors to the state and international actors.[9] Tensions arise over the content of that re-presenting and the actual wishes and desires at any one time of particular segments within popular sectors. In the case of the FISE, NGOs argued that the long-term interests of the poor would be better served with a fund that provided not just scattered public works projects, but service and investment projects and a focus on an overall reform of the social welfare sector. However valid this argument may be, it can easily contradict local community desires and needs for bridges, school buildings, and other infrastructure. Also, NGOs clearly represent themselves in their efforts to influence social policy. This makes them equally, if not more, representative of middle-class development practitioners than popular sectors.

Conversely, NGOs work to place pro-poor issues on the national social agenda; these range from insufficient health care to the negative impact of structural adjustment policies, women's issues, and polluted and unhealthy urban environments that undermine already problematic popular urban neighborhoods.[10] NGOs pressure the state (and international actors) to expand or execute commitments to popular sector programs. The Foro Permanente de Organizaciones por y con los Niños, Niñas y Adolescentes, an association of NGOs working in child welfare, produces alternative national reports to the United Nations regarding child welfare programs the government promised but has not delivered.[11] NGOs working in microenterprise development lobby for new laws and access to credit for normally excluded populations.[12]

These contradictory examples highlight the mixed reality of the representational nature of NGOs. If the direct consultation and linkage of NGOs to particular groups of popular sectors are the criteria for representation, then many NGOs will fail the test. If we broaden the concept of representation to include more abstract forms of representation, then NGOs do represent by inserting their

[9] For what is still one of the most comprehensive analyses of the varied meanings of representation, and an overview of representation theory, see Pitkin (1967).
[10] See Kathryn Hochstetler's chapter in this book for an analysis of the representative role of environmental movements in Brazil.
[11] In 1990 the government of Ecuador signed a United Nations convention over the rights of children, promising to implement the principles and norms of the UN convention in domestic policies targeting child welfare. The government is required to send a report to the UN every year stating its progress to date on child welfare policies. In order to pressure the government to actually carry out its commitment, the Foro sends an alternative document such as the 1994 'Una Promesa Incumplida a los Niños Ecuatorianos' to the UN.
[12] The Asociación de Corporaciones de Desarrollo de la Microempresa (ASOMICRO) and INSOTEC are two organizations active in promoting access and new regulations favoring microenterprise development.

interpretation of popular needs, social problems, and methods of addressing those problems into traditionally circumscribed policy arenas.

The chapter is organized into five sections. The following section reviews the theoretical ideas that gave shape to the new development model, and how to understand the emergence of a welfare network that it stimulated. Section 2 presents a brief historical overview of state–society relations regarding social policy in Ecuador. Section 3 examines and analyzes the FISE as a seminal learning experience for NGOs in their process of new identity formation as political actors in national development. Section 4 presents and analyzes the acceleration of NGO organization and voice in the wake of the FISE during the early 1990s. Finally, the conclusion summarizes the extent of the welfare net construction in Ecuador and re-examines what this construction means for who participates in social welfare and whose interests are represented.

1. Constructing a Welfare Network

The move toward a welfare network as a new structure of social service management and social policy formation is rooted in the breakdown of the developmentalist state paradigm in the early 1980s. International and national NGOs worked within Latin America and in Ecuador long before the 1982 debt crisis. However, reliance on NGOs as a significant development strategy only gained influence when trend-setting international aid agencies such as the World Bank, the Inter-American Bank (IDB), and the United States Agency for International Development (USAID) began to search for alternative channels of service delivery in the midst of state fiscal crisis and reform (Sollis 1992).

This paradigm shift is still in process. The parameters of the new model are open to policy experimentation, policy feedback, and change. For example, over the course of the decade the focus on civil society as an active partner in development became more central in the wake of negative experiences with adjustment strategies (*World Development* Special Issue 1988; Nelson 1992). This interest was paralleled, and then influenced, by work within academia regarding the role of civil associations in democracy (Schmitter 1992; Putnam 1993; Bratton 1989).[13] The combination of practical reflection of international aid actors mixed with theoretical perspectives borrowed from the academic community moved the development paradigm away from a cruder market-based model of state–society interaction that shaped development programs after the debt crisis, toward more sophisticated and deeply political analyses of the type of state and society required to sustain economic and political development.

[13]   The interaction between major organizations such as World Bank and the IDB, think tanks, and a network of academics forms the basis for an epistemic development community.

The result of this reflection was a reframing of the crisis of the interventionist state. The problem moved from one of too much state to one of too little effective governance. The World Bank was a central actor in the development of this new problem definition and its solution.[14] Focusing on the failure of the state in Africa, Bank policy analysts argued that state crisis was due not only to imprudent fiscal structures, but also to the lack of state capacity. Initially, solutions to the lack of sufficient governance focused on improving governance by technical reforms of administrative and managerial systems within the state (World Bank 1994; Williams and Young 1994).[15]

However, the concept of governance has a broader meaning not necessarily restricted to dynamics within the state. Governance can be seen as methods of management that include linkages between state and non-state actors in which a set of actors working within markets or particular policy domains 'seek to overcome scarcities of resources or information by combining degrees of cooperation and/or coordination in the context of competition' (Hershberg 1995). Peter Evans's work (1992) on successful state–industrial policy focuses on how the relationships between state planners, business groups, and corporations facilitate the formation of state policy and enhance the capacity of the state to achieve it. Although these linkages are more commonly referred to in political economy, they can easily apply to social policy. Reframing governance to include the management and distribution of welfare services entails new solutions to public problems, namely reforming and decentralizing the state in a manner that incorporates actors within civil society, and not just the market, in the management of collective goods with scarce resources.

How do these new ideas and policy prescriptions influence changes in the state's welfare role? Given the central role of international actors, the emergence of a welfare network could be explained as an outcome of the sheer pressure and power of international actors, including international structural conditions on countries such as Ecuador. By limiting the availability of external resources, international funders pressure state leaders to abandon the developmentalist state model. The remaining policy choices for restructuring the state-led model of development are influenced by a set of ideas and alliances which link domestic and international actors. In sum, the power international creditors have over policy choice is derived from the economic leverage they hold over states as new 'rules of the game' are negotiated (Stallings 1992).

Clearly, international actors wield substantial power in facilitating the emergence

[14]   For a discussion of how defining policy problems engenders new solutions and shapes policy agendas, see Stone (1989), Baumgartner and Jones (1991), Edleman 1988.

[15]   The extent to which this is explicitly or implicitly stated depends on the nature of the international actors. The World Bank presents its arguments in terms of more effective governance achievable through technical improvements in public administration. It is, however, implicitly based on a liberal state and society model. A unilateral agency such as the United States Agency for International Development (USAID) is able to be more open about its political perspectives and agendas. For further discussion see Williams and Young (1994).

and construction of a welfare network. However, the Ecuadorian case will show that although international financial actors such as the World Bank are powerful and do narrow policy choices, within those parameters state planners are relatively insulated from international actors and from societal interests. This institutional buffering gives state policy elites a relative autonomy in the manner in which they define public problems and develop solutions to them (Grindle 1991; Conaghan and Malloy 1994). Moreover, NGOs with their own interests and perspectives on development do not always conform to the expectations and pressures of international funders.

An alternative way of interpreting this dynamic is to move away from linkages that emphasize dichotomies such as state–society and international–state. The use of networks as an image is a useful way of conceptualizing these complex cross-institutional and national interrelations. Networks are boundary-crossing and fluid sets of relationships that coalesce around particular issues or policy areas. In political science, networks are used primarily in the area of policy studies. Policy networks are composed of all actors (or potential actors) that have an interest in a particular policy area, and who at various times are able to shape policy in that area. A policy community includes experts and interest groups from society and their counterparts within the state. The policy network is the 'linking process' or active relation of some, but not necessarily all, of the actors within the policy community around specific policy issues (Atkinson and Coleman 1992). For example, a health policy community would include medical associations, health policy experts, insurance companies, citizens' groups, and relevant state agencies and politicians. This community is transformed into a network regarding specific issues such as the ongoing process of health reform in the United States.

The concept of policy communities and networks reveals complex state–society linkages in two ways. First, it identifies the diverse set of actors that have interests, expertise, and input by policy area. Second, as particular policy issues arise it shows how some (or all) of those actors negotiate their positions and interests in the policy process. Policy networks form channels of communication and negotiation over policy issues and within specific policy domains. The policy literature moves closer to a more realistic and complex model of political action and can easily be expanded to incorporate international actors. Issues that are not always addressed in the American policy literature and that prove to be significant factors in understanding the Ecuadorian case are: how the network is structured, the unequal power held by its participants, and how the type of issue influences who participates and the outcomes. Finally, it is critical to note that policy networks do not operate in a vacuum and are affected by changes in the political macro-environment in which they are set.

Keck and Sikkink's work on transnational issue networks provides an innovative conceptualization of networks that routinely include international actors and stretch across national boundaries. They define transnational issue networks as 'the set of relevant actors working internationally on an issue who're bound together by shared values, a common discourse and dense exchanges of information and services' (Keck and Sikkink forthcoming). The expertise, knowledge, and information held by 'non-traditional international actors' such as environmental groups, women's networks, and human rights groups provide these organizations with the leverage enabling them to become significant actors in policy debates, within both international and domestic arenas.

The concept of a welfare network to explain change in the Ecuadorian case goes a step beyond either policy networks or transnational issue networks because it includes the element of executing social policy and administration of those services. The linkages between international, state, and domestic actors illuminated by the network concept enable us to understand how new structures of governance are being constructed in social service delivery and social policy in Ecuador.

2. Rethinking the Interventionist State in Ecuador

Ecuador was a relative latecomer to the developmentalist state model. Prior to the 1970s the Ecuadorian state primarily used its distributive powers to manage its complex and shifting relations of patronage with various sectors and regions within Ecuador. However, by the early 1970s two factors converged to alter the character and form of the state: the discovery of oil and the subsequent military coup in 1972. Fueled by state-controlled oil profits, the ensuing period of military reformism rapidly expanded the state's role in the economy, initiated social reforms, and created new social ministries.

However, by the end of the decade the military experiment to 'sow petroleum' was a failure. The linkages the military regime had created with popular sectors by expanding state social programs had not resulted in a stable political coalition. Pressure from elites had initiated a turn to the right within the regime. The military's increasing repression of newly mobilized labor and rural organizations, in turn, alienated its political supporters among popular sectors. Not satisfied by the military's more conservative path and frustrated at their continued exclusion from policy-making, the business class spearheaded a return to democracy by 1979.[16]

The transition to democracy occurred as the centrality of the state in leading development was coming under increasing criticism in the developed and developing world. State-initiated economic and social policies, once heralded as critical tools in guiding national development, were now perceived as having generated the ongoing economic crisis by promoting development strategies that created fiscal indiscipline and public deficits (Pereira *et al.* 1993). The region-wide debt crisis generated a strong consensus among key international and domestic actors over the consequent need to reduce the state's role in managing the economy and providing social welfare.

---

[16] For a discussion of the elite role in the transition to democracy see Conaghan (1988).

Since Ecuador's return to democracy in 1979, each new administration has faced a policy environment which makes stabilization measures and structural reforms almost unavoidable. The election of center-left governments traditionally sympathetic to popular sector interests has neither slowed down the move to reform the state nor greatly mitigated the social impact of structural adjustment policies on popular sectors. Yet, neither governments to the right or to the left have sufficiently overcome societal resistance to complete their policy reforms.

The inability to move beyond economic crisis while attempting to restructure the role of the state presents serious puzzles for political and state actors in Ecuador. The prolonged economic crisis, combined with policies that in the short run undermine standards of living, generates societal resistance ranging from localized protests to national strikes. The state is faced with the dual task of managing its limited resources and information to provide services while organizing a consensus regarding its project to reform the state's role in development. Moreover, if political parties traditionally sympathetic to popular sectors are unable to create an alternative project to neoliberal reform, what alternative organizations can represent the interests of the poor as the social service sector is restructured? Within these dilemmas NGOs find spaces to present themselves as one possible solution to the problems of politics and public management.

THE NGO–STATE DYNAMIC IN ECUADOR

NGOs and the state in Ecuador did not have a particularly adversarial history. In the 1960s many of the 'first generation' NGOs were initiated by the Catholic Church in order to provide technical support to recipients of Ecuador's first land reform in 1964.[17] Under the military regime in the 1970s, the rapid expansion of social services at the state level filled most of the space for service organizations. However, although the military created new social agencies and programs, these organizations often lacked information regarding the rural and urban populations they were to serve. The increased need for social analysis resulted in the growth of 'second generation' NGOs oriented towards policy research. Although NGOs opposed military rule, they supported the expansion of the state's welfare services and provided information and program analysis on an *ad hoc* basis to state social agencies.[18]

It was not until the 1980s that the NGO community experienced a rapid acceleration in growth and a significant shift in purpose. By the mid to the late 1980s

[17] I am indebted to Francisco Carrión, Assistant Director of FLACSO Ecuador, for his use of David Korten's NGO generations as a means of clarifying the development of the Ecuadorian NGO community for me.
[18] The suppression of political parties led many political advocates to work through NGOs as a means of creating a counter-critique to the military regime. This level of involvement never reached the intensity of participation as in Chile and Brazil. See Padron (1987).

the NGO community numbered over a thousand officially registered organizations. In Ecuador, the term NGO refers to a range of non-state organizations. It includes grassroots organizations; larger, more professional, intermediary NGOs that work with grassroots organizations and local communities and are normally staffed by middle-class professionals; international NGOs; and church-affiliated NGOs (Carroll 1992). The growth of Ecuador's intermediary NGO community was spurred by three primary factors: the increasing attention and resources channeled to NGOs by international organizations, the withdrawal of the state from social service provision, and rising levels of university-trained professionals who could no longer be absorbed by the state.

As the NGO community expanded in the 1980s, NGOs began to specialize along sectoral lines and increase in professional capacity. Moreover, many of the new third-generation NGO leaders were development professionals with links to the right rather than engaged in a leftist discourse. This move generated tensions within the NGO community as the professional capacity of many of the new NGOs enabled them to access national and international funds. Despite this, by the end of the 1980s there appeared a new trend to consider the position of the NGO community toward national development and a growing realization that in order to influence development policy NGOs needed to work together. The NGOs which later proved to be significant in the negotiation of the FISE and participate as leaders in the strategic planning initiatives were drawn primarily from the intermediate level.

Before turning to the case history of the FISE, I will briefly describe two models of Bank–NGO–government interaction which strongly shaped the ideas of the policy network which coalesced around the FISE's negotiation. The experience of the Bolivian Emergency Fund and the Guatemalan Social Investment Fund would prove to be particularly meaningful for the state planners, politicians, international actors, and NGOs which made up the policy network negotiating the FISE.

3. Social Investment Funds, NGOs, and the State

Social Investment Funds (SIFs) are compensatory programs funded by the World Bank and other multilateral and bilateral donors to mitigate the impact of structural adjustment on the poor. SIFs also provide incentives for governments to continue implementing unpopular adjustment policies by giving them a means of addressing social resistance to those policies. SIFs are normally temporary programs, and are not explicitly intended to shape the state's long-term social policies and programs.

The first SIF developed by the World Bank was the Bolivian Social Emergency Fund (ESF). Created in 1985 in the wake of near economic collapse and the Bolivian government's subsequent implementation of a strong macroeconomic shock treatment, the ESF's primary goal was the rapid execution of simple, demand-driven projects geared toward generating income and employment. Within its initial three-year life-span, the ESF funded over 3,000 projects in a rapid and transparent manner and generated much-needed political support for the government (Sollis 1992; Graham 1994).

Several factors accounted for the ESF's success in achieving its organizational goals. The ESF avoided bureaucratic entanglement by operating as a semiautonomous agency outside of the ministry structure. Strong support from then-President Paz Estensorro, and a capable staff drawn from the private sector enabled the ESF to come on line within a remarkably short negotiation period. One of the unexpected results for the World Bank was the level of NGO participation during the ESF's implementation. NGOs channeled over 25 per cent of the ESF's portfolio and generated over a third of its projects. Moreover, NGO projects often covered gaps in the government's regional and sectoral provision of social services (van Domelen 1992).

The high level of initially unsolicited NGO participation in the Bolivian ESF also created a new opportunity for the Bank to act on its policy goal to include NGOs in Bank-sponsored programs. The rationale for targeting NGOs focused on their ability to implement and test new methodologies and to access populations that were outside the reach of state programs. Moreover, the flexible organizational structure of NGOs made them an attractive alternative to the more cumbersome and often corrupt state social agencies in channeling resources to the poor.

However, the process of incorporating NGOs in Bank-sponsored projects often clashed with the Bank's operational culture. Operations managers were not rewarded by projects whose timetables and project preparation 'rules of the game' were slowed down or altered by the inclusion of NGOs. In contrast, by opening the fund to proposals from both public and private development organizations, as in the Bolivian case, a Bank manager could in a relatively painless manner begin to translate those policy goals into action.

The second model of state–NGO–Bank involvement which influenced the conception of NGO–state relations in the Ecuadorian FISE was drawn from the Guatemalan fund. Building from the positive experience of NGO participation in Bolivia, the World Bank sought to include NGOs more systematically when the government of Guatemala requested a SIF in 1988. The Bank worked with an NGO network, the Association of Service and Development Institutions (ASINDES), composed of national and international NGOs. The Bank was particularly interested in working with NGOs in Guatemala because it was felt that they represented closer linkages with the poor than the state. However, the highly politicized relations between the NGO community and the state complicated the project preparation and negotiation of the SIF.[19]

The entry of NGOs into the dialogue and negotiation of the SIF generated tensions between the NGO community and the state over their respective roles in leading development. In Guatemala, the NGO community was far more effective

---

[19] The Guatemalan story is presented in a case-study, Malefakis (1990).

than state social ministries in proposing projects for the fund. If the projects were approved on merit, then the NGOs would have been implementing over half of the SIF's projected resources (Malefakis 1990). The Guatemalan government felt that the loss of prestige and social capital was too high, despite the increased capacity offered by the NGOs, and negotiations were suspended.

The Guatemalan fund provided several positive and negative lessons for the Bank and the NGO community. For Bank project managers, reaching out to the NGO community had led to overruns in the Bank's time and resources, had irritated the Guatemalan government, and had fueled an NGO movement which the Bank could not control. Conversely, for the Bank NGO unit, and later for the Ecuadorian NGO community, the Guatemalan experience showed how powerful organized NGOs could be when given the opportunity to enter into negotiations with the state.

EXPLORING LINKAGES: THE BORJA ADMINISTRATION AND THE FISE

The election of the center-left government of Rodrigo Borja (1988–92) represented what was by that time a patterned swing in Ecuador's electoral cycle from right to left. Borja had campaigned on the premise that his Izquierda Democrática (ID) party would pay as much attention to the 'social debt' as to the economic one, and that his administration would counteract the aggressive free market policies of the preceding government of León Febres Cordero (1984–8). Nevertheless, when the new government found itself faced with a high inflation rate, a huge fiscal deficit, and a shortage of foreign exchange, it quickly moved to initiate orthodox stabilization and adjustment policies.

A Social Investment Fund represented a means to address popular sector criticism of the Borja government's economic policies. Moreover, the fund could also complement the longer-term impact of several major Bank-financed projects located within the areas of rural development, urban infrastructure, health, and education. These projects, while located within various social sector ministries, emphasized local participation and decentralization as a means of sharpening the state's interaction with the rural communities and urban popular sectors. Thus, state planners sought to design a FISE which targeted vulnerable populations yet was also tied into separate projects to reform the social sector's service delivery.[20]

The Borja government recognized that NGOs had played a key role during the implementation stage of other SIFs, and expressed interest in incorporating them more systematically into the FISE. However, neither the Bank nor the state had significant knowledge regarding the extent and capability of the NGO sector in Ecuador. What role could they play in national development and how ready were they to enact it?

One of the key elements in constructing a welfare network is NGO capacity to

---

[20] Interview with the Director of the Unidad Política Social (UPS) under the Borja government, 10 June 1992.

work with the state. An organizationally weak NGO community offers state planners little incentive to partner with them. In 1989 the World Bank initiated a survey of Ecuadorian NGOs and found a community that was relatively unorganized by sector, jealous of each other's contacts with international donors, and characterized by uneven levels of institutional capability. A formal NGO representational organization, CEOP, would be established in 1990 and play a role in the FISE, but at the time of the Bank's survey there was no organization dedicated to providing a means of articulating long-term NGO interests, much less of representing these interests in any systematic way.

These factors created barriers to NGOs' abilities to have an impact on social policy beyond providing contract or consulting services to state ministries on an *ad hoc* basis. First, minimal contact between NGOs inhibited the flow of information regarding successful projects, methods, and experiences. Second, the atomized nature of the NGO community prevented both the identification of significant issues by area and the development of a response to those issues by NGOs as a sector. Third, NGO relationships and information about state programs with funds earmarked for NGO participation often depended on personal contacts with various ministries rather than on public announcements. The lack of consistent patterns of interaction and information contributed to the general suspicion by NGOs about working with the state. Finally, the NGO community had little information regarding other NGO–state collaborations outside of Ecuador. The Bank felt that such knowledge was vital to the process of social learning, but there were no channels bringing those experiences to the attention of the Ecuadorian NGO community.

In short, during the initial dialogue with the Bank, the Borja government's primary concern was for a SIF that could provide compensation and address societal criticism. Yet the government also had a long-term goal to reform, sharpen, and decentralize the Social Ministries.[21] The government, therefore, was open to suggestions for new strategies to address the reform of a state beset by shrinking resources. The World Bank responded, both to the government's reformist goals and to the potential strength and current flaws of the NGO sector, with an alternative approach to project preparation and negotiation that normally occurs between the Bank and a government. Drawing on previous experiences and embedded in the policy to facilitate NGO–state partnerships, the NGO unit within the Bank initiated a process of strategic planning derived from the Guatemalan NGO sector, working with a group of Ecuadorian intermediary NGOs. This planning process had the explicit goal of strengthening the NGO community's ability to negotiate their ideas into the FISE design and implementation and implicitly to contribute to a more general interaction between NGOs and the state over social policy and service delivery.

---

[21] The UPS was an example of the Borja government's interest in rationalizing the state social sector. The UPS's mandate was to coordinate the work done by the social ministries and thereby diminish the level of duplication, overlap, and lack of internal information which characterizes interrelations between state ministries in Ecuador.

THE ECUADORIAN EMERGENCY SOCIAL INVESTMENT FUND (FISE)

The project preparation phase was placed concurrently under two teams within the Ministries of Labor and Social Welfare. As noted above, at this stage, one of the barriers to NGO participation was a lack of knowledge on the state's part regarding the expertise and capability of the NGO sector. The Bank NGO unit provided a roster of international and national consultants experienced in government–NGO partnerships to assist the Ministry of Labor's evaluation of the national NGO community. The Bank also commissioned a national intermediary NGO, Fundación Alternativa (Alternativa), to undertake an assessment of the NGO sector. Alternativa produced an institutional history of the Ecuadorian NGO community, its relations with the state, and a compilation of statistical data on NGO development investment portfolios (Mora 1992).

The assessment produced by Alternativa was not aimed only at improving the state's knowledge regarding the NGO sector. It was widely circulated within the NGO community as well. The work by Alternativa served as the basis for a series of informal meetings to discuss the growth and direction of NGOs as actors in national development. This consciousness-raising was strengthened by the move to initiate formally strategic planning after the initial identification work. The Bank, in conjunction with several international aid organizations and national NGOs, facilitated the financing and organization of an inter-institutional strategic planning workshop in Puembo, Ecuador. The workshop focused on the future of NGO–state relations and in particular on the potential NGO role in the FISE. The NGO organizers also invited key actors from the Ministries of Labor and Social Welfare and observers from the Bank to attend.

The workshop proved to be a model for a series of planning seminars by sector within the NGO community. Each seminar addressed issues shared by the NGOs regarding their respective area of expertise and discussed state action and/or gaps in these areas as well. These meetings influenced state–NGO relations by: generating an NGO consensus regarding issues to present to the state and increasing ties between the two ministries involved in formulating the FISE and the NGO community. Moreover, these ties influenced the FISE design at that time through the inclusion of several NGOs by each ministry on a consultative basis to assist in the project design.

IMPASSE AND TRANSITION TO THE SIXTO DURÁN BALLÉN ADMINISTRATION

Despite the interest of the Borja administration in a FISE, designing the fund under two ministries raised serious institutional and operational constraints which the Borja administration had not resolved by the end of its administration in 1992. The ministries essentially developed two competing fund designs which reflected the interests of each agency. The Ministry of Labor created a plan for the FISE which focused on employment issues while the Social Welfare Ministry produced a fund design which revolved around social services. The conflicting visions of the fund ultimately led to an impasse within the state which brought the negoti-ations with the Bank to a halt. The Bank pointed out that the Borja administration had created two, rather than one, FISE. Since breaking the fund into two separate components was not an institutionally feasible option, the Bank announced that it would only continue negotiations when the government had resolved the issue and presented a viable fund design.[22]

It was at this point that the NGOs that had been participating in the strategic planning process and quietly following the progress of the FISE's design stepped in. In the wake of the impasse between the two ministries and the World Bank, Alternativa and CEOP organized a meeting of over seventy NGOs with the govern-ment and the World Bank. The NGOs were concerned that the Borja government lacked sufficient time to synthesize the design of each ministry into one SIF, and that the information and relations developed between the state and NGOs over the past several years would be lost in the transition to the newly elected Durán Ballén government. In order to prevent this loss of institutional memory, the NGOs con-vinced the Bank and the Borja administration to provide them with a formal review of the final project design to date.

In the end NGO fears were justified. The Borja government did not synthes-ize a new FISE design. The competition between the two ministries prevented the merger of their separate plans. The division within the state also prevented a more coherent alliance with NGOs, despite an increasing level of knowledge regarding the NGO sector and interaction with key intermediary NGOs. State infighting under-mined a more systematic relationship because working with one ministry precluded working with another. Moreover, many of the state elites appointed by Borja felt that they had a good grasp on social policy and did not need NGOs to provide the state with information and alternative development methods, or to connect the state to popular sectors.[23]

Ironically, it was not until the entry of the new Durán Ballén administration with its strong neoliberal project to modernize the state that the NGOs were able to find an institutional home for themselves and forge a linkage regarding their role in restructuring the welfare sector. Capacity to do so was heightened by the fact that NGOs held as detailed a knowledge regarding the FISE as the incoming administration.

MODERNIZING THE STATE: THE DURÁN BALLÉN ADMINISTRATION AND ITS NEOLIBERAL PROJECT

The Durán Ballén administration (1992–6) shifted Ecuador back to the neolib-eral project espoused by the administration of León Febres Cordero (1984–8). The new Vice-President, Alberto Dahik, had been the Economic Minister under Febres

[22] Private communication with Bank operations consultant, 1992.
[23] Private communication by World Bank official, World Bank NGO unit, International Economic Relations Division, Operations Policy Department (OPRIE).

Cordero, and was a strong proponent of the new government's economic modernization plan. The modernization project, which was to become the centerpiece of the Durán Ballén administration, entailed privatizing state-owned industries, reforming trade and investment laws, and streamlining and rationalizing the bureaucracy. In conjunction with the modernization plan, the Durán Ballén administration's intention to implement a series of 'shock policies' made the formalization of the FISE politically imperative. The Consejo Nacional de Desarrollo, or National Planning Agency (CONADE), which fell under the purview of the Vice-President, was given the task of expediting negotiations with the Bank.

When the new government took power in August 1992, NGO leaders moved quickly and showed considerable astuteness in establishing connections with CONADE. The NGOs provided CONADE with a synopsis of previous design work on the fund, including their own views on how it might be improved. Moreover, they argued that a fund-orchestrating cooperation between private and public organizations dovetailed with the new government's expressed goals to streamline and rationalize the bureaucracy. This objective could be furthered by considering the FISE as not just a short-term compensatory fund, but as a mechanism to increase public/private collaboration through the creation of new institutional linkages between the state and NGOs. Partnerships could stretch state resources and provide complementary services to state programs, particularly in areas where the state had little or no presence.[24]

Drawing on consultants from the NGO sector that had organized the synopsis, CONADE quickly adapted the previous FISE designs to suit the needs of the incoming administration. CONADE argued that, contrary to the Bolivian experience, a more effective strategy for Ecuador would be to make the fund semi-autonomous, but under CONADE's wing. The Bank team was initially reluctant to place the fund under CONADE's direction. CONADE was a small agency more powerful on paper than in reality. It was responsible for producing the national plan and overseeing, in a general way, the activity of both international and national NGOs. CONADE itself did not directly execute social programs. Bank staff recommended that the fund be either completely outside the normal state structure or under the aegis of a social ministry experienced in implementing large-scale poverty alleviation programs.

However, CONADE argued that its Unidad Political Social, or United Social Policy Unit (UPS), was uniquely qualified to manage the fund. Under the Borja administration UPS had been involved in the fund design sponsored by the Ministry of Social Welfare. Moreover, with technical assistance and funding from the World Bank, UPS had also supervised a project to identify and coordinate social policy and programs among the social ministries. If one of the goals of the FISE was to complement the longer-term renovation of the social ministries, then having the UPS coordinate the fund was seen as a natural extension of its earlier experience.

---

[24] Interview, Soledad Jarrin, Fundación Alternativa, 8 Mar. 1993.

Moreover, CONADE fell under the direct administration of the office of the Vice-President and Dahik was interested in reforming the state and open to innovation.[25]

Building on the prior work of the Ministries of Labor and Social Welfare and NGO consultant contributions, the CONADE plan included several technical components to create formal mechanisms facilitating linkages between the state and NGOs. These included having an NGO–state administrator within the FISE. Having a full-time liaison officer could bring some of the concerns of the better NGOs skeptical of working with the state to the attention of the FISE staff, and thereby alleviate NGO fears of excessive state control. The liaison officer could also channel NGO feedback regarding project implementation, thereby incorporating the flexible and rapid learning characteristic of NGOs into the funding mechanism. Moreover, the FISE would also function as a means for increasing the level of organization and professionalization among participating NGOs through its technical training seminars. An increasingly capable NGO sector, it was argued, would provide a larger pool of effective partners for future NGO–state collaboration.

Over the course of three years of program design and negotiation, the FISE became a potent symbol to the diverse set of actors involved. For NGOs, it was an opportunity to define the terms on which they would be willing to work with the state. For state planners it was a means of supplementing state capacity in the face of continuing fiscal cuts within the social sectors. Finally, for the World Bank it proved to be an interesting policy experiment with new mandates within the Bank to facilitate NGO–state interactions. However, the policy network that coalesced around the FISE's design and negotiation was not set within a vacuum. The larger political environment, mainly ignored by NGOs and their allies within the state and international organizations, intervened.

A DISSENTING VOICE: THE UNITED STATES AGENCY FOR INTERNATIONAL DEVELOPMENT (USAID) AND THE FISE

Although the FISE proposed by CONADE pleased the NGOs and interested the World Bank, USAID strongly disagreed with its design. Although formally outside of the FISE's design and negotiation, AID had several direct interests in the fund. First, AID was contributing the seed money for the fund's immediate implementation once the FISE design had been agreed upon. Second, AID was working closely with the Durán government in creating the new modernization and privatization policies and viewed the FISE as a means to mitigate social resistance to those policies. Therefore, AID wanted the FISE to reflect what they thought of as the best of the Bolivian experience: demand-driven projects, rapid contract process, and implementation targeting private sector contractors. Within this context, facilitating new institutionalized working relations between NGOs and the state

---

[25] Interview with Soledad Jarrin, Fundación Alternativa, 8 Mar. 1993.

was not an AID priority. Conversations with key AID staff revealed a deep skepticism of the NGO community in Ecuador. AID staff cited the rapid growth of the NGO community in the late 1980s, the lack of transparency in funding, limited information regarding technical capacity of NGOs, and the heterogeneous nature of NGOs as reasons which made AID doubtful about creating a formal role for NGOs within the FISE.[26]

Thus, when the new CONADE design was revealed, AID began to work to influence the outcome of the fund. AID worried that placing the FISE, even loosely, under the wing of a government agency would slow down its execution and deprive the FISE of the political clout necessary to implement the fund in a rapid and transparent manner. Therefore, in January 1993, AID brought in an international consultant who had played a key role in developing the earlier Bolivian ESF. This consultant provided AID with an alternative version of the FISE to the one under negotiation between CONADE and the World Bank.

In the course of assisting the government with developing its economic modernization plan, AID had worked closely with the executive office and the President.[27] This working relationship enabled AID to lobby the president informally to favor their version of the FISE. AID stressed that placing the FISE under CONADE would slow it down, and that a more flexible institution outside of the normal channels of the state structure would enhance the President's political capital at a time when he was facing serious resistance from popular sectors and Congress alike over the proposed modernization plan.[28]

In March 1993 President Durán Ballén signed the decree authorizing the FISE. The decree placed the FISE not within CONADE, but directly under the administration of the President. The technical component targeting NGOs was moved out of the fund, and the institutional parameters were redrawn to resemble the Bolivian ESF. Formal NGO participation remained only in the form of two NGO representatives on the Administrative Council overseeing the fund. In short, the choice was made to create a FISE which reflected the Bolivian ESF model rather than initiate a more experimental fund.[29]

LEARNING TO PLAY POLITICS: ANALYZING THE FISE

The FISE represents a dramatic and visible instance of intermediary NGOs trying to insert themselves at the state level, and it has proven to be a powerful learning

[26] The AID perspective is drawn from a 3 June 1993 interview with an Ecuadorian staff officer in the AID/Ecuador Mission. The staff member had been assigned to work on developing an alternative FISE design and was traveling to Bolivia to meet with ESF workers. Shortly after our interview he left AID to work as an assistant to the new FISE Director.

[27] Interview with a consultant on the Bank operations team, 4 June 1993.

[28] Interview with Operations Consultant, 4 June 1993.

[29] The FISE did provide the administration with an effective means of channeling funds to local communities and enhancing the political capital of the President. One of the strongest and most vocal

experience for the NGOs involved. State policy elites faced the problem of addressing increasing levels of poverty with diminishing state resources. One strategy introduced to state planners through the combined influence of international actors and national NGOs was to experiment with the FISE to create a new division of labor between the state and NGOs. This process was neither smooth nor uncontested and reflects how experiential learning shapes and refines the creation of a shared set of ideas and patterns of interaction between NGOs, state planners, and international actors regarding the complementary role of state–NGO partnerships. State planners were seeking strategies that in the long run could contribute to the process of state reform and diminishing resources in the social sectors. NGOs were working to convince the state that they were indeed an important element in national development.

NGO participation provided state planners with an expanded base of knowledge regarding the needs of popular sectors and examples of new methodologies and approaches that had been successful in creating sustainable, participatory projects.[30] NGOs demonstrated that they were capable of participating in international–state projects and, by providing information and fresh methodological perspectives, contribute to CONADE's capacity to formulate the FISE design. NGOs made a strong case against the FISE's replicating 'public works' projects as had occurred with the Bolivian ESF. They pushed the FISE to consider social and income generation programs that may have a longer-lasting impact on popular sectors than the short-term construction projects of roads and other types of infrastructure.

During the process of negotiating the FISE, NGOs emerged as significant actors in the construction of a welfare network. Prior to the FISE, it can be argued that national NGOs formed part of the general policy community concerned with issues of national development. However, NGO activity regarding the FISE signified a claim for a more active, purposeful role in national programs and social policy, a key criterion for welfare network formation. Yet the experience of the FISE shows that the mere participation of NGOs did not guarantee outcomes either for themselves as organizations, or for popular sectors that they purport to represent. NGOs must, and did, learn political skills in order to manage their relationships with more powerful international and state actors. In the case of the FISE, NGOs incorrectly assumed that their alliance with and support for the World Bank, and close ties to like-minded state planners within CONADE, was sufficient to ensure their influence in the FISE. Therefore, strategies to influence the larger political environment were not considered.

opponents of the administration's reforms has been the indigenous movement. Although the FISE does not specifically target indigenous groups, its use of a national poverty map as the basis for assigning funds means that a majority of the funding goes to rural areas where indigenous peoples are the primary residents. This is not to say that the FISE has undermined indigenous mobilization. However, the large signs that mark every FISE project site are visible reminders that the state is 'listening' to local demands and needs. Interview with Santiago Bustamante, Director of the FISE, Aug. 1995.

[30]   Interview, Monica Hernandez, Director, Alternativa, 2 June 1993.

The neoliberal political environment that provided openings for NGOs also generated political pressures that led to their exclusion from the FISE. The Durán government was dogged by national strikes and protests from its earliest days in power. Although the new administration exhibited a high level of clarity in regard to its initial economic modernization package, opposition from urban popular sectors and resistance from the middle class and Congressional leaders on both the left and right undermined the government's ability to pursue its policy goals. Moreover, the Durán Ballén administration lacked an equally coherent plan for reforming the social sector. Thus, from the beginning of the Durán administration, as the promise of economic growth appeared to recede for the majority of Ecuadorians, it also seemed that the government lacked contingency plans to buffer popular sectors from the impact of reform.[31]

Given these factors, the President chose to reach directly to popular sectors by placing the FISE outside the ministry structure and under his office. The choice was not to experiment with the FISE, but to make it in the image of the proven and flexible Bolivian ESF. NGOs would still play a significant role in the implementation of the fund, depending on their ability to present projects, but the 'symbolic capital' would accrue to the president.

4. Expanding the Policy Debate: NGOs in the 1990s

The World Bank survey of the Ecuadorian NGO community in 1987 portrayed a relatively atomized set of organizations with little approximation to the capable, societal partner for the state called for in the new development model. Yet by 1995 significant segments of the NGO community belonged to sectoral and multi-sectoral umbrella organizations. The goals of these organizations are both to advance the organizational capacity of member NGOs and to produce consensus within that membership and the larger NGO community over policy positions *vis-à-vis* the state and international funders. Although many of the divisive characteristics that plagued the Ecuadorian NGO community continue into the 1990s, there has been a remarkable upsurge in inter-NGO organizing, and an increasing capacity of NGOs to engage the state.

There are several reasons for the acceleration of NGO organization and voice. As noted above, the strategic planning and learning experience of the FISE contributed to the development of new professional and political identities of key NGO actors. These new and evolving perceptions about their role in national development were coupled with the realization that working together enhances influence and political voice. This growing self-awareness escalated in the face of a dramatic transformation of Ecuador's economy and the role of the state under the Durán

---

[31] Interview, Monica Davila, Executive Director of CEOP, 2 June 1993.

Ballén administration's neoliberal modernization plan. Many NGOs were opposed to those neoliberal transformations and their exacerbation of poverty and inequality. NGOs, to the left and to the right, criticized the government's lack of a coherent social agenda. However, state reform also opened up new opportunities for NGOs to insert themselves in the process of reforming the social ministries. NGOs were able to use the language of neoliberal models, i.e. rationalizing the bureaucracy, the importance of societal participation, in order to make arguments about why they should have a voice in the way structural and administrative reforms should proceed. Thus, the neoliberal project provided new opportunities for NGO participation and organization and galvanized NGOs into action about the direction of that reform.

Ecuadorian NGOs use a range of political strategies to strengthen the organization of the NGO community and to influence the policy system. One of these new strategies is the increase in inter-organizational linkages. In the 1990s, this momentum produced a surge of NGO *foros* (fora). Fora are institutional spaces where NGOs deliberate on policy, generate consensus, and formulate policy and program recommendations. Fora may focus on specific sector issues such as health, child welfare, or the environment. There are also multi-sectoral fora that seek to build contacts and consensus across the NGO community. The Foro Nacional Ecuatoriano de Organizaciones No-Gubermentales (FONEONGs) is an example of one of the several fora created to prepare for the 1994 United Nations Social Development Conference in Stockholm. These fora continued to exist after the UN conference meeting, adapting themselves to address national development issues in Ecuador.

Policy recommendations are inserted into the social policy arena through a variety of tactics. NGO fora submit their policy proposals formally and informally to relevant state actors, and directly lobby Congress and the Executive. NGOs also use the media to publish critiques of and counter-proposals to (or support for) the overall modernization plan and/or particular poverty and social programs. Finally, many of the fora sponsor open meetings and invite state and social actors to participate.

Individual NGOs are also becoming regular actors in social policy. Two contrasting examples of how neoliberal reforms and international linkages provide openings and shape the organizational purpose of NGOs are found in the experiences of Fundación Grupo Esquel-Ecuador (Esquel) and Fundación Ecuador. Fundación Ecuador, founded in 1991 with support from USAID, was created initially to address trade and investment issues. In order to facilitate Fundación Ecuador's access to the government, USAID sought key Ecuadorian elites within business, academics, and the non-profit sector to sit on the Fundación's board of directors. When the Durán Ballén administration came to power in 1992, Fundación Ecuador began to work actively in support of the government's proposed economic reforms. By tapping national NGO think tanks for statistical studies and consulting international experts, Fundación Ecuador formed policy recommendations that clarified and sharpened the claims of the administration (and countered arguments of opposition parties) regarding the impact of economic policy reforms. Using these studies and hosting a series of seminars, Fundación Ecuador successfully lobbied Congress and state ministries and shaped public debate through television talk show appearances and newspaper editorials.[32]

In 1995, Fundación Ecuador signed a new agreement with USAID. As part of this agreement, it began to turn its skills toward social sector reform. Fundación Ecuador's Executive Director stated that by the end of 1993:

> we had achieved many of the most important economic reforms, inflation was down and the economy was growing. However, we realized that there was a dramatic problem since despite this poverty was increasing. Over two-thirds of the population live below the poverty line, and if this is not addressed then all the economic reforms, and democracy itself, will be undermined.[33]

Fundación Ecuador began to work in four areas of social reform and broadened its working relationships with other intermediary NGOs. In order to link their work on social policy to popular sectors, Fundación Ecuador also organized meetings, fora, and discussion among the local groups that its policies address. In an unusual agreement with the state, Fundación Ecuador is working in conjunction with the Ministry of Education and USAID on reforming the national education system.[34]

Clearly, Fundación Ecuador's influence is in large part due to its prestigious board of directors, its resource base, and the domestic and international expertise it is able to draw upon. However, it is important to note that Fundación Ecuador has not cut itself off from the NGO community, nor does it concentrate its efforts among particular political parties. As an organization, Fundación Ecuador has a centrist vision, yet it actively works to promote consensus among groups across a broad spectrum of political affiliation. On its own board and among its active associates, Fundación Ecuador is careful to include members of the left as well as the right. This inclusionary stance has mitigated criticism of Fundación Ecuador from the NGO community, despite its connection with USAID and the 'elitist' composition of its board. The almost total lack of criticism found in interviews with other intermediary NGOs is unusual given its recent formation and the competitive culture that still shapes the Ecuadorian NGO community.

If Fundación Ecuador is a third-generation NGO, Fundación Esquel-Ecuador, although not legally incorporated until 1991, is rooted in the first generation of Ecuadorian NGOs. In the 1970s, its founding members, a loose compilation of intellectuals and practitioners, met to discuss and criticize national development strategies that, they argued, reflected Ecuador's dependent status in the global

---

[32] Fundación Ecuador, 1993 Annual Report.

[33] 13 Feb. 1995 interview with Dr Bolívar Chriboga, Deputy Executive Director, Fundación Ecuador.

[34] One of the policy recommendations of the Fundación will be to redirect state subsidies away from the university system and toward the country's ailing primary school system. This type of reform is, however, much harder to pass politically since it undercuts the benefits of the vocal middle class for the more marginalized urban and rural poor.

economy. Working together during the 1980s in a variety of policy think tanks and academic settings, Esquel's founders formally incorporated in order to 'put what we had been thinking and writing about into practice'.[35] Thus, Esquel considers itself as an institution whose thinking about alternative models of development has been formed over twenty years.

To translate its theories of development into practice Esquel built a participatory project model into its institutional structure. The project cycle begins when community organizations present Esquel with proposals for projects such as potable water systems or a health clinic. Esquel then matches communities with local NGOs whose expertise is in the requested area. Although Esquel provides the majority of the project's financing, both the community and the participating NGO are expected to contribute financially to the project, often in kind. Finally, Esquel monitors and evaluates the projects in order to ensure that local perspectives, including criticisms, are incorporated into the foundation's institutional memory.

As in the case of Fundación Ecuador, the impact of structural adjustment policies in 1993 prompted Esquel to broaden its scope. It became particularly concerned that in the process of national reform the voices of popular sectors were almost completely excluded from national debate. In order to address this gap in January 1994 Esquel initiated the Foro de la Ciudadanía (Citizens' Forum). The Foro is a space for consensus building and the formation of opinions within civil society regarding the direction of social policy, the reform of the state, human rights, and alternative models of development. Convened by subject, these highly publicized debates (always announced in the newspapers) are both open to the general public and consist of carefully chosen NGO leaders, government officials, business people, academics, and social movement leaders. Each meeting results in a 'white paper' which is then circulated among a distribution network of over 2,000 actors in civil society and disseminated widely throughout relevant government agencies. An example of how the Foro can influence the political system concerns the political impasse between Congress and the Executive over the issue of constitutional reform. The resulting paper and policy recommendations derived from a series of Foro meetings was used as a behind-the-scenes catalyst to move the Congress and Executive forward.[36]

Conclusion

This chapter opened by arguing that the breakdown of the interventionist state model and the subsequent restructuring of the state's role in social services and social policy in the 1980s and 1990s is producing a welfare network and a new

---

[35] 21 Feb. 1995 interview with Boris Cornejo, Director of Development, Fundación Esquel.

[36] Interview with Boris Cornejo, Director of Development, Fundación Esquel, 21 Feb. 1995.

representative structure in Ecuador. However, this chapter also shows that the construction of a welfare network is a work in progress. The welfare network is not just a technical solution to state crisis, but a profoundly political restructuring of state–society and international relationships. NGOs become new political actors in social policy because they view themselves as more than organizational vehicles to which public services are contracted out. NGOs seek to structure the terms on which they work with state social agencies and to shape social policy. Although state actors need strategies to supplement and enhance state capacity, they are wary that this proactive stance by NGOs may lead to a loss of authority and legitimacy that social programs traditionally give to the state. International actors facilitating new state–society interaction are drawn more deeply into aspects of administration and implementation and into a larger policy process and political environment that they do not always control.

The case of the FISE is a good example of how prior institutional practices and relations of power shape the adoption and implementation of the new policy ideas that underlie the welfare network model. In Ecuador the Executive sets the tone for policy. Ministers of social agencies formulate policies that reflect the President's interests and present them to the President for approval. In the case of the FISE, policy design extended outside of the social ministries to include NGOs and international actors. The importance of the link with the executive in gaining support for policy innovation was overlooked. Without the support of the President, and in the face of a political logic that called for generating consensus on economic reforms, the policy experiment to incorporate NGOs in the FISE was dropped. In order to maneuver through this complex institutional and political landscape, NGOs needed to learn to be political actors. NGO participation in the identification and design stages of the FISE, and their formal exclusion from it, became a seminal learning experience for the NGO community. This experience contributed to the process of creating a new professional identity for NGOs that served to 'scale up' NGO perceptions of their role from local development actors to players on the national level.

What political implications does the emergence of the welfare network have for participation, citizenship, and representation? The Ecuadorian case contradicts the argument that including NGOs in welfare provision is leading to a privatization of social services and a depoliticization of social policy. On the contrary, constructing a welfare network has expanded the set of actors who, at least occasionally, are able to influence social policy. Coupled with the experiential evolution of their own political identity, NGO participation has kept social policy in the political as well as the technical sphere. The strategies of NGO fora and individual NGOs such as Esquel and Fundación Ecuador to forge linkages to other social actors also make social policy a focal point for national political debate.

The issue of representation is less straightforward. Fundación Ecuador, an elite and internationally created policy actor, is hardly representative of popular sectors. Fundación Ecuador formulates policy recommendations that it perceives will facilitate social development. Yet, perhaps unexpectedly, these recommendations can contradict middle-class interests in favor of popular sectors. In the area of educational reform, Fundación Ecuador advocates redistributing resources from national universities to middle and primary schools, a policy benefiting marginalized rural populations. Fundación Esquel has a more participatory structure that it uses to complement its own organizational policy agenda. However, when Esquel meets with state policy elites on issues of policy and administrative reform it acts on its own views of how reform and policy should be shaped rather than as a representative of popular sectors.

The representative role for NGOs is problematic if NGOs claim to speak directly for popular sectors, or assume that their technical expertise overrides popular sector perceptions of their needs and wants. Sometimes NGOs are pressured into a more representative role than they actually care to take. International and state actors often find it easier to consult NGOs working in popular neighborhoods rather than the series of small committees that compose popular organization in that area. Inadvertently, NGOs can 'crowd out' the participation and voice of popular sectors.[37]

The construction of a welfare network in Ecuador highlights the dual nature of the neoliberal model of state reform and societal participation. On the one hand, restructuring the state's welfare role represents a divesting of the state's obligation to provide social welfare services and consequently redefines the extent and nature of citizenship in Ecuador. On the other hand, that restructuring presents new spaces and opportunities for a wider range of societal actors to participate in the social agenda. The inclusion of NGOs and international actors is altering civil society and creating a new structure of representation in social policy. Further research is needed to analyze whether or not this transformation is indeed improving governance and breaking patterns of clientelism.[38]

---

[37] This point was made by Mario Unda of CIUDAD. See Chalmers (1992) for a discussion of NGOs as a political service sector.

[38] See the Conclusion to this volume for a provocative discussion about the emergence and nature of new patterns of representation in Latin America.

21 | Regional Integration and Transnational Politics: Popular Sector Strategies in the NAFTA Era

María Lorena Cook[1]

Introduction

On 1 January 1994, Mexico's long-awaited entry into the First World—symbolized by its alliance, through the NAFTA, with the largest economic power in the world—was quickly overshadowed by the appearance of what the *New York Times* called 'the first Latin American revolutionary movement of the post-cold war age' (Golden 1994*a*). Just as the North American Free Trade Agreement took effect, a group of Indian rebels calling themselves the Zapatista National Liberation Army occupied San Cristóbal de las Casas and several other communities in Mexico's southern-most state of Chiapas, declaring war on the Salinas government and labeling NAFTA a death sentence for indigenous peoples. Within days, journalists and observers proclaimed the end of the neoliberalism for which the Salinas administration had been applauded throughout the world, and the Mexican political landscape was turned upside down.

Much has happened since that New Year's Day when Mexicans awoke to find hooded rebel fighters on their television sets: the assassination of presidential candidate Luis Donaldo Colosio, a relatively peaceful and heavily monitored election that ended in victory for the Partido Revolucionario Institucional (PRI), another political assassination (of PRI General Secretary Francisco Ruiz Massieu) that revealed the presence of dangerous factional divisions within the ruling party, and a peso devaluation in December 1994 that ushered in Mexico's worst economic crisis in recent memory. Given this succession of events, the Chiapas uprising appears as the first in a string of shocking developments in a country that had not seen this level of armed protest and political violence for decades. The political

[1] The author would like to thank Douglas Chalmers, Michael Jiménez, Monique Segarra, Celia Toro, and Deborah Yashar for their insightful comments. A preliminary version of this essay was presented at the Center for International Studies, Harvard University, 15 Feb. 1994, and at the International Congress of the Latin American Studies Association, Atlanta, Georgia, 10–12 Mar. 1994, as well as at the Columbia University Workshop on Poverty and Inequality in Latin America, 3–5 Mar.

dynamics that the rebellion in Chiapas set into motion are still unfolding, and it may be some time before there is a final resolution to the conflict and before the full effect of the uprising can be grasped. What is clear at this point, however, is that what happened in Chiapas not only drew international attention to the exclusionary aspects of the neoliberal economic reforms implemented by the Salinas administration (and which NAFTA was to consolidate and extend), but it also catalyzed a national movement for broader political reform in anticipation of the August 1994 presidential elections and beyond (Eaton 1994: 1A; Fox 1994*a*).[2]

Chiapas also represented the first example of how the domestic and transnational networks that emerged during the pre-NAFTA-vote period (1990–3) would react to a post-NAFTA-vote crisis in Mexico. In the days immediately following the takeover of four communities by the Zapatista army, the Mexican government was slow to respond, and then did so through indiscriminate bombing of Indian communities. In contrast, Mexican civil society reacted with tremendous maturity and speed, seizing the opportunity both to push for a political solution to the conflict and to drive home the urgent need for a true democratic political reform. As one analyst noted, Chiapas revealed once again the tremendous gap (*desajuste*) that existed between civil society and the political system in Mexico (Hernández Navarro 1994). International and US-based organizations—in particular, human rights groups—also swung into action, as did members of the US Congress, both those who had voted for and against NAFTA. Whether or not events surrounding the Chiapas rebellion will be representative of reactions to future political crises in the NAFTA era, it seems clear that the political environment first generated by the NAFTA negotiation and debate period has created new interests, new resources, new allies, and new arenas for strategic action by both governmental and non-state actors.

Recent discussions of the impact of neoliberal economic reforms on popular sectors in Latin America have tended to emphasize their demobilizing effects on popular organizations and social movements, many of which showed startling vitality just a few years ago. In Mexico, many independent labor and popular organizations saw the North American Free Trade Agreement as the extension of a process of economic liberalization that had been taking place since the mid-1980s, one that had brought real wage decline, employment loss, and growing inequality. At the same time, however, the prospect of a free trade agreement with the United States and Canada breathed new life into a variety of Mexican non-governmental organizations (NGOs) and popular organizations, as they mobilized against the agreement in collaboration with Canadian and US counterparts. The result was a novel and unexpected by-product of the NAFTA process: a network of North American labor, environmental, human rights, and other citizens' organizations using international alliances to pressure their governments to modify the agreement.[3]

---

[2] For an overview of these electoral reform measures in the wake of the Chiapas uprising, see Cook *et al.* (1994).   [3] On the development of these transnational coalitions, see Thorup (1991).

In a somewhat paradoxical development, transnational coalitions of popular-sector organizations had emerged in response to what many labor unions, human rights groups, women's and community organizations, and other grassroots and civic organizations widely viewed as an anti-popular and exclusionary process—the free trade negotiations.

This chapter argues that although economic integration between the United States and Mexico had been taking place for some time, it was the *formal recognition* of this process as represented by the discussions surrounding the North American Free Trade Agreement that facilitated transnational political action by non-state actors. Whereas the globalization of the economy and the prevalence of neoliberal economic policies may be considered by some to undermine popular sector organization and actions, formal recognition of regional economic integration in North America has produced a 'transnational political arena' that has expanded the resources available to non-governmental groups, increased their leverage in domestic political arenas, and broadened their strategic options.

This chapter will examine the dimensions of this transnational political arena. What are its characteristics? How is it likely to evolve over time? How is this arena similar to or different from other 'internationalized' phenomena that a number of analysts have begun to observe and describe? How might different kinds of actors take advantage of this new environment? In particular, how does the existence of a transnational political arena affect popular organizations and social movements (including labor movements) whose activities have traditionally taken place within national borders? Will a Mexico more tightly connected to the US market offer increased opportunities for the mobilization of Mexican social movements, or will it strengthen the barriers against popular organization and activism?

NAFTA and the Emergence of a Transnational Political Arena

Mexican President Carlos Salinas de Gortari's proposal to President George Bush to extend a free trade agreement to Mexico represented for many the culmination of the liberal economic policies Salinas, and De la Madrid before him, had been following. Those who opposed NAFTA did so partly on the grounds that it would lock in economic policies that had produced further inequality and weakened the poor. NAFTA, many argued, was actually a charter of rights for multinational corporations, and ignored the needs of the majority of the population of all three of the countries involved. NAFTA would hurt the majority of citizens by constraining democratic government, limiting a country's ability to implement social programs, infringing on national sovereignty, and by further removing key decisions from citizens, forcing them to respond to the initiatives of private corporations protected by the agreement.

At the same time, some who pointed to NAFTA's possible adverse effects on the majority of the population also acknowledged a positive development: the emergence of a growing number of cross-border contacts between labor, environmental, human rights, women's, and other citizens' groups in the three countries (Grinspun and Cameron 1993). What was emerging, and what was further needed, in response to the globalization of the economy was the globalization of social movements, the transnationalization of a political and social response to corporations, capital, and goods that moved freely across international borders (Brecher and Costello 1991a, 1991b). Whereas the globalization of the economy and regional economic integration have generally been viewed as harmful to popular organizations and national labor movements, some of the political changes that have accompanied these regional and global tendencies may point to the generation of a new, transnational political arena that could, in turn, broaden the range of strategies that national social movements may adopt.

The NAFTA debate acted as a catalyst to the formation of cross-border alliances. Since 1990, there has been an explosion of contacts between Canadian, Mexican, and US non-governmental groups. These have taken a variety of forms: site visits, educational tours and workshops, meetings attended by representatives of organizations from the three countries, regular communication and exchange of information (aided by faxes and access to computer networks), joint political strategizing around NAFTA, solidarity actions with specific struggles, pressuring of government officials and politicians to concern themselves with events in the other country, and so forth. Cross-border collaboration has taken place at both the grassroots level of people-to-people contacts and among organization leaders.[4] This development of direct, people-to-people networking in the three countries has been called 'citizen diplomacy' and represents a novel dimension in US–Mexican relations. Some have argued that this citizen diplomacy can, therefore, act as an important, bottom-up check on traditional diplomatic relations and government-to-government exchanges (Thorup 1991, 1993).

This cross-border coalition formation took place in a unique historical context, one in which Mexico's economic and political future had come to depend—as never before—on a decision to be made in the US Congress. At the same time, NAFTA's passage was by no means a foregone conclusion. This meant that the political process in the United States was particularly porous on this issue. Congress was not only bombarded by the lobbying efforts of the Mexican government (producing the most expensive single-issue lobbying campaign by any foreign government thus far), but also by domestic constituencies, especially labor and environmental groups, and by the congressional testimony of Mexican citizens: representatives of popular organizations, Mexican NGOs, intellectuals, and even individuals who felt wronged by the actions of US companies in Mexico.[5] Whereas before Mexican

---

[4] For a discussion of some of these cross-border efforts, see Brooks (1992), Eisenstadt (1993), Hernández Navarro (1993), Thorup (1991, 1993), and Browne et al. (1994).

[5] In one case, a woman fired from her job at a General Electric *maquila* due to prior union organizing activities was brought to the USA to testify before the US Senate. The United Electrical Workers, Teamsters, and Jobs with Justice were instrumental in bringing her to the United States.

NGOs' international activities consisted, in the best of cases, of contacts with foundations or other social movements, now they were 'lobbying at the centers of political decision making, especially the U.S. Congress', where, increasingly, issues relating to Mexico were being decided (Hernández Navarro 1993: 10). Government officials and legislators have also crossed borders in recent years. US politicians flocked to Mexico, especially the border, to learn more about the concerns of their constituents, both those who favored and opposed the agreement. Mexican government officials have been especially active in the US political arena. Not only did they spend millions on lobbying and influential consultants in Washington, DC, but they targeted the opinion pages of major US newspapers and traveled throughout the country to campaign for NAFTA (Dresser 1993). The Mexican government especially tried to win over Hispanics in the USA in the hopes that they could act as a strong 'pro-Mexico' lobby in Washington.

The political opposition in Mexico also campaigned in the USA among Mexican immigrants, and declared its plans to lobby the US Congress and President Clinton on electoral and human rights issues (Hughes 1993a: 12). Competition between the Salinas administration and the opposition headed by Cuauhtémoc Cárdenas for the hearts and minds of Mexican citizens residing in the USA even prompted the Mexican government to respond with an international version of Solidaridad, the government's public works program targeted at the poor (Hughes 1993b: 13). However, it was in the political process and debate surrounding NAFTA that the interpenetration of the domestic politics of the United States and Mexico emerged most clearly. That domestic politics were 'internationalized' by the NAFTA debate became especially visible within Mexico. Their country long ruled by strong nationalist sentiments and mistrust for its northern neighbor, Mexico's political leaders have typically bristled at any criticism coming from the United States and felt little compunction to address its concerns. Because of its proximity to the United States and the history of US–Mexican relations, Mexico has clung more steadfastly to notions of national sovereignty than most other Latin American nations. These strong nationalist tendencies made themselves felt in the economic arena as well as in politics, even though Mexico's economy has always been strongly dependent on the United States. However, the gradual opening of Mexico's economy in the mid-1980s and President Salinas's strong support of NAFTA have made it more difficult to sustain the nationalist discourse within Mexico and with other countries. Moreover, economic liberalization and restructuring in Mexico threaten to dismantle the regime's traditional domestic support coalition, affecting organized labor in particular, which constituted the strongest pillar of support during moments of nationalist or statist retrenchment *vis-à-vis* the United States or even the Mexican private sector.

The NAFTA political process made the Mexican government uncharacteristically responsive to outside criticism of its domestic policies and helped to shape the reform process within Mexico. US concerns with Mexico's environmental problems and lax enforcement of its laws led President Salinas to revise environmental legislation and take a series of strongly visible measures aimed at assuaging these concerns. Complaints about corruption, drug trafficking, and human rights violations—issues that had led to tensions in US–Mexican relations in the past—led President Salinas to step up drug interdiction efforts, clean up the judicial police force, and appoint a former human rights advocate to the position of Attorney General. On political issues the Mexican government has been more tentative. Nonetheless, charges of authoritarianism from outside as well as pressure from domestic political opponents persuaded the regime to recognize opposition electoral victories in some states and to propose a series of electoral reforms, a process that received even greater impetus after Chiapas.

Mexico's authoritarian political system has traditionally limited the ability of domestic political opponents to influence the political process via elections or other domestic institutional means. In recent years, however, Mexican political reform was increasingly spurred and shaped by what happened in the USA. In extreme cases, a critical article in the *Wall Street Journal* or the *New York Times* could lead to a speedier change in government policy than years of domestic political pressure. It is little wonder, then, that some Mexican intellectuals, labor groups, human rights organizations, and opposition parties used the US political arena to press for change in their own country. The Mexican left, in particular, has overcome historic mistrust in order to build alliances with US and Canadian groups. Meanwhile, the NAFTA debate increased the contact points between international actors and the domestic political process in both the United States and Mexico, and it expanded the possible arenas available to non-governmental actors for strategic action on a range of issues, not all of them pertaining strictly to NAFTA.

With the initiation of government talks over NAFTA, then, several new developments emerged that have helped to define what may be termed a new transnational political arena in the North American region: (1) non-state actors began to search across borders for common interests in trying to influence the NAFTA negotiations process; (2) international actors (governmental and non-governmental alike) began to scrutinize Mexican domestic politics more intensely; (3) the Mexican government became more sensitive and more responsive to external criticism as it waited for the fate of NAFTA to be decided in the US Congress; (4) some Mexican non-state actors obtained increased bargaining leverage within Mexico because of their relationship with international allies, and increased attention internationally because of their critical position within Mexico.

The novelty of these developments becomes evident when one looks at the history of US–Mexican relations, which has largely involved government-to-government relations at the level of policy, frequently over problems shared due to geographical proximity—especially drug trafficking, immigration, pollution, and trade. While the social, cultural, and economic integration of the southwestern United States and northern and central Mexico has been a fact for some time, and Mexican political movements have at times spilled over into areas of the United States, the breadth of grassroots involvement and the intensity of Mexican government and non-governmental efforts to influence and organize public opinion in the USA are unprecedented. As Denise Dresser noted, 'For the first time in its postrevolutionary history, Mexico launched a new policy *towards* the United States *in* the United States' (Dresser 1993: 94). The novelty of these developments and of the political environment they have generated challenges us to rethink the ways in which sovereignty, domestic politics, and popular sector strategies take shape in North America.

The Internationalization of National Politics: Rethinking the Strategic Arena

Recently, many analysts seem to be wrestling with new ways to describe and conceptualize what appear to be new global developments. These have been variously described as the 'interpenetration of international and domestic spheres', 'internationalized politics', or the 'new transnationalism'.[6] Douglas Chalmers, for instance, has argued that internationalizing trends in the areas of the economy, communications, culture, and politics have introduced international actors at all points within the domestic political process, thereby 'internationalizing the politics of states' (Chalmers 1991: 6–7). According to Chalmers, these internationalizing trends are changing the way we think about the basic units in the international system, aspects of the 'nation', the significance of territorial borders, and the utility of notions of foreign policy that presume a model of separate, territorial nation-states. Sikkink (1993) has argued that 'transnational nonstate actors' such as non-governmental organizations and transnational social movements are increasingly influencing state policies, particularly in certain issue-areas, just as foreign governments, international organizations, and transnational corporations have traditionally done. For his part, Rosenau has described a 'multi-centric system of diverse types of actors [that have] emerged to rival the anarchic world of nation-states' (Rosenau 1993: 20). How does the political arena generated by NAFTA relate to some of these internationalized processes that other authors have sought to analyze?

Sikkink talks about the emergence of 'principled issue-networks': networks of international and domestic non-governmental organizations, global and regional intergovernmental organizations, and private foundations organized around shared values or principled ideas—in this case, human rights. These international human rights networks challenge traditional concepts of national sovereignty by seeking

---

[6] Benedict Anderson has referred to the efforts of foreign residents in the centers of global economic and political power to influence politics in their countries of origin as 'E-mail nationalism' ('The Origins of E-Mail Nationalism and its Consequences', presentation to the International Studies in Planning Spring Seminar Series, Cornell University, 25 Feb. 1994).

to redefine what is within the domestic jurisdiction of states and attempting to alter state practices (Sikkink 1993: 413). The targets of these international issue-networks in the area of human rights depend in part on the political context, in part on the extent and severity of the violations. In Argentina, gross human rights violations under the military government in the mid-1970s attracted the network's attention, as did rights violations in Central America during the 1980s. In Mexico, Sikkink points out, the human rights network did not become active, despite the existence of gross rights violations in earlier periods (such as the 1968 massacre of students), until after Central America had faded from the screen, more domestic human rights groups had emerged in Mexico, and the NAFTA debate had begun to focus attention on Mexico (Sikkink 1993: 428–30).

While international issue-networks have become part of the new NAFTA environment, it seems clear that they did not create it. The international human rights network, for example, predates the new political arena created by the NAFTA debate, and to some degree turned its attention to Mexico *because* of this new political environment. It may also be that the NAFTA debate process has generated new networks organized around other kinds of issues, such as the environment and labor rights. In any case, while the presence of these networks is certainly part of what the transnational political arena is about, they are different phenomena. For example, geography is relatively unimportant for the networks that Sikkink describes. The human rights network might turn its attention equally to Pakistan, Argentina, or El Salvador; indeed, proof that location is relatively unimportant is that the focus turned toward Mexico, the United States' immediate neighbor, only recently. In contrast, geography—the idea of a 'region'—appears to be central for the transnational political arena this study attempts to characterize.

One author who has advanced the discussion on how to talk theoretically about a regional arena is James Rosenau (1993), in his discussion of what he calls 'the California–Mexico Connection'. The California–Mexico Connection refers to a region marked by the overlap and flow of people, culture, and 'issues' that affect both California and Mexico. While NAFTA is not central to the Connection's existence (the Connection predates NAFTA), NAFTA is likely to expand and strengthen the ties that bind these geographic areas, and may bring them into greater 'coherence'. What distinguishes this region is the geographical contiguity of the two national areas and the social, cultural, and economic linkages that derive from this contiguity. From this perspective, it is unlikely that we would ever speak of a 'New York–Mexico Connection', even with NAFTA. For the transnational arena produced by NAFTA, geography is important, but not in the same way that it is important in the case of the California–Mexico Connection. NAFTA redraws the geographical boundary around three nation-states, not simply between regions within countries. This regional area then becomes important to the concept of a transnational political arena because of the formal recognition of economic ties, the meanings people give to these ties, and the possibilities for political action and alliances that they engender. Cultural similarities exist within this arena, but are not necessary for its existence.[7] Finally, the California–Mexico Connection is defined by the presence of unorganized phenomena (people, goods, problems) in the region, rather than by the actions of organized groups and the adaptation of their political strategies to a new terrain. The transnational space produced by NAFTA therefore differs from that of the California–Mexico Connection.

The development of regional trading blocs in the world has also begun to spur new ways of thinking about the politics that occurs within these regional blocs. Even though the European case involved a higher degree of institutionalization at the supranational level and a more explicit recognition of the need for harmonization, regional integration in both Europe and North America has involved a similar set of pressures.[8] European economic integration, with its accompanying political-institutional changes at the supranational level, has raised the question of whether domestic institutions and practices should or do converge to meet international demands during integration. Suzanne Berger, for example, observed how domestic structures and practices become the object of pressure and the subject of international negotiation during the process of integration in Europe.[9] This negotiation was being driven by market forces, but also by social and political demands for 'fair trade', which calls for 'leveling the playing field' among trading partners. Robert A. Pastor (1992) argues something similar in the case of NAFTA: what had been termed 'only' an agreement about trade and investment in fact drew attention to a range of non-trade issues, such as human rights, the environment, labor, and politics. In North America, the existence and pressure of non-governmental groups opposed to NAFTA was an important factor in extending the debate. The question of labor and environmental standards, for example, became part of the agenda due to pressure from environmental organizations and the labor movement in the United States. Much of the opposition to NAFTA and pressure to expand the debate also stemmed from the fact that such great disparities existed between the United States and Mexico in terms of levels of economic development and the character of their political institutions. Thus, the importance assigned to non-trade issues depended ultimately on the meanings that non-governmental groups assigned to the process of regional integration and what they believed its implications would be. Indeed, *asymmetry* has been an important factor in expanding the terms of the debate in the NAFTA case and in generating a transnational political arena. Mexico was in general the weaker partner in the NAFTA negotiations; its dependence on US Congressional approval drove Mexican government and party officials to lobby the US government, Congress, and public opinion and helped to shape the

[7]   Similarly, one important component of the transnational arena, that which relates to immigration and migratory circuits, is a large part of the California–Mexico Connection but also extends beyond California. The concept of 'transnational communities' used to talk about Mexican immigrants in the United States refers to Mexican village identities and networks spanning both Michoacán and Redwood City, Oaxaca and Fresno, Puebla and New York City (see R. Smith 1992).

[8]   On the creation of new institutions in Europe, see the essays in Sbragia (1992).

[9]   Presentation by Suzanne Berger to workshop on 'The Political Economy of the New Europe', Cornell University, Nov. 1992.

domestic reform process within Mexico. Different levels of economic development and different political systems sparked the concerns of the US labor movement, environmental groups, and other citizens' organizations, which saw NAFTA as lowering standards and eliminating jobs in the USA. The lack of democratic debate in Mexico also influenced the creation of a transnational arena. Unable to express dissent at home, Mexican organizations and individuals brought their dissent to the US political arena, where criticism of Mexican government practices could generate greater results.[10]

What changed with the NAFTA debate was not so much the degree of institutional development nor even of economic integration, but the political context—in particular, the strategies that became possible and the resources that became available because of it. What changed were the meanings people ascribed to developments in each country and their willingness to engage with counterparts and allies across the border. The political environment therefore changed without (or prior to) significant institutional change. What was further distinctive about the arena generated by NAFTA and about the notion of transnational politics was that they acknowledged the existence of new arenas and resources for strategic action by organizations, groups, and movements that had traditionally been bound by national borders. While one has to be careful not to underestimate the extent to which national factors continue to shape and, in many cases, determine the actions of these groups, it is important to recognize the ways in which the presence of a transnational area can shape domestic organizations' strategies.

One of the reasons why the international relations literature has proven inadequate for understanding some of the internationalizing developments described above is because these developments involve significant participation by non-state, grassroots actors. The environment and actions of these actors have been more adequately dealt with by the rich theoretical literature on social movements. Nonetheless, this literature has tended to treat social movements as nationally bounded (Sikkink 1993; McAdam and Rucht 1993). As with other sub-fields and disciplines, the social movements literature also demands reconceptualization to take into account transnational developments; in this case, it requires rethinking the political environments of movements. Within the social movements literature, one approach has focused on how changes in movement environments—the existence or absence of 'political opportunities'—facilitate or impede movements' abilities to mobilize and to act. The determinants of a particular 'structure of political opportunities' were most often found to be national, political factors.[11] The presence or absence of these factors could help to understand the timing of movement mobilization. For example, important variables in a political opportunity structure were whether institutional access existed; whether political (usually

---

[10] See Aguilar Zinser (1993) for a discussion of the political restrictions on a NAFTA debate within Mexico.

[11] Among authors writing from within this 'political process' perspective are Jenkins and Perrow (1977); McAdam (1982); Kitschelt (1986); Brockett (1991); and Tarrow (1988, 1991, 1994).

electoral) alignments were in disarray; whether there were conflicts within the political elite; and whether there were influential allies either from within or outside of the system (Tarrow 1991: 15). The relevant characteristics in this approach were typically associated with a type of polity (usually, advanced industrial democracies) rather than a country's position in a regional or global economic system. Similarly, the concept of a 'social movement sector' (the existence of a number of movements occurring more or less simultaneously and the relations among them) visualized such sectors as existing within national boundaries. In spite of the fact that this part of the social movement literature largely confined itself to discussions of national social movements, the concepts of this literature may be usefully applied to understand the contours of the transnational political arena and how movements may act within this arena. We may superimpose a set of transnational variables onto the national determinants of political opportunity structure, or simply extend these concepts to include their transnational, as well as domestic, dimension. In this way, the concept of social-movement sector may include not only the traditional, national array of social movements and domestic NGOs but also their counterparts in other countries. Influential allies may refer not only to domestic allies within or outside of the system but also to allies in neighboring states (whether from government, Congress, the labor movement, domestic NGOs, or other social movements) and to private foundations and international agencies (such as those involved in the human rights issue-network that Sikkink describes).[12] Electoral alignments and political developments in the neighboring country or in the region may become just as important to a network of movements and organizations as political conditions in their own country. And institutional access may be sought elsewhere, and may be used to pressure for increased access at home. In the language of social movement theory, the NAFTA process has created a new structure of political opportunities, one that has generated a change in expectations and an expansion of the possible strategies and resources that various actors may adopt.

A transnational political arena is, consequently, one in which non-governmental and governmental actors utilize the political process and media networks of another country, and/or attempt to form contacts and alliances with non-governmental actors of another country, in an effort to influence public opinion in that country and/or in an effort to affect the political process at home. To distinguish this arena from isolated, individual cases of cross-national activism, for such an arena to exist there must be a generalized awareness of the interrelatedness of the issues that emerge in each country, and a perception that formerly domestic issues carry repercussions for the citizens of another country, and therefore are subject to pressure by, and negotiation with, foreign actors. While these perceptions are difficult to measure, they can be observed in such statements as those by the Mexican deputy foreign minister who explained that the Mexican government's more partisan involvement

---

[12] On the importance of international allies for the human rights movement in Argentina, for example, also see Brysk (1993).

in US politics on account of California ballot Proposition 187 was 'part of the new reality of [the US–Mexican] relationship', in which greater integration was changing the political rules observed by the two countries (Golden 1994*b*). The comments of Baldemar Velásquez, president of the Farm Labor Organizing Committee, which has a close working relationship with its counterpart in Mexico, are also telling: 'Today, we have to look at ourselves as citizens in a collective economy as opposed to citizens of a particular nation' (Bryce 1993). A transnational political arena by definition challenges traditional notions of national sovereignty. While regional proximity may not be necessary for the existence of a transnational political arena, geographical contiguity may facilitate the breadth and frequency of cross-border exchanges. What further distinguishes a transnational political arena from some other kind of region with shared problems and a social and cultural overlap is that a transnational political arena is primarily about a political process: how the actors involved perceive and pursue power resources in order to gain bargaining leverage and to influence political decisions. Although cultural and social similarities and supranational institutions may exist in this arena, they are not essential for its existence. Moreover, it is an arena in which international issue-networks may operate, but these networks exist independently of a transnational political arena. Finally, although strong economic ties between Mexico and the United States had existed for some time, it was the formal recognition of these ties rather than the fact of their existence which helped to change actors' perceptions and strategies.

In the North American case, a transnational political arena was created when talks began on the North American Free Trade Agreement. What generated this arena was the effort to expand the agenda during the negotiations to include non-trade issues. The belief on the part of some actors that domestic non-trade issues then became subject to international negotiation helped to generate a political process and a set of strategies aimed at influencing this negotiation.

Asymmetry between the United States and Mexico was key in helping to forge this transnational political arena. The Canada–USA Free Trade Agreement of 1989 did not generate a similar process. The incorporation of Mexico, with its much smaller and less developed economy, its authoritarian political system, its weaker environmental protections, its lax enforcement of legislation, and its much poorer population immediately provoked the opposition of domestic interest groups in the United States, many of whom wanted to discuss the 'harmonization' of policies and standards and therefore expanded the terms of the debate. The differences in the ways that public policies are decided in each country also helped to forge a transnational arena. While in Mexico there was never any question that NAFTA would be ratified by the Mexican Senate, in the United States the executive could not ensure the outcome of the vote in the US Congress. This made the US Congress the site where NAFTA—and Mexico's economic and political future—would be decided. It also meant that congressional representatives were subject to political pressure by interest groups and constituencies, including Mexican governmental and non-governmental actors. The lack of a democratic debate within

Mexico pushed Mexican citizens' groups into the US political arena as well. In addition, the more traditional power asymmetry in the relationship between the US and Mexico has meant that the 'domestic' policies that become subject to negotiation tend to be Mexican ones (or Canadian ones) rather than those in the United States.[13]

The new transnational political arena created by the NAFTA process is therefore one in which (*a*) contacts and alliances have emerged among citizens' groups in the three countries on a range of issues; (*b*) new resources have become available to the Mexican groups, including the networks and resources of their international allies, and the possibility of funding from international sources; (*c*) the US Congress and the US public have developed a heightened awareness of Mexican issues; (*d*) the number of Mexican non-governmental organizations has expanded and they have come to play a larger role both within Mexican society and in the international arena (especially in the case of human rights, environmental, and pro-democracy groups); (*e*) some groups (such as the labor movement) have adopted new strategies in their own struggles that incorporate a transnational element.

The Transnational Arena and Labor Strategies

This section will focus on some of the actions and strategies that have developed among US, Canadian, and Mexican labor organizations. Cross-border contacts and transnational strategies have taken place among an array of groups, as was mentioned above. Nonetheless, transnational strategies among labor unions have been among the most difficult and, in some ways, among the most important. Cooperation between US and Mexican labor organizations has been difficult because of a history of mistrust, misunderstanding, and ignorance, but also because for many in the labor movement, NAFTA involved a zero-sum game in which US job losses were viewed as Mexico's job gains (Browne *et al.* 1994, ch. 3). At the same time, the principal labor organizations in Mexico, such as the Confederation of Mexican Workers (CTM), refused to oppose the Salinas government on the NAFTA issue, making it difficult for US and Mexican unions to find common ground. The relatively limited political autonomy of most Mexican trade unions was another important factor restricting their ability to adopt a more critical position.[14] Labor

---

[13]   Although the institutions established by NAFTA permit any one of the parties to file complaints or review the practices of any other, it remains to be seen how they will be used. It is also worth noting that foreign involvement in domestic politics can work both ways: the Salinas government actively opposed the November 1994 ballot initiative in California, Proposition 187, which would deny educational and non-emergency medical services to undocumented immigrants. Mexican government officials contacted Hispanic-American groups working against the proposition, prepared an advertising campaign reminding Californians of Mexicans' contributions to the state, and declared that they would hire lawyers to help fight the initiative in the US courts should it pass (Golden 1994*b*).

[14]   See Cook (1995) for a more detailed discussion of political constraints on Mexican unions under the Salinas administration.

actions have been especially important in the NAFTA context because so much of the debate surrounding NAFTA has centered on the 'labor question'—whether US workers would be forced to compete for jobs with Mexican workers on the basis of lower wages, lax enforcement of labor legislation, and greater restrictions on union autonomy and militancy.

Whereas past efforts by US labor organizations to engage in international solidarity have produced mixed results at best, it is important to ask in what ways the current context generated by NAFTA alters the prospects for political action and facilitates new strategies in this transnational arena.[15] The globalization of the economy and the formation of regional trading blocs provide an incentive for the resurgence of labor internationalism, even though numerous obstacles persist, and domestic political factors and institutions continue to weigh heavily on the actions and strategic decisions of labor movements.[16] Nonetheless, regional economic integration may make cross-border actions more politically feasible and palatable to union memberships than in the past. Meanwhile, the formation of regional economic blocs in Europe, South America, and North America has reopened the debate on whether and how to engage in cross-national collaboration on labor strategies.[17]

A number of cross-national activities in the labor arena have emerged in recent years. These vary in terms of their objectives and the nature of their collaboration with counterparts. Some of them are reviewed here.

TRANSNATIONAL COLLECTIVE BARGAINING

This strategy involves cross-border cooperation in bargaining with a common multinational employer. While there are numerous cases of cross-border solidarity between unions, more concerted strategizing is rare. Nonetheless, one case

[15] For critical accounts of past cases of labor internationalism, see Buchanan (1990) and Wedin (1991). On the Mexican experience, see Middlebrook (1992), Carr (1993, 1995), and Browne and Sims (1993).

[16] Denis McShane, of the International Metalworkers' Federation, has argued that international labor activity has changed, becoming increasingly horizontal rather than vertical: 'The traditional pyramid organization of unions with international contacts carefully controlled and monitored at the very peak runs counter to the most useful forms of international contacts which are horizontal between workers employed by the same company (or industry) in different countries. Fax, E-mail, and cheap travel also will encourage horizontal network building which contrasts with traditional trade union activity. Thus, the new development of international trade unionism will pose a challenge to existing trade union structures and international communications linkages', in 'Eight Theses on Trade Union Internationalism', presentation to Research Workshop on 'Democratic Institutions and Development in the Transition to a New International Order: The Role of Trade Unions', Graduate School of International Relations and Pacific Studies, University of California, San Diego, June 1991.

[17] For a discussion of cross-national labor collaboration in Europe, see Turner (forthcoming); on labor actions in Mercosur, see de Freitas Barbosa and Candia Veiga (1994), and Portella de Castro (1995).

that has received recent attention is that of the Farm Labor Organizing Committee (FLOC), an AFL-CIO affiliate, and the Sinaloa-based National Farm Workers' Union (Sindicato Nacional de Trabajadores Agrícolas, SNTOAC), a CTM affiliate (Nauman 1993: 14; Moody and McGinn 1992; Browne *et al.* 1994: 48; La Botz 1994: 9–10).[18] Both have agreed to work together to improve conditions in each union by assisting each other in collective negotiations with their employer, Campbell's Soup Company. According to union leaders, this strategy has proven effective in increasing wages and benefits for members in both countries, although Mexican wages remain far lower than those of their US counterparts.[19]

The FLOC took the initiative to locate its Mexican counterpart in 1987, well before NAFTA had even been contemplated, in response to Campbell's threat to buy its tomato paste from Mexico if US workers made it 'too expensive' to do so in the USA. The US union then developed a strategy that consisted of improving conditions for Mexican workers so that the company could not use the disparity in costs against US workers. Through AFL-CIO contacts, the FLOC approached CTM patriarch Fidel Velázquez to secure his assistance in contacting the SNTOAC, and obtained support from both the CTM and AFL-CIO to set up a commission for ongoing talks between the two unions. This national-level support appears to have been important in making this transnational cooperation successful. Baldemar Velásquez, president of the FLOC, explains his union's strategy: 'Let's look at it that we are becoming less citizens of the nations in which we are born, and look upon ourselves as citizens of the companies that we work for. So what we're dealing with is the development of that international worker community' (La Botz 1994: 10).

TRANSNATIONAL ORGANIZING

Some initial cases of US–Mexican cooperation in union organizing have also taken place, most notably in the *maquila* industry along the border. The *maquila* sector has the lowest union density of any other manufacturing activity in Mexico. Where unions do operate in the *maquila*, these tend to be dominated by the official confederations (Confederación de los Trabajadores Mexicanos (CTM), Confederación Revolucionaria de Obreros y Campesinos (CROC), and Confederación Regional Obrera Mexicana (CROM)). Due to the relatively high percentage of non-unionized plants, this sector is perhaps the most open to organizing. However, many obstacles remain: employers discourage unions, the workers themselves may even shun them, and the official unions can be extremely powerful and effective at stamping out any efforts to organize workers into more independent or democratic unions.[20]

Nonetheless, one independent labor federation in Mexico has begun to try to

---

[18] For a history of the Farm Labor Organizing Committee, see Barger and Reza (1994).

[19] Here the unions have been pushing for wage 'parity' by comparing the relationship between wages and cost-of-living in each country.

[20] On unionization in the *maquiladora* sector, see Carrillo (1991); Williams and Passé-Smith (1992); and Hualde (1994).

make inroads into the *maquiladora* sector. This is a relatively small labor federation, the Authentic Labor Front (Frente Auténtico del Trabajo, FAT), that has been extremely active in the transnational arena. In Mexico, it is one of the founding members of the Mexican Action Network on Free Trade (Red Mexicana de Acción Frente al Libre Comercio, RMALC), a network of approximately 100 citizens' and labor groups formed to critically evaluate the NAFTA process and to propose alternatives to NAFTA. In 1992, the FAT and the United Electrical, Radio, and Machine Workers of America (UE) entered into what they called a 'strategic organizing alliance'. They decided to cooperate in organizing *maquila* workers, targeting those runaway plants that had employed UE-represented shops in the USA (Witt 1992; Browne and Sims 1993: 5). Although the unions involved are relatively small and the results are so far mixed, the alliance has received a great deal of publicity and has inspired other forms of direct assistance to Mexican unions.

Some indication that transnational organizing is occurring in the agricultural sector has also appeared recently. As part of their cooperative strategy, both the FLOC and the SNTOAC (mentioned above) were working to organize non-union farm labor in Texas and in south-central Mexico. The International Brotherhood of Teamsters was also contacting employees of US-based agricultural industries in Mexico's south-central farm belt (Moody and McGinn 1992). Teamsters Local 912 from California was especially active in collaborating with Mexican employees of Green Giant, which transferred its vegetable canning and packing operations from Watsonville to Mexico.

US unions have also launched 'adopt an organizer' campaigns to support union organizers that have been fired for their organizing work. The program, begun by the San Diego-based Support Committee for Maquiladora Workers, funds Mexican workers who devote themselves full-time to organizing in the border plants. US unions involved in the campaign so far include the UE, Teamsters, and UAW locals. Thus far the program has been targeted at a Zenith electronics assembly plant in Reynosa and at the Ford plant in Cuautitlán, among others (NAWWN 1993: 10; Kalmijn 1994).

TRANSNATIONAL SOLIDARITY

This strategy encompasses different kinds of activities, from participation in trinational meetings to solidarity actions in response to specific conflicts, to speaking tours and site visits. In recent years, labor organizations throughout the continent have engaged in activities of this type. For most these contacts are a starting-point, leading to closer cooperation with counterparts and to the adoption of one of the transnational strategies outlined above. For others, visits and meetings do not lead to more frequent communication. In any case, the number of contacts that has occurred is significant, especially when one considers the sparse communication among Canadian, US, and Mexican unions prior to 1990, especially at the grass-roots level.

For many, a series of trinational exchanges that brought together leaders and representatives from a broad range of unions and non-labor organizations provided the initial contact with counterparts across the border. In these trinational meetings, participants discussed free trade, what positions groups should adopt, and whether and how they should cooperate in defending their interests (see Eisenstadt 1993).[21] Participants stressed that the NAFTA did not only represent a threat to jobs, wages, and working conditions, but that it was also an opportunity to develop trinational connections in order to help shape the continuing process of integration (Trinational Exchange 1991: 3). In the first meeting, the Mexican side included top representatives from some of the principal labor organizations in Mexico, including the telephone workers, the electrical workers, the airline pilots' association, and the teachers' union, as well as representatives of the FAT and of the CTM. This meeting marked one of the first in which both official and independent union representatives appeared together. From the labor movement on the US side were representatives from the Communications Workers of America (CWA), United Auto Workers (UAW), Amalgamated Clothing and Textile Workers' Union (ACTWU), International Ladies Garment Workers' Union (ILGWU), the AFL-CIO, the Coalition for Justice in the Maquiladoras, the International Union of Electrical Workers (IUE), and the Farm Labor Organizing Committee.

Several intra-industry meetings have also been set up in the auto sector, including one by the Chrysler-Ramos Arizpe union and the CTM, to which US and Canadian unions were invited (Middlebrook 1992), and another sponsored by the Transnationals Information Exchange (TIE), held in Mexico in 1991. At the TIE meeting, auto workers from the Big Three (Chrysler, Ford, and General Motors) discussed developing action plans by company and formed a trinational committee to coordinate industry-wide cooperation and networking (Moody and McGinn 1992). The Mexican Telephone Workers' Union (Sindicato de Telefonistas de la República Mexicana, STRM) also signed an agreement with the US Communications Workers of America and the Communications and Electrical Workers of Canada pledging to defend worker rights in the face of regional integration and to exchange information on changes in their industry.[22] Canadian, US, and Mexican electrical workers' unions met in Mexico in February 1994 to discuss common concerns. This meeting was especially significant given that the International Brotherhood of Electrical Workers (IBEW) and the Sindicato Mexicano de Electricistas (SME) carry more clout in their respective countries than either the UE or the FAT.[23]

Labor conflicts at US auto plants in Mexico have drawn the attention of the UAW and the AFL-CIO and have led them to lodge complaints about the handling of such conflicts. Among the most important of these cases has been the ongoing

[21] An outgrowth of these trinational meetings was a NAFTA congress held in Mexico in 1991 at the same time as official negotiations on the agreement were taking place, sponsored by the Mexican Action Network on Free Trade, during which a social charter was developed (RMALC 1992).
[22] A copy of the agreement is reprinted in *Latin American Labor News*, 5 (1992), 7.
[23] 'SourceMex—Economic News and Analysis on Mexico', Latin America Data Base, Latin American Institute, University of New Mexico, 5/7 (16 Feb. 1994).

series of conflicts at the Ford plant in Cuautitlán, outside of Mexico City. In 1990, the struggle over union representation left one worker dead at the hands of hired thugs who ambushed workers at the plant.[24] The case revealed the collusion of the Mexican government, Ford Motor Company, and the CTM in the repression of labor dissent and of union democracy in Mexican plants.[25] The publicity this case received and the degree of solidarity shown by US unions was unprecedented. The Canadian Auto Workers and some UAW locals lent their support by publicizing the events in their own countries, pressuring government officials to complain about the matter, and by organizing a trinational day of protest in which workers wore black ribbons on the anniversary of the Mexican auto worker's death. The UAW locals in St Paul and in Kansas City, Missouri, were especially active in organizing support for Cuautitlán workers; they formed a Mexico–US–Canada Solidarity Task Force and sent members to Mexico to witness union elections in 1991. The national UAW, meanwhile, was initially reluctant to engage in a nationwide campaign (Browne and Sims 1993: 6). These UAW locals and other US groups continue to follow events at Ford-Cuautitlán; with the help of the North American Worker-to-Worker Network and electronic networks, supporters have begun to adopt the kinds of international action campaigns (telegrams to Mexican labor authorities and political leaders) that Amnesty International has long engaged in to draw attention to human rights violations around the world (NAWWN 1993: 26).[26]

In the Cuautitlán case, solidarity focused primarily on supporting Mexican auto workers in their fight for union democracy rather than on trying to engage in collaborative collective bargaining or promote other kinds of demands, such as wage increases (Middlebrook 1992). Such demonstrations of solidarity nonetheless annoyed the Mexican government and the CTM, both of which threatened the workers and pressured them to abandon their external alliances.[27] In subsequent bargaining with Ford, however, the Cuautitlán union was able to draw on the added leverage gained through these alliances. It agreed not to enlist the help of US allies if Ford would meet some of its demands during collective bargaining. Authorities have discouraged auto workers at the Ford plants in Chihuahua and Hermosillo from adopting similar forms of cooperation with US allies (Middlebrook 1992).

In another case from the auto industry, workers from the Volkswagen plant in Puebla, Mexico, enjoyed the support of their German counterparts during a long strike in 1987. The German workers refused to step up production to compensate for the loss due to the strike in Mexico (Garza and Méndez 1987*b*). This solidarity helped the union to escape the fate that befell other auto unions in that year.

[24] For an account of this case, see La Botz (1992), and Americas Watch (1990: 67–70).

[25] See *La otra cara de México*, 21 (May–June 1991), 4–5.

[26] In a post-NAFTA-vote strategy session, the North American Worker to Worker Network, a coalition of local unions and labor-related NGOs, decided to support independent union organizing in Mexico through a variety of tactics, including an Emergency Response Network of people who would send faxes, telegrams, and take out newspaper ads in the event of illegal firings or harassment of Mexican independent labor organizers.

[27] La Botz (1992); 'Weekly Commentary', *ARKA Mexico Report*, 21 Aug. 1992.

Managers at the Ford-Cuautitlán auto plant, for example, fired the workers during a strike, closed down the plant, and later reopened, rehiring some of the workforce at lower benefit and wage levels and with new work rules (Garza and Méndez 1987a; Middlebrook 1989: 86, 92). However, workers at Volkswagen were finally defeated during their 1992 strike when confronted with these same tactics (Nauman 1992; Othón Quiroz and Méndez 1992).

During a strike in 1990 at the Modelo Brewery, Teamsters in Chicago supported the strike by refusing to deliver shipments of the imported beer. A boycott of the product saw limited success in the United States, but was somewhat more successful in Canada and Europe. The Modelo workers belonged to a CTM-affiliated union, and their enlistment of foreign support drew the wrath of Fidel Velázquez, who also did everything in his power to defeat the strike (La Botz 1992). Other solidarity actions included a corporate campaign by Teamsters Local 912 against Green Giant products in cooperation with striking Mexican employees of the company (Moody and McGinn 1992: 48).

The number of site visits and other kinds of exchanges and collaboration that have occurred in recent years are too numerous to mention here, but some examples include the establishment of US and Mexican 'sister schools', arranged between US teachers and Mexican teachers belonging to the National Coordinating Committee of Education Workers, a large dissident current within the National Teachers' Union (Witt 1992). Announcements for tours to Mexico for US labor groups and others cover the pages of publications such as the *Free Trade Mailing*, and the Detroit-based *Labor Notes* sponsored a Cross-Border Organizing Conference on the Mexican border in May 1994.

The *maquiladora* sector has received particularly strong attention since NAFTA was approved by the US Congress in November 1993. One *maquiladora* in Tijuana, Plásticos Bajacal (a division of Boston-based Carlisle Plastics), first received publicity prior to the NAFTA vote when a bus of US union activists and observers tried to visit the plant and were turned away by the management. In December 1994 human rights and union observers witnessed union elections at the *maquiladora* plant. The company had signed a contract with a union affiliated with the Regional Confederation of Mexican Workers (CROM); workers only learned of the existence of this union once they sought to organize themselves under the auspices of another labor organization, the Revolutionary Labor Confederation (COR). During the representation election, workers were forced to vote out in the open and in the presence of managers, and made to sign their names beside their vote. US observers expressed shock and frustration at what they witnessed. Elections were finally halted because it was feared that plant managers would retaliate against the dissident workers. US observers felt that by publicizing the case, they were at least able to prevent retaliation against the COR supporters (Bacon 1993; Kalmijn 1994).

Two other cases that received much publicity in the USA during the winter of 1993–4 were the firings of workers who had been trying to organize a union at a General Electric *maquiladora* plant in Ciudad Juárez and at Honeywell in Chihuahua.

In both cases, the organization trying to organize the workers was the independent FAT. Its allies in the USA, the UE and the Teamsters, reacted quickly to the firings. UE leaders wrote to the US Congress and pressed General Electric to reverse its position. Teamsters began carrying out leafleting campaigns at US General Electric plants. In January 1994, the unions finally succeeded in getting General Electric to reinstate six of eleven workers who had been fired in Ciudad Juárez. Efforts continued to force the company to reinstate the remaining fired workers. Teamsters president Ron Carey wrote President Bill Clinton, warning him that unless the labor violations at the Honeywell and General Electric plants were resolved, they could become 'an international symbol of the violations of human rights now that NAFTA has passed'.[28]

Perhaps most significant, on 15 February 1994, the UE and Teamsters became the first unions to file complaints to the new National Administrative Office (NAO) set up under the terms of the NAFTA labor side agreement (Rose 1994: A2). The US unions argued that by firing the union organizers, GE and Honeywell were violating the spirit of the trade agreement. In April the NAO responded by indicating that it would indeed review the complaints. This set an important precedent, especially given that the labor side accord had been criticized by labor advocates for its failure to include freedom of association and the right to organize, to strike, and to bargain collectively among those rights whose violation could subject a country to trade sanctions or to the withdrawal of NAFTA privileges.[29] (Such penalties can be applied only in the case of persistent violations of domestic labor legislation in the areas of child labor, minimum wage, and occupational health and safety.) Nonetheless, after conducting a preliminary hearing the NAO stated that it would not pursue the complaints filed by the US unions. During the hearing the Secretary of the NAO steered the spotlight away from the conduct of US corporations in Mexico to the issue of Mexican government enforcement of labor legislation and found that the NAO could not conclude that Mexico had failed to enforce its labor laws (US National Administrative Office 1995). While US corporations had condemned the NAO's decision to hear the cases in the first place, they applauded the focus adopted during the hearing. Labor unions, of course, were disappointed. Teamsters president Ron Carey said, 'The process set up by the NAFTA labor side agreement shows that fair trade was a false promise' (Bureau of National Labor Affairs 1994; *Inside NAFTA* 1994).[30]

---

[28] 'SourceMex—Economic News and Analysis on Mexico', Latin America Data Base, Latin American Institute, University of New Mexico, 5/7 (16 Feb. 1994).

[29] For a discussion of the review mechanisms set up under the NAFTA labor side accord see Compa (1995).

[30] Subsequent filings, however, moved beyond these first cases. In August 1994, a group of Mexican and US organizations filed a complaint against a Sony plant in Nuevo Laredo (Davis 1994). This case, which also concerned the issues of association and the right to organize, moved through the NAO review process to the point of ministerial consultations, the highest level to which complaints over these issues can proceed (US National Administrative Office 1995). In Feb. 1995, the Mexican telephone workers' union also filed a complaint with the Mexican NAO regarding Sprint's firing of workers during a union organizing drive in San Francisco (Pattee 1995).

POLITICAL BARGAINING IN THE TRANSNATIONAL ARENA

Another strategy that some labor groups have adopted involves political bargaining in the transnational arena. This strategy was directly linked to the NAFTA
debate, and involved both direct and indirect lobbying of US congressional representatives by Mexican groups. Indirect lobbying occurred through the exchange
of information and networking with US-based organizations, which then lobbied
members of Congress. Direct efforts included congressional testimony by individuals
and representatives of Mexican groups who reported on conditions for workers
in Mexico. The strategy was largely aimed at defeating NAFTA in the US Congress
and with the US public, although it also helped to secure support for side agreements and consideration of compensation mechanisms for likely 'losers' of free
trade.

At the same time, because of the Mexican government's sensitivity to outside criticism, Mexican coalitions such as the Mexican Action Network were able
to gain access to their own government because of the attention they received and
the role they played in the US debate on NAFTA. Under circumstances in which
the Network would not otherwise have played much of a political role within the
country, its use of transnational spaces gave it greater leverage within national boundaries. To the extent that the Network has played a role in providing information
about Mexican labor and environmental conditions to unions and other groups
in the United States and to the US Congress, it has also acted indirectly to reform
domestic politics in Mexico. This is so because the Mexican government acted to
pre-empt criticism of Mexican practices and to address the concerns of those in
the Congress who would decide NAFTA's fate.

Popular Sector Strategies in a Transnational Political Arena: Future Prospects

Several questions emerge in considering how the future evolution of a transnational
political arena is likely to affect popular sector strategies in the NAFTA era. Here
again it is important to distinguish between two phases: (1) the period prior to the
vote in the US Congress on 17 November 1993; and (2) the period after the vote,
and especially after 1 January 1994, when the NAFTA formally took effect (the
NAFTA era).

WILL CROSS-BORDER COALITIONS SURVIVE INTO THE NAFTA ERA?

A first question that emerges is whether the groups that formed during the NAFTA
debate process will survive into the post-NAFTA-vote era. The NAFTA debate
clearly signaled the coming together of diverse single-issue groups and networks

to influence the NAFTA process. The coalitions that were forged were therefore often loose and contained at times conflicting and competing interests (Trinational Exchange 1991). The split that occurred between US labor and environmental groups and within the environmental camp when the side agreements were announced was one example of the kinds of schisms that existed. It is reasonable to believe, therefore, that after the NAFTA vote these loose coalitions would drift apart, each organization tending again to its particular area of interest and to issues long neglected by the anti-NAFTA campaign.

A smaller number of groups may succeed in shifting their focus and their strategies toward monitoring the effects of NAFTA and even toward trying to extend ties to similar networks in the rest of Latin America.[31] A few new groups may emerge as well in the USA and Canada to monitor and support causes in Mexico, perhaps building on earlier contacts. Other organizations may find also that contacts initiated during the debate phase will lead to collaboration in the redefinition of more long-term strategies.

Human rights and environmental issues may continue to receive strong attention by international allies in conjunction with Mexican NGOs. The prior existence of these particular issue-area networks and the existence of multiple Mexican organizations dealing with these issues point to the likelihood of continued collaboration. Labor rights and democracy questions may still be more difficult, however. In the case of the former, strong control over and protection of this arena on the part of both the Mexican government and official trade unions in Mexico may complicate efforts to shed light on labor rights violations. During negotiations between the three governments on the labor side accord, Mexican government officials made it very clear that they considered the labor question to be a national sovereignty issue; the resulting agreement was noticeably weak on labor protections. This, combined with the resistance of US companies in Mexico, may make it more difficult for US and Mexican allies to advance in this arena, even though the few steps that have been taken so far are significant. More open intervention in support of democracy in Mexico has also been complicated, as evidenced by the considerable debate surrounding the issue of whether or not to permit foreign election observers in 1994.[32]

WILL THE RESPONSE TO CHIAPAS BE REPRESENTATIVE OF POLITICS IN THE NAFTA ERA?

The Chiapas uprising represented the first NAFTA-era political crisis. For this reason, it is important to note how domestic and international groups mobilized

[31] Indeed, one of the leaders of the Mexican Action Network mentioned these as the new tasks the anti-NAFTA coalitions would try to adopt (personal communication, Mexico City, 13 Jan. 1994).

[32] A category called 'invited foreign visitors' was finally devised in 1994. Approximately 1,000 foreigners came to observe the 1994 elections, the great majority of them from the United States.

in response to it. Domestic and international human rights, environmental, labor, and indigenous groups reacted quickly to the government and military actions in Chiapas. Mexican intellectuals and analysts carried on an important debate in the national press and forged a consensus around peaceful negotiations. The anti-NAFTA coalition in the US Congress was also mobilized, as were congressional representatives who had voted for NAFTA but who were alarmed that Chiapas might signal the advent of widespread political instability in Mexico, contrary to what many NAFTA supporters had predicted. Several congressional representatives traveled to Chiapas on fact-finding tours, and once again hearings on Mexican political affairs were held in Washington, DC. Meanwhile, Mexican political parties reached an agreement on a series of electoral reforms, raising the possibility of fair presidential elections in August 1994 for the first time. While it is certainly true that the catalyst for political reform was the events in Chiapas, and not NAFTA itself, the NAFTA era has introduced new interests and new forces that may have permanently altered the environment in which Mexican politics unfolds.[33]

Throughout 1994–5 the Mexican government also found itself caught in the midst of a political and economic transition, and therefore more vulnerable not only to US criticism (whose influence may indeed be less after the NAFTA vote), but principally to domestic pressures, in an interesting reversal of the pre-NAFTA-vote period.[34] The political context of the presidential succession and the Chiapas rebellion made the government especially vulnerable and gave citizens' groups increased bargaining leverage. Thus, while the new political environment of the NAFTA era did not necessarily create the government's crisis, it certainly may have added to the regime's vulnerability and to domestic groups' leverage.

A second question, then, is whether the intense spotlight on Mexican domestic politics and the activation of international networks that was witnessed in the immediate wake of the Chiapas uprising will remain permanent features of NAFTA-era politics. The Chiapas rebellion, political assassinations, and the presidential elections focused high levels of attention on Mexico during NAFTA's first year. Whether this heightened level of attention and intensity of interaction will persist after the presidential elections is difficult to answer at this time.[35] In any case, what the pre-NAFTA-vote period facilitated was the creation of transnational networks and the generation of a transnational political arena. The Chiapas uprising, coming as soon

---

[33]   For further elaboration of this argument, see Heredia (1994). For additional discussion on the relationship between NAFTA and democratization in Mexico, see P. Smith (1992) and R. Pastor (1992).

[34]   See the remarks of Mexican Deputy Foreign Secretary Andrés Rozental, in response to the congressional hearing convened by US Representative Robert Torricelli to determine whether the Mexican army had committed human rights abuses in Chiapas: 'The implementation of the North American Free Trade Agreement does not give anyone outside Mexico the right to sit in judgment on matters that Mexicans are solely responsible for resolving' ('Mexico Tells U.S. to Stop Meddling', *San Francisco Chronicle*, 4 Feb. 1994, p. 14A).

[35]   This chapter was written prior to the 1994 peso devaluation: an analysis of transnational interaction during the ensuing economic crisis is therefore beyond its scope.

as it did after the NAFTA vote, may have helped to consolidate these networks and to underscore their importance. Whether or not these same levels of attention are witnessed on a permanent basis, the contacts, alliances, and networks could well be in place to spring into action again should another crisis event call for it.

WHAT DIFFERENCE WILL INSTITUTIONALIZATION, OR THE LACK OF IT, MAKE?

A third question is how the presence or lack of institutionalization is likely to affect popular sector politics in a transnational arena. As mentioned earlier, NAFTA involves a relatively limited degree of institutional innovation. Among the institutions to be created under the trade agreement are the NAFTA trade commission, two secretariats (one for labor and one for the environment), National Administrative Offices (NAOs) in each country, a border commission, and the North American Development Bank. The key question for this discussion is how the environmental and labor secretariats and the NAOs will operate, and whether they will serve to complicate or to complement the efforts by grassroots organizations. As discussed above for the case of labor, the results thus far have been mixed, although it is perhaps still too early to tell what the full impact of the labor side accord will be. At the same time it is important to recognize that the procedures for filing complaints with the NAO, which require that allegations of rights violations in one country be presented before the NAO of another country, encourage cross-border collaboration. Since the labor side accord removes some of the most controversial issues (such as the right to organize, to strike, and to collective bargaining) from the scope of sanctionable violations, it may be that these kinds of rights issues must still be handled primarily through other forms of political pressure and popular-sector organizing, with the use of the institutional channels established under NAFTA serving as a complementary strategy. The use of both strategies, then, may well foster further transnational popular sector cooperation.

The relative lack of institutionalization could affect popular sector groups involved in transnational political strategies in another way. So much of what has occurred in the way of cross-border contacts has been based on the undertakings of committed activists and local union leaders, who are subject to burnout and removal, and on organizations with relatively limited resources. An important question here is the extent to which external funding for Mexico support work (for organizations in the USA and Canada) and international financing of popular organizations and NGOs in Mexico will become available. In the 1980s, a number of private foundations supported US organizations in their solidarity work with Central American groups. Will Mexico-related support work be the new focus of foundation aid in the 1990s?

Conclusion

In spite of the perceived (and real) limitations that the implementation of free trade agreements implies for popular sector groups, this chapter has argued that such regional free trade agreements may also expand the strategic options and political opportunities available to these groups through the simultaneous generation of a transnational political arena. All movements toward regional free trade appear to involve some degree of compromise of national sovereignty, as well as provide some incentive for cross-border collaboration among non-state actors. It may well be, however, that the particular characteristics of North American regional integration and of the circumstances in which the debate over NAFTA took place have generated an especially unique transnational political space in the region. The tremendous political, economic, and cultural asymmetry between the United States and Mexico helped to drive US, Canadian, and Mexican non-state actors across national boundaries in their search for allies to combat an agreement that they viewed as harmful to their interests. The alliances and networks built during this period prior to the NAFTA vote may help to make transnational politics a permanent feature of the NAFTA era, although the visibility and intensity of transnational political interaction may now assume lower levels most of the time.

The advantage of interacting in the transnational political arena for popular sector groups that are strongly constrained by national politics in what they can achieve is that they may be able to obtain greater bargaining leverage in dealing with their own governments. Whether, in the Mexican case, the ability to do so is made more permanent as a result of NAFTA or whether time and institutionalization will overtake cross-border grassroots mobilization efforts remains to be seen. What appears clear at this point is that in the complex process of economic and political change that lies at the core of the globalization of the economy and the fashioning of regional trade agreements, there are opportunities to be found. Part of the necessary task, then, is to think of new ways to conceptualize these changes so that these opportunities can be seized more readily.

Conclusion

22 | Associative Networks: New Structures of Representation for the Popular Sectors?

Douglas A. Chalmers, Scott B. Martin, and Kerianne Piester[1]

After an extended absence, the 'social question' has returned to Latin America. In contrast to the early decades of this century, however, a rising and seemingly inexorable tide of popular mobilization is not evident. Strikingly, revolutionary proposals are nowhere to be found, even though democratization, guided by an ascendant neoliberalism, thus far has dashed the widespread expectations for social justice that it raised. Occasional, sometimes large-scale street demonstrations against particular anti-popular reforms or corrupt public officials continue to dot the region's political landscape, to be sure, as popular frustration bubbles up spasmodically. Yet, there are few signs of a sustained, broad-based popular movement against neoliberalism, and much less around an alternative project. Guerrilla movements exist in a few countries, but they are either politically isolated or, like the Zapatistas in Mexico, they have used arms not to seize power but to create new opportunities for peaceful political change. Most disturbing of all, as Carlos Vilas so eloquently details in the introduction, violence is rife in many parts of the region and large numbers of its poorest citizens—whether out of hope or fear—recently have cast their electoral lot with neoliberal reformers.

Despite the dramatic absence of unified popular political 'subjects', social concerns have crept back onto the Latin American political agenda. 'Fighting poverty' —if not inequality—has become good politics even for neoliberal reformers. International development institutions have highlighted basic needs; state financial managers need to prevent popular outbursts to avoid scaring off volatile in-flows of foreign capital; and old-fashioned political expediency has its role.

If one views popular politics through an interpretive lens that looks beyond electoral contests and mass movements (or their absence), moreover, encouraging

[1] We wish to acknowledge the very helpful comments of our fellow editors as well as Robert Kaufman, Daniel Mato, Al Montero, Eric Hershberg, and the members of the Workshop on Identities, Institutions, and Representation of the Center for the Social Sciences and of the Latin America Ph.D. group, both at Columbia University.

recent signs of dynamism are ample. Many of the studies in this book point to new activity—the transformation of corporatist structures by innovative unionists in Brazil and Argentina; the reconfiguration of ties between left parties and popular movements in Venezuela and Mexico; experiments in participatory local governance under left parties in Brazil and Uruguay; and new forms of representation in social policy-making in Ecuador and Mexico. These examples reflect a trend toward a reconstruction of popular participation—redefining the identities and issues around which the popular sectors organize—and a reconfiguration of popular representation—reordering the structures through which they gain a voice in centers of political power and through which others seek to shape and control them.[2] Activists and poor people continue to 'imagine' new causes and identities (like indigenous rights or environmental protection), organize fitfully around them, and engage with public authorities in novel and proactive ways. Such developments attest to the continued capacity for reinvention of popular politics, even in hostile environments.

In this concluding chapter, we seek both to build on and look beyond the studies in this volume to sketch the outlines of an emerging model of representation. Our analytical point of departure is the notion that the ongoing reorganization and reinsertion of the popular sectors into the political process has not followed the classic model of popular incorporation in the post-Depression era. Nor does it conform to the various versions of the class-based model that popular and left leaders long espoused. Nor do conventional visions of 'modern societies' such as the liberal-pluralist framework capture or explain these new developments. Rather, we detect important signs of movement—incipient and partial, but real—towards new and substantially different structures of popular representation that we will characterize as 'associative networks'.

In order to explain how some of the developments described in this book point to a nascent type of popular representation, we first discuss the 'old' types through a schematic periodization. The first is the period of 'popular sector incorporation', lasting roughly from the 1930s to the 1960s, which was marked by the political 'coming of age' of the popular sectors and their decisive incorporation into national polities. The conditions and outcomes varied from country to country (Collier and Collier 1991) but the fact of incorporation was a constant. 'Decomposition', the second period beginning roughly in the 1960s, saw a process of either gradual erosion or dramatic dismantling of popular sector ties with the state. This is followed

---

[2] Although the term 'representation' points to the bottom-up qualities of making claims, these structures are always simultaneously channels for top-down processes of securing compliance, often through control. We mean always to refer to both dimensions. For popular actors (or any other actor for that matter), representation involves having access to decision-making processes and thus being 'heard' and 'taken into account', but not necessarily that their views or positions are reflected in the final policy outcome. In this sense, representation does not necessarily yield 'representative' outcomes, for it is inherently a process of *mediation* among competing interests, demands, and claims.

by the period of our main concern, spanning roughly the last decade, when a 'recomposition' of ties began to occur.

Based on an analysis of these periods and drawing upon the existing literature, we identify four ideal types of structures of representation central to the incorporation period—'clientelist', 'populist', 'corporatist', and 'mass-mobilizational'. The new trends differ from all of these in (1) being less tied to a single national structure of power and in (2) placing more emphasis on ties resulting from decisions to associate. Drawing on the empirical evidence from our cases and recent theoretical developments outside the study of Latin American politics, we propose a fifth type of structure of representation—the 'associative network'. Such a network links state and societal actors—sometimes including popular ones—through interpersonal, media, and/or interorganizational ties. Multiple networks process and reshape contending political claims through relatively open-ended and problem-focused interactions. They are distinctive not only in the way they link people with decision-making centers, but also by their multiplicity and relatively rapid reconfiguration over time.

Popular sectors are not the only the actors nor the most powerful within many associative networks. Indeed, some networks are created without their participation. However, popular participation in them seems to be increasing and, as we explain below, there are reasons why elites draw them in.

We attribute the rise of these more variegated and less centralized structures of representation to fundamental changes in global and domestic conditions and related shifts in the strategies of elites and popular actors. Especially crucial has been the dispersion of decision-making activity away from the centralized state of the earlier era to a more polycentric state, with multiple centers of decision-making. Associative networks are constructed around, and further the development of, these new centers.

Associative networks are transforming popular representation, but only partially as well as unequally across countries, regions, and policy arenas. The evidence is not sufficient for us to make confident statements about the degree to which this ideal-typical formulation has been approximated or realized in practice. Moreover, many poor people evidently are still linked to the polity through clientelistic and state corporatist structures and—as Panfichi suggests in his essay on Peru in this volume—a new form of populism has appeared in some countries. More seriously still, the factors explored in Carlos Vilas's introductory essay have left many individuals and groups enmeshed in situations of grinding poverty and myriad forms of violence with no effective way of engaging with, or protecting themselves from, the state.

Notwithstanding these sometimes tragic trends in the region, the evidence contained in this book leads us to conclude that there is far more movement in the direction of recomposition of popular representation through the novel forms that we propose than is perceived conventionally. Such perceptions are shared, we believe, even by those observers and participants most identified with the popular sectors, who still tend to think in terms of the recomposition of old forms, not the emergence of new ones. To be sure, substantial fragmentation and social disembeddedness continue to plague the region, but a complex evolution also is occurring that can be overlooked or dismissed as '*ad hoc*' only if we remain strictly within the confines of existing conceptual categories and analytical tools. Understanding these changes constitutes an important agenda for research.

We believe the current situation facing the popular sectors is one in which, in varying ways in different countries, associative networks slowly are becoming more relevant. These networks certainly are not inherently more democratic than the earlier forms, although they have the potential to be so. The key point, however, is that unless one understands the new forms of popular representation, it will be impossible to perceive whether progress towards democratization is occurring, or to work for it.

Reinterpreting the Historical Legacy of Popular Representation

During the populist era in Latin America, emerging patterns of popular representation were centered on a complex process of negotiation, accommodation, and confrontation between elites and the popular sectors. With time, subaltern strata were incorporated into national polities, economies, and societies as important actors (Collier and Collier 1991). Popular sector political incorporation rested on two essential conditions: (1) an expanding economy led by an interventionist state following a basic doctrine of national development and (2) a relatively harmonious—albeit temporary—fit between the political goals and strategies of elite actors, on one hand, and those of popular-sector and left leaders, on the other. Although important cross-national differences in the timing and institutionalization of incorporation existed, there was a broadly similar dynamic across all of the countries considered here except Guatemala.[3]

It is worth emphasizing the first of the two points above, the existence of a centralized, interventionist state. The state was by no means all-powerful and significant numbers of landholders, owners of extractive industries, and foreign companies, among others, retained substantial autonomy, but that autonomy was not translated into the 'colonization' of branches of government, local governments, or independent ministries. Instead, decision-making in the state was highly centralized in the hands of the President and his or her closest colleagues.

---

[3] For instance, incorporation occurred considerably earlier in Mexico, Brazil, and the Southern Cone, on one hand, than in Ecuador, Venezuela, and Peru, on the other. Moreover, Guatemala constituted a clear exception to the general rule among the countries studied here, for reformist efforts to integrate the popular sector in that Central American country were quashed decisively following the 1954 military coup.

Within a broader context of inward-oriented, state-promoted industrialization, new elites were led by a variety of motives to cultivate a political relationship with the popular sectors. The latter were believed to be an active or potential threat to political order, requiring measures to pre-empt and control. The poor also were viewed as a potentially powerful social and political base for industrialization, requiring measures to mobilize and co-opt. For their part, popular leaders sought firm relationships with emerging political elites as a propitious, and perhaps the only, way to secure access to the state. Such access was deemed crucial by these leaders not just for obtaining material and organizational benefits, but also for exercising some degree of political power and fostering progressive visions of economic and social change. Underlying the latter goals was a particular set of ideological conceptions and political practices shared by a broad spectrum of popular and left activists. In so far as state power was central to left and popular conceptions of political and economic life, political opportunism in gaining access to that state became justified and grassroots organizing was viewed largely as an instrument to gain such access. In turn, the vertical and asymmetrical nature of group–state ties tended to be replicated at the level of ties between popular leaders and 'the masses'.

Four types of structures of popular representation shaped the emerging new relationship between the popular sectors and the political systems of this era—populism, corporatism, clientelism, and political parties. Populism provided the overarching framework for appeals to a broad abstract entity, *el pueblo* or *la nación*, which cut across boundaries of class, ethnicity, gender, and region (Cardoso and Faletto 1977; Coniff 1982; Weffort and Quijano 1973). While the term 'populism' has many distinct and often competing usages (e.g. Roberts 1995), we refer to it as a personalistic relationship between leader and masses that tends to be expressed only partially in formal organizations.

Populism was often accompanied by another, more formal structure of popular representation—corporatism. This concept generally refers to structured relationships tying functionally organized groups in civil society to the state, in which the latter sanctions, oversees, and regulates group formation and activities in the former (Chalmers 1985; Collier and Collier 1977; Malloy 1977; Schmitter 1974). Latin America's state corporatism entailed few, if any, effective restrictions on dominant-class organizations like business, but strong controls on subaltern-class organizations representing workers and peasants (O'Donnell 1977).

While populism and corporatism were the central structures of popular representation, clientelism and political parties also played an important, albeit subordinate, role. Unlike corporatism, clientelism was based on direct, face-to-face encounters between individual elites and poor people characterized by little or no formal structure (Schmidt *et al.* 1977). While clientelistic practices had deep roots in earlier periods of Latin American history, they became particularly important during the populist era in mobilizing the electoral support of the poorly organized, such as recent urban migrants and peasants lying outside officially sanctioned associations. Typically, extensive patron–client networks were constructed out of many clientelistic exchanges, in which the ultimate beneficiary of the 'upward' flow of support was separated from the individuals receiving a 'downward' flow of goods and services by a series of regional and local brokers.

During the populist-corporatist era, political parties claiming to represent popular interests emerged and in many cases flourished, particularly as elections became more open and competitive. Nonetheless, parties generally played a less central role in organizing mass political participation in Latin American polities than they did in the prototypical party systems of advanced industrial democracies. In most countries under consideration here, with the major exception of Chile, parties lacked the ideological and programmatic character and well-defined class basis of their European counterparts. The mass-mobilization model long espoused on the left, whether class or more broadly based, rarely became a reality except in the opposition. Rather, parties tended to be personalistic, pragmatic, and often opportunistic. Links with popular constituents were built on varying mixtures of populist appeals and, as noted above, corporatist and clientelistic exchanges. Given the weakness of party systems and the centralization of power in the executive in many countries, parties tended to be more of an instrument for winning elections than for exercising power and mediating popular demands on an everyday basis (Chalmers 1972).

At first glance, the highly vertical and hierarchical character of these structures suggests an image of monolithic elite and state control over the popular sectors, much like that generally conveyed by studies of corporatism and incorporation in the region. To be sure, the potential for mass revolutionary uprisings was defused, at least for some time and in most of our focus countries. Yet, it is important to recognize that through the very same ties elites sought to use to encapsulate the popular sectors the latter actually found new and varied points of *access* to the political system. That is to say, through voting and partisan mobilization, corporatist and clientelistic bargaining, and relationships with populist leaders, poor people acquired an organized political voice for the first time, however limited and imperfect.

Though formally circumscribed, channels of popular representation under the classic 'populist-corporatist' model nonetheless enabled critical segments of the popular sectors to gain some leverage over elites, particularly in the more extensively industrialized countries of the region. Underlying the growth of popular sector political leverage was a style of popular demand-making and bargaining that we call 'insider pressure politics'. This style entailed the following key elements: a rhetorical emphasis on abiding loyalty to particular elites; the casting of demands in the populist language utilized and legitimized by leaders; the use of mobilization as a flexible tool alternatively to extract concessions from and express support for leaders; and, in extreme cases, threats to withdraw support or transfer it to other elites.

What are we to make of the costs and benefits for the popular sectors of this populist-corporatist model of popular representation? In recent political discourse, there is a tendency either to condemn classic popular representation for its manifest limitations or to wax nostalgic about its perceived virtues *vis-à-vis* the current state of affairs. We see truth in both views. In economic terms, benefits were selective, to be sure, generally favoring the organized working class and emerging middle strata over the unorganized poor, as well as urban-industrial over rural-agricultural interests. Yet, notwithstanding this selectivity and deepening inequalities, it is undeniable that in many countries fairly broad segments of the popular sectors gained some measure of upward social mobility through transfer payments as well as improvements in literacy, nutrition, sanitation, and health care.

In political terms, the loss of organizational autonomy and grassroots participation clearly had negative long-term consequences for the popular sectors, despite the immediate material advantages that were secured through links with the state. Nonetheless, the popular sectors acquired an important organizational presence, a crucial degree of political recognition, as well as an intangible but extremely important subjective sense—an identity—of possessing political and social rights within emerging national polities. Over time, these organizational and symbolic resources enabled popular actors increasingly to challenge and contest not only the boundaries of their incorporation, but also to some extent elite domination of the underlying political and socioeconomic systems.

THE DECOMPOSITION OF HISTORICAL STRUCTURES

From roughly the 1960s through the 1980s, various pressures contributed to what we call the decomposition of traditional, populist-era structures of representation. While we recognize that some new forms emerged and attempts were made to reform and reinvigorate old patterns during this period, the four structures of popular representation mentioned in the previous section deteriorated as channels of popular political access at a much more rapid rate than they could be reformulated or replaced by new ones. Decomposition was a gradual, though by no means steady or even, process that stemmed from pressures that were both exogenous *and* endogenous to structures of representation.

From the vantage point of the mid-1990s, it is tempting to assume that historic patterns of popular representation simply were overwhelmed by the major structural shifts that have transformed political, economic, and social systems around the globe—amounting to a sort of Latin American functional equivalent to the crisis of the Keynesian welfare state in advanced industrial countries (e.g. Offe 1984). To be sure, events and processes that are, strictly speaking, exogenous to traditional patterns of popular representation—such as military coups and governments followed by redemocratization, the end of the Cold War, economic globalization, structural adjustment and market reform, and the growing informal economy—did much to erode structures of popular representation. Yet, such structures already were experiencing considerable flux and strain *before* these global and national trends emerged. The source of these ongoing strains, evident as far back as the late 1950s in some countries, was twofold: (1) growing intra-elite rivalry and division over the political role of the popular sectors as well as (2) rising popular sector and left challenges to traditional institutions of representation. The context for these strains was growing centrifugal pressures generated by the region's model of development (O'Donnell 1973; Cardoso and Faletto 1979). We contend that it was the juxtaposition of these existing strains with subsequent 'structural' pressures—which served to exacerbate them—that together produced the decomposition of popular representation.

As suggested above, increasing pressures from below gradually began to undermine nascent or established ties of popular incorporation. Popular demands for growing wages, benefits, and rights proved difficult to accommodate. Incorporated groups became increasingly adept at playing—and pushing the limits of—insider pressure politics; groups that were excluded struggled to gain comparable access; and, all the while, economic conditions turned more and more volatile. During this period, popular leaders and their constituencies began to confront more openly the restrictive dimensions of incorporation. In part, this departure in popular sector behavior reflected strategic and ideological trends within the partisan left—namely, the decline of 'collaborationist' thinking and the rise of nationalist and radical ideologies and even guerrilla strategies, particularly following the Cuban Revolution. Together, all of these developments combined to heighten popular sector militancy and the general confrontational tone of politics.

Popular actors were not alone in challenging the established terms of their incorporation into national polities. The growing political salience of the popular sectors, along with the emerging new socioeconomic realities of state-led, dependent industrialization, also generated new dynamics among elite actors. Political and ideological divisions over the course of national development began to emerge, increasingly pitting reformers, radical nationalists, and conservatives against each other (Cohen 1994). In Brazil and the Southern Cone, where populism was most strongly rooted, an outright elite backlash against populism occurred in the form of a series of military coups between 1964 and 1976. The ensuing new authoritarian regimes closed channels of popular representation, either by dismantling popular and left organizations and the arenas in which they operated or, alternatively, by turning them into narrow instruments of coercive state control (D. Collier 1979; Schamis 1991; O'Donnell 1973). Even in those countries where existing regimes weathered similar pressures (Venezuela and Mexico) or where 'late' populist breakthroughs occurred under the auspices of reformist military regimes (Ecuador and Peru), elite counter-pressures—through coup-plotting, capital flight, and the like —narrowed the range of maneuver for distributive policies and economic nationalism. Moreover, broadly inclusionary systems, like those in Mexico and Venezuela, became more rigid, unable to accommodate smoothly the rapid expansion of social forces.

Hence, by the mid-1970s, spaces for popular representation in our focus countries could be characterized as 'forcibly closed' (under conservative military regimes), 'restricted' (under inclusionary regimes turned oligarchic), or 'nascent' and 'fragile' (under reformist military regimes). In most countries, popular representation was manifestly weak—and in some cases moribund—and had been so for a number of years when exogenous shocks, economic restructuring, and regime change subsequently began to exacerbate this process of decomposition.

Together, economic restructuring and democratization have dominated political praxis in and scholarly reflection on the region since roughly the early 1980s. Yet, it is infrequently understood that the impact of these twin processes on popular representation has been decidedly contradictory in nature. In an immediate sense, the ongoing process of decomposition reached its culmination, as major elite-dominated economic and political changes left the popular sectors more distant and disengaged from political decision-making than they ever had been since the onset of incorporation. We argue below, however, that from a long-term perspective the seeds for a new structure of popular representation were sown even in the midst of a terminal phase of decomposition of old structures.

A complex array of domestic and global forces has rewoven the economic and social fabric of the region in the past quarter-century. Among them are the oil 'shocks' of the 1970s; the post-1982 debt crisis; bouts of runaway inflation and stabilization; market and state reforms; increased integration into the world economy; the globalization of production and capital flows; and changes in the geography, social structure, and models of capitalist production. During the 1980s, these trends generally had a devastating impact on the material conditions and traditional political organizations of the popular sector. In the cities, formal-sector jobs declined in number, security, and remuneration, while the informal sector mushroomed. In the countryside, wage labor in capitalist, export-oriented agriculture generally expanded, although pay levels and security remained precarious and subsistence farming declined. Unions and peasant organizations found not only their memberships and bargaining strength diminished (if not decimated), but also their traditional access to decision-making arenas concerning social services and benefits cut off or severely eroded. More generally, claims on state resources by popular organizations generally fell on the deaf ears of increasingly austerity-minded governing elites.

As economic restructuring further undermined already weak ties of popular representation, processes of democratization were having much the same overall impact. Belying general expectations, the democratic transitions or openings that occurred in most of our focus countries neither stimulated the emergence of new patterns of popular representation advocated by many—such as social pacts and 'democratic class compromise' (e.g. O'Donnell and Schmitter 1986; Roxborough 1992*a*)—nor reinvigorated old populist-era patterns and aspirations centered on various forms of mass mobilization, as feared by many. Rather, popular actors found themselves unable to forge strong links of *whatever* type with democratizing movements and the governments of either new democracies or entrenched political systems. Among other factors, the post-transition legacy of elite-dominated regime change, the dire nature of economic realities, and the growing predominance of neoliberal thinking in domestic and international quarters all played a role in reducing the space for popular representation.

Yet, while efforts to rebuild popular _representation_ in the democratic transitions were decidedly unimpressive, popular _participation_ did show considerable signs of dynamism in some countries. Building on the lessons of earlier periods and changing left models within and outside Latin America, popular activists began to place unprecedented importance on grassroots organizing, autonomy from the state and political parties, and traditionally displaced or ignored issues and collective identities (Eckstein 1989; Escobar and Alvarez 1992). These new-found values and concerns nurtured not only struggles for greater participation within traditional peasant and labor organizations, but also the mushrooming of a vast new array of movements and associations—neighborhood-based, church-linked, gender-oriented, human rights-oriented, indigenous, environmental, and so on. Many associations began to take the novel form of non-governmental organizations, or NGOs, analytically distinct from membership-based popular organizations, social movements, and political parties.

However much civil society was growing independently of the state, the mid-1980s was generally a period of very weak structures of representation linking those groups with the state. The debt crisis, stabilization programs, and market reforms exacerbated this situation, severely undermining living standards and capacity for sustained and organized popular mobilization. In some cases, the decay of popular representation was so profound, and the conditions so hostile, that institutions became extremely fragile and, on the local level at least, order broke down.

The view that a general political 'demobilization' of popular actors took place seems to suffuse contemporary discourse in and about the region. Some observers believe that civil society has degenerated into 'anomie' and 'disarticulation' (Tironi 1986; Zermeño 1989). Traditional bases of sociability and solidarity like religion, family and community structures, and work are held to have undergone rapid decline, contributing to the destruction of capacities for collective organizing and action. A weak civil society, divided against itself, further undermines—it is argued—historically weak political institutions and provides fodder for the personalistic appeals of often unscrupulous politicians. However formally democratic they remain, their democratic content is drained by chief executives who run roughshod over rules and institutions, ruling by a mixture of decree, charisma, and old-fashioned patronage. Whether these political forms are labeled 'exclusionary', 'delegative', or 'neopopulist' (Acuña 1994; O'Donnell 1994; Roberts 1995) the common image that emerges is one in which nominally democratic rule rests on the absence—and even the active destruction—of political links both within civil society and between it and the state.

We characterize such a purported type of political system as 'socially disembedded', where remaining popular organizations are few and often politically isolated and ineffective—when not outright repressed, albeit by ostensibly legal means. The exercise of citizenship thus is reduced for the popular sectors to voting, receiving messages conveyed through the elite-controlled media, and waiting passively for the benefits of state policies to trickle down—perhaps—from on high. This commonly accepted view is a vision of the logical completion of decomposition.

Several of our chapters—Yashar on Guatemala, Burt and Panfichi on Peru, Pinheiro on Brazil, and the introductory chapter by Vilas—highlight important manifestations of disembeddedness in contemporary Latin American polities. While we agree that these are important in some countries and present in all, other chapters highlight countervailing tendencies. Moreover, we believe that there are reasonable grounds for expecting that, as medium- to long-term issues of growth, sustainability, and equity begin to overshadow largely crisis-driven macroeconomic reforms on the region's policy agenda—and in the absence of authoritarian reversals—greater opportunities will emerge for a *re*-embedding of politics linking state and societal actors.[4]

We find that there is variation in the degree of decay or reconstruction between different issue areas, producing noteworthy dissimilarities between countries, or even within a single one. For instance, macroeconomic policy-making throughout the region—on issues like trade liberalization, monetary and general fiscal matters, privatization, and deregulation of foreign investment—continues to be dominated by elite actors and technocratic styles, excluding popular sectors from all but diffuse influence through the ballot box. Yet, the chapters by Piester and Fox on Mexico and Segarra on Ecuador underline a broader, though uneven, trend toward greater involvement of NGOs and popular actors in the implementation, and sometimes the shaping, of social policy. While their involvement is unlikely to produce dramatic redistributive shifts that favor the popular sectors, it does provide opportunities for voicing claims and extending debates on social policy issues. Here and elsewhere contradictions are apparent. For instance, if we juxtapose growing popular access to decision-making in Brazil over sectoral industrial policy (Martin), environmental issues (Hochstetler), and small-town local governance (Nylen) with Pinheiro's sobering account of the absence of basic civil liberties and genuine rule of law for the poorest Brazilian citizens, we gain a vivid image of the kind of contradictory realities that may coexist within a single country. Finally, if we contrast the perverse combination of social disarticulation, personalistic rule, and decay of political institutions documented by Burt and Panfichi in Peru—a case that has been very influential for the aforementioned analyses of social

---

[4] In this connection, Haggard and Kaufman (1995*b*: 309–34) make an important distinction between the 'politics of initiation' of market reforms in developing regions like Latin America, typically involving a substantial degree of concentration of discretionary authority in the executive, and the 'politics of consolidation' of market reforms and democracy, wherein two key tasks come to the fore: first, how to 'depersonalize' executive authority and make it 'accountable' (335) and, second and more generally, how to embed liberal political and economic norms in formal and durable institutions (363–4). Of course, they also note that whether or not such tasks will be fulfilled effectively remains an open question.

disembeddedness—with trends highlighted in other countries, that Andean country seems more an exceptionally severe case of institutional and social decay than a 'paradigm' for contemporary Latin American politics.

In sum, then, violence, social disarticulation, and personalistic modes of leadership clearly are very present in today's Latin America, and particularly rife in some countries. These characteristics of Latin American societies and polities continue to cry out for scholarly reflection, normative critique, and practical solutions. Yet, they by no means exhaust the full range of recent and emerging trends in popular participation and representation as documented in this book. In order to perceive and understand these trends we need to look beyond the old structures of representation, however, and recognize the factors that are producing a new structure.

Forces Shaping the Recomposition of State–Popular Sector Links

Recomposition comes about for a variety of reasons, in part the same ones for which popular sectors mobilized in earlier periods. Popular actors participate in politics in large part in order to overcome exceptionally high rates of inequality, unemployment, and physical and economic insecurity. Political and economic elites search for ways of setting limits on popular politics because of the fear that 'the dangerous classes' will disrupt stability in the face of sacrifices demanded by economic restructuring, particularly by making skittish international and domestic investors flee.[5] Yet, these usual reasons are not producing, on any large scale, the classic responses in the form of the rise or strengthening of corporatist institutions and populist parties. Although a 'neopopulist' style does characterize some current (Fujimori and Menem) and past (Salinas and Collor) presidential leaders, these experiences of leadership seem much more media-based, election-oriented, and episodic than the *institution-building* breakthroughs associated with classic populism.[6]

Nor have traditional motives for popular mobilization yielded substantial steps towards a mass movement to counteract efforts to control popular sectors, an outcome long sought—or feared—by many. Some conjunctures do suggest the possibility of a broad mobilization, but the movements they have generated have been either transitory or narrow in scope. For example, the rioting in Caracas in 1989,

---

[5] On the increasing political and economic importance of the 'management of international expectations', see, for instance, Roxborough (1992c).

[6] The label 'neopopulist' has become increasingly commonplace in the literature (e.g. Castro Rea et al. 1992; Dresser 1991; Roberts 1995). Yet, given the ignominious political fates of the impeached Collor and the subsequently discredited Salinas, as well as the notable contrasts between their heavy-handed governing styles and the more consensus-oriented approaches of their respective successors (Franco and Cardoso in Brazil, Zedillo in Mexico) and, perhaps, the recent electoral difficulties of Menem and Fujimori at the state and/or local level, at the time of this writing (Jan. 1996) there is considerably less reason to see neopopulism—or its analytical 'cousin' delegative democracy—as an ineluctable region-wide trend than there seemed to be in the late 1980s and early 1990s.

the mobilization of support for Cárdenas in the 1988 Mexican election, and the recent civic pro-impeachment campaigns in Brazil and Venezuela were dramatic and had a substantial social base, but they did not produce enduring mass movements, party-based or otherwise. The very broad protests by the indigenous movement in Ecuador described in Selverston's essay were an important national event, but chiefly for consolidating the political role of an indigenous organization and carving out a sphere for indigenous rights. Even in cases where the appeal of a popular movement captures national and international attention, as in the 1994 Zapatista uprising in Chiapas, Mexico, the sustained popular mobilization appears to be *local*, even though its democratizing effects may turn out to be national.[7]

Despite the absence of enduring mass movements and of any large-scale reformulation of classic structures of popular representation, nonetheless, recomposition is occurring, and it is taking the specific form that we call associative networks. Changing conditions and shifting goals of elites, popular sectors, and other relevant actors are leading to the forging of links between groups of people and the state along new lines. Although there is no way at this time to predict with certainty—nor even measure with accuracy—the degree to which associative networks will become dominant, there is good reason to believe that they will be of growing prominence because the forces producing them are powerful. These forces can be summarized as follows:

- the dispersion of political decision-making,
- the impact of new resources for communicating and acquiring knowledge,
- the influence of ideas advocating greater societal and popular involvement in decision-making in order to increase competitiveness and the cost-effectiveness of public administration,
- the consequences of the internationalization of many policy spheres and political arenas, and
- political learning by elites and popular actors induced by the perceived failure of established strategies and institutions to respond to changing political and economic realities.

First, and most important, structures of representation have been shaped by the dispersion of decision-making activity from the exclusive control of the chief executive and his or her cabinet, close political associates, and advisers, and towards *multiple* decision-making centers. This movement is in three directions: to subnational units, to more or less autonomous centers within the central government, and to external arenas.[8]

---

[7] See the concluding section to the chapter by Fox, which emphasizes the national impact of the rebellion, even though direct mobilization was limited.

[8] There are many terms to describe the process and the end result. Ostrom (1990; Ostrom *et al.* 1993, 1994) uses the term 'polycentrism' to describe a system with sub-centers, and her analysis is relevant, but we have opted not to use the term because it suggests too complete a separation of the centers, and if used to describe a state, too evenly balanced centers. 'Decentralization' is useful, but often refers only to dispersion to subnational units. 'Deconcentration' is less specific and has some

The 'centralized state' model that historically characterized Latin American polities under both populist-democratic and authoritarian regimes allowed many
observers to discuss politics with reasonable accuracy as if it took place in one
singular, unified 'space'. Set geographically in the national capital, this space was
centered in the informal but widely recognized sphere dominated by the interactions (coalition-building, deal-making, intrigues, maneuvers, etc.) of the President
with a particular set of powerful cabinet members, personal advisers, party officials,
legislative leaders, and military officers who were directly tied to the President, together, under some circumstances, with foreign investors, bankers, ambassadors,
and church leaders.[9] One should not overemphasize this centralism, as there were
obviously important spheres of business activity and rural enclaves where *de facto*
public power lay in private hands. Yet, in the populist-corporatist era, the single
national arena of decision-making was *the* place where political actors, especially
from the popular sectors, directed their demands.

If we think of the state as the set of authoritative decision-making centers of a
polity backed by a legitimate monopoly of the use of coercion, along with the rules
and 'rule-enforcing' agents who regulate those arenas, there was, by and large, only
one such center in the pyramidal structure of political authority of the centralized
state. All the various structures of representation, particularly popular representation, were firmly anchored at the top of the pyramid in either direct or indirect fashion, flowing downward from it.[10]

The chapters in this volume, along with a growing body of other evidence, provide indications that—by default and by design—there has been in recent years
a significant shift of effective decision-making activity away from the executive-
centered political coterie lying at the apex of the pyramid. A variety of more or
less autonomous administrative, legislative, subnational, and external sites have
emerged and become the foci of political action.

The most straightforward examples of dispersion of decision-making activity
concern administrative and political decentralization to subnational units. Decentralization, in the sense of shifting authority over budgets and policy decisions to
state/provincial and municipal levels, is on the reform agenda of many Latin American countries and is already a significant, if incomplete, reality in some (López
Murphy 1995; Morris and Lowder 1992; Reilly 1995). Movement in this direction
flows from many wellsprings: increased political contestation at the subnational

currency in contemporary debates; we use it occasionally. Dispersion to external sites is more controversial, and phrases such as 'loss of sovereignty' come to mind. See Chalmers (1992) for a brief
discussion of sovereignty in an internationalized environment. We have settled on 'dispersion of
decision-making activity' as being the most descriptive.

[9] There always have been exceptions, of course. There are some non-trivial aspects of federalism
in Brazil and Mexico; new state agencies often have been created to allow some modest arenas of autonomous decision-making; and military institutions have, on occasion, operated as a state within the state.

[10] We do not mean to imply anything about the relative 'strength' of the state or about political
stability when referring to the centralized state. In fact, we believe that, as a general analytical category, centralized states cut across distinctions like 'strong' versus 'weak' states, stable versus unstable
regimes, and even authoritarian and democratic regime types.

level; the reformist ideas of 'good government' advocates, such as the World Bank, and neoliberals; the opportunism of national-level officials who want to rid themselves of seemingly intractable problems; and practical concerns about stimulating local economic development and responding to the greater territorial distribution of economic activities and population that now characterizes the region. Constitutional reform has played a part in decentralization in a few countries, as in the 1988 Brazilian document that mandated (the now quite controversial) revenue-sharing provisions and the new Colombian constitution's creation of elected municipal governments.

The subnational dispersion of decision-making creates a new political reality for those interested in influencing public policy. While it is conceivable that a unified national party representing the popular sectors could act in each of these centers, the essays on innovative municipal administrations in small towns in northeastern Brazil by Nylen and in the Uruguayan national capital by Winn and Ferro-Clérico suggest the difficulties attendant to such efforts. These researchers' enquiries were guided initially by a concern for what the respective national parties could accomplish when given a chance to govern and how local 'lessons' might reshape national politics. Yet two intriguing implications emerge from these chapters: (1) greater local success comes not from implementing national party decisions and doctrines but rather from developing a creative political praxis centered on local needs and (2) local progressive governments do not necessarily translate into either success at the polls or clear guidance for party platforms at the national level, nor *should* they be assessed strictly in such instrumental terms.

The relative success at the local level of these progressive experiments was predicated on the capacity of local administrations and party activists to take advantage of and further foster the autonomy of local arenas of decision-making from national control, whether exercised by central governments or by national party structures. Of course, opposition governments at the state or municipal levels are a more widespread and growing phenomenon in the region—one with, it bears emphasizing, relatively few historical precedents under the centralized state. This trend currently encompasses centrist to center-left governments in major cities and/or states in at least two additional focus countries (Argentina and—as discussed by López-Maya in this volume—Venezuela) and primarily center-right opposition governments at the state and municipal level scattered throughout much of Mexico (Rodríguez and Ward 1995).

The dispersion of state decision-making, however, entails not only a shift to subnational territorial units, but also the development of relatively distinct policy domains *within* the state, principally (but not only) at the level of the central government.[11] In these domains, a particular group of officials, often reaching out

---

[11] This aspect of dispersion is similar to Evans's (1995) notion of 'embedded state autonomy', which embodies a mixture of what he calls 'connectedness' to society and 'insulation' from particularistic pressures. Yet, we do not share Evans's strong analytical preoccupation with the issue of autonomy, although we recognize the important normative and practical issues raised by tight collaboration between private actors and public authorities.

to some societal actor or actors, makes policy with a significant degree of auto-nomy. A trend towards the establishment of independent central banks is one major example of how this may happen in a formal way (Maxfield forthcoming). Social policy (as discussed in the chapters by Segarra on Ecuador and by Piester and Fox on Mexico) has also emerged as a field in which specialized segments of the state apparatus—various agencies, ministries, legislative committees, and the like—play a central, and moderately autonomous, role in shaping policy. One could easily add other policy domains, like environmental regulation (Hochstetler in this volume) or industrial promotion (Evans 1995), in which state policy-makers some-times call on the expertise, manpower, political support, or other forms of coopera-tion that non-state actors may offer.

The broad phenomenon that is currently grouped under the broad label of 'pri-vatization' can sometimes be equated with this sort of dispersion. Privatization can mean many things, including simply selling off government-owned firms, which then become part of the market. Yet, even in these cases, states frequently main-tain leverage and influence over newly privatized firms through a variety of policy instruments, ranging from minority ownership and close ties to the new manage-ment to regulations in areas like anti-trust, trade, and labor and environmental matters. More generally, and as this example suggests, much of what is called pri-vatization entails, in fact, less the abdication of public authority than the disper-sion of public decision-making, because both major firms and 'privatized' social security entities make authoritative decisions that have public imprimatur and a force similar to that of public law. Government officials often continue to be part of the decision-making process, formally or informally.

Whether the dispersion of decision-making takes place through creating auto-nomous teams in government ministries, establishing independent agencies, or (partial) privatization, the net impact is to stimulate political actors, including those from the popular sectors, to target those varied, and often changing, centers of decision-making. Further, the relatively narrow range of policy issues being considered in any particular center suggests the importance of political strategies focused at least in part on policy debate, rather than simply making broad demands that can only be realized through electing a whole new government or, at the extreme, seizing power.

A final direction of dispersion is outwards. Chalmers (1992) refers to the US Con-gress, international organizations, and even the decision-making bodies of major foreign private organizations as 'secondary arenas' of domestic politics when they become the locus of conflict not only among the citizens or members of those for-eign institutions but also for domestic actors from the country affected by those decisions. It is clear that in some countries, most dramatically El Salvador, the decision-making processes that shape the actions of the UN peace-keeping pres-ence are an important arena for many political actors within the country. A more complicated case concerns US decision-making bodies.

In the discussion of the decision on the North American Free Trade Agreement (NAFTA) in Cook's chapter, it is clear, for example, that the US Congress was an arena for making decisions significant for Mexican citizens. This is nothing new, of course, since what goes on in 'Washington' has long been of major importance. The difference lies in the way in which politics is played out in that arena. In the classic view (and in international law), such centers as the US Congress do not become arenas of contestation for citizens of foreign countries, and their influence is limited to exchanges of notes between the heads of state and their representatives. Although this norm was ignored by many businessmen, revolutionaries, and governmental lobbyists, adherence to this formality was emphasized by many Latin American governments—Mexico in particular—as a device to prevent retaliatory intervention by US actors in their domestic politics.

In the new situation, illustrated by the NAFTA debate, not only did the Mexican government mount a very broad campaign to influence the US Congress, but so did Canadian and US NGOs and labor unions allied with Mexican groups and parties opposed to a purely market-oriented treaty. The net result was to make the US Congress a secondary arena of Mexican decision-making. Furthermore, this case illustrates the interaction of the formation of networks and the dispersion of decision-making centers, in that these actors helped to create new secondary arenas, i.e. the trinational institutional arrangements for monitoring and dispute settlement on labor and environmental issues set up through the side agreements to NAFTA.

It is important not to conflate the dispersion of decision-making activity with other related but analytically distinct aspects of the configuration of state power. For example, the distribution of decision-making activity is different from the question of where final legal authority lies. Whether a subunit has the legal authority to make the final decision, or whether it remains in the hands of the President, may or may not be important for the strategies of popular actors. The question of where, in the normal course of events, public policy is discussed, bargained over, and shaped is arguably more important for strategy than this legal issue. When political actors strive to influence decisions or gain concessions, it is to these centers that they direct their efforts, and it is around these centers that political networks are built.

Efforts to establish checks and balances among the branches of government are also important, but probably more for preserving than for shaping popular representation. Achieving a separation of powers entails structuring decision-making processes in such a way that the legislature, executive, and judiciary can check each other. Even with built-in checks and balances, this is a single process, with the three powers jointly shaping public policy through a combination of conflict, competition, and cooperation. The dispersion of decision-making concerns, instead, the fact that the actual work of forging policy out of competing demands and claims takes place in multiple centers. Establishing effective checks and balances is a major concern for popular representation because of the haunting danger of the collapse of democracy itself.[12] If Fujimori and Menem can ignore or

---

[12] Separation of powers has become a major topic, because of the serious concern that executives in some countries have been ruling by decree rather than through effective coordination with, and

manipulate Congress, then any structural changes in popular representation might conceivably be wiped out in a new wave of legalized repression. However, we are inclined to believe that, short of that outcome, the dispersion of decision-making authority is rooted at least in part in the requirements of government (and governance) in a complex society, and is likely to continue even if the separation of powers is flawed badly.

It should be clear that the trend towards multi-centric decision-making is not the same as democratization in the sense of shifting power to 'the people'. Democratization entails a change in the rules of political competition and participation. The dispersion concerns the units of decision-making, which may or may not be democratic. The transfer of policy-making to a relatively autonomous ministry or agency, in itself, is only a shift from one set of elites to another. A new sub-center of policy-making may even be less democratic than the larger system, for example, if power is devolved to state governments where a narrow group of elites monopolizes control; the 'subnational authoritarian regimes' identified by Fox are a clear example. It may even be suggested that, in some cases, the 'farming out' of policy-making may be a way to remove it from the sites likely to be influenced by popular groups. One logic of creating independent central banks, for example, is to insulate them from politically motivated decisions which might be 'too favorable' to (short-term) popular needs.

On the other hand, it is also not true that dispersion of decision-making is always non-democratic. Decentralization may bring decision-making physically closer and more accessible to concerned actors, and the disaggregation of policy areas may have the desirable effect of making policy debate more substantive and meaningful from the point of view of the particular popular groups involved—say, indigenous groups, specific sets of workers, or participants in the informal economy. There are thus important potentials for democratization.

---

coalition-forming in, the national legislature. Argentine President Carlos Menem, now in his second term, has been rather high-handed in his dealings with Congress, as was Fernando Collor of Brazil during most of his two-and-half-year presidency (cut short by impeachment in 1992); 'high-handed' would be a charitable characterization of the governing style of Alberto Fujimori of Peru, who closed Congress in 1992—to considerable popular acclaim—and then reopened it under more restrictive rules (making it more malleable) which were approved in a procedurally suspect national plebiscite in 1993. These experiences have given rise to such terms as 'delegative democracy' (O'Donnell 1994). Scholars have speculated that they may well become a permanent fixture on the region's political landscape. The same mixed record can be seen with regard to progress in strengthening the judiciary and legal system, which historically have been executive-dominated. Even in traditionally legalistic Chile, military commanders have defied openly the edicts of civilian courts and authorities. There are, however, some signs that traditionally weak legislative arenas are becoming more vibrant in Brazil and Mexico, which are reinforced by the orderliness of the unprecedented presidential impeachment proceedings in Brazil, Venezuela, and Colombia over corruption issues. Yet there seem to be contrary trends in countries like Uruguay and Chile, where traditionally strong national legislatures may have lost some ground in the post-transition era. On the Chilean case, see Garretón (1994b). On the Uruguayan, one interpretation of Filgueira and Papadópulos's chapter in this volume is that national referenda proved necessary to break political deadlocks over issues that parties could not resolve in Congress.

Besides dispersion of decision-making, another broad factor affecting the shape of popular participation concerns the lowering costs for political actors of establishing contact with others sharing similar interests, coordinating with them, exploring possible solutions, and seeking out resources for action. It is clear that the availability of less expensive mass media—print, radio, television—has had an important impact, but there now are also more specialized communication—inexpensive publication of pamphlets, books, and journals; access to discussion groups in electronic media; and less expensive telephones, fax machines, and electronic mail.

The increasing number of mass media sources and, especially, the escalating availability of more specialized media have a massive impact on political organization, though its precise nature is hard to pin down. At the very least, these developments have made possible the establishment, around relatively specialized concerns and interests, of links beyond community and organizational boundaries among diverse people located at some distance from each other. At the same time, new and expanded means of communication vastly increase access to knowledge—and misinformation—as it becomes easier and easier to obtain competing sources of information about many different kinds of issues. In addition to diffusing through more efficient and accessible technologies, information also flows more readily in today's Latin America through the activities of universities, research centers, NGOs, and many other organizations. Obviously, access to these new technologies and ideas is not distributed evenly, and the possibility for new informational inequalities is real. Overall, while diffuse, the impact of changes in communication on the shape of political organization is, nonetheless, profound.

A third force that shapes popular representation is the emerging sets of beliefs held by particular elites about how they should relate to those popular actors with whom they interact most. Traditional elitist attitudes suggesting distance, the appropriateness of clientelistic relations, or authoritarian postures no doubt are still common. Yet, there are growing currents—and not only in Latin America—that promote a different approach. An increasingly wide variety of actors perceive the need for complex social coordination to make and implement effective decisions in the particular settings of most concern to them, whether they be firms, government agencies, or other kinds of institutions. Whether the goal is sustainable development, producing competitive goods, combating extreme poverty, making efficient use of scarce state resources, or some other such social coordination—often referred to as 'governance'[13]—requires more effective cooperation between, for example, public and private actors or workers and managers.

In so far as some set of popular actors is often deemed essential to any particular instance of coordination—and can hinder it if they are excluded or coerced into participation—the search for collaborative solutions contributes, however

[13] This is a large field. See, among others, Atkinson and Coleman (1992), Campbell *et al.* (1991), Cohen and Rogers (1992), Hay and Jessop (1995), Hirst (1994), Hollingsworth *et al.* (1994), Malloy (1991*a*, 1991*b*), Nagel (1994), Ostrom (1990), Streeck and Schmitter (1985*a*, 1985*b*), Thompson *et al.* (1991).

unintentionally, to the emergence of new forms of popular representation. Such new forms, therefore, grow out of the need to solve problems of social coordination and governance, especially to provide scarce public goods and manage common-pool resources (Ostrom 1990; Ostrom *et al.* 1994). Mass participation is seldom the resulting form, but rather more *diffuse* participation focused around relatively specific purposes.

A fourth factor shaping new forms of popular representation is new patterns of the internationalization of Latin American politics. Foreigners of one kind or another long have had a direct interest in mass politics. The economic presence of multinational capital has, of course, long been emphasized by observers. In an earlier period, international solidarity movements supported mobilization by various left and center-left parties sympathetic with political movements like Communism, Social Democracy, or Christian Democracy. For its part, the United States government encouraged conservative counter-mobilization through a combination of development assistance, support for anti-Communist political forces, and covert action. Recently, Washington has promoted 'governance' and building 'free markets'. However, fiscal crises and ideological turns in the USA itself have diminished its once hegemonic impact in the region. And the collapse of the expansionist socialist bloc has changed global political competition radically.

Partisan and government influences by foreign actors on popular representation have come to be overshadowed by those of international organizations, foreign NGOs, and international corporations. These actors are pushing in a variety of political directions, but a prominent thread is the emphasis on project- or sector-specific involvements and some version of the governance doctrines noted above. The World Bank and the Inter-American Development Bank often promote some kind of participation by program beneficiaries and other local actors in order to rationalize project administration. They have been joined by other international organizations, such as the Organization of American States and various United Nations agencies, as well as semi-governmental donors such as the European foundations, the various branches of the National Endowment for Democracy in the USA, the international representatives of labor organizations, and a host of private donors. The overall impact, we believe, has shifted away from promoting mass movements and towards project-oriented mobilization focused on delimited groups of people, more particular objectives, and some form of interaction among government officials, foreign and domestic experts, and service recipients. Although there are enough reports to know that such interactions are not always successful—and, more to the point, to the satisfaction of supposed beneficiaries —the broad impact seems to entail the fostering of specialized groupings anchored within network structures.

Finally, as many countries in Latin America recently have experienced obvious failures of political institutions, a complex learning process seems to have gone on that may also contribute to nascent forms of popular representation. In Brazil and the Southern Cone, many new political organizations emerged out of the opposition to military governments. In countries in transition like Mexico or in breakdown (and transition?) such as Venezuela, groupings associated with the popular sectors have had to build outside established—but weakening—party and governmental organizations (see Fox, Bruhn, and López-Maya in this volume).

While some may argue that many new organizations were the product of special circumstances and will fade, we do not believe that is always true. NGOs emerged during the fight against authoritarian regimes, neighborhood organizations arose in response to crises such as earthquakes (especially in Mexico), and election monitoring has been important in establishing 'founding elections'. Yet, the presumption is that once the crisis is over, the groups will disappear, or be absorbed into political parties and government agencies. The evidence clearly is not definitive, but there is some ground for another conclusion, namely, that the activists from these organizations have struggled—sometimes successfully—to find new roles for themselves and/or their organizations after the immediate crisis has passed, without returning to what are often perceived to be failed or much weakened parties, electoral processes, and local governments. The legacy of earlier activism is thus sometimes both a sense of accomplishment when objectives have been achieved at least partially, and a more or less permanent capacity to acquire the knowledge, skills, and resources necessary to act politically around new issues, in new venues, or through new organizations whilst remaining independent.

With regard to learning by movements on the left, the apparent failure of mass-mobilization models seems to have led people to explore alternatives other than a return to party mobilization. There are many reasons: their re-valorization of formal democracy following the experience of repression under authoritarianism; the critique of left instrumentalism and vanguardism; the growing recognition of multiple sites of domination (gender, ethnicity, race, class, etc.); and the decline or demise of once-attractive international models (social democracy and state socialism, in particular). In addition, growing sensitivity to more 'immediate' needs as well as global shifts in progressive thinking have fostered individual identification with groups much less broad than *el pueblo* or the working class. As a result, initiatives from below typically have a more delimited focus in which collective action centers around localities, the workplace, or previously neglected problems, such as environmental degradation, gender exploitation, and racial and ethnic discrimination.

These and other factors shaping the reconfiguration of popular representation could and should be the subject of much more extensive analysis than space permits. Yet, we are convinced that the combination of trends in governance, information technology, ideas about collaboration in societal domains, internationalization, and other basic forces in contemporary society are weighty enough to go a long way toward changing political action in many Latin American countries. And if those underlying trends are broadly convergent, then the chances of seeing a strengthened new political model emerge are quite significant. We believe that that is the case, and that the associative network is the centerpiece of that model.

A New Analytical Model

We will present associative networks as an *ideal type* in the Weberian sense. That is, we are not presenting this as achieving some normative ideal, but rather as an elaboration of what the characteristics of a polity would be if the model were widespread. We recognize that in any extant polity in Latin America elements of this new structure of popular representation coexist with vestigial or modified elements of older structures like corporatism, clientelism, and populism, along with classic forms of territorial representation based on elections and political parties.

The other sense of the term 'ideal', that is, as a norm or a goal, is not irrelevant to the particular model of an associative network that we develop, as will be apparent. Every form of popular representation embodies some desirable condition that may or may not be achieved. Corporatists aspired to an ordered harmony, and even clientelism suggests a kind of caring paternalism. The norms associated with associative networks evidently will be a combination of flexible adaptation induced by sheer pragmatism together with the possibility of a more 'discursive' or 'deliberative' democracy (Dryzek 1990; Habermas 1987; Mansbridge 1983; Sabel 1995). But our goal is far from that of promoting the ideal, or even its analysis. Rather, we see the evolution of associative networks as a fact—by no means fully realized, but partially so—and our intention is to lay out those characteristics. We take no position on the desirability of this form over others, although we will call attention to its advantages and disadvantages from the standpoint of the popular actors it links to the state, and try to elucidate in the concluding sections the conditions under which these advantages may be realized more fully.

ASSOCIATIVE NETWORKS

What sorts of structures of representation connect the popular sectors with the state?[14] Increasingly, we argue, they are a particularly flexible kind that we call 'associative networks'. Let us first clarify the general category of which we see associative networks as a particular type.

By 'structures of representation' we mean, first, the sets of individuals or organizations that make claims and, second, the mediating entities that debate, reshape, and transmit claims and pressures to authoritative decision-making centers. For example, a series of NGOs and grassroots groups may be linked to social policy-making centers through a government consultative council, as in the case of Ecuador discussed by Segarra. Or agricultural workers may be organized into rural unions in north-east Brazil, as discussed by Pereira. Such unions' links to decision centers

---

[14] As indicated above, we use the term 'representation' although the linkage is always two-way and control is also a possibility, and is even strongly implied. Further, 'representation' may involve debate and discussion, and not just transmission of demands. A structure of representation specifically includes institutionalized spaces where, for example, preferences are discussed and shaped.

occur in part through the relatively formal ties of those unions with the government in Brazil's corporative labor structure, though they also participate in a network of organizations and official agencies that are involved in issues of agrarian policy; rural unions' contribution to the latter is mediated through public statements, strikes, demonstrations, and the like.

We do not mean only an 'interest group' and its channels for making demands when referring to structures of representation. We are concerned also with linking procedures and organizations which resolve conflicts between competing interests and in which debate or discussion takes place, leading to clarification of preferences, examination of the conditions affecting any policy decision that may emerge, and interpretation of the meanings of the actions to be taken. Thus we are interested not only in demand-making and bargaining but also in 'cognitive politics'. Cognitive processes relevant to politics include perception, social learning, and communication, which go beyond strategic bargaining based on fixed interests to encompass the consideration and sometimes the resolution of competing claims. A structure of representation is thus a set of actors that are linked to decision-making centers through an ensemble of procedures and organizations in which bargaining *and* cognitive exchanges occur, influencing the policies adopted by that center.

Structures of representation become institutionalized in different ways. One common, but not exclusive, basis anchors the structure of representation around a single decision center. The most obviously institutionalized structure of representation is that built around legislatures with geographic constituencies and representatives interacting through election campaigns and political debate. This is the structure of representation most likely enshrined in democratic constitutions. Legislatures are the classic representative institution, so there tends to be a presumption that they are the unique structure of representation shaping the entire polity. Yet it has long been recognized that, in all systems, a great deal goes on outside of this formal institution, particularly in highly centralized states such as those that have prevailed until recently in most of Latin America. Much of this activity is 'extra-constitutional' and sometimes ignored in looking for the institutional basis of politics. Yet, if 'institutionalization' means more than enshrining a pattern in the constitution, and encompasses more than those patterns that are legally established, then there actually are many more institutionalized structures of representation.[15]

One special but influential structure of representation that was not defined by its relationship to a single decision-making center was that made up of class-based and programmatically oriented political parties, which, particularly in Europe, became an ideal of 'mass parties'. Such parties constitute a structure of representation in themselves, in that they define a membership or constituency and establish

---

[15] This particular conception of institutionalization resonates more with current formulations in sociology (e.g. Powell and DiMaggio 1991) than with the traditional political science emphasis on the consolidation of formal state and/or regime institutions. We are indebted to Kelly Moore for helping us clarify this point.

procedures for transmitting claims and demands, organizing debate, building consensus and control, and, finally, bringing influence to bear on decisions in many decision-making arenas.[16] The 'glue' holding the structure together, in addition to the organizational commitments of the members, is the common concern with the issues and program of the party.

Beyond these structures, there are many other possibilities—not only organized around centers other than the legislature, but also around major issues that are not the exclusive domain of a political party. The notion of 'issue' or 'policy networks' (Atkinson and Coleman 1992; Heclo 1977; Katzenstein 1985; Keck and Sikkink forthcoming; Marin 1990) starts from a different point, emphasizing the personal relationships and shared commitment to ideas within the networks rather than the notion of political representation. In order to fit more closely our conception of associative networks, such formulations would have to be adjusted to pay attention to these networks' relationship with political claim-making—in this case involving the popular sectors. Yet there is a common thread between our approach and these in terms of a concern with the way in which political space is structured. From our point of view, there are many different actual or potential structures of representation in any given polity, and this is an area where significant evolution seems to be taking place not just in Latin America, but around the world.

We have already discussed a series of structures of representation that have been common in the region: clientelism, populism, corporatism, and mass mobilization. Clientelism is a structure of representation where the principal actors are individuals, and the links are exchanges with brokers and patrons. The patron resolves competing claims in this structure. Populism is one in which the actors are primarily individuals (in large clusters) and the links are found in the interplay between the leader's charisma, promises, etc. and the norms and demands of the masses. In the classic forms of populism (e.g. Perón in Argentina and Vargas in Brazil), this kind of link was strengthened by organizations (the leader's political party) and often reinforced by clientelistic 'machines'. In either case, the 'rules' of bargaining and debate are centered heavily on the populist leader. Finally, corporatism is a structure of representation in which the units are (usually) officially sanctioned labor, business, or professional associations and the links are the organizational and legal ties among them, with the state bureaucracy, as well as, in some cases, with the governing party.[17]

In the increasingly polycentric states in the region, popular representation—and political representation more generally—is increasingly taking place through a different structure of representation, the associative network. We use the term

---

[16] Such a vision is an idealized form of political party. Many parties are clearly only parts of structures of representation, or perhaps, parts of the meta-structures that regulate other ones.

[17] Corporatism may be a form of state, with rules establishing chambers of corporations as the authoritative decision-making centers, and appeared so in many idealizations of the form. As many have pointed out, however, it is almost always more important as a structure of representation relating some specific set of interests to the government, often in order to control them, rather than as a 'form of regime' (Chalmers 1985).

'associative' to call attention to the way in which these structures arise out of and rest on purposive, non-hierarchical 'acts of association'. As a particular way of coming together to form a framework of social interaction, associating or 'associationalism' is both distinct from and historically parallel in importance to the two major principles of modern social and political organization—'hierarchies' (like centralized states and corporations), with their trademark relations of authority and dependency, and ideal-typical 'markets', with their faceless competition among atomized agents (Cohen and Rogers 1992; Hirst 1994).[18] We use the term 'network', in the way that social scientists—particularly sociologists[19]—use it, to characterize social ties without making assumptions about the nature of the norms guiding participants' interaction. Within any given network, there may or may not be competition, conflict, ascriptive features, domination and dependency, or cooperation. The concept of networks also possesses the attractive feature of connoting a *purposeful* interconnectedness. The associative networks we are concerned with are structures of representation, and therefore their central purpose is that of shaping public decisions and policy. Putting the terms together, a working definition of associative networks emerges: 'non-hierarchical structures formed through decisions by multiple actors who come together to shape public policy'.

Organized around issues and one of the new decision-making centers, such networks are numerous and changing. The distinctive characteristics of this new model are the following:

- First, the form of any single associative network is likely to be characterized by a diversity of organizations, individuals, and other participants.
- Second, any particular network is likely to be reconfigured over time as issues, decision-making rules, participants, and opportunities change.
- Third, the associative network entails strong emphasis on what we have called cognitive politics, involving debate and discussion of preferences, understandings, and claims, in addition to—and potentially transforming—more conventional bargaining over demands and interests.[20]
- Finally, while associative networks can and often do involve actors with sharply

[18] In works following in the Tocquevillian tradition (e.g. Putnam 1993) as well as in those of former students of neocorporatism like Streeck and Schmitter (1985a, 1985b), the term 'association' refers more narrowly to the act, or organizational by-product, of individuals who share a similar status *vis-à-vis* the larger collectivity joining together to engage in collective action. That similar status might be, for example, a profession, a place of work, a place in the division of labor, or a common relationship with a particular public agency (e.g. welfare recipients). In this context, we extend the noun 'association' and the adjective 'associative' to characterize a particular class of interactions among individuals and groupings who have markedly *different* status and at least one of whom embodies the formal public authority of the state.

[19] For a useful critical survey of network approaches, see Emirbayer and Goodwin (1994). Among the now classic works in network analysis are White *et al.* (1976), Burt (1982), and Granovetter (1973).

[20] We note that this particular notion of the properties of an associative network seems to dovetail with a new current in network analysis labeled 'structuralist constructionism' (Emirbayer and Goodwin 1994), which emphasizes the interplay of structural and symbolic-discursive elements.

unequal resources, there are typically more chances to escape or shift the ground to avoid a direct test of strength with an unequal competitor. These chances derive, we believe, from the lesser importance of rigid, hierarchical authority relations (compared with party or corporatist forms); shifting and multiple patterns of identity (compared with clientelism and populism); and the more open-ended character of cognitive politics. This results not so much in more equality as *less rigid* inequality among the participants.

These elements apply to each associative network, but by and large they also apply to the pattern of associative networks taken together. If a whole polity were made up of associative networks, it, too, would likely be characterized by diversity, constant reconfiguration, greater emphasis on cognitive politics, and lesser prominence of rigid hierarchies.

We will discuss and illustrate these four characteristics by reference to the two basic elements of a structure of representation—the set of actors who participate in it, and the links between them and the decision-making arenas where debate and bargaining take place.

POPULAR ACTORS IN ASSOCIATIVE NETWORKS

The increasing vitality and diversity of popular sector actors is apparent, but there is also a kind of fragmentation and specialization as well. New identities have become the basis for associations, alongside the 'traditional' ones founded on class, locality, or ties to particular political leaders. As shown in the chapters by Cook, Martin, Murillo, and Pereira, well-established popular organizations such as labor unions are struggling with, but also adapting to, the new demands of more open economies. For the most part, the project of representing a broad social class in a long, historical, and potentially revolutionary process has been replaced with concerns for workers' well-being and unions' role in a rapidly changing economy.[21]

In addition, there are many more organizations based on ethnic identities, identification with ecological causes in almost all countries, gender-based groupings among all classes, neighborhood organizations in many cities, and a variety of grassroots organizations in rural areas. While some of these might be considered 'new social movements' (Escobar and Alvarez 1992), there are few signs that 'postmodern' causes are taking over, and older organizations based on 'traditional' identities are still very much with us. Diversification and a search for new forms of collective action seem more the norm than a replacement of one type of identities with another.

[21] Pereira in this volume notes that resurgent rural unionism in north-eastern Brazil has had more of a class character recently than before military rule, and that it relies on a government-sanctioned, and therefore at least quasi-corporatist, institution. He treats this as an exception to the rule, but it may also be evidence of actors who create a broad identity and utilize links to the state to deal with practical problems, a development which may have little to do with at least the old ideal of corporatism.

Government organizations and officials, as well as concerned party activists, legislators, and businessmen, are also among the potential non-popular-sector participants in associative networks. Frequently, issue-specific networks will involve those government officials responsible for that issue interacting with the organized groups who make relevant claims and stimulate discussion among them. Thus, associative networks should not be thought of as sitting in civil society, separate from the government, but rather as connecting segments of civil society with the state. The growth of associative networks is not the 'growth of civil society', but the growth of its connections with the state.

Another set of potentially participating organizations that is neither popular nor official is usually called 'non-governmental' or 'non-profit'. To this pair of negatives, one might add 'non-party', to emphasize that not only are these organizations not a part of the state apparatus or the business community, but they also do not function like a party (for example, fielding candidates for elective office).[22] Choosing the designation most common in Latin America, non-governmental organizations (NGOs), we give that term the meaning employed by Piester and Segarra in their chapters in this volume, roughly suggested by the notion of 'intermediary organizations' used by Thomas Carroll (1992) or 'grassroots service organizations'. These are organizations of professionals or semi-professionals who, when they are involved with the popular sectors, help to organize projects among them, develop policy proposals relevant to them, generate information about them, help to mobilize them, and provide many other services. They clearly are directly relevant to these sectors, although they are often neither of these sectors themselves nor directly engaged in representing their interests in the way that, say, a union organization represents its membership. The issue of the (lack of) representativity of NGOs is, in fact, often a source of tension. Yet, they certainly belong in any description of structures of popular representation because of their role in shaping claims and making it possible to bring pressure to bear on decision-making centers.

This brings us to an aspect of the model that underpins not only the diversity but also the ongoing reconfiguration of these structures of representation, which is another central characteristic of associative networks. A political party of the ideal type described above presumably does not need much reconfiguration, since the same groups within the party develop positions on a very wide range of issues; provide skills needed to mobilize support; establish bases for resolving disputes; generate a media presence; and use their local affiliates to understand how people are reacting to events. In a more polycentric state where alliances vary greatly from issue to issue, parties are less able to do this than they ever were. The electoral-representative links usually provided by parties and party systems come under even more strain. More and more individuals and organizations become involved in order

---

[22] Another term, 'private voluntary organizations', seems particularly inappropriate here, for although there are some experiences of charitable and strictly volunteer work, the NGOs we are concerned with are more likely to be staffed by paid personnel—however badly and erratically paid they may be.

to meet the demands of the political process, and to develop and use skills independent of particular interests or particular policies.

NGOs, both domestic and internationally based, have begun to play some of these diverse roles—even those that enter the field intending only to implement specific projects. They become involved in mediating between the state and grassroots organizations and begin variously to mobilize, bargain and debate, and press for action. Moreover, popular groups need and sometimes obtain from NGOs organizational resources, including spaces to meet, communications equipment, information to make strategies and formulate proposals, training, organization, openings to make contacts in the government, and funds to pay salaries and buy equipment.

To some extent NGOs have become part of a professional 'political service sector', which includes media specialists, academic policy experts, newspaper pundits, pollsters, grassroots organizers, training facilities, think-tanks, and funders (Chalmers 1992). Not only are they better trained for these things, but they often provide organizational resources to a wide range of groups. Their connections with groups may be either enduring, or on a contract basis. One of the changes in politics more generally in Latin America, as elsewhere, is the emergence of such professionals. Election campaigns have become the domain of pollsters, public relations specialists, image consultants, and all kinds of 'handlers'. Policy-making is another area of professionalization. Policy think-tanks, given a major push when they provided a space for intellectuals during periods of repression (Puryear 1994), have emerged as ongoing centers for policy discussion and formulation, sometimes linked to the government, sometimes not (Goodwin and Nacht 1995).

Many of these professionals are not, of course, oriented towards the poor—who are less likely to be able to pay. Yet, whether it is because of social commitment, a chance to use their skills, career advancement, or long-term political ambition (or all of these), there are significant numbers of such professionals working with such populations as the urban and rural poor or the indigenous. Many of the groups we identify as NGOs appear to think of themselves in this way.

A noteworthy aspect of this political service sector is the presence of a substantial number of people and organizations from abroad, perhaps because they are likely to have specialized skills and also because their non-citizen status is likely to push them away from a more 'direct' role in the political process. Pollsters and economic policy specialists, for example, may be hired international experts. International sources may remain behind the scenes as funders of projects managed by domestic actors. They may pay for local opinion or policy studies or for meetings of activists. They may arrange for publication of local experts. For good or ill—and neither can be taken for granted—the international presence has helped to change the political economy of organizing and acting for the popular sectors.

While NGOs may lower the costs of resources for political organization, technical factors do so as well. Buying time in the mass media is very expensive in Latin America as elsewhere, but the immediacy of television, together with strategies for getting free or cheap political coverage may—in those countries with uncontrolled media—make some kinds of appeals much less expensive than they might have been without the media. In general, of course, information and communication technology—crucial resources for any kind of organization—have become notoriously cheaper, even when they remain beyond the reach of many. The ease of communicating, including the enormous expansion of person-to-person communication afforded by computer networks, has played a role in shaping organizations, as is clear from the story about the building of a transnational coalition among citizens of Canada, Mexico, and the USA recounted by Cook.

The net result of the diversification of popular sector (and other) organizations, as well as the addition of new organizations that provide the resources to mobilize, articulate claims, and interact with like-minded organizations, is *not*, as some might have expected, to create a dense solidaristic web of popular organizations in a broad movement. Rather what emerges is a *highly differentiated and rapidly shifting set of popular groups struggling, and sometimes succeeding, to form a cluster of organizations equipped to recognize, analyze, debate, and bring pressure to bear on issues.* As a consequence, popular representation increasingly depends on the participation of societal and state actors in a shifting set of associative networks.

LINKAGES IN ASSOCIATIVE NETWORKS

What kinds of interactions bring these diverse actors together to debate, reshape, and transmit claims and pressures to decision-making centers? How does interaction among the organizations and individuals take place, and how is the output—a strong policy recommendation, a signal of a deep division, or readiness to accept the status quo—produced? In the formal constitutional system, representatives debate and vote on laws in legislatures. In a strict corporatist model, these processes would be found in the formal meetings among designated representatives. In the idealized party version, it lies in the deliberative bodies of the party organization.

Recalling their distinctive characteristics, the mediating processes in associative networks (a) relate diverse types of organizations and people, (b) frequently change in response to new situations, (c) generally privilege cognitive politics, and (d) rarely exhibit a sharp hierarchical form. Where does this mediation take place?

In the cases covered in this book, some networks are centered in formal institutions. If popular actors simply were co-opted into a hierarchical administrative agency or government party, this situation clearly would not fit within the notion of an associative network. However, governments in the region have been experimenting with 'demand-based' and interactive administrative forms, particularly for public works and social programs, which take some steps towards qualifying as associative networks (Graham 1994). In the face of actual or potential political unrest as a result of economic restructuring, governments have sought to reach out to the poor, as with the National Solidarity program during the Salinas administration in Mexico. The innovation that moves this in the direction of the associative network model is that local groups are established and share to some degree in setting priorities for spending on social and public works projects through local committees. While these no doubt are often manipulated by the government—and the evidence is by no means all in[23]—it is hard to believe that at least some of the local groups created will not have achieved some distinctive organizational base and identity and found ways of negotiating with—or confronting—the government or other entities, whether the program survives in some form or completely disappears. Indeed, Fox highlights the paradox that manipulatively conceived programs may end up engendering or politicizing popular claimants.

Another model centered in official bodies were the experiments in local government launched by leaders aligned with left opposition parties in Brazil and Uruguay, described by Nylen and Winn and Ferro-Clérico. There and elsewhere, local governments created political/administrative structures to involve popular organizations in both decision-making and policy implementation. Another partial example concerns the Ecuadorian experimentation with creating consultative bodies including both public and private groups (NGOs) in the Social Emergency Investment Fund program, discussed by Segarra.[24] Finally, there is the example Martin describes concerning the metalworker unions' entry into the sectoral chamber in the automobile sector in Brazil. This chamber should not be seen as reproducing the corporatism of the past, but rather to have constituted one step toward creating centers for discussion of the challenges that competition presents for all its participants. Although this took place within a formal, government-sponsored institution, the agenda and negotiating dynamics were much more open-ended than in, say, a conventional collective bargaining situation. Finally, Martin suggests that the network ties among actors in the auto sector have persisted and, in some cases, even grown in the wake of the state's formal retreat from the auto chamber, an example which illuminates nicely the adaptation and reconfiguration of networks in response to changing political and economic environments.

More typical of the associative networks than the organizational links that are generated within these formal institutions, however, is a pattern of interaction that is less formalized, and a process of producing outcomes that is less guided by formal institutions. Even those that are principally centered in an organization seem very likely to develop links beyond the organization as well.

As the term network implies, these interactions can take the form of personal links among the individual members from various organizations. Even when the network is centered in a government agency, the links seem to spread out beyond the boundaries of the organization to other group representatives, experts, and so

---

[23] A general conclusion of the volume edited by Cornelius *et al.* (1994) is that the political impact of this presidentially directed program was influenced by local and regional dynamics and varied greatly across the many program areas.

[24] Segarra notes that although the intention of the founders may have been to establish an associative network involving many kinds of groups in the Social Emergency Fund, a hierarchical and clientelistic structure eventually emerged, lacking the kind of flexibility that many had hoped for. This example highlights the need for an analysis of the dynamics of associative networks.

forth. The personal linkages are often a crucial element, particularly in the process of arriving at some formal position.

On the other hand, one of the striking characteristics of the networks we see emerging in many countries is their creation of a public space that is not sustained as much by personal contacts as by the existence of some kind of common media—journals, television, specialized publications, radio talk shows, and, increasingly, computers. Communication between computers represents a mixture of the two—with direct communication between people through e-mail, and a generalized medium with newsgroups and the rapidly growing World Wide Web.

The importance of personal communications, mass media, and electronic communication is easy enough to observe (although harder to measure). A more interesting question arises, though, when one asks how this sort of network produces an output—pressure on decision-makers, policy proposals, or other messages with political clout. There is ample research about public opinion and policy in the USA, although less in Latin America. These impacts are probably more successful in one kind of arena—involving general public opinion about highly visible public policy, mediated through elections—where research in Latin America is even more scarce.

The associative networks we see are more difficult to analyze, at least when they are not centered on a formal organizational structure. In the latter case, votes are taken or key meetings force some sort of consensus, but where the patterns of communication are personal or occur in the increasingly common public spaces created in the media, the process is more diffuse. Opinions are expressed, claims are made, ideas are put forward and challenged, assumptions are made and questioned. In some, threats are made, symbolic violence is enacted (perhaps even terrorism), dramatic public gestures are staged. And through it all, tendencies appear and become reinforced, interpreted, and rejected or adopted. It begins to be said that 'most of the activists think', 'the experts believe', or simply that 'everyone says . . .'. Through multiple actors and their links, the message—the *de facto* political output—gets assembled and delivered and, perhaps, decision-makers act on it.

We mean to emphasize the cognitive aspects of this process—the discussion of proposals and ideas—but not to exaggerate their importance. When, for example, the individuals and organizations in the network have well-established priorities and understandings, and their preferences are reasonably fixed, this interplay of ideas and interpretations may be seen as simply the confrontation of rationalizations, and the real process as a bargaining game. Or for those who see a sharp underlying conflict of interest between, say, the poor and the wealthy or some other division, the interplay of ideas may be seen as a process of overcoming false consciousness. In either case, something politically meaningful is occurring, even if it is not an intellectual debate. Yet, especially in the type of associative networks where the target is specialized decision-making centers and diverse groups, including professionals and other political service providers, participate and the questions at stake concern how to deal with serious social problems lacking simple answers, a model of cognitive politics seems appropriate, even when very real and understood interests are also present.

How should we characterize this open-ended process, which is at least a part of the linking processes of many associative networks? It is more like a conversation, the trading floor of a major stock market, or street theater than the ordered processes in a legislative body or a staff meeting. It is a kind of interactive field, in which the participants are reasonably clear but the rules according to which the outcome is determined are much less so.

Such interactive fields are not exclusive to the associative networks that we have been describing. There is a long-running show that involves public opinion at the broadest level. The selective use of violence by guerrilla activists, the political use of dramatic public events (such as soccer championships), and many other techniques require playing out a strategic game in a public space aimed at influencing policy outcomes. Moreover, populist leaders have long played on the lack of a transparent process inherent in this sort of interactive field, making the broadest possible appeals to limit their accountability. Through the force of their personality or their monopoly over public discourse, they appropriate the right to determine what 'the people' want. While modern neopopulists also clearly utilize a mass communications-driven style (Cavarozzi 1994), it seems less dangerous because of the transitory quality of its effect but more dangerous because of its volatility.[25]

We think the diffuse nature of the linking process in interactive fields is a very important feature of some associative networks and, therefore, of the emerging structure of popular representation. The fluidity allows both a maximum flexibility and room for innovation and clear thinking but, on the other hand, seems easily manipulated, making accountability difficult. There are other difficulties, too. It may be easy for experts to dominate the process, and they may be remote from the popular sectors. Certainly, popular criticism about the insensitivity of experts to indigenous values, to the poor's non-developmental economic goals, to the costs of dislocation, all suggest that a system enshrining the values and opinions of experts—a possible but not necessary outcome of associative networks—does not always benefit the popular sectors.

It is worth noting that the phenomenon to which we are pointing through the concept of associative networks is not the same as classical or interest-group pluralism. Aside from the plurality of societal actors involved, associative networks have little in common with classic understandings of political representation under pluralist approaches. Unlike the pluralist model of competition among interest groups and demand-making on the state through pressure politics, the type of interaction found within an associative network involves state and societal actors engaging in cognitive processes—of making, countering, and trying to

---

[25] Marcelo Cavarozzi also emphasizes the importance of the media to neopopulists with respect to their desire to build support or acquiescence in 'Politics: A Key for the Long Term in Latin America', in Smith *et al*. (1994*a*: 127–56).

resolve competing claims—that can in practice lead to the redefinition of interests as well as bargains among established ones. Moreover, the narrow connotation usually attached to the term 'interest groups' fails to capture the variety of analytical categories that the popular and other societal actors participating in associative networks encompass—social movements and movement organizations based upon newly politicized collective identities, non-governmental organizations, private firms, as well as the classic membership-based interest groups organized around socioeconomic categories. Lumping these categories together not only blurs the distinctiveness of each but also negates any possibility of problematizing the relationship among them, such as the often tense ties between NGOs and popular actors. Finally, the pluralist vision is of a political world made up of individual citizens and interest groups, separate from the politicians and policy-makers who aggregate their demands only through parties and elections and the apparently individualistic notion of lobbying. Classic pluralism minimizes the intermediate *structures* linking state and society aside from territorial representation and party systems,[26] to which we call attention with the notion of associative networks. Such structures fuse—or at least blur greatly the boundaries between—activities of 'interest articulation' and 'interest aggregation', of 'demand-making' and 'policy-making'.

Conclusions: Requirements for More Effective Popular Representation

What are the practical implications of this new analytical model of changing clusters of popular organizations, government representatives, businessmen, and NGOs? Does it suggest a better deal for the popular sectors than other models were able to provide? The answer, we would suggest, can be yes, but only if certain difficult conditions are met.

A 'better deal' consists of progress on three dimensions: establishing stable and effective government; overcoming the still drastic inequality in the region; and building spaces where people are able to participate effectively and have their claims taken seriously. The meanings of the first two of these are relatively straightforward,[27] but a few words about the third are in order.

---

[26] Indeed, it is precisely the absence of such 'linking structures' that led Heclo (1977) to propose the notion of 'issue networks' connecting actors across legislatures, executive agencies, and interest organizations. His work was in large part a reaction to the notion of 'iron triangles' linking such actors together for particularistic, rent-seeking purposes within American politics, which itself was also a response to the absence of intermediate institutions in pluralist formulations. Finally, of course, the whole corporatist paradigm (e.g. Schmitter 1974; Schmitter and Lehmbruch 1979; Berger 1981), particularly in the study of advanced industrial countries, was centered on an explicit critique of the absence of any acknowledgment and exploration of concrete structures of 'interest intermediation' in classical pluralist approaches.

[27] Once, discussion would have had to account for two possible scenarios—a first involving steps taken to bring down the system in anticipation of a revolutionary reconstruction and a second involving challenges from below to bring about evolutionary changes. We will not consider the former.

Progress in creating meaningful participation is obviously a democratic object-ive, but the nature of associative networks has prompted us to look for more than the opportunity to vote and express opinions freely. The notion of the associat-ive network embodies the possibility of a politics that goes well beyond—without supplanting—these traditional forms. Participation in such networks also focuses attention beyond the strength of positions in strategic bargaining to maximize interests—always important in political life but not the only dimension. In associ-ative networks, the challenging task for any group or individual is to define or re-shape its identity and goals and, through interaction with others, come to collective decisions. Democracy involves meaningful participation in that cognitive dimen-sion as well as the strategic bargaining dimension of representation.

The distinctiveness of this political style is captured by the fact that the char-acteristic political 'tools' of each set of actors in other political situations change their significance in the dynamics of associative situations. Administrative fiat by government actors has little control over others; monolithic technocratic pro-nouncements must confront those of other experts; log-rolling and compromise by politicians tends to be very visible to the participants; demand-making backed by mobilization or the threat thereof on the part of popular actors in civil society is a blunt tool. In associative networks, all these conventional political tools are more evidently in tension with the ideal of a shared search for solutions. This is not to say that such tactics no longer are used, and sometimes effectively. However, the emphasis on cognitive politics means that adopting such tactics can become counter-productive or suboptimal for both actors and the network-defined col-lectivity later, or in reconfigured associative networks.

Political encounters in associative networks hold the potential of generating new understandings of the nature of the problems confronted and, by extension, new solutions. This may be true whether the problem is how to balance sustainability and economic efficiency in the use of natural resources; how to ensure that social benefits are tailored to the specific needs of both particular groups of recipients and the labor market niches that they could fill; or how to promote greater coop-eration among workers and managers in the interest of fostering competitive-ness in higher value-added market niches. Hence, the role played by such cognitive resources as the ability to marshal information and arguments and use persuas-ive speech is crucial, which shifts the basis of inequality at least partially away from actors' structural position. If (and, of course, it is a big 'if') popular sectors in associative networks are able to develop the cognitive skills, and if elites can develop the capacity to hear what they are saying, such networks represent arenas in which outcomes will not be determined uniquely by the fundamental political resources associated with class, property, social status, or access to the means of coercion.

What, then, are the requirements that need to be met so that this new struc-ture will promote stability, redistributive justice, and democratic participation? While this is a broad topic, there are a few points that flow from the nature of the structures of representation we are describing, which we offer as the beginnings of a research agenda.

We see three sets of requirements: (*a*) organizations and procedures that coordinate the multiple decision centers and constantly changing networks, (*b*) a framework of rights that makes participation in associative networks possible, and (*c*) popular sector strategies that make the most of the opportunities and avoid the pitfalls of the new form.

INSTITUTIONS FOR COORDINATION

In the face of increasingly polycentric decision-making and multiple, diverse, and sometimes diffuse and constantly reconfiguring associative networks, the meta-institutional framework that organizes them is crucial. We might refer to these top-level institutions as constitutional, although many of the norms, rules, and monitoring devices necessary are indicated only very partially in written constitutions. Although there are many elements in this coordinating structure, we only touch on a few that require an approach somewhat out of the ordinary.

In our analytical model, the key institutional elements in liberal democracy—elections, legislatures, and party systems—should be considered as much or more as meta-institutional elements, rather than simply structures of representation. Although the rhetoric of liberal democracy is to speak of the way in which all three effectively represent their voters, constituents, or party members, in all three cases the rules and procedures governing them have a significant impact on how sensitive decision-makers are to the diverse pressures from associative networks, and how well they are coordinated in producing policy.

Recent efforts at legislative reform in the region suggest a fairly widespread concern with establishing a coordinating function for law-making bodies. The issue is not only legislative independence from the executive, but also whether legislative institutions can 'rise above' the immdiate pressures of representation (which may involve clientelism, corruption, 'special interests', and localism). The isolation of decision-makers to ponder only collective goods is also not the relevant concern here. Rather, the issue is how institutionally to tie the legislatures into the constantly changing pattern of associative networks, whether by having members of the legislature become part of the networks, or by granting members of the networks access to the legislative process. The goal is that the input from each network be given its due in the formulation of a coherent public policy.

Elections are another institution that is often thought of in terms of representation alone (e.g. whether the votes are correctly counted, or the clarity and binding quality (or lack thereof) of the mandate that emerges). These are very important issues, particularly in countries that have experienced manipulated elections for many years. Yet it is less common to address elections in the light of the problem of coordination. A classic view that is relevant here suggests that the ideal elections are those between teams of leaders in which the electorate is called upon to judge with respect to their overall competence, not so much their specific programs (Schumpeter 1942). Yet, in a polycentric state more systematic attention should probably be paid to the capacities of leaders to respond to, and perhaps generate, associative networks.[28]

Parties are even more often seen as a structure of representation. However each party, and most especially the party system, is also a major component of the meta-institutional framework that coordinates the various decision-making centers and the multiple associative networks. Mainwaring and Scully (1995)[29] have shown that there are a number of countries where parties are well institutionalized in Latin America, in the sense of having stable rules of competition and established organizational and voter bases. Beyond this minimum, however, we suggest that analyses of political parties will have to investigate how political parties are responding to the rise—and the challenge—of associative networks.

The old model in which the party took on all the aspects of a structure of representation seems pretty much dead in the rapidly changing and reconfiguring world of more polycentric states. The old pluralist vision that appropriated and made a virtue of the notion of the 'catch-all party' converges with the limited notion of democratic elections in which the main task was simply to elect competent teams. There seems little doubt that political parties need to be accessible and responsive to associative networks. Yet, as coalition builders responsible for organizing debate and bargaining among the various actors in the top-level decision-making centers, they need some way of building in not just flexibility, but meaningful interaction with constantly changing associative networks. In one sense, parties are losing (or failing to maintain) their dominance within processes of representation; yet, if they can become indispensable agents or vehicles of coordination among decision-making centers (a tall order, to be sure), they could become more central in the end.

THE RIGHTS AND RESOURCES NECESSARY FOR PARTICIPATION

If a new, more flexible, more complex, and perhaps more powerful set of structures of representation is emerging, then the conditions for popular actors becoming involved will shape strongly whether the popular sectors will be represented effectively or not. Since these are not formal institutions based on individuals, such as elections, equalization of rights to participate must go beyond any single institutional or legal change. Guarantees of rights are very important, however, and take many forms.

---

[28] This point runs parallel to Heclo's (1977) discussion of a new breed of politicians-*cum*-managers he calls 'policy politicians'. He argues that they frequently emerge from, and negotiate between, issue networks.

[29] They argue (ch. 1) that Venezuela, Costa Rica, Uruguay, Chile, Colombia, and to a 'lesser degree' Argentina have well-institutionalized party systems.

A first requirement, suggested by the chapters on the stubbornness of violence, is the guarantee of personal security. This may seem an odd place to start, but the formation of associative networks clearly requires some level of personal security, not only from state repression, but also from a breakdown of order, or from the kind of situation outlined by Paulo Sérgio Pinheiro, in which government agents and paramilitary groups behave like vigilantes.

A second set of institutional requirements for rendering an associative network just is that the formation and activities of associations, NGOs, movements, etc., be as free as possible. People should not be subject to private or public measures designed to prevent group formation, such as penalizing workers for joining a union. In addition, a legal status for organizations that recognizes their existence and gives them standing in the courts, legislative hearings, and other arenas is important. For instance, one of the relevant struggles in Latin America recently has been to find the right legal status for NGOs. Yet, the emphasis we have given to the importance of resources involves not only the legal right to exist and be heard, but also the facilitation of their access to resources, without—as Jonathan Fox points out in discussing clientelism—conditioning that access on political loyalty. These resources include the right to information from a variety of sources, particularly about the operations of government.

A third set of requirements concerns the establishment of arenas of discussion, debate, and policy formation that are accessible to popular groups. An associative network model raises not only the issue of the relative power of popular groups but also, since so much of the politics in this model takes place in the shaping of policy arenas, their ability to shape agendas. The establishment of media that are independent not only of the state but of particular economic interests and accessible and attentive to popular voices is clearly a central task. In many countries, universities have also been a place where agendas can be shaped. The growth of independent universities, research institutes, and other centers of discussion imbued with a healthy respect for popular concerns is an important requisite.

A fourth requirement relates to the waves of financial scandals that currently seem to plague the region. A challenge to the effectiveness of government clearly lies in the corruption and rent-seeking of public officials. And one can probably credit at least part of the new trend towards exposing such corruption as the grudging elite rejection of such practices as detrimental to their role—and reputation—in the world. Yet, there is an important question about distributive justice involved here, too. The old clientelistic and populist patterns sometimes actually used corruption as a tool for redistribution, but in the associative network model such a possibility is absent. Corruption becomes mere self-enrichment, not the building of a machine based on a favored clientele. In this connection, the challenge for redistributive justice in the current wave of anti-corruption efforts is that they be carried out in such a way as to establish meritocratic standards and public accountability for officials.

A fifth set of requirements centers on the need to protect group rights. If individuals continue to be subject to tacit official discrimination based on race, ethnicity, gender, sexual orientation, or other aspects of their background and beliefs, associative networks will face obstacles in both their social reach and their ability to secure greater stability, justice, and participation for the popular sectors. Specific guarantees that recognize the disadvantages faced by specific social groupings—including special provisions for the political and cultural autonomy and economic welfare of the region's many indigenous peoples—are another meta-institutional requirement for a better deal.

Some of these rights can be achieved by legislation, but this is a more complex process and its full realization will depend also on changing norms and beliefs among both citizens and officials. Any structures of representation need to be embedded in society and, as a relatively new one, associative networks require learning a new set of standards and behaviors.

POPULAR SECTOR STRATEGY: TOWARDS A NEW POLITICS OF INEQUALITY

The final set of requirements concerns the principles guiding the actions of popular actors and their political allies. The problems they face include the need to prevent the multiplicity of associative networks from becoming fragmented. Many associative networks create a serious potential for the splintering of political issues—and hence of organizations—into arenas that become disconnected, depoliticized, and narrowly circumscribed.

Further, popular sector participants enter into associative networks with unequal resources. Indigenous activists confronting government authorities and local landowners over land-tenure and development issues are less likely to have access to education budgets, land-use studies, or powerful political ties that are often important. Neighborhood organizations concerned with urban services and housing are likely to be much more limited in their ability to have access to architects and engineers, the money or social prestige to place ads or influence the local television, or the means of coercion that are available to city officials, building contractors, and local businessmen with whom they have to deal. Unions trying to organize in restructuring industries may have to develop considerable capacity to understand market trends, global commodity chains, and trade regulations in order to interact meaningfully and effectively with government economists and management. Moreover, as Carlos Vilas writes in the Introduction, there are still significant areas where actors are willing to use violence—Guatemala for much of this century, the interior of Brazil, the shantytowns of Lima. If violence becomes the norm, the formation of networks is impossible. But if violence is used selectively, as it often is, as a means of gaining tactical advantage, then unless popular sector groups are armed they will be at a disadvantage compared to the landowners, state officials, or others who can command or hire the necessary means of coercion.

In sum, although associative networks present real possibilities for improving the conditions of the popular sectors, it is clear that they will not automatically do so. Simply changing the type of structure of representation obviously does not mean that the popular sectors will be taken more seriously or that their claims necessarily will be satisfied. Even if the shift to associative networks were complete and universal, it would not necessarily mean a perfect democracy. Associative networks, like clientelistic relations, corporatist institutions, class-based parties, and populist movements, can be manipulated by elites to entrench or reinvent inequalities or mystify people about their real interests. Their fluidity and reliance on people who frame agendas and offer information present distinctive opportunities for such manipulation. Yet, we argue, when their inherent possibilities are realized by resourceful actors, associative networks do offer new ways of clarifying and reformulating strategic goals and finding new resources and allies to pursue claims; to at least some extent, popular actors are already using these emerging networks in such a way.

If our view of the dynamics of new structures of representation centered on associative networks has any validity, a new politics of inequality becomes possible. For example, the elaboration of associative networks changes the context of political action, in part because it encourages an elite view of the popular sectors as partners in finding solutions, as opposed to being either enemies or objects of all-or-nothing co-optation. This does not make them equal partners, but it opens up new opportunities. Since specific popular actors can influence decisions of particular concern to them, taken together, they have the potential to shape public decision-making more directly than ever before. In these arenas, 'experts' may become privileged, but in associative networks popular actors may seek the help of technically sophisticated allies, and further, bring their 'local knowledge' to bear.

The diversification of arenas and the weakening of broad ideological claims make it possible to do what would have been contradictory before—'having it both ways' (like the auto unionists in Brazil, who negotiated with Collor government officials on sectoral issues while continuing to be political opponents of that government and harsh critics of its overall economic policies). Despite continued diversity and discussion, there are trends within the left that are consistent with the rise of associative networks: the embrace of proactive styles; the erosion of hierarchical organizational forms like vanguardism and democratic centralism; moves away from instrumental party attitudes toward popular organizations (including the formation of movement-based parties such as the PT and the Causa R); and the valorization of formal democratic institutions. And while the broad political mobilization associated with Social Democracy has not emerged, some popular sector activists have been influenced by some of its core values, like 'concertation', 'codetermination', and 'social solidarity'. Taking other streams of ideas, 'radical democracy', with its emphasis on deepening democracy and extending it into diverse spheres of social life, and various notions of 'citizenship' generally link procedural issues of democratic rights with substantive issues of equity and equality.

Some efforts to reformulate popular strategy along these general lines have centered on 'individualistic' mechanisms of direct democracy like plebiscites and referenda. We believe that even in an ideal situation they can and should play only a supporting, rather than central, role in reformulating representation along progressive lines. They encourage a 'one-time-only', electorally centered mobilization and a 'yes or no' formulation of often complex issues, features which are in sharp contradiction with the many-sided quality of associative networks and their comparatively deeper discussions. As Filgueira and Papadópulos suggest in their chapter in this volume, in Uruguay plebiscites proved useful only in the limited—although by no means trivial—sense in which they enabled popular and left actors to mobilize public opinion to block technocratically conceived neoliberal reforms; it was simply not in the nature of these mechanisms to facilitate the proactive formulation of programmatic alternatives or social mobilization around such proposals.

The broadest implication of the growth of a polycentric state and multiple, changing associative networks is that securing redistribution and meaningful participation will not be the work of some single central popular leadership, but will be accomplished, if at all, by *many individuals and organizations operating in many different arenas*. There will be no 'popular sector strategy' to deal with the impacts of neoliberal policies, rather there will be social policy coalitions, progressive unions, indigenous and racial movements, and others, often going their own way and each calling on resources, allies, and assistance from a wide, shifting, and sometimes international range of sources. Political action based on solidarity and horizontal coordination among popular groups within and across these shifting networks and arenas—to take common action without a unified and centralized organization—remains a challenge.

Successful popular sector strategy will not depend primarily on dramatic legislation, mass campaigns, or plebiscites. It will also, and more importantly, depend on the development of the skills of many potential popular participants, enabling them effectively to create and exploit the opportunities of associative networks. The form by no means guarantees success, but much can happen if activists can build effective and accountable organizations; obtain accurate information and analysis; and develop ways of utilizing contacts with the media, government officials, and experts without becoming subordinate to them. While this task seems daunting, it places a premium on the resourcefulness and experience of popular actors in imagining and crafting new strategies and new forms of social organization.

The vitality of popular organizations that has been recounted in this volume suggests that even in inhospitable environments progress in forging new spaces for making political claims can occur. Only time will tell whether this will be enough to secure justice.

References

Acuña, Carlos H. (1992). 'Política y economía en la Argentina de los 90 (O porqué el futuro ya no es lo que solía ser)'. Presented at the conference 'Democracia, Mercados y Reformas Estructurales en América Latina'. Buenos Aires (Mar.).

—— (1994). 'Politics and Economics in the Argentina of the Nineties (Or, Why the Future No Longer Is What It Used To Be)'. In William C. Smith, Carlos H. Acuña, and Eduardo A. Gamarra (eds.), *Democracy, Markets, and Structural Reform in Latin America: Argentina, Bolivia, Brazil, Chile, and Mexico.* New Brunswick, NJ: Transaction/North–South Center, University of Miami.

Addis, Caren (1995). 'Emerging Forms of Industrial Governance: Promoting Cooperation between Small and Large Firms in Brazil'. Presented at Latin American Studies Association, Washington, DC, 28–30 Sept.

Adler Lomnitz, Larissa (1975). *Cómo sobreviven los marginados.* DF, Mexico: Siglo XXI.

Aguiar, Joaquim (1990). 'Sociedade Fragmentada e Clivagens Políticas'. *Análise social,* 25 (108–9): 545–87.

Aguilar Zinser, Adolfo (1993). 'Authoritarianism and North American Free Trade: The Debate in Mexico'. In Ricardo Grinspun and Maxwell A. Cameron (eds.), *The Political Economy of North American Free Trade.* New York: St Martin's Press.

Ai Camp, Roderick (1982). 'Family Relationships in Mexican Politics: A Preliminary View'. *Journal of Politics,* 44 (3): 848–62.

Albarrán de Alba, Gerardo (1992). 'Con Pronasol, la necesidad de la gente se usa electoralmente: Ruffo'. *Proceso,* 829, 21 Sept.

Aldrete-Haas, José A. (1991). *La deconstrucción del estado mexicano: Políticas de vivienda, 1917–1988.* DF, Mexico: Alianza Editorial.

Alesina, Alberto, and Allan, Drazen (1990). 'Why are Stabilizations Delayed'. Papers on Political Economy No. 1. Cambridge, Mass.: Harvard University.

Allen, Christopher S. (1990). 'Trade Unions, Worker Participation, and Flexibility: Linking the Micro to the Macro'. *Comparative Politics,* 22 (3): 253–72.

—— and Riemer, Jeremiah M. (1989). 'The Industrial Policy Controversy in West Germany: Organized Adjustment and the Emergence of Meso-Corporatism'. In Richard E. Foglesong and Joel D. Wolfe (eds.), *The Politics of Economic Adjustment: Pluralism, Corporatism, and Privatization.* New York: Greenwood.

Almeida, Marco Antonio de (1993). 'Estudos de Gestão: Icapuí e Janduís'. *Pólis,* 11.

Alonso, Jorge (coord.) (1986). *Los movimientos sociales en el valle de México.* DF, Mexico: Ediciones de la Casa Chata.

—— Aziz, Alberto, and Tamayo, Jaime (coords.) (1992). *El nuevo estado mexicano,* iii: *Estado, actores y movimientos sociales.* DF, Mexico: Nueva Imagen.

Altamirano, Teófilo (1988). *Cultura andina y pobreza urbana: Aymaras en Lima metropolitana.* Lima: Fondo Editorial Universidad Católica del Perú.

Altimir, Oscar (1994). 'Cambios de la desigualdad y la pobreza en la América Latina'. *El Trimestre Económico,* 241: 85–133.

ALVAREZ, SONIA (1990). *Engendering Democracy in Brazil: Women's Movements in Transition Politics*. Princeton: Princeton University Press.

ALVES, MARIA HELENA MOREIRA (1985). *State and Opposition in Military Brazil*. Austin: University of Texas Press.

—— (1993). 'Something Old, Something New: Brazil's Partido dos Trabalhadores'. In Barry Carr and Steve Ellner (eds.), *The Latin American Left: From the Fall of Allende to Perestroika*. Boulder, Colo.: Westview/Latin American Bureau.

Americas Watch (1990). *Human Rights in Mexico: A Policy of Impunity*. New York: Americas Watch.

—— (1991*a*). 'Violência Rural no Brasil'. São Paulo: Núcleo de Estudos da Violência, Comissão Teotônio Vilela.

—— (1991*b*). 'Unceasing Abuses: Human Rights in Mexico One Year after the Introduction of Reform'. New York.

—— (1993*a*). *The Killings in Candelária and Vigário Geral: The Urgent Need to Police the Brazilian Police*. New York: Americas Watch.

—— (1993*b*). *Urban Police Violence in Brazil: Torture and Police Killings in São Paulo and Rio de Janeiro after Five Years*. New York: Americas Watch.

AMES, BARRY (1994). 'The Reverse Coattails Effect: Local Party Organization in the 1989 Brazilian Presidential Election'. *American Political Science Review*, 88 (1): 95–111.

Amnesty International (1993). *Guatemala: Impunity—A Question of Political Will*. New York.

ANASTASIA, CARLA MARIA JUNHO (1994). 'Corporativismo e calculo político'. *Novos Ramos*, 9: 46–51.

ANDERSON, BENEDICT (1983). *Imagined Communities: Reflections on the Origins and Spread of Nationalism*. London: Verso.

ANDERSON, JULIE (1990). 'Legislation, Development and Legislating Development in Brazilian Rural Labor Markets'. Unpublished. Cambridge.

ANDRADE, ODORICO MONTEIRO DE, and GOYA, NEUSA (eds.) (1992). *Sistemas Locais de Saúde em Municípios de Pequeno Porte: A Resposta de Icapuí*, 2nd edn. Fortaleza: Expressão.

ANGELL, ALAN (1991). 'Unions and Workers in Chile during the 1980s'. In Paul Drake and I. Jacsik (eds.), *The Struggle for Democracy in Chile*. Lincoln: University of Nebraska Press.

ANTUNIASSI, MARIA HELENA R., MAGDALENA, CELIGRÁCIA, and GIANSANTI, ROBERTO (1989). *O Movimento Ambientalista em São Paulo: Analise Sociológica de um Movimento Social Urbano*. São Paulo: Textos, CERU.

APPENDINI, KIRSTEN (1992). *De la milpa a los tortibonos: la reestructuración de la política alimentaría en México*. DF, Mexico: EL Colegio de México.

ARAÚJO, PAULO FERNANDO CIDADE DE (1983). 'Agricultura brasileira sem subsídio'. *Revista de Economia Rural*, 21: 3–7.

ARBIX, GLAUCO ANTÔNIO TRUZZI (1995). 'Uma Aposta no Futuro: Os Tres Primeiros Anos da Câmara Setorial da Industria Automobilística e a Emergência do Meso-Corporativismo no Brasil'. Doctoral thesis, Departamento de Sociologia, Faculdade de Filosofia, Letras e Ciências Humanas, Universidade de São Paulo.

ARELLANO-LÓPEZ, SONIA, and PETRAS, JAMES F. (1994). 'Non-governmental Organizations and Poverty Alleviation in Bolivia'. *Development and Change*, 25: 555–68.

ARENDT, HANNAH (1963). *On Revolution*. New York: Penguin Books.

—— (1970). *On Violence*. New York: Harcourt Brace Jovanovich.

ARICÓ, JOSÉ (1989). 'El Marxismo en América Latina: Ideas para abordar de otro modo una vieja cuestión'. In Fernando Calderón (ed.), *Socialismo, autoritarismo, y democracia.* Lima: Instituto de Estudios Peruanos and CLACSO.

ASPE, PEDRO, and SIGMUND, PAUL E. (eds.) (1984). *The Political Economy of Income Distribution in Mexico.* New York: Holmes & Meier Publishers, Inc.

ATKINSON, MICHAEL M., and COLEMAN, WILLIAM D. (1985). 'Corporatism and Industrial Policy'. In Alan Cawson (ed.), *Organized Interests and the State: Studies in Meso-Corporatism.* London: Sage.

—— —— (1992). 'Policy Networks, Policy Communities and the Problems of Governance'. *Governance: An International Journal of Policy Administration,* 5 (2).

AVELAR, LUCIA (1991). 'As Clivagens do Voto: Eleições Presidenciais de 1989'. Presented at Latin American Studies Association Congress, Washington, DC.

AYALA MORA, ENRIQUE (1989). *Los partidos políticos en el Ecuador.* Quito: Ediciones la Tierra.

AZEVEDO, CLOVIS BUENO DE (1991). 'Leninismo e Social-Democracia: Uma investigação sobre o projeto político do Partido dos Trabalhadores'. Master's thesis for the Universidade de São Paulo, Departamento de Ciência Política.

AZEVÊDO, FERNANDO ANTONIO (1982). *As Ligas Camponesas.* Rio de Janeiro: Paz e Terra.

BACON, DAVID (1993). 'Mexican Union Election Falls Short'. *San Francisco Chronicle,* 24 Dec.: 1A.

BALBI, CARMEN ROSA (1989). *Identidad clasista en el sindicalismo.* Lima: DESCO.

—— (1992). 'Sendero en las fábricas: Encendienco la mecha'. *QueHacer,* 77. Lima: DESCO.

—— (1993). 'Del golpe del 5 de Abril al CCD: Los problemas de la transición a la democracia'. *Pretextos,* 3/4. Lima: DESCO.

—— (1997). 'Politics and Trade Unions in Peru'. In Philip Mauceri and Max Cameron (eds.), *The Peruvian Labyrinth.* University Park: Pennsylvania State University.

BALLINAS, VICTOR, and URRUTIA, ALONSO (1994). 'La imagen de Cárdenas y las alianzas, cartas del PRD en el DF'. *La Jornada* (Mexico City), 7 Aug.: 51–2, 68.

BALLÓN, EDUARDO (1986). *Movimientos sociales y democracia: La fundación de un nuevo orden.* Lima: DESCO.

—— (1990). *Movimientos sociales: Elementos para una relectura.* Lima: DESCO.

BALOYRA, ENRIQUE (1983). 'Reactionary Despotism in Central America'. *Journal of Latin American Studies,* 15: 295–319.

BANCK, GEERT A. (1994). 'Democratic Transparency and the Train of Joy and Happiness'. In Jojada Verrips (ed.), *Transactions: Essays in Honor of Jeremy Boissevain.* Amsterdam: Spinhuis.

Banco Mundial (1993). *Informe sobre desarrollo mundial.* Washington: Banco Mundial.

BARBALET, J. M. (1988). *Citizenship.* Minneapolis: University of Minnesota.

BARBIN, LUCAS (1991). 'La sociedad fragmentada'. *Nueva Sociedad,* 111: 100–8.

BARDACKE, TED (1992). 'The Lion Learns New Tricks'. *El financiero internacional,* 20 July.

BARGER, W. K., and REZA, ERNESTO M. (1994). *The Farm Labor Movement in the Midwest: Social Change and Adaptation among Migrant Farmworkers.* Austin: The University of Texas Press.

BARROS, GERALDO SANTA ANA DE, MOITINHO AMARAL, CICELY, and BARROS AMARAL, VERA L. (1983). 'Análise do Mercado de Trabalho na Agricultura Brasileira'. *Revista de Economia Rural,* 21 (3).

BARROS, ROBERT (1986). 'The Left and Democracy: Recent Debates in Latin America'. *Telos,* 68 (2): 49–70.

BARTRA, ROGER (ed.) (1975). *Caciquismo y poder político en el México rural.* Mexico City: Siglo XXI.

BARZELAY, MICHAEL (1986). *The Politicized Market Economy: Alcohol in Brazil's Energy Strategy*. Berkeley and Los Angeles: University of California Press.

BASÁNEZ, MIGUEL (1992). 'Quinta crisis?' *Folios de Este Pais*, 14: 1–8.

BASTOS, SANTIAGO, and CAMUS, MANUELA (1993). *Quebrando el silencio: Organizaciones del pueblo maya y sus demandas (1986–1992)*. Guatemala: FLACSO.

BAUMGARTNER, FRANK R., and JONES, BRYAN D. (1991). 'Agenda Dynamics and Policy Subsystems'. *Journal of Politics*, 11/91: 1044–74.

BECARIA, LUIS, and ORSATTI, ALVARO (1990). 'Precarización laboral y estructura productiva en la Argentina: 1974–1988'. In P. Galín and M. Novick (eds.), *La precarización del empleo en la Argentina*. Buenos Aires: Centro Editor de América Latina.

BEDOYA, JAIME (1989). 'Más inseguros que nunca'. *Debate*, 11 (55). Lima: APOYO.

BELTRÁN DEL RIO, PASCAL (1990*a*). 'Solidaridad, oxígeno para el PRI, en el rescate de votos'. *Proceso*, 718, 6 Aug.

—— (1990*b*). 'El memorandum de Pichardo, prueba de que el Pronasol es para servir al PRI'. *Proceso*, 730, 29 Oct.

BENJAMIN, CÉSAR (1990). 'Nossos Verdes Amigos'. *Teoria e Debate*, 12.

BENNETT, VIVIENNE (1992). 'The Evolution of Urban Popular Movements in Mexico between 1968 and 1988'. In Arturo Escobar and Sonia Alvarez (eds.), *The Making of Social Movements in Latin America*. Boulder, Colo.: Westview Press.

BERG, RONALD (1986–7). 'Sendero Luminoso and the Peasantry of Andahuaylas'. *Journal of Inter-American Studies and World Affairs*, 28: 164–96.

—— (1992). 'Peasant Responses to Shining Path in Andahuaylas'. In David Scott Palmer (ed.), *Shining Path of Peru*. New York: St Martin's Press.

BERGER, SUZANNE (ed.) (1981). *Organizing Interests in Western Europe: Pluralism, Corporatism, and the Transformation of Politics*. Cambridge: Cambridge University Press.

BERMEJILLO, EUGENIO (1995). 'Hacia la autonomía india'. *Ojarasca*, 45, Aug.–Nov.

BISHOP, EDWIN WARREN (1959). 'The Guatemalan Labor Movement, 1944–1959'. Doctoral diss., Department of Economics, University of Wisconsin.

BITTAR, JORGE (ed.) (1992). *O Modo Petista de Governar*. São Paulo: Teoria & Debate.

BITTENCOURT PASSOS, ANA TEREZA, and KHAN, AHMAD SAEED (1988). 'Política Agricola e Desigualdade Econômicas e Sociais do Setor Agricola Brasileiro'. *Revista de Economia e Sociologia Rural*, 26 (1).

BLANCO RIVERA, RAFAEL (1991). 'Oaxaca, 1980'. *Cuadernos de demografía indígena*. Mexico: INI, Dirección de Investigación y Promoción Cultural.

BOBBIO, NORBERTO (1984). *Direitos e Estado no Pensamento de Emmanuel Kant*. Brasília: Editora da Universidade de Brasília.

BOITO, Jr., ARMANDO (1991). *O Sindicalismo Brasileiro nos Anos 80*. São Paulo: Paz e Terra.

BOLLEN, KENNETH A. (1991). 'Political Democracy: Conceptual and Measurement Traps'. In Alex Inkeles (ed.), *On Measuring Democracy: Its Consequences and Concomitants*. New Brunswick: Transaction Publishers.

BONFIL, GUILLERMO (1990). *México profundo: Una civilización negada*. DF, Mexico: Grijalbo/CONACULT.

BOOTH, JOHN A., and SELIGSON, MITCHELL A. (1989). *Elections and Democracy in Central America*. Chapel Hill: The University of North Carolina Press.

BORGES, FRANCISCA NEUMA FECHINE, *et al.* (eds.) (1986). *Antología de literatura de cordel*. João Pessoa: Universidade Federal de Paraíba.

Boschi, Renato (1987). *A Arte de Asociação: Política de Base e Democracia no Brasil*. Rio de Janeiro: Vértice and IUPERJ.

Bosworth, Barry P., Dornbusch, R., and Labán, R. (eds.) (1994). *The Chilean Economy: Policy Lessons and Challenges*. Washington: The Brookings Institution.

Bourdieu, Pierre (1980). *Questions de sociologie*. Paris: Minuit.

Bourque, Susan C., and Warren, Kay B. (1989). 'Democracy without Peace: The Cultural Politics of Terror in Peru'. *Latin American Research Review*, 24 (1): 7–34.

Bourricaud, François (1970). *Power and Society in Contemporary Peru*. New York: Praeger.

Bowles, Samuel, and Gintis, Herbert (1986). *Democracy and Capitalism*. New York: Basic Books.

Brading, David A. (1991). *The First America: The Spanish Monarchy, Creole Patriots and the Liberal State, 1492–1867*. Cambridge: Cambridge University Press.

Bratton, Michael (1989). 'Beyond the State: Civil Society and Associational Life in Africa'. *World Politics*.

Brautigam, Deborah (1994). 'State, NGOs, and International Aid in The Gambia'. In Eve Sandberg (ed.), *The Changing Politics of NGOs in African States*. New York: Praeger.

Bravo, Fernando (1994). 'Del democratismo al autoritarismo: Cuando la sociedad es voluble'. *Socialismo y Participación*, 65. Lima.

Brecher, Jeremy, and Costello, Tim (1991a). 'Labor Goes Global I: Global Village vs. Global Pillage'. *Z Magazine*, Jan.: 90–7.

—— —— (1991b). 'Labor Goes Global II: A One-World Strategy for Labor'. *Z Magazine*, Mar.: 88–97.

Bresser Pereira, Luís Carlos, Maravall, José María, and Przeworski, Adam (1993). *Economic Reforms in New Democracies: A Social Democratic Approach*. Cambridge: Cambridge University Press.

Brock, P., Connolly, M., and González-Vega, C., (eds.) (1989). *Latin American Debt and Adjustment: External Shocks and Macroeconomic Policies*. New York: Praeger.

Brockett, Charles D. (1991). 'The Structure of Political Opportunities and Peasant Mobilization in Central America'. *Comparative Politics*, 23: 253–74.

Brooke, James (1994). 'Scandals Shaking Faith of Brazil in Democracy'. *New York Times*, 4 Jan.

Brooks, David (1992). 'The Search for Counterparts'. *Labor Research Review*, 19: 83–96.

Browne, Harry, and Sims, Beth (1993). 'Global Capitalism, Global Unionism'. *Resource Center Bulletin*, 30. Albuquerque.

—— —— and Barry, Tom (1994). *For Richer, for Poorer: Shaping U.S.–Mexican Integration*. The U.S.–Mexican Series 4. Albuquerque: Resource Center Press and Latin America Bureau.

Bryce, Robert (1993). 'Mexican Unions Struggle in a Tough Post-NAFTA World'. *Christian Science Monitor*, 22 Dec.: 7.

Brysk, Alison (1993). 'From Above and Below: Social Movements, the International System, and Human Rights in Argentina'. *Comparative Political Studies*, 26 (3).

Buchanan, Paul G. (1990). ' "Useful Fools" as Diplomatic Tools: Organized Labor as an Instrument of U.S. Foreign Policy in Latin America'. Working Paper No. 136. Notre Dame, Ind.: The Helen Kellogg Institute for International Studies, University of Notre Dame.

Bunuel, Jean (1992). *Pactos y agresiones: El sindicalismo argentino ante el desafío neo-liberal*. Buenos Aires: Fondo de Cultura Económica.

Bureau of National Labor Affairs (1994). *Daily Labor Report* (DLR No. 197), 14 Oct.

BURT, JO-MARIE (1995). 'Shining Path in Lima's *Barriadas*: Popular Responses and Perceptions in Villa El Salvador'. Paper presented at the International Symposium 'Shining and Other Paths: Anatomy of a Peruvian Tragedy, Prospects for a Peruvian Future', University of Wisconsin-Madison.

—— and ESPEJO, CÉSAR (1995). 'The Struggles of a Self-Built Community'. *NACLA Report on the Americas*, 28 (4).

—— and LÓPEZ RICCI, JOSÉ (1994). 'Peru: Shining Path after Guzmán'. *NACLA Report on the Americas*, 28 (3).

—— and PANFICHI, ALDO (1992). *Peru: Caught in the Crossfire*. Jefferson City, Mo.: Peru Peace Network.

BURT, RONALD (1982). *Toward a Structural Theory of Action*. New York: Academic Press.

Business Monitor International, Ltd. (1993). *Brazil 1993: Annual Report on Government, Economy and the Business Environment*. London: BMI Ltd.

CABALLERO, ALEJANDRO (1991). 'Ex-militantes de grupos de izquierda predominan en plurinominales del PRD'. *La Jornada* (Mexico City), 27, 3 May.

CABRAL, PEDRO EUGÊNIO TOLEDO (1984–6). 'O processo de Proletarização do Trabalhador Canaveiro de Pernambuco'. *Revista Pernambucana de Desenvolvimento*, 11–12 (1–1).

CALDEIRA, TERESA PIRES DO RIO (1992). 'City of Walls, Crime, Segregation and Citizenship in São Paulo'. Ph.D. diss., Anthropology, University of California at Berkeley.

CALDERÓN, FERNANDO, PISCITELLI, ALEJANDRO, and REYNA, JOSÉ LUIS (1992). 'Social Movements, Actors, Theories, Expectations'. In Arturo Escobar and Sonia Alvarez (eds.), *The Making of Social Movements in Latin America*. Boulder, Colo.: Westview Press.

CAMERON, MAXWELL A. (1991*a*). 'The Politics of the Urban Informal Sector in Peru: Populism, Class and Redistributive Combines'. *Canadian Journal of Latin American and Caribbean Studies*, 16 (31): 79–104.

—— (1991*b*). 'Political Parties and the Worker–Employer Cleavage: The Impact of the Informal Sector on Voting in Lima, Peru'. *Bulletin of Latin American Research*, 10 (3): 293–313.

CAMMACK, PAUL (1993). 'Latin American Social Democracy in British Perspective'. In Menno Vellinga (ed.), *Social Democracy in Latin America: Prospects for Change*. Boulder, Colo.: Westview Press.

CAMOU, ANTONIO (1992). 'Once tesis sobre la "transición" mexicana: Gobernabilidad y democracia'. *Nexos*, 55 (170), Feb.

CAMP, RODERIC A. (1990). 'Camarillas in Mexican Politics: The Case of the Salinas Cabinet'. *Mexican Studies/Estudios mexicanos*, 6 (1), Winter: 85–107.

CAMPBELL, JOHN L., HOLLINGSWORTH, J. ROGERS, and LINDBERG, LEON N. (eds.) (1991). *Governance of the American Economy*. Cambridge: Cambridge University Press.

CAMPOS, EDSON (1992). 'Longe das capitais'. *Teoria & Debate*, 18 (2).

CANTÚ, JESÚS (1992). 'Solidaridad, además de electorero, se manejó en Michoacán coercitivamente'. *Proceso*, 819, 13 July.

CÁRDENAS, CUAUHTÉMOC (1988). 'Llamamiento al pueblo de México'. Mexico, D.F.: Partido de la Revolución Democrática.

CARDIA, NANCY (1993). 'Percepção de Direitos Humanos, Ausência de Cidadania e a Exclusão Moral'. Unpublished. São Paulo: Núcleo de Estudos da Violência.

CARDOSO, ADALBERTO MOREIRA, and COMIN, ALVARO AUGUSTO (1993). 'Câmaras Setoriais, Modernização Produtiva e Democratização nas Relações de Trabalho no Brasil:

A Experiência do Setor Automobilístico'. Paper presented to the First Latin American Congress on Labor Sociology, Mexico City (22–6 Nov.).

CARDOSO, FERNANDO HENRIQUE (1979). 'On the Characterization of Authoritarian Regimes in Latin America'. In David Collier (ed.), *The New Authoritarianism in Latin America*. Princeton: Princeton University Press.

—— and FALETO, ENZO (1977). *Dependency and Development in Latin America*. Berkeley and Los Angeles: University of California Press.

CARDOSO, RUTH CORRÊA LEITE (1992). 'Popular Movements in the Context of the Consolidation of Democracy in Brazil'. In Arturo Escobar and Sonia Alvarez (eds.), *The Making of Social Movements in Latin America*. Boulder, Colo.: Westview Press.

CARDOZA Y ARAGÓN, LUIS (1955). *La revolución guatemalteca*. DF, Mexico: Cuadernos Americanos 43.

CARMACK, ROBERT M. (ed.) (1988). *Harvest of Violence: Guatemala's Indians in the Counter-insurgency War*. Norman: University of Oklahoma Press.

CARO, NELLY (1993). *Democracia interna y las organizaciones de sobrevivencia en Lima*. Master's thesis, Sociology Department, Catholic University of Peru.

CARPENA, RICARDO, and JACQUELINE, CLAUDIO (1994). *El intocable*. Buenos Aires: Ed. Sudamericana.

CARR, BARRY (1993). 'Hacia un nuevo internacionalismo obrero'. Presented to Coloquio Internacional sobre la Clase Obrera, los Nuevos Sujetos Sociales y las Alternativas Socialistas del Presente, Universidad de Guadalajara (10 Sept.).

—— (1995). 'Labor Internationalism in the Era of NAFTA: Past and Present'. Latin American Labor Studies Occasional Paper No. 14. Miami: Center for Labor Research and Studies, Florida International University.

—— and ELLNER, STEVE (eds.) (1993). *The Latin American Left: From the Fall of Allende to Perestroika*. Boulder, Colo.: Westview/Latin American Bureau.

—— and MONTOYA, RICARDO ANZALDUA (eds.) (1986). *The Mexican Left, the Popular Movements and the Politics of Austerity*. La Jolla: Center for US–Mexican Studies, University of California, San Diego, Monograph Series 18.

CARRASCO, ROSALBA, and PROVENCIO, ENRIQUE (1988). 'La política social 1983–1988 y sus principales consecuencias'. *Investigación Económica*, 4–6/88 (184): 95–7.

CARRILLO V., JORGE (1991). 'The Evolution of the Maquiladora Industry: Labor Relations in a New Context'. In Kevin J. Middlebrook (ed.), *Unions, Workers, and the State in Mexico*. La Jolla: Center for US–Mexican Studies, University of California, San Diego.

CARROLL, LEAH (1991). 'Repression and the Limits to Rural Democratization: The Experience of Leftist County Executives in Colombia, 1988–1990'. Paper presented at the Latin American Studies Association.

CARROLL, THOMAS F. (1992). *Intermediary NGOs: The Supporting Link in Grassroots Development*. West Hartford, Conn.: Kumarian Press.

CARVALLO, GASTÓN, and LÓPEZ-MAYA, MARGARITA (1989). 'Crisis en el sistema político venezolano'. *Cuadernos del CENDES*, 10. Caracas.

CASANUEVA, CRISTINA, and DÍAZ, ALBERTO (1991). *Vivienda y estabilidad política: alternativas para el futuro*. DF, Mexico: Editorial Diana.

CASCÃO, RODOLFO INÁCIO (1992). *Democratização do Poder Local: Uma Experiência no Araguaia*. Rio de Janeiro: FASE.

CASTAÑEDA, JORGE G. (1993a). *La utopía desarmada: Intrigas, dilemas y promesas de la izquierda en América Latina*. DF, Mexico: Joaquín Mortiz.

CASTAÑEDA, JORGE G. (1993b). *Utopia Unarmed: The Latin American Left after the Cold War*. New York: Alfred Knopf.

CASTILLO, OSCAR (1991). 'Lo que el Tsunami se llevó: Jóvenes, política y empleo en Perú' (mimeograph). Lima.

CASTORIADIS, CORNELIUS (1975). *L'Institution imaginaire de la société*. Paris: Éditions du Seuil.

CASTRO REA, JULIAN, DUCATENZEILER, GRACIELA, and FAUCHER, PHILIPPE (1992). 'Back to Populism: Latin America's Alternative to Democracy'. In Archibald R. M. Ritter, Maxwell A. Cameron, and David H. Pollock (eds.), *Latin America to the Year 2000: Reactivating Growth, Improving Equity, Sustaining Democracy*. New York: Praeger.

Causa R (1973). 'Qué nos proponemos', *Causa R*, 2 (July). Caracas.

CAVAROZZI, MARCELO (1992a). 'Beyond Transitions to Democracy in Latin America'. *Journal of Latin American Studies*, 24: 661–84.

—— (1992b). 'La política: Clave del largo plazo Latinoamericano'. Presented to the XVIth Meeting of the Latin American Studies Association, Los Angeles.

—— (1993). 'The Left in South America: Politics as the Only Option'. In Menno Vellinga (ed.), *Social Democracy in Latin America: Prospects for Change*. Boulder, Colo.: Westview Press.

—— (1994). 'Politics: A Key for the Long Term in Latin America'. In William C. Smith, Carlos H. Acuña, and Eduardo A. Gamarra (eds.), *Latin American Political Economy in the Age of Neoliberal Reform*. New Brunswick, NJ: Transaction.

CAWSON, ALAN (ed.) (1985). *Organized Interests and the State: Studies in Meso-Corporatism*. London: Sage.

—— (1986). *Corporatism and Political Theory*. Oxford: Basil Blackwell.

CENTENO, MIGUEL ANGEL, and MAXFIELD, SYLVIA (1992). 'The Marriage of Finance and Order: Changes in the Mexican Political Elite'. *Journal of Latin American Studies*, 24 (1), Feb.

Center for Justice and International Law (CEJIL) (1993). 'The Docket of CEJIL'. In *Documents for Second Meeting of the Board of Directors*. Washington: CEJIL.

Centro de Investigación para el Desarrollo (1991). *Vivienda y estabilidad política: Reconcebir las políticas sociales*. DF, Mexico: Editorial Diana.

Centro Santo Dias de Direitos Humanos da Arquidiocese de São Paulo (1993). 'Agenda Nacional de Direitos Humanos, caderno 1'. São Paulo: Centro Santo Dias de Direitos Humanos.

CEPAL (Comisión Económica para América Latina y el Caribe) (1992). *El perfil de la pobreza a comienzos de los años 90*. Santiago de Chile: CEPAL.

CERNEA, MICHAEL (1983). 'A Social Methodology for Community Participation in Local Investment: The Experience of Mexico's PIDER Program'. World Bank Staff Working Paper, no. 598. Washington, Aug.

CHALMERS, DOUGLAS (1972). 'Parties and Society in Latin America'. *Studies in Comparative International Development*, 7 (2): 102–30.

—— (1985). 'Corporatism and Comparative Politics'. In Howard Wiarda (ed.), *New Directions in Comparative Politics*. Boulder, Colo.: Westview Press.

—— (1991). 'An End to Foreign Policy: The U.S. and Internationalized Politics'. Conference Paper No. 60. New York: The Columbia University–New York University Consortium.

—— (1992). 'The International Dimensions of Political Institutions in Latin America: An

Internationalized Politics Approach'. Presented at the 1992 annual meeting of the American Political Science Association, Chicago.

CHARVET, PAOLA SILVA (1991). *La organización rural en el Ecuador*. Quito: Abya-Ayala.

CHÁVEZ, ELÍAS (1992). 'Michoacán: Cada voto costó 239,188 pesos; cada voto del PRD costó 6,916 pesos'. *Proceso*, 821, 27 July.

CHÁVEZ DE PAZ, DENNIS (1989). *Juventud y terrorismo: Características sociales de los condenados por terrorismo y otros delitos*. Lima: Instituto de Estudios Peruanos.

CHAVIGNY, PAULO (1990). 'Police Deadly Force as Social Control: Jamaica, Argentina and Brazil'. *Criminal Law Forum International*, 1 (3): 389–485.

—— (1995). *Edge of the Knife*. New York: The New Press.

CHAZEN, NAOMI (1994). 'Engaging the State: Associational Life in Sub-Saharan Africa'. In Joel S. Migdal, Atul Kohli, and Vivienne Shue (eds.), *State Power and Social Forces: Domination and Transformation in the Third World*. Cambridge: Cambridge University Press.

CLAPHAM, CHRISTOPHER (ed.) (1982). *Private Patronage and Public Power: Political Clientelism in the Modern State*. New York: St Martin's Press.

COHEN, JEAN (1985). 'Strategy or Identity: New Theoretical Paradigms and Contemporary Social Movements'. *Social Research*, 52 (4): 663–716.

—— and ARATO, ANDREW (1992). *Civil Society*. Cambridge, Mass.: MIT Press.

COHEN, JOSHUA, and ROGERS, JOEL (eds.) (1992). 'Secondary Associations and Democratic Governance'. Special issue of *Politics and Society*, 20 (4): 393–472.

COHEN, YOUSSEF (1994). *Radicals, Reformers and Reactionaries: The Prisoner's Dilemma and the Collapse of Democracy in Latin America*. Chicago: University of Chicago Press.

COLEMAN, JAMES S. (1990). *Foundations of Social Theory*. Cambridge, Mass.: Belnap Press of Harvard University Press.

COLLIER, DAVID (1978). *Barriadas y elites: De Odría a Velasco*. Lima: IEP.

—— (ed.) (1979). *The New Authoritarianism in Latin America*. Princeton: Princeton University Press.

—— (1995). 'Trajectory of a Concept: "Corporatism" in the Study of Latin American Politics'. In Peter H. Smith (ed.), *Latin America in Comparative Perspective: New Approaches to Methods and Analysis*. Boulder, Colo.: Westview.

COLLIER, RUTH BERINS (1992). *The Contradictory Alliance: State–Labor Relations and Regime Change in Mexico*. Berkeley and Los Angeles: University of California.

—— and COLLIER, DAVID (1977). 'Inducements Versus Constraints: Disaggregating Corporatism'. *American Political Science Review*, 73 (4): 967–86.

—— —— (1991). *Shaping the Political Arena: Critical Junctures, the Labor Movement, and Regime Dynamics in Latin America*. Princeton: Princeton University Press.

COLLINS, JOSEPH, and LEAR, JOHN (1995). *Chile's Free Market Miracle: A Second Look*. Oakland, Calif.: Institute for Food and Development Policy.

Comisión Económica para América Latina y el Caribe (CEPAL/ECLAC) (1991). *Magnitud de la pobreza en América Latina en los años ochenta*. Santiago: United Nations.

—— (1993). *Población, equidad, y transformación productiva*. Santiago: United Nations.

Comisión Nacional de Plan de Gobierno (1990). *Plan de gobierno de Izquierda Unida 1990–1995: Plan de acción inmediata*. Lima: Izquierda Unida.

COMPA, LANCE (1995). 'Going Multilateral: The Evolution of U.S. Hemispheric Labor Rights Policy under GSP and NAFTA'. *Connecticut Journal of International Law*, 10 (2): 337–64.

Conaghan, Catherine (1988). *Restructuring Domination: Industrialists and the State in Ecuador*. Pittsburgh: University of Pittsburgh Press.

—— and Malloy, James (1994). *Unsettling Statecraft: Democracy and Neoliberalism in the Central Andes*. Pittsburgh: University of Pittsburgh Press.

CONAIE (1989). *Las nacionalidades indígenas en el Ecuador: Nuestro proceso organizativo*. Quito: Ediciones Abya-Yala.

—— (1994). 'Proyecto político de la CONAIE'. Quito: CONAIE.

Coniff, Michael L. (1982). *Latin American Populism in Comparative Perspective*. Albuquerque: University of New Mexico Press.

Connolly, Priscilla (1993). 'The "Go-between": CENVI, a Habitat NGO in Mexico City'. *Environment and Urbanization*, 5 (1): 68–90.

Consejo Consultivo del Programa Nacional de Solidaridad (1991). *Solidaridad a debate*. DF, Mexico: El Nacional.

Convergencia de Organismos Civiles por la Democracia (1992). 'Informe de observación electoral'. *Perfil de la Jornada*, 16 Aug.

Cook, Maria Lorena (1994). 'Regional Integration and Transnational Labor Strategies under NAFTA'. In Maria Lorena Cook and Harry C. Katz (eds.), *Regional Integration and Industrial Relations in North America*. Ithaca, NY: Institute of Collective Bargaining, New York State School of Industrial and Labor Relations, Cornell University.

—— (1995). 'State–Labor Relations in Mexico: Old Tendencies and New Trends'. In Donald E. Schulz and Edward J. Williams (eds.), *Mexico Faces the Twenty-First Century*. Westport, Conn.: Praeger.

—— Middlebrook, Kevin J., and Molinar Horcasitas, Juan (1994). 'The Politics of Economic Restructuring: Actors, Sequencing, and Coalition Change'. In Maria Lorena Cook, Kevin J. Middlebrook, and Juan Molinar Horcasitas (eds.), *The Politics of Economic Restructuring: State–Society Relations and Regime Change in Mexico*. La Jolla: Center for US–Mexican Studies, University of California, San Diego.

COPRE (Comisión Presidencial para la Reforma del Estado) (1986). *Propuestas para reformas políticas inmediatas*. Folletos para la discusión No. 1. Caracas: Ediciones de COPRE.

—— (1987*a*). *Lineamientos generales para una política de descentralización territorial en Venezuela*. Folletos para la discusión No. 9. Caracas: Ediciones de la COPRE.

—— (1987*b*). *Propuestas para impulsar el proceso de descentralización territorial en Venezuela*. Folletos para la discusión No. 9. Caracas: Ediciones de COPRE.

Corkill, David, and Cubitt, David (1988). *Ecuador: Fragile Democracy*. London: Latin America Bureau.

Cornelius, Wayne (1975). *Politics and the Migrant Poor in Mexico City*. Stanford, Calif.: Stanford University Press.

—— (1987). 'Political Liberalization in an Authoritarian Regime: Mexico, 1976–1985'. In Judith Gentleman (ed.), *Mexican Politics in Transition*. Boulder, Colo.: Westview Press.

—— and Craig, Ann (1991). *The Mexican Political System in Transition*. La Jolla, Calif.: UCSD, Center for US–Mexican Studies.

—— Gentleman, Judith, and Smith, Peter H. (1989). *Mexico's Alternative Political Futures*. La Jolla, Calif.: Monograph Series, 30, Center for US–Mexican Studies, University of San Diego.

—— Craig, Ann L., and Fox, Jonathan (eds.) (1994). *Transforming State–Society Relations in Mexico: The National Solidarity Strategy*. San Diego: Center for US–Mexican Studies, University of California.

CORONEL, JOSÉ (1992). 'Violencia política: Formas de respuestas comunera en Ayacucho'. In C. I. Degregori *et al.* (eds.), *Perú: El problema agrario en debate.* Lima: Universidad Nacional de la Amazonía Peruana & Seminario Permanente de Investigación Agraria.

CORRADI, JUAN E. (1992). 'Toward Societies without Fear'. In Juan E. Corradi, Patricia Weiss Fagen, and Manuel Antonio Garretón (eds.), *Fear at the Edge: State Terror and Resistance in Latin America.* Berkeley and Los Angeles: University of California Press.

—— FAGEN, PATRICIA WEISS, and GARRETÓN, MANUEL ANTONIO (eds.) (1992). *Fear at the Edge: State Terror and Resistance in Latin America.* Berkeley and Los Angeles: University of California Press.

CORREA, GUILLERMO (1990). 'El PRONASOL, que nació como esperanza, ha generado corrupción y protestas'. *Proceso,* 727, 8 Oct.

CORREIA DE ANDRADE, MANUEL (1994). *Modernizacão e Pobreza: A Expansão da Agroindústria Canavieira e seu Impacto Ecológico e Social.* São Paulo: Editora Unesp.

CORRIGAN, PHILIP, and SAYER, DEREK (1985). *The Great Arch: English State Formation as Cultural Revolution.* Oxford: Basil Blackwell.

COTLER, JULIO (1978). *Clases, estado y nación en el Perú.* Lima: Instituto de Estudios Peruanos.

—— (1986). 'Military Interventions and "Transfer of Power to Civilians" in Peru'. In Guillermo O'Donnell, Philippe C. Schmitter, and Laurence Whitehead (eds.), *Transitions from Authoritarian Rule: Latin America.* Baltimore: Johns Hopkins University Press.

—— (1993). *Descomposición política y autoritarismo en el Perú.* Documento de Trabajo No. 51. Lima: IEP.

—— (1994). *Política y sociedad en el Perú.* Lima: IEP.

COULOMB, RENÉ (1990). 'México: La política habitacional en la crisis'. Mimeograph. DF, Mexico: 1–21.

—— and SÁNCHEZ MEJORADA F., CRISTINA (coords.) (1992). *Pobreza urbana, autogestión y política.* DF, Mexico: CENVI.

COURIEL, ALBERTO (1988). *El Uruguay empobrecido: Deuda externa y modelo neoliberal.* Montevideo: Ediciones de la Banda Oriental.

COUTO, CLÁUDIO GONÇALVES, and ABRUCIO, FERNANDO LUIZ (n.d.). 'A Dialética da Mudança: O PT Confronta-se com a Institucionalidade'. Working paper for Centro de Estudos de Cultura Contemporânea (CEDEC) (mimeograph). São Paulo.

CSE (1990). *Elecciones 1989,* i. Caracas: Ediciones del Consejo Supremo Electoral.

—— (1993). 'Elecciones 1992' (mimeograph). Caracas: Consejo Supremo Electoral.

CUÉLLAR, ANGÉLICA (1993). *La noche es de ustedes, el amanecer es nuestro.* DF, Mexico: UNAM.

CUÉLLAR, MIREYA (1991). 'CSG ha remontado la condición de "desprestigio" de 1988: PRD'. *La Jornada* (Mexico City), 10 Nov.: 12.

CUEVA, AGUSTÍN (1988). *Las democracias restringidas de América Latina.* Quito: Editorial Planeta.

—— (comp.) (1994). *Ensayos sobre una polémica inconclusa: La transición a la democracia en América Latina.* DF, Mexico: Consejo Nacional para la Cultura y las Artes.

DAHL, ROBERT (1971). *Polyarchy: Participation and Opposition.* New Haven: Yale University Press.

—— (1982). *Dilemmas of Pluralist Democracy: Autonomy vs. Control.* New Haven: Yale University Press.

DA SILVEIRA COTRIM, FERNANDO (1990). *A Geografia do Voto no Brasil: Eleições de 1989.* Rio de Janeiro: IBASE.

DAVIS, BEN (1994). 'Fund Files NAO Complaint against Mexican Government'. *Worker Rights News*, International Labor Rights Education and Research Fund, Issue No. 10 (Summer).

DAVRIEUX, HUGO (1987). *El gasto público en Uruguay*. Montevideo: CINVE-EBO.

DEERE, CARMEN DIANA (1990). *Household and Class Relations: Peasants and Landlords in Northern Peru*. Berkeley and Los Angeles: University of California Press.

DE FREITAS BARBOSA, ALEXANDRE, and CANDIA VEIGA, JOÃO PAULO (1994). 'The Role of Unions in a Transnational World: The Case of CUT in the Mercosul Integration' [text in Portuguese]. Presented at the Workshop on Inequality and New Forms of Popular Representation in Latin America, Institute of Latin American and Iberian Studies, Columbia University, New York (Mar.).

DEGREGORI, CARLOS IVÁN (1986). *Sendero Luminoso*, i: *Los hondos y mortales desencuentros*; ii: *Lucha armada y utopía autoritaria*. Documentos de trabajo No. 4 y 6. Lima: Instituto de Estudios Peruanos.

—— (1989). *Qué difícil es ser Dios: Ideología y violencia política en Sendero Luminoso*. Lima: El Zorro de Abajo Ediciones.

—— (1990). *Ayacucho 1969–1979: El surgimiento de Sendero Luminoso*. Lima: Instituto de Estudios Peruanos.

—— (1991*a*). 'Jóvenes y campesinos ante la violencia política: Ayacucho 1980–1983'. In Henrique Urbano (ed.), *Poder y violencia en los Andes*. Cuzco: Centro de Estudios Regionales Andinos Bartolomé de Las Casas.

—— (1991*b*). 'La estrategia urbana de Sendero: Al filo de la navaja'. *QueHacer*, 73. Lima: DESCO.

—— (1992). 'The Origin and Logic of Shining Path: Two Views'. In David Scott Palmer (ed.), *Shining Path of Peru*. New York: St Martin's Press.

—— and GROMPONE, ROMEO (1991). *Demonios y redendores en el nuevo Perú*, Colección Mínima No. 22. Lima: Instituto de Estudios Peruanos.

—— BLONDET, CECILIA, and LYNCH, NICOLAS (1986). *Conquistadores de un nuevo mundo: De invasores a ciudadanos en San Martín de Porres*. Lima: Instituto de Estudios Peruanos.

DEIBE, ENRIQUE, ESTEVEZ, ANTONIO, and MATHEU, PEDRO (1994). 'Productividad y negociación laboral en Argentina 1991/94'. Presented at II National Conference of Labor Studies, ASET, Buenos Aires (Aug.).

DE LA TORRE, CARLOS (1992). 'The Ambiguous Meanings of Latin American Populism'. *Social Research*, 59 (2): 385–414.

D'ELIA, GERMAN (1984). *Nuestros sindicatos*. Montevideo, Uruguay: Serie Nuestra Tierra, No. 4.

DELPINO, NENA (1991). 'Las organizaciones femeninas por la alimentación: Un menú sazonado'. In Luis Pásara, Nena Delpino, Rocío Valdeavellano, and Alonso Zarzar (eds.), *La otra cara de la luna: Nuevos actores sociales en el Perú*. Buenos Aires: Manatial.

—— and PÁSARA, LUIS (1991). 'El otro actor en escena: Las ONGDs'. In Luis Pásara, Nena Delpino, Rocío Valdeavellano, and Alonso Zarzar (eds.), *La otra cara de la luna: Nuevos actores sociales en el Perú*. Buenos Aires: Manatial.

DEL PINO, PONCIANO (1992). 'Los campesinos en la guerra: O de como la gente comienza a ponerse macho'. In C. I. Degregori *et al.* (eds.), *Peru: El problema agrario en debate/SEPA IV*. Lima: Universidad Nacional de la Amazonía Peruana & Seminario Permanente de Investigación Agraria.

DEMETRIUS, F. JOSEPH (1990). *Brazil's National Alcohol Program*. New York: Praeger.

DEMO, PEDRO (1992). 'Cidadania menor'. Petropólis: Vozes.

DE SOTO, HERNANDO (1989). *The Other Path: The Invisible Revolution in the Third World*. New York: Harper & Row Publishers.

DE SOUSA SANTOS, BOAVENTURA (1994). 'Subjetividad, ciudadanía, y emancipación'. *El Otro Derecho*, 15 (3): 7–60.

DÍAZ, ALVARO (1989). 'La reestructuración industrial autoritaria en Chile'. *Proposiciones*, 17: 14–35.

DIETZ, HENRY (1980). *Poverty and Problem-Solving under Military Rule: The Urban Poor in Lima*. Austin: University of Texas Press.

DIMAGGIO, PAUL, and POWELL, WALTER W. (1991). 'Introduction'. In Walter W. Powell and Paul J. DiMaggio (eds.), *The New Institutionalism in Organizational Analysis*. Chicago: The University of Chicago Press.

Dimensión y características de la pobreza según CASEN 1990 (1990). Santiago: Mideplan.

DINIZ, ELI (1994). 'Reformas Econômicas e Democracia no Brasil dos Anos 90: As Câmaras Setoriais como Fórum de Negociação'. *Dados*, 37 (2): 277–315.

DOIMO, ANA MARIA (1990). 'Movimentos Sociais e Conselhos Populares: Desafios de Institucionalidade Democrática'. Presented at ANPOCS (mimeograph).

DONNER, RICK, DEYO, FREDERIC, and HERSHBERG, ERIC (1994). 'Economic Governance and Flexible Production in the Developing World'. Unpublished. New York: Social Science Research Council.

DORNBUSCH, RUDIGER, and EDWARDS, SEBASTIAN (1991). *The Macroeconomics of Populism in Latin America*. Chicago: The University of Chicago Press.

DOS REIS VELLOSO, JOÃO PAULO (1994). 'Governance, the Transition to Modernity and Civil Society'. In *Redefining the State in Latin America*. Paris: OECD.

DOS SANTOS, WANDERLEY G. (1979). *Ciudadana e Justica: A Politica Social na Ordem Brasileira*. Rio de Janeiro: Editora Campus.

DOUGHTY, PAUL (1970). 'Behind the Back of the City: Provincial Life in Lima, Peru'. In William Mangin (ed.), *Peasants in Cities*. Boston: Houghton Mifflin Company.

DRESSER, DENISE (1991). *Neopopulist Solutions to Neoliberal Problems: Mexico's National Solidarity Program*. San Diego: Center for US–Mexican Studies, University of California Press.

—— (1992). 'Pronasol: Los dilemas de la gobernabilidad'. *El Cotidiano*, 49: 49–57.

—— (1993). 'Exporting Conflict: Transboundary Consequences of Mexican Politics'. In Abraham F. Lowenthal and Katrina Burgess (eds.), *The California–Mexico Connection*. Stanford, Calif.: Stanford University Press.

DRIANT, JEAN-CLAUDE (1991). *Las barriadas de Lima: Historia e interpretación*. Lima: IFEA/DESCO.

DRYZEK, JOHN (1990). *Discursive Democracy: Politics, Policy, and Political Science*. New York: Cambridge University Press.

DUARTE, ISIS, *et al.* (1995). *La cultura política de los dominicanos: Entre el autoritarismo y la democracia*. Santiago de los Caballeros: Pontificia Universidad Católica Madre y Maestra.

EAGLETON, TERRY (1991). *Ideology: An Introduction*. London: Verso.

EATON, TRACEY (1994). 'Mexico Pledges Electoral Reform in Bid for Peace'. *Dallas Morning News*, 28 Jan.

ECHEVERRÍ-GENT, JOHN (1992). 'Public Participation and Poverty Alleviation: The Experience of Reform Communists in India's West Bengal'. *World Development*, 20 (10), Oct.

ECKSTEIN, SUSAN (1977). *The Poverty of Revolution: The State and the Urban Poor in Mexico.* Princeton: Princeton University Press.

—— (1988). *The Poverty of Revolution*, 2nd edn. Princeton: Princeton University Press.

—— (ed.) (1989). *Power and Popular Protest: Latin American Social Movements.* Berkeley and Los Angeles: University of California Press.

ECLAC (Economic Commission for Latin America and the Caribbean) (1991). *Sustainable Development: Changing Production Patterns, Social Equity, and the Environment.* Santiago: United Nations, ECLAC.

—— (1993). *Panorama social de América Latina.* Santiago: ECLAC.

Economía y trabajo en Chile 1993–1994 (1994). 4th edn. Santiago: Programa de Economía del Trabajo.

The Economist (1994). Weekly Report of Economic Indicators, Sept.

EDIE, CARLENE J. (1991). *Democracy by Default: Dependency and Clientelism in Jamaica.* Boulder, Colo.: Lynne Rienner Publishers.

EDLEMAN, MURRAY (1988). *Constructing the Public Spectacle.* Chicago: University of Chicago Press.

EISENSTADT, S. N. (1966). *Los sistemas políticos de los imperios.* Madrid: Revista de Occidente.

—— and LEMARCHAND, RENÉ (eds.) (1981). *Political Clientelism, Patronage and Development.* Beverly Hills, Calif.: Sage Publications.

—— and RONIGER, LUIS (1980). 'Patron–Client Relations as a Model of Structuring Social Exchange'. *Comparative Studies in Society and History*, 22.

EISENSTADT, TODD (1993). 'Helping Grassroots Actors Find a Voice: An Interview with David Brooks'. *Enfoque* (Center for US–Mexican Studies, Spring).

ELIAS, JOHN L. (1976). *Conscientization and Deschooling: Freire's and Illich's Proposals for Reshaping Society.* Philadelphia: Westminster Press.

ELLNER, STEVE (1988). *Venezuela's Movimiento al Socialismo: From Guerrilla Defeat to Innovative Politics.* Chapel Hill, NC: Duke University Press.

—— (1993a). 'A Tolerance Worn Thin: Corruption in the Age of Austerity'. *NACLA Report on the Americas*, 27 (3): 13–16.

—— (1993b). 'Introduction: The Changing Status of the Latin American Left in the Recent Past'. In Barry Carr and Steve Ellner (eds.), *The Latin American Left: From the Fall of Allende to Perestroika.* Boulder, Colo.: Westview/Latin American Bureau.

EMIRBAYER, MUSTAFA, and GOODWIN, JEFF (1994). 'Network Analysis, Culture, and the Problem of Agency'. *American Journal of Sociology*, 99 (6): 1411–54.

EPSTEIN, EDWARD (1993). 'Labor and Political Stability in the New Chilean Democracy: Three Illusions'. *Revista de Economía y Trabajo*, 1 (2).

ERICKSON, KENNETH PAUL (1977). *The Brazilian Corporative State and Working Class Politics.* Berkeley and Los Angeles: University of California Press.

ESCOBAR, ARTURO, and ALVAREZ, SONIA E. (eds.) (1992). *The Making of Social Movements in Latin America: Identity, Strategy, and Democracy.* Boulder, Colo.: Westview Press.

Escola Superior de Guerra (1990). 'Estructura do Poder Nacional para o Ano 2001'. Rio de Janeiro: Escola Superior de Guerra.

ESPING-ANDERSEN, GOSTA (1990). *The Three Worlds of Welfare Capitalism.* Cambridge: Polity Press.

EVANS, PETER (1992). 'The State as Problem and Solution: Predation, Embedded Autonomy, and Structural Change'. In Stephan Haggard and Robert Kaufman (eds.), *The Politics of Economic Adjustment: International Constraints, Distributive Conflicts and the State*. Princeton: Princeton University Press.

—— (1995). *Embedded Autonomy: States and Industrial Transformation*. Princeton: Princeton University Press.

FAECyS (1994). 'Memorias'. Buenos Aires: Federación Argentina de Empleados de Comercio y Servicios.

FALS BORDA, ORLANDO (1992). 'Social Movements and Political Power in Latin America'. In Arturo Escobar and Sonia E. Alvarez (eds.), *The Making of Social Movements in Latin America*. Boulder, Colo.: Westview Press.

FATLyF (1993). 'XXXIV Congreso ordinario de la Federación Argentina de Trabajadores de Luz y Fuerza'. Mar del Plata.

FAUNDEZ, JULIO (1988). *Marxism and Democracy in Chile: From 1932 to the Fall of Allende*. New Haven: Yale University Press.

FAVRE, HENRI (1984). 'Perú: Sendero Luminoso y horizontes oscuros'. *QueHacer*, 31: 25–35.

FEIGENBAUM, HARVEY B., and HENIG, JEFREY R. (1994). 'The Political Underpinnings of Privatization: A Typology'. *World Politics*, 46: 185–208.

FERNÁNDEZ, JORGE (1991). 'El PRI ante su propia transición'. *Unomásuno*, 7 Nov.

FERNÁNDEZ BACA, JORGE, and SEINFELD, JEANICE (1993). 'Gasto social y políticas sociales en América Latina'. *Desarrollo Social*, 5. Lima.

FERNÁNDEZ-ORDOÑEZ, MIGUEL ANGEL, and SERVÉN, L. (1992). 'Reforma económica en la Europa del Sur: El caso de España'. *Pensamiento Iberoamericano*, 2: 22–3.

FIGUEROA, CARLOS (1991). *El recurso del miedo*. San José: EDUCA.

FIGUEROA Y IBARRA, CARLOS (1980). *El proletariado rural en el agro guatemalteco*. Guatemala: Editorial Universitaria de Guatemala.

FILGUEIRA, CARLOS (1970). 'Burocracia y clientela: Una política de absorción de tensiones'. *Cuadernos de Ciencias Sociales*, 1.

—— (1990). 'Organizaciones sindicales y empresariales ante las políticas de estabilización: Uruguay 1985–1987'. *Estabilización y respuesta social*. Santiago: PREALC/OIT.

FILGUEIRA, FERNANDO (1991). 'El movimiento sindical en la encrucijada: Restauración y transformación democrática'. *Revista Uruguaya de Ciencia Política*, 4.

FINCH, HENRY (1980). *Historia económica del Uruguay contemporáneo*. Montevideo: EBO.

FISHER, JO (1993). *Out of the Shadows: Women, Resistance and Politics in South America*. London: Latin American Bureau.

FLISFISCH, ANGEL (1987). '¿Puede la Izquierda cambiar de ideales?' *Zona Abierta*, 45: 153–74.

—— (1991). 'Estatismo, economía y democracia en la crisis actual del socialismo'. In Norbert Lechner (ed.), *Capitalismo, democracia, y reformas*. Santiago: FLACSO.

FLORES, JUAN (1991). 'Proyectos de Etnodesarrollo = los ricos más ricos y los pobres más pobres'. *Etnias*, 2 (8), Jan.

FLYNN, PETER (1974). 'Class, Clientelism, and Coercion: Some Mechanisms of Internal Dependency and Control'. *Journal of Commonwealth and Comparative Politics*, 12 (2).

—— (1993). 'Collor, Corruption and Crisis: Time for Reflection'. *Journal of Latin American Studies*, 25 (2): 251–71.

FONCODES (1994). *El mapa de la inversión social: Pobreza y actuación de FONCODES a nivel departamental y provincial.* Lima: Instituto Cuanto and UNICEF.

FONSECA, GONDIN DA (1962). *Assim Falou Julião.* São Paulo: Editora Fulgor.

FORMAN, SHEPARD (1975). *The Brazilian Peasantry.* New York: Columbia University Press.

FORTUNA, JUAN CARLOS (1990). 'El empleo público en el Uruguay, 1963–1985'. In Adrian Marshal (ed.), *El empleo público frente a la crisis: Estudios sobre América Latina.* Geneva: International Institute of Labor Studies.

FOWERAKER, JOE, and CRAIG, ANN L. (1990). *Popular Movements and Political Change in Mexico.* Boulder, Colo.: Lynne Rienner Publishers.

FOX, JONATHAN (1989). 'Time to Cross the Border: Paying Attention to Mexico'. *Radical America,* 22 (4).

—— (1992*a*). 'New Terrain for Rural Politics', *Report on the Americas,* 25 (5).

—— (1992*b*). 'Democratic Rural Development: Leadership Accountability in Regional Peasant Organizations'. *Development and Change,* 23 (2).

—— (1992*c*). *The Politics of Food in Mexico: State Power and Social Mobilization.* Ithaca, NY: Cornell University Press.

—— (1994*a*). 'The Challenge of Democracy: Rebellion as Catalyst'. *Akwe:kon Journal,* Summer: 13–19.

—— (1994*b*). 'Latin America's Emerging Local Politics'. *Journal of Democracy,* 5 (2), Apr.

—— (1994*c*). 'Political Change in Mexico's New Peasant Economy'. In Maria Lorena Cook, Kevin Middlebrook, and Juan Molinar Horcasitas (eds.), *The Politics of Economic Restructuring: State–Society Relations and Regime Change in Mexico.* La Jolla, Calif.: UCSD, Center for US–Mexican Studies.

—— (forthcoming). 'Local Democratization in Latin America: Why It Matters'. *Journal of Democracy.*

—— and HERNÁNDEZ, LUIS (1992). 'Mexico's Difficult Democracy: Grassroots Movements, NGOs, and Local Government'. *Alternatives,* 17: 165–208.

FOXLEY, ALEJANDRO (1992). 'Sustainable Development with Equity in the 1990s'. Keynote address, conference at the University of Wisconsin-Madison, May.

FRANCO, CARLOS (1991). 'La otra modernidad: De la migración a la plebe urbana'. In Enrique Urbano (ed.), *Modernidad en los Andes.* Cusco: Centro Bartolomé de las Casas.

—— (1993). 'Visión de la democracia y crisis del régimen'. *Nueva sociedad,* 128.

—— (1994). 'Ciudadanía plebeya y organizaciones sociales en el Perú (Otro camino para "otra" democracia)'. In Gerónimo de Sierra (ed.), *Democracia emergente en América del Sur.* DF, Mexico: CIIH-UNAM.

FRANK, ANDRÉ GUNDER, and FUENTES, MARTA (1989). 'Diez tesis acerca de los movimientos sociales'. *Revista Mexicana de Sociología,* Apr.: 21–43.

FREGA, ANA, and TROCHON, YVETTE (1991). 'Los fundamentos del estado empresario (1903–1933)'. *Cuadernos del Claeh,* 58–9: 115–37.

FRENCH, JOHN (1991). *The Brazilian Workers' ABC.* Chapel Hill: University of North Carolina Press.

FRÍAS, PATRICIO (1989). *El movimiento sindical chileno en la lucha por la democracia.* Santiago: Programa de Economía del Trabajo.

FRIEDEN, JEFFREY A. (1991). 'Invested Interests: The Politics of National Economic Policies in a World of Global Finance'. *International Organization,* 45 (4): 425–51.

GABEIRA, FERNANDO (1987). 'A Idéia de um Partido Verde no Brasil'. In J. A. Pádua (ed.), *Ecologia e Política no Brasil.* Rio de Janeiro: Editora Espaço e Tempo.

GACEK, STANLEY (1994). 'Revisiting the Corporatist and Contractualist Models of Labor Law Regimes: A Review of the Brazilian and American Systems'. *Cardozo Law Review*, 16: 21–110.

GALICH, MANUEL (1977). *Del pánico al ataque*. Guatemala: Editorial Universitaria.

GAMBETTA, DIEGO (ed.) (1988). *Trust: Making and Breaking Cooperative Relations*. Oxford: Basil Blackwell.

GAMERO, JULIO (1990). 'Estabilización: Gradualismo o shock?' *QueHacer*, 63: 9–12.

GAMSON, WILLIAM A. (1990). *Strategies of Social Protest*. 2nd edn. Belmont, Calif.: Wadsworth.

GARCÍA AÑOVEROS, JESÚS (1987). *La reforma agraria de Arbenz en Guatemala*. Madrid: Ediciones Cultura Hispánica, Instituto de Cooperación Iberoamericana, Imprime Gráficas.

GARCIA CANCLINI, NESTOR (1992). *Culturas híbridas*. Buenos Aires: Editorial Sudamericana.

GARRETÓN, MANUEL ANTONIO (1987). 'En qué consistió la renovación socialista? Síntesis y evaluación de sus contenidos'. *La renovación socialista: Balance y perspectivas de un proceso vigente*. Santiago: Ediciones Valentín Letelier.

—— (1992). 'Fear in Military Regimes: An Overview'. In Juan E. Corradi, Patricia Weiss Fagen, and Manuel Antonio Garretón (eds.), *Fear at the Edge: State Terror and Resistance in Latin America*. Berkeley and Los Angeles: University of California Press.

—— (1994a). 'Human Rights and Democratisation'. *Journal of Latin American Studies*, 26 (1).

—— (1994b). 'The Political Dimension of Processes of Transformation in Chile'. In William Smith, C. Acuña, and E. Gamarra (eds.), *Democracy, Markets and Structural Reform in Latin America*. New Brunswick, NJ: Transaction.

—— and ESPINOZA, M. (1992). 'Reforma del estado o cambio en la matriz socio-política? El caso chileno'. *Perfiles Latinoamericanos*, 1. Mexico: FLACSO.

GARRETT, GEOFFREY, and LANGE, PETER (1991). 'Political Responses to Interdependence: What's "Left" for the Left?' *International Organization*, 45 (4): 539–64.

GARRISON, JOHN II (1993). 'A Eco-92 e o Florescimento das ONGs Brasileiras'. *Desenvolvimiento de base*, 1: 2–11.

GARZA, MARÍA TERESA, and MÉNDEZ, LUIS (1987a). 'El conflicto de la Ford Cuautitlán'. *El Cotidiano*, 20: 384–5.

—— —— (1987b). 'La huelga en Volkswagen'. *El Cotidiano*, 20: 381–3.

GAVILANES DEL CASTILLO, LUÍS MARIA (1992). *Monseñor Leonidas Proaño*. Quito: FEPP.

GEERTZ, CLIFFORD (1973). *The Interpretation of Cultures*. New York: Basic Books.

GELLNER, ERNST (1983). *Nations and Nationalism*. Ithaca, NY: Cornell University Press.

—— (1994). *The Conditions of Liberty: Civil Society and its Rivals*. New York: Penguin Books.

—— and WATERBURY, JOHN (eds.) (1977). *Patrons and Clients in Mediterranean Societies*. London: Duckworth.

GENTLEMAN, JUDITH (1987). 'Mexico after the Oil Boom'. In Judith Gentleman (ed.), *Mexican Politics in Transition*. Boulder, Colo.: Westview Press.

GEREFFI, GARY, and KORNECIEWICZ, M. (1993). *Commodity Chains and Global Capitalism*. New York: Praeger.

GERMANI, GINO (1968). *Política y sociedad en una época de transición: De la sociedad tradicional a la sociedad de masas*. Buenos Aires: Paidós.

—— DI TELLA, TORCUATO S., and IANNI, OCTÁVIO (1973). *Populismo y contradicciones de clase en Latinoamérica*. DF, Mexico: Era.

GEUSS, RAYMOND (1981). *The Idea of a Critical Theory*. Cambridge: Cambridge University Press.

GIL, JORGE, SCHMIDT, SAMUEL, and CASTRO, JORGE (1993). 'La red de poder mexicana: El caso de Miguel Alemán'. *Revista Mexicana de Sociología*, Mar.: 103–17.

GILLESPIE, RICHARD (1989). *The Spanish Socialist Party: A History of Factionalism*. Oxford: Oxford University Press.

GLEIJESES, PIERO (1989). 'La aldea de Ubico: Guatemala, 1931–1940'. *Mesoamérica*, 17: 25–59.

—— (1991). *Shattered Hope: The Guatemalan Revolution and the United States, 1944–1954*. Princeton: Princeton University Press.

GOLDEN, MIRIAM (1990). 'A Rational-Choice Analysis of Union Militancy with Application to the Cases of British Coal and Fiat'. Occasional Paper No. 26, Western Societies Program, Center for International Studies, Cornell University.

—— and PONTUSSON, JONAS (eds.) (1992). *Bargaining for Change: Union Politics in North America and Europe*. Ithaca, NY: Cornell University Press.

GOLDEN, TIM (1992). 'Point of Attack for Mexico's Retooled Party Machine: The Leftist Stronghold'. *New York Times*, 12 July.

—— (1994*a*). 'Old Scores: Left Behind, Mexico's Indians Fight the Future'. *New York Times*, 9 Jan.

—— (1994*b*). 'Government Joins Attack on Ballot Idea'. *New York Times*, 3 Nov.: A29.

GOLTE, JURGEN, and ADAMS, NORMA (1987). *Los caballos de Troya de los invasores: Estrategias campesinas en la conquista de la gran Lima*. Lima: IEP.

GÓMEZ CALCAÑO, LUIS, and LÓPEZ-MAYA, MARGARITA (1990). *El tejido de Penélope: La reforma del estado en Venezuela*. Caracas: Ediciones CENDES-Asociación de Sociólogos y Antropólogos-IPP.

GÓMEZ LEYVA, CIRO (1991). 'Solidaridad gratuita en todas las pantallas'. *Este País*, 7, Oct.

GONDA, ALEJANDRO (1995). *Reporte de la Consultora de Investigación Sindical Independiente*. Buenos Aires: CISI.

GONZALES, JOSÉ (1992). 'Guerrillas and Coca in the Upper Huallaga Valley'. In David S. Palmer (ed.), *Shining Path of Peru*. New York: St Martin's Press.

GONZÁLEZ, ALVARO, VALDIVIA, TERESA, and REES, MARTHA (1987). 'Evaluación de los programas agrícolas del INI: Chiapas, Puebla y Oaxaca'. Paper presented to the Society for Applied Anthropology, Oaxaca, Apr.

GONZÁLEZ BLOCK, MIGUEL ANGEL (1991). 'Economic Crisis and the Decentralization of Health Services in Mexico'. In Mercedes González de la Rocha and Agustín Escobar Latapí (eds.), *Social Responses to Mexico's Economic Crisis of the 1980s*. La Jolla, Calif.: Center for US–Mexican Studies, University of California, San Diego.

GONZÁLEZ CASANOVA, PABLO (1986). 'Cuando hablamos de democracia: De qué hablamos?' *Revista Mexicana de Sociología*, Mar.: 3–6.

GONZÁLEZ DE LA ROCHA, MERCEDES, and ESCOBAR LATAPÍ, AGUSTÍN (coords.) (1991). *Social Responses to Mexico's Economic Crisis of the 1980s*. La Jolla: Center for US–Mexican Studies, University of California, San Diego.

GONZÁLEZ DE OLARTE, EFRAÍN (1992). *La economía regional de Lima: Crecimiento, urbanización y clases populares*. Lima: IEP.

—— and SAMAMÉ, LILIAN (1991). *El péndulo peruano: Políticas económicas, gobernabilidad y subdesarrollo, 1963–1990*. Lima: Consorcio de Investigación Económica y el Instituto de Estudios Peruanos.

GONZÁLEZ TIBURCIO, ENRIQUE (1991). *Reforma del estado y política social.* DF, Mexico: Instituto Nacional de Administración Pública.

GOODIN, ROBERT J., *et al.* (1987). *Not Only the Poor: The Middle Classes and the Welfare State.* London: Allen & Unwin.

GOODMAN, JOHN B., and PAULY, LOUIS W. (1993). 'The Obsolescence of Capital Controls? Economic Management in an Age of Global Markets'. *World Politics*, 46 (1): 50–82.

GOODWIN, CRAUFORD, and NACHT, MICHAEL (1995). *Beyond Government: Extending the Public Policy Debate in Emerging Democracies.* Boulder, Colo.: Westview.

GORRITI, GUSTAVO (1987). 'Sendero: Qué hacer?' *Posible.* Lima.

—— (1990). *Sendero Luminoso: Historia de la guerra milenaria en el Perú.* Lima: APOYO.

GOULD, CAROL C. (1988). *Rethinking Democracy: Freedom and Social Cooperation in Politics, Economy and Society.* Cambridge: Cambridge University Press.

GRAHAM, CAROL (1991). 'The APRA Government and the Urban Poor: The PIAT Programme in Lima's Pueblos Jóvenes'. *Journal of Latin American Studies*, 23 (1), Feb.

—— (1992). 'The Politics of Protecting the Poor during Adjustment: Bolivia's Emergency Social Fund', *World Development*, 20 (9), Sept.

—— (1994). *Safety Nets, Politics, and the Poor: Transitions to Market Economies.* Washington: Brookings Institution.

GRAHAM, LAWRENCE S. (1993). 'Rethinking the Relationship between the Strength of Local Institutions and the Consolidation of Democracy: The Case of Brazil'. In Ilpyong J. Kim and Jane Shapiro Zacek (eds.), *Establishing Democratic Rule: The Reemergence of Local Governments in Post-authoritarian Systems.* Washington: In Depth Books.

GRANADOS, MANUEL JESÚS (1987). 'El PCP Sendero Luminoso: Aproximaciones a su ideología'. *Socialismo y Participación*, 27: 15–30.

GRANOVETTER, MARK (1973). 'The Strength of Weak Ties'. *American Journal of Sociology*, 78: 1360–80.

GRIEB, KENNETH J. (1979). *Guatemalan Caudillo: The Regime of Jorge Ubico, Guatemala 1931–1944.* Athens: Ohio University Press.

GRINDLE, MERILEE (1981). 'Official Interpretations of Rural Underdevelopment: Mexico in the 1970s'. Working Papers in US–Mexican Studies, 20.

—— (1991). *Public Choices and Policy Change: The Political Economy of Reform in Developing Countries.* Baltimore: The Johns Hopkins University Press.

GRINSPUN, RICARDO, and CAMERON, MAXWELL A. (1993). 'The Political Economy of North American Integration: Diverse Perspectives, Converging Criticisms'. In Ricardo Grinspun and Maxwell A. Cameron (eds.), *The Political Economy of North American Free Trade.* New York: St Martin's Press.

GROMPONE, ROMEO (1991*a*). *El velero en el viento: Política y sociedad en Lima.* Lima: IEP.

—— (1991*b*). 'Fujimori: Razones y desconciertos'. In *Demonios y redentores en el nuevo Perú.* Lima: IEP.

GRZYBOWSKI, CANDIDO (1990). 'Rural Workers and Democratization in Brazil'. In Jonathan Fox (ed.), *The Challenge of Rural Democratization: Perspectives from Latin America and the Philippines.* London: Frank Cass.

GUARDIA, ALEXIS (1993). 'Herencia económica y reconversión'. In *Como cambiar al estado? Los casos de Chile y Perú.* Lima: Grupo Propuesta.

GUASTI, LAURA (1977). 'Peru: Clientelism and Internal Control'. In Steffen W. Schmidt, James C. Scott, Carol Landé, and Laura Guasti (eds.), *Friends, Followers and Factions: A Reader in Political Clientelism.* Berkeley and Los Angeles: University of California Press.

GUILLÉN LÓPEZ, TONATIUH (1989). 'The Social Bases of the PRI'. In Wayne A. Cornelius, Judith Gentleman, and Peter H. Smith (eds.), *Mexico's Alternative Political Futures*. Monograph Series, 30. La Jolla: Center for US–Mexican Studies, University of San Diego.

GUILLERMO, MARTIN (1990). 'El FONHAPO y la política de vivienda'. *Barrio Nuevo*, 6–7: 5–6.

GUIMARÃES, IVAN GONCALVES RIBEIRO (1994). 'A Experiência das Câmaras Setoriais: Democratizando a Política Econômica'. Unpublished manuscript. 4th version.

GUIMARÃES, ROBERTO P. (1991). *The Ecopolitics of Development in the Third World: Politics and the Environment in the Third World: Politics and Environment in Brazil*. Boulder, Colo.: Lynne Rienner Publishers.

GUNTHER, RICHARD (1986). 'The Spanish Socialist Party: From Clandestine Opposition to Party of Government'. In Stanley G. Payne (ed.), *The Politics of Democratic Spain*. Chicago: The Chicago Council on Foreign Relations.

GUTIÉRREZ ALVAREZ, CORALIA (1985). 'Los trabajadores del campo y la política agraria en la revolución guatemalteca de 1944–1954'. Tesis de Licenciatura en Sociología. Mexico: UNAM.

GUTIÉRREZ G., V. MANUEL (1964). 'Breve historia del movimiento sindical de Guatemala'. Unpublished. Mexico City.

GUZMÁN, ABIMAEL (1988). 'La entrevista del siglo'. *El Diario*, Aug.

HAAS, PETER M. (1989). 'Do Regimes Matter? Epistemic Communities and Mediterranean Pollution Control'. *International Organization*, 43: 377–403.

HABER, PAUL (1992). 'Collective Dissent in Mexico: The Political Outcome of Contemporary Urban Popular Movements'. Ph.D. diss., Columbia University.

—— (1994). 'Political Change in Durango: The Role of National Solidarity'. In Wayne A. Cornelius, Ann L. Craig, and Jonathan Fox (eds.), *Transforming State–Society Relations in Mexico: The National Solidarity Strategy*. US–Mexico Contemporary Perspectives Series, 6. La Jolla: Center for US–Mexican Studies, University of California, San Diego.

HABERMAS, JÜRGEN (1981). 'New Social Movements'. *Telos*, 49: 33–7.

—— (1987). *The Theory of Communicative Action*. Boston: Beacon Press.

HAGGARD, STEPHAN, and KAUFMAN, ROBERT (eds.) (1992). *The Politics of Economic Adjustment*. Princeton: Princeton University Press.

—— —— (1995a). 'Estado y reforma económica: La iniciación y consolidación de las políticas de mercado'. *Desarrollo Económico*, 139: 355–72.

—— —— (1995b). *The Political Economy of Democratic Transitions*. Princeton: Princeton University Press.

—— and WEBB, STEVEN B. (eds.) (1994). *Voting for Reform: Democracy, Political Liberalization and Economic Adjustment*. Washington: Oxford University Press/The World Bank.

HAGOPIAN, FRANCES (1990). ' "Democracy by Undemocratic Means?" Elites, Political Pacts and Regime Transition in Brazil'. *Comparative Political Studies*, 23 (2), July.

—— (1993). 'After Regime Change: Authoritarian Legacies, Political Representation, and the Democratic Future of South America'. *World Politics*, 45: 464–500.

HALL, MICHAEL, and AURÉLIO GARCIA, MARCO (1989). 'Urban Labor'. In Michael L. Conniff and Frank McCann (eds.), *Modern Brazil*. Lincoln: University of Nebraska Press.

HALPERN, PABLO, and BOUSQUET, E. (1991). 'Opinión pública y política económica: Hacia un modelo de formación de percepciones económicas . . .'. Colección estudios CIEPLAN. 33.

——— ——— (1992). 'Percepciones de la opinión pública acerca del rol económico y social del estado'. Colección estudios CIEPLAN. 36.

HANDY, JIM (1984). *Gift of the Devil: A History of Guatemala*. Boston: South End Press.

——— (1985). 'Revolution and Reaction: National Policy and Rural Politics in Guatemala, 1944–1954'. Doctoral diss., Department of History, University of Toronto.

——— (1986). 'Resurgent Democracy and the Guatemalan Military'. *Journal of Latin American Studies*, 18: 383–408.

——— (1988a). 'The Most Precious Fruit of the Revolution: The Guatemalan Agrarian Reform, 1952–1954'. *Hispanic American Historical Review*, 68 (4): 675–705.

——— (1988b). 'National Policy, Agrarian Reform, and the Corporate Community during the Guatemalan Revolution, 1944–1954'. *Comparative Studies in Society and History*, 30 (4). Cambridge University Press.

——— (1989). 'Reform and Counter-Reform: Agrarian Policy in Guatemala, 1952–1957'. Presented at the Latin American Studies Association XV Congress.

HARDING, COLIN (1988). 'Antonio Díaz Martínez and the Ideology of Sendero Luminoso'. *Bulletin of Latin American Research*, 7 (1): 65–73.

HARRIS, RICHARD L. (1992). *Marxism, Socialism, and Democracy in Latin America*. Boulder, Colo.: Westview.

HAUSMANN, RICARDO (1994). 'Sustaining Reform: What Role for Social Policy?' In Colin I. Bradford, Jr. (ed.), *Redefining the State in Latin America*. Paris: Organization for Economic Co-operation and Development.

——— and RIGOBON, ROBERTO (eds.) (1993). *Government Spending and Income Distribution in Latin America*. Baltimore: Johns Hopkins University Press.

HAWORTH, NIGEL (1993). 'Radicalization and the Left in Peru, 1976–1991'. In Barry Carr and Steve Ellner (eds.), *The Latin American Left: From the Fall of Allende to Perestroika*. New York: Westview Press.

HAY, COLIN, and JESSOP, BOB (eds.) (1995). 'Local Political Economy: Regulation and Governance'. *Economy and Society*, 24: 3.

HECHT, SUSANNA, and COCKBURN, ALEXANDER (1990). *The Fate of the Forest*. New York: Harper Collins Publishers.

HECLO, HUGH (1977). 'Issue Networks and the Executive Establishment'. In Anthony King (ed.), *The New American Political System*. Washington: American Enterprise Institute.

HELD, DAVID (1989). *Political Theory and the Modern State: Essays on State, Power and Democracy*. Stanford, Calif.: Stanford University Press.

——— (1992). *Modelos de democracia*. Madrid: Alianza Editorial.

HELLER, AGNES (1988). 'On Formal Democracy'. In John Keane (ed.), *Civil Society and the State*. London: Verso.

HELLIWELL, JOHN F. (1994). 'Empirical Linkages between Democracy and Economic Growth'. *British Journal of Political Science*, 24: 225–48.

HELLMAN, JUDITH ADLER (1992). 'The Study of New Social Movements in Latin America and the Question of Autonomy'. In Arturo Escobar and Sonia E. Alvarez (eds.), *The Making of Social Movements in Latin America*. Boulder, Colo.: Westview Press.

HENKIN, LOUIS (1990). 'Constitutions and the Elements of Constitutionalism'. A working paper presented for the American Council of Learned Societies Conference on Constitutionalism and the Transition to Democracy in Eastern Europe, held in collaboration with the Department of Sociology of Law, Eötvös Loránd University (Budapest), 18–20 June.

HEREDIA, CARLOS (1994). 'NAFTA and Democratization in Mexico'. *Journal of International Affairs*, 48 (1): 13–38.

HERMAN, EDWARD, and BRODHEAD, FRANK (1984). *Demonstration Elections*. Boston: South End Press.

HERMET, GUY (1983). *Aux frontières de la démocratie*. Paris: Presses Universitaires de France.

—— ROSE, RICHARD, and ROUQUIÉ, ALAIN (eds.) (1978). *Elections without Choice*. New York: John Wiley.

HERNÁNDEZ, LUIS (1988*a*). 'CDP de Durango: La conquista del futuro'. *Pueblo*, 138: 28–9.

—— (1988*b*). 'Durango: De la lucha reinvindicativa a la democracia social'. *Pueblo*, 11 (125): 29–30.

—— (1991). 'El Partido del Trabajo: Realidades y perspectivas'. *El Cotidiano*, 40: 21–8.

HERNÁNDEZ LAOS, ENRIQUE (1992). *Crecimiento económico y pobreza en México*. DF, Mexico: Centro de Investigaciones Interdisciplinarias en Humanidades, UNAM.

HERNÁNDEZ MONTIEL, NORBERTO (1991). 'El MUP: Del rechazo al sufragio a la lucha electoral'. *La Jornada* (Mexico City), 14 Aug.: 39.

HERNÁNDEZ NAVARRO, LUIS (1993). 'Mexican NGOs in Transition'. *Enfoque* (Center for US–Mexican Studies), Spring.

—— (1994). 'La nueva guerra maya'. *Reforma* (Mexico City), 9 Jan.: 14–17.

HERR, ROBIN (1993). 'A Call for Independence in Taiwan'. *Christian Science Monitor*, 5 Mar.

HERRERA, RAMÓN VERA (1995). 'Las fronteras de la enormidad' and 'La eloquencia como servicio'. *Ojarasca*, 45, Aug.–Nov.

HERSHBERG, ERIC (1989). 'Transition from Authoritarianism and Eclipse of the Left: A Reinterpretation of Regime Change in Spain'. Unpublished Ph.D. diss., University of Wisconsin.

—— (1991*a*). 'The Transformation of Socialism in Spain and Chile'. Presented to the XVth Meeting of the Latin American Studies Association.

—— (1991*b*). 'The United Left and the Future of Progressive Politics in Spain: Is There any Alternative (on the) Left?' Presented to the American Political Science Association, Washington.

HEWITT, CYNTHIA (1969). 'Brazil: The Peasant Movement of Pernambuco, 1961–1964'. In A. Henry Landsberger (ed.), *Latin American Peasant Movements*. Ithaca, NY: Cornell University Press.

HIGLEY, JOHN, and GUNTHER, RICHARD (eds.) (1992). *Elites and Democratic Consolidation in Latin America and Southern Europe*. Cambridge: Cambridge University Press.

HIRST, PAUL (1994). *Associative Democracy: New Forms of Economic and Social Governance*. Amherst, Mass.: University of Massachusetts Press.

HOBBES, THOMAS (1973). *Leviathan* (1651). London: J. M. Dent & Sons.

HOBEN, ALLAN, and HEFNER, ROBERT (1991). 'The Integrative Revolution Revisited'. *World Development*, 19 (1): 17–30.

HOCHSTETLER, KATHRYN (1994). *Social Movements in Institutional Politics: Organizing about the Environment in Brazil and Venezuela*. Ph.D. diss., University of Minnesota.

HOFFMAN, RODOLFO, and DA SILVA, LUIZ ARTUR CLEMENTE (1986). 'Contribuição ao Estudo da Concentração da Produção Agropecuária no Brasil em 1975 e 1980'. *Revista da Economia Rural*, 24 (2).

HOLLINGSWORTH, J. ROGERS, SCHMITTER, PHILIPPE C., and STREECK, WOLFGANG (eds.) (1994). *Governing Capitalist Economies: Performance and Control of Economic Sectors*. Oxford: Oxford University Press.

HUALDE, ALFREDO (1994). 'Industrial Relations in the Maquiladora Industry: Management's Search for Participation and Quality'. In Maria Lorena Cook and Harry C. Katz (eds.), *Regional Integration and Industrial Relations in North America*. Ithaca, NY: Institute of Collective Bargaining, New York State School of Industrial and Labor Relations, Cornell University.

HUGHES, SALLIE (1993*a*). 'Looking North for Support'. *El financiero internacional*, 6–12 Sept.: 12.

—— (1993*b*). 'Poverty Program Serves Up Pork'. *El financiero internacional*, 6–12 Sept.: 13.

HUIZER, GERIT (1972). *The Revolutionary Potential of the Peasantry in Latin America*. Lexington, Ky.: D. C. Heath and Co.

Human Rights Watch (1994). *Human Rights World Watch Report 1994*. New York: Human Rights Watch.

Human Rights Watch/Americas (1994). 'Final Justice: Police and Death Squad Homicides of Adolescents in Brazil'. New York: Human Rights Watch.

HUMPHREY, JOHN (1982). *Capitalist Control and Workers' Struggle in the Brazilian Auto Industry*. Princeton: Princeton University Press.

HUNTINGTON, SAMUEL (1968). *Political Order in Changing Societies*. New Haven: Yale University Press.

—— (1991–2). 'How Countries Democratize'. *Political Science Quarterly*, 106 (4), Winter: 579–616.

HURRELL, ANDREW (1992). 'Brazil and the International Politics of Amazonian Deforestation'. In A. Hurrell and B. Kingsbury (eds.), *The International Politics of the Amazon*. New York: Oxford University Press.

HURTADO, JAVIER (1993). *Familias, política y parentesco: Jalisco 1919–1991*. DF, Mexico: Fondo de Cultura Económica.

HURTADO, OSVALDO (1985). *Political Power in Ecuador*. Boulder, Colo.: Westview Press.

HYDEN, GORDEN (1992). 'Governance and the Study of Politics'. In Gorden Hyden and Michael Bratton (eds.), *Governance and Politics in Africa*. Boulder, Colo.: Lynne Rienner.

HYMAN, RICHARD (1994). 'Industrial Relations in Western Europe: An Era of Ambiguity'. *Industrial Relations*, 33 (1): 1–24.

IAA (Instituto de Açúcar e Álcool), Superintendencia Regional de Pernambuco (1987). *Quadro Comparativo de Safras, 1960–1 a 1986–7*. Recife: IAA.

IBARRA, ALICIA (ed.) (1987). *Los indígenas y el estado en el Ecuador*. Quito: Abya-Yala.

IBARRA, DAVID (1990). *Privatización y otras expresiones de los acomodos de poder entre estado y mercado en América Latina*. DF, Mexico: UNAM.

IBASE (Instituto Brasileiro de Analise Socio-Econômico) (1983). *Organização Sindical no Meio Rural*. Rio de Janeiro: IBASE.

IBGE (Instituto Brasileiro da Geografia e Economia) (1950). *Serviço Nacional de Recensamento, Censo Agrícola de 1950*. Rio de Janeiro: IBGE.

—— (1980). *Censo Agropecuário de 1980*. Rio de Janeiro: IBGE.

—— (1985). *Censo Agropecuário de 1985*. Rio de Janeiro: IBGE.

—— (1990). *Estatísticas Históricas do Brasil: Séries econômicas, demográficas e sociais de 1550 a 1988*, 2nd edn. Rio de Janeiro: IBGE.

—— (1991). *Anuário Estatístico 1991*, 51. Rio de Janeiro: IBGE.

IDL (1992). *Perú hoy: En el oscuro sendero de la guerra*. Lima: Instituto de Defensa Legal.

IDL (1995). 'Policía nacional ¿Reforma integral o retoque cosmético?' *Ideele*, 79. Lima: Instituto de Defensa Legal.

IDS (1989). *Perú: La violencia política vista desde el pueblo*. Serie: Estrategia Integral de Paz. Lima: Instituto Democracia y Socialismo.

Iguíñiz, Javier (1991). 'En medio del volcán'. *QueHacer*, 73: 18–24.

ILO (International Labour Organization) (several years). *Yearbook of Labor Statistics* Geneva: ILO.

INAPP/Inca (1991). 'Participação Popular: um Sonho Possível'. Mimeograph.

Indec (1992a). 'Síntesis: Situación y evolución social no. 1'. Buenos Aires: Instituto Nacional de Estadísticas y Censos.

—— (1992b). 'Datos proporcionados al Ministerio de Trabajo y Seguridad Social'. Buenos Aires: Instituto Nacional de Estadísticas y Censos.

—— (1993a). *Estadística mensual*, 3 (4). Buenos Aires: Instituto Nacional de Estadísticas y Censos.

—— (1993b). 'Encuesta permanente de hogares, información de prensa' (May). Buenos Aires: Instituto Nacional de Estadísticas y Censos.

—— (1994). *Anuario estadístico de la República Argentina*. Buenos Aires: Instituto Nacional de Estadísticas y Censos.

—— (1995a). *Estadística mensual*, 5 (6). Buenos Aires: Instituto Nacional de Estadísticas y Censos.

—— (1995b). 'Encuesta permanente de hogares, información de prensa' (May). Buenos Aires: Instituto Nacional de Estadísticas y Censos.

'Informe de Opinión de APOYO S.A.' (1988). *Debate*, 9 (49): 10.

Inforpress (1985). *Guatemala: Elections 1985*. Guatemala: Inforpress Centroamericana.

INI (Instituto Nacional Indigenista) (1990). *Programa nacional de desarrollo de los pueblos indígenas, 1991–1994*. DF, Mexico: INI.

—— (1991). 'Manual de operación de los fondos regionales de solidaridad para el desarrollo de los pueblos indígenos'. Unpublished. DF, Mexico.

Inkeles, Alex (ed.) (1991). *On Measuring Democracy*. New Brunswick: Transaction Publishers.

Inside NAFTA (1994). 1 (19), 21 Sept.

Isbell, Billie Jean (1992). 'Shining Path and Peasant Responses in Rural Ayacucho'. In David Scott Palmer (ed.), *Shining Path of Peru*. New York: St Martin's Press.

Izquierda Unida (1995). *1995: Plan de acción inmediata*. Lima: Izquierda Unida.

Jacobi, Pedro (1995). 'Alcances y límites de los gobiernos locales progresistas en Brasil: Las alcaldías petistas'. *Revista Mexicana de Sociología*, 2/95: 143–62.

Jaguaribe, Hélio, *et al.* (1986). *Brasil 2000: Para um Novo Pacto Social*. São Paulo: Editora Paz e Terra.

James, Daniel (1988). *Resistance and Integration: Peronism and the Argentine Working Class, 1946–1976*. Cambridge: Cambridge University Press.

Jaquette, Jane (ed.) (1989). *The Women's Movement in Latin America: Feminism and the Transition to Democracy*. Boston: Unwin Hyman.

Jenkins, J. Craig, and Klandermans Bert (eds.) (1995). *The Politics of Social Protest: Comparative Perspectives on States and Social Movements*. Minneapolis: University of Minnesota Press.

—— and Perrow, Charles (1977). 'Insurgency of the Powerless: Farm Worker Movements (1946–1972)'. *American Sociological Review*, 42: 249–68.

JESSOP, BOB (1982). *The Capitalist State*. New York: New York University Press.

JILBERTO, ALEX FERNANDEZ (1993). 'Internationalization and Social Democratization of Politics in Chile'. In Menno Vellinga (ed.), *Social Democracy in Latin America: Prospects for Change*. Boulder, Colo.: Westview Press.

JOCHAMOWITZ, LUIS (1993). *Ciudadano Fujimori: La construcción de un político*. Lima: PEISA.

JONAS, SUZANNE (1991). *The Battle for Guatemala: Rebels, Death Squads, and U.S. Power*. Boulder, Colo.: Westview.

—— and MCCAUGHAN, EDWARD J. (eds.) (1994). *Latin America Faces the Twenty-First Century: Reconstructing a Social Justice Agenda*. Boulder, Colo.: Westview.

JOSEPH, GILBERT, and NUGENT, DANIEL (1994). *Everyday Forms of State Formation: Revolution and the Negotiation of Rule in Mexico*. Durham, NC: Duke University Press.

JULIÃO, FRANCISCO (1972). *Cambão: The Yoke: The Hidden Face of Brazil*. Harmondsworth: Penguin Books.

'Jurado Nacional de Elecciónes' (1990). Lima: Peruvian Government Document.

KAHLER, MILLES (1992). 'External Influence, Conditionality, and the Politics of Adjustment'. In Stephan Haggard and Robert Kaufman (eds.), *The Politics of Economic Adjustment*. Princeton: Princeton University Press.

KAIMOWITZ, DAVID (1992). 'Aid and Development in Latin America'. *Latin America Research Review*, 27 (2): 202–11.

KALMIJN, JELGER (1994). 'U.S. Activists Support Organizing Drive: Intimidation Halts Union Vote in Tijuana'. *Labor Notes*, Feb.: 3, 14.

KARL, TERRY LYNN (1986). 'Imposing Consent? Electoralism vs. Democratization in El Salvador'. In Paul Drake and Eduardo Silva (eds.), *Elections and Democratization in Latin America, 1980–1985*. La Jolla, Calif.: UCSD-CILAS.

—— (1990). 'Dilemmas of Democratization in Latin America'. *Comparative Politics*, Oct.

KATZ, HARRY C. (1993). 'The Decentralization of Collective Bargaining: A Literature Review and Comparative Analysis'. *Industrial and Labor Relations Review*, 47 (1): 3–24.

KATZENSTEIN, PETER J. (1985). *Small States in World Markets: Industrial Policy in Europe*. Ithaca, NY: Cornell University Press.

KATZNELSON, IRA, and ZOLBERG, ARISTIDE (eds.) (1986). *Working Class Formation*. Princeton: Princeton University Press.

—— GEIGER, KIM, and KRYDER, DANIEL (1993). 'Limiting Liberalism: The Southern Veto in Congress, 1933–1950'. *Political Science Quarterly*, 108 (2), Summer.

KAUFMAN, ROBERT R. (1974). 'A Patron–Client Concept and Macropolitics: Prospects and Problems'. *Comparative Studies in Soiety and History*, 16 (3).

—— (1986). 'Liberalization and Democratization in South America: Perspectives from the 1970s'. In G. O'Donnell, P. Schmitter, and L. Whitehead (eds.), *Transitions from Authoritarian Rule*. Baltimore: Johns Hopkins University Press.

—— and HAGGARD, S. (forthcoming). *The Political Economy of Democratic Transitions*.

—— and STALLINGS, BARBARA (1991). 'The Political Economy of Latin American Populism'. In R. Dornbusch and S. Edwards (eds.), *The Macroeconomics of Populism in Latin America*. Chicago: University of Chicago Press.

KECK, MARGARET (1989). 'The "New Unionism" in the Brazilian Transition'. In Alfred Stepan (ed.), *Democratizing Brazil: Problems of Transition and Consolidation*. New York: Oxford University Press.

—— (1991). 'The International Politics of the Brazilian Amazon'. New York: The Columbia University/New York University Consortium Conference Papers, 63.

KECK, MARGARET (1992). *The Workers' Party and Democratization in Brazil.* New Haven: Yale University Press.

—— (1993). 'Equity and Justice Issues in Contemporary Brazil'. Washington: Interamerican Dialogue.

—— and SIKKINK, KATHRYN (forthcoming). 'Issue Networks in International Politics'. Unpublished.

KERN, HORST, and SABEL, CHARLES (1991). 'Trade Unions and Decentralized Production: A Sketch of Strategic Problems in the West German Labor Movement'. *Politics and Society,* 19 (4): 373–402.

KIM, ILPYONG J., and ZACEK, JANE SHAPIRO (eds.) (1993). *Establishing Democratic Rule: The Reemergence of Local Governments in Post-authoritarian Systems.* Washington: In Depth Books.

KINGSTONE, PETER (1994a). 'Shaping Business Interests: The Politics of Neo-liberalism in Brazil, 1985–1992'. Ph.D. diss., University of California at Berkeley, Department of Political Science.

—— (1994b). 'Social Democracy in the Era of Neo-liberalism: Lessons from the Swedish Case for Brazil'. Presented to the conference 'The Politics of Inequality', Institute of Latin American and Iberian Studies, Columbia University, New York City, Mar.

KIRCHEIMER, OTTO (1966). 'The Transformation of the West European Party Systems'. In Joseph Lapalombara and Myron Weiner (eds.), *Political Parties and Political Development.* Princeton: Princeton University Press.

KIRK, ROBIN (1991). *The Decade of Chaqwa: Peru's Internal Refugees.* Washington: US Committee for Refugees.

KITSCHELT, HERBERT P. (1986). 'Political Opportunity Structures and Political Protest: Anti-nuclear Movements in Four Democracies'. *British Journal of Political Science,* 16 (1): 57–85.

—— (1988). 'Left-Libertarian Parties: Explaining Innovation in Competitive Party Systems'. *World Politics,* 40 (2): 193–234.

—— (1994). *The Transformation of European Social Democracy.* Cambridge: Cambridge University Press.

KOHLI, ATUL (1987). *The State and Poverty in India: The Politics of Reform.* Cambridge: Cambridge University Press.

—— (1994). *State Power and Social Forces: Domination and Transformation in the Third World.* New York: Cambridge University Press.

KOROVKIN, TANYA (1993). 'Indians, Peasants, and the State: The Growth of a Community Movement in the Ecuadorian Andes'. Occasional Papers. CERLAC: York University.

KORPI, WALTER (1978). *The Working Class in Welfare Capitalism.* London: Routledge & Kegan Paul.

—— (1983). *The Democratic Class Struggle.* London: Routledge & Kegan Paul.

—— (1985). 'Developments in the Theory of Power and Exchange'. *Sociological Theory,* 3 (2).

LA BOTZ, DAN (1992). *Mask of Democracy: Labor Suppression in Mexico Today.* Boston: South End Press.

—— (1994). 'Making Links across the Border'. *Labor Notes,* 185: 7–10.

La Causa R (1993). *Proyecto político para una nueva Venezuela.* Caracas: Documento Base.

LACURCIA, HUGO (1990). 'El sistema de pensiones en Uruguay'. In *Regulación del sistema financiero y reforma del sistema de pensiones: Experiencias de América Latina*. Santiago: CEPAL/PNUD.

LANDIM, LEILAH (1993). 'Brazilian Crossroads: People's Groups, Walls and Bridges'. In P. Wignaraja (ed.), *New Social Movements in the South: Empowering the People*. London: Zed Books.

LARA, JR., FRANCISCO, and MORALES, JR., HORACIO (1990). 'The Peasant Movement and the Challenge of Democratization in the Phillipines'. In Jonathan Fox (ed.), *The Challenge of Rural Democratization: Perspectives from Latin America and the Philippines*. London: Frank Cass.

LARRAIN, FELIPE, and SELOWSKY, MARCELO (eds.) (1991). *The Public Sector and the Latin American Crisis*. San Francisco: ICS Press.

Latin America Data Base (1994). 'SourceMex: Economic News and Analysis on Mexico'. Latin American Institute, University of New Mexico: 5 (7).

Latin American Labor News (1992). 5. Miami: Florida International University.

LAWSON, KAY, and MERKL, PETER (eds.) (1988). *When Parties Fail: Emerging Alternative Organizations*. Princeton: Princeton University Press.

Lawyers Committee for Human Rights (1990). *Abandoning the Victims: The UN Advisory Services Program in Guatemala*. New York.

LECHNER, NORBERT (1988). 'De la revolución a la democracia'. *Los patios interiores de la democracia: Subjetividad y política*. Santiago: FLACSO.

—— (1990). *Los patios interiores de la democracia: Subjetividad y política*. DF, Mexico: Fondo de Cultura Económica.

LEFTWICH, ADRIAN (1994). 'Governance, the State and the Politics of Development'. *Development and Change*, 25 (2): 363–86.

LEHMBRUCH, GERHARD, and SCHMITTER, PHILIPPE (eds.) (1982). *Patterns of Corporatist Policy-Making*. London: Sage.

LEITE LOPES, JOSE SERGIO (1978). *O Vapor do Diabo: Trabalho dos Operários do Açúcar*. São Paulo: Paz e Terra.

LEÓN, JORGE (n.d.). 'Levantamiento indígena, levantamiento campesino: Actores, propuestas, contextos, perspectivas'. Unpublished.

LINDENBERG, MARC, and DEVARAJAN, SHANTAYANAN (1993). 'Prescribing Strong Economic Medicine: Revisiting the Myths about Structural Adjustment, Democracy, and Economic Performance in Developing Countries'. *Comparative Politics*, 25 (2): 169–82.

LINDHEIM, DANIEL NOAH (1986). 'Regional Development and Deliberate Social Change: Integrated Rural Development in Mexico'. Ph.D. diss., University of California, Berkeley.

LINDHOLM, CHARLES (1990). *Charisma*. Cambridge: Basil Blackwell.

LINZ, JUAN, and STEPAN, ALFRED (forthcoming). *Problems of Democratic Transition and Consolidation: Southern Europe, South America and Eastern Europe*. Oxford: Oxford University Press.

—— and VALENZUELA, ARTURO (1994). *The Failure of Presidential Democracy*. 2 vols. Baltimore: Johns Hopkins.

LIPSET, SEYMOUR MARTIN (1991). 'No Third Way: A Comparative Perspective on the Left'. In Daniel Chirot (ed.), *The Crisis of Leninism and the Decline of the Left: The Revolutions of 1989*. Seattle: University of Washington Press.

LITTLE, WALTER (1992). 'Political Corruption in Latin America'. *Corruption and Reform*, 7: 41–66.

Locke, John (1947). *Two Treatises on Government* (1690). New York: Hafner.

Locke, Richard M. (1992). 'The Demise of the National Union in Italy: Lessons for Comparative Industrial Relations Theory'. *Industrial and Labor Relations Review*, 45 (2): 229–49.

Loiola, Francisco Antônio (1993). 'Padrões de Gestão ao Nível das Escolas e dos Sistemas Municipais de Ensino: O caso de Icapuí-CE'. Presented at XI Encontro de Pesquisa Educaçional do Nordeste, Recífe.

Lomas, Emilio (1991*a*). 'La democracia ya no es de las cúpulas, afirma Salinas'. *La Jornada*, 13 Sept.

—— (1991*b*). 'Salinas: Nueva relación Estado–sociedad civil'. *La Jornada*, 15 Sept.

López, Arturo, *et al.* (1989). *Geografía de las elecciones presidenciales de México, 1988.* Mexico: Arturo Rosenblueth.

López, Sinecio (1991). *El dios mortal: Estado, sociedad y política en el Perú del siglo XX.* Lima: Instituto Democracia y Socialismo.

López Claros, Augusto (1989). 'Growth-Oriented Adjustment: Spain in the 1980s'. *Finance and Development.* IMF/World Bank.

López Larrave, Mario (1976). *Breve historia del movimiento sindical guatemalteco.* Guatemala: Editorial Universitari.

López-Maya, Margarita (1989). *El Banco de los Trabajadores de Venezuela ¿Algo más que un banco?* Caracas: Ediciones de la UCV.

—— (1991). 'Tensiones sociopolíticas del proceso de descentralización en Venezuela'. *Cuadernos del CENDES*, 17/18. Caracas.

—— (1993). *Auge y decadencia de Acción Democrática.* Caracas: Editorial Historiadores Sociedad Civil.

—— Gómez Calcaño, Luis, and Maingón, Thais (1989). *De punto fijo al pacto social.* Caracas: Fondo Editorial Acta Científica Venezolana.

López Murphy, Ricardo (ed.) (1995). *Fiscal Decentralization in Latin America.* Washington: Inter-American Development Bank.

López Ricci, José (1988). 'Marcha al olor a pólvora'. *La Voz.*

—— (1993). 'Las organizaciones populares en San Martín de Porres'. Informe de Investigación. Lima: Centro Alternativa.

'Los resultados del 14 de abril y el reajuste de la táctica' (1985). Lima: Second Plenary Session of the Central Committee, Partido Unificado Mariateguista.

Loveman, Brian (1976). *Struggle in the Countryside.* Bloomington: Indiana University Press.

—— (1979). 'Political Participation and Rural Labor in Chile'. In Mitchell A. Seligson and John A. Booth (eds.), *Political Participation in Latin America*, ii: *Politics and the Poor.* New York: Holmes & Meier.

—— (1994). 'Protected Militaries' and Military Guardianships: Political Transitions in Latin America, 1978–1993'. *Journal of InterAmerican Studies and World Affairs*, 36 (2): 105–89.

Lowenthal, Abraham (1991). *Exporting Democracy: The United States and Latin America.* Baltimore: The Johns Hopkins University Press.

Luckman, Thomas (1980). *The Social Construction of Reality: A Treatise in the Sociology of Knowledge.* New York: Irvington Publishers.

Luhmann, Niklas (1979). *Trust and Power: Two Works by Niklas Luhmann.* Chichester: John Wiley.

Lustig, Nora (1992). *Mexico: The Remaking of an Economy.* Washington: Brookings Institution.

—— (1994). 'Solidarity as a Strategy of Poverty Alleviation'. In Wayne Cornelius, Ann Craig, and Jonathan Fox (eds.), *Transforming State–Society Relations in Mexico: The National Solidarity Strategy*. La Jolla, Calif.: Center for US–Mexican Studies.

LYNCH, NICOLÁS (1992). *La transición conservadora: Movimiento social y democracia en el Perú, 1975–1978*. Lima: El Zorro de Abajo Ediciones.

McADAM, DOUG (1982). *Political Process and the Development of Black Insurgency, 1930–1970*. Chicago: The University of Chicago Press.

—— and RUCHT, DIETER (1993). 'The Cross-national Diffusion of Movement Ideas'. In Russell J. Dalton (ed.), *Citizens, Protest, and Democracy*. Special Edition of *Annals of the American Academy of Political and Social Science*, 528: 56–74.

MACAS, LUIS (1991). 'El levantamiento indígena visto por sus protagonistas'. In I. Almeida *et al.* (eds.), *INDIOS: Una reflexion sobre el levantamiento indígena de 1990*. Quito: Logos.

McCLINTOCK, CYNTHIA (1984). 'Why Peasants Rebel: The Case of Peru's Sendero Luminoso'. *World Politics*, 37 (1).

—— (1989). 'Peru's Sendero Luminoso Rebellion: Origins and Trajectory'. In Susan Eckstein (ed.), *Power and Popular Protest: Latin Amerian Social Movements*. Berkeley and Los Angeles: University of California Press.

—— and LOWENTHAL, ABRAHAM F. (eds.) (1983). *The Peruvian Experiment Reconsidered*. Princeton: Princeton University Press.

McCORMICK, GORDON (1990). *The Shining Path and the Future of Peru*. Santa Monica, Calif.: The Rand Corporation.

—— (1992). *From the Sierra to the Cities: The Urban Campaign of the Shining Path*. Santa Monica, Calif.: The Rand Corporation.

McCREERY, DAVID (1976). 'Coffee and Class: The Structure of Development in Liberal Guatemala'. *Hispanic American Historical Review*, 56 (3).

—— (1983). 'Debt Servitude in Rural Guatemala'. *Hispanic American Historical Review*, 63 (4): 735–59.

—— (1990). 'State Power, Indigenous Communities, and Land in Nineteenth-Century Guatemala, 1820–1920'. In Carol Smith (ed.), *Guatemalan Indians and the State, 1540 to 1988*. Austin: University of Texas.

MACERA, PABLO (1992). 'A propósito del Fujigolpe: Entrevista a Macera'. *Debates* (May–June). Lima: Apoyo SA.

MACEWAN, ARTHUR (1988). 'Transitions from Authoritarian Rule'. *Latin American Perspective*, 58: 115–30.

McGUIRE, JAMES (1991a). 'Union Political Tactics and Democratic Consolidation in Alfonsín's Argentina, 1983–89'. *Latin American Research Review*, 1993/3.

—— (1991b). 'Peronism as a Party: Where is the Center?' Presented at the XV Congress of the International Political Science Association, Buenos Aires.

—— (1994). 'Economic Reform and Political Shenanigans in Menem's Argentina, 1989–93'. Presented for the XVIII International Congress of the Latin American Studies Association, Atlanta, Ga.

—— (forthcoming). *Peronism without Perón: Unions, Parties and Democracy in Argentina*. Stanford, Calif.: Stanford University Press.

McSHERRY, J. PATRICE (1992). 'Military Power, Impunity and State–Society Change in Latin America'. *Canadian Journal of Political Science*, 25 (3): 463–88.

MAFRA, HUMBERTO (1993). 'O Movimento Ambientalista Brasileiro: Desafios e Oportunidades'. Unpublished. San Francisco.

MAINWARING, SCOTT (1988). 'Political Parties and Democratization in Brazil and the Southern Cone'. *Comparative Politics*, 21 (1): 91–117.

—— and SCULLY, TIMOTHY R. (1994). 'A Institucionalização dos Sistemas Partidários na América Latina'. *Dados*, 37 (1): 43–79.

—— —— (eds.) (1995). *Building Democratic Institutions: Party Systems in Latin America*. Stanford, Calif.: Stanford University Press.

—— O'DONNELL, GUILLERMO, and VALENZUELA, J. SAMUEL (eds.) (1992). *Issues in Democratic Consolidation: The New South American Democracies in Comparative Perspective*. Notre Dame, Ind.: University of Notre Dame.

MALEFAKIS, MICHAEL (1990). 'Steps Toward a Social Investment Fund: Negotiations Involving Non-governmental Organizations, Government of Guatemala and the World Bank'. New York: PACT.

MALLOY, JAMES M. (ed.) (1977). *Authoritarianism and Corporatism in Latin America*. Pittsburgh: University of Pittsburgh.

—— (1989). 'Policy Analysts, Public Policy, and Regime Structure in Latin America'. *Governance: An International Journal of Policy and Administration*, 2 (3): 315–37.

—— (1991*a*). 'Parties, Economic Policy Making, and the Problem of Democratic Governance in the Central Andes'. Prepared for the International Political Science Association XV World Congress, Buenos Aires.

—— (1991*b*). 'Statecraft, Social Policy, and Governance in Latin America'. Unpublished. Pittsburgh: University of Pittsburgh.

—— and CONAGHAN, CATHERINE (1994). *Unsettling Statecraft: Democracy and Neoliberalism in the the Central Andes*. Pittsburgh: University of Pittsburgh Press.

MANEIRO, ALFREDO (1986). *Notas políticas*. Caracas: Ediciones del Agua Mansa.

—— *et al.* (1971). *Notas negativas*. Caracas: Ediciones Venezuela. 83.

MANRIQUE, NELSON (1989). 'La década de la violencia'. *Márgenes*, 5: 137–82. Lima.

MANSBRIDGE, JANE (1983). *Beyond Adversary Democracy*. Chicago: Chicago University Press.

MANZ, BEATRIZ (1988). *Refugees of a Hidden War: The Aftermath of Counterinsurgency in Guatemala*. New York: State University of New York.

MARAVALL, JOSÉ MARÍA (1982). *The Political Transition in Spain*. London: Croom Helm.

—— (1993). 'Politics and Policy: Economic Reforms in Southern Europe'. In Luiz Carlos Bresser Pereira, J. M. Maravall, and A. Przeworski (eds.), *Economic Reforms in New Democracies*. Cambridge: Cambridge University Press.

MARIN, BERND (ed.) (1990). *Governance and Generalized Exchange: Self-Organizing Policy Networks in Action*. Frankfurt: Campus Verlag/Westview Press.

—— and MAYNTZ, RENATE (1991). *Policy Networks: Empirical Evidence and Theoretical Considerations*. Boulder, Colo.: Westview Press.

MARSHAL, ADRIANA (1989). 'The Fall of Labor's Share in Income and Consumption: A New "Growth Model" for Argentina?' In W. Canak (ed.), *Lost Promises: Debt, Austerity and Development in Latin America*. Boulder, Colo.: Westview Press.

—— (1990). 'Introducción: El empleo público frente a la crisis: Estudios sobre América Latina'. Geneva: International Institute of Labor Studies.

MARSHALL, T. H. (1963). *Class, Citizenship, and Social Development*. Chicago: University of Chicago Press.

—— (1965). *Class, Citizenship, and Social Development*. Garden City, NY: Anchor Books.

—— (1967). *Cidadania, Clase Social e status*. Rio de Janeiro: Zahar.

MARTIN, GUILLERMO (1990). 'El FONHAPO y la política de vivienda'. *Barrio Nuevo*, 6–7: 1–6.

MARTIN, SCOTT B. (1994). 'Forward or Backward: Corporatism and Industrial Restructuring in Brazilian Autos'. Presented at the conference 'The Politics of Inequality'. Institute of Latin American and Iberian Studies, Columbia University.

—— (1995). 'How Unions Can Learn to Innovate: Evidence from the Brazilian Auto Industry'. Presented to the Latin American Studies Association. Washington.

—— (forthcoming). 'Redefinindo o corporativismo: Sindicatos e empresários na câmara setorial da indústria automotiva Brasileira'. *Lua Nova*.

MARTUCCELLI, DANILO, and MARISTELLA, SVAMPA (1993). 'La doble legitimidad del populismo'. *Pretextos*, 3/4. Lima: DESCO.

MARTZ, JOHN D. (1992). 'Party Elites and Leadership in Colombia and Venezuela'. *Journal of Latin American Studies*, 24: 87–112.

MARVÁN, IGNACIO L., and CUEVAS, J. AURELIO (1987). 'El movimiento de damnificados de Tlaltelolco (septiembre de 1985–marzo de 1986)'. *Revista Mexicana de Sociología*, 49 (4): 111–40.

MATOS MAR, JOSÉ (1984). *Desborde popular y crisis del estado*. Lima: Instituto de Estudios Peruanos.

MAXFIELD, SYLVIA (forthcoming). *Gatekeepers of Growth: The International Political Economy of Central Banking in Developing Countries*.

MAYBURY-LEWIS, BIORN (1994). *The Politics of the Possible: The Brazilian Rural Workers' Trade Union Movement, 1964–1985*. Philadelphia: Temple University Press.

MAYORGA, RENÉ ANTONIO (coord.) (1992). *Democracia y gobernabilidad en América Latina*. Caracas: Nueva Sociedad.

MAZLISCH, BRUCE (1991). 'The Breakdown of Connections and Modern Development'. *World Development*, 19 (1): 31–44.

MEDINA, PABLO (1988). *Pablo Medina en entrevista*. Caracas: Ediciones del Agua Mansa.

—— (1993). 'Causa Radical: Entrevista a Pablo Medina'. *Motivos*, 102. Ciudad Mexico.

MED/UNICEF/CENPEC (1993). 'Todas as Crianças na Escola: A experiência de Icapuí-CE, 1989/1992'. *Educação & Desenvolvimento Municipal*, 12. Brasília: Quantum.

MEJÍA PINEIROS, MARIA CONSUELO, and SARMIENTO, SERGIO (1987). *La lucha indígena: Un reto a la ortodoxia*. DF, Mexico: Siglo XXI.

MELO, MARCUS (1993). *Financiers, Builders and Bureaucrats: The Rise and Demise of Housing Coalitions in Brazil, 1964–1993*. Working Paper No. 3. New York: The Janey Program on Latin America, The New School for Social Research.

MELUCCI, ALBERTO (1989). *Nomads of the Present*. Philadelphia: Temple University Press.

MENDES, CHICO (1989). *Fight for the Forest*. London: Latin America Bureau.

MÉNDEZ, LUIS, ROMERO, MIGUEL ANGEL, and BOLÍVAR, AUGUSTO (1992). 'Solidaridad se institucionaliza'. *El Cotidiano*, 49: 60–72.

MENÉNDEZ CARRIÓN, AMPARO (1989). 'Para una interpretación de la naturaleza del comportamiento electoral urbano en contextos de precariedad estructural: Propuesta para el caso de Guayaquil'. In Felipe Burbano and Carlos de la Torre (eds.), *El populismo en Ecuador*. Quito: ILDIS.

MERICLE, KENNETH S. (1977). 'Corporatist Control of the Working Class: Authoritarian Brazil since 1964'. In James M. Malloy (ed.), *Authoritarianism and Corporatism in Latin America*. Pittsburgh: University of Pittsburgh Press.

MERKEL, WOLFGANG (1992). 'After the Golden Age: Is Social Democracy Doomed to Decline?' In *Socialist Parties in Europe*. Barcelona: Institut de Ciencies Politiques i Sociales.

MESA-LAGO, CARMELO (1978). *Social Security in Latin America: Pressure Groups, Stratification and Inequality*. Pittsburgh: University of Pittsburgh Press.

—— (1985). *El desarrollo de la seguridad social en América Latina*. Santiago: Estudios e Informes dela CEPAL, No. 43.

—— (1993). 'Changing Social Security in Latin America and the Caribbean: Towards the Alleviation of Social Costs'. Unpublished. Pittsburgh: University of Pittsburgh.

MEYER, DAVID S., and WHITTIER, NANCY (1994). 'Social Movement Spillover'. *Social Problems*, 41 (2).

MEYERSON, ALLEN R. (1994). 'Big Labor's Strategic Raid in Mexico'. *New York Times*, 12 Sept.: D1, D4.

MIDDLEBROOK, KEVIN J. (1989). 'Union Democratization in the Mexican Automobile Industry: A Reappraisal'. *Latin American Research Review*, 24 (2): 69–93.

—— (1992). 'Transnational Industrialization and Labor Alliances: Mexican Automobile Workers Confront Industrial Restructuring and North American Economic Integration'. Presented at the Latin American Studies Association International Congress, Los Angeles.

MIGDAL, JOEL (1974). *Peasants, Politics, and Revolution: Pressures toward Political and Social Change in the Third World*. Princeton: Princeton University Press.

—— (1988). *Strong Societies and Weak States: State–Society Relations and State Capabilities in the Third World*. Princeton: Princeton University Press.

Ministerio de la Presidencia (1993). 'Lineamientos básicos de la política social'. Mimeograph. Lima.

Ministerio de Trabajo (1993a). 'Proyecto de ley de reforma al régimen de contrato de trabajo'. Buenos Aires.

—— (1993b). 'La dinámica de la negociación colectiva en el marco de la reforma laboral y algunas aplicaciones de la ley de empleo'. Buenos Aires: Comisión Técnica Asesora de Productividad y Salarios.

—— (1994a). 'Acuerdo marco para el empleo, la productividad y la equidad social'. Buenos Aires.

—— (1994b). 'Estadísticas laborales, Ministerio de Trabajo y seguridad social'. Buenos Aires: Departamento de Estadísticas Laborales.

Minnesota Lawyers International Human Rights Committee (1990). *Justice Suspended: Failure of the Habeas Corpus System in Guatemala*. Minneapolis.

MINUJIN, ALBERTO (1993). 'En la rodada'. In *Cuesta abajo: Los nuevos pobres: Efectos de la crisis en la sociedad argentina*. Buenos Aires: Losada.

MOCTEZUMA, PEDRO (1993). 'Del movimiento urbano popular a los movimientos comunitarios: El espejo desenterrado'. *El Cotidiano*, 57: 3–10.

MOE, TERRY (1980). *The Organization of Interests: Incentives and the Internal Dynamic of Political Interest Groups*. Chicago: University of Chicago Press.

MOGUEL, JULIO (1991). 'La Coordinadora Estatal de Productores de Café de Oaxaca'. In Gabriela Ejea and Luis Hernández (eds.), 'Cafetaleros: La construcción de la autonomía'. *Cuadernos desarrollo de base*, 3.

—— (1992). 'El programa nacional de solidaridad, para quién?' In *Los nuevos sujetos sociales de desarrollo rural*. DF, Mexico: Fundación Interamericana.

—— (1993). 'Banco Mundial y Pronasol: Administrar la pobreza'. *Ojarasca*, 22: 12–17.

—— and ARANDA, JOSEFINA (1992). 'La Coordinadora Estatal de Productores de Café de Oaxaca'. In Julio Moguel, Carlota Botey, and Luis Hernández (eds.), *Autonomía y nuevos sujetos sociales en el desarrollo rural*. DF, Mexico: Siglo XXI/CEHAM.

MOISÉS, JOSÉ ÁLVARO (1985). 'Poder Local e Participação Popular'. In Pedro Dallari (ed.), *Política Municipal*. Porto Alegre: Mercado Aberto/Fundação Wilson Pinheiro.

—— (1993). 'Elections, Political Parties and Political Culture in Brazil: Changes and Continuities'. *Journal of Latin American Studies*, 25 (3): 575–611.

MOLINAR HORCASITAS, JUAN, and WELDON, JEFFREY A. (1994). 'Electoral Determinants and Consequences of National Solidarity'. In Wayne A. Cornelius, Ann L. Craig, and Jonathan Fox (eds.), *Transforming State–Society Relations in Mexico: The National Solidarity Strategy*. US–Mexico Contemporary Perspectives Series, 6. La Jolla: Center for US–Mexican Studies, University of California, San Diego.

MONEY, JEANNETTE (1992). 'The Decentralization of Collective Bargaining in Belgium, France and the United States'. In M. Golden and J. Pontusson (eds.), *Bargaining for Change*. Ithaca, NY: Cornell University Press.

MONTAÑO, JORGE (1976). *Los pobres de la ciudad en los asentamientos espontáneos*. DF, México: Siglo XXI.

MONTEFORTE TOLEDO, MARIO (1965). *Guatemala: Monografía sociológica*. 2nd edn. DF, Mexico: Instituto de Investigaciones Sociales, UNAM.

MONTESINOS, VERONICA (1993). 'Economic Policy Elites and Democratization'. *Studies in Comparative International Development*, 28 (1).

MONTOYA, DAVID, and REYNA, CARLOS (1992). 'Sendero: Informe de Lima'. *QueHacer*, 76. Lima: DESCO.

MOODY, KIM, and McGINN, MARY (1992). *Unions and Free Trade: Solidarity vs. Competition*. Detroit: Labor Notes.

MOORE, BARRINGTON, JR. (1966). *Social Origins of Dictatorship and Democracy*. Boston: Beacon Press.

—— (1978). *Injustice: The Social Bases of Obedience and Revolt*. New York: M. E. Sharp, Inc.

MORA, MARIANA (1992). 'Problematica y características de las ONGs en el Ecuador'. *Report of Ministry of Social Welfare and Labor*.

MORÃES, CLODOMIR (1970). 'Peasant Leagues in Brazil'. In Rodolfo Stavenhagen (ed.), *Agrarian Problems and Peasant Movements in Latin America*. Garden City, NY: Anchor Books.

MORALES, JUAN ANTONIO, and McMAHON, G. (eds.) (1993). *La política económica en la transición*. Santiago, Chile: CIEPLAN.

MORALES DE LA CRUZ, BALTASAR (1944). *La caída de Jorge Ubico: Derrocamiento de una tiranía: Reseña de la gesta cívica de junio de 1944*. Aporte del Partido Social Democrático a la Historia de Guatemala. Guatemala: Tipografía Sánchez & de Guise.

MORIMOTO, AMELIA (1979). 'Los inmigrantes japoneses en el Perú'. Lima: Taller de Estudios Andinos, Universidad Nacional Agraria.

MORRIS, ALDON, and MUELLER, CAROL McCLURG (1992). *Frontiers in Social Movement Theory*. New Haven: Yale University Press.

MORRIS, ARTHUR, and LOWDER, STELLA (eds.) (1992). *Decentralization in Latin America: An Evaluation*. New York: Praeger.

MOSES, JONATHON (1994). 'Abdication from National Policy Autonomy: What's Left to Leave?' *Politics and Society*, 22 (2): 125–48.

MOYAO M., ELISEO (1991). 'Hay un cambio del fondo en la política social del gobierno?' *Barrio Nuevo*, 9: 1–5.

MUNCK, GERARDO (1990). 'Identity and Ambiguity in Democratic Struggles'. In Joe Foweraker and Ann Craig (eds.), *Popular Movements and Political Change in Mexico*. Boulder, Colo.: Lynne Rienner.

MUÑOZ, OSCAR, and CELEDÓN, C. (1993). 'Chile en transición: Estrategia económica y política'. In J. A. Morales and G. McMahon (eds.), *La política económica en la transición*. Santiago, Chile: CIEPLAN.

—— and SCHAMIS, H. (1992). 'Las transformaciones del estado en Chile y la privatización'. In Joaquín Vial (ed.), *Adonde va América Latina*. Santiago, Chile: CIEPLAN.

NAGEL, STUART S. (ed.) (1994). *Latin American Development and Public Policy*. New York: St Martin's Press.

NAGENGAST, CAROLE, and KEARNEY, MICHAEL (1990). 'Mixtec Ethnicity: Social Identity, Political Consciousness and Political Activism'. *Latin American Research Review*, 25 (2).

NAUMAN, TALLI (1992). 'VW Gets Its Way; Workers Get Grief'. *El financiero internacional*, 31 Aug.

—— (1993). 'Labor Solidarity Crosses the Border'. *El financiero internacional*, 9–15 Aug.: 14.

—— (1994). 'Border Plants Central to Union Efforts'. *El financiero internacional*, 17–23 Jan.: 10.

NAVARRO, ZANDER (1992). 'Democracy, Citizenship and Representation: Rural Social Movements in Southern Brazil, 1978–1990'. Unpublished. Cambridge, Mass.

NAWWN (North American Worker to Worker Network) (1993). *Free Trade Mailing*, 3 (2).

NEF, JORGE (1992). 'Chile: Redemocratization or the Entrenchment of Counterrevolution'. In A. R. M. Ritter, M. Cameron, and D. Pollock (eds.), *Latin America to the Year 2000*. New York: Praeger.

NELSON, JOAN (ed.) (1990). *Economic Crises and Policy Choice*. Princeton: Princeton University Press.

—— (1992). 'Poverty, Equity, and the Politics of Adjustment'. In Stephan Haggard and Robert R. Kaufman (eds.), *The Politics of Economic Adjustment*. Princeton: Princeton University Press.

—— (1994). *Intricate Links: Democratization and Market Reforms in Latin America and Eastern Europe*. New Brunswick, NJ: Transaction Publishers.

New York Times (1993). 'Chile Advances in a War on Poverty'. 4 Apr.: 4.

NICKSON, R. ANDREW (1995). *Local Government in Latin America*. Boulder, Colo.: Lynne Rienner.

NIETO, JORGE (1983). *Izquierda y democracia en el Perú, 1975–1982*. Lima: DESCO.

NIETO, SANTIAGO (1993). 'El problema indígena'. In Diego Cornejo Menacho (ed.), *Los indios y el estado país*. Quito: Abya-Yala.

NORDSTROM, CAROL, and MARTIN, JOANN (1992). *Paths to Domination, Resistance and Terror*. Berkeley and Los Angeles: University of California Press.

NORONHA, EDUARDO (1991). 'A Explosão das Greves na Década de 80'. In Armando Boito, Jr. (ed.), *O Sindicalismo Brasileiro nos Anos 80*. São Paulo: Paz e Terra.

North American Agreement on Labor Cooperation between the Government of the United States of America, the Government of Canada and the Government of the United Mexican States (1993). Final Draft, 13 Sept.

NOVARO, MARCOS (1994). *Pilotos de tormentas.* Buenos Aires: Letra Buena.

NUGENT, JOSÉ GUILLERMO (1992). *El laberinto de la choledad.* Lima: Fundación Friedrich Ebert.

—— (1993). 'Elites? Masas?' *Cuestión de estado*, 4–5. Lima: IDS.

NUN, JOSÉ (1993). 'Democracy and Modernization, Thirty Years Later'. *Latin American Perspectives*, 79: 7–27.

NYLEN, WILLIAM R. (1992). 'Liberalismo para Todo Mundo, Menos Eu: Brazil and the Neoliberal Solution'. In Douglas A. Chalmers *et al.* (eds.), *The Right and Democracy in Latin America.* New York: Praeger.

O'DONNELL, GUILLERMO (1973). *Modernization and Bureaucratic-Authoritarianism: Studies in South American Politics.* Berkeley and Los Angeles: Institute of International Studies, University of California.

—— (1977). 'Corporatism and the Question of the State'. In James M. Malloy (ed.), *Authoritarianism and Corporatism in Latin America.* Pittsburgh: University of Pittsburgh Press.

—— (1988). 'Challenges to Democratization in Brazil'. *World Policy Journal*, 5 (2).

—— (1991). 'Democracia Delegativa'. *Novos Estudos CEBRAP*, 31: 25–40.

—— (1992*a*). 'Transitions, Continuities, and Paradoxes'. In Scott Mainwaring, Guillermo O'Donnell, and J. Samuel Valenzuela (eds.), *Issues in Democratic Consolidation: The New South American Democracies in Comparative Perspective.* Notre Dame, Ind.: University of Notre Dame Press.

—— (1992*b*). *Delegative Democracy?* Working Paper No. 172. Notre Dame, Ind.: Kellogg Institute, University of Notre Dame.

—— (1992*c*). 'On the State and Some Conceptual Problems'. Unpublished, Working Paper. São Paulo, Notre Dame, Ind.: CEBRAP, Kellogg Institute.

—— (1993*a*). 'Estado, democratización y ciudadanía'. *Nueva Sociedad*, 128: 62–87.

—— (1993*b*). 'Acerca del estado, la democratización y algunos problemas conceptuales: Una perspectiva latinoamericana con referencia a países poscomunistas'. *Desarrollo Económico*, 130: 163–84.

—— (1993*c*). 'On the State, Democratization and Some Conceptual Problems: A Latin American View with Glances at Some Post-communist Countries'. *World Development*, 21: 1355–69.

—— (1993*d*). 'The Browning of Latin America'. *New Perspectives Quarterly*, 10 (4).

—— (1993*e*). 'Citizenship, Social Authoritarianism and Democratic Consolidations'. Working Paper No. 20. Notre Dame, Ind.: Kellogg Institute.

—— (1994). 'Delegative Democracy'. *Journal of Democracy*, 5 (1): 55–69.

—— and SCHMITTER, PHILIPPE C. (1986). *Transitions from Authoritarian Rule: Tentative Conclusions about Uncertain Democracies.* Baltimore: Johns Hopkins University Press.

—— —— and WHITEHEAD, LAURENCE (1986). *Transitions from Authoritarian Rule.* Baltimore: Johns Hopkins University Press.

OECD Economic Surveys 1992–1993, Spain (1993). Paris: Organization for Economic Cooperation and Development.

OFFE, CLAUS (1984). *Contradictions of the Welfare State.* Cambridge, Mass.: MIT Press.

—— (1985*a*). 'The Attribution of Public Status to Interest Groups'. In Claus Offe (ed.),

Disorganized Capitalism: Contemporary Transformations of Work and Politics. Cambridge, Mass.: MIT Press.

OFFE, CLAUS (1985*b*). 'Two Logics of Collective Action'. In Claus Offe (ed.), *Disorganized Capitalism: Contemporary Transformations of Work and Politics.* Cambridge, Mass.: MIT Press.

—— (1986). 'The Attribution of Public Status to Interest Groups'. In Susan Berger (ed.), *Organizing Interests in Western Europe: Pluralism, Corporatism and the Transformation of Politics.* Cambridge: Cambridge University Press.

—— (1988). *Partidos políticos y nuevos movimientos sociales.* Madrid: Editorial Sistema.

—— (1990). 'Reflections on the Institutional Self-Transformation of Movement Politics: A Tentative Stage Model'. In Russell J. Dalton and Manfred Kuechler (eds.), *Challenging the Political Order: New Social and Political Movements in Western Democracies.* Oxford: Oxford University Press.

OI, JEAN (1985). 'Communism and Clientelism: Rural Politics in China'. *World Politics,* 37 (2), Jan.

OLINDA, ERCÍLIA MARIA BRAGA DE (1991). *A Dimensão Educativa do Partido Político.* Fortaleza: Expressão.

OLIVEIRA, EDMUNDO (1993). 'O Censo Penitenciário e a Crueza Existencia das Prisões no Brasil'. Brasília: Ministério da Justiça, Conselho Nacional de Política Criminal e Penitenciária.

OLIVEIRA, FRANCISCO DE (1992). 'Fernando Collor de Mello: Perfil de un prestidigitador'. *Nueva Sociedad,* 118: 99–108.

—— *et al.* (1993). 'Quanto Melhor, Melhor: O Acordo das Montadoras'. *Novos Estudos CEBRAP,* 36: 3–7.

OLIVEIRA, MIGUEL DARCY (1992). 'Crise ou Transformação: As Respostas Mudam a Pergunta'. In IBASE/PNUD, *Desenvolvimento e Cooperação Internacional.* Rio de Janeiro: IBASE/PNUD.

OLIVERA, LUIS, and BALLÓN, EDUARDO (1993). 'Lima y su organización popular'. Unpublished, presented at the 'Foro de Iberoamérica, Participación Ciudadano y Movimientos Sociales en las Metropolis Latinoamericanos', Salamanca.

OLSON, MANCUR (1971). *The Logic of Collective Action.* Cambridge, Mass.: Harvard University Press.

OPPENHEIM, LOIS HECHT (1993). *Politics in Chile: Democracy, Authoritarianism and the Search for Development.* Boulder, Colo.: Westview Press.

OSTROM, ELINOR (1990). *Governing the Commons: The Evolution of Institutions for Collective Action.* New York: Cambridge University Press.

—— SCHROEDER, LARRY, and WYNNE, SUSAN (1993). *Institutional Incentives and Sustainable Development: Infrastructure Policies in Perspective.* Boulder, Colo.: Westview Press.

—— *et al.* (1994). *Rules, Games, and Common-Pool Resources.* Ann Arbor: University of Michigan Press.

OSZLAK, OSCAR (1988). *Diagnóstico de la administración pública uruguaya: Serie reforma del estado.* No. 3. Montevideo: INL-ONSC.

OTÁROLA PEÑARANDA, ALBERTO (1994). 'El otro desborde popular: Violencia urbana'. *PeruPaz,* 3 (18). Lima: Instituto Constitución y Sociedad.

OTHÓN QUIROZ, JOSÉ, and MÉNDEZ, LUIS (1992). 'El conflicto de Volkswagen: Crónica de una muerte inesperada'. *El Cotidiano,* 51: 81–91.

PADRON, MARIO (1987). 'Non-governmental Development Organizations: From Development Aid to Development Cooperation'. *World Development.*

PÁDUA, JOSÉ AUGUSTO (ed.) (1987). *Ecologia e Política no Brasil*. Rio de Janeiro: Editora Espaço e Tempo and IUPERJ.

—— (1991). 'O Nascimento da Política Verde no Brasil: Fatores Exógenos e Endógenos'. In H. Leis (ed.), *Ecologia e Política Mundial*. Rio de Janeiro: FASE and Editora Vozes.

PAGE, JOSEPH (1972). *The Revolution that Never Was*. New York: Grossman Publishers.

PAIGE, JEFFREY (1975). *Agrarian Revolution: Social Movements and Export Agriculture in the Underdeveloped World*. New York: Free Press.

PAIXÃO, ANTONIO LUÍS (1982). 'A Organização Policial numa Área Metropolitana'. *Dados: Revista de Ciências Sociais*, 25 (1): 83–5.

PALERMO, VICENTE (1993). 'Apoyos y resistencias'. Unpublished diss., Madrid: Fundación Ortega y Gasset.

—— and TORRE, JUAN CARLOS (1992). 'A la sombra de la hiperinflación: La política de reformas estructurales en la Argentina'. Unpublished. Buenos Aires: CEPAL.

PALMER, DAVID SCOTT (1986). 'Rebellion in Rural Peru: The Origins and Evolution of Sendero Luminoso'. *Comparative Politics*, 18 (2): 127–46.

—— (ed.) (1992). *Shining Path of Peru*. New York: St Martin's Press.

PALOMINO, HÉCTOR (1988). *Cambios ocupacionales y sociales en Argentina: 1947–1985*. Buenos Aires: CISEA.

PALOMO, ARMANDO (1988). 'Elecciones y movimiento urbano popular'. *Pueblo*, 138, Aug.: 9–13.

PANEBIANCO, ANGELO (1982). *Modelli di partito*. Bologna: Il Mulino.

—— (1988). *Political Parties: Organization and Power*. Cambridge: Cambridge University Press.

PANFICHI, ALDO (1983). 'La crisis y las multitudes: Lima 5 de febrero de 1975'. *Debates en sociología*, 9. Departamento de Ciencias Sociales: Universidad Católica del Perú.

—— (1993). 'Juventud, tradición y trabajo'. In Gonzalo Portocarrero (ed.), *Los nuevos limeños: Sueños, fervores y caminos del mundo popular*. Lima: Ediciones SUR-TAFOS.

—— and FRANCIS, CÉSAR (1993). 'Liderazgos políticos autoritarios en el Perú'. *Debates en sociología*, 18: 227–47.

—— and SANBORN, CYNTHIA (1995). 'Democracia y neopopulismo en el Perú contemporáneo'. *Márgenes*, 13/14: 43–67.

PANIZZA, FRANCISCO (1993). 'Democracy's Lost Treasure'. *Latin American Research Review*, 28 (3): 251–66.

PAPADÓPULOS, JORGE (1992). *Seguridad social y política en Uruguay*. Montevideo: CIESU.

PARODI, JORGE (ed.) (1993). *Los pobres, la ciudad y la política*. Lima: Ediciones CEDYS.

—— and TWANAMA, WALTER (1993). 'Los pobladores, la ciudad y la política: Un estudio de actitudes'. In Jorge Parodi (ed.), *Los pobres, la ciudad y la política*. Lima: Centro de Estudios de Democracia y Sociedad.

PARRY, GERAINT, and MORAN, MICHAEL (eds.) (1994). *Democracy and Democratization*. London: Routledge.

Partido de la Revolución Democrática (1989*a*). *Documentos básicos (anteproyectos)*. DF, Mexico: Partido de la Revolución Democrática.

—— (1989*b*). *Documentos básicos (proyectos)*. DF, Mexico: Partido de la Revolución Democrática.

—— (1990). *Documentos básicos*. DF, Mexico: Partido de la Revolución Democrática.

Partido Mexicano Socialista (1989). 'La situación nacional y la construcción del Partido de la Revolución Democrática'. DF, Mexico: Partido Mexicano Socialista.

PÁSARA, LUIS (1993). 'El ocaso de los partidos'. In Augusto Alvarez Rodrich (ed.), *El poder en el Perú*. Lima: Ediciones APOYO.

—— and ZARZAR, ALONSO (1991). 'Ambigüedades, contradicciones e incertidumbres'. In Luis Pásara *et al.* (eds.), *La otra cara de la luna: Nuevos actores sociales en el Perú*. Buenos Aires: Manatial.

—— DELPINO, NENA, VALDEAVELLANO, ROCÍO, and ZARZAR, ALONSO (1991). *La otra cara de la luna: Nuevos actores sociales en el Perú*. Buenos Aires: Manatial.

PASTOR, JR., MANUEL, and WISE, CAROL (1992). 'Peruvian Economic Policy in the 1980s: From Orthodoxy to Heterodoxy and Back'. *Latin American Research Review*, 27 (2): 83–118.

PASTOR, ROBERT A. (1992). 'NAFTA as the Center of an Integration Process: The Nontrade Issues'. In Nora Lustig, Barry P. Bosworth, and Robert Z. Lawrence (eds.), *North American Free Trade: Assessing the Impact*. Washington: Brookings Institution.

PATTEE, JON (1995). 'Sprint and the Shutdown of La Conexión Familiar'. *Labor Research Review*, 23: 13–21.

PEARSON, NEALE J. (1967). 'Small Farmer and Rural Worker Pressure Groups in Brazil'. Unpublished diss. University of Florida.

PEASE, HENRY (1994). *Los años de la langosta: La escena política del fujimorismo*. Lima: La Voz Ediciones, IPADEL.

PEDRAGLIO, SANTIAGO (1995). 'Violencia y pacificación'. *Ideele*, 78. Lima: Instituto de Defensa Legal.

PENDLE, GEORGE (1952). *Uruguay, South America's First Welfare State*. London: Royal Institute of International Affairs.

PEREIRA, ANTHONY (1992). 'Agrarian Reform and the Rural Worker's Unions of the Pernambuco Sugar Zone, Brazil 1985–1988'. *Journal of Developing Areas*, 26 (1).

PEREIRA, L. S., MARAVALL, J. M., and PZREWORSKI, A. (1993). 'Reformas Econômicas em Democracias Recentes: Uma abordagem Social-Democrata'. *Dados: Revista de Ciências Sociales*, 36 (2): 171–208.

PÉREZ, MATILDE (1991). 'El ejido es un sistema equitativo y eficaz'. *La Jornada*, 23 Oct.

Perú: Compendio Estadístico 1991–92 (1992). Lima: Dirección Técnica de Indicadores.

Perú en números 1992. Statistical Yearbook, Cuanto SA.

Peru Statistics 1993. PromPeru-Apoyo SA.

PETKOFF, TEODORO (1976). *Proceso a la Izquierda*. Bogotá: Editorial Oveja Negro.

PETRAS, JAMES, and LEIVA, F. I. (1994). *Democracy and Poverty in Chile: The Limits to Electoral Politics*. Boulder, Colo.: Westview Press.

PFALLER, ALFRED, GOUGH, IAN, and THERBORN, GORAN (eds.) (1991). *Can the Welfare State Compete? A Comparative Study of Five Advanced Capitalist Countries*. New York: Macmillan.

PIERSON, CHRISTOPHER (1991). *Beyond the Welfare State? The New Political Economy of Welfare*. London: Polity Press.

PINEDA, LUIS, *et al.* (1993). *Ciudadanía y democracia: Percepciones de los jóvenes en medio de la crisis*. Lima: Ediciones Alternativa-Tarea.

PINHEIRO, PAULO SÉRGIO (1992). 'São Paulo: People on the Margin and Civil Society'. Background notes for a presentation at the Seminar 'Place and Right Conference', 11–13 Sept. at Arden Homestead, New York, sponsored by The Committee on Theory and Culture.

—— (1993). 'Reflections on Urban Violence: The Urban Age'. Washington: The World Bank 1 (4).

—— (1994). 'Under the Gun'. *Hemisfile*, 5 (2).

—— (forthcoming). 'The Legacy of Authoritarianism in Democratic Brazil'. In Stuart Nagel (ed.), *Latin American Development and Public Policy*. New York: Macmillan.

—— and VIEIRA, OSCAR (1993). 'Corrupção, a Morte Anunciada dos Governos'. In José Luiz Del Roi (ed.), *Itália Operação Mãos Limpas. E no Brasil, Quando?* São Paulo: Ícone.

—— EL-CHICHINI, MALAK, and KAHN, TULIO (1993). 'Poverty, Marginalization, Violence and the Realization of Human Rights'. New York, United Nations, General Assembly, World Conference on Human Rights, Preparatory Committee, Fourth Session, Geneva, 19–30 Apr.

PINTO, ANIBAL (1973). 'Heterogeneidad estructural y modelo de desarrollo reciente de la América Latina'. In Anibal Pinto (ed.), *Inflación: Raíces estructurales*. DF, Mexico: Fondo de Cultura Económica.

PINTO, VALESKA PERES (1992). 'Prefeitura de Fortaleza: Administração Popular, 1986–88'. *Pólis*, 6.

PION-BERLIN, DAVID (1989). *The Ideology of State Terror: Economic Doctrine and Political Repression in Argentina and Peru*. Boulder, Colo.: Lynne Rienner Publishers.

—— (1992). 'Military Autonomy and Emerging Democracies in South America'. *Comparative Politics*, 25 (1), Oct.

PITKIN, HANNAH (1967). *The Concept of Representation*. Berkeley and Los Angeles: University of California Press.

PIVEN, FRANCES FOX (1992). *Labor Parties in Post-industrial Societies*. Oxford: Oxford University Press.

—— and CLOWARD, RICHARD A. (1977). *Poor People's Movements: Why They Succeed, How They Fail*. New York: Vintage Books.

PIZZORNO, ALESSANDRO (1978). *Economía y política en la acción sindical*. DF, Mexico: Cuadernos de Pasado y Presente.

PLACE, SUSAN E. (ed.) (1993). *Tropical Rainforests: Latin American Nature and Society in Transition*. Wilmington, Del.: Scholarly Resources.

POPKIN, SAMUEL (1979). *The Rational Peasant: The Political Economy of Rural Society in Vietnam*. Berkeley and Los Angeles: University of California Press.

POPPOVIC, MALAK, and ADORNO, SÉRGIO (n.d.). 'Direitos Humanos e Justiça'. Unpublished. São Paulo: Núcleo de Estudos da Violência.

PORTELLA DE CASTRO, MARÍA SILVIA (1995). 'Mercosul e Acão sindical'. Latin American Labor Studies Occasional Paper No. 19, Miami Center for Labor Research and Studies, Florida International University.

PORTES, ALEJANDRO (1971). 'Political Primitivism, Differential Socialization, and Lower-Class Leftist Radicalism'. *American Sociological Review*, 36: 820–35.

—— (1989). 'Latin American Urbanization in the Years of Crisis'. *Latin American Research Review*, 24 (3).

PORTOCARRERO, GONZALO (1993a). *Racismo y mestizaje*. Lima: Ediciones SUR.

—— (1993b). *Los nuevos limeños: Sueños, fervores y caminos del mundo popular*. Lima: Ediciones SUR-TAFOS.

POSNER, MICHAEL (1993). 'The Establishment of the Right of Non-governmental Human Rights Groups to Operate'. Unpublished. New York: Lawyers Committee for Human Rights.

POWELL, WALTER W., and DiMAGGIO, PAUL J. (eds.) (1991). *The New Institutionalism in Organizational Analysis*. Chicago: University of Chicago Press.

PRD Human Rights Commission (1992). *The Political Violence in Mexico: A Human Rights Affair*. Mexico: Human Rights Commission Parliamentary Group.

Prefeitura Municipal de Icapúi (1993). 'Plano Municipal de Desenvolvimento'.

PREVOST, GARY (1993). 'The Spanish Peace Movement'. *West European Politics*, 16 (2).

PRICE, ROBERT (1964). *Rural Unionization in Brazil*. Madison: University of Wisconsin Land Tenure Center Research Paper No. 14.

PRIETO, ANA MARÍA (1986). 'Mexico's National *Coordinadoras* in a Context of Economic Crisis'. In Barry Carr and Ricardo Anzaldúa Montoya (eds.), *The Mexican Left, the Popular Movements, and the Politics of Austerity*. Monograph Series, 18. La Jolla: Center for US–Mexican Studies, University of California, San Diego.

Pro-Aim (1990). Prefeitura do Estado de São Paulo, Programa de Informações sobre Mortalidade.

—— (1991). Prefeitura do Estado de São Paulo, Programa de Informações sobre Mortalidade.

Propuesta programática de los Socialistas para el segundo gobierno de la concertación de partidos por la democracia (1992). Santiago: Partido Socialista de Chile.

PRZEWORSKI, ADAM (1981). 'Compromiso de clases y estado: Europa Occidental y América Latina'. In Norbert Lechner (ed.), *Estado y política en América Latina*. Mexico City: Siglo XXI.

—— (1985). *Capitalism and Social Democracy*. Cambridge: Cambridge University Press.

—— (1991*a*). *Democracy and the Market: Political and Economic Reform in Eastern Europe and Latin America*. Cambridge: Cambridge University Press.

—— (1991*b*). 'The "East" Becomes the "South"? The "Autumn of the People" and the Future of Eastern Europe'. *PS: Political Science & Politics*, 24 (1): 20–3.

—— and WALLERSTEIN, MICHAEL (1982). 'The Structure of Class Conflict in Democratic Societies'. *American Political Science Review*, 76: 215–38.

PUCCI, FRANCISCO (1992*a*). 'La negociación colectiva en el gobierno neoliberal'. INF, 52/92. Montevideo: CIESU.

—— (1992*b*). *Sindicatos y negociación colectiva 1985–1989*. Montevideo: CIESU.

—— (1992*c*). 'Intermediación de intereses o conflicto privado?' Presented at the Latin American Studies Association Conference.

PURCELL, SUSAN KAUFMAN, and PURCELL, JOHN (1980). 'State and Society in Mexico: Must a Stable Polity Be Institutionalized?' *World Politics*, 32 (2).

PURYEAR, JEFFREY (1994). *Thinking Politics: Intellectuals and Democracy in Chile 1973–1988*. Baltimore: Johns Hopkins University Press.

PUTNAM, ROBERT D. (1993). *Making Democracy Work: Civic Traditions in Modern Italy*. Princeton: Princeton University Press.

PYE, LUCIAN W. (1990). 'Political Science and the Crisis of Authoritarianism'. *American Political Science Review*, 84 (1), Mar.

'Quixadá' (1993). *Tribuna do Ceará*. [Fortaleza] (4/22/93: 20B).

RADCLIFFE, SARA H., and WESTWOOD, SALLY (1993). *'Viva': Women and Popular Protest in Latin America*. London: Routledge.

RAMA, GERMÁN (1987). *La democracia en Uruguay*. Buenos Aires: Grupo Editor Latinamericano.

RAMÍREZ SÁIZ, JUAN MANUEL (1991–2). '¿Dos proyectos antagónicos de movilización?' *CISMOS*, 4–5: 103–29.

—— (1992). 'Entre el corporativismo social y la lógica electoral: el estado y el movimiento urbano popular (MUP)'. In *El nuevo estado Mexicano*, iii: *Estado, actores, y movimiento sociales*. DF, Mexico: Nueva Imagen.

—— (1993). *La vivienda popular y sus actores*. Puebla: Programa Editorial Red Nacional de Investigación Urbana.

RAMOS, PEDRO, and BELIK, WALTER (1989). 'Intervenção Estatal e a Agroindústria canaveira no Brasil'. *Revista de Economía e Sociología Rural*, 27 (2).

REAL DE AZÚA, CARLOS (1989). *El poder*. Montevideo: CELADU.

REILLY, CHARLES (ed.) (1995). *New Paths to Democratic Development in Latin America: The Rise of NGO–Municipal Collaboration*. Boulder, Colo.: Lynne Rienner Publishers.

RÉNIQUE, JOSÉ LUIS (1993). 'La batalla por Puno'. Presented at the 'Seminario sobre la violencia política en el Perú: Análisis y perspectivas'. Organized by the Centro Peruano de Estudios Sociales (CEPES) and the Instituto de Estudios Peruanos (IEP). Lima.

Resumen (1982a). 'La candidatura de Jorge Olavarría ratificada por el Plenario de la Causa Radical'. *Resumen*, 457. Caracas.

—— (1982b). 'Catia: Sucursal del infierno'. *Resumen*, 432. Caracas.

REYNA, JOSÉ LUIS, and WEINERT, RICHARD S. (eds.) (1977). *Authoritarianism in Mexico*. Philadelphia: Institute for the Study of Human Issues.

RIAL, JUAN (1988). 'El movimiento sindical Uruguayo ante la redemocratización', *Política económica y actores sociales*. Santiago de Chile: PREALC/OIT.

RIOFRÍO, GUSTAVO (1978). *Se busca terreno para próxima barriada*. Lima: DESCO.

RIVERA CUSICANQUI, SILVIA (1990). 'Liberal Democracy and *Ayllu* Democracy: The Case of Northern Potosí, Bolivia'. In Jonathan Fox (ed.), *The Challenge of Rural Democratization: Perspectives from Latin America and the Philippines*. London: Frank Cass.

RMALC (Red Mexicana de Acción Frente al Libre Comercio) (1992). *Memoria de Zacatecas: La opinión pública y las negociaciones del Tratado de Libre Comercio: Alternativas ciudadanas*. Mexico City: RMALC.

ROBERTS, KENNETH (1995). 'Neoliberalism and the Transformation of Populism in Latin America'. *World Politics*, 48 (1): 82–117.

ROCHABRÚN, GUILLERMO (1994). 'Crisis de representatividad? O crisis de intermediación?' *Cuestión de Estado*, 6. Lima: IDS.

RODRÍGUEZ, HECTOR (1986). *Nuestros sindicatos*. Montevideo: Centro de Estudiantes de Derecho.

RODRÍGUEZ, VICTORIA E. (1992). 'Mexico's Decentralization in the 1980s: Promises, Promises, Promises . . .'. In Arthur Morris and Stella Lowder, *Decentralization in Latin America: An Evaluation*. New York: Praeger.

—— and WARD, PETER M. (1995). *Opposition Government in Mexico*. Albuquerque: University of New Mexico Press.

RODRÍGUEZ KAUTH, ANDRÉS (1994). 'Sobre los discursos entrecruzados de la pobreza, la riqueza y la violencia'. *Realidad Económica*, 127: 23–33.

RODRIGUEZ RABANAL, CESAR (1989). *Cicatrices de la pobreza: Un estudio psicoanalítico*. Caracas: Editorial Nueva Sociedad.

RODRIGUEZ REYNA, JOSÉ IGNACIO (1993). 'La "privatización" de la política'. *Expansión*, 619: 54–79.

ROJAS, CARLOS, *et al.* (1991). *Solidaridad a debate*. Mexico: El Nacional.

ROJAS, ROSA (1992). 'Indígenas de Chiapas piden se libere a 3 funcionarios del INI'. *La Jornada*, 21 Mar.

ROMERO, GUSTAVO, *et al.* (1986). 'Las cooperativas de vivienda ante los movimientos urbanos y la problemática habitacional'. In *Los movimientos sociales en el Valle de México*, i. DF, Mexico: Ediciones de la Case Chata.

RONIGER, LUIS (1990). *Hierarchy and Trust in Modern Mexico and Brazil*. Westport, Conn.: Greenwood.

—— and GUNES-AYATA, AYSE (eds.) (1994). *Democracy, Clientelism and Civil Society*. Boulder, Colo.: Lynne Rienner.

ROSE, ROBERT L. (1994). 'Labor Unions File First Tests of NAFTA Office'. *Wall Street Journal*, 15 Feb.: A2.

ROSENAU, JAMES N. (1993). 'Coherent Connection or Commonplace Contiguity? Theorizing about the California–Mexico Overlap'. In Abraham F. Lowenthal and Katrina Burgess (eds.), *The California–Mexico Connection*. Stanford, Calif.: Stanford University Press.

ROSENBERG, TINA (1991). 'Beyond Elections'. *Foreign Policy*, 84, Fall: 72–91.

ROSPIGLIOSI, FERNANDO (1989). 'Izquierdas y clases populares: Democracia y subversión en el Perú'. In Julio Cotler (ed.), *Clases populares, crisis y democracia en América Latina*. Lima: Instituto de Estudios Peruanos.

ROTHSTEIN, BO (1992). 'Labor-Market Institutions and Working-Class Strength'. In Sven Steimo, Kathleen Thelen, and Frank Longstreth (eds.), *Structuring Politics*. New York: Cambridge University Press.

ROUQUIÉ, ALAIN (1978). 'Client Control and Authoritarian Contexts'. In Guy Hermet, Richard Rose, and Alain Rouquié (eds.), *Elections without Choice*. New York: John Wiley & Sons.

—— (1982). 'El análisis de las elecciones no competitivas: Control clientelista y situaciones autoritarias'. In Guy Hermet, Alain Rouquié, and Juan J. Linz (eds.), *¿Para qué sirven las elecciones?* DF, Mexico: Fondo de Cultura Económica.

ROXBOROUGH, IAN (1989). 'Organized Labor: A Major Victim of the Debt Crisis'. In Barbara Stallings and Robert Kaufman (eds.), *Debt and Democracy in Latin America*. Boulder, Colo.: Westview Press.

—— (1992*a*). 'Inflação e Pacto Social no Brasil e no México'. *Lua Nova*, 25: 197–224.

—— (1992*b*). 'Inflation and Social Pacts in Brazil and Mexico'. *Journal of Latin American Studies*, 24: 639–64.

—— (1992*c*). 'Neo-liberalism in Latin America: Limits and Alternatives'. *Third World Quarterly*, 13 (3): 421–40.

—— (1994). 'What Future for Social Democracy in Latin America?' Presented at the conference 'The Politics of Inequality'. Institute of Latin American and Iberian Studies, Columbia University, New York City.

RUESCHMEYER, DIETRICH, HUBER-STEPHENS, EVELYNE, and STEPHENS, JOHN D. (1992). *Capitalist Development and Democracy*. Chicago: University of Chicago Press.

RUÍZ-TAGLE, JAIME (1993*a*). 'Desafíos del sindicalismo chileno frente a la flexibilización del mercado de trabajo'. *Revista de Economía y Trabajo*, 1 (1).

—— (1993*b*). 'Tareas pendientes: Reducción de la pobreza y distribución de los ingresos en Chile'. *Mensaje*, 425: 640–3.

RUSTOW, DANKWART (1970). 'Transitions to Democracy'. *Comparative Politics*, Apr.: 337–63.

SABEL, CHARLES (1981). 'The Internal Politics of Trade-Unions'. In S. Berger (ed.), *Organizing Interests in Western Europe*. Cambridge: Cambridge University Press.

—— (1992). 'Studied Trust: Building New Forms of Co-operation in a Volatile Economy'. In Frank Dyke and Werner Sengenbergers (eds.), *Industrial Districts and Local Economic Regeneration*. Geneva: International Institute for Labour Studies.

—— (1995). 'Design, Deliberation, and Democracy: On the New Pragmatism of Firms and Public Institutions'. Paper presented to the conference on 'Liberal Institutions, Economic Constitutional Rights, and the Role of Organization', European University Institute, Florence.

SADEK, MARIA TERESA E ARANTES, and BASTOS, ROGÉRIO (1994). 'A crise do Judiciário e a Visão dos Juízes'. *Revista da USP*, 3–5/94: 39.

SADER, EMIR (ed.) (1986). *E Agora P. T.? Caráter e Identidade*. São Paulo: Brasiliense.

—— (ed.) (1991). *A Transição no Brasil: Da Ditadura a Democracia?* São Paulo: Atual Editora.

SALDAIN, RODOLFO (1987). 'El Social Welfare en el Uruguay'. Unpublished. Montevideo.

—— (1993). 'Seguridad social en el Uruguay: Un análisis en proección y bases de cambio'. *Revista de la Seguridad Social*, BPS 1 (1): 67–104.

SALGADO, LÚCIA HELENA (1993*a*). 'Câmaras Setoriais e Concorrência'. *Linha Direta*, weekly publication of the São Paulo regional directorate of the Workers' Party 9–15 July: 6–7.

—— (1993*b*). 'Política de Concorrência e Estratégias Empresariais: Um Estudo da Indústria Automobilística'. Série Seminários No. 10/93, Instituto de Pesquisa Econômica Aplicada. IPEA, Brasília (June).

SALINAS DE GORTARI, CARLOS (1982). 'Political Participation, Public Investment, and Support for the System: A Comparative Study of Rural Communities in Mexico'. Research Report Series 35. La Jolla, Calif.: UCSD, Center for US–Mexican Studies.

SANBORN, CYNTHIA (1991). 'The Democratic Left and the Persistence of Populism in Peru: 1975–1990'. Ph.D. Diss., Harvard University.

SÁNCHEZ PÁRGA, JOSE (1990). *Etnia, poder y diferencia*. Quito: Abya-Yala.

SANTESMASES, ANTONIO (1988). 'Cesión y claudicación: La transición política en España'. *Pensamiento Iberoamericano*, 14 (July–Dec.).

SANTOS, WANDERLEY GUILHERME (1993*a*). 'Mitologias Institucionais Brasileiras: Do Leviatã Paralítico ao Estado de Natureza'. *Estudos Avançados*, 7 (17). São Paulo: Universidade de São Paulo /IEA.

—— (1993*b*). *Razões da Desordem*. Rio de Janeiro: Rocco.

SARÁCHAGA, DARÍO, and VERA, TABARÉ (1989). *Sector externo: Oportunidades y riesgos*. Montevideo: FESUR.

SARMIENTO, SERGIO (1991). 'Movimiento indio y modernización'. *Cuadernos agrarios*, NS 2.

SAUCEDO, FRANCISCO (1988). 'La asamblea de barrios en las elecciones'. *Pueblo*, 11 (125): 33–4.

SBRAGIA, ALBERTA M. (ed.) (1992). *Euro-Politics: Institutions and Policymaking in the 'New' European Community*. Washington: Brookings Institution.

SCHAMIS, HECTOR (1991). 'Reconceptualizing Latin American Authoritarianism in the 1970s: From Bureaucratic-Authoritarianism to Neoconservatism'. *Comparative Politics*, 23 (2): 201–20.

SCHARPF, FRITZ (1991). *Crisis and Choice in European Social Democracy*. Ithaca, NY: Cornell University Press.

SCHERER-WARREN, ILSE, and KRISCHKE, PAULO (eds.) (1987). *Uma Revolução no Cotidiano? Os Novos Movimentos Sociais na América do Sul*. São Paulo: Brasiliense.

SCHMIDT, STEFFEN W., *et al.* (eds.) (1977). *Friends, Followers, and Factions: A Reader in Political Clientelism.* Berkeley and Los Angeles: University of California Press.

SCHMITTER, PHILIPPE C. (1971). *Interest Conflict and Political Change in Brazil.* Stanford, Calif.: Stanford University Press.

—— (1974). 'Still the Century of Corporatism?' *Review of Politics,* 36: 85–131.

—— (1988). *The Consolidation of Political Democracy in Southern Europe.* Stanford, Calif.: Stanford University, Instituto Universitario Europeo.

—— (1992). 'The Consolidation of Democracy and Representation of Social Groups'. *American Behavioral Scientist,* 35 (4/5).

—— (1993). 'La consolidación de la democracia y la representación de los grupos sociales'. *Revista Mexicana de Sociología,* Mar.: 3–30.

—— and KARL, TERRY LYNN (1991). 'What Democracy is . . . and is Not'. *Journal of Democracy,* 2 (3), Summer.

—— and LEHMBRUCH, GERHARD (eds.) (1979). *Trends toward Corporatist Intermediation.* London: Sage.

SCHNEIDER, CATHY (1992). 'Radical Opposition Parties and Squatters Movements in Pinochet's Chile'. In Arturo Escobar and Sonia E. Alvarez (eds.), *The Making of Social Movements in Latin America.* Boulder, Colo.: Westview Press.

SCHNEIDER, RONALD M. (1958). *Communism in Guatemala, 1944–1954.* New York: Praeger Publishers.

SCHÖNWÄLDER, GERD (1993). 'Estado y sociedad civil: Nuevas formas de vinculación, experiencias con el gobierno local en Lima'. *Socialismo y Participación,* 62: 47–59.

SCHTEINGART, MARTHA (1991). 'Aspectos teóricos y prácticos de la autogestión urbana'. *Sociológica,* 5 (12).

—— and PERLÓ, MANUEL (1984). 'Movimientos sociales urbanos en México'. *Revista Mexicana de Sociología,* 46 (4): 105–25.

SCHUMPETER, JOSEPH A. (1942). *Capitalism, Socialism, and Democracy.* New York: Harper & Brothers.

—— (1950). *Capitalism, Socialism and Democracy.* New York: Harper & Row.

SCHVARZER, JORGE (1993). 'El proceso de privatizaciones en Argentina'. *Realidad Económica,* 120: 79–143.

SCOTT, JAMES C. (1969). 'Corruption, Machine Politics, and Political Change'. *American Political Science Review,* 63 (4), Dec.

—— (1972). *Comparative Political Corruption.* Englewood, NJ: Prentice-Hall.

—— (1976). *The Moral Economy of the Peasant: Rebellion and Subsistence in Southeast Asia.* New Haven: Yale University Press.

—— (1985). *Weapons of the Weak: Everyday Forms of Peasant Resistance.* New Haven: Yale University Press.

—— (1990). *Domination and the Art of Resistance: Hidden Transcripts.* New Haven: Yale University Press.

Secretaría de Desarrollo Social (1993). *La solidaridad en el desarrollo nacional.* DF, Mexico: SEDESOL.

Secretaria de Estado da Saúde de São Paulo (1993). 'Mortalidade por Homicídio no Município de São Paulo'. Informe Técnico 2. São Paulo: Centro de Vigilância Epidemiológica.

SELBY, HENRY A., MURPHY, ARTHUR D., and LORENZEN, STEPHEN A. (1990). *The Mexican Urban Household: Organizing for Self-Defense.* Austin: University of Texas Press.

SELIGMAN, ADAM (1992). *The Idea of Civil Society.* New York: The Free Press.

SELVERSTON, MELINA (1993). 'Politicized Ethnicity as Social Movement: The 1990 Indigenous Uprising in Ecuador'. Paper Series No. 32, Institute of Latin American and Iberian Studies, Columbia University.

SEN, AMARTYA (1993). 'The Economics of Life and Death'. *Scientific American*, May.

SENÉN GONZÁLEZ, SANTIAGO (1978). *El poder sindical*. Buenos Aires: Editorial Plus Ultra.

SESTO, FARRUCO (1992). *Tres entrevistas con Andrés Velásquez (1986–1990–1991)*. Caracas: Ediciones del Agua Mansa.

SHAPIRO, HELEN (1994). *Engines of Growth: The State and Transnational Auto Companies in Brazil*. Cambridge: Cambridge University Press.

—— (1996). 'The Mechanics of Brazil's Auto Industry'. *NACLA Report on the Americas*, 29 (4): 28–33.

SHEAHAN, JOHN (1980). 'Market-Oriented Economic Policies and Political Repression in Latin America'. *Economic Development and Cultural Change*, 28: 267–91.

—— (1987). *Pattern of Development in Latin America*. Princeton: Princeton University Press.

SHEFTER, MARTIN (1978). 'The Electoral Foundations of the Political Machine: New York City, 1884–1897'. In Joel Silbey *et al*. (eds.), *The History of American Electoral Behavior*. Princeton: Princeton University Press.

SHENON, PHILIP (1992). 'It's Business as Usual in Thailand (Votes for Sale)'. *New York Times*, 18 Mar.

SIERRA, MANUEL FELIPE (1989). 'La evolución política (1974–1989)'. In Pedro Cunill Grau *et al*. (eds.), *Venezuela contemporánea*. Caracas: Fundación Eugenio Mendoza.

SIGAUD, LYGIA (1980). *Greve nos engenhos*. Rio de Janeiro: Paz e Terra.

SIKKINK, KATHRYN (1991). *Ideas and Institutions: Developmentalism in Brazil and Argentina*. Ithaca, NY: Cornell University Press.

—— (1993). 'Human Rights, Principled Issue Networks, and Sovereignty in Latin America'. *International Organization*, 47 (3): 411–41.

SILVA, EDUARDO (1992). 'Capitalist Regime Loyalties and Redemocratization in Chile'. *Journal of Interamerican Studies and World Affairs*, 34.

—— (1993). 'Capitalist Coalitions, the State and Neoliberal Economic Restructuring: Chile 1973–1988'. *World Politics*, 45: 526–59.

SILVA, ELIZABETH BORTOLAIA (1991). *Refazenda a Fábrica Fordista: Contrastes da Indústria Automobilística no Brasil e na Grã-Bretanha*. São Paulo: Hucitec.

SILVER, HILLARY (1994). 'Social Exclusion and Social Solidarity: Three Paradigms'. Geneva: ILO, DP/69.

SILVERT, KALMAN H. (1969). *Un estudio de gobierno: Guatemala*. Seminario de Integración Social Guatemalteca, Publicación 26, editorial 'José de Pineda Ibarra'. Ministerio de Educación, Guatemala, trans. from the 1954 edn., New Orleans: Middle American Research Institute, Tulane University.

Sindicato de Trabajadoras del Hogar del Cusco (1983). *Basta: 23 testimonios de empleadas domésticas*. Cusco: Centro Bartolome de las Casas.

SLATER, DAVID (ed.) (1985). *New Social Movements and the State in Latin America*. Cinnaminson, NJ: FORIS Publications.

—— (1989). *Territory and State Power in Latin America: The Peruvian Case*. New York: St Martin's Press.

—— (1994). 'Power and Social Movements in the Other Occident: Latin America in an International Context'. *Latin American Perspectives*, 81: 11–37.

SMITH, ANTHONY (1989). *The Ethnic Origins of Nations*. Oxford: Basil Blackwell.

Smith, Carol (1990a). 'Introduction: Social Relations in Guatemala over Time and Space'. In Carol Smith (ed.), *Guatemalan Indians and the State, 1540 to 1988*. Austin: University of Texas Press.

—— (1990b). 'The Militarization of Civil Society in Guatemala: Economic Reorganization as a Continuation of War'. *Latin American Perspectives*, 17 (4): 8–41.

—— (1992). 'Maya Nationalism'. *Report on the Americas*, 25 (3): 29–33.

Smith, Michael (1992). 'Shining Path's Urban Strategy: Ate-Vitarte'. In David Scott Palmer (ed.), *Shining Path of Peru*. New York: St Martin's Press.

Smith, Peter (1979). *Labyrinths of Power: Political Recruitment in Twentieth-Century Mexico*. Princeton: Princeton University Press.

—— (1992). 'The Political Impact of Free Trade on Mexico'. *Journal of InterAmerican Studies and World Affairs*, 34 (1): 1–25.

Smith, Robert (1992). 'New York in Mixteca; Mixteca in New York'. *NACLA Report on the Americas*, 26 (1): 39–41.

Smith, William (1992). 'Hyperinflation, Macroeconomic Instability, and Neoliberal Restructuring in Democratic Argentina'. In *The New Argentine Democracy*. New York: Praeger.

—— (1993). 'Neo-Liberal Restructuring and Scenarios of Democratic Consolidation'. *Studies in Comparative International Development*.

—— Acuña, Carlos H., and Gamarra, Eduardo A. (eds.) (1994a). *Latin American Political Economy in the Age of Neoliberal Reform: Theoretical and Comparative Perspectives for the 1990s*. New Brunswick, NJ: Transaction.

—— —— —— (eds.) (1994b). *Democracy, Markets, and Structural Reform in Latin America: Argentina, Bolivia, Brazil, Chile, and Mexico*. New Brunswick, NJ.: Transaction.

Solares, Jorge (1993). *Estado y nación: Las demandas de los grupos étnicos en Guatemala*. Ciudad de Guatemala: FLACSO/Friedrich Ebert Stiftung.

Sollis, Peter (1992). 'Multilateral Agencies, NGOs, and Policy Reform'. *Development in Practice*, 2.

Stallings, Barbara (1992). 'International Influence on Economic Policy: Debt, Stabilization and Structural Adjustment'. In Stephan Haggard and Robert Kaufman (eds.), *The Politics of Economic Adjustment*. Princeton: Princeton University Press.

—— (ed.) (1994). *The New International Context of Development*. Cambridge: Cambridge University Press.

Stanley, William (forthcoming). *The Elite Politics of State Terrorism in El Salvador*. Philadelphia: Temple University Press.

Starn, Orin (1991). 'Sendero, soldados y ronderos en el Mantaro'. *QueHacer*, 74: 60–8.

—— (1992). ' "I Dreamed of Foxes and Hawks," Reflections on Peasant Protest, New Social Movements and the *Rondas Campesinas* of Northern Peru'. In Arturo Escobar and Sonia Alvarez (eds.), *The Making of Social Movements in Latin America*. Boulder, Colo.: Westview Press.

Starr, Paul, and Immergut, Ellen (1987). 'Health Care and the Boundaries of Politics'. In Charles S. Maier (ed.), *Changing Boundaries of the Political*. New York: Cambridge University Press.

Stavenhagen, Rodolfo (1990). 'America Latina: derechos humanos y desarrollo'. *IFDA Dossier*, 10–12/90: 42–52.

Stearns, Katherine, and Otero, Maria (1990). *The Critical Connection: Governments,*

Private Institutions, and the Informal Sector in Latin America. Cambridge: ACCION International.

STEIMO, SVEN, THELEN, KATHLEEN, and LONGSTRETH, FRANK (eds.) (1992). *Structuring Politics*. New York: Cambridge University Press.

STEPAN, ALFRED (1978). *The State and Society: Peru in Comparative Perspective*. Princeton: Princeton University Press.

—— (1985). 'State Power and the Strength of Civil Society in the Southern Cone of Latin America'. In Peter Evans, Dietrich Rueschmeyer, and Theda Skocpol (eds.), *Bringing the State Back In*. Cambridge: Cambridge University Press.

—— (1988). *Rethinking Military Politics: Brazil and the Southern Cone*. Princeton: Princeton University Press.

—— (ed.) (1989). *Democratizing Brazil: Problems of Transition and Consolidation*. New York: Oxford University Press.

—— and LINZ, JUAN (forthcoming). *Problems of Democratic Transition and Consolidation: Southern Europe, South America and Eastern Europe*.

—— and SKACH, CINDY (1994). 'Presidentialism and Parliamentarism in Comparative Perspective'. In Juan Linz and Arturo Valenzuela (eds.), *The Failure of Presidential Democracy*, i: *Comparative Perspectives*. Baltimore: Johns Hopkins University Press.

STEPHENS, EVELYNE HUBER (1983). 'The Peruvian Military Government, Labor Mobilization, and the Political Strength of the Left'. *Latin American Research Review*, 43 (2): 57–93.

STERN, STEVE (ed.) (1987). *Resistance, Rebellion, and Consciousness in the Andean Peasant World, 18th to 20th Centuries*. Madison: The University of Wisconsin Press.

STIEFEL, MATHIAS, and WOLFE, MARSHALL (1994). *A Voice for the Excluded: Popular Participation in Development: Utopia or Necessity?* London: Zed Books.

STOKES, SUSAN (1991*a*). 'Hegemony, Consciousness and Political Change in Peru'. *Politics and Society*, 19 (3): 265–90.

—— (1991*b*). 'Politics and Latin America's Urban Poor: Reflections from a Lima Shantytown'. *Latin American Research Review*, 26 (2): 75–102.

STONE, DEBORAH (1989). 'Causal Stories and the Formation of Policy Agendas'. *Political Science Quarterly*, 104 (2).

STREECK, WOLFGANG (1984). 'Neo-corporatist Industrial Relations and the Economic Crisis in West Germany'. In J. Goldthorpe (ed.), *Order and Conflict in Contemporary Capitalism*. New York: Oxford University Press.

—— and SCHMITTER, PHILIPPE C. (1985*a*). 'Community, Market, State and Associations? The Prospective Contribution of Interest Governance to Social Order'. In Wolfgang Streeck and Philippe C. Schmitter (eds.), *Private Interest Government: Beyond Market and State*. Beverly Hills, Calif.: Sage.

—— —— (eds.) (1985*b*). *Private Interest Government: Beyond Market and State*. Beverly Hills, Calif.: Sage.

STRICKTON, ARNOLD, and GREENFIELD, SIDNEY (eds.) (1972). *Structure and Process in Latin America: Patronage, Clientage and Power Systems*. Albuquerque: University of New Mexico.

SULMONT SAMAIN, DENIS (1994). 'Ajuste sin reestructuración: El trabajo en el Perú de hoy'. *Cuadernos Laborales*, 100: 8–12.

SUPE (1993). 'Sociedades comerciales conformadas por personal desvinculado de YPF S.A.'

and 'Emprendimientos en formación (Estudio de factibilidad)'. Unpublished. Buenos Aires.

Supremo Tribunal Federal, Banco Nacional de Dados do Poder Judiciário (1992). 'Quadros'. Brasília: Supremo Tribunal Federal.

SUTTON, ALISON (1994). 'Slavery in Brazil'. London, Anti-Slavery International, Human Rights Series no. 7: 24. Quoting interviews with directors of CONTAG, Confederação Nacional dos Trabalhadores na Agricultura.

TAMAYO, JAIME (1990). 'Neoliberalism Encounters *Neocardenismo*'. In Joe Foweraker and Ann Craig (eds.), *Popular Movements and Political Change in Mexico*. Boulder, Colo.: Lynne Rienner.

TARROW, SIDNEY (1967). *Peasant Communism in Southern Italy*. New Haven: Yale University Press.

—— (1988). 'National Politics and Collective Action: Recent Theory and Research in Western Europe and the United States'. *Annual Review of Sociology*, 14: 421–40.

—— (1989). 'Struggle, Politics and Reform: Collective Action, Social Movements and Cycles of Protest'. Occasional Paper no. 21, Western Societies Program. Ithaca, NY: Center for International Studies, Cornell University.

—— (1991). '"Aiming at a Moving Target": Social Science and the Recent Rebellions in Eastern Europe'. *PS: Political Science and Politics*, 24 (1): 12–20.

—— (1994). *Power in Movement: Social Movements, Collective Action and Politics*. Cambridge: Cambridge University Press.

TEFFEL, REYNALDO (1969). *El infierno de los pobres*. Managua: Ediciones El Pez y la Serpiente.

TENDLER, JUDITH (1982). 'Rural Projects through Urban Eyes: An Interpretation of the World Bank's New-Style Rural Development Projects'. Working Paper 532. Washington: World Bank.

TENTI, EMILIO (1993). 'Cuestiones de exclusión social y política'. In Alberto Minujin (ed.), *Desigualdad y exclusión: Desafíos para la política social en la Argentina de fin de siglo*. Buenos Aires: UNICEF/Losada.

THELEN, KATHLEEN (1993). 'Beyond Corporatism: Towards a New Framework for the Study of Labor in Advance Capitalism'. Unpublished. Princeton: Princeton University.

THOMAS, CLYVE (1984). *The Rise of the Authoritarian State in Peripheral Societies*. New York: Monthly Review Press.

THOMPSON, G., et al. (eds.) (1991). *Markets, Hierarchies and Networks: The Coordination of Social Life*. London: Sage.

THORUP, CATHRYN L. (1991). 'The Politics of Free Trade and the Dynamics of Cross-Border Coalitions in U.S.–Mexican Relations'. *Columbia Journal of World Business*, 26.

—— (1993). 'Redefining Governance in North America: Citizen Diplomacy and Cross-Border Coalitions'. *Enfoque*. Center for US–Mexican Studies, Spring.

TILLY, CHARLES (1978). *From Mobilization to Revolution*. Reading, Mass.: Adison Wesley.

—— (1986). *The Contentious French*. Cambridge, Mass.: Harvard University Press.

TIRONI, EUGENIO (1986). 'Para una sociología de la decadencia: El concepto de disolución social'. *Proposiciones*, 6: 12–16.

TORRES, ALFREDO (1993). 'Los cambios en la opinión pública'. In Augusto Alvarez Rodrich (ed.), *El poder en el Perú*. Lima: Ediciones Apoyo SA.

TORRES, BLANCA (comp.) (1985). *Descentralización y democracia en México*. DF, Mexico: El Colegio de México.

TOURAINE, ALAIN (1981). *The Voice and the Eye*. Cambridge: Cambridge University Press.

Tovar, Teresa (1986a). 'Barrios, ciudad, democracia y política'. In Eduardo Ballón (ed.), *Movimientos sociales y democracia: La fundación de un nuevo orden*. Lima: DESCO.
—— (1986b). 'Nuevas prácticas sociales en Villa el Salvador'. Unpublished. Lima: DESCO-CLACSO.
Trejo, Guillermo, and Jones, Claudio (coords.) (1992). *Contra la pobreza: Por una estrategia de política social*. DF, Mexico: Cal y Arena.
Trinational Exchange (1991). 'Popular Perspectives on Mexico–U.S.–Canada Relations', Summary Report, Chicago, 26–8 Apr.
Trudeau, Robert H. (1993). *Guatemalan Politics: The Popular Struggle for Democracy*. Boulder, Colo.: Lynne Rienner Publishers.
Tuesta, Fernando (1989a). 'Villa El Salvador: Izquierda, gestión municipal y organización popular'. Unpublished. Lima: CEDYS.
—— (1989b). *Pobreza urbana y cambios electorales en Lima*. Lima: DESCO.
—— (1994). *Perú político en cifras*. 2nd edn. Lima: Fundación Friedrich Ebert.
Turner, Bryan S. (1993). 'Contemporary Problems in the Theory of Citizenship'. In Bryan S. Turner (ed.), *Citizenship and Social Theory*. London: Sage.
Turner, Lowell (forthcoming). 'Beyond National Unionism? Cross-National Labor Collaboration in the European Community'. In Richard Locke and Kathleen Thelen (eds.), *The Shifting Boundaries of Labor Politics*. Cambridge, Mass.: The Massachusetts Institute of Technology Press.
UNDP (United Nations Development Programme) (1991). *Human Development Report 1991*. New York: Oxford University Press.
—— (1993). *Human Development Report, 1993*. New York: Oxford University Press.
Unión Ferroviaria (1993). 'Acta de la 10a. Asamblea General Extraordinaria de Delegados'. Proceedings, Córdoba, Argentina.
United Nations Document A/50/482 (1995). Annex, English version, *Third Report of the Director of the United Nations Mission for the Verification of Human Rights and of Compliance with the Commitments of the Comprehensive Agreement on Human Rights in Guatemala (MINUGUA)*. 12 Oct.
US Department of State (1994). 'Brazil'. *Country Reports on Human Rights Practices for 1993*. Washington: US Government Printing Office.
US National Administrative Office, North American Agreement on Labor Cooperation (1995). *Public Report of Review: NAO Submission No. 940003*. Washington: Bureau of International Labor Affairs, US Department of Labor.
Urban, Gregg, and Scherzer, Joel (1991). *Nation-States and Indians in Latin America*. Austin: University of Texas Press.
USP (Universidade de São Paulo) (1993). *Núcleo de Estudos da Violência, NEV e Comissão Teotônio Vilela, CTV: Os direitos humanos no Brasil*. São Paulo: NEV/CTV.
Vacs, Aldo (1993). 'Between Restructuring and Impasse: Liberal Democracy, Exclusionary Policy Making and Neoliberal Programs in Argentina and Uruguay'. Presented at the conference 'Deepening Democracy and Representation in Latin America', Pittsburgh: CLAS, University of Pittsburgh.
Valentín, Isidro (1993). 'Tsunami Fujimori: Una propuesta de interpretación'. In Gonzalo Portocarrero (ed.), *Los nuevos limeños*. Lima: Sur-Tafos.
Valenzuela, Eduardo (1991). 'La experiencia nacional-popular'. *Proposiciones 20*. Santiago: SUR.
van Domelen, Julie (1992). 'Working with Non-governmental Organizations'. In Steen

Jorgensen, Margaret Gross, and Marc Schacter (eds.), *Bolivia's Answer to Poverty, Economic Crisis and Adjustment.* Washington: World Bank Regional and Sectoral Studies.

VAN GUNSTEREN, HERMAVANN (1994). 'Four Conceptions of Citizenship'. In Bart Steenbergen (ed.), *The Condition of Citizenship.* London: Sage.

VANHANEN, TATU (1990). *The Process of Democratization: A Comparative Study of 147 States, 1980–1988.* New York: Crane Russak.

VARAS, AUGUSTO (ed.) (1988). *El Partido Comunista en Chile.* Santiago: CESOC-FLACSO.

VELLINGA, MENNO (1993). *Social Democracy in Latin America: Prospects for Change.* Boulder, Colo.: Westview Press.

VERGARA, PILAR (1994). 'Market Economy, Social Welfare and Democratic Consolidation in Chile'. In William Smith, C. Acuña, and E. Gamarra (eds.), *Democracy, Markets and Structural Reform in Latin America.* New Brunswick, NJ: Transaction Publishers.

VILAS, CARLOS (1992). 'Latin American Populism: Towards a Structural Interpretation'. *Science and Society.*

—— (1993). *Back to the Dangerous Classes? Capitalist Restructuring, State Reform and the Working Class in Latin America.* The Institute of Latin American and Iberian Studies Paper Series No. 34. New York: Columbia University.

—— (1994). 'Entre el Estado y la globalización: La soberanía de la sociedad civil'. *Sociológica,* 25: 31–51.

—— (1995a). *Between Earthquakes and Volcanoes: Market, States and Revolutions in Central America.* New York: Monthly Review Press.

—— (1995b). 'Entre la democracia y el neoliberalismo: Los caudillos electorales de la post-modernidad'. *Socialismo y Participación,* 69: 31–43.

—— (1995c). 'Estado, actores y desarrollo: Los intercambios entre política y economía'. *Investigación Económica,* 212: 177–95.

VILLAR, ROBERTO (1995). 'Lacking Jobs and Hope, Landless Gauchos Occupy Farms'. *Real Brazil,* 1: 6–8.

VIOLA, EDUARDO (1987). 'The Ecologist Movement in Brazil (1974–1986): From Environmentalism to Ecopolitics'. *International Journal of Urban and Regional Research,* 12 (2).

VULLIAMY, ED (1993). 'A Culture of Corruption'. *Guardian Weekly,* 4 Apr.: 12.

VUSKOVIĆ, PEDRO (1993). *Pobreza y desigualidad en América Latina.* DF, Mexico: CIIH-UNAM.

WACQUANT, LOIC J. D. (1992). 'Redrawing the Urban Color Line: The State of the Ghetto in the 1980s'. In Craig Calhoun and George Ritzer (eds.), *Essay on Race and Ethnic Relations.* New York: McGraw-Hill.

WADE, ROBERT (1990). *Governing the Market: Economic Theory and the Role of Government in East Asian Industrialization.* Princeton: Princeton University Press.

WAISMAN, CARLOS H. (1987). *Reversal of Development in Argentina.* Princeton: Princeton University Press.

WALKER, IGNACIO (1990). *Socialismo y democracia: Chile y Europa en perspectiva comparada.* Santiago: CIEPLAN.

WARD, PETER (ed.) (1986). *Welfare Politics in Mexico.* London: Allen & Unwin.

—— (1993). 'Social Welfare Policy and Political Opening in Mexico'. *Journal of Latin American Studies,* 25 (3): 613–28.

—— (1994). 'Social Welfare Policy and Political Opening in Mexico'. In Wayne Cornelius, Ann Craig, and Jonathan Fox (eds.), *Transforming State–Society Relations in Mexico: The National Solidarity Strategy.* La Jolla, Calif.: Center for US–Mexican Studies.

WARREN, KAY B. (1993). 'Interpreting *La Violencia* in Guatemala: Shapes of Mayan Silence & Resistance'. In Kay Warren (ed.), *The Violence Within: Cultural and Political Opposition in Divided Nations*. Boulder, Colo.: Westview.

Washington Office on Latin America (WOLA) (1989). *The Administration of Injustice: Military Accountability in Guatemala*. Washington.

WASSENBERG, ARTHUR F. P. (1982). 'Neo-corporatism and the Quest for Control'. In Gerhard Lehmbruch and Philippe Schmitter (eds.), *Patterns of Corporatist Policy-Making*. London: Sage.

WATERBURY, JOHN (1992). 'The Heart of the Matter? Public Enterprise and the Adjustment Process'. In Stephan Haggard and Robert Kaufman (eds.), *The Politics of Economic Adjustment*. Princeton: Princeton University Press.

WEAVER, R. KENT, and ROCKMAN, BERT A. (1993). 'Assessing the Effects of Institutions'. In Kent Weaver and Bert Rockman (eds.), *Do Institutions Matter?* Washington: Brookings Institution.

WEBER, MAX (1963). *Essays of Sociology*. Cambridge: Oxford University Press.

WEDIN, AKE (1991). *La 'solidaridad' sindical internacional y sus víctimas: Tres estudios de caso latinoamericanos*. Instituto de Estudios Latinoamericanos de Estocolmo, Monografía No. 22.

WEFFORT, FRANCISCO (1984). *Por Quê Democracia?* São Paulo: Editora Brasiliense.

—— (1992). *Qual Democracia?* São Paulo: Editora Schwartz.

—— (1993). 'The Future of Socialism'. In Larry Diamond and Marc F. Plattner (eds.), *Capitalism, Socialism, and Democracy Revisited*. Baltimore: Johns Hopkins University Press.

—— and QUIJANO, ANIBAL (1973). *Populismo, marginalización y dependencia: Ensayos de interpretación sociología*. San José: Editorial Universitaria Centroamericana.

WEINER, MYRON (1967). *Party Building in a New Nation*. Chicago: University of Chicago Press.

WEINTRAUB, SIDNEY (1993). *Transforming the Mexican Economy: The Salinas Sexenio*. Washington: National Planning Association.

WEYLAND, KURT (1997). ' "Growth with Equity" in Chile's New Democracy?' *Latin American Research Review*, 32 (1) (Spring).

WHITE, HARRISON C., BORMAN, SCOTT A., and BRIEGER, RONALD L. (1976). 'Social Structure from Multiple Networks: I. Blockmodels of Roles and Positions'. *American Journal of Sociology*, 81: 730–80.

WHITEHEAD, LAURENCE (1992). 'Alternatives to Liberal Democracy: Perspectives from Latin America'. *Political Studies*. Special Issue on Democracy, edited by D. Held.

—— (1993). 'Introduction: Some Insights from Western Social Theory'. *World Development*, 21 (8).

—— (1994). 'The Science—and Art—of Comparative Politics: Democratisation Studies'. Presented at the XVIth World Congress of the International Political Science Association, Berlin.

WIARDA, HOWARD (1981). *Corporatism and National Development in Latin America*. Boulder, Colo.: Westview.

WILKIE, JAMES W., and CONTRERAS, CARLOS ALBERTO (eds.) (1992). *Statistical Abstract of Latin America*. Los Angeles: UCLA Latin America Center.

WILLIAMS, DAVID, and YOUNG, TOM (1994). 'Governance, the World Bank and Liberal Theory'. *Political Studies*, 42: 84–100.

WILLIAMS, EDWARD J., and PASSÉ-SMITH, JOHN T. (1992). *The Unionization of the Maquiladora Industry: The Tamaulipan Case in National Context*. San Diego: Institute for Regional Studies of the Californias, San Diego State University.

WILLIAMS, ROBERT G. (1994). *States and Social Evolution: Coffee and the Rise of National Governments in Central America*. Chapel Hill: University of North Carolina Press.

WILLIAMSON, JOHN (1993). 'Democracy and the "Washington Consensus"'. *World Development*.

WILSON, FRANK L. (1983). 'Interest Groups and Politics in Western Europe: The Neo-corporatist Approach'. *Comparative Politics*, Oct.: 105–23.

WINOCUR, MARCOS (1980). *Las clases olvidadas de la revolución cubana*. Barcelona: Grijalbo.

WITT, MATT (1992). 'Labor and NAFTA'. *Latin American Labor News*, 5.

WOLF, ERIC (1972). *Las guerras campesinas del siglo XX*. DF, Mexico: Siglo XXI.

WOLFE, MARSHALL (1994). 'Some Paradoxes on Social Exclusion'. Geneva: ILO, DP/63.

WOO, JUNG-EUN (1991). *Race to the Swift*. New York: Columbia University Press.

WOOLLACOTT, MARTIN (1993). 'World Wide Corruption Feeding on Itself'. *Guardian Weekly*, 21 Mar.

World Bank (1993). *The East Asian Miracle: Economic Growth and Public Policy*. New York: Oxford University Press.

—— (1994). *Governance: The World Bank's Experience*. Washington: World Bank Publication.

WOZNIAK, LYNN (1991). 'Industrial Modernization and Working Class Protest in Socialist Spain'. Working Paper No. 165. Notre Dame, Ind.: Kellogg Institute.

WRIGHT, ANTHONY (1986). *Socialisms: Theories and Practices*. Oxford: Oxford University Press.

YAÑEZ COSSIO, CONSUELO (1991). *'Macac'—teoría y práctica de la educación indígena: Estudio de caso en el Ecuador*. Cali: Celater.

YASHAR, DEBORAH J. (forthcoming). *Demanding Democracy: Reform and Reaction in Costa Rica and Guatemala, 1870s–1950s*. Stanford, Calif.: Stanford University Press.

YATES, CHARLOTTE (1992). 'North American Autoworkers' Response to Restructuring'. In M. Golden and Jonas Pontusson (eds.), *Bargaining for Change*. Ithaca, NY: Cornell University Press.

YÉPEZ SALAS, GUILLERMO (1993). *La Causa R: Origen y poder*. Caracas: Fondo Editorial Tropikos.

ZAMOSC, LEON (1990). 'The Political Crisis and the Prospects for Rural Democracy in Colombia'. In Jonathan Fox (ed.), *The Challenge of Rural Democratization: Perspectives from Latin America and the Philippines*. London: Frank Cass.

—— (1993). 'Protesta agraria y movimiento indígena en la Sierra Ecuatoriana'. In CEDIME (eds.), *Sismo étnico en el Ecuador: Varias perspectivas*. Quito: Aby-Yala.

—— (1994). 'Estadística de las areas de predominio étnico de la Sierra Ecuatoriana'. Unpublished. San Diego: University of California.

ZAPATA, FRANCISCO (1993). *Autonomía y subordinación en el sindicalismo latinoamericano*. DF, Mexico: Fondo de Cultura Económica/El Colegio de México.

ZEITLIN, MAURICE, and RADCLIFF, RICHARD EARL (1988). *Landlords & Capitalists: The Dominant Classes of Chile*. Princeton: Princeton University Press.

ZERMEÑO, SERGIO (1989). 'El regreso del Líder: Crisis, neoliberalismo y desorden'. *Revista Mexicana de Sociología*, 4. DF, Mexico: UNAM.

ZUCKER, LYNNE G. (1983). 'Organizations as Institutions'. In S. B. Bacharach (ed.), *Research in the Sociology of Organizations*. Greenwich, Conn.: JAI Press.

Index

638 **Index**

Cubatão, Brazil 212
Custódio, Brazil 443

da Silva, Luis Inácio ('Lula') 107, 436
da Silva, Vicente Paulo 48, 68
da Silva Ramos, José Augusto 442
Dahik, Alberto 505, 507
de Andrade Vieira, José Eduardo 53
de la Madrid, Miguel 148–9, 484–5
  policies of 469–70, 473–4, 476n., 478–80,
    518
de León Carpio, Ramiro 39, 256–8
debts/debt crisis 313, 338, 492, 495, 551–2
  in Ecuador 498; in Uruguay 385;
    in Venezuela 140
decentralization/'deconcentración' 65, 545–6,
    556–61, 565–6
  in Brazil 428, 433; in Ecuador 491, 502; in
    Mexico 476n.; in Uruguay 456–65, 467;
    in Venezuela 118–22, 130, 132, 140–1
'decretismo' 341
democracy 8–10, 21, 223, 266, 417–18, 559
  in Brazil 262–4, 268, 274–5, 279–80;
    in Chile 328–9; definition of 21, 137,
    199; 'delegative' 26–7, 552; in Ecuador
    498–9; in Uruguay 363–5; in Venezuela
    138
Democratic Left, the 181
Democratic Popular Movement (MPD) 176
Democratic Rural Union (UDR: União
    Democrática Ruralista)
Democratic Workers' Party (PDT) 428
democratization/transition to democracy 6,
    8, 11–14, 18, 29, 192, 199–200, 240–60,
    313–14, 338–59, 391–4, 417–20, 421,
    546, 551, 560
  in Brazil 111; in Peru 218–19; in Venezuela
    139
Directorate for Bilingual Intercultural
    Education 187
Dominican Republic 27n., 34n.
Dulci, Luis 436–7
Durán Ballén, Sixto 186, 505–8
  policies of 170, 182–3, 510–11
Durango, Mexico 407, 482n.

Earth Summit 198, 206, 213
Ecuador 9, 170–91, 489–515, 572
  indigenous people of 38, political
    organization in 33
education:
  bilingual 171–2, 179–82, 186
  in Ecuador 493, 502
  in Mexico 474
  policy 138–9, 353
El Augustino (Peru) 288, 306

El Cerro/El Cerrito (Uruguay) 451
El Diario 282–3, 291
El Matancero 124
El Salvador 5, 417–18, 523, 558
Emergency Social Investment Fund (FISE)
    492–4, 500, 502–10, 514, 572
environmental movement 524–5, 537–8, 552
  in Brazil 192–216
ethnicity 14, 16, 19, 24
Europe 64, 66, 121, 524, 565
European Economic Community (EEC) 189,
    257, 342, 344, 346, 417
Evangelical Federation of Indigenous
    Ecuadorians (FEINE) 185

Farm Labor Organizing Committee (FLOC)
    527, 530–2
Favier, Denis 126
Febres Cordero, León 502, 505–6
Federação dos Trabalhadores na Agricultura
    do Estado do Pernambuco (FETAPE) 96,
    104, 108, 110
Federal District of Mexico 157, 167n. *see also*
    Mexico City
Federal District of Venezuela 132–3 *see also*
    Caracas
Federation of Commerce Employees 88
Federation of Electricity Workers (FATLyF)
    86–7, 88
Federation of United Unions of State Oil
    Workers (SUPE) 86, 88
Feldmann, Fábio 206
Fermín, Claudio 135
FETRAMETAL 125
Fontanele, Maria Luiza 423–4
Força Sindical 52, 63, 68
Ford Motor Company 48, 51, 67, 532–3
  Ford–Cuautitlán 531, 533–4
Foro Multi-Sectoral Social (FMS) 256
Foro Nacional Ecuatoriano de Organizaciones
    No Gubernamentales (FONEONGs)
    511
Fortaleza (Ceará, Brazil) 423–5, 436, 440, 445
Foxley, Alejandro 342, 356
Franco, Francisco 344, 348
Franco, Itamar 51, 55, 56, 111n.
Frei, Eduardo 355
Frente Amplio (Broad Front) 447–59, 461–8
Frente Democrático Nacional (FDN) 481–2
Frente Democrático Nueva Guatemala
    (FDNG) 36, 37, 258
Frente Popular Tierra y Libertad 166
Frente Zapatista de Liberación Nacional
    (Zapatistas) 30, 38, 482, 516–17, 543,
    555
FREPASO 90